THE END OF THE WORLD

THE END
OF THE WORLD

A History

by

Otto Friedrich

Fromm International Publishing Corporation

NEW YORK

Published in 1986 by Fromm International Publishing Corporation, 560 Lexington Avenue, New York, N.Y. 10022

THE END OF THE WORLD: *A History*

"The Kingdom of Auschwitz" appeared in *The Atlantic Monthly* and "The Great War" in *Playboy,* both in somewhat condensed form.

The author gratefully acknowledges permission from the following sources to quote from material in their control:

Harcourt Brace Jovanovich, Inc., for lines from "Four Quartets" and "Choruses from 'The Rock'" by T. S. Eliot.

Robert Jay Lifton and International Creative Management for excerpts from *Death in Life: Survivors of Hiroshima* by Robert Jay Lifton. Copyright © 1967 by Robert Jay Lifton.

Robert Payne and Bertha Klausner International Literary Agency, Inc., for lines of poetry by Ivan Kaliayev reprinted from *The Fortress* by Robert Payne. Copyright © 1957, 1967 by Robert Payne. All rights reserved.

Penguin Books Ltd. for lines from *The Cherry Orchard* and *Uncle Vanya,* pages 244, 245, 350, 364, 367, 384, 395, 397, and 398, in *Plays* by Anton Chekhov, translated by Elisaveta Fen, Penguin Classics, 1954. Copyright © 1951, 1954 by Elisaveta Fen.

Schocken Books, Inc., for lines of poetry by Foulques of Marseille and Peire Cardenal reprinted from SONGS OF THE TROUBADORS by Anthony Bonner. Copyright © 1972 by Schocken Books, Inc.

The University of Chicago Press for verse from the Gilgamesh Epic reprinted from *The Gilgamesh Epic and Old Testament Parallels* by Alexander Heidel. Copyright © 1946, 1949 by The University of Chicago. All rights reserved.

The University of Texas Press for poetry by Guilhem IX reprinted from the *Anthology of Troubador Lyric Poetry,* Volume III of the Edinburgh Bilingual Library, translated by Alan R. Press. Copyright © 1971 by Alan R. Press.

Printed in the United States of America

Library of Congress Cataloging in Publication Data

Friedrich, Otto, 1929–
    The end of the world.

    Reprint. Originally published: New York: Coward, McCann & Geohegan, c 1982.
    Bibliography: p. 357
    Includes index.
    1. Disaster.   I. Title.

D24.575   1986   904   86-12157
ISBN 0-88064-062-6

To Priscilla

Contents

The Great Flood

". . . the windows of heaven were opened."

And the Lord said, I will destroy man whom I have created from the
face of the earth; both man and beast, and the creeping thing, and
the fowls of the air; for it repenteth me that I have made them.
—GENESIS 6:7

The tiny island of Santorini, rising out of the Aegean Sea about sixty miles
north of Crete, takes its name from Saint Irene of Salonika, who was burned
alive in A.D. 304 for refusing to abjure the Christian faith. Greek nationalists
prefer to call the place Thera, after the first Spartan commander who ventured
to land there after the disaster. Originally, before that disaster, it was called
Kallistê, the most beautiful island, and sometimes Strongulê, the circular island. Still beautiful, it is circular no longer. It is now shaped rather like a new
moon, its tips pointed toward the west. In the center of the circle, when there
was a circle, rose a mountain about five thousand feet high. Where the mountain once stood, there is now a lagoon eight miles wide, more than two hundred
fathoms deep, so deep that none of the luxurious cruise ships that stop here can
anchor. They can only tie up at mooring buoys that have been chained to the
depths. In the center of the lagoon, covered now with an armor of dark vegetation that quickly turns black when the sun sets behind it, lies the hulk of the
volcano that destroyed Santorini nearly four thousand years ago.

We have learned only recently how gifted and sophisticated the civilization
on these Cycladic Islands in the Aegean must have been. As early as the mid-
nineteenth century, archaeologists had found several sites indicating that Santorini was an outpost of the Minoans, who were already enjoying the decadence of eye makeup and indoor plumbing more than a thousand years before
Rómulus and Remus were first suckled by a she-wolf. But most of Santorini
still remains covered, at depths of up to 150 feet, by layers of tephra, pumice
and ash that poured forth from the volcano in the great eruption. Only on the
southern tip, where wind and sea have eroded and thinned this smothering
blanket over the course of centuries, could an archaeologist named Spyridon
Marinatos have unearthed, in 1967, the treasures of Akrotiri.

These treasures are not gold and precious stones—the inhabitants (estimated
to number as many as thirty thousand) apparently had enough warning to escape with their riches—but rather a series of wonderfully preserved frescoes.

Now proudly exhibited at the National Archaeological Museum in Athens, these frescoes portray with matchless grace and charm the life of the Aegean islanders in what we patronizingly term the Bronze Age. One entire room, for example, is covered on three sides with a panorama of lilies flowering on red-and-blue mountainsides. Above the lilies, two swallows with black-and-white-striped wings encounter each other in a kind of courtship, their open beaks nearly but not quite touching. And here are other splendid creatures, like the blue monkeys, a species known only to the artists of Santorini, leaping through the air as carelessly as any swallow. Here is the young fisherman, carrying in each hand a string of blue-and-yellow mackerel, and here the priestess with the long black hair, her cheeks rouged and her breasts bare. Here are the young boxers, two boys of about twelve, stripped to loincloths, their right hands encased in boxing gloves, jabbing at each other with a childish intensity as timeless as that of Keats's lovers, "for ever panting and for ever young." And here, finally, is the magnificent naval expedition, a kind of sea saga in which a procession of needle-prowed warships, each propelled by a dozen or more oarsmen, sets forth from a walled city on some mysterious mission, escorted by blue sea fowl and frolicking blue porpoises.

The rumbling of an earthquake apparently provided the people of Santorini with their warning. The whole island shook. In Akrotiri and other such towns perched on the sides of the mountain, walls of stone split open and fell to earth. There may have been several earthquakes. They may have extended over a number of months. The first warnings may not have been sufficient. There are indications at Akrotiri that some of the fugitives returned to the ruined city and tried for a time to rebuild it. Then, in about 1500 B.C., the warnings were vastly fulfilled. In what was probably the most violent explosion in all of human history, the whole Santorini volcano blew up. An estimated thirty-two square miles of the island (about four times as big an area as that destroyed in the celebrated Krakatoa eruption of 1883) simply dissolved in a holocaust. The storm of rock and ash darkened the skies for hundreds of miles—indeed, the debris can still be found on the floor of the sea over an area of about 115,000 square miles, most of the eastern Mediterranean. The fiery ruin of the volcano, the whole center of the island of Santorini, then sank beneath the sea. And the sea rushed in, and began to boil and steam. The cataclysm started a tidal wave of almost unbelievable size and violence that smashed onto the northern shore of Crete. Estimates of its colossal height range from two hundred to three hundred feet, and it may have rolled forth at a speed of more than one hundred miles per hour. When the rain of ash and debris ended, Santorini was an island of death. Nothing could live there.

Even today, the place has a fearful reputation. "The smell of sulphur and the pit still seem to hang in the air," Lawrence Durrell wrote in *The Greek Islands.* "The yachtsman feels uneasy when he decides to anchor for a few nights—to wait for full moon, say, when Santorin glimmers like the City of the Dead in Cairo under the cold, flaring white light. It also smells of the devil, and consequently it is no surprise that in the modern folklore of Greece peasant superstition has picked on the island as a specially favored home for the vampire. . . ."

*

Something like that. Something like that moonlit landscape, the cliffs and
craters of the dead land, seems to haunt the contemporary imagination. Perhaps it is the approach of the year 2000 that revives speculation about what the
apocalyptic tradition calls "the Final Days." The threat of nuclear war inspires
student demonstrations, prayer meetings, and even a "bicycle marathon."
Books claiming Biblical authority for prophecies of disaster sell millions of
copies. Crowds flock to movies that speculate on the possibilities of destruction
and salvation, if not through a Messianic coming, or a global war, then through
voyages of flight to distant galaxies.

Although these fears and illusions have been with us for centuries, they have
acquired a new violence because of the new power of scientific technology, its
terrifying power both to create and to destroy. We have not yet really understood and accepted the technological horrors of World War II—the accidental
firestorm in Hamburg that set the air itself ablaze and suffocated everyone
within its reach, or the actual detonation over Hiroshima of a bomb so awful
that those who were spared death by burning could feel their own faces melting
in their clutching hands—and yet we have repeatedly been informed that the
weapons used against Hamburg and Hiroshima were mere toys compared to
what is now available and ready for firing. A ton of TNT is in itself an explosive force of almost unimaginable horror; a kiloton represents a thousand tons
of TNT; the Hiroshima bomb was twenty kilotons; a megaton represents a
million tons of TNT, fifty times the size of the Hiroshima bomb, and weapons
of this size are considered small and limited when compared to the 25-megaton
weapons that have already been built. The so-called SALT treaty, which was
supposed to restrict our capacity for destruction, limited us to 2,200 such weapons on each side of that vulnerable frontier that used to be called the Iron Cur-
tain.

A World War III fought with nuclear weapons—a war, as Soviet Premier
Nikita Khrushchev once said, in which the living would envy the dead—has
filled a whole generation with a sense of dread. And yet as the years go by, our
sense of a coming apocalypse has taken other forms as well. The possibility of
natural catastrophe—a choking cloud of polluted air, an earthquake under an
atomic plant, a melting of the polar ice caps—that now inspires books and
movies, astrological forecasts and underground newspapers. In a sense, these
anticipated catastrophes are much the same as a nuclear war. On the one hand,
such a war would be the ultimate pollution, the ultimate ecological disaster, for
many of the victims would probably die not by direct attack, as in past wars,
but by the poison of radioactive fallout. On the other hand, many of the natural
catastrophes that seem to threaten us are not really natural but rather
man-made assaults, distortions and perversions of the balance of nature. Faust
is at large again in the form of the scientist who asks too much of God's universe.

This moral element connects still more closely the possibilities of nuclear
war and natural cataclysm. Either way, the prophecies imply, the end of the

world will be the fault of sinning mankind, the repudiation of God's covenant with Noah after the great flood. We no longer believe in Noah, of course, but we do believe in the metaphor of a covenant that gives meaning to our existence, and in the danger of its repudiation. The end of the world is, in a way, a pun. The end can mean not only the conclusion but also the purpose of the world. Just as it has been said that a man's life can be understood only at the moment of his death, so the end of the world, the destruction of the world, seems to imply that there is some higher purpose in the world's existence. Thus, the end of the world makes manifest the end of the world.

That implies, in turn, that there really is a God, and that he has a purpose. To believe such an idea today is an act of pure faith, as it was an act of faith for Albert Einstein to keep repeating, while he pursued his doomed effort to find a coherent set of mathematical laws governing the universe, that "God does not play at dice." Living now in the shadow of World War III, to be fought with the weapons that Einstein conceived, we are more inclined to suspect that perhaps God does play at dice after all, or perhaps simply that he once did, and then abandoned the game and left the cosmic dice lying forgotten in some far corner of the universe. Stephen Crane, who was not a scientist, foresaw the central problem of the twentieth century: "When it occurs to a man that nature does not regard him as important . . . he at first wishes to throw bricks at the temple, and he hates deeply the fact that there are no bricks and no temples."

Since the apocalypse is an essentially religious idea—perpetuated for nearly two millennia now by Christ's prophecy of wars and famines and earthquakes leading to a moment when "the sun shall darken . . . and the stars of heaven shall fall"—it is difficult for anyone who cannot believe in God to imagine the end of the world, or even to imagine the world itself as a unitary whole. Most of us have been trained to believe only the evidence of our senses, so we believe only in the world that we can see around us, and the end that we dread in our prefigurings of World War III is really nothing more than an extension of our own death, the prospect that the city where we now live will suddenly be reduced to a heap of radioactive rubble. The idea that life might continue at the edges of the rubble seems small consolation.

If we start seeking a historic framework for these apocalyptic anxieties, as this book will attempt to do, we soon find that the idea of the end of the world goes back to mankind's earliest beginnings, to the fear that the sun might never return in the spring, or even at dawn. And there is evidence that even before mankind was here to worry about a supernatural disaster, disaster came. Fossils and fragments of bone show that great lizards once roamed the earth, and that they were mysteriously destroyed at the end of the Mesozoic Age about 65 million years ago. Schoolboys studying Darwinian theory used to be told that the dinosaurs' brains were too small for them to adapt to a changing climate, that they died because they were not as intelligent as modern schoolboys. In the past few years, a different and less comfortable theory has suggested that the dinosaurs died because the earth collided with a meteorite, that vast clouds of dust arising from the collision darkened the sky and killed the vegetation on which the dinosaurs lived. An occasion, it would seem, on which God did play at dice.

We can contemplate such distant calamities with considerable tranquillity, and even a legendary catastrophe like the explosion of Santorini can easily be transformed into romance. But when we reach the era of written and remembered history, the agents of disaster assume human form and become correspondingly more murderous. A bolt of lightning may be a sign of God's anger, but it may also strike at random, whereas the men who come in arms against you are aiming specifically at you, and their purpose is to destroy you. Hence, from earliest times, the fear of the barbarians at the gates, the fear that the stoutest walls around the highest pinnacles of human civilization remain always vulnerable to brute force. Eternal Rome was not eternal, except in that it could be rebuilt after being sacked. Troy was not rebuilt, nor, after the writing on the wall, was Babylon. Over a long span of time, we can view such ravages as a series of collisions between cultures, collisions in which the defeated saw their world destroyed but the victors went on to create new worlds. As the destruction comes closer, and we consider Hiroshima rather than vanished Babylon, the bloodshed seems more real, more cruel and more ominous.

The warriors who come to sack a city can often be resisted, or evaded, or ultimately civilized. Thus the descendants of the Visigoths became builders of cathedrals. Far more terrifying, because more reasoning and more implacably determined, is the destructive force that becomes embodied in the state itself, and in the state religion. When the Romans decided to destroy a city, they generally took no prisoners, except for a few to be killed for sport, or sold into slavery. When the Holy Inquisition began interrogating suspects, there was no escape by flight, nor by protestations of innocence, nor even by suicide. The Inquisition lived by gathering knowledge and pursuing error; it did not err. From its wisdom ultimately grew the Gestapo and the Ministry of Love.

The modern spectator continues to be fascinated by natural catastrophe. Though he no longer sees the hand of God in an epidemic of the bubonic plague or in an earthquake that shatters a city, though the victims are soon treated with antibiotics and plasma, the suddenness and randomness of such disasters still have the power to fill even the most skeptical witness with a sense of awe. Perhaps this, writ large, is the way the world will end. In even the worst such natural disasters, however, the sense of finality is limited, and the victims are far outnumbered by the survivors. It is the modern police state that proclaims to an entire society that no one is beyond its reach, and that the various forms of mass death are now a matter for the state to decide. The technology of the nuclear missile extends that proclamation of possibilities across the world.

Whether or how those possibilities will be fulfilled remains, of course, unknowable. "What experience and history teach," said Hegel, "is . . . that people and governments have never learned anything from history."

*

If the world ends in a cataclysm—in contrast to T. S. Eliot's prediction of a mere whimper—no end that we can imagine can be more violent than the beginning. The Book of Genesis describes the event with magnificent serenity, but the scene is one of awesome upheaval: "In the beginning God created the heaven and the earth. And the earth was without form, and void; and darkness was upon the face of the deep. . . . And God said, Let there be light: and there was light." Scientists have translated these superb verses into more exact circumstances. "In the beginning there was an explosion," according to Professor Steven Weinberg of Harvard, in *The First Three Minutes*. This was not an explosion that began at some central point and burst outward but rather "an explosion which occurred simultaneously everywhere, filling all space from the beginning, with every particle of matter rushing apart from every other particle." Science claims to know the smallest details. In the first one hundredth of a second of the universal explosion, the temperature was about one hundred thousand million (10^{11}) degrees Centigrade, a temperature so great that nothing that we know as matter, no atoms nor even the nuclei of atoms, could survive. Only the most mysterious fragments, like the neutrino and perhaps the quark, flew outward through space in the waves of that primeval explosion.

"And God said, Let there be a firmament in the midst of the waters, and let it divide the waters from the waters. . . . And God said, Let the waters under the heaven be gathered together unto one place, and let the dry land appear: and it was so." This too, one day in God's creation, modern scientists have translated into more specific terms. About 2.5 billion years ago, the earth tore away from the sun and began to congeal from blazing gases into a blob of matter and finally into a core of molten iron encircled by a wrinkled crust. It is almost impossible to imagine the millions of years that passed, millions of years for the crust to cool from bubbling liquid into quaking mass, millions more years of cracking and surging turmoil, millions more years before the first clouds formed over the bleak wasteland. And then, in some magical moment of chemical combination, the first raindrop fell. "Never have there been such rains since that time," as Rachel Carson wrote in *The Sea Around Us*. "They fell continuously, day and night, days passing into months, into years, into centuries. They poured into the waiting ocean basins, or, falling upon the continental masses, drained away to become sea."

From that sea, we all came, all of us, and in all of us there remains a kind of evolutionary memory that is more fundamental than the collective memories of any tribe or nation or race. The salty blood that flows through our bodies still contains such elements as sodium, potassium and calcium in about the same proportions as they exist in seawater. And beyond that, we must, each one of us, reexperience our rebirth from the sea in the terrifying hours of birth itself. We cannot remember—but must remember—the awful expulsion from the warm sea that has nurtured us, the awful passage down the narrow channel from safe darkness into blinding light. Seized and held upside down, dripping wet, whacked on the rear end, gasping for breath, the naked baby cries out in terror and protest.

*

The land around us can be tamed, by which we mean chopped and dug and furrowed and seeded and torn and mined, but the sea remains itself, never still, always threatening. "The sea howl/ And the sea yelp . . .," as Eliot wrote in *The Dry Salvages,* "The menace and caress of wave that breaks on water,/The distant rote in the granite teeth, and the wailing warning from the approaching headland/ Are all sea voices. . . ./ And under the oppression of the silent fog/ The tolling bell/ Measures time not our time. . . ."

The sea in flood, the sea enraged, is part of the mythology of almost every race or tribe that lives near its shores. The first of these sagas of deluge occurs in the Gilgamesh Epic, which appears on a dozen cuneiform tablets dug up in 1872 from the ruins of the Assyrian capital of Nineveh. These tablets date back to the seventh century B.C., but the epic itself is thought to be much older, originating in about 2000 B.C.

The hero Gilgamesh, seeking the secret of eternal life after the death of his friend Enkidu, encounters Utnapishtim, who seems to have become immortal even though he resembles an ordinary man. "Thou art like unto me," says Gilgamesh. When Gilgamesh asks him his secret, Utnapishtim begins to tell him the story of the terrible flood. It had been decreed by the gods that the human race was to be wiped out. In contrast to Genesis, which ascribes a similar disaster to human wickedness, the Gilgamesh Epic gives no reason for the great flood. There are other versions of the same legend, however, and in one fragment known as the Atrahasis Epic (that being a Babylonian variant of Gilgamesh's name) it is explained that the warrior god Enlil decreed the flood because the human race was making so much noise that it interfered with his sleep. As a preliminary punishment, Enlil sent a series of plagues to reduce the population, and the noise, but mankind kept on breeding, and bearing children, and shouting and singing. The final solution, Enlil decided, was utter destruction.

In the Gilgamesh Epic too, though Enlil's rage against the human race remains unexplained, it seems to have been decisive. None of the other gods had the courage or authority to oppose his plan for a deluge. But one of them, Ea, an ancient, fish-scaled deity variously regarded as the god of wisdom and subtlety, the lord of the sea, the creator and teacher of the human race, decided to save one or two of his creatures. He appeared outside the wattled hut where Utnapishtim lay sleeping and spoke to him in such a way that Utnapishtim seemed to hear his words in a dream. "Tear down [thy] house, build a ship!" said Ea. "Abandon possessions, seek life!/ Disregard goods, and save life!/ [Cause to] go up into the ship the seed of all living creatures./ The ship which thou shalt build."

Utnapishtim was perfectly willing to build an ark, but he worried about what his neighbors would say. "Tell them," said Ea, "that the high god Enlil has taken a dislike to you . . . and that you have therefore decided to leave his domain and take yourself to the sea, which belongs to your lord Ea, who will feed you on fish and fowl." Ea's instructions to Utnapishtim required an enormous boat, shaped like a cube, and measuring 120 cubits on each side, thus about one acre across and seven stories high, with everything caulked and oiled. "Bullocks I slaughtered . . . ," Utnapishtim tells Gilgamesh. "Sheep I killed every day. . . ./ Red wine, oil, and white wine/ I gave the workmen as if it were river water. . . ./ Whatever I had of silver I loaded aboard her;/ Whatever I had of gold I loaded aboard her;/ Whatever I had of the seed of all living creatures

[I loaded] aboard her./ After I had caused all my family and relations to go up into the ship,/ I caused the game of the field, the beasts of the field . . . to go."

The God of the Old Testament, having decided to destroy mankind, apparently hesitated. "Yet his days shall be an hundred and twenty years," according to one enigmatic verse in Genesis, which seems to record a period of grace in which the world's sinners might, if they understood their destiny, repent. The Babylonian gods left no period of grace, for Enlil's deluge was not to reform man but to destroy him. There were to be no survivors.

Utnapishtim, of course, had been secretly warned. "In the evening," he told Gilgamesh, "the leader of the storm caused a destructive rain to rain down./ I viewed the appearance of the weather;/ The weather was frightful to behold./ I entered my ship and closed my door." Inside his great box of a ship, he heard the gods of darkness rage. Adad, the lord of storms, sent thunder; Irragal, lord of the underworld, tore out the masts of ships; Ninurta, lord of walls and irrigation, caused the dikes to give way; the Anunnaki, judges of the underworld, raised their torches, and lightning flickered over the waters of the flood. Even the principal gods were terrified by the tempest. "They cowered like dogs and crouched in distress," Utnapishtim went on. "Ishtar cried out like a woman in labor . . . ,/ 'How could I command such evil in the assembly of the gods!/ How could I command war to destroy my people. . . .' "

"Six days and six nights," Utnapishtim recalled, "the downpour, the tempest and the flood overwhelmed the land./ When the seventh day arrived, the tempest, the flood/ Which had fought like an army, subsided in its onslaught./ The sea grew quiet, the storm abated, the flood ceased./ I opened a window, and light fell upon my face./ I looked upon the sea, all was silence,/ And all mankind had turned to clay. . . ./ I bowed, sat down, and wept,/ My tears running down over my face."

The sorrowing survivor looked in all directions for "the boundaries of the sea," but he found nothing until his giant boat was caught on the tip of Mount Nisir. There it was held fast for seven days, and on the seventh day Utnapishtim sent forth a dove, which could find no resting place, and so it returned to him. Then he sent forth a swallow, which could find no resting place, and so it returned to him. Then he sent forth a raven, "and when she saw that the waters had abated,/ She ate, she flew about, she cawed, and did not return./ Then I sent forth everything to the four winds and offered a sacrifice. . . ./ The gods smelled the savor,/ The gods smelled the sweet savor,/ The gods gathered like flies over the sacrifice."

Ishtar, the repentant goddess, held up her necklace of lapis lazuli in the light of the sun and swore that she would "remember these days," and that Enlil should not receive the sacrifice "because without reflection he brought on the deluge/ And consigned my people to destruction!" Enlil himself soon arrived, however, and, far from repenting the catastrophe, he was outraged that anyone had survived his condemnation. "Has any of the mortals escaped?" he cried. "No man was to live through the destruction!" The other gods guiltily pointed at Ea, who had saved his protégé, and though Ea was deferential toward his accuser ("O warrior . . ."), he also defended his own act of mercy. More important, he attacked Enlil for making no moral distinctions in his act of destruction. "How couldst thou without reflection bring on this deluge?" Ea demanded. "On the sinner lay his sin; on the transgressor lay his transgression!" Enlil accepted his rebuke, and accepted the survival of the human race, and made his peace with Utnapishtim. "He took my hand," Utnapishtim concludes his tale, "and caused . . . my wife . . . to kneel down at my side./ Standing between us, he touched our foreheads and blessed us:/ 'Hitherto Utnapishtim has been but a man;/ But now Utnapishtim and his wife shall be like unto us gods.' "

✻

This story appears, almost beyond question, to be the original version of the story told in Genesis. The only fundamental difference is that the assembly of Babylonian gods have become the one Jehovah, and that this Jehovah decides on the flood as a moral punishment, a means to wash away his mistake in having created man. The exact nature of man's sin is not explicitly stated, but it seems to have been sexual. Genesis tells us only that "the sons of God saw the daughters of men that they were fair; and they took them wives of all which they chose. . . . And God saw that the wickedness of man was great in the earth, and that every imagination of the thoughts of his heart was only evil continually. And it repented the Lord that he had made man on the earth."

The rest of the tale is familiar, of course, to every Sunday school: How only Noah was "a just man" who "walked with God," how God gave him detailed instructions on how to build an ark, three hundred cubits in length, and how he was told to fill it with two animals of every kind, even of "every creeping thing of the earth," and how, in the six hundredth year of Noah's life, "the windows of heaven were opened," and it rained for forty days and forty nights. "All in whose nostril was the breath of life . . . died. And every living substance was destroyed . . . and Noah only remained alive, and they that were with him in the ark. And the waters prevailed upon the earth an hundred and fifty days." Exactly like Utnapishtim, Noah came to rest upon a mountain. Exactly like Utnapishtim, he sent forth a bird three times, and when the bird found dry land, Noah emerged from his ark and built an altar and made a sacrifice, and Jehovah, just like the Babylonian deities, "smelled a sweet savor."

There is naturally no counterpart to the argument among the Babylonian gods, to the accusation that the deluge was an unjust act and the decision that the survivor should be granted immortality. Yet if Jehovah can be imagined to suffer internal conflicts, he seems to have been afflicted with some similar form of self-accusation, and he came to a similar conclusion in announcing his covenant with Noah, and in declaring, "in his heart," that he would never again decide to destroy mankind. "Neither will I again smite any more every thing living, as I have done." That was a reassuring promise, delivered as a rainbow arched across the sky. But it was a promise that Noah's myriad descendants, Jew and Gentile alike, would repeatedly come to doubt.

✻

While the parallels between the Gilgamesh Epic and Genesis are striking, it is even more remarkable how the legend of a primordial flood appears all over the world, and not just a flood but the building of an ark and the landing on a mountain and the repopulation of the devastated earth. Sir James G. Frazer collected many of the legends in *Folklore in the Old Testament:*

In Greece, Zeus decided to destroy mankind by a flood, but the Titan Prometheus warned his son Deucalion to build a large chest, and so he was saved, together with his wife Pyrrha. After floating on the seas for nine days and nine nights, they landed on Mount Parnassus. Hermes offered them a wish, and they wished for people, and so it was granted to them that when Deucalion threw a stone over his head, the stone became a man, and when Pyrrha threw a stone, it became a woman. . . .

In central India, jungle tribesmen known as the Bhils tell of a pious man who was warned by a fish that mankind would be destroyed by a deluge and that he should save himself by boarding a large box. He climbed into the box with his sister and a cock. When the god Rama discovered that they had survived the flood, he ordered the man to marry his sister, and they had seven sons and seven daughters. Rama also ordered the fish's tongue to be cut out for having given the warning. . . .

In Burma, the Chingpaw tribesmen recall a great flood in which the only survivors were Pawpaw Nan-chaung and his sister Chang-hko, who set out in a large boat with nine cocks and nine needles. When the storm was over, they turned loose one bird every day and dropped one needle overboard. When they heard the last cock crow and the last needle hit a mountaintop, they knew it was safe to leave their boat. . . .

In Sarawak, in Borneo, some women looking for bamboo shoots sat down on what they thought was a fallen tree and began cutting off shoots. They were startled to see the tree bleed where they cut. Some men passed by and saw that the fallen tree was actually a giant serpent, so they killed it and cut it up and carried it home to eat. As the women were frying the pieces of the serpent, a great rain began to fall, and the waters rose, and the whole world drowned, except for one woman, a dog and a rat. From the dog, the woman learned how to make fire, and, as the Victorian chronicle has it, "the woman took the fire drill for her mate, and by its help she gave birth to a son. . . ."

In Arizona, the Papagos Indians say that a coyote warned the hero Montezuma of the coming of the flood, and the coyote even created the ark of salvation by chewing down a large cane on the bank of a river and hollowing it out. The floods came and receded, and Montezuma sent the coyote forth to see where he could find dry land. . . .

In the Hudson Bay region, the Tinneh Indians recall a sage named Kunyan, which means wise man, who built himself a large raft, and when his wife asked him why, he said, "If there comes a flood, as I foresee, we shall take refuge on the raft." Other men mocked him, saying that they could take refuge in the trees, but when the flood came, all the trees were inundated, and all the earth disappeared, and Kunyan alone floated on the waters. Kunyan took pity on the animals and invited them aboard his raft, and when it came time to search for the vanished earth, he sent the muskrat to dive down and try to find it. The muskrat dived, and found nothing, and gasped out his message, "There is no earth." Kunyan sent him to dive again, and this time, when he rose to the surface, he said, "I smelled the smell of the earth, but I could not reach it." Then Kunyan sent the beaver to find the earth. The beaver dived deep, and stayed a long time under the water, and when he returned to the surface he held in his paw a tiny clot of mud. Kunyan took the mud and breathed on it and said, "I would there were an earth again!" And the clot of mud began to grow and grow until it became an island. . . .

It is perfectly possible, of course, that flooding is simply a commonplace occurence, at one time or another, and that all primitive peoples regard the inundation of their immediate region as the engulfing of the world. The flood in the Gilgamesh Epic, to cite one specific example, is generally thought to represent nothing more cataclysmic than an overflowing of the Tigris and Euphrates rivers. Still, there is something haunting about this recurring tale, in every region on earth, of a universal flood that destroyed all but one good family, or one couple, or one woman. The simplest explanation, perhaps, is the obvious one, that there really was once such a flood. That is the theory that the Russian cosmologist Immanuel Velikovsky argued in *Worlds in Collision,* which first appeared in the 1950s. According to Velikovsky, all these flood myths are half-remembered recollections of a cataclysmic period about 3,500 years ago when a passing comet nearly collided with the earth, interrupted its rotation, and caused it to capsize on its own axis. The comet, said Velikovsky, eventually turned into the planet Venus. It is an engaging theory, but more orthodox scientists have been remarkably unable to find much corroborating evidence. Besides, even if there once was a universal flood, how is one to account for the remarkable similarities in the way the various tribes found their salvation— the warnings and mockeries, the building and sealing of an ungainly ark, the flights of birds in search of land? For that matter, how is one to explain the fact that the mythical flood usually marks not the end of a sinful world, as in Genesis, but the end of a golden age in which men and animals spoke to one another and helped one another to the moment of survival?

"O Solon, Solon, you Hellenes are never anything but children," the aged Egyptian priest complained to the visiting Athenian statesman. The reason, said the priest, was that the Greeks had no sense of time, no sense of history, no records of past disasters. "Just when you . . . are beginning to be provided with letters and the other requisites of civilized life, after the usual interval, the stream from heaven, like a pestilence, comes pouring down, and leaves only those of you who are destitute of letters and education; and so you have to begin all over again like children, and know nothing of what happened in ancient times. . . . You remember a single deluge only, but there were many previous ones."

The accusation was set down about two centuries later by one of Solon's kinsmen, Plato, who used it as an introduction to his marvelous account (or invention) of the lost continent of Atlantis. "Beyond the straits [of Gibraltar] which are by you called the Pillars of Heracles," the Egyptian priest continued in Plato's *Timaeus*, "the island [of Atlantis] was larger than Libya [Africa] and Asia put together.... In this island of Atlantis there was a great and wonderful empire which had rule over the whole island and several others.... This vast power endeavored to subdue at a blow our country and yours ... and then, Solon, your country shone forth, in the excellence of her virtue and strength.... She defeated and triumphed over the invaders, and preserved from slavery those who were not yet subjugated, and generously liberated all the rest of us.... But afterward there occurred violent earthquakes and floods; and in a single day and night of misfortune all your warlike men in a body sank into the earth, and the island of Atlantis in like manner disappeared in the depths of the sea."

The plausibility of Plato's tale was somewhat reduced in his subsequent dialogue, *Critias,* in which he undertook to provide the history and geography of Atlantis. The gods had given the island to Poseidon, said Critias, and the sea god fell in love with an orphaned girl who lived there and was named Cleito. To guard the hill where she lived, Poseidon tore up the island and enclosed the hill with five concentric rings of land and water. Cleito bore him five sets of male twins, and Poseidon divided up the island among them. The oldest and most important of these was named Atlas, and he and his children acquired "such an amount of wealth as was never before possessed by kings and potentates, and is not likely to be ever again."

The land was rich in fruits and grains and minerals and every kind of animal, even elephants. Every five or six years, the ten kings gathered together to make laws and pass judgments, but first they had to sacrifice a bull to Poseidon. "The ten kings, being left alone in the temple, after they had offered prayers to the god that they might capture the victim which was acceptable to him, hunted the bulls, without weapons, but with staves and nooses; and the bull which they caught they led up to the [sacred] pillar and cut its throat over the top of it so that the blood fell upon the sacred inscription." For many generations, the kings and citizens of Atlantis obeyed all the laws of Poseidon, their progenitor. "But when the divine portion began to fade away, and became diluted too often and too much with the mortal admixture, and the human nature got the upper hand, they then, being unable to bear their fortune, behaved unseemly and ... grew visibly debased.... To those who had no eye to see the true happiness, they appeared glorious and blessed at the very time when they were full of avarice and unrighteous power." Zeus gathered all the gods to decide on a punishment, but just as he began to speak, Plato's manuscript broke off in midsentence. *Hermocrates,* once planned as the conclusion to the series begun by *Timaeus* and *Critias,* was never written at all.

There is no evidence that Plato's contemporaries took his tale of Atlantis with any great seriousness. His claim that the island was as big as Africa and Asia combined, and that the disaster took place nine thousand years earlier, made the empire's end seem as mythological as its beginning in Poseidon's passion for Cleito. There is hardly a mention of Atlantis in any other Greek writing (and none in any Egyptian record), and one of the few is a scornful dismissal by Plato's pupil Aristotle. "He who invented it," Aristotle remarked of the island's mysterious fate, "destroyed it." The mystery of Atlantis was not, in other words, a matter of much concern in classical times, or in the Middle Ages. And yet there was something about it—not least its origin in the work of Plato—that kept the tale alive. It became part of a folk tradition of vanished islands in the western seas, the Welsh kingdom of Avalon, the Breton city of Ys, the Portuguese Antilia, or Island of the Seven Cities. Medieval maps often showed several of these places lying in the waters that surround *terra incognita.*

Columbus' discovery naturally strengthened the various legends, and Sir Francis Bacon, among others, wondered whether the new lands of America might not ultimately prove to be Atlantis. But it was only in the nineteenth century, the age of electricity and railroads and Darwin's evolutionary progress, that Atlantis finally emerged as a citadel of the occult. Madame Blavatsky lectured on it to her Theosophical Society. Rudolf Steiner believed. In the United States, the principal enthusiast was a political maverick named Ignatius T. Donnelly, lieutenant governor of Minnesota, two-term Congressman, and unsuccessful Populist Party candidate for Vice-President. In his immensely popular book *Atlantis: The Antediluvian World* (1882), Donnelly argued not only that Atlantis really existed but that it was the site of all past Utopias, the Garden of Eden, the Elysian Fields. The inhabitants of Atlantis, he declared, were "the founders of nearly all our arts and sciences; they were the parents of our fundamental beliefs; they were the first civilizers, the first navigators, the first merchants, the first colonizers of the earth. . . ."

This sense of the lost Utopia has inspired many of the estimated two thousand books that have been written about Atlantis in the past century or so. Various experts have claimed to find traces of the lost continent in Brazil, in Iraq, in Ceylon, in the Caspian Sea, in Venezuela, in Belgium, in Spitzbergen. One unfortunate German found what he was seeking in the North Sea and published a book in the 1930s entitled *Atlantis-Helgoland, Motherland of Aryan-German Racial Thoroughbreeding and Colonization.* And if Utopia can be rediscovered, that rediscovery may come at the expense of less worthy lands. Edgar Cayce, who was regarded by his admirers as a peerless soothsayer, prophesied in the 1950s that Atlantis would rise again by the end of the following decade, but in a series of accompanying upheavals New York City would "in the main disappear," the West Coast would be "broken up," and most of Japan would "go into the sea."

*

To scientists, of course, all efforts to find the lost continent of Atlantis are utter nonsense. But it seems increasingly likely that the riddle has at last been solved, that there never was a gigantic island just beyond the Straits of Gibraltar, but that Plato's seductive story is a rather garbled account of a very real disaster—the explosion of Santorini, the sinking of the volcano, and the devastation wrought by that cataclysm upon the Minoan palaces of Crete.

Various ingenious efforts have been made to reconcile this hypothesis with the details of Plato's fable. It has been suggested, for example, that the description of the island as being as big as Asia and Libya (meaning Africa) could be interpreted as meaning an island halfway between Libya and Asia (meaning Asia Minor). And that Solon misunderstood Egyptian numbers by a factor of ten, which would make many of the stated dimensions of the island more reasonable and would also change the date of the catastrophe from an impossible nine thousand years earlier to nine hundred years earlier, i.e., 1500 B.C., which was approximately the date of the Santorini explosion.

Instead of torturing Plato's story to such an extent, however, it is much simpler to conclude that Plato's account of Critias' report of what Solon had heard in Egypt two centuries earlier can hardly be more than approximately or symbolically true. From an Egyptian point of view, Crete itself was indeed a very large island, located far off to the west. Like the Atlantans, the Minoans did use bulls in their religious ceremonies, which could well have been dedicated to Poseidon. The Minoan merchants may have impressed the Egyptians as "ful' of avarice and unrighteous power," and they certainly were rivals, if not attackers, of "our country and yours." Then came the "violent earthquakes and floods," which undoubtedly spread darkness and destruction as far as Egypt itself, and though the Egyptians may not have received accurate reports on the exact damage to Crete, they must have heard alarming stories of at least part of the Minoan empire suddenly sinking, as the center of Santorini did, beneath the seas.

Unfortunately, one must keep repeating that this is all largely conjecture— not only what might have happened to Atlantis, if there was an Atlantis, but what did happen to Crete. We know that the Minoan civilization was stricken not once but several times. The first devastation occurred in about 1700 B.C. The great palace at Knossos fell in ruins, and so did most of the lesser palaces in eastern Crete, Mallia, Phaistos, Kata Zakro. Though no one knows exactly what happened, the virtually simultaneous ruin of such separate citadels leads most scholars to believe that it was an earthquake that devastated the island. But the most important consequence was that the Minoans rebuilt their fallen palaces, restoring Knossos, in particular, to an even greater grandeur than before.

The tidal wave created by the Santorini explosion struck Crete in about 1500 B.C., perhaps as late as 1470, and it may have inundated the whole north shore of the island. Yet as nearly as archaeologists can determine, the second great collapse of the Minoan palaces occurred not in 1470 but in 1450, and Knossos, just inland from the north shore that faces Santorini, was the only major palace that did not fall. This may seem to show that the Santorini explosion was not what destroyed the Minoan empire after all, but that too is conjecture. And the Santorini explosion may have worked in a number of ways. One theory is that it was not the tidal wave but the rain of ash, blanketing the fields of Crete, that inflicted a slower but equally inexorable ruin. Another theory, perhaps more plausible, is that the explosion caused a political and social havoc even more devastating than the physical shock. If the Minoans' defensive warships and commercial fleets were wrecked, their fields and cities choked with volcanic debris, their entire social network smashed to pieces, then the ruin of the palaces must inevitably follow, either from the riots of starving survivors or from the attack of foreign invaders on the vulnerable kingdom. The consequence of the second fall of the palaces, in contrast to the first one, was that the Minoans never rebuilt them, never again occupied them. Knossos still stood, but the evidence indicates that the stricken citadel was now occupied, in about 1450 B.C., by Mycenean warriors from mainland Greece, the forefathers of King Agamemnon. About a century later, in 1380 B.C., Knossos itself was destroyed for the last time. Once again, nobody knows how. But by this time the Minoan civilization that had blazed across the Aegean for more than a thousand years was utterly dead.

The Santorini volcano lived on. It erupted over and over, creating new islets in the lagoon, joining them to the main island or tearing them apart again. One major eruption in 236 B.C. separated from the northwestern tip of Santorini a fragment now known as Therasia. In 196 B.C., the islet of Hiera rose from the sea. In A.D. 46, the islet of Thia similarly rose but then sank out of sight again. Stuart Rossiter's *Blue Guide* is eloquent in its nonchalant listing of more recent upheavals: "In 1570 the south coast of Thera, with the port of Eleusis, collapsed beneath the sea. Three years later Mikra Kaimeni appeared, and in 1711–12 Nea or Great Kaimeni. In February 1866 there began a violent eruption that . . . produced the George I volcano in the south of Great Kaimeni, and the islet of Aphtoessa, which disappeared in 1868. Another eruption began in July 1925, and lasted till May 1926; this joined Mikra and Nea Kaimeni. . . . An earthquake in July 1956 caused great damage; over half the buildings on the west coast were destroyed. . . ."

The cliffs that surround the old wound still rise nearly one thousand feet straight up out of the sea, and their shrieking layers of rock and ash still record the history of the explosion. "Where has one ever seen such colours," as Durrell wrote, "seen rock twisted up like barley-sugar, convoluted and coloured so fancifully . . . ? Mauve, green, putty, grey, yellow, scarlet, cobalt, . . . every shade of heat from that of pure molten rock to the tones of metamorphic limestone cooling back into white ash. And off the crest, like the manes of horses, little spurts of white ash drift down into the bay from the silent white houses."

One arrives in Santorini to survey the island of death, and one finds that the fabled cliffs tell a story of more than ash and lava, for as they rise they begin to slope. And as they slope, the volcanic debris softens into volcanic soil, and seeds begin to take hold, and the upper half of the dead cliffs sprout green with life. And yellow, for the grass that clings to these cliffs is speckled with daisy-like flowers known as wild chrysanthemums. The spring air is hazy, and the sea melts into the sky, and the far tip of the island seems to float in an infinity of blue. Far below, down where the ships are moored, two seagulls drift in aimless circles.

But as one looks down from the town of Fira, perched on the top of the cliffs, one cannot help seeing a blue plastic bag, filled with garbage and flung into a ravine, where it split open and spilled its rotting insides onto the hillside. Santorini, the dead island, is alive, and life in our time, perhaps in any time, means garbage among the flowers. People live here, and eat, and work, and go to church. There is a pumice mine, which grinds up the debris and ships it to Athens as an ingredient in concrete, and a factory that makes frames for spectacles. The fields around Fira are terraced with black volcanic rock and planted with grape vines that produce a brisk red wine, and the vintners provide it with legendary names: Volcan, Atlantis, Lava.

The main business of the island, of course, is to receive visitors. Almost every day, new cruise ships tie up in the lagoon, and the delegations of gray-haired Germans board the waiting donkeys and work their way up the twisting concrete stairway that climbs the cliffs to Fira, and then they descend like locusts on the row of little shops that wait to sell them Santorini T-shirts or hand-painted replicas of the volcano. Or anything else. VOLCAN DISCO, says one sign; ATLANTIS RENTACAR, says another, and then LAVA BOUTIQUE and ACHILLES FUR AND JEWELRY. Smaller signs on the doors announce that American Express cards are welcomed, also Carte Blanche, Visa, Eurocard.

It is easy enough to mock this commercialism, this guileless exploitation of a terrible disaster (which just might recur some day, strongly enough, at least, to send the souvenir shops and tavernas and jewelry boutiques plunging down the cliffs into the lagoon), and yet all of that too is part of the reassertion of the green force that survives volcanoes. Where once there was a mountain on which goats grazed, there is now a lagoon filled with plump crayfish and silvery mullet, and people can flourish at the edge of either, digging and building, selling and trading. But ghosts survive, too, and possibly vampires as well, and when one goes to sleep next to the window that looks out over the dark lagoon, one feels just a faint twinge of wonder at what strange things might occur during the moonlit night. When the sun's first rays touch the lagoon, the first sound of the morning in Santorini is the mighty crowing of a cock, somewhere on that hillside, hurling forth his challenge to the universe.

BOOK I

—

BARBARIANS

AT

THE GATES

—

On the day Gog attacks ... the fish in the sea and the birds of heaven, the wild beasts and all the reptiles that crawl along the ground, and all men on earth, will quake. Mountains will fall, cliffs crumble, walls collapse, and ... this is how they will learn that I am Yahweh.

—EZEKIEL 38:18–23

The Sack of Rome

A.D. 410

"Antichrist has already been born"

Saint Jerome, born Eusebius Sophronius Hieronymus, the greatest Christian scholar of his day and the first to translate the Bible into Latin, was working on his commentary on Ezekiel in a hillside cell near Bethlehem in the year of our Lord 410 when he heard that the city of Rome had been besieged, assaulted, conquered and sacked by barbarians, by Alaric, King of the Visigoths. Rome, where Jerome had studied poetry and rhetoric and the philosophy of Plato, where he had attended the courts of law and listened to skilled advocates pleading their cases in the Forum, was an impregnable citadel no longer. The fall reverberated from one end of the Mediterranean to the other. *"Quid salvum est si Roma perit?"* Jerome wrote to a friend. What is safe if Rome perishes?

Many of the early Christians anticipated the Second Coming of Christ as an imminent apocalypse, as Christ himself had foretold, and they saw this event inextricably associated with the destruction of Rome. "The fall and ruin of the world will soon take place," Lactantius Firminianus confidently predicted in his *Divinae Institutiones* early in the fourth century, "but it seems that nothing of the kind is to be feared as long as the city of Rome stands intact." When the invulnerability of the city began to seem less certain, the prospect of universal ruin began to acquire a terrifying reality. After the Goths annihilated the imperial army at Adrianople in 378, Saint Ambrose of Milan, who clearly identified the Goths with Ezekiel's Gog, proclaimed that "the end of the world is coming upon us." Saint Martin of Tours, laboring in vain to suppress the paganism that still flourished in the forests of Gaul, wrote anxiously of the coming of Antichrist, whose reign would signify the Last Days. *"Non est dubium, quin antichristus ...* There is no doubt that the Antichrist has already been born. Firmly established already in his early years, he will, after reaching maturity, achieve supreme power."

When Saint Martin died in 397, King Alaric of the Visigoths, having already broken away from Roman sovereignty and ravaged the countryside of Greece, established his armies in what is now Yugoslavia and prepared his first invasion of Italy. Scarcely more than a decade later, he was to stand in the burning city of Rome, the Gog prophesied by Ezekiel, the Antichrist of Saint Martin, and to all Romans of the old faith the incarnation of barbarism triumphant. Centuries later, Edward Gibbon still shuddered at the disaster. "Rome, the imperial city, which had subdued so considerable a part of mankind," he wrote, "was delivered to the licentious fury of the tribes of Germany and Scythia." The image lingers to this day—the imperial fortress besieged by barbarians, the gates stormed, women and children put to the sword, palaces plundered of their treasures, and all of the destruction lit by the ravenous flames of a city ablaze. If Rome perishes, what is safe?

✳

Rome itself had been built, of course, on the ruins of other cultures. The Etruscans, the Samnites, the Aequi and the Volsci—all the rival peoples of Italy were destined to be obliterated. When the Romans conquered Syracuse, Saint Augustine noted in *The City of God,* Marcus Marcellus wept at the fate that he felt obliged to impose: "[He] shed his own tears over it before he spilt its blood . . . yet the city was sacked according to the custom of war." The three Punic Wars against Carthage lasted a full century, and the Romans would settle, finally, for nothing less than total destruction. *Delenda est Carthago.* After three years of siege and a house-to-house battle from the outer walls to the central citadel, only about fifty thousand of the half-million Carthaginians survived to be sold into slavery in the year 146 B.C. Not only was the city razed, and all human habitation forbidden, but Roman priests solemnly dedicated the ruins to the gods of the underworld.

The Roman passion for conquest was insatiable. The Greek commercial center of Corinth, which had fought beside Athens at Thermopylae and Salamis, undertook the leadership of an Achaean League in resistance to Roman expansion. By order of the Roman Senate, the entire city was burned down. Ancient Thebes, once the capital of upper Egypt, ventured to rebel against Roman tax-gatherers, and it too was reduced to rubble. Pax Romana, the imperial authorities called it, a peace based on splendid roads, a code of law, and slavery. "To robbery, slaughter, plunder they give the lying name of empire," a noble Briton named Galgacus warned his countrymen, according to Tacitus' *Agricola.* "They make a desert and call it peace."

By the time of Christ, the Caesars ruled a territory so vast that they could almost equate it with the known world. Spreading outward in all directions from the sea that the Romans called Mare Nostrum, it extended roughly two thousand miles from Scotland south to the headwaters of the Nile and about three thousand miles from the Pillars of Hercules eastward to the sands of Persia. Its citizens and subject peoples numbered perhaps eighty million. One of the last and least important acquisitions of this giant empire was the coastal strip sometimes known as Palestine or Israel, actually the four disparate territories of Judea, Samaria, Galilee and Peraea. As had happened more than once in the region's past, two rivals were fighting for the position of high priest. Both appealed to the nearest Roman commander, Gnaeus Pompey, and Pompey responded by seizing Jerusalem in 63 B.C.

A series of inept and corrupt Roman procurators then ruled over the quarreling factions in Palestine. The Romans were relatively tolerant toward their new subjects, permitting them to continue their incomprehensible religious rituals and exempting them from such Roman innovations as the worship of each new emperor as a divinity. There were endless conflicts, however, and when the procurator Gessius Florus demanded a bribe of seventeen talents from the priests of the Temple of Herod, the Jews resisted. A bellicose nationalist group known as the Zealots killed a number of Roman soldiers and seized control of the Temple in May of A.D. 66. The Roman governor of Syria, Cestius Gallus, led a punitive expedition against Jerusalem, nearly recaptured the Temple, but then fled, losing about five thousand of his soldiers' lives in the flight. This was an affront that no Roman ruler could accept. The Emperor Nero, who only two years earlier had connived in the week-long burning of Rome and then, as Tacitus wrote, "fastened the guilt and inflicted the most exquisite tortures on a class hated for their abominations, called Christians," now decreed that the revolt in Jerusalem was to be ruthlessly suppressed.

In the last week of his life, Jesus Christ had heard someone praising the beauty and magnificence of the Temple, and he warned his disciples that within the coming generation it would be destroyed. "There shall not be left one stone upon another that shall not be thrown down," he said, according to Saint Luke. The disciples asked what signs would foretell this impending destruction, and Christ answered that all kinds of disasters would soon occur. "Nation shall rise against nation, and kingdom against kingdom," he said. "And great earthquakes shall be in divers places, and famines and pestilences; and fearful sights and great signs shall there be from heaven. . . . And when ye shall see Jerusalem compassed with armies, then know that the desolation thereof is nigh. . . . For these be the days of vengeance, that all things which are written may be fulfilled."

On the eve of Nero's invasion, there were, in fact, a whole series of omens and portents of the kind Jesus had foretold for Jerusalem. "First a star stood over the city, very like a broadsword, and a comet that remained a whole year," according to Flavius Josephus in *The Jewish War*. Then just at Passover in the year 66, Josephus went on, a light shone around the altar of the Temple at three in the morning, a light "so bright . . . that it might have been midday." This lasted for half an hour. "The inexperienced took it for a good omen, but the sacred scribes at once gave an interpretation which proved right." A few days later, an even more awesome event occurred: "When the priests had gone into the Inner Temple at night to perform the usual ceremonies, they declared that they were aware, first, of a violent movement and a loud crash, then of a concerted cry: 'Let us go hence.' " Josephus, himself born to the Judaic priesthood, interpreted this literally as God's public announcement that he was abandoning his chosen people.

Josephus also heard of another supernatural prophecy that sounded more promising, for it predicted that a man from Palestine would soon "become monarch of the whole world." Suetonius recorded a similar report: "There had spread all over the Orient an old and established belief, that it was fated at that time for men coming from Judea to rule the world." And Tacitus: "Rulers coming from Judea were to acquire universal empire." Interpreters of a later age might have considered this a prophecy of the coming triumph of Christianity, but many of the Jewish rebels apparently considered it a promise that they could defeat the Romans. Josephus even called that illusion "their chief inducement to go to war." Josephus and the two Roman historians emphatically declared that the prophecy obviously applied to Vespasian, the future emperor whom Nero had sent to command the invasion of Palestine, and to his son and deputy, Titus.

Vespasian, the victor in several campaigns for the conquest of Britain, undertook his new assignment with professional efficiency. His three legions, the fifth, tenth and fifteenth, together with some allied forces, totaled about 45,000 men, far fewer than the Jews had mobilized, but the Jews were little more than a rabble in arms; the trained and disciplined Roman legions were the panzer divisions of their day. Crossing the northern frontier of Galilee, Vespasian struck first at Gabara, captured it with his first assault, slaughtered the inhabitants, and burned everything.

This was the Roman policy throughout the four-year campaign: no pardons and no prisoners of war. In Japha, for example, Josephus recorded that "when the fighting men had been expended, the rest of the population were butchered in the open and in the houses, young and old together. For no male was left alive apart from infants in arms, who with the women were sold into slavery. Those who had been slaughtered . . . totaled 15,000, the slaves 2,130." In Samaria, where the defenders assembled on Mount Gerizim, the Romans "fell upon them and slew them all to the number of 11,600." And in Jotapata, where Josephus himself was the commander, the Romans spent several days searching through the ruins and killing anyone they could find. Josephus estimated the dead at 40,000, the enslaved women and children at 1,200. It is noteworthy that he wrote down these statistics not as an accuser but as an admirer, for he himself escaped execution by joining and serving the Romans; he survived to write his history as a pensioner of the Emperor Vespasian.

While the pacification of Palestine continued, the capital of the world was shaken by a series of political convulsions. In the year 68, when the legions in Spain and Gaul mutinied, the Senate and the Praetorian Guard threw their support to the governor of Spain, Sulpicius Galba. The terrified Emperor Nero fled with only four attendants, one of them a boy named Sporus whom Nero had castrated and ceremonially "married." After much faltering, the hated Emperor finally stabbed himself in the throat before the pursuing soldiery could seize him.

Galba lasted just seven months. Then a faction of the Praetorian Guard, complaining that the parsimonious new Emperor had failed to distribute the customary largesse, assassinated him and installed on the throne one of Nero's intimates, Marcus Salvius Otho. He, in turn, lasted only four months. The legions of Germany claimed for themselves the right to name emperors, and so they marched south to overthrow Otho and install as their creation a swinish official named Aulus Vitellius. "Prayers for either would be impious . . . ," Tacitus wrote in his *History,* "when from their conflict you can only learn that the conqueror must be the worse of the two." When Otho's forces were defeated near Cremona, he committed suicide.

The Senate duly recognized Vitellius as emperor, but now the legions of the East rebelled and swore allegiance to their own Vespasian. Vitellius tried at the last moment to hide in a doorkeeper's lodge, with a couch barricading the door, but Vespasian's soldiers dragged him out, tied a noose around his neck, and dragged him through the streets while the Romans jeered and threw dung at him. His mutilated body was flung into the Tiber.

Vespasian, the fifth Roman emperor in two years, left his son Titus to complete the subjugation of Palestine, which by now required only the conquest of Jerusalem. At thirty years of age, Titus was a man of heroic cast. Tacitus wrote glowingly of "the mingled beauty and majesty of his countenance," and Josephus repeatedly described him besting ten or twenty opponents in hand-to-hand combat. He also wrote verses in Greek and played the harp with considerable skill. (Mozart later celebrated the Emperor's legendary magnanimity in his last opera, *La Clemenza di Tito*.)

Jerusalem was a challenge worthy of all his abilities. Built on the crest of two hills, it was protected on the north by three mighty walls nearly forty feet high and on all other sides by steep ravines. Behind its fortifications, King Herod the Great had recently rebuilt the Temple of Solomon into a marvel of Hellenistic extravagance. Its double colonnades of white marble were nearly a mile in circumference. Its massive gates were plated with gold and silver, its walls hung with rich Babylonian tapestries. Herod had also built himself a luxurious palace, with huge banqueting halls and guest rooms with a hundred beds. "Its magnificence and equipment were unsurpassable . . . ," Josephus wrote. "The open spaces between [the colonnades] were all green lawns, with coppices of different trees traversed by long walks, which were edged by deep canals and cisterns everywhere plentifully adorned with bronze statues."

This fortress city, swollen by refugees to a population of more than a million, had been plagued for some time by fighting among its defenders. The two factions headed by John of Gischala and Simon ben Gioras not only battled each other in and out of the Temple but extorted support from the citizenry with floggings and torture. Once Titus set up his camp outside the north wall, however, the Zealots united for a fierce defense of the capital. Titus brought up huge battering rams to attack the walls; the Jews beat them back with a storm of arrows, rock and flaming pitch. Titus built seventy-five-foot wooden towers from which to bombard the defenders; the Jews charged forth and set them afire. The Jews fought with almost suicidal courage, but Titus' legions were not to be stopped. After two weeks of fighting, the outer wall was breached, and four days later the second gave way. Titus then suspended the attacks while he called on the Jews to surrender to Roman mercy.

Inside the besieged city, food was running out. "When hunger reigns, restraint is abandoned," Josephus wrote. "Thus it was that wives robbed their husbands, children their fathers and—most horrible—mothers their babes." The Zealots broke into houses in search of food and tortured anyone suspected of hiding it. Some of the starving citizens tried to slip out of the city by night, and a few of them swallowed gold coins to provide for future needs. When some of the Romans' auxiliaries discovered this ruse, they began eviscerating

any refugees they could catch. Titus deplored such murders, according to Josephus, but he encouraged his soldiers to gloat over their food rations in sight of
the famished defenders. When more refugees kept fleeing from the city, the
Roman commander began having them crucified and put on display outside
the walls. "Titus indeed realized the horror of what was happening, for every
day five hundred—sometimes even more—fell into his hands," the fawning
Josephus explained. "However, . . . to guard such a host of prisoners would tie
up a great proportion of his troops. But his chief reason for not stopping the
slaughter was the hope that the sight of it would perhaps induce the Jews to
surrender." When this tactic failed, the Romans tried another one. "Many of
the prisoners Titus ordered to have their hands cut off, that they might not be
thought to have deserted and might be believed . . . ," Josephus wrote. "Then
he sent them to Simon and John, urging those two to put an immediate end to
their resistance and not compel him to destroy the city."

The Jews still refused to surrender, and it took three months of fighting and
famine before Titus' troops ultimately forced their way to the gates of Herod's
Temple. Though Titus ordered that the holy sanctuary be saved, according to
Josephus, one of his soldiers, "urged on by some unseen force, snatched up a
blazing piece of wood and climbing on another soldier's back hurled the brand
through a golden aperture." The Jews gave a cry of horror and tried to quench
the fire, but within a few minutes the whole Temple was ablaze. The Romans
plunged on through the adjoining streets, slaughtering and plundering anyone
they encountered. Then they raised their battle standards in front of the flaming Temple, performed their pagan sacrifices and hailed Titus as *imperator.*
The priests of the Temple begged Titus to spare their lives, but he said the time
for pardons was past and ordered them executed. The last defenders behind the
walls of the upper city offered to abandon Jerusalem if they could simply depart with their wives and children. Titus refused. His soldiers stormed the last
wall and killed everyone they could find. They even invaded the sewers to root
out the last fugitives, among them John and Simon. Then they burned the city
to the ground.

Josephus estimated the total of dead at 1.1 million. Of the surviving prisoners, some of the handsomest were saved for display at Titus' prospective triumph in Rome, some of the strongest were sent in chains to hard labor in
Egypt, and others were used as human sacrifices at the ceremonies that the
Romans called games. Titus himself, before returning to Rome, celebrated his
younger brother's birthday at Caesarea by having 2,500 of his Jewish prisoners
die in combat with each other, by being fed to wild animals or by being burned
alive.

*

"And I stood upon the sand of the sea, and saw a beast rise up out of the sea,
having seven heads and ten horns . . . and upon his heads the name of blasphemy. . . . And they worshiped the beast, saying, Who is like unto the beast?
Who is able to make war with him?"

Throughout the centuries, the great Beast of the Apocalypse has seemed to symbolize all that is fearful and monstrous, the Rome of the Inquisition, the marching armies of Nazi Germany, but to the prophet known as John of Patmos the beast that he saw in his vision represented the Roman Empire, and specifically that emperor who first persecuted the Christians—Nero. There was a legend in those days (indeed, it lasted until the twelfth century) that Nero had not really committed suicide. He would reappear in the East, at the head of an army from the Parthian Empire, to reestablish his tyranny in Rome. At least three impostors who claimed to be Nero attempted insurrections in various provinces. Hence John's report that the beast had a "deadly wound [that] was healed," and that it was a creature "that was, and is not, and yet is."

About John of Patmos himself there is considerable mystery. It is generally thought, though, that he was a preacher exiled to the Aegean island of Patmos for his public avowals of Christianity, and that he wrote his Book of Revelation during the reign of Titus' cruel younger brother, Domitian, probably in about the year 95. Though John's poetic images of beasts and dragons lend themselves to many interpretations, his clear purpose was to warn his contemporaries in Asia Minor of coming persecutions, to rally the threatened Christians against any surrenders to Roman force, and to reaffirm the coming triumph of the true faith.

The beast appears, in John's vision, only after an awesome series of disasters. First the Lamb of God opened the seven seals on the holy book, and each opening of a seal brought war, famine, death, "and the sun became black as sackcloth . . . and the moon became as blood, and the stars of heaven fell unto the earth, even as a fig tree casteth her untimely figs, when she is shaken of a mighty wind." Then came seven angels with trumpets, and each trumpet call brought earthquakes, storms of fire, the sea turning to blood, darkness everywhere, and swarms of locusts emerging from the bottomless pit. "And in those days shall men seek death, and shall not find it."

The beast represented Roman might—"power was given him over all kindreds, and tongues and nations"—and that was why his worshipers claimed that no one was "able to make war with him." But the greatest crime of the Roman emperors, in John's eyes, was their blasphemous insistence that all their subjects in various lands worship them as divine, together with the goddess they called Roma. John transformed Roma into the great Whore of Babylon, who rode on the beast, adding to its brute strength her own powers of seduction. "The woman was arrayed in purple and scarlet color," he wrote with passionate loathing, "and decked with gold and precious stones and pearls, having a golden cup in her hand full of abominations and filthiness of her fornication." The kings of the Roman world all took part in this fornication, and all the merchants "waxed rich through the abundance of her delicacies," and she herself became "drunken with the blood of the saints."

John prophesied that the beast would have power for only forty-two months, and then he would have to confront the Lord and his 144,000 saints (twelve thousand for each of the twelve tribes of Israel) at "a place called . . . Armageddon." And thus would destruction come to the city that John called Babylon but apparently intended as Babylon's successor, Rome. John saw an angel, and the angel cried, "Babylon the great is fallen, is fallen, and is become the habitation of devils, and the hold of every foul spirit, and a cage of every hateful and unclean bird." The great beast would then be cast alive into a lake of burning brimstone, and Satan would be bound for a thousand years, and Christ would return to earth. And after a thousand years, Satan would be loosed again, and defeated again, and cast into the lake of fire to be "tormented day and night for ever and ever." And then, finally, the New Jerusalem would descend from heaven and God himself would reign over his people. "And God shall wipe away all tears from their eyes," John wrote, "and there shall be no more death, neither sorrow, nor crying, neither shall there be any more pain: for the former things are passed away."

At about the time that John saw his vision, in the first century of the Christian era, the Germanic tribes were starting to break through the Roman barricades along the Rhine. And far behind those border wars, there began the long southward migration of the Goths. They seem to have come from Sweden, possibly from the Baltic island still known as Gottland. Their first historian, a sixth-century monk named Jordanes, described their homeland as an island, Scandza, but he said that its western shores faced an impassable ocean, so he may have been referring to the whole Scandinavian peninsula. "Now, from this island of Scandza, as from a hive of races or a womb of nations," Jordanes wrote in *De Origine Actibusque Getarum,* "the Goths are said to have come forth long ago under their king, Bering by name. . . ."

They landed on the coast of Pomerania, near what was one day to become the city of Danzig, or Gdansk. They roamed more than a thousand miles southward along the banks of the Vistula, across what is now Poland, and the Ukraine. By the third century, they had established themselves on the northwestern shores of the Black Sea, in the region known as Scythia. From there, they could observe the rich harvests in the neighboring Roman province of Dacia, now Romania. The Goths had their own cattle and their own plows, but they were a warlike people, and they began to forage along the edges of the Empire. Tacitus had observed long ago that the Germanic tribes "think it tame and stupid to acquire by the sweat of toil what they might win by blood."

These were violent times—as, in different ways, all times are. The Goths roamed as far as Greece and Asia Minor, not thieves and murderers, really, but warriors, who took what they wanted. It fell to the Emperor Decius to challenge the marauders, in the year 251, and so the two forces clashed in a Bulgarian swamp. The first two of the three Gothic lines buckled and turned, but the third stood fast. It was the Romans who finally fled from that dark forest. The Emperor Decius' son was killed by an arrow. The body of Decius himself was lost forever in the swamp. The Goths thereafter occupied the province of Dacia and charged Rome an annual tribute in corn to stay north of the Danube.

There, about a century later, they came into conflict with the Huns, originally named Hiung-nu, or slaves, by the Chinese, who invaded their Mongolian grazing lands and drove them westward across the steppes of central Asia.

Jordanes, the Gothic monk, seems to have been unable to imagine such an origin for these tribal enemies. They were actually descended, he wrote, from certain Gothic women whom King Filimer decreed to be witches. "He expelled these women from the midst of his race and compelled them to wander in solitary exile afar from his army," Jordanes wrote. "There the unclean spirits, who beheld them as they wandered through the wilderness, bestowed their embraces upon them and begat this savage race, which dwelt at first in the swamps, a stunted, foul and puny tribe, scarcely human, ... fiercer than ferocity itself."

Despite Jordanes' epithets, the "foul and puny" Huns were such expert cavalrymen that they were eventually hired to serve in the vanguard of the so-called Roman legions, which already consisted mainly of Germans and Slavs. The Huns' first victims, however, were the tribes that had settled along the Black Sea. In A.D. 372 they collided with the Alani and sent them fleeing westward. They smashed the Ostrogothic King Hermanric, who killed himself in the desperation of defeat. The Visigoths, then led by Athanaric, marched to the banks of the Dniester River to challenge the invaders and were utterly routed.

The remnants of the whole Gothic nation, perhaps 100,000 (though Gibbon estimated the total as high as one million), fled south to the Danube and pleaded with the border guards for permission to settle within the confines of the Roman Empire. "Standing upon the river bank in a state of great excitement," according to the chronicle of Eunapius, they "stretched out their hands from afar with loud lamentations and earnestly begged that they might be allowed to cross over the river...." The Emperor Valens, who had already waged two bloody campaigns against the Goths, hesitated briefly, then granted his permission—on two conditions. The Goths were to surrender all their weapons, and the Gothic chiefs were to give up their children as hostages, for resettlement in various towns throughout the empire. The Goths accepted their degradation and then began paddling their crude boats and rafts across the mile-wide estuary of the Danube. These were scarcely the invading barbarians of legend but rather a swarm of starving refugees.

The Romans treated them accordingly. The corrupt military governors of Thrace, Lupicinus and Maximus, imposed heavy taxes on the newcomers, and, as Jordanes wrote, "sold to them at a high price not only the flesh of sheep and oxen but even the carcasses of dogs and unclean animals." When the Goths complained, their new leader, Fritigern, was summoned to a conference with Lupicinus. The Romans fed him a sumptuous dinner, and then ambushed him in his tent. Fritigern fought his way out with his sword. "That day put an end to the famine of the Goths and the safety of the Romans," Jordanes wrote with some pride, "for the Goths, no longer as strangers and pilgrims, but as citizens and lords, began to rule." The Goths, in other words, rose in revolt, defeated the provincial forces sent against them, and then attacked the city of Adrianople, less than 150 miles from the capital, Constantinople.

The Emperor Valens marched forth, at the head of an army of about sixty thousand men, to destroy them. Up to the last minute, Fritigern offered to make peace if the Goths could only be allowed to settle in some deserted lands in Thrace, with an allowance of corn and cattle. The Emperor Valens refused the offer and launched his attack, August 9, A.D. 378. It was a disastrous decision. Fritigern's Goths routed the Roman cavalry, then surrounded the infantry and slaughtered them. Valens, wounded by an arrow, fled to a nearby cottage. A band of Goths pursued him there, only to be driven back by Roman archers who had established themselves on the roof of the cottage. The Goths set the cottage on fire. "And thus," as Jordanes put it, "he was cremated in royal splendor. Plainly it was a direct judgment of God." If so, it was also a direct judgment of God that about two thirds of Valens' army, some forty thousand men, should die on the battlefield of Adrianople, and that the whole Empire of the East should lie helpless before the victorious Visigoths.

The Goths did not take great advantage of their victory. Perhaps they did not realize the extent of what they had won. They were still looking for a land to settle in, with their cattle and their wagons and what remained of their children, and when Fritigern died soon after the victory at Adrianople, his people simply roamed across northern Greece, a vast straggling tribe of marauders. The Romans did not rally to defend their lands, but reacted with characteristic guile. In all the towns throughout the empire where the Gothic children had been resettled at the time of the crossing of the Danube, they were now ordered to assemble in the main marketplaces. They were told that they were to be resettled once again, with gifts of land and money. Once these barbarian children had been assembled in the various forums and marketplaces of the civilized world, they were attacked by Roman soldiers and slaughtered.

Valens' successor, the Spaniard Theodosius, did his best both to reorganize the imperial forces and to placate the Goths. He discovered their former leader, Athanaric, who had been pushed aside after his defeat by the Huns, and invited him to a consultation within the walls of Constantinople. The Gothic chieftain was overwhelmed. "I now behold what I never could believe," he said, according to Jordanes' chronicle, "the glories of this stupendous capital. . . . Indeed, the Emperor of the Romans is a god upon earth, and the presumptuous man who dares to lift a hand against him is guilty of his own blood." The overawed Athanaric thereupon committed the whole Gothic army to the service of the empire. He stayed on in Constantinople and attended a series of imperial banquets, and shortly thereafter he died. It was never actually proved that the Romans had poisoned him, but such an act would hardly have violated either the Roman practice of politics or the Roman sense of hospitality to barbarians. In any case, they staged a splendid funeral for Athanaric, erected a monument to his memory, and enrolled his armies as *foederati,* or allies, under the imperial banners of Rome.

So the Goths were finally pacified and settled, a decade after their crossing of the Danube, within the empire, in the province of Moesia, now known as Bulgaria. But although they swore fidelity to the empire, they refused to disperse and become simple Roman subjects. They stayed together, establishing their own camps and villages. They spoke their own language. They clung to their barbarian custom of voting on who should be their chief. When it came to fighting, however, they were ready to do battle for Theodosius. In 392, a distinguished Roman general named Arbogastes, of Frankish origin, rebelled against the Western Emperor Valentinian, and had him strangled, and put forward the imperial claims of a pagan usurper named Eugenius. The Goths, some twenty thousand warriors, rallied to Theodosius. Among them was a young nobleman named Alaric, of a family known as Balthi, meaning bold. With the Visigoths fighting for Theodosius, the Emperor was invincible. The usurper Eugenius' head was cut off as he lay begging for mercy from the Emperor; Arbogastes fell on his own sword. The statues of Jupiter that Eugenius had installed at a number of mountain passes were cast down and desecrated by the Christian imperial troops and their Gothic allies.

Scarcely four months later, in January of the year 395, the Emperor Theodosius, known for both his military prowess and his religious orthodoxy as Theodosius the Great, died of dropsy. He left the empire divided between his two incompetent young sons, Arcadius, aged seventeen, Emperor of the East, and Honorius, aged eleven, Emperor of the West. Neither of the new emperors had any real authority, either political or military, and in the camp of the imperial allies Alaric demanded to know why the victorious Gothic armies should remain subject to the rule of boys. "He took counsel with his men," as the Gothic historian Jordanes briefly reported this decisive change in his people's fortunes, "and persuaded them to seek a kingdom by their own exertions rather than serve others in idleness."

The fourth century was not only an age of tribal warfare but also one of intense religious conflict. Indeed, the two are inseparable. To many of the most gifted and passionate men of that era, the task of defining Christian orthodoxy was the most important issue confronting Roman civilization, and the defense of that orthodoxy was the most compelling element in the defense of Rome itself. And since orthodoxy governed the writing of history for the next millennium, it taught all subsequent generations to judge the combatants of the fourth century by criteria that many of them never accepted, never even knew.

One of the main reasons why the Visigoths have traditionally been regarded as invading barbarians rather than as soldiers of the Lord is that they followed the teachings of a saintly man named Ulfila, or Wulfila (meaning Little Wolf). His parents had lived in the Roman province of Cappadocia, in Asia Minor, and had been carried off as prisoners during the Gothic attacks in the time of the Emperor Decius. So Ulfila was born and raised among the Goths, but with a sense of Roman parentage, and when he was about twenty, in the year 332, he came to Constantinople as either an envoy or a hostage from the Goths.

In the capital of the East, Ulfila turned to the study of theology. Indeed, it was difficult to do otherwise. "This city," according to a contemporary account by Gregory Nazianzen, "is full of mechanics and slaves, who are all of them profound theologians, and preach in the shops and in the streets. If you desire a man to change a piece of silver, he informs you wherein the Son differs from the Father." This question of the difference between the Son and the Father was of overwhelming concern to the intellectual caste of the fourth century.

The Alexandrian monk Arius argued that it was incredible for God the Father, creator of the universe, to have become incarnate in the form of Jesus Christ, that Jesus must have been a creation of God, imbued with the Logos but hardly identical with his creator.

The Council of Nicea, summoned by the Emperor Constantine to resolve this dispute, decided in the year 325 that Arius was wrong. The Father, the Son and the Holy Ghost were one, in all ways, now and forevermore. This ruling failed to settle the dispute, however. At the Council of Rimini, in the year 359, the assembled theologians decided the exact opposite, and their decision was confirmed the following year at the Council of Constantinople. At both of these gatherings, Jesus was decreed to be "like" (*homoios*) God the Father but not "of the same essence." In Constantinople, therefore, the Arians remained convinced of their own logic, and their own orthodoxy, and when Ulfila was ordained by a bishop and sent northward to convert the Goths in 341, he carried with him what the Catholic Church later condemned as the plague of the Arian heresy.

In the wilderness north of the Danube, these theological distinctions were of relatively little importance. Athanaric, King of the Visigoths, was still a pagan—that is, a believer in the god of his fathers, the Norse god Odin. He responded to the Christian teachings of Ulfila by sending his own priests from tent to tent and demanding obedience to the rituals of animal sacrifice. Anyone who refused was confined within his tent, and the tent was then set afire. Ulfila retreated back across the Danube in 349, but now he brought with him what a contemporary chronicler called "a great body of the faithful," and this migration of persecuted Gothic Christians may have had an important influence on the Emperor Valens when the rest of the Goths subsequently pleaded for refuge from the Huns.

Valens too was an Arian. One of his priests, Eudoxius, urged the migrating Goths to take communion with the Emperor, and though they hesitated, they finally agreed to do whatever Ulfila advised. "Their bishop Ulfilas was implicitly obeyed by them," according to the *Ecclesiastical History* by Theodoretus, bishop of Cyprus, "and they received his words as laws, which none might break. Partly by the fascination of his eloquence and partly by the bribes with which he baited his proposals, Eudoxius succeeded in inducing him to persuade the barbarians to embrace communion with the Emperor, so Ulfilas won them over on the plea that the quarrel between the different parties was really one of personal rivalry and involved no difference in doctrine. The result is that up to this day the Goths assert that the Father is greater than the Son."

Poor Ulfila devoutly went his way, converting more and more of the Goths, in the course of his long life, to a form of Christianity that was to be branded heresy, and heresy, in the view of the church, was worse than paganism. Ulfila seems not to have known that. To bring Christianity to his people, he determined to translate the entire Bible into Gothic (or most of it; he left out the violent chronicles of the Books of Kings on the ground that such accounts might inflame the warlike Goths to unchristian acts). And since the Goths had no written language, Ulfila invented one for them, devising an alphabet of twenty-four characters and adapting the Greek script to the spoken sounds of the Gothic tongue. He was, in other words, not only the Saint Jerome of the Goths but also their Homer. His Bible, which antedates any other known Germanic text by about three centuries, spread the Gothic language among the Vandals and other neighboring tribes and made Gothic the lingua franca, if that is the right term, of Central Europe.

In the year 380, three years before Ulfila died, the Emperor Theodosius finally pronounced anathema on that form of Christianity to which Ulfila had converted the Goths. "It is our pleasure," he decreed, "that all nations which are governed by our clemency and moderation should steadfastly adhere to the religion which was taught by Saint Peter to the Romans. . . . And as we judge that all others are extravagant madmen, we brand them with the infamous name of heretics." Ulfila, the uncanonized saint of the Goths, may enjoy a saint's revenge. His Bible was copied and recopied enough times so that one version—painted in silver on pages of purple vellum, but only a fragment, actually, consisting of the four books of the Gospels, the Pauline letters, and three books of the Old Testament—survived. Survived Theodosius and all the other Roman emperors and all the orthodox bishops and all the barbarians of all sorts, survived and reappeared, finally, in the seventeenth century, in a monastery at Werden, near Cologne. And was taken from there to Prague, and then was seized by the Swedes, who were once again ravaging Germany during the Thirty Years' War. And was presented by these Swedes to their Queen Christina, and ultimately brought to rest at the University of Uppsala, in the land of Scandza, from which the Goths first came, two thousand years ago.

Of the young Alaric we know so little that he seems almost eponymous, like Cain or Achilles, a mere symbol of the tribe that was destined to conquer Rome. He is said to have been born in about A.D. 360, on the island of Peuce in the Danube delta. We know nothing of his parentage except that his family, the Balthi, was considered to be one of the most noble among all the Visigothic clans, descended from the god Balder, one of the lords of Valhalla. His original name of Ala-Reiks meant Master of All, but he himself wanted to be known by the Latin name of Alaricus.

Historians live on suppositions, inferences, guesses pieced together from old coins and inscriptions. They have supposed that Alaric was born into what the Goths considered their aristocracy, that he somehow survived without undue hardship the tribal crossing of the Danube. They have supposed that he grew to be a powerful young warrior, tall and red-haired, a master of sword and bow and battle-ax. And that the clansmen who had pledged themselves to the imperial army as *foederati* took the youth with them on a series of campaigns in Gaul and Spain. And that he acquired a Roman education, and a knowledge of Greek and Latin literature. And that he rose, at about the age of thirty, to the rank of officer during Theodosius' victorious struggle against the pagan usurper Eugenius. And that he and his troops were sent home, for some mysterious reason, perhaps the jealousy of other officials, to the tribal camp in Moesia.

There, perhaps in the very year that Theodosius died, A.D 395, the Visigoths are said to have lifted Alaric onto a shield and thrown him into the air with shouts of *"Thiudans! Thiudans!"* (The King! The King!). Thus Alaric was crowned and enthroned, but his was a throne without a kingdom. The Goths were a people but a people divided (there were Goths already high in the imperial service and Goths still living along the Black Sea), a people who had spent more than three centuries searching for a homeland.

The tribal reservation in Moesia that had been assigned to the Visigoths was not what they wanted. They were warriors. They complained to Alaric, their new king, that they had fought the battles of their Emperor Theodosius and that they deserved some future better than they could see in the fields of Moesia. Alaric could hardly disagree. He himself may have had visions of his own future as *magister militum,* commander of the imperial army. He probably thought of himself, in other words, not as a barbarian invader but as a tribal ruler who had earned a higher imperial authority for himself and his people.

Such ambitions would hardly have been unusual, for the Roman Empire, which was still referred to as a republic, had become less an empire than a disheveled confederation of warlords. Rome itself had been abandoned as an inconvenient center for imperial rule since the era of Diocletian, and the two inept young sons of Theodosius the Great now maintained their courts in the two capitals of the divided empire, Milan and Constantinople. In both of these courts, the true power was exercised not by the boyish emperors but by generals from the far provinces. In Constantinople, this unofficial ruler was an infinitely corrupt Spaniard named Rufinus; in Milan, the Emperor Theodosius had bequeathed his authority, though not his throne, to a warrior named Stilicho, son of a Vandal chieftain. Theodosius had also bequeathed to Stilicho his niece Serena as a bride. Stilicho, in turn, gave his daughter Maria in marriage to the Emperor Honorius, then fourteen. Stilicho undoubtedly had ambitions of taking command of the imperial throne. So did Rufinus. So, perhaps, did Alaric. At the very least, he could look southward from his camp in the mountains of Moesia and observe the lands of the Caesars spread out before him like a banquet table. Alaric has been viewed for centuries as a lord of rapine and plunder, but perhaps he more nearly resembled the eternal provincial regarding the impregnable city with a sense of awe and yearning, the Balzacian hero scraping his muddy boots at the crossroads of Montparnasse.

King Alaric saw the possibilities, and he attacked. Late in the year 395, the year of the death of the Emperor Theodosius and the year of his own election as King of the Visigoths, the year in which he had persuaded his people "to seek a kingdom by their own exertions," Alaric led his bristling tribesmen out of the hills of Moesia and through the undefended crossroads of Thessaly. His objective may have been Constantinople itself, and although he could hardly have hoped to conquer the strongly fortified capital, the threat brought forth Rufinus, chief minister at the imperial court. Rufinus ordered his forces to a halt a few miles from the Goths, then asked for a private meeting with Alaric. To the dismay of his lieutenants, Rufinus took off his imperial uniform and went to the meeting wearing the leather and furs of the Goths. What happened at that encounter can only be inferred from the fact that Alaric forthwith turned away from Constantinople and marched southward to plunder Greece. Some kind of compact had obviously been made. Rufinus claimed to have saved the imperial capital; his enemies charged him with betraying its richest province.

Stilicho, the Vandal who commanded the armies of the West, augmented by a number of Eastern legions left behind from the campaign against the usurper Eugenius, decided to challenge Alaric's invasion of Greece. He may have thought, as his enemies suggested, that a victory over Alaric would enable him to march on and seize control of the Eastern Empire. At the least, he apparently hoped to assert the Western Empire's authority over the disputed province of Illyricum (Yugoslavia), which had become the empire's richest area for the recruitment of troops. (Recruitment is the polite and customary term, but Brooks Adams was probably more accurate when he described the process as "really slave hunts on a gigantic scale.")

Stilicho marched his legions as far as Thessaly, and there he came face to face with Alaric's Visigoths. Both sides prepared themselves for battle, the outnumbered Goths behind their traditional circle of wagons, the Roman legions assembling into their thick ranks. Trumpet calls and the swinging of swords and the chanting of battle cries. Then, at the very hour of battle, a horseman suddenly galloped in from Constantinople with a letter from the Emperor Arcadius, a letter reflecting all the Eastern court's suspicions of Stilicho's ambitions. The general was ordered to halt his campaign immediately, to send his Eastern troops back to Constantinople by themselves and to take his own troops back to Italy. Stilicho and his soldiers, reined in at the very edge of victory over the outnumbered Goths, hesitated for a moment of bitter disappointment, then obeyed.

This maneuver, like so many before it, seems to have been the work of Rufinus. The suspicious chief minister at Constantinople did not want his Western counterpart, Stilicho, to assert his authority in the East, for he was doing his best to persuade the Emperor Arcadius to make him co-emperor. Indeed, Rufinus had already minted coins that celebrated his own accession, and in a dream a spirit told him, "High above the people shalt thou be raised." But as Rufinus and Arcadius reviewed the returning troops, who had been marched back to Constantinople under a Gothic commander named Gainas, the chief minister did not realize that a number of the discontented legionaries had encircled him, and that they were steadily tightening the circle around him. When the Goth's troops had surrounded Rufinus, one of them stepped forward with raised sword and shouted, "With this sword Stilicho strikes thee!" And stabbed him. The other soldiers hacked Rufinus' body to pieces. They chopped off his head and, as the spirit had foretold, carried it through Constantinople on the tip of a spear.

So Alaric was free to march southward, past the province of Olympus, past the defile of Thermopylae, and right to the outskirts of Athens. There, mysteriously, he stopped. According to *Historia Nova* by Count Zosimus, a guileless advocate of the pagan faith and also one of the few surviving sources of information on this period, Alaric was about to strike when he was deterred by a vision of Athena herself. "He beheld Athene Promachus, just as she is represented in her statues, clothed in full armor, going round about the walls," Zosimus wrote, without the slightest sign of skepticism about Alaric's vision. Achilles too appeared, displaying an "aspect of divine rage and thirst for battle." Neither of these two classic spirits actually did anything, but their appearance had its effect. "Awestruck at the sight," Zosimus continued, "Alaric desisted from his warlike enterprise . . . and concluded a treaty with the Athenians. After which he entered the city in peaceful guise with a few of his followers, was hospitably entertained by the chief inhabitants, received presents from them, and departed."

This was neither the first nor the last time that the pagan gods suddenly materialized to save civilization from the Christian attacker from the north. Though the Emperor Constantine had encountered little opposition in establishing Christianity as the state religion early in the fourth century, there were still many pagans among Rome's powerful and conservative old families, and thus among the judges and teachers and civil servants. Despite the laws that Theodosius had decreed, forbidding any practice of their religion, they regarded the invasion of Alaric as a punishment for the public abandonment of the traditional religion, and for the official establishment of a strange sect from the Middle East as the only legal form of worship. The evidence for that dark view was strong, and it would take all the rhetorical power of Saint Augustine to convince the citizens of the crumbling empire that the pagan critics were "ungrateful men who blasphemously impute to Christ the calamities which they deservedly suffer in consequence of their own wicked ways."

In the following year, A.D 396, while Alaric was still at large in Greece, Stilicho once again set forth from Italy with an army organized to destroy him. This time, his fleet landed in the Peloponnesus and soon trapped the Visigoths in the mountains of Arcadia. Stilicho was reluctant to fight, however, reluctant to commit himself and to risk severe casualties. Instead, he waited for hunger to ravish the encircled Goths. He underestimated Alaric. The King of the Visigoths found an unguarded point in the Roman circle, struck at it with all his force and broke free. He marched northward, not only with his army intact but with his wagons filled with the riches of Greece. It was such a stunning escape that the chroniclers of the time could not believe that Stilicho had not conspired to permit it. The Spanish prelate Paulus Orosius used the word "treason," and Zosimus charged, perhaps more accurately, that Stilicho was "wasting his time with harlots and buffoons when he should have been keeping close watch on the enemy."

It is much simpler to regard Alaric as a master of guerrilla warfare, a master of the feint and the surprise attack. Having broken through Stilicho's encirclement, he marched northward with his wagonloads of booty and reestablished himself in the foothills of the Balkans. From that haven, he imperiously informed the court of Arcadius that he would be willing to make peace. His terms were simple. He was ready to accept a commission as the Roman commander for the disputed territory of Illyricum, and to settle there with his Goths. The imperial court groveled and agreed. Alaric thus acquired what he had long sought—a land for his people and imperial authority for himself. But the court of Constantinople had its own reasons, aside from its desire to keep Alaric out of Greece, for giving in so easily to his demands. Since Illyricum was border territory claimed by both East and West, Arcadius, in presenting it to Alaric, was simply inviting him to defend it against Stilicho.

This Eastern strategy was fully understood in the West, as we can tell from the verses of one of Stilicho's courtiers. Claudian was his name. He was an Egyptian, one of the last exemplars of Latin poetry and one of the last secular chroniclers of Rome's downfall. He produced state poetry, panegyrics on various consulships, even an epithalamium on Honorius' marriage to Maria, and in these florid verses historians have had to pan and sift for what few fragments of fact might be discovered. How to translate them is yet another problem. The standard version by Maurice Platnauer (1923) relies simply on antique prose, but Thomas Hodgkin, fellow of University College in London and author of the luxurious chronicle entitled *Italy and Her Invaders* (1880–89), believed that Claudian's incorrigible unreliability might best be conveyed by presenting him in the fustian of rhymed couplets. Thus the Victorian version of the Roman poet decrying, in *De Bello Getico,* the Eastern Empire's surrender of Roman territory to Alaric:

> And in law's name he sways the trembling crew
> Whose wives he ravished and whose sons he slew.

Hodgkin's suspicion of Claudian is validated when the poet presumes even to imagine what Alaric might have said to himself at this moment of triumph in Illyricum:

> So fate was with me, So the Emperor gave
> The very race I plundered as my slave.

*

In the year 400, King Alaric suddenly repudiated his role as imperial governor of Illyricum and launched his first invasion of Italy. His motive is unknown. To those who regard the Goths simply as barbarian invaders, the tempting weakness of Italy was cause enough; those who view the Goths more sympathetically can only guess at what the Roman provocation may have been. Or perhaps the prospect of such an invasion was the Eastern court's main purpose in establishing Alaric in Illyricum, on the border of the Western Empire.

In any case, Alaric led his fur-clad warriors and their women and their wagons down from the mountains of Croatia and onto the Venetian plain. He encountered a Roman army under the walls of Aquileia and scattered it. (Aquileia was then the fortress city at the head of the Adriatic, though Attila's Huns burned it to the ground a half century after Alaric's passage, and the survivors fled into the marshes to found the city that would eventually replace it, Venice.) He marched south toward the fortified city of Ravenna, where he may have thought the Emperor Honorius was to be found. And then, after reconnoitering the swamps and marshes that surrounded Ravenna, turned completely around and marched westward toward Milan, the true residence of the cowering Honorius.

At this same time, another Gothic army, headed by a chieftain named Radagaisus, marched through what we now call the Brenner Pass and descended upon the plains of Lombardy. And although we do not know the exact relationship between Alaric and Radagaisus—there may well have been none at all—we do know that Stilicho mistakenly considered Radagaisus' invasion the more threatening of the two. "Cease your unmanly lamentations," he told the Romans, according to Claudian's verses. "The Goths have . . . perfidiously stolen into our country . . . , but Italy has borne and overborne worse shocks of fate than this."

Stilicho was apparently alone in his bravado. At the imperial court in Milan the fainéant Emperor Honorius and his frightened favorites consulted the oracles. There had been showers of stones and eclipses of the moon and unseasonal swarms of bees. When Honorius went to inspect some troops, two wolves suddenly appeared and attacked the soldiers. The soldiers fought back, and killed the wolves, and cut them open. Inside each one they found a human hand, one right hand and one left hand, and both still pink, as though alive.

Honorius and his ministers in Milan thought only of flight. Perhaps to Corsica or Sardinia, where a number of nobles had by now established sanctuaries for themselves, perhaps even to the banks of the Rhone. It would be interesting indeed to know the state of mind of the threatened Romans, to know whether they saw themselves at the edge of disaster, but virtually no written evidence on this question has survived. One letter by a wealthy landowner named Q. Aurelius Symmachus, for instance, does not even mention the Gothic invasion, only that Symmachus had made a long detour, because of unsafe roads, to reach the court at Milan. Occasionally, there are references to the dangers of brigandage, but that was almost commonplace.

Stilicho apparently rallied the court to a semblance of courage and set off to defend the empire. Heading north to Lake Como, he mobilized a number of garrisons into an improvised army and pushed Radagaisus' Goths back into what is now Austria. "From dreadful doom," sang the poet Claudian, "he, in those Alpine huts, redeemed thee, Rome." And then marched south again to find that Rome, far from having been redeemed, was much more gravely threatened by Alaric.

The King of the Visigoths had cut his way across northern Italy and was now besieging Pollentia, a thriving city some twenty miles southeast of Turin. According to Claudian's fanciful account, a number of Gothic elders felt profound misgivings about this invasion. One of them, says Claudian, "shook his white and shaggy locks" as he recounted that thirty years had passed since the Goths' crossing of the Danube. "But never, believe me in this, O Alaric, did the weight of adverse battle lie so heavy on us as now. . . . Why talk to us perpetually of the fruitful vines of Etruria, of the Tiber, and of Rome? If our fathers have told us aright, that city is protected by the immortal gods." Alaric scolded the old warrior for his superstition and then told of a vision that he himself had experienced. He had been walking in a grove of sacred oaks, he said, when he had heard a chorus of voices, as from the trees themselves, promising him the conquest of Rome that very year. *"Hoc impiger anno/ Alpibus italiae ruptis, penetrabis ad urbem. . . ."* (Thou shalt penetrate to the city itself).

It was nearly Easter of the year 402 when Stilicho's legions marched up to confront Alaric at Pollentia. Marched up and then once again paused and reconnoitered. They found the barbarian Goths at prayer, at their services commemorating Good Friday. An excellent time for an attack, said one of the Romans' chief cavalry officers, Saulus by name, one of those Alani who had learned their tactics in their losing struggle against the Huns. He led his cavalry on a wild charge that stampeded through the tents of the surprised Goths. Saulus himself, however, was unhorsed and killed as the Goths scrambled up from their prayers and ran for their horses and organized a counterattack. Only then did Stilicho's infantrymen march onto the center of the field, expecting an easy victory, finding an enraged enemy slashing back at them.

What happened next is somewhat confused. According to the verses of Claudian, Stilicho's protégé, the Roman legions swept all before them, routed the Gothic wagons, freed their captives, and recaptured the booty that the Goths had brought all the way from Greece, including even the tattered purple robes of the Emperor Valens, slain at Adrianople. "Never," cried Claudian, "was the sword of Rome plunged so deep in the Scythians' throat." According to the Gothic historian Jordanes, on the other hand, the Goths quickly recovered from the Romans' impious attack. "Soon regaining their courage and arousing each other by brave shouting, as is their custom," Jordanes wrote, "they turned to flight the entire army of Stilicho and almost exterminated it." From these contradictory accounts, which agree only on the fact that many thousands were slaughtered, judicious historians have concluded that the battle of Pollentia was one of those clashes that prove bloody but inconclusive. Or rather, decisive only in that an invasion is halted. Did Meade really win at Gettysburg or Pétain at Verdun?

One of the most interesting elements in the confusion is Claudian's report that Alaric returned to his camp during a break in the battle and found that his wife and children had been seized and borne into captivity by the Romans. "That wife of thine," Claudian gloated, "who . . . demanded in her madness the jeweled necklaces of Italian matrons for her proud neck and Roman girls for her servants." It would be pleasantly romantic to think that Alaric had been forced by this capture of his family to enter into truce negotiations, and that it was for them that he halted his invasion of Italy. The surviving records provide no previous mention of this unnamed wife and children, however, and we never hear of them again. All we know is that there was some kind of negotiation between Alaric and Stilicho, and that it ended with the King of the Visigoths leading his army, still intact, back across the Po, across the plains of Lombardy as far as Verona (where another battle may have occurred), then back to his sanctuary in Illyricum.

"Thou and thou alone, Stilicho, hast dispersed the darkness that enshrouded our empire and hast restored its glory," cried the faithful Claudian. "Thanks to thee, civilization, all but vanished, has been freed from the gloomy prison and can again advance." Other observers of that period were less euphoric. Orosius, the disciple of Saint Augustine, referred sarcastically to "King Alaric with his Goths, often defeated, often hemmed in, and always allowed to escape." His implication was that the barbarians on both sides of the battle line indulged each other at the expense of Imperial Rome. While that implication seems unfair to the loyalty of Stilicho, it was perhaps true that the mercenary armies of Rome had already acquired the self-preserving philosophy that was to become characteristic of the *condottieri* of a later age. When two wolves meet in combat, they do not ordinarily fight to the death; the one that feels its antagonist's teeth upon its throat makes a gesture of surrender, and then the tribal struggle for survival goes on.

∗

Poor Honorius, now twenty, an apparently pious and simpleminded youth interested mainly in the raising of exotic poultry in his new sanctuary of Ravenna, chose or was prevailed upon to choose this ambiguous victory over the Goths as the occasion for the celebration of an imperial triumph in the streets of Rome. It was actually only the third time in the past century that a Roman emperor had ever appeared in Rome, but the Romans were delighted to evoke once again their magnificent traditions of imperial chariots leading captives in chains. They seem to have had no sense of their impending ruin. "The matrons admired the fresh-glowing cheeks of Honorius," according to Claudian's account, "his hair bound with the diadem, his limbs clothed with the jeweled consular robe, his strong shoulders, his neck, which might vie with that of Bacchus, rising from amid Arabian emeralds." The Roman senators were pleased that he did not make them march before him, as some of his predecessors had done, and they noted, too, that he was closely surrounded by his wife, Maria, and her father, Stilicho, and her brother Eucherius, whose eventual coronation as emperor was said to be the principal goal of all of Stilicho's policies.

The capital of Christianity still cherished its pagan traditions of human sacrifice in the form of circuses and gladiatorial games. The Emperor Constantine, in his decrees establishing Christianity as the official religion, had abolished the gladiatorial games almost a century earlier, but Constantine's regulations were sometimes hard to enforce, and in the abandoned capital of Rome the cruel entertainments were periodically revived. For this celebration of the triumph over the Goths, in the year 404, the young Honorius took his place in the imperial stand, and the Colosseum that had been built by Vespasian and Titus on the site of Nero's palace echoed once again to the roars of the Roman mob. Down on the sandy floor of the great arena, the hacking and stabbing had already begun when people began to notice the figure of a robed monk named Telemachus who worked his way through the crowded ranks of spectators and down into the arena. The monk, unarmed, forced himself between two gladiators, waving them apart, insisting on halting their combat. When the Roman crowd realized what Telemachus was doing, they howled their rage and began bombarding him with stones. The monk fell bleeding to the floor of the arena, down there with the gladiators, and so he died. The Emperor Honorius was so shaken that he proclaimed Telemachus a saint and martyr, and he ordered that the gladiatorial games be ended forever.

✳

The year after Honorius' official triumph over the Goths, the Goths returned. These were not the armies of Alaric but rather those of Radagaisus, the enigmatic figure whose first attack on Italy coincided with Alaric's first invasion. Radagaisus may not actually have been a Goth at all (Gibbon subscribed to this theory), and his army included many Vandals and Alani and Suevi. Most contemporary chroniclers, though, describe him as "Radagaisus the Goth." He was a pagan and, in the view of Saint Augustine's friend Orosius, "the most savage of all past or present enemies of Rome." That very paganism, however, inspired revived hopes among the old families of Rome, who still expected, somehow, to be liberated from the shackles of the new state religion of Christianity. "It was being told to us at Carthage," Saint Augustine recalled in *The City of God,* "that the pagans were believing . . . and boasting that he, on account of the gods friendly to him, . . . would certainly not be conquered by those not performing such sacrifices to the Roman gods."

Radagaisus' mighty army, estimated at more than 200,000 men, took a wrong road, however, and soon found itself struggling through the mountain passes of the Appenines. Stilicho, commanding an army reinforced by mercenary Goths and Huns, managed to trap the invaders there, just north of Florence, and to cut off their food supplies. When Radagaisus' forces were near starvation, he tried to break through the besiegers' lines, but he was captured and beheaded. His soldiers were sold into slavery. It was, said Augustine, a "marvelous defeat of the worshipers of demons."

But after every defeated invasion came new invaders. The Rhine, that traditional barrier protecting Roman Gaul, froze solid in the winter of 406, and across it streamed an army of Vandals. They marched to Rheims and Amiens and eventually as far as Bordeaux, butchering anyone who resisted their advance. Farther east, the Alemanni, pressed from behind by the fierce Burgundians, attacked and conquered the Roman outposts at Worms, Speyer and Strasbourg. In remote Britain, the rebellious legions proclaimed one of their own soldiers, Constantine by name, to be emperor. The usurper promptly set sail for Gaul and marched unopposed as far as Arles. In the fortified marshlands of Ravenna, the Emperor Honorius trembled.

To Stilicho, who was chiefly responsible for defending the crumbling ruin that still considered itself an empire, King Alaric began to acquire a new significance. Instead of being an invader and an enemy, perhaps he might become an ally against worse invaders. Stilicho reflected. Emissaries suggested possibilities. Alaric, who had originally entered Illyricum as the champion of the slain Eastern minister Rufinus, weighed the possible advantages of becoming the deputy of the powerful Western minister, Stilicho.

Alaric suddenly marched back into northern Greece in the year 408, then halted, then mysteriously turned northward and once again appeared on the frontier of Italy. In the course of these maneuvers, Alaric's prospects in the

West changed drastically. Stilicho, who originally had attached great importance to gaining control of Illyricum, now saw that such ambitions were a luxury, that he had to devote his forces principally to suppressing the usurper Constantine and the rebellious legions in Gaul. He soon devised his own version of the classic imperial strategy of setting one enemy against another. What would Alaric require to lead an attack against Constantine?

Alaric by now had learned to mistrust Roman strategy. *Timeo Romani et dona ferentes.* The Gothic warlord demanded that Rome pay him for his expedition into Greece—specifically, four thousand pounds in gold. When the Roman Senate was convoked to debate this extravagant request, Stilicho surprised the senators by acknowledging that Alaric had "faithfully asserted the just pretensions" of Rome and had acted "for the best interest of the Emperor." But there had been palace intrigues. Stilicho's own wife, Serena, a niece of Theodosius the Great and thus a cousin of both Eastern and Western emperors, had apparently interfered in Stilicho's designs on Illyricum and won a halt to Alaric's invasion in order to end the fratricidal conflict. The senators reluctantly agreed that Alaric had a right to complain about the contradictory messages from the imperial court, and they voted him the money he demanded. They voted it grudgingly. *"Non est ista pax sed pactio servitutis.* This is not a treaty of peace but of servitude," declared the Senator Lampridius.

It was a strange tradition, this Roman custom of buying off the Goths. Ever since the wars of Emperor Decius, a century and a half earlier, the Romans had regularly paid the Goths their stipendia in corn and cloths and other goods in an effort to make them keep the peace. The Romans liked to regard this as a welfare subsidy to the troublesome poor, a form of charity. The Goths considered it a tribute from the cowardly to the brave, hardly different from the tribute that Rome exacted from its conquered provinces. There were usually no definite time limits on these subsidies. When the Romans felt secure, as they periodically did, they stopped paying. Then the fighting began anew.

In retrospect, it is easy to see that Stilicho was doomed. He undoubtedly thought otherwise. Not only had he defeated Radagaisus and bought off Alaric, but he had strengthened his personal hold on the Emperor Honorius. When his young daughter Maria, whom he had married to the fourteen-year-old Emperor ten years earlier, died—and died, it was said, a virgin—Stilicho persuaded Honorius to marry his second daughter, Thermantia.

And now in that same spring of 408, the imperial court at Ravenna received word that Honorius' brother Arcadius, emperor of the East, had died. His son and heir, Theodosius, was a boy of seven. Honorius announced that he would go to Constantinople and take charge of his brother's empire. Stilicho argued strongly against such a voyage. With Gaul overrun by barbarians, with the usurper Constantine established at Arles, Honorius' entire empire would be imperiled if he now abandoned his capital for the sake of political intrigues in the east. This was quite true, though the same arguments could be used against

Stilicho's own plan, that he himself journey to Constantinople to settle the heritage of the Emperor Arcadius.

Honorius, ever vacillating, agreed to Stilicho's proposals. But while Stilicho prepared for his own voyage to the East, some of his enemies filled Honorius with suspicions about his powerful minister. Stilicho's true ambition, said a Greek courtier named Olympius, was to murder the young Theodosius and to seize control of the Eastern Empire, if not for himself then for his own son, Eucherius. This Eucherius, the ostentatiously Christian courtier continued, was secretly a pagan who hoped to suppress the true faith. Honorius listened and doubted and wavered.

Olympius apparently spread similar tales among the soldiers garrisoned at Ticinum (now Pavia, just south of Milan), where the Emperor and his court were visiting. And these soldiers, who like many of the once disciplined legions were by now little better than an armed mob, soon rose in surly revolt. They had long resented, among other things, having a Vandal as supreme commander, and they suspected a pro-German bias in all his policies and promotions. The mutineers murdered several of their principal officers, who had been appointed by Stilicho, then began rampaging through the streets of the town, plundering their victims more or less at random. The magistrates responsible for keeping order all fled. Olympius and some other courtiers persuaded the Emperor Honorius to don the short tunic of a private citizen and let himself be thus paraded through the town, a gesture that seems to have been intended and accepted as an imperial plea for mercy and order. The sated legionaries straggled back to their quarters.

When the first confused accounts of these disturbances reached Stilicho, still preparing to sail from Ravenna to the East, they reported that Honorius had been put to death by the mutineers. Stilicho gathered what loyal officers he could, most of them Germanic tribesmen of one sort or another, and they decided to march on Ticinum and punish the Emperor's assassins. When subsequent messages proclaimed that the Emperor was still alive, the Germanic *foederati* wanted to march anyway, but the loyal Stilicho now held back. "He did [not] think it either honorable or safe," according to the chronicle of Count Zosimus, "to incite barbarians against the Roman army."

Stilicho's caution was ill-conceived and ill-repaid. The courtier Olympius, seeking a scapegoat for the mutiny that he himself had incited in Ticinum, persuaded Honorius that Stilicho had been plotting a coup d'état and should be arrested on suspicion of treason. Stilicho, the supreme commander of the Western Empire for more than two decades, knew what he might expect. He fled to a church and took sanctuary. There he was discovered the following day by an imperial officer named Heraclian, leading a band of Honorius' soldiers. They took an oath before the bishop of Ravenna that they had been ordered only to take Stilicho into custody, not to injure him or even to put him in chains. On the basis of that oath, Stilicho gave himself up. No sooner was he removed from the sanctuary of the church than Heraclian brought forth a new letter from Honorius ordering that Stilicho be executed for crimes against the commonwealth. Even at this late hour, Stilicho could have fought back. His barbarian officers and friends urged him to resist or flee. Stilicho wearily refused, and refused to permit them to do violence on his behalf. Instead, as Zosimus put it, he "calmly submitted his neck to the sword. . . . He was the most moderate and just of all the men who possessed great authority in his time."

The death of Stilicho in August of 408 was the signal for Honorius' minions to attack everyone who had supported the fallen minister. His son, Eucherius, the supposed pagan usurper, was pursued as far as a church in Rome, lured out of the sanctuary by promises, as his father had been, then executed. His daughter, Thermantia, was divorced by Honorius and sent home to her mother, Serena (Thermantia, like her sister, was later said to have died a virgin). An imperial decree ordered that all men who had held office under Stilicho should surrender all their property to the state. And with or without an imperial decree, the Roman soldiery once again assaulted the wives and children of the Goths and other barbarian *foederati* who had undertaken to serve the empire. "On hearing of the death of Stilicho," Zosimus wrote, the soldiers "fell upon all the women and children in the city who belonged to the barbarians. Having, as by a preconcerted signal, destroyed every individual of them, they plundered them of all they possessed." Some thirty thousand of these barbarians, thus rewarded by Rome, forthwith deserted the imperial standard and marched north to join forces with Alaric.

*

King Alaric, however, seemed to have become strangely pacific. Perhaps he was shaken by the death of Stilicho; perhaps he had dreams of replacing the Vandal as the commander and even the chief minister of the Western Empire. In any case, he sent messengers to Honorius offering a treaty of peace. In exchange for a moderate subsidy in gold and corn—he left the amount to Honorius' decision—Alaric proposed to keep his men in the mountainous Adriatic province of Pannonia. Honorius, having been offered his salvation, refused even to negotiate with Alaric. He and his ministers were busy purifying the realm. Decree after decree poured forth from Ravenna, promising retribution against all Manicheans, Montanists, Priscillianists and all manner of heathens. "We forbid those who are enemies of the Catholic sect to serve as soldiers in our palace," said one of these pronouncements. "We will have no connection of any kind with any man who differs from us in faith."

Rejected, Alaric finally decided to march back into Italy, and now that there was no Stilicho to oppose him, the road to Rome was clear. Descending from the Julian Alps in the autumn of 408, Alaric bypassed all the major Roman fortresses. He ignored the Adriatic citadel of Aquilea. He led his caravans across the Po, unopposed, then south to Rimini and then inland to Bologna. He did not even stop to reconnoiter Honorius' sanctuary at Ravenna. Rome was his goal. According to one of the legends that survive from this time, a robed monk came to Alaric's tent to plead with him to halt his march on Rome and his plundering of the countryside. Alaric is supposed to have replied by citing the prophecy he had heard in the grove of sacred oaks: "I am impelled to this course in spite of myself, for something within me urges me every day irresistibly onward, saying, Proceed to Rome and make that city desolate." *"Penetrabis ad urbem.* You shall penetrate to the city," the voices had said.

Alaric reached Rome in about September of 408, seized control of the port of Ostia and cut the supply line to the sea. His siege was total. The Romans, who had not been attacked at their own city gates for nearly a thousand years, not since the Celts had come and seen and conquered in 389 B.C., were horrified. Unable to defend their city, they began worrying about espionage and searching for traitors. Their most notable victim was a defenseless woman, Serena, the widow of Stilicho and cousin of the Emperor. The Roman Senate, according to Zosimus, voted that she must be a spy, because of her barbarian connections, and therefore she must be put to death. The chronicler quoted the Senate as deciding that "Alaric, upon Serena being removed, will retire from the city, because no person will remain by whom he can hope the town to be betrayed into his hands."

Zosimus, himself a pagan, declared that the Senate's suspicion "was in reality groundless, as Serena never had any such intentions." But to this political exculpation he promptly added a religious indictment, charging that Serena "suffered justly for her impieties toward the gods." More than a decade earlier, at the time of Theodosius' triumph over the pagan usurper Eugenius, there had been a great wave of repression of the pagan rituals. Theodosius, arriving in Rome, had ordered the dismissal of many priests and forbidden the use of public funds for pagan ceremonials. The young Serena, joining in these Christian victory celebrations, took part in a mocking desecration of a temple dedicated to Rhea, the mother of Zeus. On a statue of the goddess she saw a necklace that appealed to her, and so she took it off and draped it around her own neck. An aged priestess in the temple scolded Serena for her impiety, and Serena ordered her attendants to chase the old woman away. The old woman then put a curse on Serena. "She prayed," according to Zosimus' account, "that whatever was due to such impiety might fall on Serena, her husband and children." And so he considered it entirely appropriate that the woman who had once stripped a necklace from the statue of a goddess should ultimately be, by a vote of the Roman Senate, strangled.

King Alaric quite possibly never knew of Serena's fate, may never even have known of her existence, certainly did not alter in any way his plans to starve the proud Romans into submission. Inside the walls, the citizens' daily ration of three pounds of bread was cut in half, then to one third, then to one fifth. The old people began to starve. Children wasted away. Corpses lay in the streets, rotting. The stench spread through the whole city. Pestilence was everywhere. The citizens of Rome, more than a million of them, huddled within their houses, afraid even to set foot outside to forage for food, and knowing there was no food to be found. Two officials, John, the chief of the imperial notaries, and a Spanish provincial governor named Basil, were finally chosen to go and plead for mercy. They attempted, in the usual manner, to proclaim that the citizens of Rome were ready to fight. "The Roman people," a contemporary chronicler quotes them as saying, "were prepared to make peace on moderate terms, but were yet more prepared for war. They had arms in their hands, and from long practice in their use had no reason to dread the result of battle."

King Alaric laughed. He heard those pronouncements and looked at the gaunt faces of the ambassadors and considered the prospect of the Romans sallying forth to do battle and laughed. Perhaps he recalled his days of exile in the fields of Moesia. "The thicker the hay, the easier it is mowed," he said.

The ambassadors tried a new tactic—the standard Roman tactic, in these imperial times, of trying to buy off all enemies. What, they asked, was Alaric's price?

"Deliver to me all the gold that your city contains," said Alaric, "all the silver, all the movable property that I may find there, and all your slaves of barbarian origin."

The ambassadors were shocked. All their gold? All their barbarian slaves? (There were as many as thirty thousand of these slaves held captive in the capital of the civilized world.) "If you take all these things," said one of the Roman ambassadors, "what do you leave to our citizens?"

"Your souls," said Alaric.

The ambassadors returned to the besieged city and reported the besieger's terms. The Romans heard them with despair. Without their gold and their silver and their slaves, what would become of their great city? It was a punishment, many said, for their abandonment of the old religion. And in this crisis, the prefect of the city, Pompeianus, discovered that the old religion might yet be invoked to drive off the barbarians. Two refugees from the north reported that when the Goths had approached the town of Narnia, in Tuscany, some priests had performed the ancient rites and animal sacrifices and called on the old gods for salvation. And there had come thunder and lightning, so fierce that the invaders had retreated from the town and left it unharmed. Perhaps, said the refugees, the same rituals could save Rome.

These rituals, however, were strictly forbidden. Anyone who participated in them was liable to the confiscation of all his property. Still, Pascal's wager was known to mankind long before Pascal ever formulated it, and Pompeianus, though a Christian, was also a politician. To protect himself, he decided to appeal to the Pope, Innocent I, and to ask his special dispensation for a performance of the pagan rites. Innocent, despite his name, had not become a pope by accident, and his decision was spendidly pontifical. "Preferring the safety of the city to his own private opinion," as a contemporary account put it, Innocent gave his permission for a performance of the forbidden rites—on condition that they be done in secret. When the prefect Pompeianus reported this verdict to the priests of the old religion, they insisted that secret rituals would have no effect. The ceremonies had to be performed in public on the Capitoline Hill, with the whole Senate as witnesses. Confronted with this new demand, Pope Innocent gave way and agreed even to a public ceremony, perhaps because he knew the temper of the Senate, which finally balked at the prospect of a new pagan revival. Or the senators may simply have doubted the efficacy of any religious offering. They decided to produce whatever Alaric demanded. A new delegation went to pay court at Alaric's camp and to determine what he wanted of

Rome. After much negotiation, specific figures were reached: 5,000 pounds of gold, 30,000 pounds of silver, 4,000 silken tunics, 3,000 hides dyed scarlet, and 3,000 pounds of pepper.

The Romans accepted, even though they did not know how they could pay. The public treasury was nearly empty. Lists of leading citizens were drawn up, and everyone was assessed his share, but even that did not suffice. The city officials then decided to start stripping down the statues of the gods they had once worshiped. "And since it was fated that . . . everything should concur to the ruin of the city," said the horrified Zosimus, "they not only stripped the statues of their adornments but they even melted down some of those which were composed of gold and silver, among which there was one of Valor (which the Romans call Virtue). And when this was destroyed, all that was left of Valor and Virtue among the Romans perished with it."

On these terms, Alaric agreed to make peace—these terms and one other, which may have been more important to him than the extortion of Rome's gold. He wanted, once and for all, some legal and official declaration of his own position and his people's position within the framework of the empire. The principal officials of Rome were willing to oblige him, but this matter lay solely within the authority of the Emperor Honorius. The Emperor, still confronting the rival claims of the usurper Constantine, strongly established in Gaul, was said to concern himself mainly with the raising of his prize chickens in the imperial poultry yard at Ravenna. A delegation from Rome pleaded with the Emperor to negotiate some kind of arrangement with Alaric and his Gothic army, now swollen by the thousands of freed slaves. Honorius refused even to discuss the problem. It was beneath the dignity of Rome, or Ravenna. The Emperor may have acted at the behest of Olympius, that Greek courtier who had inspired the overthrow of Stilicho. Olympius, however, soon demonstrated his incompetence as chief minister among the eunuchs and flatterers at Ravenna, then fled to a remote country retreat. He was replaced by an even more devious courtier named Jovius.

This Jovius had known Alaric during the Goth's first ventures into Greece, and now he took it upon himself to invite the barbarian King to a peace conference at Rimini, just north of Ravenna. There, with representatives of the Pope in attendance, Jovius asked what Alaric wanted as the price of a final settlement. In view of the fact that Alaric had just compelled the surrender of Rome and now commanded the most powerful military force in Italy, his demands were relatively modest. He wanted a yearly payment of gold and provisions— the exact amount to be negotiated later—and a large rectangle of frontier land, roughly from Venice to Munich to Vienna to Dubrovnik, where the Goths could finally establish an autonomous homeland within the empire. Jovius sent these demands back to Ravenna and accompanied them with a suggestion of his own, that Alaric might settle for a lot less land if he were granted the personal honor of the empire's chief military title, *magister utriusque militiae,* or commander of cavalry and infantry. He may have been right, though it is not clear whether this designation was meant to imply a mere title or the power that Alaric really wanted, supreme command of all imperial forces. While the eunuchs at the anarchic court of Ravenna considered these questions, Jovius remained in Rimini, and the negotiations went on. It happened that Alaric and Jovius were talking together when the Emperor's answer came, and it happened that Jovius, perhaps assuming that the pliant Emperor had accepted his suggestions, unwisely began reading Honorius' letter aloud to the assembled Goths. The Emperor agreed to unspecified "payments of gold and subsidies of corn," but he rejected, in the most disdainful terms, any idea of naming a Goth to the highest military command in the empire. "I hold it unfitting," Honorius wrote, and Jovius read aloud, "that such offices as you name should ever be held by Alaric or any of his race."

Alaric was outraged. He broke off all negotiations and swore vengeance. He would make Rome pay for this insult. Jovius scuttled back to Ravenna and tried to inspire the imperial court to prepare for war. He persuaded Honorius to take an oath that he would never make peace with Alaric. Then he and the chief ministers took a similar oath, swearing on the Emperor's own head that they would never make peace. The Emperor did very little to carry out his oaths, however. He recruited ten thousand Huns to reinforce his armies, brought in some cattle and sheep to increase the supplies in Ravenna, and sent a few scouts to watch over Alaric's march on Rome.

Alaric, now stricken by some mysterious doubt, delayed that march. It was as though he sensed that his prophesied mission to conquer Rome would also lead to his own death. Something, in any case, held him back, even when all of Italy lay prostrate before him. He sent new emissaries to Ravenna, again offering peace and on much easier terms than before—no titles for himself, no gold for his treasury, only basic rations for his troops and a settlement for his people in two provinces of what is now Austria. Once again, the minister Jovius ruined all prospects of peace. The Emperor's oath of perpetual war on Alaric, and the similar oath of the ministers who had sworn on the Emperor's own head, could not, he claimed, be violated. Alaric's new offer was rejected.

The King of the Visigoths forthwith began his second siege of Rome. He again captured the port of Ostia, again seized all the supplies of grain on which the city lived. This was hardly a siege, though, for the Romans offered no resistance whatever. Having been starved and ruined by the first siege, they wanted only to know what terms Alaric would set for their surrender. This time, Alaric had an entirely new strategy. Since the Emperor Honorius simply sat behind the marsh-encircled walls of Ravenna and refused to negotiate, Alaric proposed to the Romans the creation of a new and more understanding Roman emperor—their own Pretorian prefect, Priscus Attalus. This Attalus was of Greek origin, a wealthy man of some rhetorical skill and political influence but also a man of overweening vanity. The Romans at this point would accept anything. The Senate formally renounced all allegiance to Honorius and bestowed all power on Attalus, and Attalus formally made peace with Alaric, granting him, finally, that cherished imperial title of *magister utriusque militiae.* He also paraded to the Senate and addressed it in terms worthy of an Augustus, promising, in this hour of its humiliation. that he, Priscus Attalus, would "bring the whole world back under the dominion of Rome."

Alaric was more shrewd. Now that he was master of Rome, actually established inside the city, creator and counselor of the new Emperor, he soon realized that no new shipments of grain were arriving from Africa. The provincial governor, Heraclian, who had been promoted to his post in Africa as a reward for having carried out the execution of Stilicho, remained stoutly loyal to the Emperor Honorius. And without its customary shipments of African grain, Rome was blockaded as effectively as by any Gothic siege. Alaric urged Attalus to send a powerful Gothic army to Africa to overthrow Heraclian, but Attalus was already drunk with the imperial powers to which Alaric had elevated him. He pompously declared that it would be unfitting for a barbarian force to be sent to attack a Roman province. Instead, he sent a small Roman force under a Roman commander, who, in his view, should be able to require obedience to the new Emperor. Attalus' main goal, however, was the obvious one that Alaric, perhaps overawed by the imperial traditions, had tried to avoid—a march on Ravenna and the destruction of Honorius. Alaric, again mysteriously compliant to his new Emperor, agreed.

No sooner had Honorius learned of the usurper's approach than he sent his minister Jovius out with a message. "Let us divide the empire," said Honorius. "You reign at Rome, I at Ravenna, only let me still be Augustus here." The treacherous Jovius apparently read this message as what it was, a virtual capitulation, and promptly went over to Attalus' side. He may even have taken part in composing Attalus' extraordinary answer. "Not a particle of Italian soil, O Honorius, not a vestige of the imperial dignity, not even thy own body will we allow thee to preserve unmutilated," the former prefect, the creature of King Alaric, replied to the Emperor Honorius. "Thou shalt be maimed, thou shalt be banished to some island, and then, as a favor, we will concede to thee life."

The Emperor was terrified. He knew that he had no army worthy of the name. His only hope, he decided, lay in fleeing by sea from his coastal fortress of Ravenna to the sanctuary of the court at Constantinople. But even as Honorius made his preparations for flight from Attalus' advancing forces, an almost miraculous event occurred. On the horizon there suddenly appeared sail after sail, an armada of warships flying the standards of Constantinople. When the ships tied up at the waterfront in Ravenna, a whole army marched ashore—six legions totaling forty thousand men, reinforcements that had been requested for some now-forgotten crisis two years earlier. It had taken that long for the request by Stilicho, now dead, executed, to be answered. Honorius was saved.

Alaric, still reluctant to challenge Honorius in Ravenna, marched northward up the Adriatic coast and then up the Po Valley, demanding and obtaining oaths of loyalty, everywhere he went, to his new Emperor Attalus. But Attalus' feeble expedition against Africa had been defeated, and starvation was again threatening Rome. At one public spectacle in the Flavian Amphitheater, there had even been a disgraceful outcry challenging the Emperor to set a market price for human flesh. *Pretium pone carni humanae!* Alaric soon tired of his experiment. He commanded his Emperor to present himself at Rimini. There, in front of the entire army, the King of the Visigoths contemptuously deposed the Roman Emperor whom he had created less than a year before. He stripped off Attalus' purple robe, his diadem and badges of office, and flung them to one side. Attalus, reduced to the rank of a private citizen, asked only to be allowed to follow in the Visigoths' caravan. Alaric granted him that permission.

Yet again, Alaric tried to reopen negotiations with Honorius. He sent the imperial insignia that he had torn from Attalus to the court at Ravenna, a gesture indicating that he accepted Honorius' rule and that he wanted mainly some region in which the Goths could settle themselves. This time, it was another Goth who sabotaged and destroyed that possibility. Sarus was his name, and he was a prince of one of the noble families of the Gothic nation. He had once been a friend and supporter of Stilicho, but had turned against him when Stilicho had refused to suppress the mutiny at Ticinum. Since then, Sarus had remained a kind of dissident warlord, nominally loyal to Honorius but under no imperial control. Now, for mysterious reasons of his own, perhaps a fear that an alliance between Alaric and Honorius would work against his own interests, Sarus and some three hundred of his warriors suddenly staged a surprise attack on the Gothic camp.

Alaric easily beat off the raiders, but he felt a dark suspicion that Sarus had acted not as a dissident at all but as an agent for the untrustworthy Emperor. He may even have been right. In any case, he considered this the end. To be treacherously attacked by Roman mercenaries in the midst of peace negotiations with the Roman Emperor—there could be no clearer illustration of the Romans' perfidy, or of the Emperor's contemptuous attitude toward the Goths. Once again, Alaric broke off all negotiations, once again he headed for Rome. This time, the third time, he was determined to carry out the prophecy that he had tried for so long to evade. And Rome by now was prepared for its destiny. Besieged for the third time in three years, it hardly resisted at all.

To present the drama of Alaric's final onslaught, one might perhaps turn to the pages of Marcel Brion, whose biography *Alaric the Goth,* published in 1932, is a model of its kind. Having brought his hero to the gates of Rome, Brion conjures up a splendid scene in which Alaric once again strips the cringing Attalus of his imperial regalia, then whips him across the shoulders and sends him back to the servants' quarters. Then, while the awed citizens of Rome watch from their walls, Alaric stages a fierce ceremony of renunciation. He tears off, piece by piece, his Roman uniform, his corselet and coat of mail, his helmet with its scarlet plume. All of these symbols of the Roman command that he had tried so long to achieve he flings to the ground. Finally, in a prophetic gesture, he slowly puts on the tribal costume of the Goths, the leather jacket, the bronze helmet with the ox horns, the long sword and battle-ax. The sack of Rome is ready to begin.

It was the night of August 24, in the year 410, exactly two years after the humbling and execution of the Vandal Stilicho. Brion describes vividly the eruption of a thunderstorm. Gusts of wind. Lightning. The Roman sentries cower under the torrents. The Goths smash their bronze battering rams against the Salarian Gate, just east of the Pincian Hill. It splinters. The Goths swarm in. A few Roman militiamen attempt a resistance. The former slaves who had escaped to join Alaric's army now demand vengeance. They set fire to the Palace of Sallust, near the Salerian Gate, and the flames soon spread to neighboring houses.

But let Brion tell his story in his own words: "The tumult of galloping hoofs resounds in the Forum. The palace of the emperors is invaded. The doors of convents and dwellings are broken open. The unloosing of barbaric rage on the city of the Caesars causes terrible panics, in which children are crushed to death and women trampled underfoot. . . . Excited by the guttural cries of their chiefs, the Goths gallop through the vast empty squares . . . smashing precious mosaics, shivering to pieces portals carved in wood, tearing down silken curtains, and lashing beautiful marble effigies with their whips. Some among them hold a disheveled woman . . . on the pommels of their saddles, and snatch up in passing any object that appeals to their greed, a golden vase, an ivory statuette, some precious weapon dedicated to the gods of yore, or the humble family treasure a trembling young girl hugs to her breast. Trampling the corpses, dispatching the wounded, flinging themselves with savage howls on the bodies of the women who resist and shriek, the Goths pass through the appalled city like a horde of demons."

This is worthy, in some ways, of the extravagant ceremonial verses of Claudian and the credulous folk tales of Zosimus. But while these chroniclers lived at some proximity to the events they described, and therefore may have had some reason for even the most improbable passages in their works, Alaric's only recent biographer seems to have relied heavily on his own imagination. The Gothic hoofbeats, the women sprawled across their saddles, the family treasures snatched from trembling girls—all this is pure fantasy.

We do not actually know any of the circumstances of how the Goths entered Rome. There is a traditional tale that the Salarian Gate was thrown open from inside, possibly by some Gothic slaves still held within the city, possibly by Goths sent inside as slaves solely for that purpose. But what is really startling is that in a disaster of such magnitude, the conquest of the capital of the civilized world, not one contemporary account by an eyewitness has survived. For the details of what actually happened we can only elaborate on a few inspirational anecdotes in various ecclesiastical histories. Claudian's epic poems end in 404. Even the blundering Count Zosimus mysteriously breaks off just as Alaric is approaching the capital. It is as though future historians searching for the exact circumstances of World War III found that the microfilmed files of *The New York Times* abruptly ended in 1978, and the destruction of Washington was only episodically referred to in some evangelical tracts published on a commune in northern California.

Contemporary accounts agree that the Goths did somehow enter Rome on the night of August 24 through the Salarian Gate, where earlier citizens had once brought in the capital's supply of salt. And that the city was sacked. Such an assault must always be an ugly spectacle, for an army turned loose upon a civilian population soon becomes quite different from an army on a battlefield. Despite all orders commanding restraint, an army easily turns into an animal. The helplessness of its victims seems only to provoke the animal to ferocity. The Goths, nearly 100,000 strong, long anticipating the spoils of war, probably behaved much like a hundred other armies in a hundred other conquests, from the Romans at Jerusalem to the Russians at Berlin. They looted, they plundered, they seized whatever attracted their attention, and beat or stabbed anyone who resisted them. And if Alaric maintained command over his Gothic soldiers, he was probably less successful in controlling the former slaves who thirsted for revenge. Even those Romans who escaped attack were reduced to the degradation of terror. "Rome, the mistress of the world, shivered, crushed with fear, at the sound of the blaring trumpets and the howling of the Goths," the British monk Pelagius wrote to a friend. "Where, then, was the nobility, where were the certain and distinct ranks of dignity? Everyone was mingled together and shaken with fear; every household had its grief, and an all-pervading terror gripped us. . . . The same specter of death stalked before us all."

This was partly shock and hysteria at the mere fact of the Gothic conquest. It is difficult to find more than a few recorded instances of rapine. The Palace of Sallust, near the Salarian Gate, was the only major building that caught fire; there was no general conflagration of the kind that swept the city in the reign of Nero. And in such sources as the letters of Saint Jerome, we find only a few ambiguous cases of assault. Jerome tells, for example, of a noble widow named Marcella, who lived on the Aventine Hill in a house that she had turned into a convent. A band of Goths banged at her door, demanding her money. When she showed them her humble robes and told them of her vows of poverty, they ruthlessly beat her and whipped her, but when she insisted on her poverty the attackers seem to have relented and taken her to the Basilica of St. Paul, where she chanted her immunity to all physical torment "because she was filled with all the fullness of Christ." A few days later, she died of her injuries. Orosius, the friend of Saint Augustine, provides even fewer details about a nameless young matron who was assaulted by a nameless Gothic soldier. When she cried out that she preferred death to dishonor, the soldier drew his sword. She willingly bowed her head. The soldier hacked at her. She fell to the ground, bleeding profusely. The soldier hacked at her again. The woman lay prostrate but still alive. The Goth, stricken by remorse, led her to a church, paid some attendants to take care of her, then marched on.

One element that made this barbarian conquest of Rome quite different from the Roman conquests of enemy cities was Alaric's order that Christian churches be respected as sanctuaries. Thousands of Romans apparently took shelter there, and even Alaric's fiercest troops obeyed his command. Saint Augustine, for one, was astounded. He cited Julius Caesar's account of the customary practices—"that virgins and boys are violated, children torn from the embrace of their parents, matrons subjected to whatever should be the pleasure of the conquerors, temples and houses plundered, slaughter and burning rife." Alaric's Goths, by contrast to Caesar's legions, spared at least the temples. "What was novel," as Augustine put it, "was that savage barbarians showed themselves in so gentle a guise, that the largest churches were chosen and set apart for the purpose of being filled with the people to whom quarter was given, and that in them none was slain, from them none forcibly dragged."

One of the most extraordinary episodes in this upheaval occurred at the home of an aged lady who had been entrusted with the treasures of Saint Peter.

(Orosius tells the story, and again there are no names.) A Gothic officer rapped on her door and demanded her gold and silver. She set out before him a stupe-fying array of crosses and chalices and other riches. The astonished Goth asked her where they had come from. "They are consecrated to the service of the Apostle Peter," the old lady said. "I am not strong enough to defend them from you. Take them if you are not afraid to do so. You will have to answer for the deed." The Gothic officer sent a messenger to Alaric's headquarters to ask what should be done. Alaric sent back orders that the old woman and her treasure should be officially escorted to sanctuary in the Basilica of St. Peter. And so in the middle of this barbarian sacking of Rome, a strange procession formed: the old woman and her treasures, lifted on high by platoons of fur-clad Gothic warriors, and followed by various friends and neighbors, Christians and pagans alike, who felt a momentary sense of safety in this official procession. And they began to sing. Hymns, ritual chants, whatever one sings at a time of exhausted exaltation. And the hymns attracted new marchers and singers, frightened citizens watching from their windows or hiding behind barred doors, wondering how to find sanctuary. The resounding chorus promised them that, and so they fled to join it, to join in the desperate singing and in carrying the old woman's riches to the Basilica of St. Peter.

After three days of disorder (or six days, according to some accounts), Alaric decided to march his troops out of the humbled city. His principal reason was apparently neither moral nor military but simply the lack of food supplies from Africa. This was a problem that could never be solved, he determined, until he marched southward and established forever the security of the empire's harvests. When Alaric decided, his will was done. Out of the fallen city, fallen and humiliated but hardly destroyed, the Goths reassembled their wagons and their horses and began wheeling south. With them they took whatever treasure they could carry, probably including at least some of the spoils that the Emperor Titus had brought from the smoking ruins of Jerusalem. There was nothing now to stop the Visigoths on their march, nothing but the simple shape of the land and the sea.

Africa cannot easily be invaded by an army marching southward from Rome. Alaric and his myriad tribesmen marched as far as Reggio, just a few miles across the Strait of Messina from Sicily. The Sicilians had no defense except another appeal to the old gods. They cherished a sacred statue, according to the historian Olympiodorus, that contained holy water in one of its feet and perpetual flame in the other, and they appealed to this ancient deity to preserve them from invasion. Though Sicily is a natural bridge to Africa, Alaric may not have been planning to invade it at all. He ordered his forces in Reggio to build a vast fleet of sailing vessels to transport the entire Gothic nation across the Mediterranean. And it was done, and the fleet set out to sea, a motley assortment of rafts and dugouts, leather-skinned coracles and crude sailboats. The Goths had almost no experience with the sea, only a deep tribal sense that they had once sailed in three vessels from Scandza, their lost home in the north, and that their centuries of wanderings had brought them to this southernmost tip of Italy.

We must not attach any importance, of course, to the primitive statue that guarded the Sicilians from invasion—a few years after the passing of Alaric, it was officially cast down and destroyed on orders from the imperial court at Ravenna—and it was undoubtedly a coincidence that, on the very day of the sailing of Alaric's fleet, one of those sudden Mediterranean storms turned the sky black and lashed the strait into a froth and utterly swamped the Goths' invasion fleet. Alaric may have sensed some curse upon him, whether from Sicily or who could say where. Crying out against the fate that had brought him to this godforsaken tip of the earth, he suddenly fell ill with a mysterious fever. It lasted only a few days. Raging, tossing, sweating, shouting in a delirium, surrounded by lieutenants and counselors who could do nothing for him or for themselves, the King of the Visigoths died.

The Goths could not take Alaric back to his homeland for burial. They could only bury him where he lay, but they determined that this spot should never be violated. They ordered some of their Roman captives to dig a vast trench, near the town now known as Cosenza, to divert the Busento River from its course. In the emptied riverbed they dug a royal grave for King Alaric, and they buried him in it with his crown and his broadsword and his Gothic uniform of leather and fur, and a rich collection of the treasures he had brought from Rome, golden crosses, silver chalices, necklaces of rubies and emeralds, and who knows what further riches. The Goths then ordered their captives to resume their digging, to send the river back into its original course, to flood the grave of the fallen king. They slaughtered all of those captives so that no one should ever know where King Alaric and his riches lay buried. Then they reassembled all their forces and marched north again, past cursed Rome, out of cursed Italy, until they finally settled themselves in southwestern France, making their capital in Toulouse. And no one, to this day, has ever discovered the spot that contains the grave of Alaric and the spoils of Rome.

In the unworldly imperial court at Ravenna, according to a story by the malicious Procopius, a story so implausible that no historian can authenticate it but so peculiar that no historian can resist repeating it, a royal chamberlain came running to the Emperor to report that Rome had perished.

"Rome perished!" cried the childish Honorius. "It is not an hour since she was feeding out of my hand."

The imperial chamberlain had to explain that he meant the city of Rome, not the chicken that the Emperor had named after the former capital. The Emperor was relieved. "But I thought, my friend," he said, "that you meant that I had lost my *bird*, Rome."

There are modern historians too who argue that the sacking of Rome was no epochal event. The Goths came, the Goths went, and the barbarian wanderings had been going on for so long—some three centuries by now—that the Romans themselves no longer saw any clear division between an era of past security and of present devastation. Burned villages were rebuilt, burned again and rebuilt again; ruined fields soon grew new crops. The traditional and imminent date for the "fall" of the Roman Empire in the West, A.D. 476, merely marked the replacement of the last Emperor, Romulus Augustulus, by a Germanic military commander, Odovacar, who declined the imperial title. The empire had been disintegrating for many years, and the evolution of its constituent parts would continue for many years to come. To those historians who concern themselves with patterns of trade or shifts of population, no mere emperor stands very commandingly above the tidal flows of time.

To religious-minded Romans of the fifth century, however, the sacking of the great city was an event of both moral and supernatural significance. "It is through our sins that the barbarians are strong," Saint Jerome wrote. The pagans, still powerful and still resentful of the way their rituals had been suppressed, declared that the destruction was a perfectly fitting consequence of the dethroning of the old gods. Against this widely held view, the Christians had to mobilize every argument, and every casuistry, that they could devise.

The most distinguished of these controversialists was, of course, Saint Augustine, the bishop of Hippo, who devoted twenty years to refuting every argument the pagans ever proposed, and some that they had never even imagined. From the very start of *The City of God*, Augustine adopted a tone of belligerence. "O infatuated men," he cried, "what is this blindness, or rather madness, which possesses you?" He too argued that the sack of Rome was a divine punishment, not because the Romans had turned to Christianity but because they had not become Christian enough. The calamities inflicted by the Goths, he said, "they deservedly suffer in consequence of their own wicked ways." Augustine acknowledged that some of the most pious of Christians were among the slain, but he simply shrugged. "Well, if this be hard to bear," he wrote, "it is assuredly the common lot of all who are born into this life." He was equally serene about those who had been tortured to disclose their hidden treasure (it was not demonstrated that this ever happened). "They should have been reminded," he said, "that ... they should endure all torment, if need be, for Christ's sake; that they might be taught to love Him rather [than] silver and gold."

And what of those virgins who were said to have been ravished by the Goths? (Once again, there is no evidence that even one Roman virgin ever suffered such a fate.) Augustine devoted several of his most celebrated pages to an almost morbid examination of the moral issues involved. He started by acquitting the virgins of any sin so long as they did not acquiesce in any assaults upon them. But when he came, as any theologian must, to the question of why God had permitted such assaults, he demanded that the victims "interrogate your own souls, whether ye have not been unduly puffed up by your integrity, and continence and chastity." Did they not, in other words, provoke the attacks upon them? Even if the women denied such provocation, even if they were, as Augustine put it, "unconscious of any undue pride on account of their virtuous chastity," the saint charged that they might nonetheless suffer "some lurking infirmity which might have betrayed them into a proud and contemptuous bearing, had they not been subjected to the humiliation that befell them."

These few excerpts may convey the tone of Augustine's extended polemic. Arguing against all religious orthodoxy that preceded his own, he recounted all manner of pre-Christian misfortunes, from the fall of Troy to various floods and epidemics, and demanded to know why Jupiter or Apollo had not intervened. "Where were they when, during ten successive years of reverses, the Roman army suffered frequent and great losses among the Veians . . . ? Where were they when the Gauls took, sacked, burned and desolated Rome? Where were they when that memorable pestilence wrought such destruction, in which Furius Camillus too perished? . . . Nay, during this plague they introduced a new pestilence of scenic entertainments, which spread its more fatal contagion, not to the bodies, but to the morals of the Romans. Where were they when another frightful pestilence visited the city—I mean the poisonings imputed to an incredible number of noble Roman matrons." And so on.

The saint's first charge against the Roman gods, or "demons," as he preferred to call them, was that they "took no steps to improve the morals of their worshipers." And no matter where his endless arguments led him, he repeatedly returned to the charge of Roman immorality. He cried out against obscenities in the theater. He even complained about "iron bedsteads and expensive carpets" as "the luxury of Asia, more destructive than all hostile armies." But his chief argument against Rome's long history of barbaric violence was that the pagan gods had obviously failed to protect the Roman people from their enemies or their rulers or themselves. Why should any virtuous Romans care, then, about the sack of the imperial city when the new religion promised them a far higher realm? "Incomparably more glorious than Rome," Augustine wrote, "is that heavenly city in which for victory you have truth; for life, eternity." As for their recent sufferings, he offered the Romans the example of Job and urged them to rejoice in their survival. "That you are yet alive," he wrote, "is due to God, who spares you that you may be admonished to repent and reform your lives."

Saint Augustine may have been right in a way that he never intended, for the Goths' sack of Rome was indeed a kind of retribution, not against the Romans' religious shortcomings, much less their fondness for the lewdness of the theater, but for their long history of attacking and oppressing their neighbors. Alaric's personal grievances against the Romans were relatively petty. But when he finally assaulted them, he acted as the sword for generations of Goths, and, beyond that, for generations of forgotten peoples whose swords had been turned into chains. The sacking of the city was retribution, though not intended as such, for all those Gothic children who had been taken captive at the crossing of the Danube and forced into slavery and eventually slaughtered by the Roman legionaries. It was retribution for the killing of the wives and children of the Gothic *foederati* after the death of Stilicho. It was retribution for all the barbarian captives who had died in the Colosseum to entertain the Roman mob. Rome, the maker of laws, builder of roads, was the capital of the world, but the world that it ruled was a world of rapacity, corruption and utterly casual brutality. Alaric's attack was retribution for all of that.

There is a deeply believed principle, though, that a man who leads a moral life will be treated morally by his state and his god; that the state knows and cares who does right and who does wrong; that it will defend the right and punish the wrong. And that if the state fails in this basic function, some god will make up for its failure, punish wrongdoers whom the state rewarded and reward the virtuous whom the state betrayed. The sack of Rome—no matter what the past sins of the city had been—seemed to violate that principle. The innocent suffered along with the guilty, and, though Augustine tried to evade the problem by arguing that there were no innocent, the fact was that the supreme secular authority in the world had failed to defend its law-abiding citizens from the ravages of indiscriminate violence, and that the supreme religious authorities who now occupied the throne of Saint Peter had been equally unable to protect the virtuous, except by holding open the sanctuaries that the conqueror permitted to them. Neither the old gods nor the new had guarded their faithful. Neither the old gods nor the new had shown any sign of knowing or caring who the faithful were. In that divine indifference to a supreme crisis lay the terrible message of the sack of Rome.

∗

Augustine said that the survivors of the sacking had been spared so that they might repent and reform, but they did not repent or reform. And Rome survived, survived to be sacked again and again. Less than half a century after Alaric's passage, King Gaiseric of the Vandals sailed north from Africa and spent a leisurely two weeks stripping the city of whatever gold and silver could be found, even the copper roof on the Temple of Jupiter Capitolinus. It was Gaiseric, according to one report, who seized the seven-branched candlestick and other sacred vessels that Titus had taken from Herod's Temple, Gaiseric who loaded these treasures aboard one of his ships and then saw the vessel founder on the voyage back to Africa.

Charlemagne came to Rome to force his own coronation as emperor, and Otto the Great came to demand imperial approval of every papal election. When Otto encountered resistance, in the year 966, he turned his soldiers loose to sack the city once more. A century later, in 1083, it was the Emperor Henry IV who was besieging Pope Gregory VII in the Castel Sant' Angelo. Gregory called in the Norman adventurer Robert Guiscard to rescue him, and no sooner had the Normans expelled the imperial troops than an outburst of rioting led to yet another three-day sacking of Rome.

Those were the so-called Dark Ages. The worst sacking of Rome, however, occurred during the Renaissance, in the year 1527, when Michelangelo and Titian were at the height of their powers. The invading army of about 25,000 Spaniards, Germans, Italians and Swiss nominally represented Charles V, the Holy Roman Emperor. The issues involved have been forgotten; only the record of barbarism remains. "The squares before the churches were strewed with the ornaments of the altar, relics, and other sacred things," according to the classic account by J.-C-.L. de Sismondi, "which the soldiers threw into the streets after having torn off the gold and silver which adorned them. Men, women and children were seized, whenever their captors could flatter them-

selves that they had concealed some treasure, or that there was anyone sufficiently interested for them to pay their ransoms. Every house resounded with
cries and lamentations of wretched persons thus subjected to the torture; and
this dreadful state of crime and agony lasted not merely days, but was prolonged for more than nine months." It was ended only, in fact, by an outbreak
of the plague, so severe that the torturers fled northward in terror.

And again, Rome survived. The Rome of the Caesars, the Rome of Saints
Peter and Paul, of Innocent III and the Borgias—these are now simply historical categories in the guidebooks that have welcomed Goethe, Keats and
Stendhal, Napoleon and Hitler. And today, on the Pincian Hill overlooking the
Salarian Gate that opened to the Visigoths, German ladies in flowered silk
dresses sit idly by the fountains in the café just across the street from the Villa
Medici and savor an exotic spring delicacy, a slice of pineapple with vanilla ice
cream. In the pocked and pitted ruins of the Colosseum, where the monk Telemachus was stoned to death in the last recorded demonstration of the Roman
gladiatorial spirit, an official sign proclaims that this grim amphitheater is a
monument to all the nameless Christian martyrs who died here. The walls
around this ancient scene of terror are now daubed in black paint with symbols
of rage, the hammer and sickle, slogans warning of death to rival political
forces and their leaders. Inside, though, the endless game goes on. Guides in
sweat-stained blue shirts and raffish sunglasses offer to provide graphic details
on the deaths of the martyrs. Postcards are for sale. Also color slides.

So Augustine was right, in a way, in arguing that the sacking of Rome did
not mean the end of the world. Rome lives on, and two millennia of destruction
and rebirth have only made her, soft and tawny in the spring sunlight, more
glorious than ever.

The Birth of the Inquisition

1209–44

"Kill them all . . ."

Of all the regions of France, there is none more beautiful than the proud and remote land that still bears the name of Languedoc. The name speaks its own language, meaning that land where the Provençal tongue softened the Latin word for "yes" from *hoc* into *oc* (in contrast to the northern regions where the French spoke the *langue d'oil,* now *oui*). Languedoc has no fixed boundaries, but it extends roughly from the dark mountains of Auvergne to the snowy Pyrenees, from the marshy delta where the Rhone pours into the Mediterranean to the estuary where the Garonne confronts the Atlantic. It is the land of the sun, the Midi, the midday zenith.

Languedoc is the province with the oldest civilization, and the most diverse. The Phoenicians established colonies here, and the Greeks. Gallia Narbonensis was one of the seventeen provinces of Augustus' empire, and Narbonne was by then already a flourishing city, as were Toulouse and Béziers. Cicero called the region "the boulevard of Latinism," for it served to connect Spain and Italy, and from its rich farmlands Rome imported wine and oil, flax and hemp and fragrant cheeses.

The Visigoths found their homeland here after their conquest of Rome, and although the Gothic reign was the reign of heresy, it eventually extended deep into Spain, and it endured for two centuries before being engulfed by the advancing Saracens. King Pepin of the Franks expelled the Saracens from their strongholds at Arles and Narbonne in the middle of the eighth century, establishing Frankish sovereignty and Catholic orthodoxy as far as the Pyrenees. The Franks' dominion also proved transitory, however, for there was no central authority that could protect the coasts of France from the ravages of the Norsemen. By the middle of the tenth century, we find the region west of the Rhone ruled by autonomous counts of Toulouse, descendants of a Carolingian official named Fulguald, who called themselves "princes of Gothia" and owed only nominal fealty to the distant kings of France. When the one-eyed Count Raymond IV answered the call to the First Crusade, he marched to the Holy Land as an independent prince, his army the largest European force in the field, his authority subordinate to no one.

Tolosa, as the city was then known, lay athwart the route of the great pilgrimages to the shrine of Santiago de Compostela at the northwestern tip of Spain, and in the Garonne Valley that connected the Atlantic and the Mediterranean; and when international commerce began to revive after the dark years of Saracen and Viking plunder, Toulouse provided the central market for the natural riches of Languedoc. Its merchants shipped cloth and leather to the trade fairs outside Paris, and the wines of the Bordeaux region to England. Peasants from the outlying fields carted their wheat and barley to the mills that wheeled in the Garonne. The sea captains of Genoa and Pisa appeared, bringing the silks and spices of the Levant in exchange for Toulouse's oil and wax, rope, lumber and fish.

Capitals of commerce tend to favor diversity, and so Toulouse, a busy metropolis of perhaps 25,000 souls in A.D. 1200, welcomed Normans and Sicilians, Catalans and Jews. The Third Lateran Council of 1179 formally outlawed usury, by which it meant any interest charged on any loan, but Toulouse understood the uses of money, and although the devout might follow the rules of Christian piety, Jewish moneylenders were not only tolerated but respected. They even held official positions as advisors and administrators under the counts of Toulouse, a situation almost without parallel in twelfth-century Christendom.

Commerce also tends to demand independence, and the merchants of Toulouse managed to equate their interests and their liberties in a way that would have done credit to the Hancocks and the Cabots of eighteenth-century Boston. They paid the counts of Toulouse for exemption from certain taxes, they demanded and won the right to try their own citizens in their own courts. In 1152, they wrote a charter that circumscribed the counts' once-absolute rights, and in 1189 they established a city government of twenty-four consuls or *capitouls.* The consuls came from the leading commercial families, of course, but they asserted a republican authority almost unknown in the north of France. A citizen of Toulouse—even an alien, even a Jew—could not be claimed by any outside feudal authority, could not be arbitrarily taxed, could not be prevented from freely going about his business.

And commerce, in bringing diversity and toleration and independence, brings, almost as a byproduct, art. Under the twelfth-century sun of Languedoc, there occurred one of those almost miraculous flowerings of cultural life, of grand Romanesque citadels and cloisters at Carcassonne and Cahors and Moissac, of infinitely sophisticated sculpture such as the tympanum of Ste.-Foy at Conques, and of the lyric poetry by those enigmatic figures known as the troubadors. The Provençal poets, who sang in what Dante called the *lingua materna,* which Ezra Pound translated as "the fostering tongue," not only created great art but provoked the creation of great art in Italy and Spain and even Germany. As the first lyric poets since those of antiquity, the troubadors were the forefathers of Marlowe and Kleist and Verlaine and all that followed. Languedoc was their vineyard. *"Ab l'alen tir vas me l'aire/ qu'en son venir de Provensa . . . ,"* wrote Peire Vidal, the son of a furrier in Toulouse. "With each breath I draw in the air I feel coming from Provence; I so love everything from there that when people speak well of it, I listen smiling."

No one has ever explained how such a brilliant shoal of poets could suddenly emerge out of nothing, appearing first in the form of Guilhem IX, Count of

Poitiers and Duke of Aquitaine, of whom his anonymous contemporary biographer observed that he "knew well how to sing and make verses, and for a long time he roamed all through the land to deceive the ladies." *"Companho,"* cried the Duke, in one of the dozen of his poems that still survive, *"faray un vers . . ./ Et er totz mesclatz d'amor e de joy e de joven . . .* My friends, I'll make a poem . . . and it will be all mingled with love and joy and youth."

It seems almost an explosion of self-discovery, but no combustion is entirely spontaneous. One theory is that Provençal poetry had been developing as a form of popular art, and that Guilhem was simply the first whose rank made his creations appear worth preserving. The troubador poetry that has come down to us is passionately aristocratic poetry (about half of the four hundred known troubadors were noblemen, and twenty-three of them were reigning princes), an art allied with falconry and dance in the enjoyment of courtly life. It flourished in Languedoc under the generous patronage of Count Raymond V of Toulouse, that "Coms Raymon" who appears in so many Provençal songs as a hero of *valors.* And Toulouse by now was a capital at least as powerful as the crude northern city of Paris, and its holdings were somewhat larger. From the borders of Aquitaine, claimed by the Plantagenets of England, all the way to the waterfront of Marseille, Count Raymond, and not the King of France, was master.

There is another theory, though, that the outburst of troubador poetry was not purely a local inspiration of the courts of Languedoc but rather a movement powerfully influenced by a school of Arab lyric poets flourishing in Spain and North Africa. Guilhem of Poitiers, who went on crusade to the Holy Land in 1101, might have encountered there the Arabic prosody of the *zadjal* that is said to govern five of his eleven surviving poems, or he might have learned it simply as part of the tumultuous commerce in new ideas that the traders of the Mediterranean were bringing into Languedoc. Yet other sources can be suggested. Ezra Pound, in *The Spirit of Romance,* argued that the whole region still retained the touch of ancient Greece. "Provençal song," he wrote, "is never wholly disjunct from pagan rites of May Day. . . . The troubadors . . . have, in some way, lost the names of the gods and remembered the names of the lovers. Ovid and the *Eclogues* of Virgil seem to have been their chief documents."

The equation of song and paganism can be ominous. There is yet another theory, most eloquently argued by Denis de Rougemont in *Love in the Western World,* that many of the troubadors' lyrics of love were not simple songs to various court ladies but elaborately symbolic hymns to the condemned divinities of the Cathar Church. "O high and glorious King, O Light and Brightness true!" Guiraut de Bornheil prays while supposedly waiting for his lady. Bernart de Ventadour, having been parted from his love, writes of her in tones that could easily represent religious anguish: "She has taken my heart, she has taken my self, she has taken me from the world, and then she has slipped away from me, leaving me with only my desire and my parched heart."

Whatever the exact degree of entanglement between the poets and the heretics, it was generally acknowledged that the city of Toulouse and the rich lands of Languedoc formed not only the commercial and cultural center of southwestern Europe but also the center of a cursed and forbidden religion. As early as 1145, when Saint Bernard of Clairvaux came to Toulouse to argue with the dissidents, whom he likened to Arians, he was horrified to find "churches without congregations, congregations without priests, priests without proper reverence. . . . Prayers and offerings for the dead were ridiculed, as were the invocations of saints, pilgrimages by the faithful, the building of temples . . . , and in a word, all the institutions of the church were scorned." Thirty years later, Count Raymond V described the collapse of the true church in even more desolate terms. He was hardly an objective witness, of course, having supported the German Emperor Frederick Barbarossa and the Antipope Victor during one of the church's periodic convulsions, and now he needed to establish his religious orthodoxy by appealing to the French crown for help against the church's enemies. "The heresy has penetrated everywhere," he wrote. "It has sown discord in every family, dividing husband from wife, son from father, a man's wife from his mother. Even priests yield to the temptation. The churches are abandoned and falling into ruin."

The Lateran Council of 1179 responded to Count Raymond's plea by approving in principle a campaign against the heretics of Languedoc. They were to be hunted down and forced into slavery. Nothing much came of this plan, however, which probably suited Count Raymond. About twenty years later, at the dawn of the thirteenth century, the Vatican was still complaining about "the insolence of the heretics" in Languedoc, but now it attached much of the blame to the corruption of the clergy, particularly the clergy under Berengar II, the archbishop of Narbonne. "This man knows no other God but money," declared the Pope, "and keeps a purse where his heart should be." The archbishop openly sold the clerical offices of the province, and his subordinates behaved accordingly. "Regular monks or canons have ... taken wives or mistresses," the Pope raged on, "and are living by usury; some indeed have set up as lawyers, *jongleurs* or doctors." As for their ardor in propagating and defending the true faith, "they are blind creatures, dumb hounds who can no longer bay."

What made these latest accusations more than a matter of rhetorical lament was that they came from Lotario de' Conti di Segni, newly elected, at the age of thirty-seven, Pope Innocent III. A small, dark, stern figure, Innocent was determined to assert the powers of the Papacy on a scale hardly more than imagined by his predecessors. *"Petro non solum universam ecclesiam, sed totum reliquit saeculum gubernandum,"* he declared. "To Peter was left the governance not only of the universal church but of the whole world." Innocent soon intervened decisively in the election of a new Holy Roman Emperor. To enforce his will on King John of England, he laid the entire island under interdict and ultimately made it a fief of the Holy See. He launched the Fourth Crusade to reconquer the Holy Land from the Mohammedans, and when the Crusaders strayed off to seize Christian Constantinople, Innocent calmly made use of their assault to take command of the Orthodox Church, expressing the hope that East and West would henceforth be "one fold under one shepherd." This was the Pope who sent the Teutonic Knights northward along the Baltic to "convert" the Letts and the Livonians, so when Innocent III confronted the specter of heresy among the rich and complacent lords of Languedoc, there was little doubt in his mind about how to respond to it. Had not Jesus Christ himself said, "I come not to bring peace but the sword?"

*

Like most ruined and destroyed religions, Catharism remains a somewhat mysterious faith. Its rites and beliefs have survived mainly in the denunciations of its enemies, and in the confessions extorted from the prisoners of the Inquisition. At its height, however, it seems to have been a true rival to the Church of Rome, proclaiming its own apostolic tradition and its own ecclesiastical hierarchy, its own version of Christian theology and morality.

It seems to have derived from Manicheanism, which was itself a ruined and destroyed religion. As a philosophical doctrine, Manicheanism generally means little more than a mild belief in the duality of good and evil, and in an eternal conflict between the two. Mani himself was a more impassioned prophet. Roving from Babylon as far as western China, he taught that the material world was the creation not of God but of Satan, that Satan controlled man's physical existence (it was Satan, in fact, who created Eve for Adam and fathered on her both Cain and Abel). Mani declared that he himself was the last and greatest of the prophets, who could lead a few of his most spiritual followers into the kingdom of light, when the world was consumed, as must soon happen, by fire.

Mani was executed—flayed alive—by the Persians in A.D. 276, but his beliefs, infected with the mysticism of the Gnostics, spread like a plague among the bewildered citizens of the dying Roman Empire. As early as the reign of Valens, that Arian Emperor who was killed by the Goths at Adrianople, Manicheanism was decreed to be a crime, and by the time of Justinian it was punishable by death. But it survived, particularly in the Eastern Empire, under a series of different names and formulations. It appeared in the fifth century among the Paulicians, named after the Patriarch Paul of Samosata, who flourished in Asia Minor and Armenia. It reappeared in the tenth century among the Bogomils, a movement apparently founded by a priest of that name, which spread through the Gothic land once known as Moesia, now Bulgaria. By this time, Manicheanism had acquired dense accretions of Gnosticism and Zoroastrianism and simple folklore. The Bogomils declared that God had two sons, of whom the elder was Satanail, who rebelled and was exiled to the lower heavens. And it was he who created man and held him in bondage until God sent his second son, Michael, as a redeemer who could break the bond....

The infection spread across Italy, where the heretics were known as Patarini, and France, where the Waldensians preached a life of holy poverty, and into Languedoc, where they acquired the name of Albigensians, after one of their first strongholds in the city of Albi. They themselves used the name of Cathars, after *cathari,* the Greek word for pure. Or, more simply, they called themselves the *bons hommes.* They believed, as did the early Christians whom they claimed as their models, that the impending destruction of the earth required each of them to preach and practice the virtues of austerity. They lived in poverty and chastity, and they ate no meat or other animal products, not even cheese. Saint Bernard, who preached in vain against them, confessed to a sense of futility. "As to their conversation, nothing can be less reprehensible," he wrote, "and what they speak, they prove by deeds. As for the morals of the heretic, he cheats no one, he oppresses no one, he strikes no one; his cheeks are pale with fasting, . . . his hands labor for his livelihood."

The Cathars called themselves Christians, but their version of Christianity challenged the most fundamental theses of the Roman Church. They believed that the Jehovah of the Old Testament, creator of the universe, was actually Lucifer, the fallen angel. They regarded all material things as evil, and human life itself as a kind of purgatory. The imprisoned soul could only pass from one body to another until it found release. Christ had appeared not as a redeemer, the incarnation of God in man, but rather as an angelic messenger, sent to teach the way of salvation. His crucifixion represented, once again, the triumph of the evil world.

The Cathars openly defended their beliefs, to the amazement of the orthodox, at a public debate in 1165 in the town of Lombers, near Albi, and they defended all the implications of those beliefs. They rejected the cross as a symbol not of redemption but of torture and degradation. They rejected all veneration of dead saints and martyrs, whose relics they regarded as hardly different from sticks and stones. They rejected all the traditional sacraments, from baptism to extreme unction. They rejected, above all, the Church of Rome, which they attacked as the betrayer of Christianity. They likened it to the Antichrist, and to the Whore of Babylon.

These criticisms may seem purely destructive, but the Cathars claimed the authority of the New Testament for their own version of Christianity. Did Christ not attack the orthodoxy of his time, and was he not accused of blasphemy? The Cathars not only preached from the New Testament but preached it in the Provençal language, which was forbidden by Rome. Their main prayer, repeated over and over, was exactly what Christ had said it should be: *"La nostre paire qui es els celo . . ."* Like the early Christians, and in contrast to the great financiers and engineers of Catholicism, the Cathars had no churches at all. They wandered from town to town in their black robes, preaching, tending to the sick, working in the fields, administering the sacraments of their faith.

The Cathars had only four basic rituals. The simplest and most common was the blessing of bread, a kind of eucharistic ceremony, performed daily. After the recitation of the Lord's Prayer, the highest-ranking person at table asked for grace, broke the bread, and distributed it. *"Benedicite,"* said the others. The senior celebrant answered, *"Dieus vos benesiga."* Almost equally simple was the *melioramentum,* or act of veneration, by which the faithful asked for and received a blessing whenever they encountered one of their wandering priests. The believer bowed down three times and said, "Pray God to make a good Christian of me and bring me to a good end." The priest answered in kind: "May God make a good Christian of you, and bring you to a good end." Somewhat more elaborate was the *apparelhamentum,* a monthly communal confession of sins. "For many are the sins," the petitioners chanted, "by which we offend God night and day in thought, word and deed, whether willfully or in spite of ourselves—by means of the will which evil spirits bring to the flesh wherewith we are clothed." The priest, after hearing the confessions, would prescribe penances, fasting and recitations of the Lord's Prayer.

The most complex ritual was that which transformed the common believers, or *credentes,* into the priesthood of the *perfecti.* It was known as the *consolamentum,* or baptism by the Holy Spirit. It was traditionally preceded by a year of fasting and study. Only after these preparations was the candidate led into a brightly lit room and made to stand before a table where the New Testament lay on an immaculate white cloth. The priest, flanked by two assistants and accompanied by other *perfecti,* conducted a ritual interrogation.

"Do you give yourself to God and the Gospel?"

"I do."

"Do you promise that henceforth you will eat neither meat nor eggs nor cheese nor fat, . . . that you will not tell lies, nor take oaths, nor lend your body to any indulgence?"

"I do."

The candidate was told, finally, that he "must keep all the commandments of Christ," and that Christ had commanded "that man may not commit adultery, nor kill, nor lie, nor take oaths, nor steal, nor do anything to others that he would not wish done to himself. . . . And equally you must hate this world and its works and the things that pertain to it."

The demands of the *consolamentum* were so stern that many of the *credentes* took the pledge only on their deathbeds. But those who were able to commit their lives to the faith entered the priesthood of the *bons hommes* or *perfecti.* They abjured all sexual relations, for the creation of children meant the perpetuation of evil, and they fasted often, for days at a time. That was, as they understood it, the message of Christ, and they preached it all through Languedoc, and because their austere and dedicated lives so visibly exemplified their teaching, they acquired a moral prestige that was quite absent among the princes of the Roman Church. They built no towering cathedrals, but their organization reached into every parish. Each Roman diocese was also a Cathar diocese, with Cathar bishops headquartered at Toulouse, Carcassonne and Albi. Each bishop had two deputies designated as sons, the *filius maior* and *filius minor,* who would eventually replace him, and who would themselves be replaced by a vote of the *perfecti.*

The most important element of Catharism, however, was neither ceremony nor organization but rather the sense of mission. The Cathars claimed to be the only true followers of Christ, and of the apostolic tradition. There are legends that they based this claim on gospels that have now been lost, and even that the Cathar treasure stored in the fortress of Montségur contained the Holy Grail itself. Whether these legends be true or not, Rome recognized the Cathars not merely as a band of heretics who had strayed from the true faith but as deadly enemies. They had established themselves in the Balkans, in France and, worst of all, in Italy itself. The anticlerical magistrates of Milan openly defied Rome's attempts to suppress the Cathars, and there were colonies of heretics in Florence, Verona, Brescia, Orvieto and Ferrara. The Church of Rome, they all insisted, was the Beast of the Apocalypse, and if the beast threatened violence, so be it. True Christians had known martyrdom long before the popes had come to sit on their gilded throne.

"*Roma,*" as one of the troubadors, Guilhem Figuera, son of a Toulouse tailor, was to write,

> *Roma, tant es grans*
> *La vostra forfaitura,*
>   *Que dieus e sos sans*
> *En gitatz a non cura,*
>   *Tant etz mal renhans,*
> *Roma falsa e tafura. . . .*

"Rome," as the translator tries to express the troubador's fury, "so great is your evil doing that God and his saints you regard not, so little are you restrained, Rome false and deceitful. . . ."

*

In the youth and upbringing of Domingo de Guzmán, there seems to have been nothing in any way unusual. He was born in 1170, son of a minor Spanish nobleman, then educated in the home of an uncle who was a priest, then sent at the age of fourteen to study at a school in Palencia, where he took courses in art and theology for ten years. The only sign of his future sanctity occurred during a famine in 1191, when the young scholar is said to have sold all his books to buy food for the poor. "I do not want to study on parchment when men are dying of hunger," he said.

Domingo, better known to history as Dominic, needed a hero. He found him in Diego de Azevedo, bishop of Osma, who made the youth his subprior. Diego seems to have been an extraordinary figure, both devout and worldly, a future cardinal, perhaps a future pope. The King of Castille sent him to Denmark to negotiate a marriage between his thirteen-year-old son, Ferdinand, and one of the nieces of King Waldemar II. When these negotiations failed, Diego, always accompanied by the young Dominic, voyaged to Rome to ask Pope Innocent III to assign him to a new mission. He wanted, he said, to travel beyond the farthest reaches of Hungary and to preach among the Kuman Tartars and convert them to the true faith. Innocent was impressed by such dedication. He approved of Diego's vocation, but he told him to go not among the Tartars but among the heretics of Languedoc. There, said Innocent, Diego and his prior could best serve the Vicar of Christ.

Diego was by no means the first missionary whom Innocent had sent among the Cathars. The Pope had decided almost from the start of his reign that the clergy of Languedoc was hopelessly compromised. "The corruption of the people has its chief source in the clergy," he declared. "From this arise the evils of Christendom: faith perishes, religion is defaced, liberty is restricted, justice is trodden underfoot, the heretics multiply, the schismatics are emboldened, the faithless grow strong."As early as 1198, Innocent had sent a Brother Rainier as his legate to Languedoc to suppress the Cathar heresy. When Rainier fell ill, he was replaced by the haughty archdeacon of Manguelone, Pierre de Castelnau. Nothing availed. Innocent wondered whether he might not destroy heresy by invoking the armed forces of King Philip Augustus of France. In May of 1204 and again in February of 1205, he wrote to inquire. Philip Augustus balked. He was engaged in territorial disputes with King John of England, and he wrote back to ask whether Innocent could guarantee the security of his northern frontiers, and pay the costs of a campaign against the south.

Innocent continued to hope that intellectual arguments might triumph. He turned to Arnaud-Amalric, the abbot of the Cistercians, and appointed him chief legate to Languedoc. Arnaud-Amalric and Pierre de Castelnau did their best, but their strategy was the traditional strategy of a foreign army in a rebellious colony. "Look," as one chronicler quotes a Cathar priest describing the legates of Rome, "at the ministers on horseback representing a God who went on foot, the rich missionaries of a God who went penniless, the envoys laden with honors representing a God who was humble and despised."

Bishop Diego and his young prior saw the difficulty immediately and proposed the obvious solution. They would wander barefoot through the province, begging for just enough food to sustain them, living on the same terms of Christian poverty as their adversaries, and arguing, wherever they could find anyone to contest them, the claims of the Roman faith. From the fragmentary chronicles of the time, we hear an occasional outburst of the Cathar faith, as in the declaration of the Cathar Deacon Arnaud Othon during the public debate at Montréal in 1207: "The Roman Church is not holy. It is the church of the devil. It is that Babylon that John, in the Apocalypse, calls mother of fornication and abominations, drunk on the blood of the saints." The same chronicles urge us to hear the voice of saintly orthodoxy when Dominic is threatened with violence. "I beg you not to inflict immediately a mortal wound," he is said to have answered, "but to prolong my martyrdom by mutilating, one by one, my arms and legs . . . and then to tear out my eyes, and to let my body bathe in its own blood . . . so that I shall deserve the crown of the greatest martyrdom." The rhetoric of hagiography is supported by tales of miracles. According to the *Hystoria Albigensis* of Pierre des Vaux-de-Cernay, the Cathars seized one of Dominic's declarations and threw it into a fire. The paper, according to the good monk, "leaped out of the fire absolutely undamaged."

Of such stories is sainthood made—Fra Angelico's painting of the miracle can be seen at the Louvre—and Dominic was undeniably destined for sainthood. He was pious, zealous, and passionately dedicated to his faith. He and Bishop Diego soon realized that the power of the Cathars lay largely in their control of the young, in their network of schools and convents where the generations of the future received an education in the false faith. They determined to create a rival network, starting, in 1206, with a school for girls at Prouille. Diego returned to Spain to raise money, and there he soon fell ill and died.

Dominic, left alone among the heretics of Languedoc, preached and traveled and argued and recruited. All to little effect. The heretics remained convinced of the truth of their faith. Dominic, the future saint, became increasingly insistent. "For many years I have exhorted you in vain," he declared, "with gentleness, preaching, praying, weeping. But according to the proverb of my country, 'where blessing can accomplish nothing, blows may avail.' We shall rouse against you princes and prelates, who, alas, will arm nations and kingdoms against this land. . . ."

✳

The process had already begun. Pope Innocent III had demanded that the lords of Languedoc root out and expel the heretics from their lands. The papal legate, Pierre de Castelnau, organized a coalition of lords to carry out that order. He invited Count Raymond VI of Toulouse to join in the campaign. Count Raymond respectfully declined to enforce orthodoxy upon his people. Pierre de Castelnau promptly excommunicated him, laid his lands under interdict and freed all his vassals from all obligations to their lord. Count Raymond, always equivocal and never above duplicity, soon capitulated and joined the legate's coalition. But he must have made known his anger at the legate's threats. Pierre de Castelnau was a marked man.

On the morning of January 14, 1208, on the fog-covered bank of the Rhone, not far from Beaucaire, a group of monks and other travelers waited for the ferryboat to take them across the river. Out of the fog came a knight on horseback, his face masked in armor. He seemed to know exactly what he was searching for—one of the men in monks' robes. He soon recognized his victim, Pierre de Castelnau. He stabbed the priest through the chest with his spear, then rode off into the fog, back along the road to Beaucaire. "May God forgive thee, for I forgive thee," Pierre said as he died.

Nobody has ever determined who this knight was, or who, if anyone, had ordered him to murder the papal legate. It has generally been assumed that the knight was carrying out the wishes, spoken or unspoken, of Count Raymond, much as those knights who murdered Thomas à Becket in the Canterbury Cathedral were carrying out the wishes of King Henry II. "We realized that this was our duty," as the third knight says in T. S. Eliot's brilliant epilogue to *Murder in the Cathedral*, "but . . . we know perfectly well how things will turn out. King Henry—God bless him—will have to say, for reasons of state, that he never meant this to happen; and there is going to be an awful row."

"*Sapcatz que nolh fa bela . . .*" So wrote an obscure cleric named Guilhem de Tudela in the wonderful epic poem known as the *Canzon de la Crozada,* or *The Song of the Albigensian Crusade,* a chronicle that all subsequent historians of the struggle have used as their basic source of information. "Know that it was not agreeable to him," Guilhem was writing here, meaning that Pope Innocent III was displeased at the news of the murder of Pierre de Castelnau. Guilhem was indulging himself in poetic understatement. Innocent III was not just displeased but outraged. Arguments over the nature of Christ might be analyzed in scholarly conclaves, disputes over clerical prerogatives might be submitted to the arbitration of learned jurists, but the murder of a papal legate, the legal and spiritual representative of the Vicar of Christ, had to be avenged.

The Pope sent messages to all the priests in Languedoc, ordering them to excommunicate everyone who might have conspired in the murder of Pierre de Castelnau and to place under interdict all the lands of Count Raymond of Toulouse. And to the rulers of the surrounding lands, most notably King Philip Augustus of France, Innocent appealed for a crusade to destroy once and for all the foul heresy of the Cathars. "Brother," he said to Arnaud-Amalric, the chief abbot of the powerful Cistercians, "you will lead the armies against that perfidious race. . . . Preach to them, exhort them to drive out the heretics from among the good Christians."

The wily King Philip Augustus, embroiled in a territorial quarrel with King John of England, declined once again the honor of a crusade against Languedoc unless the Pope promised him large sums of money. The Pope refused. The Abbot Arnaud-Amalric nonetheless managed to recruit an impressive army of crusaders. The Duke of Burgundy, Eudes II, was among them, and the counts of Nevers and St.-Pol and Auxerre. To all of them and their followers the church promised, for only forty days in the field, both forgiveness of all sins and safety from all creditors. The offer was almost irresistible, and the forces that gathered at Lyon in June of 1209 were awesome. They came from as far away as Bremen, Lombardy and Lithuania. "This was a marvelously grand army," wrote Guilhem de Tudela. "Twenty thousand knights in full armor, and more than 200,000 peasants, and I am not even counting the merchants and the clergy."

Count Raymond saw the oncoming tidal wave that would destroy his nation. He sent a message to Pope Innocent to beg for mercy. Innocent was suspicious. Raymond was a sensualist, married five times, and if he was not a heretic it was probably because he had very little religion at all. One of the church's pious chroniclers, Pierre des Vaux-de-Cernay, described the Count as "a son of perdition, firstborn of Satan, enemy of the cross, . . . minister of damnation." Innocent was equally harsh. He called the Count "impious, cruel tyrant, creature both pestilent and insane." He ordered Raymond to surrender seven major castles as a token of his good faith before any negotiations could even begin. Raymond surrendered the seven castles. He was told to present himself at the Church of St.-Gilles, where the corpse of the martyred Pierre de Castelnau lay buried in the crypt. He obeyed. Stripped to the waist, Count Raymond had to submit to the new papal legate, Milo, who put a halter over the Count's neck and led him like a barnyard animal to the altar, while his subordinate priests scourged the count's bare back. At the altar, Count Raymond had to swear by the relics of Saint Gilles, an eighth-century Greek who had sailed to Provence and lived as a hermit in a cave, that he would obey any order that the Holy Father chose to give. He even enrolled himself in the impending crusade against his own people.

The papal legate remained suspicious. "As for the Count of Toulouse, that enemy of truth and justice," Milo wrote back to Rome ". . . be not moved by his tongue, skillful only in his slanders, but let him, as he deserves, feel the hand of the church heavier day by day." Innocent was not easily deceived. "Let us follow the example of the Apostle who said, 'I was cunning, I won you over by guile,' " the Pope wrote to his legates. He urged them to "attack those who have imperiled the unity of the church separately and one by one, so as to divide their forces. . . . Practice wise dissimulation. Leave [Count Raymond] to one side at first. . . . If he persists in his evil designs we can—once he is isolated and dependent on his own forces alone—deal with him last of all and strike him down without much difficulty."

Marching down the Rhone Valley in their tens of thousands, then turning westward, the crusaders stopped briefly in Montpellier, which had always been loyal to the church, then followed the old Roman road toward their first major objective, the flourishing coastal city of Béziers. The Viscount of Béziers and Carcassonne, Raymond-Roger Trencavel, warned his people of the coming attack and told them that he could not let himself be trapped inside the city. He withdrew to his impregnable capital of Carcassonne, taking with him several notable heretics and Jewish advisers whom he knew the crusaders would try to seize. He left the leaderless people of Béziers "grieving," according to Guilhem de Tudela, but they were not unduly alarmed. Their city was well fortified and well supplied. From their ramparts and turrets high over the valley of the Orb River, they could withstand a prolonged siege.

On July 21, 1209, the mass of crusaders—including the humbled Count Raymond of Toulouse, with his scarlet cross sewn to his tunic—arrived outside Béziers and began erecting their tents along the river. The bishop of Béziers, Renaud de Montpeyroux, set out to confer with them, then returned to his cathedral and assembled his flock and told them of the crusaders' proposition. The crusaders agreed to spare the city, but only if all known heretics were surrendered to them. The bishop happened to have drawn up a list of these heretics, totaling 220. The citizens of Béziers, secure behind their walls, declined the offer of salvation. They said, according to one chronicler, that they "would rather eat their children." The bishop mounted a mule and rode out of the city to join the crusaders.

On the very next day, the feast day of Saint Mary Magdalene, there occurred one of those episodes that seem almost accidentally to change the course of history. The papal legate, Arnaud-Amalric, was to describe it as "a miracle." What happened was that a crowd of citizens decided to sally forth from their fortifications and engage in a skirmish with the idled crusaders. Not even crusaders, really, but *ribauds,* riffraff, those valets and thieves and camp followers and despoilers of corpses who formed a major part of any crusading army. Guilhem de Tudela becomes indignant when he tries to describe the folly of these attackers—"these peasants," he calls them, "crazier and more foolish than whales."* They shouted, they waved scraps of linen banners. They thought, says Guilhem, that they could frighten the crusaders, "the way one

* A learned footnote in the three-volume version of the *Canzon* edited by Eugène Martin-Chabet and published between 1931 and 1961 informs us that no scholar of Provençal verse has managed to explain the meaning of this rather charming metaphor.

frightens birds in a field of oats." This marauding mob encountered one lone crusader near a bridge and beat him savagely and then threw his corpse into the moat that surrounded the city. That attack seems to have galvanized the *ribauds*. Snatching up clubs and stones and whatever other weapons they could find, they launched a wild charge. They were hardly more than a rabble, barefoot and without armor, but they had the courage of numbers. They pursued the marauders from Béziers back up the hill, back to the gate of the city.

They found that the gate was still open, or at least unbarred, to permit the marauders to return. Guilhem tells us simply that the pursuers smashed it open. And suddenly found themselves, to their amazement, inside the once-impregnable city. And saw the terrified citizens running for cover.

> *Li ribaut foren caut, no an paor de morir:*
> *Tot cant pogron trobar van tuar e ausir....*

"Being inflamed," Guilhem is saying, "the *ribauds* had no fear of death. They killed and massacred everyone they encountered." This almost accidental skirmish, this almost accidental breaching of the gate to the fortress, was the miracle that so impressed the papal commander, Arnaud-Amalric. The triumphant crusaders came to him, according to legend, and asked him whom they should kill: "Lord, what shall we do? We cannot distinguish the good from the wicked." And the ruling abbot of the Cistercians, heir to Saint Bernard of Clairvaux, said, "Kill them all! God will recognize his own."*

The knights of the crusading army, clambering up the hill in the wake of their servants and scavengers, found the proud city of Béziers already aflame. Crowds of citizens, women and children, had flocked to take refuge in the Church of Saint Mary Magdalene, whose feast day this was. They had locked the doors and begun to sing a requiem mass for the souls of the dead. The French set the locked church on fire, then watched as the flames crackled upward. "And all those who had taken refuge in the church were killed," Guilhem wrote. "Nothing could save them, neither cross nor altar nor crucifix ... *Que nols pot gandir crotz, ni cruzifis....*"

The French knights seem to have been appalled mainly at the plundering by their own forces of the riches that they expected to seize for themselves. They tried to establish some sort of order, beating back the *ribauds* from their looting. The *ribauds* responded by putting the rest of the city to the torch. Both knights and valets killed anyone they felt like killing. Arnaud-Amalric, the papal legate, proudly wrote to Pope Innocent that the crusaders had exterminated some fifteen thousand people, "showing mercy neither to order nor age nor sex." The number, like most statistics of the Middle Ages, has been dis-

---

* This most famous of all statements made during the Albigensian Crusade, illustrating the whole spirit of the campaign, may never have been made at all. It originally appeared in an account by a German Cistercian monk named Caesarius of Heisterbach, who reported it in about 1220–23 (i.e. more than ten years after the fact), in his *Dialogue on Miracles*. It should be noted that he reported Arnaud-Amalric's declaration as a thoroughly admirable statement of Christian faith.

puted. Estimates of the true casualty figures range from seven thousand to 100,-000. The numbers hardly matter now. The spirit of the crusade was one of total destruction. The crusaders burned even the Cathedral of Béziers. "So fierce were the flames," according to Guilhem, "that it burst asunder, cracked down the middle, and collapsed in two halves."

Leaving behind the smoking wreckage of Béziers, the crusaders turned inland toward the citadel of Carcassonne, some fifty miles to the west. Carcassonne, founded by the Romans, conquered and fortified by the Visigoths, abandoned to disintegration under the Capets and the Bourbons, then magnificently restored by the Roman antiquarians of the nineteenth century—"There can be nothing better than this," wrote the wandering Henry James after a moonlight stroll on the ramparts—Carcassone, like Béziers, perches high and impregnable over one of Languedoc's valleys. More exactly, it is the walled fortress of the Visigoths, *La Cité*, that perches there. Down on the banks of the River Aude, a mile or so to the west, lies the city itself, and here the victorious crusaders arrived on August 1, 1209.

Here, chanting their battle hymn, *"Veni Sancte Spiritus,"* they swept through the commercial center on the banks of the river, driving the defenders up into the hilltop fortress. The thirty towers and the thick walls of this fortress were unassailable, according to Guilhem's chronicle, but the crusaders were able to cut off the water supply from the Aude. "And in the great heat of that scorching summer the wells dried up," the chronicler goes on. The besieged citizens of Carcassonne "were plagued by many things: the stench of the sick, and of the numerous cattle within the walls, . . . the weeping and wailing of women and children . . . and swarms of flies, that bred in the heat and tormented them."

Once again there were negotiations. The King of Aragon, Pedro II, who claimed the fealty of Raymond-Roger Trencavel, the young Viscount of Béziers and Carcassonne, appeared on the scene and asked the crusaders to be lenient to his vassal. The papal legate, Arnaud-Amalric, contemptuously agreed to let Raymond-Roger go free, along with eleven companions of his own choice, if he agreed to surrender his capital of Carcassonne to the crusaders. Raymond-Roger angrily refused the offer. Then, apparently as a kind of gesture of self-sacrifice—the aristocrats of Languedoc believed passionately in *paratge,* a concept only approximated by the French term *courtoisie* and the English "chivalry"—Raymond-Roger gave himself up as a kind of hostage for the lives of his people. "In my opinion," says the wary Guilhem, "he acted like a madman."

The papal legate responded by conducting Raymond-Roger to a prison cell. And the citizens of Carcassonne were spared only in the sense that the crusaders allowed them to flee from the citadel, naked, taking with them, as one Catholic chronicler jeered, "nothing but their sins." Without the loss of a single life—except that of Raymond-Roger, who soon died in captivity, supposedly of dysentery—the crusaders achieved their second major victory. Carcassonne was to become their headquarters, and later the headquarters of the Inquisition that the crusaders established in the conquered land.

*

The crusaders had pledged themselves to only forty days of campaigning, however. Though they had achieved a series of quick successes, they would soon return home. Arnaud-Amalric needed a warrior lord whom he could assign to rule over the territory that had been newly acquired. The principal leaders of the crusade demurred. They felt wary about taking possession of lands that had been seized from one of their peers, Count Raymond, who had, after all, committed no crime against them. The Count of Nevers declined the legate's offer. So did the Count of St.-Pol. "There was no one," according to Guilhem de Tudela, "who would not consider himself dishonored if he accepted this fief."

No one but Simon de Montfort. He was one of those mighty warriors who seem destined to found dynasties—and yet also destined, like a Cortez, a Wallenstein, a Napoleon or, for that matter, an Alaric, to see their destiny elude them. Montfort was a heroic figure, large and powerful, dark, descended from an old and noble Norman family. *"Un riche baron, qui fu pros e valent ... ,"* wrote Guilhem, who had no reason to admire him. "A powerful baron, who was brave and strong, bold and combative, wise and experienced, a true knight, generous and attractive, gentle and frank, agreeable in manner and dedicated in spirit."

Montfort had inherited some land outside Paris, in the Île de France, but that was not enough to satisfy him. He set out with Count Thibaut de Champagne on the Fourth Crusade, the campaign that was subverted by the Venetians and bribed to assault the Christian outpost of Zara. Montfort was one of the few who resisted the easy subversion. "I did not come here to attack Christians," he said. He campaigned for a year in the Holy Land, then returned to France, still restless. He was skeptical about joining the Albigensian Crusade, but he fell under the spell of one of its most ardent preachers, Guy des Vaux-de-Cernay. He tried one of the favorite tests of that era, a random opening of the Scriptures. He went to church, opened the Bible, and found that his finger had landed on the Ninety-first Psalm: "For He shall give His angels charge over thee, to keep thee in all thy ways. They shall bear thee up in their hands, lest thou dash thy feet against a stone."

That sense of invulnerability may have inspired Montfort in one of the first battles of the crusade, the siege of Castelar. A knight had fallen at the base of the wall, badly wounded, and anyone who tried to rescue him would have to pass through a storm of arrows and rocks. Montfort, accompanied only by one quaking servant, raced through that storm and lifted up the fallen knight and carried him to safety. There was talk of a miracle. But now, when the papal legate offered him the command of the crusade and the possession of all the heretics' lands, Montfort was possessed by doubts. "I will do it on one condition," he said, according to Guilhem's chronicle, "on condition that all the princes here present swear an oath to me, that if I come to be in peril, they will all come to answer my call, to aid and defend me." And the leaders of the crusade all agreed: "We grant you that."

Terrified by the sack of Béziers and the fall of Carcassonne, the smaller fortresses of Languedoc surrendered with scarcely any resistance at all. Fanjeaux, Limou, Alzonne, Montréal, Lombers all opened their gates to the crusaders. Montfort installed garrisons in each of his main conquests, but he soon ran out of men. The forty days of the crusade had expired. Count Raymond of Toulouse was among the first to return home, then the Count of Nevers, then the Duke of Burgundy, and by September of 1209 only twenty-six knights out of that vast army of crusaders still remained in the field under Montfort's command. When the crusaders finally reached Toulouse and demanded that the city give up its heretics, the consuls of the city simply refused. *"Que de totas ciutatz es cela flors e roza,"* Guilhem boasted. "Of all cities, that one is the flower, the rose." The soldiers of Toulouse sortied out from their walls and attacked Montfort. The crusaders promptly withdrew.

Count Raymond, having taken part in the crusade, now decided that it was time to repair to Rome, to persuade Innocent III to leave Languedoc in peace. He took a circuitous northern route, soliciting the support of both King Philip Augustus of France and Emperor Otto IV of Germany, and managing to irritate both of them, since they were feuding with each other. When he finally reached Rome, however, he seemed to achieve a reconciliation with Innocent. "The Pope," Guilhem de Tudela reported, "gave him a princely cloak, a fine gold ring of which the stone alone was worth fifty silver marks, and also a horse. They immediately became very good and cordial friends. The Pope showed him the cloth with which Saint Veronica had wiped the brow of our Lord, he made him touch the image of the face, which seems to be that of a living man, and he gave him complete absolution for all the sins he had committed."

The price of this reconciliation, though, was the total submission of Languedoc to the forces of orthodoxy. Under the auspices of Count Raymond, therefore, the city of Toulouse, which had just rejected the demands of Simon de Montfort, now opened its doors to Arnaud-Amalric, that papal legate who had presided over the sack of Béziers. With Arnaud-Amalric came the enigmatic figure once known as Foulques of Marseille. He was the son of a rich merchant, and he became one of the most brilliant of the troubador poets, a protégé of Count Raymond V and of King Richard of England. *"En chantan m'aven a membrar* . . . In singing I sometimes remember/ what, through song, I tried to forget,/ Yet I go on singing to forget my grief/ and unhappy love. . . ."* It is said that Foulques, in later life, heard someone singing one of the erotic songs of his youth and made himself do penance for having heard it. This Foulques, though married and the father of children, abandoned the world and became a Cistercian monk, then abbot of Le Thoronet and finally Archbishop Foulques of Toulouse. There he organized the orthodox into vigilante groups known as the White Brothers and sent them off in pursuit of the phantoms of heresy—and of usury, which may be taken as a euphemism for the Jews who enjoyed the civil liberties of Toulouse. "The brotherhood prevailed to such an extent that the usurers were compelled to answer in person to those who denounced them, and to give satisfaction for their hostility," according to the chronicle of Guillaume de Puylaurens. "Otherwise, people took up arms and ran to the houses of those who did not appear and destroyed and pillaged them." Foulques and his supporters campaigned with such ferocity that one of his victims ultimately declared to Rome that the archbishop *"sembla mielhs Antecritz que messatges de Roma.* He seems more the Antichrist than the representative of Rome." To the faithful, on the other hand, Foulques seemed an angel of the lord. Dante had no scruples about assigning him a place in his Paradiso, where, according to the poet, the archbishop's "voice gladdens heaven ceaselessly."

Simon de Montfort's wife, Alix, belonged to one of the great families of the north, the Montmorencys, and she was proud to help her husband by recruiting new forces. In the spring of 1210, Simon renewed the crusade by attacking the half-dozen great fortresses that dominated the hills of Languedoc. He besieged the Château of Minerve, and when it finally surrendered he seized 140 of the Cathar *bons hommes* who had taken refuge there and burned them. "Obstinate in their wickedness," wrote Pierre des Vaux-de-Cernay, "they all threw themselves joyously into the flames." Montfort then besieged and conquered the fortress of Cabaret, then the Château of Termes. When Count Raymond VI heard of these successive disasters, he once again begged the church for mercy. If the Count's protestations of loyalty and orthodoxy could be believed, there was no reason why Rome could not accept his promises to extirpate heresy in his domains, but the papal legates, Arnaud-Amalric and Milo, were convinced that the Count would say anything to save his possessions, and that the church would prevail only if he were deposed.

In response to Raymond's request for a chance to purge himself, the papal legates summoned him to a new conference of bishops and nobles in St.-Gilles in September of 1210. Raymond seems to have been ready to promise anything, and to have believed that his promises would save him. When the bishops refused to accept his promises of expiation, Raymond burst into tears. Summoned to another conference in Arles the following February, he was handed a charter outlining the legates' terms: that the Count must observe the peace, that he must dismiss all mercenary troops from his service, that he must restore to the clergy all the property that they claimed, that he must banish from his protection all Jews, that he must turn over to the clergy everyone whom they designated as heretics, "so that they can do with them what they will." Furthermore, the Count and his vassals must demolish all their castles, must abandon the cities and live in the countryside, "like peasants," must wear crude brown cloaks, must not eat more than two kinds of meat, and must not oppose Count Simon de Montfort and his crusaders galloping through their fields, or "taking what belongs to them." And furthermore, the Count of Toulouse must go on crusade to the Holy Land and must stay there as long as Rome wished, and after that he must enter one of the knightly orders of the Temple or of Saint John of Jerusalem. And if any of these terms were rejected, he "will be driven out from all his lands, and nothing will be left to him."

Count Raymond rode through his territories and read the church's terms aloud to his vassals and asked them what he should do. His knights, according to Guilhem, said they would rather die than accept such terms. And so Count

Raymond was excommunicated, and Toulouse placed under interdict, and so the crusade went on.

Montfort's next great objective was the Château of Lavaur, about twenty miles east of Toulouse. Montfort was particularly angry at Lavaur because it was defended by Aimeri de Montréal, one of those lords of Languedoc who repeatedly broke their oaths to the invaders. Aimeri had surrendered Montréal when the crusaders assaulted it, then barred his gates when the crusaders' ranks were depleted. Now he had come to the aid of his sister, Dame Giraude, the widow of the lord of Lavaur, who had declined the crusaders' demand that the town be surrendered. Montfort's revenge, when he finally conquered Lavaur, was terrible. He took four hundred citizens, accused of being Cathars, and burned them in a field outside the city. He took eighty knights, including the unfortunate Aimeri, and inflicted on them the degradation of a public hanging. He then had Aimeri's corpse tied to a horse's tail and dragged through the streets. As for Dame Giraude, she was flung into a pit—" screaming and weeping and shrieking," as Guilhem put it—and buried alive under a shower of stones. This was "a misfortune and a crime," Guilhem observed, but he added that the massacre at Lavaur, like the sack of Béziers, was supposed to fulfill a purpose. "My lords! This was to serve them as a lesson, to the Albigensians. If they had to suffer so much, as I have seen and heard, it is because they did not do what the clerics and the crusaders demanded of them."

This was, indeed, the season in which all atrocities were committed and all atrocities justified. It is difficult to say who began, or who was responsible for the multiplication of crimes. Traditionally, it is the weak who cut the throats of the police, since terrorism is their only power of retribution against the rulers' monopoly on firing squads and gas chambers. In the Languedoc of the thirteenth century, though, the strong and the weak changed with every season. In the spring, the crusaders seemed an irresistible force; in the fall, they seemed a mere handful of colonial occupiers, "flies," in John Steinbeck's memorable phrase, "occupying more and more flypaper." And both sides employed large numbers of mercenaries, or *routiers,* pitiless cutthroats who neither gave nor received quarter.

This is typical of what happened: Two French knights were captured by the Albigensians, who gouged out their eyes and then sent them back to their companions as objects of fear and shame. Simon de Montfort heard of this while he was besieging the fortress of Bram, and when the fortress surrendered, after a resistance of only three days, he took the entire garrison of about one hundred men and had all of their eyes gouged out, and their noses and upper lips cut off. He left just one of them with just one eye to lead them to the château that was next on his list of targets. This was the strategy of the baron who had been appointed by the Vicar of Christ to command the crusade against the heretics of Languedoc.

Montfort's brutality had its effect, as brutality often does. *"Si deus me benazia!"* cries Guilhem. "God bless me! I never saw less defeats suffered and more châteaux abandoned and captured." The crusaders seized and razed St.-Marcel, then St.-Antonin. "You wouldn't have had the leisure to boil an egg,"

Guilhem wrote of the second assault, "in the short lapse of time it took them to capture it that night."

✳

By the autumn of 1212, Montfort felt himself so strongly in control of Languedoc that he summoned a kind of constitutional convention known as the Assizes of Pamiers. Before this assembly of bishops, nobles and merchants, Montfort proposed a charter for his new order. To the church, he promised the restoration of all plundered lands and all special privileges; to the general populace, he promised a reduction in taxes and certain legal rights of due process. Most important, perhaps, he ostracized all the barons tainted by heresy and rebellion and then transferred their lands to his own loyal commanders. This imposition of French colonial rule extended to the smallest details. The widows of the new French overlords, for example, were forbidden to remarry anyone but a Frenchman. In disputes great and small, French law was to replace Roman law.

Count Raymond and his lords recognized the threat, that what had begun as a crusade against heresy had become a foreign conquest. Raymond appealed to his brother-in-law and nearest ally, King Pedro of Aragon, a sovereign of unimpeachable orthodoxy who had just won a decisive victory over the Moors at Las Navas de Tolosa. King Pedro in turn appealed to Pope Innocent, and by January of 1213 the Pope was scolding Montfort: "Not content with rising against the heretics, you have carried crusading arms against the Catholic population. You have spilled innocent blood.... We order you to restore to [Pedro] and his vassals all the seigneuries you have invaded, for fear that if you unjustly retain them it will be said that you have labored for your own advantage and not for the cause of the faith." But Innocent, who had so often claimed the right to impose the right of Saint Peter upon the princes of the world, proved remarkably unable to control his own legates. Under the leadership of Arnaud-Amalric, the bishops of Languedoc met in ruined Lavaur and decided once again that there could be no peace with Count Raymond. By May of that year, they had persuaded Innocent to write to King Pedro to abandon his interventions in the affairs of Languedoc. "You have acted ill, both toward Us and Yourself. . . . ," Innocent declared.

King Pedro ignored the Pope's warnings. He decided that the only way to deal with the usurpations of Simon de Montfort was to march into Languedoc and attack him. "Count Raymond," he declared, "is not guilty of any wrong or crime against anyone in the world. I am going to help him against those cursed people who want to disinherit him."* Having made that decision, Pedro as-

---

* At this point, we must sadly part company with Guilhem de Tudela. He has been wearying of his task ("What good does it do to tell you more and to make a long story of it," he remarks near the end), and shortly before the battle of Muret he lapses into silence. The last two thirds of the *Canzon* were written by someone else, an anonymous Toulousain who may have been a retainer at the court of Count Raymond VII. He has Guilhem's talent for creating dialogue among great princes, and he is far more righteous about the sins of the crusaders, but he lacks the Leporello quality that makes Guilhem's narrative so engaging.

sembled a formidable army. A renowned warrior himself, he gathered about a thousand knights from Aragon and Catalonia, veterans of the campaigns against the Moors. From among his other vassals, and from the rebellious regions of Languedoc, he and Count Raymond recruited perhaps two thousand more. To these were added about forty thousand militia from Toulouse, not professional soldiers but good men determined to defend their land.

No sooner had the militia joined forces with King Pedro outside the besieged fortress of Muret, some twenty miles south of Toulouse, than they swarmed over the walls and drove Montfort's feeble garrison of thirty knights into the main tower. King Pedro ordered them to withdraw, however, so that Montfort could be lured into a trap. Montfort promptly rode to the rescue of Muret with about a thousand knights on horseback, their banners flying. With Montfort, too, came Dominic de Guzmán, and Archbishop Foulques of Toulouse, and on entering Muret on Sept. 11, 1213, the crusaders paused to pray. "O good Lord, O gentle Jesus!" Montfort said, according to the pious chronicle of Pierre des Vaux-de-Cernay. "You have chosen me to wage your wars in spite of my unworthiness. . . ."

King Pedro and Count Raymond and their attendant lords gathered in a nearby field to plan their strategy. King Pedro exulted in the prospect of combat. "I want to warn you that there will be a battle before nightfall," he said. "Be ready to attack and to hit them hard." Count Raymond was more cautious. Since Montfort would have to emerge from Muret, why not wait for his attack, ambush him with crossbows, then force him back into the château? Miguel de Luesia, an Aragonese baron who had commanded a victorious force against the Moors at Las Navas de Tolosa, was contemptuous of Raymond's devious strategy. "It is really too bad that when you have a domain to live on, you let yourself be despoiled of it because of your own cowardice," he said. Count Raymond was cut to the bone. All he could bring himself to say was, "Let it be as you wish."

And so the Toulouse militia charged, with such vehemence that the French barely got the gates of Muret, all reddened with blood, shut. The militia thereupon returned to their tents, like any medieval army, and began eating lunch. But Montfort, with his unique talent for the unexpected, gathered his knights, led them out of the fortress by a gate that could not be seen from the Spaniards' camp, and then struck directly at King Pedro's headquarters.

King Pedro had taken the customary precaution of outfitting one of his knights in his royal regalia. One of Montfort's knights, Alain de Roucy, confronted this false king and struck him to earth, then shouted, "This isn't the King! The King is a better fighter!" King Pedro could not resist the challenge. Standing nearby in the armor of anonymity, he cried, "I am the king!" And was immediately assaulted by Roucy and a half dozen of Montfort's knights. They cared little for chivalry. They gave no quarter. "Pedro was so badly wounded," the *Canzon* records, "that his blood spilled out all over the ground, and he instantly died there, stretched out at full length."

When the Aragonese knights saw their king cut down, they faltered, then turned to run. When the Toulouse militia saw the Spanish knights fleeing, they too turned. At this point, Montfort threw every man he had onto the flank of the wavering attackers, and victory became rout. With Montfort's horsemen hacking at them, the Toulousains fled like sheep toward the Garonne, which was running fast and deep. And like sheep they drowned, by the thousands (about fifteen thousand, according to modern estimates). "Great was the loss!" cried the author of the *Canzon.* And Simon de Montfort, having rendered his respects to the corpse of King Pedro, and having given Pedro's horse and armor to the poor, betook himself to a nearby church and gave thanks for the salvation of the crusade. Was not the victory at Muret, like the conquest of Béziers, a miracle?

When Count Raymond VI saw his countrymen fleeing to their death in the Garonne, he simply rode back to Toulouse. "In sorrow and in mourning," as the *Canzon* puts it, "he told the consuls to negotiate an agreement as best they could." And so the citizens of Toulouse bowed to Simon de Montfort and swore him their allegiance, and Archbishop Foulques reentered the city in triumph. Montfort ordered all fortifications torn down and destroyed forever.

Count Raymond sought once more to save himself by going to Rome. There, in November of 1215, Innocent III convened some 412 bishops and eight hundred abbots and priors, along with ambassadors from Constantinople, Jerusalem, England, Spain, Hungary and the Holy Roman Empire, to the grand conclave known as the Fourth Lateran Council. On the council's agenda were all the problems of Christendom, ranging from the ratification of Frederick II as emperor to the possibilities of a new crusade to the Holy Land to the authorization of the new order of friars organized by Brother Dominic to the promulgation of new restrictions on the Jews. The author of the *Canzon,* however, tells the story of the council purely as a drama of Languedoc.

Pope Innocent was indeed much concerned about the Cathars, whom he regarded as "strong and emboldened." He had had a dream recently in which he thought he saw the Lateran Basilica crumbling and about to collapse. Then he dreamed that he saw the whole building lifted and supported on the shoulders of the obscure Spanish monk, Dominic, who had come with Archbishop Foulques to petition him for the approval of his mendicant friars. But Innocent seems also to have felt sympathetic, once again, to Count Raymond's plea that he and his eighteen-year-old son, Raymond VII, were being persecuted by the papal legates. "On the Count of Toulouse," said the Pope, "there weighs not a single accusation that would require him to lose his lands, or that he has been a heretic." There followed then an angry exchange between the Count of Foix, who strenuously denied that he had ever supported or assisted heresy, and Archbishop Foulques of Toulouse, who retorted that the count had "inspired, favored and welcomed the heretics." When the archbishop went on to complain of the atrocities committed against the noble crusaders from the north, the Count of Foix declared that he only wished that he had blinded and mutilated yet more of "these brigands, these traitors and perjurors, who, bearing the cross, came to ruin me." It was in the heat of this exchange that the Count of Foix laid on Archbishop Foulques the famous curse, that he was responsible for the 500,000 casualties already suffered by the bleeding province of Languedoc, and that he "seems more the Antichrist than the representative of Rome."

"Friend," said Pope Innocent, according to the *Canzon,* "justice will be done." With that, he retired to his palace, and went to walk in the garden, "to suppress his irritation and to divert himself." In his garden, however, he was immediately surrounded by importunate priests from Languedoc, who argued that the crusaders' conquests must not be returned to Count Raymond. "My lords," the Pope answered, "how can I, without right or reason, commit such a great injustice as to deprive the Count, who is a sincere Catholic, of his heritage?" He then tried to escape from his petitioners by the traditional device of opening the Scriptures at random. All he found there was that Count Raymond "could arrive at a safe harbor."

When the priests persisted, Innocent attempted a compromise. Count Raymond could keep his lands, but Montfort should keep the properties of heretics. The question then, of course, was, who was a heretic? If such rebels as the Count of Foix were considered good Catholics, Archbishop Foulques argued when the council sessions resumed, then Montfort would get nothing. "Give him," Foulques insisted, "the entire country, without any exception." Otherwise, the archbishop added darkly, "I should prefer that the entire land be put to the torch, and to a bloody death."

The Pope was dismayed. "Of your cruel sentiments," he said, "I know nothing. . . . My lords, the church opens its arms to repentant sinners. . . . The Count is Catholic and has behaved himself loyally." Someone in the crusader faction then argued that Montfort deserved the lands he had conquered. "What counterbalances his merit," answered the Pope, "is that he has ruined Catholics as much as heretics."

A group of barons gathered around the Pope to argue for Montfort's rights. Innocent accused them of "pride and malice." And yet he gave in. For a man who claimed Rome's right to name even the Emperor of Germany, *principaliter et finaliter,* Innocent once again showed an astonishing inability to rule over his own bishops. Or perhaps he was simply weary of the struggle. His surrender sounds irritated, even peevish. "Let Simon possess the land and govern it!" he finally declared. "Since it is not possible for me to take it from him, let him guard it well, if he can!" When a loyal bishop urged him to reconsider, he could only say, "All my bishops are against me."

Count Raymond and his young son were, quite understandably, appalled. They asked for an audience with Innocent, and the Pope received them with what the author of the *Canzon* calls "an air of affliction."

"Lord Pope, I am utterly stupefied," said Count Raymond. "I put myself in your power in order to regain possession of my land, and now here I am in the middle of the sea, [required] to go out into the world to beg for a living. . . . Do not abandon me."

The Pope was grandly equivocal. He asked for time to reflect. He said that God's will would prevail over even his own errors. "If I have despoiled you," he said, "God can give you back your lands." He spoke angrily of "the wicked," who had opposed his wishes, and promised to be "avenged on them." He asked Raymond to leave his young son in Rome so that he could "deliberate on how I can let him have a territory." Count Raymond agreed. Innocent finally decided to give young Raymond a small territory known as Venaissain, between Provence and the Rhone. Young Raymond impetuously demanded his entire inheritance. "Let me have my land if I can conquer it," he said. The Pope's response was, as usual, enigmatic. He looked at the youth, according to the *Canzon*, "and heaved a sigh, and then he kissed him and gave him his benediction." He asked the young count to mark his words, and then he said, "May Jesus Christ permit you to begin well and to end well, and may you meet with good luck."

Like a Greek hero returning from the mysteries of Delphi, Raymond VII interpreted the Pope's words as a license to reconquer his patrimony from the crusaders whom that same Pope had sent to ravish his father's lands. He rode northward from Rome, met his father at Genoa, and then they both set sail for Marseille, where a crowd met them with what the *Canzon* calls "joy and happiness." Thus a kind of triumphal procession began. The two counts proceeded to Avignon, where crowds turned out into the streets to greet them with cries of *"Tolosa!"* and *"Joia!"* and "God be with us!" There were songs and dances, and *jongleurs* performed tricks, and three hundred lords of the region vowed to follow young Raymond in the reconquest of all his father's possessions. The two Raymonds reveled in the prospect of revenge. While the old Count went to Aragon to raise fresh troops, young Raymond laid siege to Beaucaire, not far from where that papal legate had been murdered nearly a decade earlier. And so the war that had just been settled began all over again. It was hardly a religious war any longer but rather a war of nationalist resistance against foreign dominion.

When the siege of Beaucaire began, Simon de Montfort was in Paris, winning the approval of King Philip Augustus. "We have received our beloved and loyal Simon, Count de Montfort," the King declared on April 10, 1216, "as liege man for the Duchy of Narbonne, the County of Toulouse, and the Viscounties of Béziers and Carcassonne . . . which have been won from the heretics and the enemies of the Church of Jesus Christ." It seemed the culmination of Montfort's ambition to create a new state in Languedoc, to be ruled by the Montfort dynasty, and when he heard the news from the south, according to the *Canzon*, it "filled him with sorrow and anger." He gathered a few loyal knights and raced to Beaucaire, but by the time he reached the besieged fortress it was all but lost. Count Raymond held the city, and he was well supplied, "with beef," the author of the *Canzon* reports, "with cows, pigs, sheep, geese, chickens, partridges, capons, wheat, flour, and wine of Genestet." Montfort's garrison, besieged in the tower above the city, was near starvation. Montfort, besieging the besiegers, tried furiously to batter his way in, but he was beaten back each time by the nineteen-year-old Count Raymond. After three months, he had to accept a humiliating compromise. In exchange for the lives of his garrison, he abandoned the siege of Beaucaire and left the young Count victorious. It was Montfort's first military defeat.

Montfort had to withdraw from Beaucaire because he heard that Count

Raymond VI had raised an army in Aragon and was marching over the Pyrenees to recapture his old capital at Toulouse. Montfort had to hurry to get there first. He succeeded; the vacillating Count Raymond avoided a confrontation and retreated back into Spain once more. But if Count Raymond was weak-spirited, the people of Toulouse were not. Though the walls of the city had been torn down, the Toulousains greeted their new Count with wooden barricades across the main streets. Montfort retaliated by setting fire to three districts of the city. The citizens fought back, attacking the French knights with sticks and stones. It was a brave but hopeless resistance, and Archbishop Foulques soon persuaded the consuls of the city to disarm. Once the citizens had been disarmed, Montfort ordered the leaders of the rebellion arrested and exiled, and all fortified areas of the city demolished. "Forth from the gates went the banished ones, "the *Canzon* records, "knights, burghers, bankers, the flower of the citizenry, escorted by a troop of armed and angry soldiers, who belabored them with blows, threats, curses. . . . Then might you have seen houses and towers, walls, rooms, fortifications, all collapsing together. They demolished living quarters and workshops, colonnades, frescoed chambers. . . . All through the city rose the sound of wailing and lamentation. . . . 'Ah, God,' they cried, one to the other, 'what cruel masters! O Lord, see how you have delivered us into the hands of brigands.' "

Having more or less sacked the city that was theoretically his own capital, Montfort told the consuls that he would pardon the city upon payment of the huge sum of thirty thousand silver marks. While the consuls were pondering that extortionate offer, Montfort set out to subjugate the nearby county of Foix, leaving his wife, Alix, and a modest garrison to hold the shattered city of Toulouse. While he was thus engaged, Count Raymond VI finally returned, one misty morning in September of 1217, and forded the Garonne just below the water mills that ground the city's wheat. "And when the count made his entry into the city through the arched gateway," says the *Canzon,* "all the people ran to meet him, young and old, knights and ladies, husbands and wives, and they knelt before him, kissing his garments, his feet, legs, arms and fingers. . . . And they said to each other, 'Now Jesus Christ is with us, and the morning star. . . .' "

True to their traditions, the Toulousains thereupon seized stones and knives and slaughtered every Frenchman they could find, driving the rest to find sanctuary in the Château Narbonais. When Montfort heard of this new outburst in his capital, he vowed to return and subdue it once and for all. And the inhabitants of the unfortified city desperately began building moats and improvising walls out of wooden stakes. These may seem feeble preparations for a siege, but it was actually Montfort who was outnumbered and on the defensive. He had to send his wife, Alix, to Paris to plead with the King for more troops, and Archbishop Foulques through France to preach a new crusade. All winter long, there were only forays and skirmishes. The spring brought crusaders from Flanders to reinforce Montfort, but it also brought Count Raymond VII with reinforcements from Provence. In June, in the ninth month of the siege of Toulouse, Montfort decided to build a *chatte,* a sort of mobile tower that could be pushed up against any rampart in order to storm it. The Toulousains sallied forth to attack this machine before it could threaten them.

Montfort was at mass, according to the admiring account by Pierre des Vaux-de-Cernay, when a messenger came to tell him of the battle. "But the very devout man replied, 'Let me first hear the divine mysteries and behold the Sacrament of my Redemption.' He was still speaking when a second messenger arrived, who said, 'Quickly, quickly, the battle is raging, our men cannot hold out.' The very Christian man replied, 'I shall not come before I have seen my Redeemer.' As the priest raised the Host, according to custom, the very devout man knelt down and stretched his arms toward heaven, crying, 'Now, Lord, let your servant go in peace. . .' And he added, 'Let us go and let us die, if need be, for him who deigned to die for us.' This having been said, the invincible man sped toward the battle."

The destiny that Montfort had just invoked awaited him, though not in the form that he probably expected. There was to be no heroic confrontation with Count Raymond, no duel on the ramparts. If it was true that Montfort had started the crusade by looking at a random page of the Bible, and if it was true that the page he read was the psalm that predicted that the angels would bear him up lest he dash his foot against a stone, then the psalm had a strange irony to it, for the women of Toulouse were now operating the artillery that fired rocks at the crusaders' camp, and one of those rocks, flung through the air on that morning of June 25, 1218, smashed Simon de Montfort squarely in the head. "His eyeballs, brains, teeth, skull and jawbone all flew into pieces," the author of the *Canzon* exulted, "and he fell down upon the ground dead, blackened and bloody."

Toulouse rejoiced. "The town and the very pavingstones rang," the *Canzon* goes on, "to the sound of horns, trumpets, church bells ringing and hammering, . . . drums, gongs and bugles." The crusaders were, to exactly the same degree, horrified. They virtually abandoned their siege the moment that Montfort died. They carried his body to Carcassonne and celebrated an elaborate funeral service at the Monastery of St.-Nazaire and declared that the slain Count was a martyred saint who had richly earned his place in heaven. The author of the *Canzon* remained implacable. "If one may seek Jesus Christ in this world by killing men . . . ," he wrote, "by setting the torch to great fires, by destroying the barons and dishonoring *paratge,* by winning lands through violence, and working for the triumph of vain pride . . . , by slaughtering women and slitting children's throats—why, then [Montfort] must wear a crown and shine in heaven."

There was a simpler and even more passionate exultation in an anonymous poem that soon appeared under the title "The Death of a Wolf":

> *Montfort*
> *Es mort*
> *Es mort*
> *Es mort!*
> *Viva Tolosa*

> *Ciotat Gloriosa*
> *Et poderosa!*
> *Tornan lo paratge et l'onor!*
> *Montfort*
> *Es mort!*
> *Es mort!*
> *Es mort!*

"Montfort is dead, is dead, is dead! Long live Toulouse, glorious and mighty city! Return chivalry and honor! Montfort is dead, is dead, is dead!"

If Simon de Montfort was unworthy of his crusade, his sons and heirs and followers were unworthy of him. His oldest son, Amaury, could think of nothing except to raise the siege of Toulouse and appeal to King Philip Augustus of France for help. King Philip, who had once balked at all papal efforts to involve him in the crusade against the south, now enjoyed a quite different position. At the battle of Bouvines, in 1214, he had decisively defeated the coalition organized against him by King John of England and John's nephew the Emperor Otto IV of Germany. Thus freed of threats from the north and the east, Philip sent southward his warlike son, Prince Louis, followed by an army that included six hundred knights and ten thousand archers, not to mention twenty bishops. Prince Louis joined Amaury de Montfort outside the walls of Marmande, a Garonne River town roughly halfway between Toulouse and Bordeaux, and there, just like the first crusaders who had sacked Béziers a decade earlier, they indulged in one of those slaughters that they hoped would convince all of Languedoc of its doom. "Men and women, barons, ladies and little children, were all stripped and despoiled and put to the sword," the chronicler of the *Canzon* reports. "And their flesh, their blood, their brains, their bodies, their arms and legs, disfigured and cut to pieces . . . , lay around in the public square as if they had rained down. Streets, fields and riverbanks were red with the blood that ran there. Neither man nor woman, young or old, survived. Not a single person escaped. . . . *La vila es destruita.*"

About five thousand people died in that slaughter, but the people of Languedoc were by now accustomed to terror. When Prince Louis marched on to Toulouse, where Count Raymond VII had established his capital and organized a force of a thousand knights, the citizens prepared for a third siege. Prince Louis, who had apparently thought that French prestige and French terror would win him an easy victory, gave up after only six weeks and marched northward again. And Count Raymond then sortied forth to recapture the castles still occupied by French forces. He captured Lavaur and slaughtered the entire garrison; he captured Montréal and executed Alain de Roucy, that knight who had tricked and killed King Pedro at Muret. Having recaptured most of his father's domains, just as the late Pope Innocent had said he would if God were on his side, Count Raymond VII now sought the endorsement of both King and church. He offered his allegiance to the very man who had just tried to destroy him, King Philip Augustus of France.

In this moment of his son's triumph, in August of 1222, the old Count Raymond VI lay dying. Dying, he wanted only to be reconciled to the church. Dying, he wanted salvation. He had made out a will leaving major legacies to the Knights Hospitallers of Toulouse, saying that he hoped to enter their order and wanted to be buried among them. On his last day, he went twice to the Church of Notre-Dame-la-Daurade, on the banks of the Garonne, then returned home to die. The abbot of St.-Sernin came to him and administered the last sacrament. Count Raymond could no longer speak. A Knight Hospitaller flung a cloak, marked with the cross of the order, over the body of the dying count to claim it for burial. A devout follower of the abbot of St.-Sernin pulled the cloak off again, and so, while the rival orders of the church fought over his corpse, Count Raymond VI died. He was sixty-six.

And in these same years, almost all the main characters of the Albigensian Crusade suddenly disappeared. It was as though the first phase of the struggle had been decreed ended. Pope Innocent III, who had originally proclaimed the crusade, died in July of 1216. Simon de Montfort fell in 1218, Saint Dominic in 1221, Count Raymond in 1222, and on July 14, 1223, King Philip Augustus of France succumbed to a raging fever.

All but Count Raymond received a Christian burial. Count Raymond remained, as he had been on his deathbed, an object of controversy. The abbot of St.-Sernin insisted that the body could not be removed from his parish; the Knights Hospitallers insisted that it must be. The cadaver remained in a coffin in a garden while Count Raymond VII petitioned Rome for a decision. Rome said it had to investigate the old Count's spiritual orthodoxy. By the year 1247, some 120 witnesses had testified that Raymond was a devout Catholic, untainted by heresy. The church decided to investigate further. By now twenty-five years had passed since the Count's death. The coffin was not inviolable. Rats found their way in. The Count's bones began disappearing. By the end of the seventeenth century, all that remained was the count's skull, an object of public curiosity. The church's investigations never ended. The skull eventually disappeared.

King Philip Augustus might conceivably have accepted the fealty of the triumphant young Count Raymond VII. His oldest son, the butcher of Marmande, now King Louis VIII, was less likely to be magnanimous. Particularly since Amaury de Montfort had offered to surrender to the French crown all of his family's claims to Languedoc. Particularly since Pope Honorius III, pretending that the struggle for Languedoc still involved nothing more than the extirpation of heresy, was appealing to him for yet another renewal of the crusade.

King Louis needed theological justification. To provide it, the Pope summoned three hundred French prelates to a council at Bourges to weigh the rival claims of Count Raymond VII and Amaury de Montfort. Not surprisingly, they decreed Raymond to be a heretic, and they acknowledged Amaury's surrender of his claims to King Louis. The King began his southward march the following June, leading an army of fifty thousand men, and by now the principal cities of Languedoc could endure no more. Béziers was the first to offer its surrender, as soon as it heard that the King was on the march. Then came Nîmes, Carcassonne, Albi, Marseille . . .

The King encountered resistance only at Avignon, which was officially a fief of the German Emperor, and which had not previously been involved in the war. Louis resolved to besiege it. Avignon held out for three months, and though the royal army finally prevailed, tearing down the city walls and imposing a huge fine on the citizenry, the troops were themselves beset by a mysterious fever. The army staggered westward, accepting the surrender of cities too exhausted to fight further, but harassed by local guerrillas. Its losses, without any major fights, were estimated at twenty thousand dead. The King reached Toulouse in October of 1226 and prepared yet another siege. The effort was too great. The King himself could already feel the first clawing of fever. He lifted the siege and ordered his army to turn northward. He died on the road a few days later. The crusaders sewed up his body in an oxhide and carried it back to Paris.

If the French could not win on the field of battle, they had other tactics in reserve. The Seneschal Humbert de Beaujeu, who had been assigned to Carcassonne as the viceroy of the dead King Louis, established a camp to the east of Toulouse and began a systematic uprooting and burning of crops and orchards. "The Crusaders heard mass at dawn," Guillaume de Puylaurens wrote, "then . . . began their work of destruction on the vineyards nearest to the town. . . . They repeated this maneuver daily for something like three months, till the devastation was more or less complete." Archbishop Foulques heartily approved, declaring, "We thus triumph in ways over our enemies."

At the same time, King Louis' widow, Blanche of Castile, let it be known that she was ready to make peace if only Count Raymond would be reasonable. She sent the abbot of Grandselve, Élie Guérin, to offer her terms, which were harsh. The French crown was to take over the Trencavel lands around Carcassonne and all the territories of Provence to the east of the Rhone; Count Raymond was to keep Toulouse and the region surrounding it. In his own territory, Raymond was to surrender nine fortresses to the French for ten years, and to dismantle thirty others. He was also to restore the properties taken from Simon de Montfort's crusaders. Most important, as it finally turned out, Raymond was to "deliver" his only child, the Princess Jeanne, born in 1220 and still a child, to be married to one of the late King Louis' brothers. There was scarcely any mention of the heretics who were supposed to have been the cause of the war.

Though the terms were hard, Raymond agreed to accept them as a basis for further negotiations. On that understanding, he proceeded to a peace conference at Meaux, some thirty miles north of Paris. He brought with him a large delegation of southern nobles and bishops. Queen Blanche produced an even larger assemblage, headed by the papal legate, Romanus de San Angelo. Raymond soon found that he had walked into a trap. The peace terms, which he had hoped to ease by negotiation, had become, on the contrary, even more severe. Considerable importance was now ascribed to the pursuit of heretics. Raymond had to agree to search them out, to pay two silver marks to anyone who caught one, to bar all suspected heretics and Jews from public office, and even to finance (for four thousand silver marks) a college of orthodox theology at Toulouse. The city of Toulouse, moreover, was to tear down its walls once more and to surrender its main fort, the Château Narbonais, to the crown. Large indemnities (fifteen thousand marks) were to be paid to various churches that claimed to have suffered war damages, even Citeaux in far-off Burgundy. And the marriage of Princess Jeanne to Prince Alphonse of France was to take precedence over the claims of any children that Raymond might have in the future. In other words, Count Raymond was to abdicate the independence of his own dynasty. Having abandoned all worldly pretensions, Raymond was to proceed to Palestine, and to serve there as a crusader for five years.

Historians have often wondered why Raymond accepted such humiliating terms. They amounted to a complete surrender after a war that he had not lost. Raymond was undoubtedly weary of combat, as were his people, but the simplest explanation is the most obvious one, that the French knew nothing of *paratge* and made it clear that they were quite prepared to seize and imprison Raymond if he did not sign. And so, on April 12, 1229, on the steps of the luminous new Cathedral of Notre-Dame-de-Paris, Count Raymond signed away everything for which he and his father and his people had fought for twenty years. "Having long waged war against the Holy Roman Church and our well-beloved liege lord, Louis King of the French, ... we have made what efforts we could ... to conclude a peace," said Raymond, his hand on the Bible. "The King has graciously consented to receive from us our daughter ... to be given in marriage to one of his brothers; and to leave us Toulouse and the diocese thereof...."

The political humiliation was not enough for the church. It demanded of Raymond, as it had demanded of his father, the degradation of a public scourging. "It was a great pity to see so noble a prince ... thus led to the altar," wrote Guillaume de Puylaurens. Stripped to his shirt and breeches, barefoot, he had a rope tied around his neck and was led to the holiest spot in the Cathedral of Notre-Dame, there to be whipped by the Legate Romanus. Even that was not enough. Having come to Paris as a sovereign prince, and having signed away most of his sovereignty, Raymond was now conducted to the Louvre and confined there until the most important elements of the Treaty of Meaux were put into effect—until the walls of Toulouse were destroyed, until the Château Narbonais was turned over to the French, and until the nine-year-old Princess Jeanne was brought to France. It was six months before Count Raymond was released from the Louvre and allowed to return to his devastated homeland.

*

Now that peace had been imposed, the Inquisition could begin.

Heresy was not unique to Languedoc, of course, and the church had already made several fitful attempts to enforce uniformity among its children. In Germany, particularly, a half-mad priest named Conrad of Marburg had been commissioned in 1227 to root out and punish all the heretics he could find, a task that he pursued with such zeal that he was finally assassinated in 1233, whereupon the German Inquisition came to an abrupt halt. Conrad's search had been little more than an erratic sort of witch-hunt, however. In Languedoc, even after two decades of crusading, the forces of heresy remained strong and well organized. In 1223, it was reported that the Cathars of Bulgaria, Croatia, Dalmatia and Hungary had held a conclave and elected a Cathar pope. In 1225, the Cathars of Languedoc held a council of their own, at Pieusse, to settle various organizational questions, creating a new diocese of Razès and electing a bishop to head it.

The Treaty of Meaux heralded the end of such impertinences. A church council at Toulouse in 1229 decreed a broad series of new regulations. Every citizen of Languedoc—boys at the age of fourteen, girls at twelve—was required to take an oath swearing loyalty to Rome, and pledging to join in the pursuit of heresy. The oath was to be renewed every two years. Anyone who failed to take this oath would come under suspicion. Anyone who failed to attend church and receive Catholic communion at least three times a year would come under suspicion. Anyone found to possess a Bible in the vernacular language of Languedoc would come under suspicion. Anyone accused by his neighbors of irregular or unusual behavior would come under suspicion. Anyone who came under suspicion could clear himself only by confessing his errors and publicly denouncing everyone else who had shared in them. That was essential, that public denunciation of one's accomplices; that was the only proof of sincere repentance. All those who confessed were punished, of course, but punishments varied widely—fines, floggings, pilgrimages to holy places, the wearing of penitential crosses sewn to one's clothes, or, more and more frequently, imprisonment for many years, sometimes for life. Those who refused to confess, on the other hand, were turned over to the secular authorities for what Pope Lucius III had termed, in 1184, "fitting punishment." This customarily meant burning at the stake. *"Car avetz d'andelh/ Ab simpla guardadura . . ."* wrote the troubadour Guilhem Figueira in his tirade against Rome. "You have the face of a lamb with a simple look, within you are a ravenous wolf, a crowned serpent engendered of a viper; therefore the devil calls to you as to his dear friend. . . . And if you make an outcry against them [the priests], they will become your accusers, and you will be excommunicated. . . ."

The new rules gave to the Roman bishops of Languedoc an awesome power over the daily lives of their parishioners, but the rules were not easy to carry out. How was a parish priest to record all these oaths of loyalty, to gather all the evidence of heresy and to interrogate everyone suspected of it? Year after year, Rome had ordered its bishops to destroy heresy, but the local priests had proved as helpless as the crusaders in defeating the Cathars. Now, however, the Vatican had a new weapon at its disposal, the robed armies of the mendicant orders, and particularly the teaching friars organized by Saint Dominic. Officially approved only in 1215, the Dominicans had organized sixty monasteries in seven countries by the time of the founder's death, in saintly poverty, in 1221. All of them were totally dedicated to fulfilling the wishes of the Papacy. Scarcely a decade later, on April 20, 1233, the Dominicans received their orders from Pope Gregory IX. Wherever they might find either a heretic or any priest or lord who tolerated heresy, said Gregory, "you are empowered to proceed against them and all others, without appeal, calling in the aid of the secular arm, if necessary, and coercing opposition, if requisite, with the censures of the church, without appeal." In a separate bull addressed to all bishops, Gregory declared: "We beg, warn and exhort you, ordering you as you reverence the Holy See, to receive them [the Dominicans] kindly and treat them well, giving them in this, as in all else, favor, counsel and aid, that they may fulfill their office."

Wherever the Dominicans tried to carry out their good works among the people of Languedoc, however, they encountered resistance and even violence. In Albi, Brother Arnaud Catala tried to arrest a suspected heretic, but a crowd swarmed around him and beat him. When Brother Ferrier, the chief inquisitor for Narbonne, tried to arrest a suspect, a crowd not only resisted him but started a local insurrection that afflicted the city for more than a year. The most dramatic conflict between the inquisitors and their antagonists occurred in Toulouse, and was recorded by Guillaume Pelhisson, a young Dominican monk.

The Dominicans took their inspiration from Master Roland of Cremona, who had come from Paris, where he was a master in theology at the cathedral, to teach at the new university that had been ordained by the Treaty of Meaux. The monks who preached against heresy were summoned to the city hall of Toulouse and ordered to desist, on the ground that there were no heretics in Toulouse. On hearing this, Master Roland urged the monks "to preach more and more against heretics," and when he heard that a cathedral canon named A. Peter had sworn the oath of heresy on his deathbed and been buried in the cloister, he "went to the spot with friars and clerics and had the body dug up, dragged to the fire, and burned."

So it began.

There was a heretic named Galvan. When he died, Master Roland led a band of monks to Galvan's house and burned it down. Then they went to the cemetery of Villeneuve and dug up the corpse. "In a great procession," Brother Guillaume wrote, they "dragged his body through the town and burned it in the common field outside the town. This was done in praise of our Lord Jesus Christ and the Blessed Dominic and to the honor of the Roman and Catholic Church, our mother, in the year of the Lord 1231."

After Master Roland returned home to Paris, the formal title of inquisitor was assigned to two men: Peter Seila, a wealthy citizen of Toulouse, and Guillaume Arnaud, a lawyer and monk from Montpellier. They made little progress. "The chief men of the region, together with the greater nobles and the burghers and others, protected and hid the heretics," Brother Guillaume wrote. "They beat, wounded and killed those who pursued them." But the pursuit went on. The inquisitors summoned every suspect to appear before them, and among these was a prominent citizen named Jean Tesseire. He protested that he had nothing to do with the ascetic Cathars. "Gentlemen, listen to me!" he cried. "I am not a heretic, for I have a wife and I sleep with her. I have sons. I eat meat, and I lie and swear and I am a faithful Christian. So don't let them say these things about me. . . . They can accuse you as well as me. Look out for yourselves, for these wicked men want to ruin the town."

Such appeals began to arouse the citizens of Toulouse against the inquisitors who had come to purge them. When Tesseire was convicted and condemned to the stake, despite the testimony of several notables in his defense, a crowd gathered and prevented the execution. The monks retreated and put Tesseire in prison. "The town was now very much stirred up against the friars," Brother Guillaume wrote. "There were even more threats and speeches against them than usual, and many heretical persons incited the people to stone the friars and destroy their houses." It happened that some other suspected Cathars were seized near Lavaur and put into prison with Tesseire, and he gave himself up to them. The Cathars were put on trial, and they denied nothing. Tesseire said he agreed with the Cathars in all things. "All who had previously defended him were now covered with confusion," the young Dominican chronicler gloated, "and they damned and cursed him . . . and he was burned at the same time as the others. In all things, blessed be God."

So the hunt continued. In 1234, the canonization of Saint Dominic was finally proclaimed in Toulouse, and Bishop Raymond du Fauga was washing his hands in preparation for dinner when he heard a rumor that a fever-ridden old woman in a nearby house was about to undergo the Cathar ritual. The bishop hurried to her bedside and managed to convince her that he was a friend, then interrogated her on her beliefs, then denounced her as a heretic. He called on her to recant. She refused. The bishop thereupon had her bed carried out into a field, and there she was burned. "And after the bishop and the friars and their companions had seen the business completed," Brother Guillaume wrote, "they returned to the refectory and, giving thanks to God and the Blessed Dominic, ate with rejoicing what had been prepared for them."

The prisoners of the Inquisition, who could exculpate themselves only by naming other heretics, seem to have thought they could escape by accusing the dead. The Dominicans were relentless in digging up the accused, dragging the bones through the streets, and then burning them. "The whole town was excited and aroused against the friars," Brother Guillaume recorded. The people appealed to Count Raymond against these desecrations of the graveyards, and Raymond asked the inquisitors to stop. "This they refused to do," said Brother Guillaume. By now, in fact, the inquisitors were ready for a frontal assault against the whole political hierarchy of Toulouse. Brother Guillaume Arnaud, one of the two chief inquisitors, issued orders that twelve prominent lords of the city be brought before him. The twelve refused to appear. "They uttered threats and dire warnings," wrote Brother Guillaume, "to make him desist from his activities." In this resistance, said Guillaume, they were acting "at the wish and with the assent of the Count of Toulouse." It was a grave and never-proven charge, since Count Raymond had sworn to cooperate with the church in the pursuit of heresy. In any event, the twelve notables refused to give in. Neither did Arnaud and his monks.

"Thereupon," wrote Brother Guillaume, "the consuls of Toulouse and their accomplices took direct action and expelled the friar inquisitor from the convent and the town, manhandling him as they did so. The entire convent accompanied him in procession to the head of the Daurade Bridge over the Garonne. There the consuls announced that they would allow him to stay in the town with the other friars if he would give up the Inquisition; otherwise, on behalf of the Count and themselves, they enjoined him strictly to leave the Count's lands without delay." The inquisitor refused, of course, to give up his mission. Yielding temporarily to superior force, he took himself to Carcassonne. Once there, he sent word to his subordinates that he wanted the same twelve notables of Toulouse summoned to appear before him in Carcassonne. The subordinate priests did as they were told. The consuls of Toulouse were outraged. The priests were arrested and taken to the city hall and held there for most of the night. "Then they expelled them from the town," Brother Guillaume reported, "with the declaration and threat that if anyone issued summons for them in this affair in the future, he would be killed at once."

At the same time, the consuls sent heralds throughout the city of Toulouse to declare that the Dominicans were to be treated as outlaws. No one was to give, sell or lend them anything. Anyone who violated these new regulations was subject to fines and beatings. Bishop Raymond left the city, but Brother Guillaume and his fellow Dominicans stood fast within their monastery. "We friars," he wrote, "did have the essentials in sufficient supply from friends and Catholics who, despite the danger, handed us bread, cheese and eggs over the garden walls. . . . When the consuls of the town learned of this, they set their guards at our gates. . . . They even cut us off completely from the water of the Garonne. This was a more serious blow to us because we were unable to cook our vegetables."

The inquisitor, Guillaume Arnaud, was not to be dissuaded. From Carcassonne, he wrote once again that the twelve notables whom he wanted to interrogate were to be summoned before him. If anyone who served such a summons was to be threatened with death, then let him take pride in the prospect of martyrdom. "The prior ordered the bell tolled," Brother Guillaume wrote, "and, when the friars had gathered, said with joyful countenance, 'Now, brethren, rejoice and be exceeding glad, for I am now to send four of you by martyrdom to the court of the Highest King.' " The prior said he wanted four volunteers to serve the summonses, even if it meant instant death, as promised. "I want those who are so prepared to prostrate themselves as for pardon," said the prior. "At this," Brother Guillaume reported, "all, acting as one, prostrated themselves." The prior was delighted. "Blessed be the Lord that I find you ready," he said. He then picked four volunteers, one of whom was Brother Guillaume.

The four made full confession and received absolution and set forth to summon the notables of Toulouse to appear before the Inquisition. At one of the very first houses they entered, they were assaulted. Two of their prospective victims, wrote Brother Guillaume, "came running and hustled the friars out of doors, heaping abusive words on them, dragging them by the hair and thrusting them out of the house, shouting as they struck them, and trying to slash them with knives." Despite all this resistance, the monks managed to serve the summonses.

The consuls of the city regarded this as a violation of their commands, and, in order to maintain their version of peace and quiet, they determined to expel the Dominican monks, just as they had expelled the inquisitor. No historian could improve on Brother Guillaume's account of the confrontation that followed: "When the friars, numbering about forty, were at table the consuls arrived with a great crowd, their sergeants crying out for the doors to be opened at once or they would be broken down. . . . The prior rang the bell, the friars all rose from the table and in procession entered the chapel, singing, '*Miserere mei Deus* . . .' The consuls sternly ordered the prior and his whole convent to depart from the town at once; if not, they would expel them by force. The prior told them that under no circumstances would he do so. . . . The prior took the cross and the coffer containing relics that was at the foot of the cross and seated himself in the cloister, the cross in his hands, and the whole convent sat down there in front of the consuls and their confederates. . . . Then some men took the prior by the arms and dragged him roughly out of the cloister. The other hangers-on and sergeants of the consuls dragged all the friars in the same way out of the cloister. . . . And thus they expelled all the friars, dragging and driving them outside the town. . . . The prior, and with him the convent, began to chant loudly the symbol of faith as it is sung in the mass, the Te Deum, and, when they were in front of the Church of Notre-Dame-la-Daurade, the Salve Regina. . . ."

∗

In theory, the Inquisition was a perfectly legal and orderly procedure. According to the prevailing principles of civil law, there were three standard methods for the prosecution of crimes: *accusatio,* in which a plaintiff formally accused a defendant; *denunciatio,* in which a public official denounced a criminal; and *inquisitio,* in which a judicial official undertook to investigate various reports of crime, to summon witnesses, to hear rebuttals. It is the same system that survives in much of Europe to this day, and although the investigating magistrate was a figure of great authority, the defendant had and still has the right to engage a lawyer and the right to appeal. Indeed, it was the revived study of Roman law in the early thirteenth century that helped make it possible for the church to codify the new regulations that would supersede the irregularities of local feudal law.

Upon this system of law, the church slowly built a system of organized terrorism. The first step was to define heresy as a crime, subject to clerical judgment, then to make that judgment enforceable by secular punishment. In this, the church gained invaluable support from a series of edicts by the Emperor Frederick II, who was trying in the early years of his reign to placate the church that would ultimately condemn him as a heretic and a sorcerer. Under these imperial decrees, issued between 1220 and 1239, all heresy was forbidden, and anyone who aided or defended heretics was liable to punishment. Nor need heresy be proved. Suspicion of heresy was enough to justify prosecution. Anyone who confessed and repented was to be punished. Anyone who refused to confess was to be judged impenitent, then turned over to the secular authorities for execution. Anyone who recanted a confession, or said that his confession had been given under coercion, was to be judged a relapsed heretic, and therefore executed. The house of any condemned heretic was to be destroyed forever; all his property was confiscated; all his children were barred from public office. There was to be no dissent. Every secular ruler must obey the church's demands for the hunting of heretics—or forfeit all rights to his own lands.

These decrees were not immediately enforced, but the church treated them as a model, to be established everywhere. In 1234, Bishop Raymond du Fauga of Toulouse drew up a similar code of rules for Languedoc, and Count Raymond was compelled, on threat of excommunication, to sign it. The Dominicans had already developed a method for carrying out these new decrees, and their method was codified as early as 1248 in a manual entitled *Processus Inquisitionis,* by Bernard de Caux and Jean de St.-Pierre, who were both based in Carcassonne. The first step, they said, was to go to the central town of a province and tell the parish priest to summon the citizens. They even provided the proper forms of address: "The inquisitors of heretical depravity send greetings in the Lord to so and so, parish priest. We enjoin and strictly instruct you, in virtue of the authority we wield, to summon in our name and by our authority all the parishioners of such and such a church or inhabitants of such and such a place, men from the age of fourteen, women from the age of twelve, or younger if by any chance they shall have been guilty of an offense, to appear before us on such a day at such a place to answer for acts which they may have committed against the faith and to abjure heresy."

This summons was generally followed by a period of grace, ranging from two weeks to a month, during which repentant heretics were allowed to confess their sins under a promise of relatively mild punishment. No such confession was considered sincere, however, unless the sinner named others who had shared in his sins. The inquisitors thus quickly accumulated dossiers of accusations, while among the townspeople nobody could be sure who had accused whom, or of what. The temptation to accuse an unfriendly neighbor or an unfaithful wife often proved irresistible. The inquisitors carefully recorded everything but kept all their records secret. Once the period of grace was finished, it came time to summon some of those who had failed to confess. Bernard de Caux and Jean de St.-Pierre once again provide detailed instructions for their colleagues: "The person is diligently questioned about whether he saw a heretic ..., where and when, how often and with whom, and about others who were present; whether he listened to their preaching or exhortation and whether he gave them lodging or arranged shelter for them, ... whether he ate or drank with them or ate bread blessed by them ... or learned anything from them ..."

These interrogations can be imagined. On the one side, the robed inquisitor, a monk, supported by all the authority of church and state, of God and dungeon. Next to him sat a notary, writing down every question and every answer for the archives of the Inquisition. On the other side stood the defendant, often an illiterate peasant, usually alone and without counsel. Yet the inquisitors managed to persuade themselves that they were unfairly matched against the sophistry of the forces of Satan. Bernard Gui, the chief inquisitor at Toulouse from 1308 to 1322, wrote a detailed *Practica Inquisitionis* in which he left us a matchless example of how these interrogations might go.

Q: You are accused as a heretic, and that you believe and teach otherwise than the Holy Church believes.

A: Lord, thou knowest that I am innocent of this . . .

Q: Do you believe in one God the Father, and the Son, and the Holy Ghost?

A: I believe.

Q: Do you believe the bread and wine in the mass performed by the priests to be changed into the body and blood of Christ by divine virtue?

A: Ought I not to believe this?

Q: I don't ask if you ought to believe, but if you do believe.

A: I believe whatever you and other good doctors order me to believe. . . .

Q: I ask whether the body there is of the Lord, who was born of the Virgin, hung on the cross, arose from the dead, ascended, et cetera?

A: And you, sir, do you not believe it?

Q: I believe it wholly.

A: I believe likewise.

Q: You believe that I believe it, which is not what I ask, but whether you believe it.

A: If you wish to interpret all that I say otherwise than simply and plainly, then I don't know what to say. I am a simple and ignorant man . . .

Q: If you are simple, answer simply, without evasions.

A: Willingly. . . .

As we read such testimony, we must keep remembering the alternatives that confronted the prisoner. If he confessed his sins, he faced fines, flogging or long imprisonment. If he refused to confess, he faced torture or burning at the stake, or both. Torture was actually rare in the early days of the Inquisition. The church moved slowly, and it was not until other methods of coercion had been tried for about two decades that Pope Innocent IV finally recommended, in his bull of 1252, *Ad Extirpanda,* the fire, the irons and the rack.

These same prolongations animated the real torture of the early Inquisition: imprisonment, interminable imprisonment. If an inquisitor judged a suspect's answers unsatisfactory, his contrition and repentance inadequate, he simply ordered him returned to his cell for three months, or six months, or a year, to await another interrogation. These terrible places can still be seen today in the fortress of Carcassonne, tiny cages, only a few feet wide, with barred entrances, and shrouded in perpetual darkness. According to the rule of *murus largus,* the prisoners confined in these dungeons could emerge from their cells at fixed intervals and at least talk to other prisoners; according to *murus strictus,* they had to stay in their cells indefinitely; according to *durus carcer et arcta victa,* they had to remain not only confined but chained, and fed only on bread and water. These confinements could last for years before the Inquisition even bothered to renew its inquiries, much less to reach a decision. One suspected heretic named Guillem Salavert confessed his sins to the inquisitors of Toulouse in 1299, but his confession was judged unsatisfactory, and so he was returned to the dungeons. Seventeen years later, he was allowed to confess again, but once again his confession was judged unsatisfactory, and once again he was sent back to his cell. Finally, at the auto-da-fé of 1319, he confessed yet again, and so, after twenty years of incarceration, he was finally released to perform the perpetual penance that Saint Dominic had invented, the wearing of a yellow cross on his breast.

"Churchmen pass for shepherds/ but they're murderers ...," wrote the troubador Peire Cardenal, who had been a secretary to Count Raymond VI and who went on fulminating against the Count's enemies until he died at the age of nearly one hundred. "Kings and emperors .../ used to rule the world;/ but now I see/churchmen holding sway/with their thefts and treachery/ and their hypocrisy,/ their violence and their preaching. ... And the mightier they are,/ the less is their virtue,/ and the greater their folly/ the less their truthfulness. ..../I say this of false/clergymen, for never/ did God have such enemies/ since time immemorial."

Languedoc died slowly. Over and over again, its doomed nobles rose in doomed revolt. Raymond Trencavel, the exiled Viscount of Béziers, who had been an infant when his father died after the first siege of Carcassonne, had grown up in Aragon, learning the skills of war in combat against the Moslems of southern Spain. In the autumn of 1240, he led an army across the Pyrenees and was welcomed as a returning hero in the rebellious towns of Alet, Limoux and Montréal. He laid siege to his father's citadel of Carcassonne, and the ferocity of that siege can be judged by the fact that Trencavel granted safe-conduct to thirty-three priests to leave the city, then butchered them. The assault on Carcassonne failed. A French relief force drove Trencavel away, besieged him in Montréal, then forced him to return to Aragon, leaving Montréal to be sacked by the victorious French.

Both sides called on Count Raymond VII to help them, but Raymond, just like his father, equivocated. His sympathies were with the invaders, but he dreaded any further retribution from the French, and from the church. Raymond was pursuing a Quixotic theory that if he could marry a new wife and produce a son, he could renegotiate that onerous clause in the Treaty of Meaux by which he had bequeathed all his lands to his daughter Jeanne and her French prince, Alphonse of Poitiers. To the dismay of Raymond's wife, Sanchia of Provence, the Count went before the bishop of Albi and testified that his wife was the goddaughter of his father, Raymond VI, and the bishop agreed that this spiritual consanguinity made the marriage invalid. So Raymond was free to remarry. A few months later, his ally, King Jaime of Aragon, stood proxy for Raymond at his wedding to Sanchia's grandniece, who was also called Sanchia—a wedding conditional only on a papal dispensation, which King Jaime promised he could obtain. Unfortunately, Pope Gregory IX died shorty afterward. Gregory's successor, Celestine IV, survived only two weeks in office, and then the papal throne stood vacant for nearly two years. So there could be no papal dispensation for Count Raymond's new marriage. Sanchia's father, Count Raymond Berengar of Provence, grew tired of these delays, re-married his daughter to a brother of King Henry III of England, and left Count Raymond once again without any prospect of a male heir.

Count Raymond persisted in believing that he could save Languedoc from the French by diplomatic intrigue. He helped to organize an alliance among various enemies of King Louis IX, notably King Henry III of England, Count Hugh de la Marche, various barons of Gascony, and the citizens of Bordeaux and Bayonne. It was never a very cohesive alliance. King Louis whipped a small force of English invaders at Taillebourg in July of 1242, Count Hugh de la Marche sued for peace, and Raymond was left alone to make what terms he could. The terms of the Peace of Lorris were a new humiliation. Raymond agreed to make all the nobles of Languedoc swear loyalty to France, and to join in a renewed hunt for heretics.

These heretics, though, were somewhat more resolute than Count Raymond. As one great gesture of defiance, they determined to kill the chief inquisitor himself. Guillaume Arnaud, that same stern figure who had refused to bow to the consuls of Toulouse nearly a decade earlier, was still making sweeps through the countryside, and when he sent word that he planned to spend the night in the town of Avignonet, the bailiff of that town sent word to the Cathar citadel of Montségur, fifty miles away, that the opportunity for vengeance for all the burnings had finally arrived. The commander at Montségur, Pierre-Roger de Mirepoix, sent fifteen knights and about forty-five men-at-arms to carry out that vengeance. As they went, they picked up supporters all along the way, sturdy peasants armed with axes. It was as though the whole countryside had silently determined to make an end to the Inquisition.

On May 28, 1242, the eve of Ascension Day, the men from Montségur gathered in a leper house on the outskirts of Avignonet. There they received periodic messages from Raymond d'Alfaro, the bailiff whom Count Raymond had assigned to guard the town. They heard that Brother Guillaume and his ten followers had eaten dinner, that they were going to bed, that all was darkness. The men from Montségur filed out of the leper house and marched to the gates of the town. The gates were opened to them. Raymond d'Alfaro, who had welcomed the eleven inquisitors, now welcomed their murderers and lighted their way with torches. The men of Montségur smashed down the inquisitors' door with their axes. The inquisitors must have known, from the first awful sounds of the axes on the door, what their fate was to be. *"Va be, esta be!"* cried Raymond d'Alfaro. "This is it!" Two servants who were traveling with the inquisitors tried to flee to the rooftop, but they did not escape. The inquisitors fell to their knees and began singing. *"Salve Regina,"* they sang. Singing, they died. Singing, they were hacked to pieces. The murderers then ransacked the inquisitors' room, dividing up clothes, books, even a box of ginger. They took the inquisitors' horses and rode off into the night. "Good luck as you go!" Raymond d'Alfaro shouted after them.

*

The assassins seem to have thought that their attack would be part of a general uprising, but the vague maneuverings of Count Raymond were already collapsing. So the murder of the inquisitors, like the murder of Papal Legate Pierre de Castelnau more than thirty years earlier, could have only one result: the outrage and vengeance of the Roman Catholic Church. The fortress of Montségur, which had long been tolerated as a sanctuary, difficult to attack, impossible to capture, was now condemned to destruction. In April of 1243, the royal seneschal of Carcassonne, Hugues des Arcis, assembled some ten thousand troops and laid siege.

Montségur appears to be invulnerable. It is an isolated limestone mountain that rises almost perpendicularly out of the Ariège Valley to a height of about 3,500 feet. Nobody knows exactly how or why the fortress on top of the mountain was first built, probably in the ninth century, for the pinnacle is so inaccessible that it serves no military purpose. It may have been, from the beginning, some kind of Druid temple, and there is a theory that the east window was so designed that the rising sun could shine directly through the building on June 21, the day of the summer solstice. Another mysterious peculiarity is the entry gate, nearly two yards wide, far more vulnerable than anything that one would expect to see in a mountain fortress, far more like a doorway for religious processions.

The mysteries of Montségur are intensified by the fact that the whole fortress collapsed in 1204, and nobody knows exactly what was altered in the process of rebuilding. It was rebuilt, however, and reinforced, and only then did it gradually become not just the sanctuary of the Cathars but their shrine and holy place, or, as Rome called it, "the synagogue of Satan." Here the legendary treasure of the Cathars was stored, sacks of gold coins and jeweled crosses bequeathed to them by their converts, and carefully preserved Scriptures that were said to date back to the days of the Evangelists. Here the hunted *perfecti* came to meditate, and here their followers came to worship, to receive the *consolamentum* and to be buried. Several hundred of these pilgrims lived in tiny huts that clung to the sides of the mountain, just below the fortress. The guiding spirit of Montségur was Esclarmonde, sister of the Count of Foix, and a *perfecta* in the Cathar Church, but the reigning seigneur at the time of the siege was one of her brother's vassals, Raymond de Perella, and Raymond's right arm was his son-in-law, Pierre-Roger de Mirepoix, who had just directed the massacre at Avignonet. Now they were all to die.

The besieged Cathars apparently did not realize, at the beginning, that this was their destiny. Though they were vastly outnumbered, they knew that the besiegers were too few to cut them off. Messengers continued clambering up and down the mountain. There were promises of help from the outside. And, in any case, the citadel of Montségur was amply supplied with food and water, more than enough to last throughout the summer, and no siege during the three decades of the Albigensian Crusade had ever lasted more than a summer. September came, and the leaves began to turn, but the besiegers did not go away. On the contrary, they hired some Basque mountaineers to start working their way up the steep slopes. The men of Montségur were too complacent, or perhaps too stoical. One day in October, they peered down from their mountaintop and saw that the Basque mercenaries had established themselves on a narrow ledge just eighty yards below the fortress.

Here the Basques were able to install a machine that could fire rocks against the walls of Montségur, and sometimes even into the courtyard. But their noose around the mountain was still so loose that the defenders could send for an engineer of their own, who slipped through the besiegers' lines and built a rival machine that could fire rocks at the Basques on the ledge. Snow began falling, and the mountain winds clawed at the Basques on their ledge. Their crude barrages of rocks had no effect on the fortress, and there seemed no way to advance farther. Between them and the nearest outlying tower of the fort there was only one closely guarded path, about six feet wide, and on both sides of that path the rocky sides of the mountain fell away for hundreds of feet. One dark night at about Christmastime, a band of guerrillas crept along those precipices below the path, working their way upward and forward by a series of precarious handholds on the rock (they said afterward that they wouldn't have dared to make the climb by daylight, when they could have seen the terrible risks).

As they neared the defenders' tower, they called upward for help, and the defenders, assuming that they must be messengers or supporters from the world below, let them in. The Basques slaughtered every one of them and flung their bodies into the abyss. When dawn broke, the lords of Montségur could see that their defenses had been breached. Now that the Basques controlled both ends of the path, they could bring up French reinforcements and advance their artillery. Every part of the fortress was now vulnerable to French cannonades. Those few pilgrims who still huddled in their outlying huts had to take refuge in the overcrowded citadel, and nowhere in that citadel was there any refuge any longer. "No rest was given to the besieged," according to the chronicle of Guillaume de Puylaurens, "either by day or by night."

The suffering on both sides must have been intense. Bitter cold. Snow. Hunger. No rest, no safety, no security, no hope of reprieve. Every day, the siege machines hurled boulders into the crowded fort, and the defenders just as resolutely flung them back. Both sides clung to their positions all through that frozen January, and then all through February, until finally the defenders decided on a desperate gamble. They determined to creep out at night, and along the sheer walls of the mountain, and to surprise the besiegers as they themselves had been surprised. At the end of February, a band of their bravest soldiers made that hazardous foray, but the French were not surprised. They seem to have been expecting it, perhaps from the beginning. They beat back the raiders, flung many of them off the cliff, and then staged their own charge against the fortress itself. The walls of Montségur are not more than about ten feet high. The French vanguard managed to storm over them and reach the forecourt of the citadel, but, in one last spasm of survival, the defenders overwhelmed them, killed many, drove the others back.

But now the court of the mountain temple had been desecrated. There were corpses lying everywhere, their blood seeping out, and wounded men groaning in their agony, and children sobbing in terror as they witnessed the carnage all around them. And there was no hope of salvation, not here, no hope of reinforcements, no hope that the crusade that had been launched more than a generation ago would ever abandon its determination to destroy this ultimate capital of heresy, not now or ever. On the morning after that last battle, on March 1, 1244, the defenders of Montségur sent a herald out onto the rampart to sound his horn. It was the signal of surrender.

The French royal seneschal, Hugues des Arcis, was prepared to be lenient. The defenders of Montségur were to be pardoned for all past crimes, including even the massacre of the inquisitors at Avignonet. The fortress' men-at-arms would be allowed to retire honorably, keeping their weapons. But all of them and all of the other inhabitants of Montségur, would have to submit themselves to the Inquisition. There would be no torture and no prolonged incarceration, and if they confessed their sins and repented their heresy and swore allegiance to the true church, then only mild penances would be imposed on them. But they would have to confess and repent. If they refused, they would be burned at the stake. A two-week truce was declared so that they would have time to consider their decision.

The Cathars seem to have spent those two weeks in dignified preparation for their fate. Many of them received the *consolamentum*, that sacrament of dedication that was customarily taken only on the deathbed. They exchanged gifts. They made their peace. And though there was no attempt at a breakout, they did apparently manage to save the Cathar treasure. This treasure, a hoard of gold and jewels, ancient Scriptures and sacred relics, is said to have been lowered down the mountain on ropes just before or just after the surrender, but since no trace of it has ever been found, it may never have existed at all.

At the end of two weeks, the decision had to be made. Many of the Cathars, inevitably, submitted themselves to the Inquisition, but about two hundred of the five hundred defenders of Montségur stoically accepted their doom. They were roughly chained and then dragged down the mountain to their place of execution. On the southwest side of the foot of the mountain, on a sloping field, the crusaders had already built a large four-sided stockade, which they had filled with a mountain of brushwood. The two hundred chained prisoners were herded into this stockade, and shut in there, and left to their prayers. The crusaders then set fire to all four corners of the stockade, then watched the faggots smoke and catch and burn, then drew back to a safer distance as the stockade and everything in it became a holocaust.

＊

Five years later, on the eve of his departure for his long-promised crusade in the Holy Land, Count Raymond VII fell ill and died, at the age of 52, still unmarried and thus without any heir who might wrest Languedoc from the French crown. One of his last efforts to ingratiate himself with the unforgiving Church of Rome was to order and witness the public burning at Agen of eighty citizens accused of being Cathars. In death, he asked only that his body be shipped to Fontevrault, that Loire Valley tomb of the Plantagenets, so that he could lie near his grandmother, Eleanor of Aquitaine. And so it was done, and a barge containing the embalmed body of the last true Count of Toulouse drifted slowly down the Garonne. "It was pitiful . . .," wrote Guillaume de Puylaurens, "to see these people lamenting and weeping for their natural lord, who had left absolutely no one else of his race. It was thus that it pleased our Lord Jesus Christ to make it manifest to all, that God, in taking away a generous master, had punished the whole country, on account of the heresy with which it was infected . . ."

＊

And the Inquisition continued. In the year 1252, in the papal bull known as *Ad Extirpanda,* Pope Innocent IV finally ordered all Christian princes to cooperate in the pursuit of heresy or be suspected of heresy themselves. And there was to be no more dialectic. *Ad Extirpanda* not only permitted the torture of suspects, as had actually been approved by the Fourth Lateran Council of 1215, but recommended it, virtually urged it. By this time, torture was already becoming increasingly common. There were still some rules, though. The suspect was shown the terrible instruments and urged to confess before the instruments were applied; he could not be tortured more than once; he still had a right to a lawyer. But as the Inquisition became more and more a self-fulfilling institution, all the rules that limited its authority gradually disintegrated. At the Council of Albi, in 1254, it was agreed that any advocate who defended a suspected heretic was himself liable to a charge of complicity in heresy. In 1256, Pope Alexander IV abolished the rule that the inquisitors could not themselves take part in the torturing of suspects. His edict permitted the inquisitors to absolve each other of any violence in which they had participated, and though torture could not be applied more than once, it could be "suspended" and then "continued." This same Pope reissued *Ad Extirpanda* in 1259, and Pope Clement IV reissued it again in 1265.

By this time, the Inquisition was uncontrollable. The inquisitors themselves were appointed for life, and anyone who interfered with them, or criticized them, or even questioned them, was subject to arrest, incarceration and torture. There were powerful economic reasons for the continuing pursuit of heresy, since the Inquisition by now claimed a large share, usually one third, of all the property of anyone condemned as a heretic. And the definition of heresy had gone far beyond theology, beyond even the suspicions of witchcraft and magic. The Inquisition, according to one account, regarded as suspect anyone "differing in life or manners from the ordinary faithful." And since the inquisitors' first demand of their victims was confession, and since the sincerity of a tortured defendant's confession could be proved only by his denunciations of his friends, neighbors and accomplices, the inquisitors' search proved unending, their field of battle unlimited. As early as 1248, in the *Processus Inquisitionis* of Bernard de Caux and Jean de Saint-Pierre, the death sentence itself had been reduced to a formula, with blanks to be filled in: "We, the inquisitors aforesaid, having heard and carefully weighed the crimes and defaults of [so and so], named above, . . . adjudge [so and so], named above, to be a heretic, because he believed in the errors of heretics and is proved still to believe them and because, when examined or when convicted and confessing, he flatly refused to be recalled and to give full obedience to the mandates of the church. We relinquish him now to secular judgment. . . ."

It has become customary, in secular times, to regard the Inquisition as a kind of organized madness, in which evil-minded and sadistic authorities tortured the innocent to make them confess and then burned them at the stake for crimes that they had not committed. In the thirteenth century, however, the salvation of a Christian's immortal soul was considered the supreme goal of both church teaching and secular power. In the view of most Christians, and perhaps even most heretics, there could be little question of any "right" to dissent, any more than a modern official would grant anyone the right to walk the streets while suffering from smallpox or the bubonic plague. To permit a heretic to continue preaching heresy meant the eternal damnation of everyone infected by his preaching. To confine such a carrier of pestilence in the dungeons of Carcassonne would hardly have shocked a citizen of Languedoc any more than a Californian might be shocked by the incarceration of a bank robber in San Quentin. And the inquisitors themselves rather resembled federal judges, not zealots and fanatics but stately men well trained in the intricacies of philosophy and jurisprudence. Even Saint Thomas Aquinas, who devoted page after page of his *Summa Theologica* to the analysis of ethical niceties, approved and justified the execution of all heretics.

Those few who tried to resist the Inquisition generally argued not that heresy should be tolerated but that the Inquisition was persecuting the innocent. The most heroic figure of the early fourteenth century, a Franciscan named Bernard Délicieux, acted on the theory that a combination of virtue, courage and Christian orthodoxy could bring the Inquisition to a halt. "The inquisitors' power comes from people not daring to stand up to them," he preached. "We must dare—and not worry about the consequences." For a time, Bernard Délicieux profited from the fact that King Philip the Fair was at odds with Pope Boniface VIII, and so he won such victories as the royal decree that the prisons of the Inquisition were to be used solely for keeping suspects in custody, not torturing them (*"ad custodiam, non ad poenam"*). But as time passed, King Philip moved on to other problems, and the Inquisition never forgot. Bernard Délicieux was denounced, arrested, tortured, sentenced to incarceration for life, on bread and water, in one of those dark cages in Carcassonne. He died there, at some unknown date.

The Inquisition never forgot, never relented, never gave up. The Cathar network managed to survive the capture of Montségur, and the capture a decade later of the heretics' last small fortress at Quéribus, but the nobles of Languedoc gradually abandoned the struggle. Catharism became, more and more, a religion of the forests, and of the poor. The *bons hommes* survived only in the mountain villages. Even there, the inquisitors pursued them. One of the last of the Cathar trials involved a wandering priest named Guilhem Belibasta, who spent years hiding in the mountains behind Valencia, was lured back into Languedoc, trapped, put on trial before the archbishop of Narbonne and burned at the stake in 1321. The last known group of Cathars were discovered at about this same time in the caves of Lombrives, near Pamiers. Bishop Jacques Fournier, who was to become Benedict XII in the Papacy that Philip the Fair had lured to Avignon, ordered them walled up inside their cave forever. All that survived of them and the others was the careful record of the Inquisition concerning each execution: "For straw, 2 sols 6 deniers. For four stakes, 10 sols 9 deniers. For ropes to tie the convicts, 4 sols 7 deniers . . ."

It has been argued that the Inquisition destroyed not heresy but the church itself. That any force that could burn Saint Joan of Arc and compel Galileo to deny his own discovery that the earth goes around the sun was a force that represented, as the Cathars had said from the beginning, the triumph of Antichrist. On a more modest level, though, the Albigensian Crusade and the destruction of Montségur and the victory of the Inquisition provide sad evidence that oppression and persecution do serve their purposes. By the middle of the fourteenth century, the Inquisition in Languedoc came to an end because even the inquisitors could find no more victims. There were no more Cathars, no more troubadours, no more traces of heresy of any kind, or of that rebellious civilization that had once been the glory of Languedoc.

Today, seven centuries later, the citadel of Montségur still perches on its mountaintop, a hollow shell of stone, infinitely remote, and when one clambers up the mountain to see what remains of its mysteries, one finds only a profound stillness, faintly reverberating with the echoes of the violence that once occurred there. And Toulouse, stripped of its stone walls, stripped of its independence—Toulouse is just a raffish provincial city, a center of aircraft production, where the stores and the cafés and the television shows are much like those in Bordeaux or Lyon or anywhere else, where, on moonlit summer nights, the Place du Capitole resounds to the roar of young motorcyclists racing their machines around the dark and empty city hall that once was the headquarters of the defiantly independent consuls. Thus was Rome avenged upon the Goths.

BOOK II

—

THE EYE

OF

GOD

—

Are not two sparrows sold for a farthing? And one of them shall not fall on the ground without your Father [seeing]. . . . Fear ye not therefore, ye are of more value than many sparrows.

—MATTHEW 10:29, 31

The Black Death

1347–50

"A vast, dreadful solitude"

The Genoan traders who occupied the fortress of Kaffa on the eastern coast of the Crimea guarded the overland routes to Turkestan and China. There they did a brisk trade in horses and furs and Russian slaves, and there they saw the Tartars in the surrounding countryside begin to succumb to a mysterious plague. Within a few months, toward the end of the year 1346, the pestilence killed an estimated 85,000 people in the Crimea alone.

The Tartars blamed the disaster on the Genoans. It is tempting to suspect that they regarded the alien Genoans as Christian scapegoats, but perhaps the Genoans were simply victims of intrigues by the Venetians, who also wanted to establish themselves as masters of the trade routes to China. In any case, there was a collision. The Tartar ruler known as Kipchak Khan Janibeg seized on a street brawl between some of his men and the Genoans as a pretext to lay siege to Kaffa. But even as the Khan waited for the besieged Genoans to surrender, his own forces began falling ill with the plague. "The Tartars . . . were stupefied and amazed," according to the contemporary chronicle of Gabriel de Mussis, a notary in Piacenza, "observing themselves dying without hope of health . . ."

In a rage, Janibeg Khan ordered that the victims' corpses, all blackened and swollen and putrefying in the sun, be loaded onto siege guns and catapulted like missiles over the stone walls of the encircled city. The horrified Genoans gathered up the decaying bodies and hauled them to the wall nearest to the Black Sea and flung them into the water. But as the plague continued to ravage the Tartar army, the ghastly cannonade continued. "Thus were projected mountains of dead," de Mussis' chronicle went on. "Nor could the Christians hide or flee, or be freed from such disaster. . . . And soon all the air was infected and the water poisoned, corrupt and putrefied, and such a great odor increased . . ."

The Genoans inevitably began falling sick. The terrible signs were always the same—the egg-sized swellings known as buboes in the groin and the armpits, the fever and the spitting of blood, then, usually within a week, often less, death. The boldest of the Genoans decided that they could save themselves only by flight. They abandoned the dying city of Kaffa and clambered aboard four of their galleys and began rowing desperately across the Black Sea toward the imperial capital of Constantinople. They brought with them, of course, the bubonic plague. Emperor John VI Cantacuzene, who was to lose his son Andronicus to the epidemic, left a mournful account of the disaster. "The plague attacked almost all the seacoasts of the world," he wrote, "and killed most of their people."

Where did it come from, this devastating disease, and how did it spread so far? Nobody knows for certain, but there are remote areas of the world where the plague bacillus now known as *Pasteurella pestis* seems to be endemic, where all its victims have either died or developed an immunity. Of all these remote areas, one of the most utterly forlorn is the region around Lake Issyk-Kul, where the Soviet territory of Kirghiz now abuts the western border of Sinkiang. Nobody knows, again, what routed the plague out of this obscure land, but Chinese chronicles of the early fourteenth century report a disastrous series of natural convulsions beginning in 1333 and 1334. Violent earthquakes shook the capital of Kiangsai, several mountains of Ki-ming-chan collapsed, and floods ravaged the region around Canton. There were droughts, famines, swarms of locusts. The more fanciful chroniclers wrote of deluges of frogs, lizards and scorpions.

From such semimythological accounts, it can only be guessed that these natural cataclysms drove the rats and other rodents of central Asia out of their natural habitat and forced them to migrate in search of food and shelter. With them they carried the flea known as *Xenopsylla cheopsis,* the chief carrier of the plague bacillus. By the year 1346, there were already reports in Europe of devastating pestilence in China, where thirteen million people were said to have died, then India, then the Middle East. There too the pestilence was heralded by earthquakes. "Between Cathay and Persia, there rained a vast sea of fire, falling in lakes like snow and burning up mountains . . . ," according to one Italian account," and then arose vast masses of smoke; and whoever beheld this died within the space of half a day." "India was depopulated," according to another report, "Tartary, Mesopotamia, Syria, Armenia were covered with dead bodies . . ."

Though these reports were written like factual accounts—granted a certain amount of exaggeration based on thirdhand information—contemporary scientists had virtually no idea what was happening. That was what made it so terrifying. The plague bacillus itself was not isolated and identified until 1894, and the physicians of the fourteenth century knew nothing about the role of rats and fleas, knew nothing about what caused the epidemic or what could be done to stop it. They knew that the plague was highly contagious, but they attributed its spread to some noxious quality in the air, possibly caused by earthquakes. Its workings remained mysterious. A man suddenly struck down by boils and fevers was simply a man struck down by God's will—or, worse, God's anger. There appeared to be no difference in meaning between this plague and the eruption of Mount Etna in 1333, the severe thunderstorms that ruined French harvests in 1336, the swarms of locusts that attacked crops in 1337 and 1338, the great floods of the Rhine in 1342, the earthquakes that devastated Italy in 1347, no difference except that an unappeased God seemed to have become more wrathful than ever. As William Langland wrote in *Piers Plowman,*

"God is deaf now-a-days and deigneth not hear us,/ And prayers have no power the Plague to stay."

There were precedents, not simply medical precedents like the so-called Plague of Justinian that had ravaged Europe in the sixth century, but theological precedents fully described in Genesis. In the land of the pharaohs, as every good Christian knew, God had turned the waters of the Nile into blood, and sent swarms of frogs and lice and flies, and loosed a plague of boils and sores. And as Judgment Day approached, as good Christians also knew from Revelation, an angel would take a key and unlock the bottomless pit, and clouds of dark smoke would issue forth. "And there came out of the smoke locusts upon the earth: and unto them was given power, as the scorpions of the earth have power. And it was commanded them that they should not hurt the grass of the earth ... but only those men which have not the seal of God in their foreheads."

From infected Constantinople, the Genoans sailed westward, still hoping to reach safety. By now, they were not the only plague carriers. About a dozen Genoan galleys from various ports in the eastern Mediterranean were working their way homeward, "fleeing," according to the chronicle of the Franciscan Michael of Piazza, "from the vengeance which our Lord was taking on account of their nefarious deeds." They reached the Straits of Messina and then apparently could go no farther, for, as Michael put it, "they bore in their bones so virulent a disease that anyone who merely spoke to them was seized with a mortal illness." The people of Messina, knowing nothing of this, welcomed the Genoans hospitably. And so the plague reached Western Europe in October of 1347.

It was virulent beyond anything in anyone's memory, and the most terrifying effect of this mysterious virulence was not only that it killed so many people but that it turned them against one another, cutting all the bonds that held society together. "As the number of deaths increased in Messina," Michael's chronicle continued, "many desired to confess their sins to the priests and to draw up their last will and testament. But priests and lawyers refused to enter the houses of the diseased.... Soon men hated each other so much that, if a son was attacked by the disease, his father would not tend him. If, in spite of all, he dared to approach him, he was immediately infected.... Soon the corpses were lying forsaken in the houses. No priest, no son, no father and no relation dared to enter, but they paid hired servants with high wages to bury the dead.... Soon there was a shortage of servants and finally none at all. When the catastrophe had reached its climax the Messinians resolved to emigrate ..."

First they turned on the surviving Genoan seamen, beating them and driving them back into their galleys and ordering them to finish their voyage home. Then they began to flee their stricken city. Many of them simply wandered out into the fields and vineyards and camped there, waiting for death to find them, as it generally did. Others, more resolute, trekked down the mountainous coast to the next main town, Catania, some sixty miles to the south. The Catanians treated the first refugees kindly, took the sick into their hospitals, just as the Messinians had done for the Genoans. But just as the Messinians had realized that their hospitality had doomed them, so the Catanians soon began barring all travelers from the north. "So wicked and timid were the Catanians," said Friar Michael, "that they refused even to speak to any from Messina, or to have anything to do with them, but quickly fled at their approach."

The Messinians refused to depart. Their goal was to persuade the Patriarch Archbishop of Catania, Gerard Othos, to cure their epidemic by loaning them the relics of Saint Agatha. She was a powerful intermediary, a pious Catanian virgin of the third century who had resisted the advances of a Roman official named Quintian and had consequently been arrested and tortured to death. As part of her martyrdom, her breasts had been cut off, and this inspired the local hagiologists to make her the patron saint of bell-founders and to have new loaves of bread blessed in her honor on her feast day, the fifth of February. The Patriarch agreed to the Messinians' plea, but the Catanians were outraged at the prospective departure of their martyr from their cathedral. "They tore the keys from the sacristan," Michael reported, "and stoutly rebuked the Patriarch, saying that they would rather die than allow the relics to be taken to Messina." The Patriarch agreed, in turn, to the wishes of the Catanian mob. Leaving the remains of Saint Agatha in their place, he contented himself with dipping some of the relics in water and then setting forth with the newly sanctified water for the plague-infested city of Messina. He found there a nightmarish spectacle.

"In that city," according to Michael's chronicle, "there appeared demons transfigured into the shape of dogs, who wrought grievous harm upon the bodies of the citizens; so that men were aghast and dared not go forth from their houses." Despite these raging animals, the surviving citizens of Messina agreed to join the Patriarch in a parade through the city, reciting litanies as they marched. They then encountered an even more extraordinary spectacle. "While the whole population was thus proceeding around the streets," said Michael, "a black dog, bearing a drawn sword in his paws, appeared among them, gnashing his teeth and rushing among them and breaking all the silver vessels and lamps and candlesticks on the altars and casting them hither and thither. . . . So the people of Messina, terrified by this prodigious vision, were all strangely overcome by fear."

The water into which the relics of Saint Agatha had been dipped produced no effect, so the citizens of Messina invoked one last resource, a statue of the Virgin Mary at a shrine six miles outside the city. A barefoot procession of Messinians marched out to the shrine and loaded the statue onto a horse, but even this desperate act of piety was doomed. "This aforesaid Mother of God, when she saw and drew near unto the city, judged it to be so hateful and so profoundly stained with blood and sin that she turned her back on it," Michael wrote, "being not only unwilling to enter therein, but even abhorring the very sight thereof. For which cause the earth yawned open and the horse which bore the image of God stood fixed and motionless as a rock." When the petitioners finally got the horse and the statue into the city of Messina, it did as little good as the water that had been sanctified by the relics of Saint Agatha. The heroic Patriarch of Catania returned home and died.

By then, death was everywhere. The Genoans brought the plague home to Genoa in January of 1348, but Venetian sailors brought it to Venice at just about the same time. From Sicily it followed all the major trade routes—probably because the ships that sailed those trade routes carried with them the black rat, known to science as *Rattus rattus,* which carried the fleas that carried the plague bacillus—to Tunis, to Corsica, to Barcelona, to the coast of Languedoc. For the Italians, who had recently endured earthquakes from Naples to Venice, then floods, droughts and famines, this mysterious epidemic was worse than anything ever recorded. The chroniclers of the time reported 63,000 people dying in Naples within the space of two months, and more than 100,000 in Florence. In Venice, the toll was said to be six hundred per day. Pisa was reported to have lost four fifths of its inhabitants and Verona three quarters. Modern historians have disputed these figures, arguing that the medieval chroniclers were prone to exaggeration, to hearsay, round numbers and Scriptural prophecies. Indeed, the widespread reports of the death of one third of the population—*"Bien la tierce partie du monde mourut,"* Jean Froissart simply stated it—coincided remarkably with the tolls prophesied in Revelation, when the angels sounded their trumpets, and thus "was the third part of men killed."

Still, the fourteenth-century chroniclers were doing their best to describe a disaster of almost unimaginable magnitude. And even after modern historians have pored over all available parish records and tax receipts and other fragmentary documents, they come to somewhat similar conclusions. They estimate the death toll throughout Europe, with many local variations, at about thirty percent, or 25 million out of a population of about 80 million. The scholarly estimates of worldwide casualties remain little more than medieval guesses: perhaps 75 million dead out of a total population of perhaps 500 million.

The chroniclers themselves knew that their reports were beyond all reckoning. In Siena, where the great new cathedral had to be left forever unfinished, one of them told of deep pits piled up with corpses, and of dogs devouring them, and finally he compressed the whole story into his own misfortune: "And I, Agnolo di Tura, called the Fat, buried my five children with my own hands, and so did many others likewise. . . . And nobody wept no matter what his loss because almost everyone expected death. . . . People said and believed, 'This is the end of the world.' "

"O happy posterity, who . . . will look upon our testimony as a fable," wrote Petrarch. The poet nonetheless felt that the events of "that dreadful year 1348" must be recorded for the very posterity that would not believe the testimony. "Will posterity believe," he wrote from Parma in the late spring of 1349, "that there was a time when, with no deluge from heaven, no worldwide conflagration, no wars or other visible devastation, not merely this or that territory but almost the whole earth was depopulated? When was such a disaster ever seen, even heard of? In what records can we read that houses were emptied, cities abandoned, countrysides untilled, fields heaped with corpses, and a vast, dreadful solitude over all the world?"

One reason that posterity can believe in this devastation is that Petrarch's friend Giovanni Boccaccio wrote a vivid description of it in the preface to his *Decameron*. Being a realistic observer rather than a poet, Boccaccio began with a simple description of the plague's symptoms, the growths in the thighs, "roughly the size of the common apple," then the "dark blotches and bruises on the arms, thighs and others parts of the body." (Though the bubonic form of the plague was the most common, the Black Death included two even more lethal variants: pneumonic, in which the plague bacillus invaded the lungs, and septicemic, in which it entered directly into the bloodstream.) He emphasized, however, that nobody had any idea what had caused the epidemic. "Some say that it descended upon the human race through the influence of the heavenly bodies," he wrote, "others that it was a punishment signifying God's righteous anger at our iniquitous way of life."

One of Italy's most eminent doctors, Gentilis of Foligno, who was himself to die of the plague, left a record of the remedies he prescribed: bleeding, purging, repeated bathing in vinegar, and much burning of odoriferous wood to purify the air. All such remedies, Boccaccio said, were "profitless and unavailing." Everyone was left to choose his own way. Some, of course, simply went on with their daily lives, enduring what they must and praying for deliverance. Others, like the storytellers of the *Decameron,* retired from all contact with the plague-ridden world. "Having withdrawn to a comfortable abode where there were no sick persons," Boccaccio wrote, "they locked themselves in and settled down to a peaceable existence, consuming modest quantities of delicate foods and precious wines and avoiding excesses. They refrained from speaking to outsiders, refused to receive news of the dead or sick, and entertained themselves . . ." To still others, debauchery was the road to salvation, or, if there was to be no salvation, to happiness in the few days that remained. These profligates abandoned all work and drifted from house to house, drinking, stealing, fornicating. "People behaved as though their days were numbered," Boccaccio wrote, "and treated their belongings and their own persons with equal abandon. Hence most houses had become common property, and any passing stranger could make himself at home. . . . In the face of so much affliction and misery, all respect for the laws of God and man had virtually broken down. . . . Those ministers and executors of the laws who were not either dead or ill were left with so few subordinates that they were unable to discharge any of their duties. Hence everyone was free to behave as he pleased."

The freedom to behave as one pleases traditionally seems a license for saturnalia. Describing a plague that had struck Athens nearly two thousand years earlier, Thucydides wrote: "Men who had hitherto concealed their indulgence in pleasure now grew bolder. For, seeing the sudden change, how the rich died in a moment . . . , they reflected that life and riches were alike transitory, and they resolved to enjoy themselves while they could, and to think only of pleasure." Pleasure soon gave way, however, to more rudimentary needs, not even sex or self-indulgence but mere survival. "This scourge had implanted so great a terror in the hearts of men and women," Boccaccio wrote, "that brothers abandoned brothers ... and in many cases wives deserted their husbands. But even worse, and almost incredible, was the fact that fathers and mothers refused to nurse and assist their own children, as though they did not belong to them."

As usual, the sacrifice of all else to survival could not ensure survival. The plague impartially killed the moralist and the immoralist, the ascetic and the epicure, killed those who tried to save others and those who tried to save themselves. The most vivid illustration of this, to the fourteenth-century mind, was not the shutting down of markets or other commercial enterprises but the threat that there soon might not be enough living to bury the dead. Boccaccio was shocked that neighbors were no longer willing to accompany the corpses to the graveyard. Instead, there suddenly materialized, "from the lower orders of society," a corps of professional scavengers. "These people assumed the title of *becchini* [gravediggers], and demanded a large fee for their services, which consisted in taking up the coffin and hauling it swiftly away, not to the church specified by the dead man in his will, but usually to the nearest at hand." Even these misfortunes marked only the despoliation of the wealthy. The poor simply lay where they fell. "Many dropped dead in the open streets, both by day and by night," Boccaccio wrote, "while a great many others, though dying in their own houses, drew their neighbors' attention to the fact more by the smell of their rotting corpses than by any other means. And what with these, and the others who were dying all over the city, bodies were here, there and everywhere." And then there were no more graves, no more consecrated ground. "So when all the graves were full, huge trenches were excavated in the churchyards, into which new arrivals were placed in their hundreds, stowed tier upon tier like ships' cargo, each layer of corpses being covered over with a thin layer of soil till the trench was filled to the top.... No more respect was accorded to dead people than would nowadays be shown toward dead goats."

Death on such a scale made all the traditional forms of life meaningless. Family responsibilities became meaningless, work became meaningless, money and property became meaningless. Farmers not only failed to plant their fields but failed even to harvest the crops that were already growing there. "Peasants and their families ... collapsed by the wayside," Boccaccio wrote, "in their fields and in their cottages at all hours of the day and night, dying more like animals than human beings.... Moreover, they all behaved as though each day was to be their last, and, far from making provision for the future by tilling their lands ..., they tried in every way they could think of to squander the assets already in their possession. Thus it came about that oxen, asses, sheep, goats, pigs, chickens and even dogs ... were driven away and allowed to roam freely through the fields, where the crops lay abandoned."

Sober-minded historians have argued, as sober-minded historians customarily do, that Boccaccio was exaggerating. It can certainly be demonstrated that various civic authorities did take various steps to combat the plague. Committees were appointed and regulations issued. Streets were cleaned, markets regulated, travel limited, and sins that might have angered God, like gambling, were prohibited. And the hundreds of thousands of corpses were, one way or another, buried. Still, one has a sense that Boccaccio's portrait of anarchy and helpless despair was essentially accurate. The officials who were supposed to govern Italy understood nothing and could do nothing. In the course of a year, the plague killed everyone who was vulnerable and then simply burned itself out, like a forest fire. The Florentine historian Giovanni Villani died in the middle of a sentence, *"E dure questo pistolenza fino a*— And during this pestilence there came to an end—"

As the plague moved on to the north, Pope Clement VI demonstrated the misguided faith of the highest authorities in Christendom by decreeing 1350 to be a holy year, a jubilee. The first of these ceremonials had been held in 1300, and they were intended as centennial events, but the Pope succumbed to the idea that summoning hundreds of thousands of pilgrims from all over plague-stricken Europe to the altars of Rome would be a worthy commemoration of the fact that two thirds of God's children had survived his chastisement. Among the estimated one million pilgrims who crowded into Rome to celebrate that dark jubilee was Saint Bridget of Sweden, who arrived early in 1349 and offered her prescription for dealing with the plague: "Abolish earthly vanity in the shape of extravagant clothes, give free alms to the needy and order all parish priests to celebrate mass once a month in honor of the Holy Trinity."

∗

The Rome of Saint Bridget was far different, of course, from the Rome of the Caesars, or even the decaying imperial citadel that King Alaric had stormed. "Rome . . . was once the head and is now the rump of the civilized world," as one of Boccaccio's characters offhandedly remarked. Deprived of its imperial splendors, the city had sunk into banditry and anarchy during the so-called Dark Ages, and the emergence of the imperial Papacy in the twelfth and thirteenth centuries proved an ambiguous blessing. Pilgrims of all stations brought wealth from the farthest corners of Europe, and the papal court provided a great deal of employment, but Rome's unique position failed to stimulate the development of the manufactures that were beginning to enrich Florence and Milan. Rome's physical location provided none of the trading opportunities enjoyed by the Genoans and the Venetians; even its immediate surroundings, the long-neglected Campagna, no longer provided food.

Rome's dependence on the Papacy blighted not only its economic life but its political development. The middle classes that supported the emerging republics of Florence and Pisa and many other prospering northern towns scarcely existed in Rome. Local power remained the object of furious battles among the rival bands of cutthroats who pledged allegiance to the Colonnas and the Orsinis and the other great clans that called themselves noble. When a commune actually did establish itself in Rome in the mid-twelfth century, inspired in part by Arnold of Brescia's passionate preachings against secular power for the clergy, it was soon subverted by the nobles and constrained by the Vatican.

But now, in these plague years, the popes no longer lived in Rome. For almost half a century they had been established in Avignon, victims partly of the political demands of the French monarchy, partly of the ceaseless brawling and rioting in Rome itself. Whatever the effects of the seventy-year "Babylonian Captivity" on the church, and the effects were mostly bad, the consequences to the city of Rome were devastating. Its economic difficulties worsened, its turbulence continued unchecked, and its very reason for existence was fading. Yet even in Rome's darkest days, when it was not only powerless but an object of pity and contempt, the Romans cherished an illusion of their city as the capital of the world, of both universal empire and universal church.

It was in this spirit that the relic still known as the Roman Senate invited Petrarch, in the year 1340, to be crowned at the Capitol as the poet laureate, successor to Virgil and Horace. And in this spirit Petrarch journeyed from the new center of power in Avignon to the Capitoline Hill, where, surrounded by phalanxes of aristocratic youths in green and scarlet robes, he delivered a discourse on a text by Virgil and a sonnet in praise of the great city, and then bowed down to receive his laurel crown, and then heard the Roman citizenry chorus his praises ("Long life to the Capitol and the poet!"), and then led a procession to the abandoned Vatican so that the laurel wreath could be hung before the shrine of Saint Peter.

The proud city of Avignon, which the French had besieged and conquered and stripped of all its fortifications because of its defiant support of Count Raymond of Toulouse, had grown large once again since the Papacy had moved there from faction-ridden Rome in 1309, grown large with papal bureaucrats and wandering petitioners and moneylenders and prostitutes. It had grown so large so rapidly—its population of eighty thousand was about four times that of depleted Rome—that a pestilential smell of sewage hung perpetually over it. The poet Petrarch—poet but also courtier and retainer to Giovanni Cardinal Colonna—spent as much time as he could in the more salubrious atmosphere of Vaucluse, where he mused and wrote sonnets upon the beauties of Laure de Sade. He regarded the stench of Avignon as a kind of symptom. "This is a sewer," he wrote, "to which all the filths of the universe come to be reunited. Here people despise God, they adore money, they trample underfoot both human laws and divine law. Everything here breathes falsehood: the air, the earth, the houses and, above all, the bedrooms." And again: "I will not speak of adultery, seduction, rape, incest; these are only the prelude to their orgies . . ."

When Clement V brought the Papacy here, a move that he originally considered temporary, it was partly in deference to the political demands of the French crown, but Avignon was not actually part of France. It was a fief of the kingdom of the Two Sicilies, which was in turn a fief of the church. The location of Avignon not only made Pope Clement independent of Roman upheavals but brought him nearer to the geographical center of Christendom. The building of the new Babylon required large sums of money, however, and Avignon soon filled with prelates who were expert at devising new forms of taxation. The "annate," for example, was a fee paid for a clerical office, usually one year's revenues; the "expectative" was a fee paid for an office that was not yet vacant but soon might be. Then there was the disposition of lands and titles; the d'Este family, for one, paid ten thousand gold florins a year for the duchy of Ferrara. And then the little fees and charges, the *servitia communia,* the *servitia minuta,* the *visitationes ad limina.* Clement's successor, John XXII, justified these exactions as necessary for a new crusade to reconquer the Holy Land, but the crusade never took place, and the money simply poured into Avignon. John inherited a fortune of seventy thousand gold florins and bequeathed his successors a hoard of seventeen million, as well as seven million worth of jewels and gold plate and other treasures. "Every time I went to the apartment of the Lord Pope's chamberlain," according to one contemporary witness, "I inevitably found bankers, money changers, tables loaded with gold, and clerks weighing and counting out florins."

"My predecessors did not know how to be popes," declared Clement VI, the urbane archbishop of Rouen, on his election to the throne of Saint Peter in 1342. By which he meant that they had been niggardly in their fund raising and in their spending. Clement proceeded to squander everything those predecessors had accumulated. He ordered a vast expansion of the papal palace. Since he loved hunting, he commissioned magnificent frescoes of scenes of the chase. He filled the papal stables with white thoroughbreds and lined the terraces with exotic flowers. His library overflowed with the works of Homer, Plato, Horace, Seneca, Terence. He often welcomed to his bedchanber the young ladies of Avignon, and also, some said, the young men. Pope Clement was to die, in good time, of venereal disease.

He knew, as he had promised, how to be pope. At one dinner in his honor, he was served a pastry castle containing a roasted stag, roebucks and hares. This was only one of nine courses, and each course had three parts. To wash down the food, there was a fountain, built of peacocks, pheasants and partridges, and it spewed forth five kinds of wine. In between courses, there were a tournament, a concert, repeated exchanges of gifts. The Pope was given a white charger worth four hundred florins, and two rings, an enormous sapphire and an enormous topaz. The sixteen cardinals present also received jeweled rings. The dessert consisted of two trees, a silver one bearing gilded apples, pears, peaches, figs and grapes, and a green one bearing various candied fruits.

Among Clement's many purchases was the city of Avignon itself, which he acquired for a relatively modest eighty thousand florins from the twenty-one-year-old Queen Joanna of Naples, who badly needed papal exculpation from the rumors that she had connived in the assassination of her husband, Prince Andrew of Hungary. By the time Joanna arrived in Avignon for her spectacular trial in March of 1348, the city was already infected with the plague. The epidemic had taken only a month or so to leap from Italy to France. Following in the wake of the Italian coastal vessels, it had killed about fifty thousand people in Marseille. Moving west into Languedoc, the disease ravaged Montpellier and Narbonne and Toulouse. It reached Bordeaux in August and struck down Princess Joan of England, who had stopped there on her voyage south to marry Prince Pedro of Castile. It simultaneously moved northward through the eastern provinces, invading Lyon in May and Paris in June. But Avignon was the headquarters of the holy church, and it was shocking to all Europeans, and to the leaders of the church itself, that God's scourge should strike so fiercely the new citadel of Christ's vicar on earth.

Nearly two thousand deaths were reported in Avignon within the first few days, during the middle of Lent. By the end of April, Canon Louis of Beeringen wrote to some friends in Bruges that more than half the inhabitants were dead. "Within the walls of the city, there are now more than seven thousand houses shut up; in those no one is living, and all who have inhabited them are departed; the suburbs hardly contain any people at all. A field near 'Our Lady of Miracles' has been bought by the Pope and consecrated as a cemetery. In this, from the 13th of March, eleven thousand corpses have been buried. This does not include those interred in the cemetery of the Hospital of St. Anthony, in cemeteries belonging to the religious bodies, and in many others which exist in Avignon."

Pope Clement was confounded. Almost a quarter of the Papal Curia succumbed to the disease. Seven of the most powerful cardinals collapsed, among them Petrarch's patron, Giovanni Colonna. Clement responded with the weapons of his time. He proclaimed plenary absolution for everyone who had confessed and then died of the plague. He not only consecrated a new cemetery but finally consecrated the Rhone River itself so that the heaps of corpses could be dumped into its waters. He even ordered, in violation of all the traditions of the church, that the bodies of plague victims be dissected in a vain effort to find a medical explanation for the disaster. There was no explanation. On December 20, a pillar of fire appeared for an hour at sunrise over the Pope's palace. There was no explanation.

The Pope's own physician, Guy de Chauliac, one of the most eminent and enlightened scientists of the day, was convinced that the principal cause of the plague was a grand conjunction of the three superior planets, Saturn, Jupiter and Mars, in the sign of Aquarius. This had occurred on March 23, 1345, and had started the dangerous corruption of the earth's atmosphere. To guard against that corruption, Chauliac warned his principal patient to remain secluded in his chamber and to keep a fire constantly lit, even throughout the summer. Pope Clement did as instructed. He also rubbed and turned one of his rings, an emerald, which he had been told would keep pestilential spirits at bay.

He reflected on his church, his palace, his courtiers, and the results of these reflections would burst forth three years later when a delegation of bishops and priests asked him to suppress the troublesome mendicant orders, the Franciscans and the Dominicans. The Pope refused. Turning on the petitioners, he asked them what they would preach if the mendicants were no longer there to share in the church's mission. "Of humility? But you, above all the prelates in the world, are mighty, proud, puffed-up and pompous. . . . Of poverty? But you are so grasping, avaricious and covetous that all the benefices in the world are not sufficient for you. Of chastity? Concerning this, we keep silence, for God knows how each of you conducts himself . . ."

So Clement, who knew how to be pope, survived the great plague. But Petrarch's beautiful Laure, whom the poet had loved from a discreet distance for more than twenty years while she bore eleven children to her trusting husband, suddenly fell ill and died. "That chaste and lovely body was laid to rest in the church of the Brothers on the very day of her death, at evening," Petrarch wrote. "But her soul has returned, I am persuaded, to the heaven whence it came . . ." And in *terze rima,* he wrote of the Triumph of Death:

> . . . She closed her eyes; and in sweet slumber lying,
> her spirit tiptoed from its lodging-place.
> It's folly to shrink in fear, if this is dying;
> for death looked lovely in her lovely face.

✳

In Paris, in the summer of 1348, the coming of the plague was heralded by a large and exceptionally bright star in the western skies. "It did not seem, as stars usually do, to be very high above our hemisphere but rather very near," Jean de Venette wrote in his chronicle. "As the sun set and night came on, this star did not seem to me or to many other friars who were watching it to move from one place. At length, when night had come, this big star, to the amazement of all of us who were watching, broke into many different rays and, as it shed these rays over Paris to the east, totally disappeared and was completely annihilated. Whether it was a comet or not . . . I leave to the decision of astronomers. It is, however, possible that it was a presage of the amazing pestilence to come."

The amazing pestilence reached Paris that June, and it was to afflict the city for a year and a half. The number of deaths reached a height of eight hundred per day, and the estimates of the total range as high as eighty thousand. "The multitude of people who died in the years 1348 and 1349 was so large that nothing like it was ever heard, read of, or witnessed in past ages . . . ," according to Venette. "In many places there did not remain two alive out of every twenty." Like so many witnesses to the disaster, Venette records the priests' abandonment of their flocks—"in many towns, small and great, priests retired through fear"—but, unlike others, he also records the heroism of the nuns at the great public hospital on the Île de la Cité. "So great was the mortality in the Hôtel-Dieu of Paris," he wrote, "that for a long time more than fifty corpses were carried away from it each day in carts to be buried. And the devout sisters of the Hôtel-Dieu, not fearing death, worked piously and humbly, not out of regard for any worldly honor. A great number of these said sisters were very frequently summoned to their reward by death, and rest in peace with Christ."

That remained one of the most baffling and terrifying aspects of the plague, its indiscriminate slaughter of the devout as well as the sinful. If this was God's anger, how could it be understood, much less appeased? The shadow fell upon the royal palace, and Queen Johanna of Burgundy sickened and died. King Philip VI fled to Normandy. The plague went with him. At Rouen, one probably exaggerated account put the death toll at 100,000, and over many stricken towns a black flag flew from the church tower.

King Philip asked the medical faculty of the University of Paris for an explanation of the disaster. The professors reported that a disturbance in the skies had caused the sun to overheat the oceans near India, and the waters had begun to give off noxious vapors. The medical faculty offered a variety of remedies. Broth would help, for example, if seasoned with ground pepper, ginger, and cloves. Poultry, water fowl, young pork and fatty meat in general were to be avoided. Olive oil could be fatal. Bathing was dangerous, but enemas could be helpful. "Men must preserve chastity," the doctors warned, "if they value their lives."

The King still worried about the divine wrath. He issued an edict against blasphemy. For the first offense, the blasphemer's lip would be cut off; a second offense would cost him the other lip, and a third the tongue. But was King Philip, like another Oedipus, himself to blame? He had virtually seized the throne on the death of his childless cousin Charles IV, and King Edward III's challenge to that seizure had brought English invaders to pillage much of northern France. Less than two years before the coming of the plague, the two kings had confronted each other outside the village of Crécy, and though the French outnumbered the English by nearly three to one, the fortunes of war had been cruel. As the French knights charged into the setting sun, the English longbows cut them down, row by row. King Philip himself, wounded in the neck by an arrow, had fled to Amiens. The next morning, when the English prowled through the fog-shrouded battlefield with their long knives, they found more than ten thousand French dead. It was the luxurious Pope Clement VI who intervened then to arrange a truce on behalf of "the poor, the children, the orphans, the widows, the wretched people who are plundered and enduring hunger ..." The Hundred Years' War had just ended its tenth year.

The plague, though, killed far more than the war. "It is impossible to credit the mortality throughout the whole country," wrote Gilles Li Muisis, abbot of Saint-Martin's in the Flemish border town of Tournai. "Travelers, merchants, pilgrims and others who have passed through it declare that they have found cattle wandering without herdsmen in fields, towns and wastelands; that they have seen barns and wine cellars standing wide open, houses empty, and few people to be found anywhere. So much so that in many towns, cities and villages, where there had been twenty thousand people, scarcely two thousand are left. ... And in many different lands, fields are lying uncultivated." Li Muisis was writing from distant hearsay, but the tide of death was moving straight at him. In Amiens alone, some seventeen thousand people died. By August of 1349 the plague was in Tournai, and the bells were tolling for twenty or thirty deaths every day.

The town authorities reacted with a series of stern measures to halt the spreading panic. They ordered the tolling of the bells to cease. They outlawed the wearing of black clothing. They forbade the gathering of more than two people at a funeral, or any display of grief in public. And to placate the angry God who had brought this affliction, they banned all work after noon on Saturdays, all gambling and swearing, and they demanded that everyone living in sin get married immediately. Li Muisis recorded happily that the number of marriages increased considerably, profanity was no longer heard, and gambling declined so much that the makers of dice turned to making rosaries. He also recorded that in this newly virtuous place 25,000 citizens died of the plague and were buried in large pits on the outskirts of the town.

All in all, throughout France, the richest, strongest and most populous kingdom in Europe, there is no counting the number of people who were struck down by the Black Death. From contemporary chronicles, church archives, tax records, historians keep returning to the traditional estimate of about one third of the population. The population itself is unknown, but the best estimates run to about twenty million, so the number of dead was probably more than six million.

If the inhabitants of Britain thought that the English Channel would protect them, and they probably did, their illusion did not last long. Since the plague traveled along trade routes, the Channel was less a protection than a gateway. "In this year 1348, in Melcombe, in the county of Dorset, a little before the Feast of Saint John the Baptist, two ships ... came alongside," according to *The Grey Friars' Chronicle.* "One of the sailors had brought with him from Gascony the seeds of the terrible pestilence, and, through him, the men of that town of Melcombe were the first in England to be infected." The Feast of Saint John the Baptist occurred on June 24, and within a few weeks the plague was in Bristol. "There died, suddenly overwhelmed by death, almost the whole strength of the town," according to the chronicle of Henry Knighton. In Lincoln, the pestilence halted the building of the cathedral nave, and in Winchester, where two of the cathedral towers had been torn down for a remodeling, the authorities had to erect a temporary west front that still stands there to this day. Parliament was to reconvene in London in January of 1349, but King Edward prorogued it because "the plague of deadly pestilence had suddenly broken out in the said place." The Archbishop of Canterbury, John Stratford, died in August of 1348, and his successor in May of 1349, and yet another successor that following August. Of these two disastrous years, which killed perhaps 1.5 million of the English, one despairing chronicler wrote that there "is little to be written, nothing being done abroad, in effect, through the great mortality of the plague that raged all over the land."

And Germany. From Padua and Verona the plague made its way up the Adige Valley, and through the Brenner Pass, and by the summer of 1348 it was in the Bavarian Alps. By November it was laying waste to the Austrian province of Styria. "Men and women, driven to despair, wandered around as if mad ...," according to the anonymous author of the *Neuburg Chronicle.* "Cattle were left to stray unattended in the fields, for no one had any inclination to concern himself about the future."

By the following summer, Vienna was prostrate. The daily death toll climbed into the hundreds, and on one day it reached 1,200. "Because of the odor, and horror inspired by the dead bodies, burials in the church cemeteries were not allowed," according to one contemporary account, "but as soon as life was extinct the corpses were carried out of the city to a common burial place called 'God's acre.' " As these huge pits filled, with as many as five thousand corpses in each, the terrified Viennese spread tales of a *Pest-Jungfrau* (Plague Virgin), who could be seen flying over the city in the form of a blue flame. On one occasion, a pestilential ball of fire was said to have descended on the city, but a bishop went to exorcise it, and a commemorative statue of the Virgin Mary was built on the spot.

That autumn of 1349, the plague swept the length of the Rhine. It appeared in Cologne in December, killing as many as half the inhabitants. By now, the deaths are simply lists of numbers everywhere in the ruined land. Weimar reported five thousand lives lost, Bremen seven thousand, Lübeck nine thousand. This carnage by now passed all understanding. In Lübeck, according to one account, "the confusion was so great that the citizens, as if deprived of their senses, took leave of life and willingly renounced all earthly possessions. They bore their treasures to the monasteries and churches to lay them on the steps of the altars. But for the monks the money had no attraction, for it brought death. They closed their gates, but the people threw their money over the walls of the monasteries . . ."

In the countryside the devastation was even worse. "Savage wolves roamed about in packs at night and howled round the walls of the towns," one witness recorded. "In the villages they did not slake their thirst for human blood by lurking in secret places . . . , but boldly entered open houses and tore children from their mothers' sides. Indeed, they did not only attack children but armed men, and overcame them. . . . They seemed no longer wild animals but demons. Other creatures forsook their woods. . . . Ravens in innumerable flocks flew over the towns with loud croaking. The kite and the vulture were heard in the air. . . . On the houses the cuckoos and owls alighted and filled the night with their mournful lament."

If mankind was guilty of having provoked this divine punishment, then mankind must expiate its guilt, and the convulsive movement toward that expiation suddenly erupted in Germany. Religious flagellation had its precedents, of course. The anchorites of the early Christian era made their sufferings a form of worship, and the tradition flickered on in various monastic communities. The first public demonstration of self-scourging as a means of appeasing divine wrath seems to have been led by a Perugian hermit named Raniero in 1260, and the strange practice soon spread all over Italy. That too had been a time of famine and pestilence. It had also been the year when, according to the widely circulated prophecies of Joachim of Fiore, the world was destined to pass through the reign of Antichrist and enter its third and last great epoch, the Age of the Holy Spirit. The relatively uneventful passage of the apocalyptic year dulled the fever of anticipation, but flagellation survived north of the Alps as a somewhat furtive and almost heretical ritual. With the coming of the plague, it was furtive no longer.

The Brotherhood of the Flagellants first appeared in Dresden, in Lent of

1349, then in Lübeck, Hamburg, Magdeburg, all over central Europe. They seemed to have no single leader, but they subscribed to a strict discipline, and their processions often numbered as many as five thousand, sometimes more. They marched two by two, the men separated from the women, and as this serpentine parade of penitence neared a town the church bells would sound, and all the citizens would gather to watch the spectacle. There were elements of pure theater in these demonstrations, and also of tormented eroticism, but most citizens regarded the flagellants, at least in the early days, much as the flagellants regarded themselves, as lambs of God bearing the sins of the earth. A flagellant who undertook to whip himself and implore God's mercy on behalf of less courageous sinners could only be viewed as a hero, rather as modern observers might view some dedicated doctor who entered a plague-ridden slum to bring medicine to infected victims.

They marched barefoot. They wore ankle-length white linen underclothing and cloaks of penitential black, and on their cloaks they had sewn red crosses. Their heads were covered with hoods, surmounted by gray felt hats. They carried banners of purple velvet, also bearing the emblem of the cross. They never spoke, but they sang almost incessantly:

> *"Our journey's done in the holy name.*
> *Christ Himself to Jerusalem came.*
> *His cross He bore in His holy hand,*
> *Help us, Savior of all the land. . . ."*

Twice every day and once every night, they performed their rituals of expiation, sometimes in a church, sometimes in a crowded market place. They took off everything except their white underclothes, then marched in a circle, beating themselves until they bled, and singing.

> *"Come here for penance good and well,*
> *Thus we escape from burning hell. . . ."*

They knelt down and stretched out their arms as if being crucified and then fell to the ground. They assumed different positions of supplication, representing different sins for which they were doing penance, real or symbolic. The murderer lay on his back, the adulterer on his stomach, the perjurer on one side with three fingers stretched above his head. Two elected masters passed among the penitents, delivering one blow to each and offering absolution:

> *"By Mary's honor free from stain,*
> *Arise and do not sin again."*

The flagellants arose, but only to resume scourging themselves for the sins of those citizens who crowded around and groaned at their ordeal. These were not merely symbolic demonstrations. "Each scourge," according to one chronicler, Heinrich of Herford, "was a kind of stick from which three tails with large knots hung down. Through the knots were thrust iron spikes as sharp as needles, which penetrated about the length of a grain of wheat or a little more beyond the knots. With such scourges they beat themselves on their naked bodies so that they became swollen and blue, and blood ran down to the ground and spattered the walls of the churches in which they scourged themselves. Occasionally they drove the spikes so deep into the flesh that they could only be pulled out by a second wrench."

When the scourging was done, the flagellants once again chanted their hymn, "Our journey's done in the holy name . . ." Then their master led them to the cross, where they fell to their knees while the master intoned the words "Hail Mary, sweet Mother Mary, have pity upon thy miserable Christendom." And again: "Hail Mary!" And again: "Hail Mary, rose in the kingdom of heaven, have mercy upon us and upon all faithful souls." After this series of incantations, the master read aloud the "flagellant sermon," a thirteenth-century document that purported to be a letter written by Jesus Christ on a marble tablet. This tablet was said to have fallen from heaven onto the altar of the Church of the Holy Sepulcher in Jerusalem.

"O ye children of men, ye of little faith," Christ's letter began, "ye have not believed My words. . . . Therefore did I send against you the Saracens and heathen people, who have spilt your blood and led you into bondage. Further, I have sent tribulation upon you, earthquake, famine, beasts; serpents, mice and locusts; hail, lightning and thunder, and severe disease; but ye closed your ears and would not hearken to My voice. . . . I thought to exterminate you from the earth, but My host of angels, falling at My feet, besought Me to turn away wrath, and I have shown mercy. . . . I swear to you by My raised hand, if ye are not converted and observe My commandments, My wrath will be vented on you. . . . I will send upon you wild beasts such as have never been seen and wild birds, I will convert the light of the sun into darkness so that one may slaughter the other, and there will be great wailing, and I will smother your souls with smoke, send terrible peoples against you, who will not spare you, and devastate your land, all because ye have not kept my Sabbath."

The flagellants began as a kind of monastic order, a kind of crusade. They pledged themselves to these wanderings for thirty-three and a half days, a symbolic re-creation of Christ's years of wandering on this earth. They also pledged themselves to absolute obedience in a search for sanctity. "We undertake to avoid every opportunity of doing evil to others to the best of our ability," according to one version of the Statutes of the Order of Flagellants preserved in the chronicle of Hugo von Reutlingen, "to repent of all sins of which we are conscious and to make a general confession thereof; to dispose by legal will and testament of all legally acquired possessions; . . . to pay all debts and restore all wrongfully acquired possessions; to live in peace, to improve our lives and show restraint toward others; to stake life and limb, goods and chattels for the defense and preservation of the rights of the Holy Church . . ."

Anyone joining this crusade had to have the permission of husband or wife, had to bring enough money to pay for bread and shelter (about ten pennies per day), had to agree to a life of absolute austerity, no bed at night, only a layer of straw, no bathing, no shaving, no washing of the head, no change of clothing, no conversation with any member of the opposite sex. And endless prayer: three Paternosters and three Ave Marias on arising in the morning, five more before and after each meal, and five more before sleep, and five during each scourging. . . .

This yearning for suffering, for wild excess, for passion, for religious experience beyond anything taught or advocated by the church, caused both the cancerous growth and the eventual supression of the flagellants. Despite their talk of preserving the rights of the church, the flagellants were a lay movement, and by threatening implication an anticlerical movement. The masters of the march were laymen, and their chants were the first vernacular hymns that the Germans had ever heard. And though the flagellants conducted their rituals in churches, they did so more or less by force, as riotous invaders whom the parish priests were too frightened to resist. Two Dominicans who tried to halt a flagellant ritual near Moisson were stoned by the worshipers, one of them to death.

These demonstrations soon acquired a radical political coloring. Many terrified Germans were living in expectation of an imminent restoration of the Emperor Frederick II, who had been widely regarded a century earlier as the man destined to become the universal ruler and to chastise the church on the eve of the apocalypse. Many other citizens simply wanted to vent their anxiety and anger against the clergy, the rich, the established authorities. So thousands of people flocked to the flagellant movement, and it spread outward into Bohemia, Hungary, Flanders. In the summer of 1349, a procession of flagellants at Constance was said to number 42,000, and a march through Brabant at Christmas was reputed to total more than eighty thousand. In Strasbourg, new troops of flagellants kept arriving to stage their rituals every week for six months.

The church could hardly help being alarmed. When Pope Clement first heard of the flagellants, he agreed to attend a parade in which two thousand of them marched through Avignon. He even blessed them. But he soon began to receive disturbing reports from his bishops that these bloodstained penitents were undertaking to perform the sacramental functions of the church itself. And in defending their actions, the flagellants spoke with the voice of heresy, a voice rather like the one that had caused the church to lay waste to Languedoc. "When the flagellants were asked," according to one account, " 'Why do ye preach, having received no mission . . . ?' they replied, turning the tables, 'Who, then, gave you a mission, and how do ye know that ye consecrate the body of Christ or that what ye preach is the true Gospel?' If they were told that the church could not err as it was guided by the Holy Ghost, then they replied that they received their instruction and mission most directly from the Lord and the spirit of the Lord." The itinerant flagellant masters began to perform sacraments, hear confessions, grant forgiveness. They claimed, in some instances, to be able to cast out evil spirits and to heal the sick. Their bloodstained rags were preserved and venerated as holy relics. In Strasbourg, they tried and failed to bring a dead child back to life. They claimed, more and more insistently, that their movement must last thirty-three and a half years, and then end in the Second Coming. And people believed them. "Many persons, and even young children, were soon bidding farewell to the world," according to one chronicle, "some with prayers, others with praises on their lips."

The established powers have always resisted such passions. King Philip of France forbade all flagellants to enter his kingdom, and provincial authorities appealed to the theologians of the Sorbonne for an authoritative opinion on this outbreak of self-mortification. The Sorbonne disapproved, and expressed its disapproval by sending a Flemish monk named Jean da Fayt to Avignon to argue the case before Clement. From Germany itself, Emperor Charles IV petitioned the Pope for counsel. The Pope understood; his sympathy for these zealots had been a mistake. In a papal bull issued in October of 1349, Clement denounced the flagellants and banished them from all Christian communities. "Already," he declared, "flagellants under pretense of piety have spilled the blood of Jews, which Christian charity preserves and protects, and frequently also the blood of Christians, and, when opportunity offered, they have stolen the property of the clergy and laity and have arrogated to themselves the legal authority of their superiors. . . . We therefore command our archbishops and suffragans that in their dioceses they declare in our name as godless and forbidden all societies, meetings, uses and statutes of the so-called flagellants, which we at the advice of our brethren have condemned . . ."

It was so ordered and so carried out. Although popular protests prevented the reading of the bull in some towns, the united opposition of the Pope, the Emperor, and the King of France was invincible. The chroniclers' accounts of flagellant processions fade into passing mentions of flagellants hanged in Westphalia, burned in Breslau, beheaded in Trier. Some of them appeared in Rome during the Jubilee of 1350 to expiate their heresy by being lashed before the altar of Saint Peter, but most of them simply disappeared into the countryside, "vanishing as suddenly as they had come," in the words of one chronicler, "like night phantoms or mocking ghosts."

Pope Clement was right in charging the flagellants with the persecution of Jews. In Frankfurt-on-the-Main, for example, they had marched directly to the Jewish quarter and inspired the mob to light the torches. This seems, however, to have been an almost fortuitous conjunction of two rather different manias. The mania for attacking Jews originally derived not from the expiation of collective guilt but from the turbulent launching of the First Crusade in 1096, from the emotional feeling among an ignorant peasantry that a campaign to reconquer the Holy Land from the infidel might well begin with an attack on those who had persecuted Christ. An ill-disciplined army headed by a brigand named Count Emich of Leisingen began its crusade in the Rhineland by murdering twelve Jews who refused to become Christian converts in the town of Speyer. The bishop of Speyer placed the rest of the town's Jews under his protection and even managed to punish several of the killers by having their hands cut off. Emich's forces marched on to Worms, where the citizenry was agitated by a rumor that the Jews had drowned a Christian and used the water in which he died to poison local wells. The bishop of Worms took all the Jews into his palace for protection, but Emich's crusaders led a mob in breaking down the gate and slaughtering about five hundred of the fugitives. Then came the massacre at Mainz, in which about one thousand Jews died.

The church was quite resolute in resisting these first outbreaks, but the hostility toward the Jews kept shifting into new forms. To the familiar complaints of usury, and the counterfeiting of currency, there was added, in the supposed martyrdom of William of Norwich in 1144, the first recorded accusation that Jews had murdered a Christian in order to make ritual use of his blood. At the Fourth Lateran Council of 1215, the church renewed its insistence that no Jew should be employed in any position of authority over Christians; it also forbade Jews to live among Christians, thus founding the ghetto system; and because "it happens at times that through error Christians have relations with the women of Jews," all Jews were ordered to wear distinctive clothing, such as a badge of yellow cloth. In the early thirteenth century came the first accusation that the Jews desecrated the Host, and for this the entire Jewish population of Belitz, near Berlin, was burned in 1243.

Reasonable historians have tried to find reasonable explanations for this intermittent frenzy. The Jews were hated as moneylenders, for example, because church law forbade Christians to loan money at interest, and loans were essential to the irresistible growth of capitalism. They were hated as tax collectors because their royal protectors often assigned them to that obnoxious duty. Reasonable explanations, however, cannot account for the wild fantasies that inspired the persecution of the Jews, the absurd legends of poisoned wells and ritual murders. The greatest poet of the fourteenth century, Geoffrey Chaucer, never even questioned the plausibility of the loathsome Prioress' Tale, which he set in a city where there was "a Jewerye,/ Sustened by a lord of that contree/ For foul usure . . ./ Hateful to Christ and to his companye." Through this ghetto passed a widow's son, seven years of age, who liked to sing loudly on his way to school such Christian hymns as "O Alma Redemptoris." Satan, according to Chaucer's prioress, "hath in Jewes herte [heart] his waspes nest" and therefore said to them, "O Hebraik people, allas!/ Is this to yow a thing that is honest?" In answer to Satan's question, "the Jewes han conspyred" to murder the pious boy. One of them, more villainous than the rest, accosted the youth with a knife, then "heeld him faste,/ And kitte his throat, and in a pit him caste." The widowed mother went searching for her child "among the cursed Jewes," and though they denied their guilt, a miracle occurred. The murdered boy's voice emerged from the sewage pit, relentlessly singing "O Alma Redemptoris." This enabled the authorities to inflict the appropriate vengeance. The provost had the murderer torn apart by "wilde hors" and "after that he heng hem."

When Edward I came to the throne of England, he issued new regulations permitting the Jews to engage in commerce, crafts and agriculture, but a papal bull of 1286 renewed the church's demand for segregation. Edward decided in 1290 to solve the problem by expelling all Jews. King Louis IX of France, the pious Crusader who ultimately became Saint Louis, had already condemned the Talmud to the flames and ordered the expulsion of all Jews before his departure for the East in 1249. This order was not carried out, however, until his grandson Philip the Fair applied his own characteristic touches. In 1306, on the anniversary of the destruction of the Temple of Jersualem, Philip ordered all the Jews in France arrested. Once they were in prison, he informed them that they were being banished and all their property confiscated. As for their usurious claims against citizens to whom they had loaned money, the King took those over for himself on behalf of the state. Even in exile, though, the Jews were regarded as a menace. When a pestilence afflicted Languedoc in 1320, there were widespread rumors that the Jews had enlisted lepers to poison the wells, and so all the lepers in Languedoc were burned.

The coming of the Black Death naturally revived all the wild tales. New rumors in Languedoc reported that all Jews took their orders from a secret council of elders headquartered in Toledo. These elders had decided that the time had come to destroy Christendom. They had concocted the plague poison out of spiders, owls, frogs, snakes, scorpions, to which they added, in various accounts, blood, urine, female hair, and a powder crushed from sacramental wafers. They packed this lethal mixture into little pouches and shipped it to Jewish agents all over Europe.

A number of French Jews had evaded the expulsion orders, and in both Narbonne and Carcassonne all Jews who could be found were rounded up and killed. As the plague and the passion for revenge moved northward during the summer of 1348, there were murderous attacks on Jews in various towns in Burgundy. In Brussels, six hundred Jews were slaughtered. Pope Clement, who was presumably a humanitarian but who also needed the Jews for his vast constructions in Avignon, was outraged. He issued two papal bulls in July and September of 1348, both forbidding the persecution of Jews and threatening excommunication to anyone who engaged in it. His edicts had as much effect as those of King Canute.

It was the Swiss, with their love of order, who converted the crude pogroms of Languedoc and Burgundy into an official legal procedure. In the town of Chillon, on the beautiful eastern rim of Lake Geneva, the authorities arrested a Jewish surgeon named Balavignus, who lived across the lake at Thonon, and subjected him to the torture of the rack for what they subsequently called "a short time." On being taken down, the official report continued, Balavignus confessed, "after much hesitation," that a Rabbi Jacob of Toledo had sent him poison in a leather pouch hidden in a mummified egg. It consisted, he said, of ground-up pieces of a basilisk. "In conformity with [the] command of the Jewish rabbis and doctors of the law," the report said, "he, Balavignus, distributed the poison in several places, and acknowledged having one evening placed a certain portion under a stone in a spring on the shore at Thonon. . . . He further deposed that Mussus [another Jew] informed him that he had also laid some of the poison under the stones of the custom house in Chillon. Search was accordingly made in this well, and the poison found: some of it was given to a Jew by way of trial, and he died in consequence. . . . Balavignus was conveyed over the lake from Chillon to Clarens to point out the well into which he confessed having thrown the powder. On landing, he was conducted to the spot; and, having seen the well, acknowledged that to be the place, saying, 'This is the well into which I put the poison.' The well was examined in his presence, and the linen cloth in which the poison had been wrapped was found in the water pipe of a notary public named Heinrich Gerhard, in the presence of many persons. . . . He [Balavignus] also declared that none of his community could exculpate themselves from this accusation, as the plot was communicated to all; and that all were guilty of the above charges."

Having recorded the confession of Dr. Balavignus, and then having burned him for his supposed crimes, the authorities of Chillon proudly forwarded their document to other cities of Switzerland and the Rhine Valley. The documents seemed to legitimize a process that was already under way. The city of Zurich voted to ban all Jews forever. The burgomasters and senators of Basel resisted the demands for punishment, but the guilds and the townspeople marched on the city hall with banners. Then they herded hundred of Jews into a large wooden building and set it on fire. An official resolution decreed that no Jews would be allowed into Basel for two hundred years.

Strasbourg was worse. Though the city's legislators at first refused to act against the Jews, a new election replaced them, and the craft guilds demanded action. On Saint Valentine's Day of 1349, some two thousand Jews were rounded up and driven toward a wooden scaffold that had been built in the Jewish cemetery. As the Jews neared the field of slaughter, the Christian mob clawed at them, tore the clothes off their backs in search of hidden gold. "The money was indeed the thing that killed the Jews," according to the chronicle of Jacob von Königshofen. "If they had been poor and if the feudal lords had not been in debt to them, they would not have been burned." As it was, the city nullified all debtors' pledges to Jews, confiscated all the Jews' property and divided it among the Christian citizens, who were urged to donate their shares to the church. The Jews themselves, on their scaffold, were offered a last chance for salvation. Some converted; a few young women and children were reprieved. The rest were burned. Then the graveyard itself was destroyed, as were the homes of the Jews, and the stones were used to repair and expand the city's churches.

In most of the great cities of Germany, in the summer of 1349, the flames broke out again and again. In Frankfurt, where the flagellants incited the mob, a great bonfire consumed the Jewish quarter. In Nuremberg, the Christians murdered every Jew they could find. And so it was in the Thuringian towns of Gotha and Eisenach and Arnstadt and Herbsleben. In Mainz, where the Jewish community of twelve thousand was the largest in Germany, it was again the flagellants who provoked fights. Here the Jews fought back. They killed about two hundred Christians. The Christians' revenge was total. The entire Jewish community was annihilated, and the heat of the fire was so intense that it melted the lead in the windows of the Church of St. Quirius.

In some towns, Jews threatened with forced conversion chose to die by their own hands. "Mothers hurled their children first into the fire, that they might not be baptized, and then leaped in after them to burn with their husbands and children," Jean de Venette wrote. The entire Jewish community of Esslingen gathered in its synagogue and then set the building afire. At Speyer, where many Jews set their own homes on fire, the charred bodies were later dragged out and stuffed into empty wine barrels and floated down the Rhine so that the city would not be polluted. Sometimes the mobs were willing to spare a Jew who converted at the last minute, and sometimes they seized Jewish children to convert them by force, but sometimes they cared nothing for the religion of their victims. In the wilds of East Prussia, where the Teutonic Knights ruled, and where no practicing Jews were allowed to live, the mobs hunted down every Jewish convert and killed every one.

When the fires died down and the slaughter ended, it ended, in most places, because there were no more Jews to kill. All in all, there were about 350 massacres in Germany, and they totally destroyed sixty large Jewish communities and 150 smaller ones. The survivors thought not of rebuilding but only of escape. To the east they went, to Poland, where King Casimir the Great, who was reputed to have a Jewish mistress named Esther, offered sanctuary and even welcome, to Poland, where their terrible destiny at the hands of the Germans had yet to be fulfilled.

And the plague reached to the north. An English ship bearing a cargo of wool set out from London for Norway in May of 1349. Its crew, all unknowing, was already afire with the pestilence. All of them died before ever reaching land. The ship of death wallowed onward across the North Sea until it ran aground on the coast of Norway, near Bergen. Some innocent Norwegians clambered aboard to see if they could help, and then they saw, as the Sicilians had seen, that they were welcoming a curse. In neighboring Sweden, King Magnus II issued a proclamation warning his people that "God for the sins of men has struck the world with this great punishment of sudden death." He urged them to eat nothing but bread and water on Fridays and to flock to their churches in bare feet to worship the relics there.

And to the south, to Spain, where the forces of Christ confronted those of Islam. The Arabs were the first to suffer from the plague, which had swept across all of North Africa, and Christian chroniclers claimed that this shook their faith in Allah. The plague knew no such distinctions. King Alfonso of Castile, leading his army in a siege of Gibraltar, succumbed to the pestilence and died on Good Friday of 1350. In neighboring Aragon, the plague took from King Pedro IV his wife, daughter and niece.

And to the east. The plague entered Poland and Hungary in 1349, then surged across Russia to the Black Sea, whence it had come. It was to return, though, again and again. In England there were epidemics of the plague in 1361, 1369, 1375, 1390, and then eight more attacks in the fifteenth century. Paris suffered twenty-two different visitations between 1348 and 1596. Each of the first two major recurrences carried off an estimated five percent of the European population. Only after ravaging London in 1665 and Marseille in 1720 did the disease virtually disappear from Europe, as mysteriously as it had first appeared. One theory is that the common black rat was vanquished by the larger brown rat, which also harbored the plague flea but was more inclined to live out of doors, away from mankind. Another is that the gradual replacement of wooden houses by buildings of stone and brick—and of thatched roofs by tiles—helped guard the inhabitants against infection. Yet another is that a milder mutant form of the plague bacillus caused its victims to develop immunity to the plague itself. One theory will serve as well as another.

One would think that any disaster that killed 25 million people in Europe alone would leave the entire Continent paralyzed for at least a generation. If the streets of New York City were suddenly littered with a corresponding number of corpses, roughly two million, or if the United States as a whole suffered more than fifty million deaths by bubonic plague within three years, the process of recovery would be hard to imagine. And so it is that we retain from the chronicles of the fourteenth century an image of deserted cottages falling in ruins and untilled wheat fields reverting to wilderness. Thousands of villages all across the face of Europe did simply disappear. The buried remnants are faintly visible in aerial photographs, spectral outlines of a vanished people, and in England alone more than two thousand such ruins have been recorded. The Germans even have a word, *Dorfwüstungen,* for the process of villages turning into wilderness. The depopulation of the cities was no less remarkable. In Toulouse, to take only one example, the number of inhabitants not only shrank from an estimated 30,000 in 1335 to 26,000 in 1385 but continued shrinking to 20,700 in 1398 and 8,000 in 1430. Virtually no city anywhere regained its population of 1300 in less than two centuries.

No aspect of this cataclysm is completely certain, however. If the population figures of the fourteenth century are largely a series of guesses inferred from surviving records of hearth taxes and clerical funerals, the economic statistics are so fragmentary that they resemble those stray chips of blue paint from which Greek antiquarians reconstructed some of the magnificent frescoes of Santorini. To what extent, then, was a change in wheat prices, if there was one, directly attributable to the plague, or did it derive from the incessant burning and plundering of The Hundred Years' War? Or both? Or neither? To what extent, for that matter, were the long-range consequences of the plague caused not simply by the Black Death but by the subsequent recurrences of the disease? No sooner does one scholar arrange the chips of questionable data into a sequence that seems to document his thesis than a rival scholar rearranges them to support a rival thesis.

There does seem to be widespread agreement, however, on two remarkable aspects of the disaster. One is that the enormous depopulation of the Continent began well before the plague ever reached Sicily. The twelfth and thirteenth centuries had been a period of sustained economic prosperity, of population growth, and the cultivation of more and more land. Some of these new lands were being colonized in the east by the Germans; many others were marginal areas wrested from the forest and the marsh. The turning point apparently came in the summer of 1314, when heavy rains ruined the harvest in much of northwestern Europe. The price of grain rose despite official efforts to control it. Hunger, which was always a danger in those years, tightened. The climatic change the following year was worse. From April on, it rained all summer. A

French invasion of Flanders ground to a halt in the mud. Again the harvests were ruined, and by the following year the famine was cruel. In Ypres alone, about 2,500 people died of hunger during the summer of 1316. The chronicles of the time begin to report wild tales of Irish villagers digging up corpses from churchyards to cook them as food, of cannibalism in Poland, of crowds cutting down executed criminals from the gallows in order to devour them. No less important, the overall birth rate began to decline. It is difficult to determine the exact date when the decline started, but it seems to have roughly coincided with the great famines that lasted from 1314 to 1319. That may have been because the shortage of food caused a decrease in fertility, or it may have been that the people sensed, in some unconscious way, that the land could not support all those who now inhabited it. It is also possible that the food shortages weakened the survivors of the famine and made them more vulnerable to the coming plague.

The second remarkable aspect of the cataclysm was that the survivors began to prosper. They were the survivors, after all, of a kind of triage. The plague had struck almost everywhere, but it killed a disproportionate share of the old, the children, the weak and infirm, the least-productive people. Having buried the dead, finally, the survivors turned to divide up what remained and found that there was more of everything for everyone. This applied not only to physical property but to the continuing value of labor. There was a shortage of workers, and so their wages went up, often doubling between 1347 and 1350. An English thresher who earned two and a half pence a day in 1348 made sixpence in 1349. "The world goeth fast from bad to worse, when shepherd and cowherd for their part demand more for their labour than the master bailiff was wont to take in days gone by," an English country gentleman named John Gower complained in 1375. "Labour is now at so high a price that he who will order his business aright must pay five or six shillings now for what cost him two in former times. . . . Ha! age of ours . . . the poor and small folk . . . demand to be better fed than their masters."

It was true. The increase in wages after the plague was not simply the usual inflation that now seems so commonplace but rather part of a gigantic social and economic shift that lasted for more than a century. In terms of prices, it was a recession. The decline in population brought a decline in food prices, and therefore the abandonment of marginal lands that had come under cultivation during the growth of the thirteenth century. "A man could have a horse, which before was worth 40s., 6s. 8d.," Henry Knighton reported, "a fat ox for 4s., a cow for 12d." This decline in prices meant a decline in the rental value of land, which supported most of the upper classes. The land around Saint-Germain-des-Prés that rented for eighty-four deniers in 1350, for example, fell to fifty-five over the following century. The prices of cloth and many other manufactured goods generally followed the downward movement. The chief exception was iron, which was needed for the endless warfare that scarred the century. A chronic shortage of gold and silver, caused by a depletion of the mines, exacerbated the contraction of the economy. But although there was a decline in the gross national product, if such a modern concept can be applied to the fourteenth century, the decline in population meant that per-capita GNP, the best indicator of personal prosperity, increased.

The increase in cash wages and the fall in prices represented, at least for a time, a kind of invisible social revolution. It not only improved the lot of the peasants but narrowed the gap between them and their increasingly hard-pressed lords. It both drove them from the land and attracted them toward the cities. The feudal lords responded in the only way they knew, by passing laws to forbid the changes. The English Parliament passed a Statute of Labourers in 1349, and again in 1351, and again in 1360, all demanding in vain that wages remain at the levels they had been before the plague. The French attempted a similar measure in 1351 with equally little result. Local coercions took other forms. Along the Rhine, for example, many landlords demanded that their peasants labor for them not six but twenty days per year. In Bohemia, a series of decrees forbade peasants to leave the land without providing a replacement and ordered towns to yield up runaway peasants to their masters. Such decrees were widely resisted and evaded, however, not only by the peasants but by other employers who were ready to pay for the work they needed done. "The labourers were so lifted up and obstinate that they would not listen to the king's command," Knighton reported, "but if anyone wished to have them he had to give them what they wanted, and either lose his fruit and crops, or satisfy the lofty and covetous wishes of the population. . . . And afterwards the king had many labourers arrested and sent them to prison; many withdrew themselves and went into the forests and woods."

"Be fruitful and multiply, and replenish the earth," God had said to Noah and his sons after the earth had been laid waste. Jean de Venette noted in his chronicle that there was a marked increase in marriages among the survivors of the plague, and although there are no reliable statistics to support him, he noted an unusual number of births and even of twins and triplets. The replenishing of the earth required about a century and a half, but it did inexorably take place. "But woe is me!" the chronicler added, "the world was not changed for the better but for the worse by this renewal of population. For men were more avaricious and grasping than before, even though they had far greater possessions. They were more covetous and disturbed each other more frequently with suits, brawls, disputes, and pleas. Nor by the mortality resulting from this terrible plague inflicted by God was peace between kings and lords established. On the contrary, the enemies of the king of France and of the Church were stronger and wickeder than before and stirred up wars on sea and on land."

Aside from all economic and political consequences, the death of a large part of the human race must have had profound effects on the psychological perceptions and religious beliefs of the survivors. Yet it is one of the characteristics of human nature to deny any disaster that denies life, to distort or simply to forget what actually happened. It is left to succeeding generations to invent theories.

Theories about the indirect effects of the Black Death touch on almost every aspect of life. There is a theory that the death of so many educated men who had been accustomed to the use of Latin led to the relatively sudden flowering of the vernacular languages in the dawn of the Renaissance. There is a theory that the death of so many nobles led to an aristocracy of parvenus, and therefore to the spread of gaudy costumes and extravagant jewelry. There are theories to account for almost everything, and there is much to be accounted for.

If anything had been learned during the Black Death, it was that the church and its priests were helpless in fighting the plague. Some attribute to this revelation the erosion of the Scholastic system newly apotheosized by Saint Thomas Aquinas and the rapid spread of mysticism in the Dominican convents of the Rhineland. Some attribute to it the proliferation of charlatans, witch doctors and seers. Some attribute to it not only the general decay in papal authority but the growth of the Lollards and the Hussites and all the other dissenters and rebels whose impassioned demands for a new way ultimately burst forth in the Reformation.

That way could not yet be seen. If there was one image that exemplified the religious obsessions of the late fourteenth century, it was the grinning specter of death, which now became almost the patron saint of the age, the master of ceremonies at an awesome new ritual known as the *danse macabre*. The figure first appeared in France in a folk tale of three young noblemen who encounter three walking corpses. The dead warn the living that their end is near. *Memento mori.* Artists took up the theme, portraying it in murals at the Church of the Innocents in Paris and at the Campo Santo in Pisa and in hundreds of miniature copies and woodcuts derived from such murals. In the early versions, the dead men who warn the living are transformations of the living men themselves, the living men as they soon will be, putrescent. Eventually, these warning images merge into the lordly figure of Death itself, all-powerful, inviting his victims to the dance.

"The macabre vision . . . is self-seeking and earthly," as the Dutch historian Johann Huizinga wrote in *The Waning of the Middle Ages.* "It is hardly the absence of the departed dear ones that is deplored; it is the fear of one's own death, and this only seen as the worst of evils. Neither the conception of death the consoler, nor that of rest long wished for, of the end of suffering, of the task performed or interrupted, have a share in the funereal sentiment of that epoch. . . . The dominant thought [was] of Death hideous and threatening." This was the triumph of the great epidemic.

The strange reappearances of the plague have helped to keep alive its fearful reputation. Though doctors by now have solved the riddle of its causes and even claim a cure through antibiotics, mankind's historic memory endows the plague with almost supernatural qualities. It is still God's scourge, still a force of moral retribution, still incomprehensible and irresistible.

As the actual plague recedes into history, though, the memory of it becomes increasingly symbolic, like something from a dream, a subject for mythological interpretations. The French Surrealist poet Antonin Artaud, inventor of what he called "the theater of cruelty," suggested a profound connection between the destructiveness of the plague and the emotional catharsis that he sought in theater. "Once the plague is established in a city," he wrote in *The Theater and Its Double* (1938), "the regular forms collapse. There is no maintenance of roads and sewers, no armies, no police, no municipal administration. . . . The dead already clog the streets in ragged pyramids gnawed at by animals around the edges. The stench rises in the air like a flame. Entire streets are blocked by the piles of dead. Then the houses open and the delirious victims, their minds crowded with hideous visions, spread howling through the streets. . . . The dregs of the population, apparently immunized by their frenzied greed, enter the open houses and pillage riches they know will serve no purpose or profit. And in that moment, the theater is born. . . ."

Artaud professed skepticism about all medical theories of how the plague spread, all rats, fleas and viruses. The plague was too mysterious for that, too godlike in the "spiritual freedom" with which it selected its victims. "If the essential theater is like the plague," Artaud wrote, "it is not because it is contagious but because like the plague it is the revelation, the bringing forth, the exteriorization of a depth of latent cruelty by means of which all the perverse possibilities of the mind, whether of an individual or of a people, are localized. . . . The theater, like the plague, . . . releases conflicts, disengages powers, liberates possibilities, and if these possibilities and these powers are dark, it is the fault not of the plague, nor of the theater, but of life."

Before publishing his essay, Artaud gave a lecture on it at the Sorbonne and suddenly began trying to act out the effects of the plague on himself. "His face was contorted with anguish, one could see the perspiration dampening his hair," according to Anaïs Nin, who was watching in the audience. "His eyes dilated. . . . He was in agony. He was screaming. He was delirious. He was enacting his own death, his own crucifixion." Artaud's listeners gasped at this exhibition, then broke into laughter, and then began noisily walking out, banging the door as they left. Artaud seemed unconcerned. "I want to awaken them," he told Miss Nin afterward in a café. "They do not realize they are dead." Poor Artaud was already half mad by then, and his deterioration seemed inexorable. He went to Ireland, carrying what he insisted was Saint Patrick's own cane and searching for the occult secrets of the universe. He became convinced that the world would end in 1940, as, in a sense, it did. By the time Hitler's armies entered Paris, Artaud was confined in a mental institution, uniformed and with shaven head, and there he was to remain throughout the war.

The German invasion aroused new images of the plague in the mind of a twenty-seven-year-old Algerian journalist, Albert Camus. He had read Artaud, but he entirely disagreed with Artaud's view of the plague. It was in no way liberating. In his journal Camus wrote: "Moral of the plague: It was of no use to anything or anyone." To Camus, though, the plague was of immense use. It was a metaphor for the disaster that had overwhelmed France. It was a test by which to analyze men's reactions to disaster and thus to judge their whole lives.

"I want to express by means of the plague the stifling air from which we all suffered and the atmosphere of threat and exile in which we lived," he wrote in his *Notebooks, 1942-1951.* "I want at the same time to extend that interpretation to the notion of existence in general. The plague will give the image of those who in this war were limited to reflection, to silence—and to moral anguish."

There is very little plot to *The Plague,* which Camus wrote mainly during the occupation and published in 1947. A mysterious disease begins killing the rats in the Algerian port of Oran. A number of citizens become stricken with fever and then with the lethal buboes in the groin and the armpits. The authorities are reluctant to accept the verdict of plague, but when they do, the entire city is sealed off under quarantine. For nearly a year then it lies prostrate under the plague, which kills and paralyzes, which becomes a kind of sovereign power, which changes and dominates all its victims' perceptions and judgments. At the end, it simply fades away, and the city is reopened, to the accompaniment of a fireworks display.

All this is narrated through a half-dozen characters, who are not really characters so much as embodiments of moral attitudes and ideas. The most important of them, Dr. Rieux, fights against the plague as a kind of revolt against death, a struggle against "creation as he found it." His friend Tarrou, who is rebelling against his father's position as a public prosecutor, organizes a volunteer sanitation service because "there are pestilences and there are victims, and it's up to us, so far as possible, not to join forces with the pestilences." Father Paneloux preaches the traditional view that God is punishing Oran for its sins. Cottard, a fugitive from prosecution for some unspecified crime, organizes a black market. Rambert, a visiting journalist trapped by the quarantine, tries to get himself smuggled out but then joins Rieux in combating the plague. "Until now I always felt a stranger in this town . . . ," he declares. "But now that I've seen what I've seen, I know that I belong here whether I want it or not. This business is everybody's business."

Perhaps because every French reader would naturally interpret *The Plague* as a parable of the German occupation, Camus never mentions the Germans or the war. The analogy lies not only in the pervasive power of the alien bacillus, not only in the varying ways in which the victims resist the infection, but in the physical circumstances of the struggle. Oran under siege is a city of wailing sirens, of shortages and rationing, of official announcements that may be lies, of enforced detainment in quarantine camps, and finally of mass cremations. "An oily, foul-smelling cloud of smoke hung low upon the eastern districts of the town [to] remind them that they were living under a new order . . ."

Since all his readers would immediately see the swastika, Camus takes an almost perverse pleasure in suggesting other meanings. "*The Plague* has a social meaning *and* a metaphysical meaning," he wrote in the *Notebooks.* "It's exactly the same." Camus' only specific political analogy is not to Nazism but to Communism, though even that is not named. Tarrou says only that he "became an agitator, as they say," for an unspecified group that was "fighting the established order," and that "there's not a country in Europe in whose struggles I haven't played a part." Only when Tarrou saw an execution in Hungary did he see the connection to his father's role as prosecutor, and only then did he realize "that I had had the plague through all those long years in which, paradoxically enough, I'd believed with all my soul that I was fighting it." To Father Paneloux, on the other hand, even after the death of a child makes him discard the idea that the plague is a punishment for the victims' sins, the catastrophe remains a kind of divine test. "We must believe everything or deny everything," he says in his second sermon. "And who among you, I ask, would dare to deny everything?" To one of Rieux's patients, a nameless old man, Camus assigns a more final judgment: "All those folks are saying: 'It was plague. We've had the plague here.' You'd almost think they expected to be given medals for it. But what does that mean—'plague'? Just life, no more than that."

Camus' own life played a remarkably large part in the formation of his idea of the plague. He had been tubercular since his youth, and so he inevitably acquired the sense of illness as both an affliction and a metaphor. He set his story in Oran because that was where he had found work as a schoolteacher after the Nazi invasion drove him from Paris. He wrote most of the novel in 1942 and 1943 after a new tubercular attack forced him to live with some in-laws in the Auvergne mountains. And it is probably because the Allied invasion of Algeria cut him off from his wife and home in the fall of 1942 that *The Plague* is dominated by an emphasis on loss, separation and exile. All the main characters in Camus' novel are philosophical alter egos, all busy with their journals and letters and sermons, all separated from their women. There are, in fact, hardly any women in Camus' Oran, which seems odd in view of the documentary tone. There are also no Arabs. And though there is a melodramatic scene at the opera, in which the singer playing Gluck's Orpheus falls dead of the plague on stage, there is almost no sign of anyone working at an ordinary job, tending store, cooking dinner or performing any of the routine functions of life that continue even during a plague. Camus was more interested in having his characters engage in philosophical speculations. He had been reading, and been greatly impressed by, a French translation of *Moby Dick*.

As a parable of the occupation, finally, *The Plague* has certain fundamental deficiencies. The main one, of course, is that the invading bacillus has none of the moral coloring of the Nazis. When Camus speaks of Rieux's chronicle, at the end, as "evidence regarding what was a sort of crime" and "some memorial of the injustice and outrage," he is forgetting what Melville so strongly emphasized in the chapter on the whiteness of the whale, the moral neutrality and indifference of nature. To imbue the medical and sanitary measures taken against the plague with the moral complexities and physical dangers of resisting the Nazi occupation is almost absurd. Dr. Rieux, who speaks of his labors as a revolt against death, is, after all, doing little more than the routine tasks by which he has always earned his comfortable living. And when Tarrou and Rambert and the others join in providing sanitary services, they are simply doing what self-interest dictates.

Not only is the resistance to the plague less than heroic, Rieux and his comrades are themselves the occupation authorities in the quarantined city. It is they who issue the orders, they who remove the victims from their homes and confine them in camps, and finally burn the corpses. There is nothing wrong with these actions, of course, but it remains puzzling that they inspired Camus to see a moral victory here, or "to state quite simply what we learn in time of pestilence: that there are more things to admire in men than to despise." The France that emerged from the plague of the occupation was a nation that yearned for such a message, yearned to be told that it had not been stained by cowardice, treachery and moral corruption, that it had actually resisted, sacrificed and triumphed. That was how *The Plague* could be read, though that was not all it said. What it said, ultimately, was that "the plague never dies or disappears for good," and that the day may come when it will "rouse up its rats again and send them forth to die in a happy city."

Even as Camus was writing his parable, laboratory research was making his story scientifically obsolete. The sulfa drugs developed during World War II proved highly effective in treating cases of the plague. The antibiotics, aureomycin and the tetracyclines, were even more impressive, reducing death rates to about four percent. The ancient threat of a return of the Black Death seemed finally over.

Yet the legendary destructiveness of the plague retained another kind of significance, one that inspired the Atomic Energy Commission in 1965 to commission the Rand Corporation to conduct still another study of the fourteenth-century disaster. This study, written by Jack Hirshleifer, begins with a standard legal notice declaring that nobody in the AEC "makes any warranty . . . with respect to the . . . usefulness of the information contained in this report" or "assumes any liabilities with respect to the use of . . . any information, apparatus, method or process disclosed in this report." Its purpose is soon obvious, however, when it declares that although no past disaster is "fully comparable" to the possibilities of World War III, "the Black Death of 1348–50 . . . perhaps approached a hypothetical nuclear war in geographical extent, abruptness of onset, and scale of casualties." There was one major difference, and that was the absence of physical destruction during the plague, but that only prompted Hirshleifer to observe that "thus, the Black Death is a closer analog to bacteriological than to nuclear war."

The question that interested the Atomic Energy Commission, then, was not simply what happened but how the disaster had affected organized society, and how difficult it had been for society to recover. Hirshleifer's researches were heartening. Although many chronicles of the time described "extremes of socially disruptive behavior," he wrote, there were others that "emphasize the continuity of established forms and institutions." Economic recovery, as modern historians have shown, was "rapid." And the planning for a renewal of The Hundred Years' War made it "evident . . . that paralysis of government in England, if it occurred at all, was limited to the period when the plague was actually raging." Hirshleifer was reluctant to infer from this that the consequences of a nuclear attack might be ephemeral, but he did end on a note of modest optimism: "We can state the negative conclusion that this historical record provides no support for contentions that social collapse or an economic downward spiral are necessary or likely consequences of massive disaster."

Still, the AEC wanted to explore one more aspect of the plague. Since the plague bacillus remains endemic among rats and nearly forty other species of rodents of the Far West, what would happen to these rodents and their fleas in the chaos of nuclear attack? The Rand Corporation assigned this question to Dr. H. H. Mitchell, who reviewed the success of treatment with antibiotics but wondered about the anarchic conditions of what he called "the post-attack environment." Would doctors and medical supplies be available? Would the infected rodents spread out of control? Dr. Mitchell remained cautious. "One is hard put," he declared, "to make any predictions about the way the ecological upsets will go and what the subsequent behavior of the wild rodents will be." Despite all the advances in medicine and in pest control, he said, "there is only a thin protective wall which guards the human population against this disease."

That wall was enough, however, for Ronald Reagan to remain completely nonchalant, during his first summer in the presidency, at the news that animals carrying the plague bacillus had been found roaming near his Rancho Cielo outside Santa Barbara, California. At one of those rustic press conferences by which vacationing Presidents pretend they are still guiding the affairs of state, a diligent reporter asked Reagan, "Have you seen any evidence of the plague?"

"No, no," said the President. "I don't know where that was found. They say some place a mile from the ranch here, but you know that—we all have to recognize that that is not something that's terribly new in California."

The President had just been photographed, beaming, with his gaudy cowboy boots resting on top of a table, so the diligent reporter persisted, "Do you tuck your pants in your boots as a precaution?"

"No," said the President.

The reporters pressed on to ask how Mrs. Reagan was enjoying herself at the ranch. She was having, the President said, a fine time.

The New Jerusalem

1525–35

"False prophets shall rise"

The traditional image of the Reformation is young Martin Luther boldly nailing his Ninety-five Theses to the church door in Wittenberg on All Saints' Day of 1517, but in Switzerland the first open defiance of the Roman Church was the eating of sausages during Lent of the year 1522. The sacrilegious act occurred at the home of a Zurich printer named Christoph Froschauer, who had been working hard to produce a new edition of the letters of Saint Paul for an impending Frankfurt Fair. After his labors, he liked to eat heartily. Fish was permitted but expensive, so Froschauer told his wife to get some sausages. He had a dozen guests in his home, among them three priests.

One of these priests was Huldreich Zwingli, who for three years had been preaching on the Gospels in the great minster of Zurich. Zwingli declined the offer of sausages but raised no objection when the others ate. But somebody informed the magistrates of Zurich, and the magistrates expressed concern. Zwingli replied with a sermon based on Saint Paul, in which he argued every man's freedom from mere ritual. "Do you, of your own free will, wish to abstain from meat?" he asked. "Then do not eat it! But allow your brother his liberty."

Just as Saint Peter did not know that he had established the Roman Catholic Church and Saint Dominic did not know that he had started the Inquisition, the founding fathers of Protestantism never thought, in these first years, that they were creating a new religion. Reformers there had been before this, and the greatest of them had finally won supreme power in Rome during the Cluniac movement of the eleventh century. Schisms there had been, too, with rival popes pronouncing anathema upon one another. Even after Martin Luther had been condemned in 1520 by the papal bull *Exsurge Domini* ("Arise, O Lord . . . A wild bear has invaded thy vineyard . . ."), he affected to think that the condemnation was a forgery and wrote an indignant reply entitled *Against the Execrable Bull of Antichrist*. Even after he learned that the verdict of Pope Leo X was authentic, he publicly burned the offending document in a public bonfire, and even then, on appearing for interrogation before the Imperial Diet of Worms the following year, he insisted that he was speaking the Word of God and his universal church, that he would recant nothing "unless I am convicted by Scripture and plain reason."

Pope Leo X, the sybaritic patriarch of the Medici tribe, suddenly died the following year at the fairly youthful age of forty-six. Not only had he failed to suppress heresy, and to unite the warring kingdoms of Europe for a new crusade against the Turkish conquerors of Constantinople, he had lived long enough to see the newly crowned Sultan Suleiman the Magnificent reopen the offensive and capture Belgrade. "I wanted to make you all happy," Leo sighed on his deathbed. His successor at the Vatican, Adrian VI, was an ascetic reformer from the Netherlands. He immediately asked the Swiss Cardinal Matthäus Schinner, a good friend of Zwingli's, to outline a program of reforms that would quiet all those irritating controversies in Germany. There would be, in other words, no Reformation. Then came a new visitation of the plague, the mysterious force that still seemed to many people a manifestation of God's will. It struck down Cardinal Schinner and, the following year, 1523, Pope Adrian. And so the throne of Saint Peter reverted to the Medicis, in the form of Clement VII, and Germany to the Reformation.

Germany means, of course, not the divided and quasi-paralyzed nation of today, nor yet the Prussian monarchy headquartered in Berlin, but rather the ramshackle collection of powers and principalities, of duchies, margravates, electorates, bishoprics and free cities known as the Holy Roman Empire. The Emperor himself, Charles V, spoke no German and had never even been to Germany until after his election to the throne of Charlemagne. Charles had been born in Ghent in 1500 and thus was ruler first of the Netherlands, which then formed part of the duchy of Burgundy. By virtue of his Spanish blood, he became king of Spain at the age of eighteen, and because of his Hapsburg lineage he succeeded to the Empire at nineteen, and promptly plunged into war against France for the domination of Italy.

In theory, Charles was also nominally sovereign over Switzerland, where the Hapsburg family had originated, but Switzerland too was far different from the somnolent banking center of today. It was, on the contrary, extremely warlike. The Swiss prided themselves on their descent from the rugged Suevi and Alemanni, Teutonic tribesmen who had resisted all missionary forays into their Alps until Saint Gallus wandered in from Ireland and converted them to Christianity in the seventh century. The Swiss infantry, organized in phalanxes of pikemen, was renowned and feared all over Europe. When Pope Leo X appealed for help against the invading French, Zurich sent a contingent of 1,500 troops, with young Zwingli as chaplain, to help Leo capture Parma and Piacenza. From there, they went on to smash the French at the battle of Novara. But Switzerland also represented an idea, the idea of independence and self-government. Ever since the three forest cantons of Schwyz, Uri and Unterwalden had beaten off the Hapsburgs at Morgarten in 1315, they had exerted a magnetic attraction for every neighboring land. Lucerne joined them in 1332, Zurich in 1351, Berne in 1353, Basel and Schaffhausen in 1499—all told, there were thirteen cantons in the Swiss Confederation at the start of the sixteenth century, and they served as a beacon to all of southern Germany.

Within the fragmented Empire, then, Zwingli's Zurich was a much larger, stronger and more important city than Luther's Wittenberg, but the spread of ideas had been revolutionized during the preceding few decades by the invention of the printing press. That crude machine suddenly brought the Bible and every other book within the reach of any citizen. In Basel, in 1516, Erasmus published his annotated Greek text and authoritative Latin translation of the New Testament, and the printing press soon dispersed it all across the Continent. Luther declared that every man was his own priest, for the source of all truth lay in Scripture, and the printing press spread the word. And when Luther, hiding in the Wartburg castle after the Diet of Worms, translated those Scriptures into German, he created a language and a nation as well as a religion.

But when the people began reading the Scriptures, hearing Christ speak to them as he had not spoken to their fathers, they heard new ideas that they were not accustomed to hearing from their priests. They heard Christ say that he had come to save the poor and the afflicted, and that he would come again, in a time of plague and famine and war, a time threatened with the appearance of Antichrist, a time much like the present. Albrecht Dürer portrayed its very image in his *Four Horsemen of the Apocalypse*. And in this time of trouble, Christ had said, "Many false prophets shall rise, and shall deceive many."

Of all the major reformers, Zwingli was the most practical, the most good-tempered, the most devoted to common sense. A humanist well versed in both Greek and Hebrew, he had met Erasmus in 1515, and four years later he had begun reading Luther with admiration. He too preached vehemently against the sale of indulgences, by which the Vatican was draining gold from the north. He was also tough, physically tough. He survived even a bout with the plague of 1519, which killed about a quarter of Zurich's seven thousand inhabitants, among them Zwingli's beloved younger brother. And he was patriotic. His service as a chaplain with the Swiss infantry in Italy filled him with both misgivings about Rome and fervor for his native land. The church he envisioned was a *Volkskirche*. And just as he decided that every man should be free to eat what he chose, even in Lent, he decided that it was useless to pretend chastity.

A report of his lapses, in fact, had almost prevented his appointment to the Zurich Minster, but Zwingli manfully confessed his fault, adding that he had never seduced a virgin, a married woman or a nun; besides, a similar investigation disclosed that his chief rival for the Zurich appointment had six illegitimate children. ("Ah, God!" Zwingli wrote in the margin of his copy of Saint Augustine's *City of God*, "if only Adam had eaten a pear!"). Now in April of 1522, scarcely a month after the scandal of the sausages, Zwingli secretly married Anna Reinhart, widow of one of the city's notables. This was a violation of church law, of course, though not of Zurich civil law, so Zwingli formally petitioned the bishop of Constance, Hugo von Hohenlandenburg, to permit priests to do what he secretly had already done. The bishop declined even to answer. Zwingli became more assertive. "What is my crime?" he wrote. "For four years, I have done nothing but preach the New Testament.... The nearer ancient customs are to the Gospel, the more shall we honor them."

The bishop refused to debate Zwingli's views, and he disciplined several priests who sympathized with the reformer. The Zurich city council, however, decided to convene a public meeting on its religious future. The councilors invited not only Zwingli and the bishop but delegates from all the other Swiss cantons. Zwingli prepared the agenda by drafting sixty-seven theses for reform. They argued that Christ, not the Pope, is the supreme authority in the Christian church, that Scripture must be the source of church law, and that there is no Scriptural requirement for such traditions as fasting, celibacy, pilgrimage, clerical dress, monastic orders, church statuary or the invocation of saints. Like Luther, Zwingli declared that all Christians stand equal and alone before God, and that salvation must be found through faith alone. In contrast to Luther, however, he insisted that the Eucharist was not a miraculous reappearance of God's body but simply a symbolic commemoration of his Last Supper.

"O men of Zurich," Zwingli declared to the crowd of more than six hundred citizens gathered in the city hall on January 29, 1523, "you may take the matter into your own hands. It is a great honor that God has bestowed on you." The city council agreed. Though it balked at any immediate change in church rituals, it voted its endorsement of Zwingli. And so he became the founder of the Swiss Reformed Church, the first alternative to both Rome and Wittenberg and an alternative that depended not on the goodwill of various German princes but on the self-reliance of a town's own citizens.

Among Zwingli's young followers and disciples, however, there were several who took the message of the Gospel more literally, who believed that every word in the Scriptures must be taken as law, and conversely that no other law was important. At a time when Christ would soon return to earth, as he had prophesied, they saw no merit in simply replacing the state church with another state church. The most prominent of these radicals were Conrad Grebel, son of one of the Zurich city councilors, and Felix Manz, illegitimate son of the canon of the Zurich minster. Now in their midtwenties, both had attended universities, both studied Greek and Hebrew with Zwingli, both began to organize weekly discussion groups to debate the dawdling progress of reform. They soon attracted to their meetings several country priests who expressed the peasants' anger at the continued imposition of tithes for church expenses. They also attracted iconoclasts determined to smash the statues in the minster. They demanded action. "Zwingli, the herald of the word, has cast down the word," Grebel wrote angrily to a friend, "has trodden it underfoot, and brought it into captivity."

The radicals' principal target was the ceremony of the mass, which was still being sacramentally performed in the minster, still in Latin, despite Zwingli's public disapproval. The radicals denounced it as an abomination. Zwingli was determined, however, to proceed slowly and steadily, always maintaining the support of the Zurich council. That was the only force that stood, like Luther's princes, between the reformers and the Inquisition. The radicals persuaded the council to convene a public debate that October on their demands for abolition of the mass and of religious images. The central issue behind these demands arose almost by accident.

"My lords will decide," Zwingli said offhand, "whatever regulations are to be adopted in the future in regard to the mass."

"You do not have the right to place the decision on this matter in the hands of my lords," protested one of the radicals, a Franciscan named Simon Stumpf, "for the decision has already been made. The Spirit of God decides."

The radicals were few in number—scarcely more than half a dozen came to the regular meetings in Manz's home near the minster—but their zeal was remarkable. They kept growing. They corresponded not only with Luther but with two of his more extreme rivals in Germany, Thomas Müntzer and Andreas Carlstadt. A radical pastor from a village outside Zurich, Wilhelm Reublin, seems to have been the first to raise the argument that there was no Scriptural justification for baptizing infants. Grebel and Manz agreed. All those whom the apostles had baptized were adult believers. It was not in itself an important issue, but it would soon come to have important implications. Zwingli, like Luther, regarded the baptism of infants as a sign of their entry into the universal church; the radicals insisted that the true church consisted only of true believers. Three families, swayed by Reublin's preaching, not only withheld their children from baptism that summer but interrupted a church service and smashed the baptismal font. The Zurich council dutifully investigated and then ruled that infant baptism was fitting and proper. Anyone who refused to have a baby baptized would be fined one silver mark.

The radicals' preaching evolved erratically, not from one leader's decrees, not from one book or one moment of revelation. There were several principles, however, that seem to have been fundamental from the start: That Scripture was the ultimate authority and that all of it should be taken literally as God's word. That man was free to choose his own destiny, and that the choice of Christianity was a rebirth, a total commitment to Christ. That there should be no church organization of any kind; anyone could preach, and any groups of believers could make their own rules, and they should support their pastor by voluntary donations. That rendering unto Caesar meant paying taxes and obeying the law, when it did not conflict with God's law, but that true Christians would take no part in government, would take no oaths, would insist on separation of church and state. And that Christ forbade all violence, all war.

The clearest statement of the radicals' views was a long letter that Grebel wrote to Müntzer in September of 1524 (it was also signed by Manz and a half-dozen others who called themselves "seven young 'Müntzers' "). Grebel did not know Müntzer but had read two of the German's pamphlets, and these moved him to declare that he and his comrades were "wonderfully happy to have found someone who was one with us in a common Christian understanding." The letter indicates that while Grebel and his friends were still arguing with Zwingli about the sacrificial mass, they had already begun celebrating a far different ritual. "Common bread shall be used," Grebel wrote, "with no idolatry and no additions: for these introduce a make-believe reverence and adoration of the bread. Also a common drinking vessel shall be used...." Grebel said he was happy to hear that Müntzer was moving in the same direction, but he was not reluctant to criticize. "We understand and have noted that you have translated the mass into German, and have begun to use German hymnody," he wrote. "That cannot be right, when we find no teaching in the New Testament about singing. . . . The only command Christ gave his ambassadors . . . was to preach the Word."

The most striking aspect of Grebel's letter, though, is his insistence that Christians must never use force. He seems to have heard mistaken reports "that this is also what you believe," and so he went on to declare his faith: "True Christian believers are sheep among wolves, sheep for the slaughter; they must be baptized in anguish and affliction, tribulation, persecution, suffering and death. They must be tried with fire, and must reach the fatherland of eternal rest not by killing their bodily but by mortifying their spiritual enemies." A few days later, Grebel heard for the first time that Müntzer had actually preached in favor of the sword. "The ungodly have no right to live," he had said. Grebel could not believe it. "Is that true?" he protested. "If you wish to defend war . . . or other things which you do not find in express words of Scripture . . . I admonish you by the common salvation of us all that you desist from all notions of your own both now and henceforth."

Zwingli met twice with Grebel and Manz later in 1524 in an attempt to reconcile their differences. When this attempt failed, he published shortly before Christmas a denunciation, *Those Who Give Rise to Rebellion*. He charged, falsely, that the radicals opposed all government and all organized religion; he charged truly that they refused all compromises and refused to stop proselytizing. Grebel did not disagree. On New Year's Day of 1525, his wife gave birth to a baby girl, named Rachel, and Grebel wrote shortly afterward that "she has not yet been baptized in the Romish bath." Grebel's friends were equally assertive. When one of the radicals loudly interrupted a sermon on baptism, the Zurich council once again called for a public debate. By now, the arguments had been made several times. The radicals declared again that there was no Scriptural justification for baptizing infants, that the ritual must be a sign of faith, and that Zwingli himself had once said much the same thing; Zwingli's answer now was that baptism had replaced circumcision as a mark of God's covenant, and that nothing in the Scriptures contradicted the centuries-old tradition of administering it to infants. On January 18, the council emphatically ruled for Zwingli. Anyone who henceforth refused to have a child baptized would be subject not to a one-mark fine but to banishment, and any pastor who refused to baptize a child would be imprisoned. Manz and Grebel were forbidden to hold any more meetings or discussions on these matters; Reublin, Stumpf and other outsiders were ordered to leave Zurich within a week.

It was characteristic of Grebel and his friends simply to ignore the authorities' commands. That same week, on the night of January 21, at a meeting of about fifteen people in Manz's house, they arrived at what was apparently a spontaneous climax. "Because God wished to have his own people, separated from all peoples," according to an account of this meeting in *The Large Chronicle of the Hutterite Brethren*, "he willed for this purpose to bring in the right true morning star of his truth to shine in fullness in the final age of this world." This anonymous account was probably written by Georg Cajacob, a monk from Graubünden who had acquired the nickname of Blaurock. Afflicted by fear, he said, the group knelt down and prayed for divine mercy "since they well knew what they would have to bear and suffer." After the prayer, Blaurock suddenly rose to his feet and asked Grebel, since there was no ordained priest there, to baptize him "with the true Christian baptism upon his faith and knowledge." Grebel did so, and then, when the others asked for a similar benediction, Blaurock baptized them all. "Thus they together gave themselves to the name of the Lord ..." the chronicle concludes. "Therewith began the separation from the world and its evil works." And so was born the first of the evangelical groups that would soon acquire the derisory name of Anabaptists; they themselves simply called one another brethren. Both Catholic and Protestant authorities, Lutheran and Zwinglian alike, would harry and persecute them as though they were the apostles of the Apocalypse, as, in a way, they were.

The week after these first baptisms, the group concentrated its activities in the outlying village of Zollikon. Manz and Blaurock conducted several baptisms there, and Grebel officiated at a series of communion suppers, a simple sharing of bread and wine, in various farmhouses. The following Sunday, Blaurock arose in the village church and loudly demanded of the pastor what he intended to do. "I will preach the Word of God," said Pastor Niklaus Billeter. "Not you but I have been sent to preach here," Blaurock retorted. Billeter mounted the pulpit and tried to start his sermon, but Blaurock kept interrupting. "It is written, 'My house shall be called a house of prayer,' but you make it a den of robbers," he shouted, banging his walking stick violently against the pew before him. A bailiff who happened to be in the congregation warned Blaurock that he would be arrested if he didn't stop interfering, and so, for the time being, he stopped.

The very next day, Zurich police officials appeared in Zollikon and arrested all the Anabaptists they could find: Manz and Blaurock for administering baptism (Grebel apparently eluded the police) and twenty-five local farmers for accepting it. Since the Zurich prison in the Wellenberg tower was too small to hold such a crowd, the overflow was confined in the Augustinian monastery, from which Zwingli had expelled the monks just six weeks earlier. Stern punishments had been decreed, but the authorities at first proved reluctant to apply them. After holding their prisoners a week, they fined and released them. The Anabaptists went right back to their forbidden meetings, and soon the authorities were dismayed to see bands of them parading defiantly through the marketplace, chanting grim warnings of divine judgment: "Woe to Zurich!"

To avoid new arrests, the Anabaptist leaders began dispersing. Grebel, for one, spent several rather fruitless weeks in Schaffhausen, just north of Zurich, then moved eastward to St. Gallen, where the saint from Ireland had founded what became an abbey and a great center of learning. Grebel's brother-in-law, Joachim von Watt, known as Vadian, was now the burgomaster of St. Gallen, and he sympathetically provided a sanctuary for the Anabaptists. They soon began making converts, lots of them. On Palm Sunday, Grebel led a crowd of several hundred new followers down to the Sitter River for a mass baptism.

The Anabaptists conducted their meetings in the open fields. Soon they were estimated to number eight hundred. The churches of St. Gallen were deserted.

Despite their subsequent reputation as wild-eyed zealots, these first Anabaptists were generally people of deep piety and strict morals. They worked hard, wore simple clothes, abhorred drinking and blasphemy. Even Zwingli, in one of his denunciations of the Anabaptists, wrote that "if you investigate their life and conduct, it seems ... irreproachable, pious, unassuming, attractive, yea, above this world. Even those who are inclined to be critical will say that their lives are excellent." Yet among the Swiss who flocked to join the Anabaptists, there was a streak of wildness, even madness, that soon appeared at the prayer meetings in St. Gallen. Johannes Kessler, a St. Gallen pastor who recorded the converts' behavior in a chronicle entitled *Sabbata,* said he repeatedly witnessed Anabaptists in the throes of ecstasy. They would sigh and groan and twist their fingers, and sweat would pour down their cheeks, and finally they would crumple to the ground and writhe about or fall unconscious. They called this "dying," as Saint Paul had meant it when he said, "I die daily."

Just two months after Grebel arrived in St. Gallen, the town council banned the Anabaptists. Grebel and his friends soon moved on to other Swiss towns, but the mania that had struck St. Gallen did not depart with them. Kessler's chronicle tells of the new believers cutting off their hair and babbling like children and tearing up their Bibles or throwing them onto bonfires, crying out Saint Paul's warning that "the letter killeth but the spirit giveth life." Others simply sat motionless, waiting for the spirit to move them or tell them what to do. Still others gave each other rings and tore off their clothes and began fornicating in the fields. On February 15, 1526, the town council recorded that five couples had "taken to one another" in the choir of a church. The following month, the councilors interrogated seven people who had run around in their underclothes and then engaged in sexual relations. "Why do you judge, you hypocrites?" one of the culprits answered. "We have died to the flesh and passed through death. Whatever we do is done by the Father, in spite of us."

A servant named Verena Baumann announced that she was Christ. She and a friend, Wybrat Vonwilerin, who had been imprisoned for Anabaptism in Zurich, took the names Mary Magdalen and Martha and established themselves in a house outside St. Gallen. Throngs of believers came there to confess their sins. Verena announced that she would give birth to the Antichrist. Then she announced that she was the woman described in the twelfth chapter of Revelation, "a woman clothed with the sun, and the moon under her feet, and upon her head a crown of twelve stars." At one point, she appeared naked before a crowd of pilgrims. She said she was the great whore of Babylon. She said she was the son of God. The abbot of St. Gallen finally had her arrested, and as she was led through the streets to the town hall she cried out, "Do penance, do penance, the Day of the Lord, the ax has already been laid to the roots of the tree." The authorities locked her up for six weeks, then expelled her from the town.

Even more strange was the case of Thomas Schugger and his brother Lienhart, who seem to have believed that they had been called to enact their own form of martyrdom. On February 6, 1526, Lienhart suddenly appeared in the marketplace and insisted on exchanging his coat and his sword for the staff belonging to one of the guards. "This is a staff of authority, but it is not the right one," he shouted. "There will be another." The next morning, he ritually broke the staff into three pieces and burned them in the presence of some friends. This signified, in his mind, the destruction of the forces of earthly power. That evening, Thomas tested Lienhart's faith by beating him with a club, then tying his feet together and twisting them over a staff, then threatening three times to blind him with his sword, then feeding him gall and vinegar until he threw up. At the climax of the ritual, in the presence of their parents and several other relatives, Lienhart asked Thomas to cut off his head. They both seem to have believed that if their faith was great enough, the sword would pass through Lienhart's neck without doing him any harm. They both prayed.

"Father, if thou be willing, remove this cup from me," Lienhart said, kneeling. "Nevertheless, not my will but thine be done."

"Father, thy will be done," said Thomas, standing behind his kneeling brother.

"Amen," said Lienhart.

Thomas then cut off his head.

The authorities of St. Gallen were outraged. They put Thomas Schugger on trial for murder, sentenced him to death, and executed him a week later. They once again forbade any Anabaptist meetings, but the believers were by now in a state of frenzy. According to Kessler's chronicle, they began running through the streets and shouting that the Last Day would arrive in exactly one week. This persuaded many more to become baptized, and finally great flocks of them, some 1,200 in all, stopped work, abandoned their homes and set off into the hills, singing and praying at the top of their lungs. Only after a week had passed, with no sign of the Last Day, did hunger and cold send the faithful straggling back to their homes.

Grebel had long gone his way, of course, and the sober historians of Anabaptism insist with some justice that such frenzies were never really part of the movement. Certainly Grebel and Manz and Blaurock preached nothing of the sort, nothing but the simplest and most austere kind of Christian piety. Yet there was something about the movement, or perhaps something about the spirit of the times, that infected at least some of the Anabaptists with what Melville called "all that most maddens and torments; all that stirs up the lees of things . . . all that cracks the sinews and cakes the brain; all the subtle demonisms of life and thought." To the Swiss authorities, to Zwingli and the Zurich councilors alike, the Anabaptist movement and the passions it aroused were utterly mysterious, and therefore threatening. "The issue is not baptism," Zwingli wrote to Vadian, "but revolt, faction, heresy."

Grebel's way took him back to Zurich, where he tried both to preach and to stay hidden. "I believe it is known that I am in my house, that I receive the Brethren there," he wrote to a friend. "However, I do not go out, in order to protect my asylum here against a possible imprisonment by Zwingli, who according to the Apocalypse will himself go into captivity." Grebel's way took him then to Waldshut to consult the noted reformer Balthasar Hübmaier, and then to Grüningen, just east of Zurich, where Grebel had spent much of his boyhood. Manz and Blaurock, who had been preaching in the mountains, joined Grebel in Grüningen, and their appearances attracted such crowds that the authorities decided once again that something must be done. A magistrate named Berger rode up to one of their prayer meetings and announced that they were forbidden to preach. The irrepressible Blaurock greeted this announcement by starting to sing. The crowd began swarming threateningly around the magistrate, but Grebel insisted that there be no violence, so the magistrate succeeded in arresting the Anabaptist leaders in what he later called "a remarkable day for all."

Once again there was a public disputation between Zwingli and the Anabaptists, once again all the familiar arguments about baptism were offered on both sides, but this time Zwingli also accused the Anabaptists of political radicalism. According to various secondhand reports, Zwingli claimed that the Anabaptists were concerned only with "the security of the saints," that they had said "that there should not be any magistracy," and "that all things should be held in common." Grebel, specifically, was accused of speaking "just as if the Messiah were alread·· at hand." Grebel denied all this as best he could. He admitted that "whoever is covetous, a usurer, a gambler, or in other ways guilty of vice, should ... in no case be considered among the Christians," but he insisted that he had "never taught that one should not be obedient to the authorities." Manz similarly denied having preached communism or anarchy and argued only "that those who desired to accept Christ and ... to follow his example should seek to unite themselves by the sign of baptism and should leave the others with their own faith."

There never was much doubt of the outcome. After three days of argument, the councilors once again declared Zwingli triumphant. On November 18, 1525, Grebel, Manz and Blaurock were all sentenced "because of their Anabaptism and their unbecoming conduct to lie in the tower on a diet of bread and water ... as long as God should please and as seems good to my Lords." They remained in solitary confinement in the tower throughout that winter, and since they gave no sign of recanting, they were retried in March and sentenced to life imprisonment. The day after their resentencing, however, a new law was passed. Citing the penalty that the Emperor Justinian had imposed on the Donatist* heretics a thousand years earlier, it made adult baptism a capital crime, punishable by drowning. On March 21, almost as though a trap were being set, the three prisoners learned that they could escape through an unlocked window and then down a rope to the drawbridge over the moat surrounding the tower. At first they were reluctant to make the escape. Someone persuaded them.

Soon there came reports of new baptisms in various towns around Zurich.

---

* The Donatists originally argued that a sacrament was invalid if administered by a sinner, specifically by those priests who had collaborated in Diocletian's recent persecution of Christians. From this they derived the view, later to be held by the Anabaptists, that the church is a society of the righteous.

Grebel preached in Appenzell and Graubünden, then headed into the mountains. There, probably in the town of Maienfeld, probably in about August of 1526, he suddenly was stricken by the plague. In a few days he was dead. Manz and Blaurock managed to continue preaching and baptizing. Wherever Manz went, according to one account, "he was accompanied on all sides by men and women, as though he were a visible divinity, and they hung on his lips as though in a trance and enchanted. He loved the fields and woods, the secure refuges of heresy. Whatever he said and commanded was held to be a divine oracle." In December, Manz and Blaurock were captured again in a forest near Grüningen and shipped back to Zurich. There was no question of their guilt, and the crime of adult baptism, which had been punished by a fine of one silver mark just two years earlier, was now to be expiated by drowning.

On the morning of January 5, a crowd gathered in the Zurich fish market as Manz was led from the Wellenberg tower down to a boat tied up near what is today the Rathaus Bridge across the Limmat River. "His mother and brother came to him and exhorted him to be steadfast," according to the chronicle by Heinrich Bullinger, Zwingli's eventual successor, "and he persevered in his folly even to the end. He praised God that he was about to die for his truth; for Anabaptism was right, and founded upon the word of God. . . . When he was bound upon the hurdle and was about to be thrown into the stream by the executioner, he sang with a loud voice, '*In manus tuas, Domine, commendo spiritum meum . . .*'"

Blaurock was not a citizen of Zurich, and so the law on baptisms did not apply to him. Instead, on the same day that Manz was drowned in the Limmat, Blaurock was taken to the fish market, bound and stripped to the waist and then flogged through the streets all the way to the Niederdorf Gate. There he was ordered to leave Zurich and to take an oath that he would never return. Bleeding from his wounds, Blaurock managed to gasp that oaths were forbidden by Scripture. They gave up then and simply expelled him, and so Blaurock wandered through the mountains, preaching the new faith. He was arrested again in Appenzell, then expelled again, and then he moved across the frontier into the Austrian Tyrol. This was Hapsburg territory, Catholic territory, and the authorities cared very little about the origins or citizenship of Anabaptist heretics. When they caught Blaurock, toward the end of 1529, they burned him at the stake.

Grebel's appeal for nonviolence may never have reached Thomas Müntzer. When the messenger carrying it could not find Müntzer at his parish in Allstedt, he brought the letter back to Zurich (it somehow reached Vadian, in St. Gallen, who saved it, and so it has been preserved to this day). Müntzer had already left Allstedt by night in that summer of 1524 to command the rising tides of the Great Peasants' War.

As early as 1499, a mathematician in Tübingen had foreseen that all of the planets would meet in the sign of Pisces in the spring of 1524, and he predicted that this disastrous conjunction would bring a flood that would inundate the world. This prophecy was generally rejected, on the ground that such a flood would violate God's covenant with Noah, but the anxiety remained. In the year 1523, printing presses in various parts of Germany spewed out no fewer than fifty-one pamphlets speculating on the impending disaster.

The spring of 1524 was a time of portents, as spring often is, and the dreaded figure of Antichrist seemed incarnate in the Turkish Sultan, Suleiman the Magnificent, who now appeared ready to advance from the captured citadel of Belgrade and to attack the Hungarian city of Buda. But while Suleiman was distracted by a revolt in Egypt, the convulsion that shook Germany that spring began because the Countess von Lupfen wanted some snail shells upon which she might wind some woolen yarn.

There had been periodic uprisings among the German peasantry for the past half century, outbreaks generally inspired not by hunger and want so much as by rage at the landlords' repeated incursions against the peasants' rights. One force behind these incursions was the rediscovery and increasingly widespread application of Roman law, which tended to transfer to the authorities the common ownership of woods and streams, which had been inherent in Germanic tradition. Another was the growth of capital—money, silver—as the only measure of the peasants' labor and possessions. The sporadic outbursts of peasant anger generally ended in some feudal court of appeal, in some arbitration of the disputed rights, and only occasionally in bloodshed. In that same spring of 1524, some peasants in the vicinity of Nuremberg had burned their crops rather than pay them as tithes, but the disturbance had soon been suppressed.

The Countess von Lupfen's snail shells were, for some reason, different. When she insisted that her peasants spend a holiday searching out and collecting shells for her, they balked. And to this trivial but intolerable new affront they began adding a list of unsettled grievances: the enclosure of woods, denial of their fishing rights, the ruin of their crops by noble hunters—there were sixty-two charges in all. About one thousand rebellious peasants gathered in the Stühlingen district some twenty-five miles northwest of the Swiss border and chose an aging *Landsknecht* named Hans Müller as their commander. Müller soon went south to Waldshut to gather more support and there recruited not only a fair number of armed peasants but also their preacher, Balthasar Hübmaier. All that summer, the disturbances spread from the shores of Lake Constance across southern Germany, to the Allgäu and the Klettgäu, to the Iller Valley of Upper Swabia, to the Donauried northwest of Augsburg. There were stonings and burnings and refusals to pay tithes, but no great bloodshed; the nobles were as disorganized as the peasants.

In March of 1525, finally, various self-appointed peasant leaders assembled at Memmingen and combined their various demands in a document known as the Twelve Articles. Partly under the influence of Hübmaier, who helped draft the document, the familiar peasant complaints now acquired a religious framework. The very first demand was that every congregation should have the right to elect and dismiss its own pastor. And it was because God had created all men that all should be free to hunt in the woodlands and fish in the streams, and it was because Christ had redeemed all men that serfdom should be abrogated. Similar arguments supported the demands for the abolition of the death fee that the lords imposed on widows, and of the tithes on livestock. The final article declared that if any of the peasants' arguments could be demonstrated to be contrary to the Bible, it would be dropped. The peasant leaders presented these demands to the lords of the Swabian League, but the lords were now gathering their forces under the generalship of Georg von Waldburg Truchsess. While negotiations dragged on, sporadic skirmishes took place.

The messianic leader whom the peasants needed had not yet joined their cause, but everything in his life was driving him toward it. Born to a middle-class family in the Harz Mountains in 1488 or '89, Thomas Müntzer read widely in the Bible and the church fathers at the universities of Leipzig and Frankfurt, and though he wanted to be a priest, he seems to have suffered torments of unbelief. In later years, he even argued that such crises were an essential prerequisite to true faith. "He who does not wish to accept the bitter Christ will eat himself sick of honey," he wrote. He encountered Luther at the Leipzig debate of 1519, and that brought him to the Reformation. At Luther's recommendation, he was invited the following year to preach at Zwickau, once a center of the persecuted Waldensian heresy but now a booming silver-mining town swollen with migrant workers. Here Müntzer not only began accusing the local Franciscans of greed but turned violently against Luther. What could salvation through faith mean to a miner or weaver unable to feed his family? "In the face of usury, taxes and rents," Müntzer declared, "no one can have faith."

Müntzer's new hero was a bizarre and almost Waldensian preacher named Nicholas Storch, a former weaver who had made himself an expert on the Bible. Storch dressed himself in a long gray robe and broad-brimmed hat and warned groups of workers that all of Christendom would soon be destroyed by the Turks. Storch preached other unusual views—in favor of polygamy, and the sharing of all worldly goods, and against the baptism of children. In support of these views, he quoted not just the Bible but God himself, who spoke directly to Storch through dreams and visions. "Those in authority live only in lust," cried Storch, "consume the sweat and blood of their subjects, eat and drink night and day, hunt, run, and kill. . . . Everyone therefore should arm himself and attack the priests, [then] the land-grabbers and noblemen." When the Zwickau magistrates asked Storch to appear and defend his unorthodox opinions, he went instead to Wittenberg with two of his disciples to carry the word to the capital of Lutheranism. Luther's friend Melanchthon was deeply impressed by the visionary, as were several other Wittenberg leaders. Luther himself, on his reemergence from his hiding place on the Wartburg, conceded nothing. He contemptuously dismissed "the Zwickau prophets" as "illiterate weavers" and condemned their messages from heaven as delusions inspired by Satan. The Zwickau authorities refused to allow Storch to return, and so he disappears from history at the end of 1522.

The Zwickau authorities also ordered the dismissal of Müntzer, who thereupon went to Prague, the center of the crushed Hussite heresy that had anticipated so much of Luther's work. Müntzer seems to have imagined that he might turn Prague into a new center of the Reformation, and he began referring to himself as the "messenger of Christ." He startled his hosts, on All Saints' Day of 1521, by the Lutheran gesture of posting on the doors of various churches a manifesto that violently attacked the nobles and the rich. "I, Thomas Müntzer," he began, ". . . have made greater efforts to attain or possess a higher instruction of the invincible and holy Christian faith than any other man." He announced the formation of a new church of the chosen, who "will be instructed in prophecy . . . so that they might really experience how amiably God speaks with his elect." As for the godless, they were all doomed. "The time of harvest is at hand," Müntzer declared. "That is why God himself has hired me to labor in his harvest. I have sharpened my sickle." If anyone resisted his preaching, finally, "God will have you slain by the Turks when they come next year." Expelled from Prague, Müntzer wandered across southern Germany, and even into Switzerland, until he finally found himself a church in 1523 in the Thuringian town of Allstedt. Here he translated Latin hymns into German and created a German liturgy and preached to growing crowds the radical sermons that aroused attention as far away as Grebel's Zurich.

Müntzer was not really an Anabaptist. Though he disapproved of infant baptism, he was willing to perform it, since he considered it relatively unimportant. Nor did he really share the Anabaptists' total belief in the Bible. It was the Holy Spirit that animated his passionate vision of the injustice of the world, and of its imminent end, yet this was a vision that was to exert considerable influence on the erratic development of the Anabaptist movement. In the throes of his vision, Müntzer imagined that he might make even Allstedt into a magnet to rival Wittenberg. He excoriated Luther as "Meister Lügner" (Master Liar) and "Bruder Mastschwein" (Brother Hog) and "Sanftleben" (Easy-Living). "The princes bleed the people with usury," he wrote, "and count as their own the fish in the stream, the bird of the air, and the grass of the field, and Dr. Liar says 'Amen.' What courage has he . . . , Dr. Easychair, the basking sycophant? He says there should be no rebellion because the sword has been committed by God to the ruler, but the power of the sword belongs to the whole community. . . . They [the rulers] shall be cast down from their seats. The fowls of the heavens are gathering to devour their carcasses." Luther was equally scornful toward his accuser: "He has swallowed the Holy Ghost, feathers and all."

Müntzer believed in action. In the spring of 1524, a crowd apparently acting on his instigation marched to the nearby town of Mallerbach and burned a miracle-working portrait of the Virgin. Müntzer denied his responsibility, but he was already organizing a revolutionary brotherhood that he called the League of the Elect. The Saxon authorities ordered it disbanded. Duke John of Saxony, interested in learning more, summoned Müntzer to the ducal palace to preach a sermon. Müntzer boldly chose as his text that vision of the future, the Book of Daniel, and he quickly made it clear that the age of prophets was by no means past. The Lutherans, he said with comtempt, "teach and say that God no longer reveals his divine mysteries to his beloved friends by means of valid visions or his audible word." It was hardly surprising that Luther, "Brother

Fattened Swine and Brother Soft Life," should reject such signs, but it was the mark of every "truly apostolic, patriarchal and prophetic spirit to attend upon visions .... For God speaks clearly, like this text of Daniel, about the transformation of the world. He will prepare it in the Last Days in order that his name may be rightly praised."

The four parts of the statue that Daniel had seen in Nebuchadnezzar's dream were traditionally understood to be the kingdoms of the Babylonians, the Persians, the Greeks and the Romans, but Müntzer interpreted the clay feet of the statue as a fifth kingdom, "that which we have before our eyes." This kingdom of clay was a kingdom of mud, of ordure, Müntzer cried out to the startled dukes, a kingdom of eels and vipers all writhing in a heap. It was up to the dukes, he said, to break away from "your hypocritical parsons," and to accept Müntzer, a "new Daniel," as the prophet in the coming crusades. "O beloved lords," he said, "how handsomely the Lord will go smashing among the old pots with his rod of iron." If the dukes declined their duty, Müntzer went on, a revolutionary populace, "the enraged people," would take on the challenge. He quoted Moses saying, "Break down their altars, smash up their images," and Christ saying, "I am not come to send peace but a sword," and then he went into a frenzy of rhetorical bloodletting: "The godless person has no right to live ... God says: Thou shalt not suffer evildoers to live. ... The sword is necessary to wipe out the godless."

The Saxon lords, somewhat bemused by Müntzer's apparent demand that they should be the ones to lead the scattered peasant forces, asked him not to leave Allstedt. Müntzer agreed, then climbed over the town wall by night and set out to lead the crusade himself. In the nearby free city of Mühlhausen he recruited the local paupers to join him in parading through the streets, bearing before them a red crucifix and a naked sword. The town council suppressed these unseemly demonstrations by the League of the Elect and banished Müntzer. He next appeared in Nuremberg and issued two revolutionary appeals. The Nuremberg council confiscated them and expelled their author. Müntzer wandered as far as Switzerland, to Zurich, where he may have met Grebel and Manz, then back to Mühlhausen, where a newly elected council was more tolerant of Müntzer's activities. By now, Müntzer was referring to himself as "the hammer" and "the sword of Gideon." "Now go at them, and at them, and at them ...," he wrote to a friend. "We must sleep no more. ... At them, at them, while the fire is hot! Don't let your sword get cold. ... God goes ahead of you, so follow, follow!"

Müntzer's hallooing may seem to border on hysteria, not to say madness, but he was not alone in his cries for blood. Even as he was appealing to the peasants to rise, Martin Luther was appealing to the princes to suppress those peasants. "Let everyone who can smite, slay and stab, secretly or openly," he wrote in a tract entitled *Against the Murderous and Thieving Hordes of Peasants*, "remembering that nothing can be more poisonous, hurtful or devilish than a rebel. It is just as when one must kill a mad dog; if you don't strike him, he will strike you, and the whole land with you." And again: "These are peculiar times, so peculiar that a prince who sheds blood earns heaven much more than many a man who prays." As for Müntzer, he was "a tree . . . bearing no other fruit than murder, rebellion and bloodshed."

Müntzer did not create the peasant revolt, nor did his appeals arouse the peasant armies he dreamed of. He commanded only a force of about three hundred ragged marauders with scythes and pitchforks on a series of raids for supplies. But as the swarms of insurgents roamed to and fro across Thuringia, Müntzer almost inevitably found himself lifted into a position of leadership. He relished it. He designed for himself a white banner decorated with the rainbow that God had shown to Noah as a sign of his covenant. A more plebeian view of these excitements was expressed in a popular verse:

> He who does not die in 1523,
> In 1524 does not drown,
> And is not beaten to death in 1525
> Can truly claim miracles in his life.

On May 15, 1525, as a peasant army of about eight thousand was encamped outside the walled town of Frankenhausen, the Lutheran Landgrave Philip of Hesse attacked with a smaller but stronger force of two thousand cavalrymen, reinforced by artillery. In an opening skirmish, the peasants stood their ground. The twenty-year-old Landgrave decided to be magnanimous. He promised the peasants that they could go free if they would surrender Müntzer and then quietly disperse. Some of the peasants apparently were tempted, but Müntzer responded with a final blaze of oratory. He declared that God had promised him victory and that all who had true faith would be impervious even to Philip's artillery. And as he spoke, there suddenly appeared in the sky a rainbow, God's emblem and his own. The peasants began singing, "Veni Sancte Spiritus . . ." as Philip's artillery sent cannonballs crashing into the wagons that they had drawn together for their defense. Then Philip's cavalry charged. The peasants broke and ran. The cavalrymen pursued, slashing and stabbing at the fleeing mob. When the slaughter ended, the dead numbered about five thousand. Philip's force lost six men.

Müntzer was found hiding in a bed in an attic in Frankenhausen, then taken to a nearby fortress to be interrogated. His captors applied thumbscrews during the questioning. In the course of two weeks of interrogation, Müntzer confessed everything, including the names of everyone who had ever helped him, and recanted everything. "You should beg the dukes for mercy," he declared in writing to whatever followers he might still have. "This is my last desire for the sake of removing from my soul the burden of being blamed for another rebellion. There should be no more shedding of innocent blood."

Müntzer even struggled through communion according to the Catholic rite, and though he was too weakened by torture to repeat the Nicene Creed, it was said for him by one of his captors. Then his head was cut off and displayed on a stake for more than five years as a warning to all rebels. "Since Thomas Müntzer has failed," Luther observed, "it is evident that he preached and worked through the Devil."

*

The ruthless persecution of the Anabaptists, by both Catholic and Protestant authorities, was formally proclaimed throughout the Empire at the Diet of Speyer in 1529, the same diet that grudgingly endorsed the toleration of Lutheranism in all territories where the Lutherans had already become strong.* "We decree," said the new edict, "that every Anabaptist or rebaptized person, of whatever age or sex, be put to death by sword, or fire, or otherwise. All preachers and those who abet and conceal them, all those who persist in Anabaptism, or relapse after retraction, must be put to death. In no case must they be pardoned." Exactly how many of the Anabaptists perished at the hands of the executioners remains, as in all such slaughters, unknown. Hundreds of these killings were recorded in 1570 in a compendium entitled *The Bloody Theater, or Martyrs' Mirror,* by Thielman van Braght, but these were only the best known. The forgotten souls who were burned and drowned and beheaded—not to mention those wanderers who died of cold and hunger—can only be estimated at four or five thousand.

This killing did not stop the spread of Anabaptism through Germany, into Poland and the Low Countries. On the contrary, after Luther's condemnation of the insurgent peasants, the working classes turned away from Lutheranism to some extent, and it was Anabaptism that became increasingly the religion of the poor, of the downtrodden and the desperate. Zwingli's disciple, Bullinger, complained of the Anabaptists in 1531 that "the people are running after them as though they were the living saints." The Count of Alzey, in the Palatinate, was reported to have exclaimed, after the execution of 350 Anabaptists, "What shall I do? The more I kill, the greater becomes their number!"

The persecution did have a powerful effect, though, on the Anabaptist movement itself. By repeatedly killing off the Anabaptist leaders, particularly the educated clerics, the authorities caused the leadership to devolve onto self-created prophets like Hans Hut, a follower of Müntzer's, who preached that "the subjects should murder all the authorities," for Christ would return exactly three and a half years after the start of the Peasants' War, in 1527. Some were even wilder. Hans Römer, for example, insisted that Christ was coming within the year, so he organized an armed band to attack Erfurt on New Year's Day of 1528 (he was betrayed and arrested). A few who called themselves Anabaptists were little better than criminals. In the region of Fulda, for example, an adventurer named Hans Krug murdered at least five people and raped a woman who refused to submit to baptism.

The execution of the Anabaptist leaders also altered their followers' beliefs. The Anabaptists had never had a uniform doctrine—the priesthood of all believers and the autonomy of each congregation formed part of their creed—but their dispersion increased the differences between the scattered groups. Some Anabaptists accepted the use of force, while others insisted on nonviolence;

* It protected the rights of the Catholic minority in Lutheran lands, however, while denying similar rights to Lutherans in Catholic lands, an inequity that prompted the Lutherans to make the formal protest that earned the movement the name of Protestants.

some preached strict piety, while others were extremely libertarian; some demanded a sharing of all goods, while others limited that sharing to the support of the poor; some argued that the Bible was the only source of divine law, while others believed passionately in dreams and visions and other manifestations of the Holy Spirit. Since each little cluster of believers felt free to debate and divide, the number of doctrinal variations is beyond counting, but one serious estimate suggests about forty different groupings.

One of the most interesting and important changes in the persecuted movement was an increasing emphasis on the end of the world and the Second Coming of Christ. The Anabaptists had always believed in an imminent apocalypse—as, indeed, did Martin Luther—for Christ himself had foretold it. But though Christ had refused to set an exact time, the Anabaptists' need for a day of reckoning became so strong that they would heed anyone who promised them, as Hut did, a definite date for their deliverance.

The most influential of these half-educated prophets of apocalypse was Melchior Hofmann, a Swabian furrier by trade, who had converted to Lutheranism in 1522, at the age of twenty-seven, and become a wandering preacher. His wanderings took him as far as Riga and Stockholm and there he published in 1526 a pamphlet explicating the twelfth chapter of Daniel and declaring that the world would end in seven years, at Easter of 1533. Hofmann divided this seven-year era roughly into two parts. In the first period, the two promised witnesses to the apocalypse, Elijah and Enoch, would appear on earth to overthrow the Pope. This would take them, as Daniel had foretold, 1,290 days. The two witnesses would be martyred, as described in Revelation, and all of the saints would be persecuted by Gog and Magog. Then, after the forty-two months of Revelation, Christ would appear.

Asked to leave Sweden, Hofmann wandered southward, preaching, entering into public disputations. He had to flee for his life from Lübeck, and he was expelled from Denmark, but in the summer of 1529 he finally reached Strasbourg, the great crossroads of the upper Rhine, a city by now so tolerant of religious diversity, it was said, that views punished on the gallows elsewhere were dismissed here with nothing worse than a public flogging. Hofmann's eccentric views kept changing. Though he still considered himself a Lutheran, he had already adopted the Zwinglian view of the Eucharist as a symbolic remembrance. Other elements of his preaching were entirely his own. He insisted that Christ had not been born of human flesh, and that no prayers should be addressed to him. And though he was not yet an Anabaptist, he startled the Strasbourg authorities by publicly demanding that this most despised of sects be given a church of its own. Hofmann not only poured forth his own views in a stream of pamphlets but transcribed and published the visions of two other Strasbourg seers, Lienhart Jost, who was generally regarded as insane, and his wife, Ursula, who spoke passionately of scorpions, rainbows and Turks.

Shortly after Melchior Hofmann formally underwent rebaptism in April of 1530, the Strasbourg city council ordered him arrested. He immediately fled to the North Sea port of Emden, where he soon baptized three hundred converts in the vestibule of the Grosse Kirche. One of these, a Dutch refugee named Jan

Volkerts, he sent back to Amsterdam as his missionary to the Netherlands, and so the Melchiorite version of the Anabaptist movement finally reached the region that had been waiting for it. Ever since the turn of the century, the growth of maritime commerce had afflicted the Low Countries with a ravenous inflation, and sporadic warfare with the Danes and the Hanseatic cities of Germany aggravated the economic problems of the region. In the early 1530s its textile exports were blocked, its fishing fleet threatened. Floods and pestilence both struck in the same year. Gangs of jobless beggars roamed the countryside. The devastation of the region was a fulfillment, in a way, of the nightmarish prophecies that had been painted two or three decades earlier by Hieronymus Bosch. And now came Hofmann's emissaries predicting the imminent end of the world.

The Catholic authorities in Amsterdam reacted fiercely. Volkerts was seized and beheaded, and so were eight of his first converts. Hofmann, an inherently gentle soul in spite of his wild preachings, was so shocked by these executions of the Melchiorites that he ordered a temporary suspension of all rebaptisms. To him, the rite of rebaptism was never more than peripheral to the momentous event on the horizon, the apocalypse. By now, Hofmann spoke openly of himself as Elijah, one of the witnesses of the Last Days, and he was deterred only by the prophecy that Elijah and Enoch were to be martyred. "The beast that ascendeth out of the bottomless pit . . . shall kill them," as John had written in Revelation. "And their dead bodies shall lie in the street of the great city."

When an old man in East Frisia prophesied to Hofmann that he would be imprisoned in Strasbourg for half a year and would then lead the 144,000 saints to victory, Hofmann seized on the prospect of a purely symbolic martyrdom. He promptly returned to Strasbourg, sent some of his pamphlets to the city council, and paraded barefoot through the streets until his inevitable arrest. Quite apart from Hofmann's provocations, the Strasbourg authorities had decided to establish some sort of theological consensus among the quarrelsome factions that had flocked to the city, and in June of 1533 they began trying to chart common ground at a prolonged synod. Hofmann duly appeared before the synod and passionately preached his views, that the divine Christ was not born of woman, that the freedom of will lost by Adam could be regained by divine illumination and rebaptism, and that Jesus would soon appear in Strasbourg. After hearing his views, the synod sentenced him to life imprisonment and ordered the expulsion of all Melchiorites from the city.

Hofmann lived in a windowless prison cell, refusing to eat anything but bread, occasionally chanting a psalm and crying out, "Woe, ye godless scribes of Strasbourg." He managed nonetheless to keep scribbling his preachings and to smuggle them out to loyal disciples who published them and spread them among his surprisingly numerous followers. By now, the coming apocalypse was Hofmann's obsession. As early as 1530, with the publication of an exegesis of Revelation, and then in an analysis of the Epistle to the Romans, Hofmann had worked out an elaborate theory that God had ordained three great awakenings. The first came at the time of Christ, and Saint Paul was the angel who then bound Satan for a thousand years. The second awakening was the preaching of Jan Hus, and it was perfectly fitting that Hus had been betrayed by the Emperor Sigismund's false promise of safe-conduct, then condemned by the Council of Constance and burned at the stake in 1415, for each glorious awakening had to be followed by what Hofmann called a "spiritual crucifixion." The forces of Antichrist, too, had their eight appointed kingdoms: Egypt, Babylon, Greece, Macedonia, Judea, Rome, the Papacy and the Holy Roman Empire. "At Constance everything was quite clear," Hofmann wrote, "since the Gospel was damned, the witness of God was burned, and the dragon Sigismund kissed the Pope's feet."

Now that God had given the world more than a century to repent, in vain, the time for the third awakening had arrived. Martin Luther had begun the process but "for his own honor and gain has delivered Christ to crucifixion." The New Jerusalem was to be Strasbourg, and it was Hofmann, as the Witness Elijah, who would lead the 144,000 apostles to save the world. Not to save it, actually, but rather to prepare it for Christ's coming. There would be grief and violence, Hofmann predicted, for "the innocent blood cries to the Lord and will not remain unavenged," but the imprisoned prophet urged his followers to keep the peace. "The true Israelites shall not avenge themselves and return evil to someone who has done evil to them," he wrote in 1533. It was the Turks, he said, who represented Gog and Magog, and God would use them to destroy the papal and imperial forces of Antichrist. "So God punishes enemy with enemy."

These preachings were too pacific for one of Hofmann's principal followers in Amsterdam. Jan Matthys, a baker from Haarlem, was a violent man, filled with dreams of future glory. He had been in trouble with the authorities as early as 1528, when he was publicly scourged for taking part in an outbreak of iconoclasm. His wife expressed doubts about his visions, so he put her aside and married a beautiful girl named Divara, who had been a nun at the Convent of St. Agnes in Haarlem. Though a convert to Melchiorite Anabaptism, Matthys refused to accept Hofmann's suspension of rebaptisms in the face of persecution. On the contrary, he went right on baptizing converts himself. Twelve of these he ordained and sent forth as his apostles, including a youth from Leyden named Jan Beukels, who was soon to become his deputy, his heir, his whirlwind.

Conceding to Hofmann the role of Elijah, Matthys declared that God had assigned to him the role of Enoch, the second witness to the coming apocalypse. This announcement bewildered the Melchiorite faithful because they considered Hofmann's leading disciple to be another Dutchman named Cornelius Polterman. "When Matthys learned of this," according to a contemporary chronicle, "he carried on with much emotion and terrifying alarm, and with great and desperate curses cast all into hell and to the devils for eternity who would not hear his voice ... and accept him as the true Enoch." The frightened parishioners shut themselves up in a room and fasted and prayed for guidance, and then, says the chronicle, "they attached themselves to Jan Matthys and became obedient."

In Matthys were united the dark strains of zealotry, rage and violence that the brethren who had first baptized each other in Zurich could scarcely have recognized as a variant of their faith. In slightly different circumstances, Matthys might have spent his life in turbulent obscurity, but his passionate sense of mission was exactly the force needed to create the new Jerusalem in the German city of Münster.

On a sandy plain in Westphalia, about halfway between Bremen and Cologne, the town of Münster was originally known as Mimegardevoord. Charlemagne made it the seat of a bishopric in about 800, but it was not until the thirteenth century that it prospered as a member of the Hanseatic League. Its ruling bishop, ecclesiastically subordinate to the archbishop of Cologne, was also a prince of the Empire, and his independent territory occupied about half the province of Westphalia. Bishop Friedrich managed to suppress the first stirrings of the Reformation, as well as all support for the Great Peasants' War, but Münster, by now a commercial center of about fifteen thousand souls, kept encountering new troubles. In the fall of 1529 there was an epidemic of a deadly fever known as the "English sweating sickness." The harvest was ruined, the price of rye tripled, and famine was everywhere. Yet the imperial authorities demanded new taxes to resist the Turks. "The misery," the archbishop of Dortmund wrote to his superior, "is appalling and indescribable."

The coming of the Reformation in Münster, as in many of these autonomous German principalities, was largely the story of one man. In this instance, it was a blacksmith's son named Bernhardt Rothmann. With money secretly provided by the craft guilds, he had studied theology at the University of Deventer, then returned home as a schoolmaster, then became a chaplain, then was dismissed for preaching what sounded like the Lutheran heresy. The rituals of the mass, he declared, were less important than faith in Christ and brotherly love. Like many incipient and uncertain rebels, Rothmann went to Wittenberg in the spring of 1531 and then on to Strasbourg. He returned in July, determined on reform. Barred from his old church, he tried preaching in the yard outside, and the townspeople flocked to hear him. Bishop Friedrich demanded his expulsion, but the city council, which had the legal authority to appoint and depose all priests, demurred. When Rothmann and his followers proclaimed a basically Lutheran statement of faith in January of 1532, the council granted him the use of the Church of St. Lamberti and of a guild house as his residence. One reason for this shift in power was that several council members, notably a prosperous and influential cloth merchant named Bernhardt Knipperdolling, had become infected by Lutheranism. Another was that the Catholic forces were in considerable disarray. Bishop Friedrich abdicated and sold his office for forty thousand gulden in March of 1532; his successor, Erich of Osnabrück, died suddenly after some heavy drinking in May, and several more weeks passed before the installation of yet another bishop, Franz von Waldeck.

Rothmann and Knipperdolling formed a powerful alliance, Rothmann as religious leader of the reform movement and Knipperdolling as its political leader. With the backing of the craft guilds, they not only dominated the wavering city council but they also could call up the noisy and stone-throwing crowds that often proved a decisive force in German local politics of the early sixteenth century. On Christmas night, a force of about one thousand citizens even surprised and seized a group of clerics and held them hostage. In February of 1533, Bishop Waldeck gave way and agreed to a formal treaty by which all of Münster's ten churches except the cathedral became Lutheran.

The reform leaders had already moved beyond Lutheranism, however. Rothmann presided over a Lord's Supper at which he freely distributed bread sprinkled with wine. He also denounced infant baptism. "It is not possible for someone to receive Christian baptism," he declared, "unless he repents his sins, has faith, and asks for [baptism], thereby showing his wish henceforth to live a new life of obedience to God." While the reform leaders were moving toward Anabaptism—they did not yet urge the crime of rebaptism—reports of the turmoil in Münster spread through Westphalia and even into the Netherlands. These reports brought to Münster first a trickle and then a stream of Melchiorite Anabaptist refugees and a variety of other persecuted radicals and visionaries. When the Lutherans on the city council finally joined forces with the Catholics in November to order the immediate expulsion of the increasingly radical Rothmann, the preacher gathered his armed followers into the marketplace and refused to leave. The council backed down and said he could stay if he gave up his controversial preaching. Rothmann refused to be silent. "The godless papists ... demanded violently that the ministers should be exiled, their noses and ears cut off and hung up between two dogs," Rothmann later recalled, "but God prevented that."

On January 6, 1534, the eve of Epiphany, two wandering preachers named Bartholomäus Boekbinder and Willem de Kuiper appeared at the gates of Münster. They announced that God had sent a new prophet to herald the coming end of the world. He was known as Jan Matthys of Haarlem, but he was truly the Enoch whose coming had been foretold in Scripture. Münster, they said, was the chosen city, and all its inhabitants should be baptized in the new faith. They rebaptized Bernhardt Rothmann, and then wandered off again. Rothmann took on the mission. Within a week, he and his helpers rebaptized no less than 1,400 of the citizens of Münster. At the end of that week, another important newcomer arrived: one of Jan Matthys' twelve apostles, Jan Beukels. Just twenty-five years of age, handsome and eloquent, Beukels was the illegitimate son of a Dutch mayor and a woman from Münster. He had worked as a tailor and innkeeper in Leyden, but his ambitions went far beyond that. He had traveled to Flanders, England, Portugal. He had a talent for theatrics, street spectacles that he wrote and staged himself. He also liked flirting, and no sooner had he arrived in Münster than he began courting the daughter of the reform leader, Bernhardt Knipperdolling.

The Catholic bishop and the Lutheran councilors were equally appalled by this sudden infestation of the Anabaptist heresy. The council once again ordered Rothmann to leave Münster, and Rothmann once again refused. On the contrary, bands of Anabaptists attempted an uprising and seized control of several main streets. The council quieted them by promising religious liberty for everyone. On February 9, however, a traveler from Dortmund brought a report, which later proved false, that Bishop von Waldeck had assembled a force of three thousand soldiers and intended to recapture control of Münster. The Anabaptists took up arms to defend themselves. After closing the gates of the city, a band of five hundred men seized control of the marketplace and part of the city hall. The legal authorities clung to the rest of the city hall and sent out an appeal for help to neighboring towns. They also managed to arrest and imprison Knipperdolling and twenty-five other Anabaptists. The Anabaptists began tolling the bell of St. Lamberti's. Crowds of the faithful rushed to the city hall, where they sang and prayed and prophesied the imminent arrival of a legion of angels.

It was a new report that Bishop von Waldeck was bringing troops, however, that reestablished a truce inside the city. The Lutheran councilors suspected with good reason that if the bishop entered Münster with an armed force, he would do his best to repress the entire Reformation. The Anabaptists, for their part, knew they were not strong enough to fight all their enemies at once. Besides, they understood that the chief burgomaster, Hermann Tylbeck, was sympathetic to their cause. By the time the bishop reached the city walls, the Lutherans and the Anabaptists had reached an agreement: complete religious freedom, a general amnesty and the release of all prisoners. Burgomaster Tylbeck told the bishop to stay away. In this triumph Rothmann saw the influence of supernatural forces. "Three suns shone at the same time," he later wrote, "and fiery clouds arose around and over the city,"

And the Anabaptists from the surrounding towns of Germany and Holland kept pouring in. The Münsterites were promising them both safety from Hapsburg persecution and the rewards of the coming apocalypse. "He who seeketh his everlasting salvation," Rothmann declared in a circular letter to other Anabaptist communities, "let him forsake all worldly goods, and let him with wife and with children come unto us here to the New Jerusalem, to Zion, to the Temple of Solomon!" They came with their wagons and on foot, in large clusters and one by one, praying and chanting, "Hosannah!"

Jan Matthys himself, a tall man with a thick black beard, arrived with his beautiful bride, Divara. And with the Anabaptists came not only refugees from persecution but also the unemployed and the destitute and even a certain number of criminals, "all fugitive, banished and evildoing citizens," as an official report in Cologne put it. The faithful saw this as a time of omens and portents. Bands of women threw themselves to the ground, writhed and shrieked and stretched out their arms to form crosses. Some claimed to see clouds of black and blue fire descending from heaven. Matthys appeared at St. Lamberti's with two stone tablets and announced that he had just spoken with God. "Almighty be our doctrine and our power," he declared, "and praised be the will of our father, who has sent us here to found the New Jerusalem."

As these newcomers swarmed into Münster, an outward tide was also running. City councilors, wealthy merchants, the orthodox and the respectable began disappearing. Many of them went furtively, leaving behind not only their possessions but their families until they could establish new homes in safer territory. Such flight had its hazards. Johannes van der Wieck, the town syndicus and a leading Lutheran, was caught and beheaded by the troops of the bishop. With the city government disintegrating, it fell time, on February 23, for the election of a new city council. In the prevailing state of excitement, the result was foreordained. Knipperdolling became the new burgomaster and head of an Anabaptist majority on the city council, but the real ruler was the prophet Jan Matthys. The Anabaptists thus acquired, more or less legally, a territory of their own. At the very least, they thought it would be a citadel and a sanctuary, what Wittenberg had been to Luther and Zurich to Zwingli. But when Christ returned to earth, as he soon would, Münster would become the holy city of the world. "O Saints of God," as Melchior Hofmann wrote to his followers from his prison cell in Strasbourg, "raise your heads, your hearts, your eyes, your ears. Your salvation is before the door. All the plagues have been fulfilled save that of the seventh angel of vengeance."

The angel soon appeared. The day after the election, a crowd sacked the cathedral and burned all its works of art, its books and manuscripts. Matthys talked darkly of killing all the godless. "His head became twice as big as before," as Knipperdolling recalled, "and he began to shout, 'Murder! Kill!' " Knipperdolling, officially the lord mayor, could only persuade Matthys to allow dissenters one week, until March 2, in which to be baptized or to leave. Everything they left behind was to be confiscated. The new authorities were soon administering as many as three hundred baptisms a day in the market-place, but those who stubbornly refused had to face expulsion. On the Friday before the deadline, Anabaptists with pikes and clubs drove even old women and children through the snow-covered streets and out the city gates in weather so bitter that, according to one account, "one ought not to have hunted a dog from the town."

When the week expired, Münster had committed itself, as totally as Montsé-gur, to its heresy. The citizens who considered themselves the vanguard of the 144,000 saints of Revelation all stood subject to the imperial death penalty, and it was with imperial sanction that Franz von Waldeck laid siege on Febru-ary 28 to the city of which he was legally the bishop. His troops, raised by feu-dal levy and reinforced by mercenaries, began the laborious process of throw-ing up earthworks. But Münster was stoutly fortified, with eighty-two cannons, and the saints labored as hard as the mercenaries in strengthening their de-fenses. The spirit and tenacity of these defenders, many of them women, has puzzled orthodox historians who regard them merely as visionaries. After a decade of ruthless persecution, after a decade of faithful reliance on the prom-ises of Christ's return to earth, the Anabaptists had now found a sanctuary to be guarded, and they guarded it in full knowledge that it had already become a trap. Under sentence of death, they lived in a kind of exaltation, passionately loyal to the men who called themselves their prophets.

Just as the Anabaptist leaders felt entitled to confiscate the possessions of ev-eryone who had left the city, they now decreed the abolition of all money. All gold and silver was to be delivered to the city council. "A Christian should have no money . . . ," said Rothmann. "All that Christian brethren or sisters have belongs to the one as much as the other. The brethren shall possess no other thing but their food, clothes, house and home." Over even these necessities the prophets soon claimed authority. Three deacons in each parish entered every house and noted down how much beef or corn had been stored and how much the owner might keep for his own needs. Once the authorities had impounded great stores of food, they decreed that the citizens should eat it together. Next to each city gate they designated one house as a communal dining hall, and ordered that each meal be accompanied by Bible readings and hymns. All work was henceforth paid for in kind, but the goal, as Beukels put it, was that "all things were to be in common, there was to be no private property, and nobody was to do any more work, but simply trust in God."

These measures seem to have been accepted willingly, but there was undeniably an element of coercion. One day early in the siege, the prophets summoned all citizens to the cathedral, singled out those who had not been baptized until the final Friday before the deadline, then ordered them to take off their armor, lie on their faces, and pray to God to grant them grace. After nearly four hours of prayer, during which the prostrate citizens began to fear that they might be summarily executed, Beukels finally strode to the high altar and announced, "Dear brethren, it is God's will that I make known to you that you have received grace from God, and shall remain with us and be his holy people."

There were cries of rejoicing and prayer, for by these strange theatrics Matthys and Beukels were not only threatening the laggard but unifying their disparate followers into a commune capable of withstanding the bishop's siege. When the prophets saw a need for harsher measures, they did not hesitate. A blacksmith named Hubert Rüscher ventured to criticize the Anabaptist leaders and suggest that they might have "a devil in their bodies." A citizen who heard him informed the authorities. The smith was haled before a general assembly, which condemned him to death forthwith. Matthys thereupon shot him with a musket, and Beukels finished him off with a halberd. Tylbeck, the former burgomaster, protested against such summary justice and was immediately imprisoned for his impertinence.

The struggle for Münster naturally caused great excitement all across Germany and the Netherlands. Anabaptist groups incited one another to new demonstrations of faith, and the authorities responded to every such demonstration with new arrests and punishments. From Münster itself the besieged saints kept appealing for help, still promising sanctuary. "God has made known to us," said one such message, "that all should get ready to go to the New Jerusalem, the city of saints, because he is going to punish the world. . . . Flee out of Babylon, and deliver every man his soul . . . for this is the time of the Lord's vengeance."

The focal point of this agitation was Amsterdam, which was believed to harbor no fewer than five thousand Anabaptists. One of their prophets, Dirck Tasch, predicted that "there will be a darkness in the city for three days, and then the Lord will turn it over to his saints without bloodshed." On March 22, five of these saints went marching naked through the streets, brandishing swords and crying out, "Repent" and "Woe to the godless." They were promptly arrested, tortured, and burned. One of their followers went to identify the corpses but could not do so, he later wrote, because "they were so frightfully changed by fire and smoke, and those on the wheels were not recognizable either." In Deventer, Campe, and Zwolle, the authorities staged house-to-house searches for Anabaptists, and in Utrecht some five hundred of the faithful were imprisoned.

To escape all this, the Anabaptists organized a great pilgrimage to Münster. They urged refugees from all over Holland to gather at noon of March 24 at the Bergklooster near Hasselt in the province of Overijssel, where the prophet Jeremiah would meet them and lead them to the New Jerusalem. At the appointed time, twenty-seven boatloads containing about three thousand Anabaptists, including many women and children, converged on the Bergklooster (another three ships sank en route). They were met not by the prophet Jeremiah but by a handful of local police. Though the Anabaptists had armed themselves with about 1,500 weapons, they offered no resistance. The police executed half a dozen men whom they took to be leaders, then confiscated all arms and money and ordered the pilgrams to return home. Münster remained under siege.

Inside the city, shortly before Easter, Jan Matthys invited his disciples to a last supper. It seems to have been pure theater, but Matthys' sincerity can be judged only by the outcome. In the middle of the supper, Matthys suddenly turned grave. He seemed to be listening to a voice from above. After a few minutes, he threw up his arms and rose to his feet and said, exactly as in Matthew's account of Christ at Gethsemane, "O Father, not as I will but as thou wilt." Then he moved around the table, shaking each guest by the hand and kissing him on the mouth and saying to each one, "God's peace be with you all." Then he went home with his wife, Divara, leaving his disciples to wonder at his behavior. What Matthys seemed to foresee was not exactly condemnation and crucifixion, for Matthys was no lamblike imitator of Christ, but rather the final struggle foretold by all the prophets, including Melchior Hofmann and himself. The next day, therefore, he assembled some twenty of his armed followers to do battle. Though they were few in number, he assured them, they would be invulnerable because they were fulfilling the Lord's great plan. He then led them out the city gate and attacked the camp of the bishop's mercenaries. The battle did not last long. One of the bishop's men stabbed the bearded prophet with a pike, and the prophet's followers were slaughtered. The bishop's mercenaries cut off Matthys' head and hacked his body to pieces and then called out to the watching citizens of Münster to come out and collect what remained of their prophet.

Jan Beukels did not waste a minute mourning the fallen leader. "God willed that Matthys should die," the handsome young Dutchman declared to the crowd he had summoned to the cathedral. "His time had come, and God has let him die, to the end that you should not place all your faith in him. . . . God shall raise up unto us another prophet who shall be greater and higher than was even Jan Matthys." Beukels left little doubt that he himself was this new prophet, and, before any other leaders could assert a rival authority, he announced that God had appeared to him in a vision and instructed him to reorganize the entire government of the New Jerusalem. He thereupon declared the elected city council abolished. In its place he named twelve "elders," representing the twelve tribes of Israel. "All things which the elders determine," said the new tables of the law that Beukels drew up, "the prophet Jan of Leyden shall, as the true servant of the Almighty and of his holy authority, proclaim to the congregation." Chief among his deputies was Knipperdolling, once the political leader of the movement but now notable chiefly as Beukels' father-in-law. Beukels' constitution made Knipperdolling "guardian of public order" and assigned him four attendants.

The public order was sternly administered in the New Jerusalem. "If we are sons of God and have been baptized in Christ, then all evil must disappear from our midst," said Beukels. His new regime decreed the death penalty not only for murder and sedition but for blasphemy, spreading scandal, adultery, avarice, fraud, lying, criticizing one's parents, or even complaining. The first men on whom these laws were demonstrated were a band of mercenaries, apparently deserters from the bishop's army, who got drunk in a Münster tavern and threatened the tavernkeeper. Arrested and brought before the twelve elders, they begged for mercy. The elders singled out two of them as examples and ordered them tied to a pair of lime trees in the cathedral close and then shot. The next day, four more were tied to the lime trees and shot. From then on, Beukels' orders were obeyed with alacrity.

He organized all of the town's resources for its defense. Even the church bells and the metal coating on the church roofs were melted down into ammunition. On Whitsunday, May 24, after three months of siege, Bishop von Waldeck sent a formal demand for surrender. Beukels rejected it. The bishop then ordered his mercenaries to storm the walls. Beukels' sentries spotted the attackers' first movements and sounded the alarm to bring hundreds of defenders scrambling to the walls. Even women and children joined in loading the cannon with shrapnel and throwing hot pitch at the attackers. The Anabaptists' resistance was so spirited that the bishop's forces abandoned their attack after a loss of about two hundred dead and wounded.

Beukels took advantage of his victory to impose the most radical of his innovations on the New Jerusalem. Rothmann announced in the cathedral that, in keeping with the Biblical injunction to be fruitful and multiply, and following the precedents of Solomon and David and other kings of ancient Israel, polygamy was henceforth not only permitted but ordered. Everyone without a spouse was given three days in which to find one and get married. Beukels himself led the way by marrying Divara, the beautiful widow of the slaughtered Jan Matthys, as well as two other young women. Ultimately, he would acquire a harem of fifteen wives, none over twenty-one. Rothmann also found himself three new brides (he eventually acquired nine). When Knipperdolling's wife objected to the invasion of stepwives into her home, she was forced to stand for hours in the marketplace, begging forgiveness.

The Anabaptists' enemies immediately seized on this polygamy as evidence of the whole movement's folly and depravity, but it can be argued that Beukels was simply using his customary flair to deal with a serious problem. Ever since the flight of the respectable burghers on the arrival of the Anabaptists, the women left behind had greatly outnumbered the men. Casualties in the repeated skirmishing outside the walls made the imbalance worse. Out of Münster's current population of about 12,000, the adult men now numbered no more than perhaps 2,500. Quite apart from the question of sexual irregularities, all the laws and customs of the sixteenth century decreed that a woman could not simply live by herself; she had to be cared for by a father, a husband, or an institution. Although polygamy sounds scandalous, the laws of the New Jerusalem still decreed the death penalty for all adultery, fornication or lewd behavior.

Most of the single women of Münster accepted their fate with stoicism. It was among the men that the new law sparked revolt. A blacksmith and former alderman named Heinrich Möllenbecke organized a group of about two hundred dissidents, many of them relatives of women who had been coerced into marriage. At midnight of July 30, a week after the polygamy decree, they broke into the homes of Beukels, Rothmann and Knipperdolling, tied them all up and took them as prisoners to the city hall. Möllenbecke summoned all citizens to the city hall to support his putsch, and he told them that he was going to surrender the city to the bishop; but though his speech was greeted only with shrugs and mutterings, he overconfidently decided to wait until morning to throw open the city gates. When Möllenbecke's drumbeats sounded in the morning, however, a large crowd loyal to Beukels surrounded the city hall and bombarded it with cannon until the rebels surrendered.

Beukels, freed from captivity, was not merciful. He ordered Möllenbecke and seven accomplices bound to the cathedral lime trees by iron bands around their necks. After pronouncing the death sentence, he invited witnesses from the crowd to take turns shooting at the condemned men. Once these eight had been executed, Beukels ordered Knipperdolling, the guardian of public order, to deal with the rest. Knipperdolling, outfitted with the great sword of state and the red mantle of the executioner, beheaded the rest of the conspirators, fifty-eight men in all.

The bishop's army, reinforced with troops provided by the Landgrave of Hesse and the ecclesiastical authorities of Cologne and Cleves, had spent the summer months digging trenches and bringing up cannon. On August 31, after three days of fierce bombardment, they tried again to storm the city walls. This time, they managed to breach the outer breastworks, but only because Beukels had planned it that way. Once the bishop's vanguard filled the area between the breastworks and the main wall, the defenders swept them with gunfire, arrows and stones. The women joined in, with boiling water, quicklime and wreaths of burning pitch. After three vain assaults, the bishop's forces once again withdrew to their camp, leaving the battleground outside the walls strewn with bodies and debris. "Dear brethren," cried Beukels to his jubilant forces, "have we not a strong God? Let us now be joyful and give thanks to the Father."

Beukels might now have marched out of Münster and broken the siege forever, but instead he again used his victory to expand his own authority. This time, he made himself king, not just of Münster but of the whole world. The event was elaborately staged. A limping goldsmith named Johann Dusentschur appeared in the marketplace and declared that he had had a vision. God had told him that Beukels should be crowned king of the world, heir to King David of Israel, and that he should reign until Jesus returned to earth to take the crown for himself. The prophet called upon the twelve elders to resign their offices, which they promptly did, and he thereupon handed the sword of office to Beukels. "In the face of the whole people of God, I hereby declare you King of the New Zion," he said. Beukels accepted gracefully. "God has chosen me to be king over the whole world," he told the citizenry. "But I tell you, brethren and sisters, I would rather tend the swine or follow the plow than be king."

Beukels then began to create for himself a royal court more grandiose than his pious subjects had ever imagined. He had the town craftsmen make him, from the money that had been confiscated at the start of the siege, an imperial crown and a royal crown, both of gold and precious stones. He wore a gold chain bearing a golden globe ornamented with the crossed swords of divine and secular justice and inscribed with the words "A king of righteousness everywhere." He carried a jewel-studded golden scepter. He wore his sword in a golden sheath on a golden belt. He minted gold medallions inscribed "One king over all, one God, one faith, one baptism."

He rode a white horse to his new throne in the marketplace. He surrounded himself with a retinue of wives and courtiers, all dressed in new costumes of red and blue silk. He gave out royal offices to his main supporters. Rothmann became royal orator and steward, Knipperdolling vice-steward. Hermann Tylbeck, the former burgomaster whom Matthys had thrown in jail, became master of ceremonies. Divara became queen, and Beukels' fourteen other young wives all had to do her homage. The King reserved for himself the office of public executioner.

Whether the purpose of all this pageantry was to impress and inspire the besieged citizens or to distract them from the dangers that surrounded them or simply to satisfy Beukels' megalomania is a question that remains unsettled. Visions of divine revelation now became almost a commonplace method of government. The prophet Dusentschur announced one day that God had told him that the citizens of Münster had too many clothes. All that the men really needed, he said, was one coat, two pairs of trousers and three shirts; for the women, one skirt, one mantle and four chemises. Beukels immediately assigned a squad of deacons to go from house to house and enforce the divine rationing. They collected eighty-three wagonloads of "surplus" clothing.

Knipperdolling, apparently resentful of his son-in-law's usurpations, tried to adopt the new tactics himself. He suddenly appeared before Beukels' throne and began leaping around, crying, "Holy, holy, holy," and declaring that he too had had a divine vision. He said God had commanded him to become the court fool, so he continued prancing around until he sprawled over a bench. Then he picked himself up, announced that the Holy Spirit had passed through him, and began kissing various courtiers on the lips, saying to each, "God has made you holy." Beukels tried to silence his father-in-law by disbanding the whole court for the day, but Knipperdolling returned the following morning and sat in the royal throne before Beukels got there. "It is I who of right should be the king here, since it is I who made you what you are," he announced. Beukels angrily walked out and went home, then returned and told his followers, "Brethren and sisters, pay no heed to what Knipperdolling has said, for he is not in his right mind." He then delivered an emotional speech on the glorious prospects that God had promised the saints of Münster, and he concluded by ordering Knipperdolling arrested. After three days in prison, Knipperdolling won his release by begging forgiveness and saying he had been led astray by the Devil.

Challenged in his authority, Beukels invited the entire population to a feast and then announced that God had appeared to him in a vision and told him to abdicate. The faithful Dusentschur rose to say that he too had seen a vision in which God had told him that Beukels must remain king. The crowd at the feast cheered as Beukels agreed to accept Dusentschur's vision as more authoritative than his own. In the midst of all these theatricals, though, Beukels knew perfectly well that his New Jerusalem could not withstand the bishop's siege indefinitely. For the first few months the siege had not been complete, and smugglers passed fairly regularly between the lines. All through the autumn of 1534, however, the twice-rebuffed bishop kept strengthening his earthworks and tightening his cordon. Beukels knew that the city's food supplies would hardly last through the coming winter.

In mid-October, Dusentschur announced another vision: twenty-seven apostles should be sent out in all four directions, north to Osnabrück, east to Warendorf, south to Soest, west to Coesfeld, to summon to the defense of the New Jerusalem the rest of the 144,000 saints of Revelation. He, Dusentschur, would lead the way. And let there be no secrecy. Let the apostles announce themselves in each town they visited and warn that any attempt to interfere with the gathering of the saints would immediately bring down God's wrath. And so it was done. The apostles set forth in all directions, announced their mission, and were promptly arrested and executed. Only one of them returned to Münster, a former schoolmaster named Heinrich Graes, who said he had miraculously escaped, still in chains, from the bishop's prison. He did not say that he had agreed, in exchange for his freedom, to become the bishop's spy.

In these waning months of 1534, Rothmann published and smuggled out into the world two pamphlets entitled *Restitution* and *Announcement of Vengeance* to proclaim the triumph of the saints of Münster. God had decreed three ages of man, Rothmann explained—the age of sin, which ended in the Flood, the age of persecution, which was just ending,* and now the age of vengeance. It was Christ himself who had established the kingdom of Münster in preparation for his own imminent return to earth. "The glory of all the saints is

---

* Since the Babylonian Captivity of 70 years had lasted 20 times as long as God's traditional punishment of 3½ years, Rothmann estimated, 20 times 70 amounted to 1,400 years, and since the church had gone astray about 100 years after the Crucifixion, the end of the era was clearly at hand.

to wreak vengeance . . . ," Rothmann wrote. "Revenge without mercy must be taken of all who are not marked with the Sign."

Beukels' next messengers went out in secret, or so he thought, just before Christmas. Perhaps because of the messengers' instructions, or perhaps because of Graes's spying, a whole series of Anabaptist plots suddenly came to light early in 1535. In Utrecht, Maastricht and Wesel, the authorities charged the Anabaptists with arming themselves for revolution. In Leyden and Groningen there was street fighting, and several fires broke out before the Anabaptists could be taken to prison. And when they asked the imprisoned Melchior Hofmann what he made of all this, he could only repeat that Christ would soon come to Strasbourg, to liberate him and the world. It was a message that he was to go on repeating throughout ten years of captivity until he died in his cell in 1543.

The only successful Anabaptist insurgent was a former mercenary named Jan van Geelen, who led two hundred of the faithful in a victorious skirmish against the Stadtholder of Frisia, Georg Schenk van Toutenburg. That triumph late in March immediately attracted more followers. Within a week, van Geelen commanded a force of three hundred men, accompanied by several hundred women and children. With this he seized the Old Cloister at Bolsward and sent out an appeal for support: "As you value the Gospel and love God, come to us in the cloister without fail, for God has given it as a place of refuge for his people." The Stadtholder mobilized a force of two hundred mercenaries, reinforced by local militia, and though van Geelen beat off the first attacks, the Stadtholder's cannon finally broke down the walls of the cloister. The mercenaries swarmed in to slaughter most of the defenders. One of the few who escaped was van Geelen.

With an audacity that verged on folly, van Geelen slipped into Amsterdam and proceeded to organize the seizure of the city hall. He seems to have thought that if he could strike in secret he could seize the whole city government, and that such a coup would inspire other Anabaptists to a general uprising. On the night of May 10, during a dinner staged for one of the city's guilds, van Geelen charged in with sixty armed men, shouting, "Kill! Kill the godless!" They cut down a burgomaster and one watchman of the guard, but the assembled diners fled to safety. A crowd of citizens soon surrounded the city hall, and the skirmishing ended with the Anabaptists trapped inside the building they had captured. Twenty of van Geelen's own men slipped away during the night, and when morning came, the counterattack began. Van Geelen saw his men being picked off, one after another, then decided that his only remaining hope was to escape the torture that inevitably awaited him. He climbed out onto the roof of the city hall, exposed himself to the besiegers' gunfire, and plunged to the street. Only twelve surviving Anabaptists were captured and executed.

Inside Münster, after a year of siege, the stores of food were finally running out. "At first, the people ate horses, head and feet as well," wrote one of the survivors, Heinrich Gresbeck. "They ate cats, dogs, mice, rats, slugs, fish, frogs, and grass." Beukels resorted to still stranger tactics in an effort to keep up his followers' morale. One night, he ran barefoot along the city wall, crying, "Israel rejoice! Thy deliverance is near!" He renamed all the streets and public places to obliterate their Catholic origins. He divided the whole world into twelve dukedoms and staged elections of the twelve dukes who should someday rule beyond the walls of Münster. He offered hope of salvation by Easter, and when Easter passed he said that God could not be held to fixed times. "Do you want to set a deadline for God?" he cried. "No, God will tolerate no deadlines. You must be free from all sin, from all sins, then God will rescue us."

Beukels talked grandly of making a sortie and fighting his way to the Netherlands, but the only people who actually emerged from Münster in April were several hundred famished refugees. As soon as the bedraggled refugees reached the bishop's lines, however, four men were promptly executed and hung up as a warning. The women and children were ordered to remain in the fields between the lines. The bishop sought the advice of his allies, the archbishop of Cologne and the Prince-Bishop of Cleves, and they both urged him to drive the refugees back into the city. When the bishop's troops ordered them back, however, they lay down and refused to move. The bishop kept them trapped there for a month, then interned the starving survivors in neighboring villages.

Inside Münster, Beukels' rule was hardly less Draconian. Hoarding food was punished by death. One woman was beheaded for denying her husband in bed, another for insulting a preacher. On one day there were no fewer than fifty-two executions. Beukels executed one of his own wives for disobedience, and all the others fled the city, leaving only Queen Divara behind. Sometimes the bodies of the executed were quartered and nailed up on display. Still the famine worsened. People boiled and ate old shoes and the bark of trees.

It was treachery, though, that finally undermined the New Jerusalem. Two dissidents, Gresbeck and Hans Eck, the latter a member of Beukels' bodyguard, escaped from the city and gave the bishop's forces a detailed report on gaps in the city's defenses. On the night of June 24, in the midst of a thunderstorm, they guided a specially picked force of four hundred men over the narrowest moat to the most weakly defended gate, the Kreuztor. With scaling ladders, the attackers stormed the watchhouse, found most of the defenders asleep, and slaughtered them. From one they first extorted the password, "Earth."

The attackers advanced as far as the cathedral before the Anabaptists roused their forces and counterattacked. There were perhaps eight hundred of them still able to fight. They trapped most of the bishop's men in one narrow street, but one of the mercenaries' captains found a doorway that permitted an escape. The street fighting surged back and forth until three in the morning. Then the bishop's forces asked for a truce. Beukels was willing to talk. But while they parleyed, one of the bishop's men slipped off to an unguarded wall and signaled for reinforcements. Just as dawn was breaking, a relief column managed to break through one of the city gates. That reopened the fighting all around the cathedral.

One of the invaders, Johann Reichel, smashed his way into Beukels' palace and nearly captured the king himself. Beukels threw his helmet at Reichel and then fled through a secret door in the wainscotting. Reichel searched through the rest of the palace and found Queen Divara in bed. He forced her to give him the keys to all the city gates, and thus the New Jerusalem was finally thrown open on every side.

Still the Anabaptists fought on. Some three hundred of them fell back on the marketplace and took shelter behind a defensive ring of wagons. They still had two or three cannons that held off the attackers, but when they were offered a safe-conduct they finally laid down their arms. By midmorning, the battle had turned into a rout. The bishop's men stormed the city hall and slaughtered everyone who had taken refuge there. The last resistance endured in the St. Lamberti Church, where four Anabaptists installed themselves in the tower and killed anyone who tried to enter. The attackers managed to kill three of them, then burst into the tower and threw the last defender out the window.

It was noon, June 25, 1535, the 482nd day of the bishop's siege. Once the fighting ended, the butchery began. The bishop's troops ignored any safe-conducts that had been given. They murdered and plundered as they pleased. Almost all the men were killed and about half the women, between three and four thousand in all. Hermann Tylbeck, who had once been burgomaster, was found in the Aegidi Monastery. The troops killed him and flung his corpse into a sewer. Beukels was found hiding in a tower near the Aegidi Gate and held for trial. Queen Divara was beheaded. Of all the Anabaptist leaders, only Pastor Rothmann escaped. At least, no trace of his body was ever found. When Bishop von Waldeck arrived in his city after four days of carnage, his troops presented to him the keys to the city and the golden chain of its deposed king.

"Are you a king?" the bishop asked his prisoner.

"Are you a bishop?" retorted Beukels.

The bishop asked what right Beukels had had to usurp power over the citizens of Münster, and Beukels asked the bishop who gave him the right to rule the city. The Pope and the Emperor, said the bishop. "And I have been called to the leadership by God and his prophets," said Beukels.

It was apparently Beukels' own idea that the bishop could retrieve the expenses of his campaign by putting his captive in a cage and exhibiting him for one gulden in the various towns of the diocese. The bishop agreed, and so it was done. After this demonstration of orthodox authority, Beukels was thrown into the dungeon of one of the bishop's castles. There, while he lay in chains, scholarly theologians came to interrogate him and induce him to recant. He apparently did offer a partial recantation, and he even offered to devote the rest of his life, if it were spared, to persuading other Anabaptists to return "silent and obedient" to the Church of Rome. His recantation was judged inadequate, or else the bishop was simply unprepared to accept any recantation as a substitute for execution.

Beukels was taken back to Münster on January 19, together with Knipperdolling and another Anabaptist leader named Bernard Krechting, for the rituals of trial. The execution came three days later, on a platform in the marketplace. The bishop and his officers watched in satisfaction. "The executioners first of all enclosed the King in a collar of iron," according to a contemporary chronicle, "and bound him to a stake. Thereupon they seized glowing pincers and proceeded to pinch the king in all parts of his body, in such a manner that flames blazed out from every part that was touched, until nearly all who were standing in the marketplace were sickened by the stench that arose." Beukels apparently suffered in silence, but the chronicle records that the other two "made known their pain with much lamentation and crying." Knipperdolling even tried to strangle himself on the collar around his neck. When the executioners saw this, they restrained him by passing a rope through his mouth and tying his head more tightly to the stake. Then they tore out the three men's tongues and stabbed them to the heart with daggers.

The three bodies were placed in cages and hoisted to the tower of St. Lamberti's Church, and there they hung on display for many years. In fact, they remained there until the end of the nineteenth century, when the tower was judged to be structurally unsafe and torn down. The three cages had by then become such a part of the city's traditions that they were reinstalled in the rebuilt tower, and, even through the bombings of World War II, they hang there to this day.

*

The rise and fall of the Anabaptists do not figure prominently in most historians' accounts of the early sixteenth century. Like Charles V himself, they have devoted more attention to the Emperor's endless wars with King Francis I of France. This was, besides, the age of Henry VIII, of Cortez and Magellan, of Michelangelo and Copernicus. It was also an age of global exploration and burgeoning technology, the start of the slave trade and capitalism ascendant.

But it is still known as the age of Martin Luther. The great survivor, hidden away in the Wartburg until his safety could be assured, protected for the rest of his life by the princely politics of Germany, outlasted all rivals and enemies, even that Pope whom he had denounced as Antichrist. And when Zwingli was cut down in battle against the Catholic cantons in 1531, cut down by a spear wound in the thigh, then clubbed on the head, then offered the services of a priest, which he declined, and so was recognized and killed, his body quartered and the fragments mixed with dung and ceremonially burned—when this happened to Zwingli, with whom he had debated on the Eucharist just two years earlier, Luther gloated to a friend, "Such is the end of the glory which they sought through their blasphemies against the Lord's Supper." And to another: "I was a true prophet when I said that God would not suffer [their] impious blasphemies."

In his old age, the true prophet went on railing. In *Against the Jews and their Lies,* he demanded that the Jews be forcibly converted or else expelled from Germany. "Their schools or synagogues should be set on fire," he wrote, "and whatever does not burn up should be covered with dirt. . . .Their homes should likewise be broken down and destroyed. . . .They ought to be put under one roof or in a stable, like gypsies, in order that they may realize that they are not masters in our land, as they boast." As for the Anabaptists, Luther formally endorsed execution for all of them, not, he said, because of their religious views but for blasphemy and sedition—the refusal to take an oath being itself seditious. "Although it seems cruel to punish them with the sword," said Luther, "it is crueler that they condemn the ministry of the Word . . . and in this way seek to subvert the social order."

That was never really true, and yet the Anabaptist moveme
and dishonored by Münster. In the mockery and contempt c
had acquired a quality of both cruelty and lunacy. In the eyes
ers, it had lost its innocence, its passionate belief in the imitati
fering, its simple and all-justifying commitment to Conrad Gr
"true Christian believers are sheep among wolves, sheep for the slaugh
first taking up arms against their persecutors, the Anabaptists had denied their
best principles, and in laying their arms down again they had made their own
denial in vain.

The movement lost its messianic vitality forever, but it did survive in other
forms. Its principal savior was Menno Simons, a Catholic priest from Utrecht,
who had not even come to Anabaptism at the time of Münster but whose younger brother was one of those executed after Jan van Geelen's seizure of the Old
Cloister at Bolsward. "The blood of these people, though misled, fell . . . hot on
my heart," Menno later wrote. "I reflected upon my unclean, carnal life, also
the hypocritical doctrine and idolatry which I still practiced daily in appearance of godliness, but without relish. I saw that these zealous children, although in error, willingly gave their lives and their estates for their doctrine
and faith." That vision survived Münster, and it inspired Menno Simons to
collect the debris of Münster, to organize and rebuild in the spirit not of revenge but of compassion. In that spirit, the Mennonities have flourished, and
so, in their stubbornly independent fashion, have the other inheritors, the
Brethren, the Hutterians, the Moravians, the Amish, all making their way
through various migrations to England, to Russia, to Canada, to the unsettled
prairies of the American West, regarded, generally, as somewhat eccentric but
industrious and respectable and essentially harmless.

The Anabaptists' original ideals were much grander than that, and they have
spread far. The idea of adult baptism into a church of believers, and of the supreme authority of the Scriptures, was taught by Dutch Mennonites to John
Smyth, the founder of the Baptist Church that is now the largest Protestant de-
nomination in the world. The insistence on nonviolence reappeared in Quak-
erism, in Thoreau, Tolstoy and Gandhi. Not the least important, the separation
of church and state, an idea as alien to Luther and Zwingli as it was to Rome,
an idea that deprived the Anabaptists of political defenders and thus of political survival, is now fundamental to American society. Yet because of Münster,
the Anabaptists are still regarded as zealots. The ultimate cruelty of history is
that it has denied them the ideas for which they died.

Since Christ never returned, Antichrist too remained only a prophesied possibility. The Turks, who seemed to so many Germans the instrument of God's
wrath, never got beyond the outskirts of Vienna (and never persecuted either
Christians or Jews within their domain). And though the popes kept preaching
a crusade against the Islamic East, the barbarians who imprisoned Clement VII
in the Castel Sant' Angelo while they sacked and plundered Rome throughout
most of the year 1527 were the imperial armies of Charles V. The false prophets predicted in Scripture were yet to come.

The Lisbon Earthquake

1755

"There is evil upon the land"

The omens seemed unmistakable, but very few people could believe what they foretold. In the town of Louriçal, for example, a nun named Maria Joanna reported that she had seen a vision of Christ, and that he had told her the citizens of Lisbon would soon be punished for their wickedness. Another nun told her confessor five times that Lisbon was doomed, that its people must pray for salvation. Still another prophet, a Sebastianist, one of those devout believers in the miraculous restoration of the twenty-four-year-old King Sebastião, who had been cut to pieces two centuries earlier while leading a bedraggled band of crusaders against the infidels of Morocco—this Sebastianist proclaimed that a great event would occur in Lisbon on All Saints' Day, November 1, 1752, heralding the return of Sebastião as the Messiah the following spring.

The Portuguese awaited their destiny. When nothing happened on All Saints' Day, the word spread that the great event would actually take place on the same holy day in 1753, and then in 1754. On the very morning of November 1, 1755, Father Manuel Portal of the Oratory woke up out of a nightmare, for he had dreamed that Lisbon was being ravaged by two successive earthquakes, and something had warned him that he would never again see the crucifix on the wall of his cell. He went to mass and prayed. A few hours later, his monastery fell in ruins, just as he had dreamed. One of the priest's legs was crushed in the collapse, but he resolutely set forth to hear confessions and give absolution. The doomed city was already in flames.

Perched on seven hills near the mouth of the mighty Tagus River, Lisbon had seemed eternal. Ulysses was said to have wandered here after the sack of Troy, and the Romans called the place Olisipo, hence Lisbon. Once a citadel of the Visigoths, then of the Moors, the Lisbon of 1755 was still one of the great capitals of the world, but it had sunk deep in decay. The Enlightenment that was transforming the rest of Europe had been kept out by the Inquisition, and the state of public knowledge was so low that even commercial accountants had to be hired from abroad. The great exploits of Henry the Navigator and Vasco da Gama were scarcely more than a memory. The nation had not really recovered from the so-called "Sixty Years' Captivity," when, shortly after the death of King Sebastião, it had fallen under Spanish rule. Independent again only since 1640, Portugal had become a political appendage of Spain and an economic colony of Britain. But although it produced neither food nor clothing enough for its own needs, it could still live handsomely on the riches of Brazil. Gold had been found there in 1680 and diamonds in 1734. The King claimed one fifth of everything, as well as all diamonds of more than twenty carats. "Merchants who have lived in Portugal inform us," John Wesley wrote in terms of hushed indignation, "that the king had a large building filled with diamonds; and more gold stored up, coined and uncoined, than all the other princes of Europe together."

King João V, who reigned throughout the first half of the century until his mind gave way, united in himself his subjects' piety and decadence, their love of splendor and their indifference to commercial reality. "This monarch's gaieties were religious processions," Voltaire wrote of him. "When he took to building, he built monasteries, and when he wanted a mistress, he chose a nun." The epigram was not an exaggeration. When King João decided to turn the convent at Mafra into a palatial institution, the ceremony of laying the foundation stone alone cost £40,000, and the army of workmen assigned to the project grew to forty thousand. In the convent at Odivella, the King discovered a nun named Donna Magdalena de Miranda, who duly became, in all probability, the mother of the illegitimate Prince Gaspar, later archbishop of Braga. In the same convent, the King encountered another handsome nun named Sister Paula, who became the mother of the illigitimate Prince José, ultimately to serve as grand inquisitor. King João guiltily donated such enormous treasures to the Holy See, estimated at about £150,000 a year, that the Pope rewarded him and his heirs with the title of *Fidelissimus*. And granted his wish that Lisbon become, alone among all Western capitals, the seat of not a mere archbishop but a patriarch. When the saintly Jesuit missionary Gabriel Malagrida returned from Brazil and appeared at the royal palace, the King himself placed the missionary's hands on his own forehead. "Bless the King, thy servant," Father Malagrida said as he looked upward toward the heavens. "Do not call me king, call me sinner," said King João.

The treasures of Brazil provided lucrative employment for the goldsmiths of Italy and the stonecutters of Flanders, and made Lisbon the third-busiest port in Europe, exceeded only by London and Amsterdam, but most of the Portuguese derived little immediate benefit from this trade. They continued to lead a life not greatly different from that of the Middle Ages. There were perhaps 250,000 people in Lisbon, clustered together in about twenty thousand houses that nestled on the sides of the seven hills. A few of these buildings were made of marble, but most of them were of brick and wood. The climate was serenely vernal, as always, and the simple ingredients of life were abundant. Good red wine cost only two sous per pint, and the Tagus was so full of sardines that they could be bought in Lisbon's bustling fish market for only three sous per hundred. The unlit streets were paved, but they were swept only once every three or four days, and the better sort of people were carried about in sedan chairs. They liked to gather at the Ruccio and to chatter from one chair to another until sundown. After that, it was not safe to be out. Those who ventured forth generally wore knee-length capes, both as a covering for their illegal side arms and as a protection against the trash and filth that people customarily threw from their windows. "The Portuguese," wrote a sharp-eyed French traveler named Gaillardie, reporting many such details in a charming little book entitled simply *Description de la villo de Lisbonne* (1730), "are large, well built and robust, but most of them are rather indolent, partly because of the climate and still more because of the intermixture with blacks, which is quite common. They are jealous to the highest degree, secretive, vengeful, sarcastic, vain and presumptuous without cause, since most of them have only a very mediocre education. . . . They are also faithful friends, generous, charitable . . ."

Their greatest passion, said Gaillardie, as did many others, was their fervor for religion. Lisbon bristled with religious institutions, from the twelfth-century patriarchal cathedral to the network of local oratories that numbered not less than 121. The Franciscans alone had five homes for their monks and four for their nuns, the Dominicans three of each, and there were nearly 150 different brotherhoods in the city. In Portugal as a whole, fully 200,000 out of a population of two million were enrolled in one religious order or another.*

Lisbon's churches and monasteries boasted great hoards of sacred relics, and reports of miraculous interventions were almost commonplace. At least twenty different images of Christ were reputed to have the power to heal the sick, and at least two of them had been heard to speak. In front of one of them, bees had built a large altar out of honey, which was itself venerated as a demonstration of sanctity. There were hundreds of sacred portraits of Saint Anthony of Padua, patron saint of Portugal, and Saint Vincent, patron saint of Lisbon, whose ship had been guided to the city by two ravens late in the third century (two ravens still lived in the cathedral, and were regularly fed, and it was said that whenever one of them died another appeared instantly, without human intervention). The quantity of relics would have defied credibility in less pious cities. At the Carmelite convent alone, a cross-shaped reliquary contained a collection of fragments that were purported to include a piece of the Infant Jesus' crib and a lock of his hair, as well as the hair of the Virgin Mary, John the Baptist and Mary Magdalene; a thorn from Jesus' crown, with traces of blood still on it; a chip from a column in Pilate's tribunal; a piece of the rope that bound Jesus to the cross; one of the nails that had been driven into him, a bloodstained strip of cloth that had wiped his brow; a piece of the lance that had stabbed him in the side; a piece of the signboard on the cross; a shred of Christ's burial shroud; and autographed letters from all of the four Evangelists.

This medieval piety was quite alien to the commonsense spirit of the Enlightenment. Even to such an enthusiast as George Whitefield, the great evangelist of the Methodist Awakening in England, the spectacle of the Portuguese

---

* Foreign ship captains, coming from less pious lands, had to sign a document pledging that they and their crews would not only take off their hats to all clergymen and kneel at every elevation of the Host but also would "in no way insult the Cross, wherever set up, by making [water], but however urgent their necessities may be, will retain the same till a proper and lawful distance." This requirement prompted a touring Scots lady named Janet Schaw to observe in her *Journal of a Lady of Quality:* "It will not be easy for the sailors to observe strictly the articles of not affronting the cross, for they [the crosses] are so close on each other that it will hardly be in their power to keep clear of offense."

worshiping their icons and relics seemed almost pagan. On his way to preach to the colonists in darkest Georgia, Whitefield was stranded in Lisbon for a month at Easter of 1754, just a year before the earthquake, and he sent home a series of outraged accounts of the religious processions that the Portuguese cherished. He described with something akin to horror a parade of Carmelite friars holding lighted tapers and followed by a crowd of thousands. "Among them was carried, upon eight or ten men's shoulders, a tall image of the Virgin Mary, in a kind of man's attire, with a fine white wig on her head, and much adorned with jewels and glittering stones. . . . These processions, from one convent to another, were made daily, for the purpose of obtaining rain." A few days later, he described with no less revulsion a series of tableaux "intended to represent the life and death of St. Francis, the founder of one of their religious orders." Once again, priests carried through the awed crowds a series of statues—the young Saint Francis, "very gay and beau-like, as he used to be before his conversion," then Saint Francis converted, Saint Francis tormented, Saint Francis angelically dying, and finally "brought forth lying in his grave, the briars and nettles under which he lay being turned into fine and fragrant flowers."

Most loathsome of all, to the Protestant eye and the Protestant conscience, were the traditional processions of the penitents, all dressed in white linen robes that covered even their faces. "One night, about ten o'clock," Whitefield wrote back to London, "I saw a train of near two hundred penitents, making a halt, and kneeling in the street, whilst a friar, from a high cross, with a crucifix in his hand, was preaching to them and the populace, with great vehemence." When the sermon was finished, the penitents marched slowly forward, beating their breasts and slapping their faces and chanting the word that their leader sounded through a trumpet: *"Penitentia."* "All were bare-footed, and all had long heavy chains fastened to their ankles, which, when dragged along the street, made a dismal rattling," Whitefield wrote. "Some carried great stones on their backs. Others had in their hands dead men's bones and skulls. Some bore large crosses upon their shoulders. . . . Most of them whipped and lashed themselves, some with cords, and others with flat bits of iron. . . . The whole scene was horrible." Whitefield's reaction to such dismal spectacles was characteristic. "O happy England!" he wrote. "O happy Methodists!"

The French voyager Gaillardie, who had witnessed similar scenes two decades earlier, attributed a touch of hypocrisy to this Portuguese passion for public piety. The penitent who marched through the streets in chains, he wrote, was quite likely to wear at the same time "a ribbon on his shoulder to be recognized by his mistress." And though the women were seated in segregated areas of the church, he said, they "slip love notes very adroitly" to their admirers. Once every year, though, despite such touches of frivolity, public announcements summoned the faithful citizens of Lisbon to the Dominican Church of São Domingo, where the names of those condemned by the Holy Inquisition were posted and read aloud, and where those condemned were still subjected to the rituals of the auto-da-fé.

The term itself is Portuguese, meaning an act of faith, but the Inquisition came late to Portugal, long after the fires of Languedoc had died out. Nor was there any heresy among the Portuguese; they were the most orthodox of believers. The conflict came from Spain, where King Ferdinand and Queen Isabella had celebrated their conquest of the last Moorish stronghold at Granada in 1492 by ordering the expulsion of all Jews. Some ninety thousand of them fled across the Portuguese border, bringing great riches with them. King João II received them civilly but ordered that each of them pay a tax of one crozada and then move on in eight months aboard ships that he would provide. When these ships failed to appear, the King angrily blamed the victims and decreed that all Jews who could be found be reduced to slavery and their children exiled to the desolate island of São Tomé in the Gulf of Guinea.

João's brother Manoel succeeded him in 1495 and freed the Jews from their slavery, but when he undertook to marry the Spanish Princess Isabella he was told that he must stop providing sanctuary to anyone of whom the Spanish Inquisition disapproved. King Manoel decided to solve the Jewish problem once and for all by ordering every Jew to be converted or sail to Africa. But as many of them prepared to depart, he ordered that all their children under the age of fourteen be separated from their parents, forcibly converted, and raised as Christians. Some Jews, it is said, killed their children and then committed suicide; others went quietly into exile; still others subscribed unhappily to the rituals of Christianity.

They were called *conversos*, or "new Christians," but there was no safety in conversion. At Easter of 1506, one of these *conversos* apparently expressed some doubt about the miraculous powers of a crucifix in a Dominican church in Lisbon. He was seized by the hair, dragged out into the street and beaten to death. The Dominican monks then led the crowds on a three-day rampage through Lisbon. They killed every Jew they saw, converted or not, and after the slaughter of what history records only as "several thousand," the massacre ended mainly because no more victims could be found. The authorities remained suspicious. When the twenty-year-old King João III came to the throne, he demonstrated his zeal for the faith by petitioning Rome, in 1531, to provide his kingdom with a Holy Inquisition modeled on that of Spain.

More than two centuries later, while nations to the north celebrated their enlightenment in one form or another, the Portuguese Inquisition still inflicted its punishments before the Church of São Domingo. The sentences on Portuguese sinners consisted mainly of various kinds of public penance, but the "new Christians," whose newness still made them objects of suspicion, periodically had to suffer the traditional purification of burning at the stake. King José Manuel, who succeeded his demented father in 1750, was interested mainly in hunting and opera, but he felt it his duty to bring his Spanish Queen María Anna to the Ruccio to attend the annual burnings. George Whitefield was there in 1754 and remarked that the Dominican friars "sang most surprisingly sweet," but as he stood watching, not far from the golden altar, he observed that "my very inmost soul was struck with a secret horror, when, upon looking up, I saw over the front of the great window of the church, the heads of many hundred Jews, painted on canvas, who had been condemned by what they call the Holy Inquisition, and carried out from that church to be burnt." As recently as the past May 19, in the year 1755, less than six months before the earthquake, King José Manuel and his Queen had gone to the Ruccio and watched a "new Christian" named José Ramos condemned as *"confitente, revogante e impenitente,"* and consigned to the flames.

Tens of thousands of these pious citizens were on their knees in their churches on that All Saints' Day of 1755, listening to the familiar exhortations to rejoice in praise of their Lord, when they felt the first faint shuddering of the earth beneath them. The priests in the choir in the great marble Basilica of São Vicente de Fora had just reached the words of the introit, *Gaudeamus omnes in Deo,* when the whole church began to sway like a ship at sea. The lights on the altar flickered. It was about nine-thirty in the morning (subsequent accounts vary widely on the exact moment), a clear, sunny morning without a cloud in the sky. "There was never a finer morning seen than the first of November," a visiting British merchant named Braddock later wrote home to the chancellor of Norwich.

Braddock was not at church but in an apartment, where he sat writing to various associates about a lawsuit that he had recently won. "I [was] just finishing a letter," he said, "when the papers and table I was writing on began to tremble with a gentle motion, which rather surprised me, as I could not perceive a breath of wind stirring. While I was reflecting with myself what this could be owing to ... the whole house began to shake from the very foundation; which I at first imputed to the rattling of several coaches in the main street. ... On harkening more attentively [I heard] a strange frightful kind of noise under ground, resembling the hollow distant rumbling of thunder; all this passed in less than a minute, and I must confess I now began to be alarmed."

Braddock hesitated for a moment, trying to decide whether to flee into the streets or to stay where he was. There seemed to be no prospect of safety anywhere. The second shock of the earthquake was even louder and more ferocious than the first. "The house I was in shook with such violence that the upper stories immediately fell," Braddock wrote, "and though my apartment (which was on the first floor) did not then share the same fate, yet every thing was thrown out of its place in such a manner that it was with no small difficulty I kept my feet, and expected nothing less than to be soon crushed to death, as the walls continued rocking to and fro in the frightfullest manner, opening in several places; large stones falling down on every side from the cracks; and the end of most of the rafters starting out from the roof. To add to this terrifying scene, the sky in a moment became so gloomy, that I could now distinguish no particular object; it was an Aegyptian Darkness indeed."

This darkness was caused by the thick clouds of dust spewed out by the collapse of so many buildings. When the dust settled, the sky was seen to be as cloudless as ever, the sun shining brightly on the wreckage. And still the city heaved (the third great shock came about a quarter of an hour after the first). One Portuguese witness, Antonio Pereira, observed with terror how the church bells clanged all by themselves, tolling the devastation, until their towers cracked open and the bells fell into the street with a great clatter. "The whole tract of country about Lisbon was seen to heave like the swelling of the billows in a storm," according to Pereira's account, "sometimes from east to west and again from north to south; those walls which were not yet thrown down waving backward and forward with alternate pulsations, and the thunderings under- ground continuing, the city seemed not only to be shaken but to be violently torn from the very deepest foundations."

The first two shocks had a cumulative effect, the first one weakening even the strongest foundations, the second completing the destruction of walls and towers that had survived the first attack. "You may guess at the prodigious havoc . . . ," wrote another English witness, "by the single instance I am going to mention. There was a high arched passage, like one of our city gates, front- ing the west door of the ancient cathedral; on the left was the famous church of Saint Anthony and on the right some private houses, several storeys high. . . . At the first shock, numbers of people, who were then passing under the arch, fled into the center of the area; those in the two churches, as many as could possibly get out, did the same. At this instant, the arched gateway, with the fronts of the two churches and the two contiguous buildings, all inclining one towards the other with the violence of the shock, fell down and buried every soul as they were standing there crowded together."

The earthquake was apparently centered just offshore, perhaps within twenty-five miles of Lisbon, but the upheaval extended for hundreds of miles. It ravaged the whole southwest of Portugal, leveling such towns as Setúbal and Sácavem and the Algarve coastal villages of Lagos, Faro and Tavira. It ex- tended across Spain, from Cádiz, which suffered heavy damage, to Madrid, which felt much lighter tremors. In North Africa, there was tremendous de- struction around Fez, and the shocks reached as far east as Algiers. Even in central and northern Europe, the tremors were recorded in Switzerland, Nor- mandy, Ireland. Inland waters as far away as Loch Ness, in Scotland, suddenly rose to unusual heights. The tidal wave reached the West Indies eight hours after the first tremor.

But the center of the disaster was the proud city of Lisbon. "The first shock began about a quarter before ten o'clock in the morning, and, as far as I could judge, lasted six or seven minutes," according to the dry account of British Consul Edward Hay. "There was then an interval of about five minutes before the second shock, which lasted about three minutes. So that in a quarter of an hour this great city was laid in ruins. . . . The part of the town towards the water, where was the royal palace, the public tribunals, the Custom House, India House, and where most of the merchants dwelt for the convenience of transacting their business, is so totally destroyed that it is nothing but a heap of rubbish, in many places several stories high."

This collapse of so many buildings took thousands of lives, but few individ- ual casualties were ever recorded. The Spanish ambassador, Count Peralada, for one, was trying to flee from his embassy when the stone emblem of the Spanish crown fell off the facade of the building and killed him as he ran down the steps. The French ambassador, Count de Baschi, saw the accident, ran into the building, rescued the Spaniard's son, and carried him off to safety in the countryside. Mr. Braddock, the British merchant, saw a more typical tragedy, and he never even learned the victim's name. He was leaving his apartment when he encountered a woman, pale and trembling, all covered with dust, and carrying a baby in her arms. "The poor creature asked me, in the utmost agony, if I did not think the world was at an end," Braddock wrote to his friend the chancellor of Norwich. He led the woman out of the house and into the street, which he found blocked by rubble nearly two stories high. He helped the woman part of the way, then had to stop. "As there was one part I could not well climb over without the assistance of my hands, as well as feet," he wrote, "I desired her to let go her hold, which she did, remaining two or three feet behind me, at which instant there fell a vast stone, from a tottering wall, and crushed both her and the child in pieces."

The dead lay where they fell, the injured cried aloud and struggled for help. "In some places lay coaches, with their masters, horses, and riders almost crushed to pieces," wrote another English survivor. "Here mothers with infants in their arms: there ladies richly dressed, priests, friars, gentlemen, mechanics: some had their backs or thighs broken: others vast stones on their breasts: some lay almost buried in the rubbish . . ." A Bridgetine nun named Kitty Witham wrote to her mother that she had survived because "I up and took to my heells, with Jesus in my mouth, and to the quire I run," but she added that "the poor presedent of the English College was killed as he was preparing for Mass. Tis thoute he lived about four and twenty hours in that misery for when they found him he was nowhere brused by reason he was under a bench."

The heaving of the earth and the collapse of the great buildings marked only the beginning of the catastrophe. Almost as soon as the dust of the first upheaval had settled, fires broke out at half a dozen different spots. One of the first of these, as a number of English witnesses noted with pious satisfaction, started at the Church of São Domingo, the headquarters of the Inquisition. But all the altars in Lisbon's dozens of churches had been ablaze with candles that morning, and thousands of housewives had left their kitchen braziers untended. Fire soon appeared in the ruins of the Carmo and Trinidade convents. A northeast wind fanned the flames. The blazes spread from São Domingo down toward the Tagus River, then over the western and southern slopes of the Castle Hill, then through the whole center of the city.

They were to rage for five days. In many areas where some buildings had at least partially survived the shock of the earthquake, the fire devoured everything. In the Rua Nova dos Mercadores and the Rua da Confeitaria, for example, storekeepers made a valiant effort to drag their property out of their damaged shops. They organized a salvage area in the nearby Terreiro do Paço. All of it was reduced to ashes. Even in such badly damaged buildings as the royal palace and the new opera house and the patriarchal church, much might have been saved after the shocks of the earthquake, but the fire swept everywhere. Holy relics, priceless libraries, tapestries, furniture, altar cloths, everything ended in the flames. In the royal palace alone, seventy thousand books were destroyed; in the palace of the dukes of Bragança, the entire royal-family archives disappeared; in the palace of the Marquis of Louriçal, the fire ravaged two hundred paintings, including works by Titian, Correggio and Rubens, as well as eighteen thousand books and one thousand manuscripts, among them a history handwritten by the Emperor Charles V.

In the midst of the collapse and the conflagration, about an hour after the first shock, there struck yet another catastrophe, perhaps the most terrifying of all. As the stricken citizens looked out into the harbor of the Tagus, the waters suddenly seemed to be ebbing out to sea. There are even reports that the entire waterfront was laid bare, down to its muddy bottom, but other accounts insist that this did not happen, could not have happened. What did happen was that the mighty Tagus suddenly rose to an overwhelming, impossible height, about thirty feet above its ordinary level, and all within the space of a few minutes. "Several boats passing in the river were seen to twirl around as in a whirlpool," an English merchant recorded, "and then, with their sterns pointed out of the water, plunged head foremost beneath it, without rising up any more." This seems somewhat exaggerated. According to a British captain who was actually aboard his ship in the harbor, the tidal wave rose three times in five minutes, but it damaged mainly small ships trapped near the shore. The ships near the shore, he wrote to *Gentleman's Magazine* in London, were "in a minute or two left dry, and again set afloat and dash'd against one another, and the tide so quick eastward and westward, that the ships turning fast around, ran foul of each other. . . . The whole river was overspread with boats, timber, masts, household goods, casks, etc."

But even to a captain caught in the tidal wave, the horror was clearly on shore. "The water rose to such a height that it overcame and overflow'd the lower part of the city," he wrote, "which so terrified the miserable and already dismayed inhabitants, who ran to and fro with dreadful cries . . . , that it made them believe the dissolution of the world was at hand; every one falling on his knees, and intreating the Almighty for his assistance." The merchant Braddock was standing near the waterfront, not far from the spot where the crowded new royal quay abruptly disappeared from sight. "On a sudden I heard a general outcry, 'The sea is coming in, we shall all be lost.' Upon this, turning my eyes towards the river, which in that place is near four miles broad, I could perceive it heaving and swelling in a most unaccountable manner, as no wind was stirring; in an instant there appeared, at some small distance, a large body of water, rising as it were like a mountain, it came on foaming and roaring, and rushed towards the shore with such impetuosity that we all immediately ran for our lives, as fast as possible; many were actually swept away, and the rest above their waist in water at a good distance from the banks. For my own part, I had the narrowest escape, and should certainly have been lost, had I not grasped a large beam that lay on the ground, till the water returned to its channel, which it did almost at the same instant, with equal rapidity . . ."

The chaos was such that nobody has ever determined how many people died that terrible morning. There was no way of telling how many lay buried under vast heaps of rubble, how many had been trapped there and burned to death, how many had been swept out to sea. "It is not to be express'd by human tongue how dreadful and how awful it was to enter the city after the fire was abated," wrote the English captain who had witnessed the disaster from the harbor, "and . . . one was struck with horror in beholding dead bodies by six or seven in a heap, crush'd to death, half buried and half burnt; and if one went through the broad places or squares, nothing to be met with but people bewailing their misfortune, wringing their hands, and crying the world is at an end." After a time, the city's parish churches were asked to draw up lists of the missing and dead among their parishioners, but these were only approximations. The estimates of the death toll range from about 15,000 to more than 75,-000. Modern historians incline to believe that the correct figure is probably about 30,000, which would be more than ten percent of the city's population, the equivalent of nearly a million in contemporary New York.

Among the survivors, haunted by fears of famine and plague, the most terrifying consequence of the disaster was that the crevices in the social order began to crack open. Looters and plunderers appeared. They started by scavenging in the ruins, and then, growing bolder, like rats atop a mound of garbage, they began attacking anyone who appeared weak or vulnerable. Several prisons had collapsed during the general devastation, including the notorious *galera,* where the galley slaves captured off the coasts of Africa were kept in chains, and so an army of convicts and criminals emerged from their cells and ran loose through the stricken city. But there seemed to be more criminals in the streets than had ever been confined in the city's prisons. Spanish deserters were blamed for several cases of arson that kept the fires spreading out of control. Much of the robbery and assault may have been simply a fight for survival, or simply an outburst of the lust for acquisition and power. Voltaire described one such villain in his portrait of the sailor who survived the sinking of the ship that brought Candide and Dr. Pangloss to Lisbon on the eve of the earthquake. "Whistling and swearing, the sailor said, 'There'll be something to pick up here . . .' The sailor immediately ran among the debris, dared death to find money, found it, seized it, got drunk and, having slept off his wine, purchased the favors of the first woman of goodwill he met on the ruins of the houses among the dead and dying."

The government, in effect, had also collapsed. All political authority, all social order, had disintegrated. In these afflictions, the citizens of Lisbon turned to their priests for protection and absolution. The various British chroniclers, who regarded the Portuguese devotion to miraculous relics with contempt, were astonished at the rituals that now took place on almost every street corner. Braddock, for one, reported that a number of "the poor bigotted creatures" held out their wooden crucifixes for him to kiss, and when he pushed aside one man's offering, "giving him to understand that I desired to be excused this piece of devotion, he asked me, with some indignation, whether I thought there was a God." One English eyewitness reported that the newly arrived chaplain to the English community was suddenly surrounded by a crowd, which he feared would do him harm, but which wanted only to have him baptized, and did so. "The poor misguided zealots expressed so wonderful a regard and fondness for their fancied proselyte that the priests even proceeded to kneeling down before him and embracing his knees." The Portuguese were not to be deprived of their miracles. They considered it miraculous, for example, that the image of Nossa Senhora do Carmo had been saved from her burned-out convent, and they thronged to worship before her in her new location in a tent on the Campo Grande. They heard tales that the flames ravaging the Church of Ingreja da Sé had suddenly died down before a statue of Nossa Senhora a Grande, not even singeing her robes or the flowers in her hand. They even heard that a figure of the Virgin in the Hieronymite Church at Belém had cried out to a nearby figure of Jesus, "It is enough, my Son, it is enough."

∗

The Messiah who saved Lisbon from devastation and anarchy was not the pious King Sebastião of the prophecy but the very worldly Sebastião José de Carvalho e Mello, later titled and generally known to history as the Marquis of Pombal. He was fifty-six years of age at the time of the earthquake, and in retrospect it is possible to say that his whole life had been spent in preparation for this moment of crisis. He had been born into a family of impoverished provincial gentry, and his parents destined him for the study of law. Carvalho rebelled and ran off to join the army. He was a large, strong youth, quite fearless, endowed with a combative temper, but the enlisted ranks of the army provided no future for his ambition. He resigned and went to Lisbon to seek his fortune. He eloped with a rich and well-connected widow, then used those connnections to win an appointment as minister plenipotentiary to London. His wife died there, but when Carvalho was transferred to the Portuguese Embassy in Vienna, he remarried even more successfully. His Austrian wife, Countess Daun, was a friend of the Austrian princess who had become Queen María Antonia of Portugal, and when King João's mind began to disintegrate, Queen Maria Antonia became regent. A place could be found for Carvalho. The Regent's son, the new King José Manuel, confirmed the ambitious courtier as one of his three secretaries of state, charged with responsibility for foreign relations.

Carvalho thus had no official responsibility for dealing with the catastrophe that leveled Lisbon, but when he arrived at the Belém Palace late in the morning of All Saints' Day, he found the hapless young King in tears and his courtiers distraught. The King's chief concern seemed to be whether he should abandon Lisbon entirely and move his court north to Coimbra. There occurred then one of those exchanges that may be apocryphal but seem to epitomize a moment in history.

"What is to be done," wailed the King, "to meet this infliction of divine justice?"

"Bury the dead and feed the living," said Carvalho. (*"Enterrar nos mortos et cuidar nos vivos."*)

The King assigned him to do what he could, and Carvalho immediately clambered into a coach and set out to make himself master of the ruined city. For three days and three nights he lived and worked in his carriage, driving from one crisis to another, scribbling out one decree after another, sometimes simply holding the paper across his knees and then signing it with a bold stroke, then driving on. There were to be some two hundred of these decrees, and they provided a remarkable framework for the autocratic imposition of order on chaos. Nobody else seemed to know where to begin; Carvalho seemed to know everything. His first step was to order the army to take up positions at the gates to the city and to halt the flow of terrified refugees into the countryside. This served to stop the removal of plunder and also to keep skilled labor in the city. Next he ordered a series of seven large gallows erected in the main public squares. Looters caught with their booty were executed on the spot. Thirty-four of these jackals—and quite possibly a number of men merely suspected of robbery—were left hanging from the gibbets for the edification of the public. They included ten Spaniards, five Irishmen, one Pole and one Moor.

Having reasserted royal authority, Carvalho proceeded to deal with what he had originally declared to be the two chief problems. To bury the dead, by now rotting in the streets, he negotiated an agreement with the church making it permissible to tow the carcasses out to sea and dump them into the ocean. To feed the living, he opened public granaries and meat markets and soup kitchens. To prevent profiteering, he decreed that all ships in the harbor must disgorge their cargoes of beef and corn and other provisions at the prices that were in effect on the day before the earthquake, and no ships could leave Lisbon without their crews and cargoes being checked for both food and booty. He decreed that all "idlers"—that is, anyone without a regular occupation—be put to work digging out the rubble and rebuilding. Lime kilns and brick ovens were established. Supplies of wood were requisitioned. So were wagons. The aqueducts were repaired. The slow process of rebuilding began.

The terror was by no means over. New shocks repeatedly struck the city— there were estimated to be five hundred during the eighteen months after the original earthquake—and though none of them did much damage, they kept the population in a state of great anxiety. Indeed, there were widespread rumors—which Carvalho blamed chiefly on the Jesuits and their preachings of future retribution—that the first anniversary of the earthquake would bring a new catastrophe. But help too came pouring in. The British Parliament voted a handsome disbursement of £100,000 in aid, half in gold and silver, half in supplies, 6,000 barrels of beef, 10,000 quarters of flour, 4,000 firkins of butter, cases of shoes, axes, spades. The Spanish provided a more modest amount, four wagons loaded with gold and silver, and even the citizens of Hamburg sent two ships filled with timber, tiles, lead and tools. Within a year, one thousand houses in Lisbon had been repaired and made habitable again. And when the first anniversary of the disaster occurred, Carvalho again called out the troops to prevent any panic, but there was none.

From the rescue of a ruined city, Carvalho progressed to ever more ambitious strategies. In 1756, he forbade all unapproved rebuilding in central Lisbon and imposed a master plan, partly inspired by the example he had seen in London's Covent Garden. Hills were leveled, medieval alleys straightened, and sewers installed underneath them. The grid of streets that Carvalho built to the north of the ruined Terreiro do Paço is still admired today as a model of eighteenth-century urban planning, one of the finest in Europe. The rebuilding was

symbolic of Carvalho's increasingly fierce reorganization of the entire kingdom, whose King by now could deny his authoritarian minister nothing. He
built up silk, shipping and other industries to end the nation's long dependence
on Britain. He streamlined the judiciary, founded a system of secular education, reduced the bureaucracy, strengthened both army and navy, outlawed
slavery, and took steps to end discrimination against the Jews. But if he regarded himself as an enlightened despot, bringing Portugal out of the Dark
Ages and into the sun of modern life, his enemies saw him as a tyrant, cruel and
morbidly suspicious, maintained in power only by his spies and his dungeons.

Carvalho's two principal antagonists were the aristocracy and the Jesuits,
both of whom were accustomed to ruling Portugal in their own ways. To combat the Jesuits was not easy, particularly in Portugal, where they not only
served as confessors to the royal family but followed the explorers out to build
great commercial empires out of their missionary networks in Latin America
and the Indies. But Carvalho skillfully took advantage of the secular spirit that
had invaded the Holy See. He sent his cousin Francisco de Almada e Men-
donça to serve as ambassador to Rome, and the ambassador soon discovered
that there was an anti-Jesuit faction in Rome, and also that certain cardinals
welcomed gifts of colonial sugar and wine. Pope Benedict XIV was dying. It
was a time of opportunity. Carvalho accused the Jesuits of exceeding their authority and carrying on illegal commerce in both Portugal and Brazil, and these
charges were duly turned over to Cardinal Saldanha, patriarch of Lisbon, for
investigation. The cardinal understood the value of cooperating with Carvalho,
who by now had installed his own brother Paul as the head of the Portuguese
Inquisition. In the spring and summer of 1758, a series of decrees from the cardinal ordered the Jesuits to stop all their commerce, then forbade them even to
preach on Portuguese territory.

Later that same year, Carvalho struck against the nobility. His opportunity
came after an assassination attempt against King José Manuel, who was out
riding one night with a companion named Pedro Teixeira when their coach
was ambushed by two bands of masked horsemen. One of them fired a musket
shot that wounded the King in the right shoulder and arm. Carvalho managed
to keep the whole affair secret until his spies and informers brought him the
names of the assassins. Then he intercepted their mail to gather further evidence. Then he sent troops to arrest the culprits. His targets, open opponents of
his own rule, were among the richest and proudest nobles in the land. The two
most important were Dom Francisco de Assis de Tavora, aged fifty-five, third
Marquis of Tavora and former viceroy of India, and his brother-in-law Dom
José de Mascarenhas, aged fifty, eighth Duke of Aveiro, eighth Count of Santa
Cruz, fifth Marquis of Gouveia, hereditary grand marshal of the royal household. Arrested with them were their wives and children, a half dozen of
their noble friends, a number of servants involved in the conspiracy, and
their spiritual advisors, the celebrated Father Malagrida and a dozen other
Jesuits.

They were brought before a special tribunal, and although the evidence
against them was already strong, they were subjected to the rack to make them

provide complete details. From a few of these details, we can infer a motive that has little to do with either politics or religion. King José Manuel was having an affair with the wife of the Marquis of Tavora's son, and the family apparently decided to inflict a symbolic revenge on the King's companion, Teixeira. It was his coach that they ambushed in the dark, and they had no reason to know that the King was inside it. Carvalho may have had personal motives as well. It was rumored that he had once presumed to ask for the hand of one of the Marquis of Tavora's daughters, and had been rejected with contempt by the Marquis' wife.

She was the first to suffer the tribunal's nine sentences of death. On a gray and rainy dawn, she was carried in a sedan chair to the public square at Belém, allowed to make her confession, then led up onto a large scaffold, shown the instruments that would be used on the rest of her family, and finally beheaded. The next five of the condemned were brought onto the scaffold and tied to X-shaped timbers. The executioners broke their arms and legs with hammers and then strangled them. The Duke of Aveiro and the Marquis of Tavora were similarly treated, except that they were not strangled but kept alive while the last of the conspirators, a servant, was burned alive. Then, at the end of the long day, the entire scaffold was burned and the debris cast into the Tagus. The young Marquise of Tavora, whom the King was supposed to have visited on the night of the attempted assassination, was confined for the rest of her life in the Convent of Santos. And it was said that when the King's barge was sighted on the Tagus, the other nuns rushed to the windows to see it, but the young Marquise just wept.

Now that Carvalho had restored order, he officially expelled the Jesuits from Portugal early in 1759 and seized all their possessions. But he was not permitted to prosecute Father Malagrida and the twelve other friars who had been arrested for the Tavora conspiracy. So he kept them in the dungeon beneath the Belém Tower. After several months in a dark cell below the water level, Father Malagrida was removed to Junqueira Prison, and by now he seemed totally mad. He said he heard angelic voices commanding him to perform painful acts of mortification. He knelt for hours with his forehead pressed to the stone floor of the prison, praying for the martyrdom that still eluded him. During his intervals of lucidity, he began writing down the words of the angelic voices and producing a book of revelation. He called it "The Heroic and Wonderful Life of the Glorious Saint Anne, Mother of the Holy Virgin Mary, Dictated by This Saint, Assisted by and with the Approbation and Help of This Most August Sovereign, and of Her Most Holy Son."

✳

At about this same time, there spread through Europe a new awareness of another great upheaval, a cataclysm that had not only destroyed a city but buried and obliterated it. The very location of the buried city had been forgotten, so when the first traces of its ruins came to light, no one had any idea what they were.

The process of rediscovery, which took the better part of a century, began in

1709 in the village of Resina, a few miles south of Naples. A peasant's well ran dry, and he recruited some neighbors to deepen it. In the course of their digging, the peasants found no water, but they did find several square blocks of marble, which they offered for sale. Word of the discovery spread. The Austrians, who had expelled the Spanish from Naples in 1707, were in the process of establishing themselves as the new rulers of the Kingdom of the Two Sicilies. Among these Austrian occupiers was a cavalry officer named Maurice de Lorraine, Prince d'Elboeuf, who married an Italian princess of the house of Salsa and decided to build himself a grand seaside villa near Portici. He needed marble. When he heard that some peasants in the nearby village of Resina had discovered several marble blocks while digging a well, he shrewdly decided to buy not just their marble but their whole property. He then hired workmen of his own to continue digging.

They cut outward from the well, and by mere luck they soon found themselves in the midst of a classic Roman theater, perfectly preserved. The Prince d'Elboeuf was not particularly interested in antiquities, only in marble. He ordered his workmen to dismantle the theater and to bring up the marble for the terraces of his new villa. And so it was done. In the course of these ruinous excavations, the Prince's workmen unearthed a statue of Hercules and then three beautiful female figures. The Prince was not a Philistine. He knew that he had discovered something important, but he had no idea exactly what the site represented, or how extensive it might be.

He also knew that he needed more money to pursue his excavations, so he sent the three female statues to Vienna to his cousin Prince Eugene of Savoy. When Prince Eugene died in 1736, his heirs sold off his various possessions, slender Milanese daggers, Irish horses, hand-copied manuscripts, heraldic tapestries, and so the three statues from the Prince d'Elboeuf, which had mysteriously come to be identified as vestal virgins, passed into the possession of Friedrich August II, Elector of Saxony and King of Poland. Friedrich August installed the three statues at his palace in Dresden, where they apparently were much admired by his daughter, Maria Amalia. In Naples, meanwhile, the Austrians had once again ceded power to the Spaniards, and the new King Carlos II ventured north in 1738 to marry Princess Maria Amalia of Saxony. As soon as she returned with him to the south, she inquired about the excavations where the three vestal virgins had been discovered.

D'Elboeuf's labors had long since been abandoned. There had been fierce eruptions of the nearby Mount Vesuvius in 1717 and again in 1737 (indeed there have been more than seventy major eruptions since the early days of the Roman Empire), and underground excavation seemed dangerous as well as expensive. Prodded by Maria Amalia, King Carlos ordered the work resumed. He assigned the project to Colonel Roque Joaquín de Alcubierre of the Neapolitan Army Engineers, and although subsequent scholars have cursed Alcubierre's relentless destruction of the site, he did manage to bring to light the first great treasures of the lost city of Herculaneum—a bronze quadriga, statues of emperors, quantities of jewelry. And just as the results of the digging began to thin out, a local antiquarian urged the colonel to abandon Herculaneum and start anew at a nearby village where peasants had recently found a number of inscribed marble blocks. In the spring of 1748, Colonel Alcubierre ordered his twenty-four workmen, who included twelve convicts in chains, to begin digging at a spot that would eventually turn out to be the site of the Temple of Fortuna Augusta in the buried ruins of Pompeii.

The civilized world had always known about Pompeii, of course, for its end during the reign of the Emperor Titus was one of those epochal acts of divine destruction, like the fall of Nineveh or Babylon. Martial had written of it in his fourth book of epigrams, first describing the slopes of Vesuvius, "shaded with green vines," beloved by both Bacchus and Venus. "And all was consumed in the flames," he wrote, "all covered with the gray ash, and the gods themselves wished that they did not have such power." The world knew but the world forgot, through some strange process of historical amnesia, exactly where the buried city lay, forgot even whether it was a real city or one of those legendary places like Troy and Atlantis. It appeared in various places on Renaissance maps, but these were maps that showed Tritons blowing their trumpets at the edges of *terra incognita.* Even when a workman dug up an inscription bearing the words *Decurio Pompeis,"* scholars convinced themselves that this was a reference to a villa belonging to the Triumvir Pompey.

Still, the legend survived in two letters of Pliny the Younger, written some years after the disaster at the request of his friend Tacitus. On the sunny morning of August 24, in A.D. 79, the earth began shaking for miles around Vesuvius, and then the mountain exploded. Pliny's uncle, Pliny the Elder, a stout figure of fifty-six, commanded a fleet at Misenum, about thirty miles north of Pompeii, and as soon as the commander heard from his wife that a strange cloud had appeared on the horizon, he wanted to investigate it. The cloud had a shape that any observer in the age of Hiroshima would instantly recognize, but Pliny struggled to find the right image. "Its general appearance can best be expressed as being like an umbrella pine," Pliny wrote to Tacitus, "for it rose to a great height on a sort of trunk and then split off into branches. . . . In places it looked white, elsewhere splotched and dirty, according to the amount of soil and ashes it carried with it. . . ." Pliny the Elder, who had devoted much of his life to recording such things in his *Natural History,* determined to set sail across the bay so that he could see more. He invited his nephew to accompany him, but the eighteen-year-old youth declined, saying that he had studying to do. As Pliny was leaving his house, he received a message from a woman named Rectina, who lived near the foot of the mountain and pleaded for a ship to rescue her. "What he had begun for love of science," the younger Pliny wrote, "he now continued out of humanity."

"He hurried to the place which everyone else was hastily leaving," Pliny's letter continued, "steering his course straight for the danger zone. He was entirely fearless, noting down each new phase of the phenomenon exactly as he observed them. Ashes were already falling hotter and thicker as the ships drew near, followed by bits of pumice and blackened stone, charred and cracked by the flames. Then suddenly they were in shallow water, and the shore was blocked by the debris from the mountain. For a moment, my uncle wondered whether to turn back, but when the helmsman advised this he refused, telling him, 'Fortune favors the brave.' He ordered him to make for the home of Pomponianus at Stabiae . . . [My uncle] embraced his terrified friend, cheered and encouraged him. Thinking he could calm his fears by his own composure, he gave orders that he was to be carried to the baths. After his bath, he lay down and dined. He was quite cheerful, or at any rate he pretended he was, which was no less courageous.

"Meanwhile on Vesuvius broad sheets of fire and leaping flames blazed at several points, their bright glare emphasized by the darkness of the night. My uncle tried to allay the fears of his companions by repeatedly declaring that these were nothing but bonfires left by the peasants in their terror, or else empty houses on fire in the districts they had abandoned.

"Then he went to rest and certainly slept, for as he was a stout man, his breathing was rather loud and heavy and could be heard by people coming and going outside his door. By this time the courtyard giving access to his room was full of ashes mixed with pumice stones, so that its level had risen, and if he stayed in the room any longer he would never have got out. He was wakened, came out and joined Pomponianus and the rest of the household, who had sat up all night. They debated whether to stay indoors or take their chance in the open, for the buildings were now shaking with violent shocks, and seemed to be swaying to and fro as if they were torn from their foundations. Outside, on the other hand, there was the danger of falling pumice stones. . . . After comparing risks, they chose the latter. . . . As a protection against falling objects they put pillows on their heads, tied down with cloths.

"Elsewhere there was daylight by this time, but they were still in darkness, blacker and denser than any ordinary night, which they relieved by lighting torches and various kinds of lamps. My uncle decided to go down to the shore and investigate on the spot the possibility of any escape by sea, but he found the waves still wild and dangerous. A sheet was spread on the ground for him to lie down, and he repeatedly asked for cold water to drink. Then the flames and smell of sulphur, which gave warning of the approaching fire, drove the others to take flight and roused him to stand up. He stood leaning on two slaves and then suddenly collapsed, I imagine because the dense fumes choked his breathing. . . . When daylight returned on the twenty-sixth, two days after the last day he had been seen, his body was found intact and uninjured, still fully clothed and looking more like sleep than death."

Pliny's letter was remarkably silent about his own fortunes, however, and Tacitus apparently wrote back to ask for more details. Pliny then wrote a second time to describe how he and his mother had fled from their home. At their very door, they encountered a swarm of fugitives, and saw that the greatest danger in any catastrophe comes from the fellow victims. "The panic-stricken crowds followed us," Pliny wrote, "obeying that instinct of fear which makes it seem prudent to go the way of others. In a long, close tide, they harassed and jostled us. Once clear of the houses, we stopped, and there encountered fresh prodigies and terrors. The chariots which we had taken were, though on level ground, knocked about in every direction and even with stones could not be kept steady. The sea appeared to have shrunk into itself, as if pushed back by the tremors of the earth. At all events, the banks had widened, and many sea creatures were beached on the sand. In the other direction gaped a horrible black cloud torn by sudden bursts of fire in snakelike flashes, revealing elongated flames similar to lightning but larger.

"And now came the ashes, though as yet sparsely. I turned around. Ominous behind us, a thick smoke spreading over the earth like a flood followed us. 'Let us get into the fields while we can still see the way,' I told my mother, for fear of our being crushed by the mob around us in the road in the midst of this darkness. We had scarcely agreed on this when we were enveloped in night, not a moonless night or one dimmed by clouds, but the darkness of a sealed room without lights. Only the shrill cries of women, the wailing of children, the shouting of men were to be heard. Some were calling to their parents, others to their children, other to their wives, knowing one another only by voice. Some wept for themselves, others for their relations. . . . Many lifted up their hands to the gods, but a great number believed that there were no more gods, and that this night was the world's last, eternal one. . . . I imagined that we were going to perish, one with all and all with one, a wretched but strong consolation in my dying. But . . . . finally a genuine daylight came, the sun even shone, but pallidly, as in an eclipse. And then before our still-stricken gaze, everything appeared changed and covered, as by an abundant snowfall, with a thick layer of ashes."

Pliny was thirty miles to the north of the exploding volcano. Pompeii and Herculaneum lay at its very foot. Herculaneum was engulfed by a torrent of lava and mud, Pompeii by a smothering blanket of pumice and ash, twelve to fifteen feet deep. The steaming lava was slow enough for most of the citizens of Herculaneum to escape. Only about thirty corpses were found there.* The suffocating rain of pumice and ash trapped the Pompeiians, in the midst of life, in their kitchens and their doorways and their cellars. About two thousand of them died that afternoon, and as Colonel Alcubierre's convicts began their excavations they stumbled on the pitiful evidence of the attempts at escape.

In the House of Menander, ten slaves had tried to flee by way of the roof. Their bodies were found on the stairway. Their leader was still clutching the bronze lantern that he had hoped would lead him through the darkness. Downstairs, the doorkeeper and his young daughter had tried to protect themselves with pillows, and so they died. The doorkeeper held a purse that contained two gold coins, ninety of silver and thirteen of brass and copper. In the garden behind the House of Cryptoporticus, a woman was found with her daughter in her arms, near the skylight through which she must have thought she had escaped. Outside the House of Sallust, a woman lay surrounded by the money and jewelry she had tried to carry away. She had also tried to take a silver mirror. Nearby lay the bodies of her three maids, all following her to her

---

* Four more were found in the summer of 1980, and another dozen in 1982, leading Professor Giuseppe Meggi, the archaeologist in charge of the continuing exploration of the Vesuvius area, to speculate that the death toll may have been much higher than previously believed.

ruin. In the Gladiators' Barracks, the bodies of sixty men were found. Also one richly dressed woman who had apparently come to visit them. Also, two prisoners with their hands manacled. Dogs too died in agony, their teeth bared, their necks stoutly chained to the nearest wall.

Not everything was discovered at once, of course. The first of Pompeii's skeletons, clutching some gold coins, was found in 1748, but King Carlos wanted the discoveries kept secret. Only in 1755, the year of the Lisbon earthquake, did the Neapolitan court's inept archivist issue the first catalogue of what had been found: 738 frescoes, 350 statues and 1,647 lesser objects. That same year, Vesuvius erupted again. Not until 1763 did the excavators of Pompeii unearth an inscription bearing the words RES PUBLICA POMPEIANORUM, and thereby realize that what they were excavating was, in fact, Pompeii. Even today, about half of Pompeii has yet to be excavated. But the discovery of the two towns buried at the foot of the volcano, this discovery being announced at almost the very moment of the Lisbon earthquake, aroused a sense of dread and fascination among the intellectuals of the north. Like the disaster at Lisbon, it posed in a new context the terrible question of why God seemed so indifferent to human suffering, so willing to let thousands die for no apparent reason at all.

Among the first to appear on the scene was Johann Joachim Winckelmann, the great German art historian, a protégé of the court of Dresden in Queen Maria Amalia's native Saxony. He came to Naples to inspect the excavations in the spring of 1758. He was appalled to find Colonel Alcubierre and his chained Neapolitan convicts simply poking around for treasure and moving the dirt from place to place as they shuffled along, burying old sites with the debris from new ones. On one occasion, Colonel Alcubierre had found some bronze letters on the wall of a house and pried them off and presented them to the King in a basket without ever recording what the letters had said. The Neapolitans, on the other hand, did not welcome the German's inspection of what was, after all, a private royal preserve. They refused even to let him sit on the committee of local bureaucrats who evaluated each new discovery.

Winckelmann vowed to carry his complaints to the King and Queen, but at almost this very moment came news of the death of King Carlos' insane half brother, Fernando VI of Spain. Carlos had to take his place, and since the diplomatic agreements of that time forbade any union of the thrones of Madrid and Naples, the latter was abandoned to Carlos' scapegrace son, also named Fernando, then a boy of eight. By the time Winckelmann returned to Pompeii in 1762, he found only eight of the chained convicts still jabbing at the debris, still covering up as much as they uncovered. And for every treasure that reached the royal museum at Portici, others ended in the hands of thieves and smugglers. *Sendschreiben von den Herculanischen Entdeckungen (Open Letter on the Discoveries at Herculaneum)* was the title of Winckelmann's public protest in 1762 over the bungling of the Vesuvian excavations. And he was heard. Diderot took up the cause in Paris; so did Goethe in Weimar, and the Society of Dilettanti in London. The court of Naples shamefacedly promised reforms. The cities under the volcano became a kind of international memorial to nature's destructive force.

Voyagers from the far north came to inspect the murderous volcano. Horace Walpole, inevitably, was one of the first. "Have you ever heard of a subterranean town?" he wrote to Benjamin West. "A whole Roman town with all its edifices remaining under ground. . . . ? This underground city [Herculaneum] is perhaps one of the noblest curiosities that ever has been discovered. . . . They have found among other things some fine statues, some human bones, some rice, medals, and a few paintings extremely fine. . . . There is nothing of the kind known in the world."

In due time, Winckelmann reported the arrival of *"ein junger Schottländer"*—James Boswell, of course—who labored his way up Vesuvius and then recorded in his journal nothing more than "monstrous mounting. Smoke; saw hardly anything." Boswell viewed Naples as "a delicious spot," but he did not approve of the Neapolitans, "the most shocking race, eaters of garlic and catchers of vermin—an exercise which they scruple not to perform on the public streets." And John Wilkes, the radical politician in flight from London, who had picked up in Paris a Bolognese dancer named Mademoiselle Corradini. He wrote to his daughter Polly that he had climbed the mountain: "I had five men to get me up: two before, whose girdles I laid hold of; and three behind, who pushed me by the back. I approached quite to the opening from whence issues the sulphurous smoke; . . . I lay on my belly against the side on the edge and looked down, but could see very little . . ." And then Gibbon, fresh from the moment of revelation on the steps of the Roman monastery where "the idea of writing the decline and fall of the city first started to my mind." Of his six-week sojourn in Naples, during which he was almost certainly taken to survey the ruins of Pompeii, he left only a few contemptuous observations: "What a mixture of pride, vice, slavery and poverty have I seen in the short time I passed at Naples."

Others were more explicit, and more admiring. Goethe came and was moved. *"Das Ort inspiriert Nachlässigkeit,"* he wrote. Schiller came and was even more moved. "What miracle is this. . . ?" he wrote. "O Earth! what gifts are these thy silent womb has nursed?/ Does life yet stir in the abyss?" And Madame de Staël came and wrote a novel, *Corinne, ou l'Italie*. Robert Adam came and studied the ruins and then began introducing specifically Roman forms into English architecture. Josiah Wedgwood did not come, but he understood fashions, and soon he was producing "Pompeian" vases. And Shelley came, and expressed more perfectly than all the others what all the others had felt:

> I stood within the City disinterred;
> And heard the autumn leaves like light footfalls
> Of spirits passing through the streets; and heard
> The mountain's slumbrous voice at intervals
> Thrill through these roofless halls. . . .
> I felt that Earth out of her deep heart spoke. . . .

The cicerone for most of these visitors, French and German and English alike, was Sir William Hamilton, the seemingly perpetual British ambassador from 1764 to 1800. Hamilton has suffered the unhappy fate of being known to history as the husband of Lord Nelson's mistress. Before he ever met the famous Emma, however, he was happily married to Catherine, a skilled harpsichordist, and he himself was a notable diplomat, scholar, and collector of classical art. And a passionate observer of Mount Vesuvius. So when it suddenly erupted, in the middle of all these visits, in the fall of 1767, he hired a peasant guide and set off for the mountaintop to see for himself the same kind of apocalyptic explosion that had killed the worthy Pliny.

"I was making my observations upon the lava . . . ," Sir William later wrote to the Royal Society in London, "when, on a sudden, about noon, I heard a violent noise within the mountain, and at the spot about a quarter of a mile off the place where I stood, the mountain split; and, with much noise, from this new mouth a fountain of liquid fire shot up many feet high, and then, like a torrent, rolled on directly toward us. The earth shook, at the same time that a volley of pumice stones fell thick upon us; in an instant clouds of black smoke and ashes caused almost total darkness; the explosions from the top of the mountain were much louder than any thunder I ever heard and the smell of sulphur was very offensive. My guide, alarmed, took to his heels . . . I followed close, and we ran near three miles without stopping . . ."

But what was the meaning of these cataclysms? It is obviously too simple to say that the early eighteenth century was an era in which everyone believed in the orderly workings of a benevolent God—every century has its mystics and its misanthropes—but that was certainly the prevalent teaching and the prevalent creed. The Lisbon earthquake, smashing down churches at the moment of high mass on the morning of All Saints' Day, dealt that creed a devastating blow.

Goethe, writing in his sixties about his recollections of boyhood (in *Dichtung und Wahrheit*), vividly remembered hearing about the "most dreadful calamity" which had occurred when he was six, the heaving earth, the collapsing buildings, the fires and tidal waves and swarms of marauding criminals. "Quicker than the authentic news," he wrote, "intimations of this event spread over wide regions; in many places slighter tremblings were noticed; many springs, especially those with health-giving properties, ceased to flow . . . Perhaps the demon of fear had never so quickly and powerfully diffused his terror over the earth." The future author of *Faust* was, as a six-year-old boy, appalled. "God, the Creator and Upholder of Heaven and Earth," he later wrote, "whom the explanation of the first article of the Creed declared to be so wise and merciful, insofar as He had abandoned the just and the unjust to a like destruction, had in no way shown Himself to be fatherly. In vain did my young mind seek to fortify itself against such impressions. This was all the less possible as the wise men learned in the Scriptures could not agree as to the way in which such a phenomenon should be regarded."

The controversy was, of course, as old as the record of human disasters, but the optimists of the early eighteenth century took as their scripture Gottfried Wilhelm Leibnitz' *Essais de Théodicée sur la bonté de Dieu, la liberté de l'homme, et l'origine du mal,* published in 1710. This work had been commissioned by the Queen of Prussia as a refutation of Pierre Bayle's *Réponse à un provincial,* in which the French Calvinist, having forgotten the fires of Languedoc, argued that the manifest evils of life necessarily implied the existence of two ultimate principles, good and evil. Leibnitz categorically denied all such arguments. This was, he declared, in a phrase that was to acquire somewhat different sonorities, "the best of all possible worlds." Logically, his argument was irrefutable. If God was omniscient and omnipotent, then he must have considered all the possibilities and chosen the best of them. If any evidence appeared to contradict this logic, then the apparent contradiction represented simply a failure to understand God's grand design. It was in a commentary on Leibnitz' *Théodicée* that a French critic coined, in 1737, a new word: "optimism."

Alexander Pope taught the same roseate doctrine to the coffeehouses of London. "Respecting Man, whatever wrong we call,/ May, must be right, as relative to all," he wrote in his *Essay on Man* (1733). Not even an earthquake could shake the poet's sublime confidence. "But errs not Nature from this gracious end . . ./ When earthquakes swallow, or when tempests sweep/ Towns to one grave, whole nations to the deep?/ 'No,' 'tis replied, 'The first Almighty Cause/ Acts not by partial but by general laws.'" And finally: "And spite of Pride, in erring Reason's spite,/ One truth is clear. *Whatever is, is right!*"

There could hardly be a more immoral principle of morality, but as long as the view from London seemed sunny, its markets filled with food and its harbor with merchant vessels, the chief objection to Pope's view was theological. "If it be true . . . that whatever is, is right," as Voltaire summarized the orthodox objections—Voltaire having been an admirer and even a translator of Pope's "immortal verse"—"it follows that human nature is not degenerated. If the general order requires that everything should be as it is, human nature has not been corrupted, and consequently could have had no occasion for a Redeemer." The Lisbon earthquake swept aside all such academic arguments. It raised the most fundamental questions about God: How could he permit such things to happen? Or if they simply happen without his willing them, then does he exist at all? Is there, in fact, any moral force of any kind that governs the universe?

To the partisan clerical eye, the answer must lie in the faults of God's own victims. "O that all who were lately destroyed in Portugal had known the Divine Redeemer," wrote George Whitefield, who had been so shocked by the evidence of Lisbon's superstitious Popery, and who assumed that the flames following the earthquake were inevitably the commencement of hellfire. "Then the earthquake would have been only a rumbling chariot to carry them to God. Poor Lisbon! How soon are all thy riches and superstitious pagentry swallowed up!" Whitefield's colleague John Wesley was less charitable. It was not mere pageantry and superstition but the Holy Inquisition that had provoked God's just wrath. "Is there indeed a God that judges the world?" Wesley demanded in *Serious Thoughts Occasioned by the Late Earthquake at Lisbon.* "And is he now making Inquisition for blood? If so, it is not surprising, he should begin there, where so much blood has been poured on the ground like water. Where so many brave men have been murdered, in the most base and cowardly, as well as barbarous manner, almost every day . . . How long has their blood been crying from the earth . . . ? *And shall I not visit for these things, saith the Lord? Shall not my soul be avenged of such a city as this?"* Among the Catholic orthodox, on the other hand, the earthquake was to be considered an occasion for repentance, and if the Inquisition was considered as a force of divine chastisement, then its only sin was its lenience. It should have rooted out more of Lisbon's sinners, and it should have treated them more harshly. God, in sum, had punished Lisbon for its failure to obey his principles.

Voltaire, as in so many instances, understood the challenge more subtly, and responded more radically. It was not a question of which orthodoxy was right or wrong but whether any orthodoxy could be believed at all. Voltaire had already abandoned Pope during the 1730s and Leibnitz during the 1740s, and as he drifted in search of a new metaphysical anchorage, the Lisbon earthquake served, as Dr. Johnson said of Joseph Baretti's prospective execution, to concentrate the mind powerfully. His dramatic *Poème sur le désastre de Lisbonne*, which he finished in draft form within a month after the cataclysm, began with a vivid evocation of the destruction and then proclaimed the paradox that was later to be declared in even more passionate form by Ivan Karamazov: "*Quel crime, quelle faute ont commis ces enfants/ Sur le sein maternel écrasés et sanglants?/ Lisbonne, qui n'est plus, eut-elle plus de vices/ Que Londres, que Paris, plongés dans les délices?/ Lisbonne est abîmée, et l'on danse à Paris.*" Tobias Smollett's contemporary translation fails to capture Voltaire's vehemence, but it is probably the best expression of the eighteenth-century view. "And can you then impute a sinful deed," he renders these same lines, "to babes who on their mothers' bosoms bleed?/ Was then more vice in fallen Lisbon found,/ Than Paris, where voluptuous joys abound?/ Was less debauchery to London known,/ Where opulence luxurious holds her throne?/ Earth Lisbon swallows; the light sons of France/ Protract the feast, or lead the sprightly dance."

The destruction of Lisbon clearly represented a kind of microcosmic version of the end of the world, and Voltaire just as clearly saw its prophetic aspects. *Mors stupebit* . . . The Smollett version again: "Approach in crowds and meditate awhile/ Yon shattered walls, and view each ruined pile,/ Women and children heaped up mountain high,/ Limbs crushed which under ponderous marble lie;/ Wretches unnumbered in the pangs of death,/ Who mangled, torn, and panting for their breath,/ Buried beneath their sinking roofs expire,/ And end their wretched lives in torments dire./ Say, when you hear their piteous, half-formed cries,/ Or from their ashes see the smoke arise,/ Say, will you then eternal laws maintain,/ Which God to cruelties like these constrain?"

Having raised these questions, Voltaire did not know how to answer them. There are, obviously, only three answers: that there is no God, that the God who created the universe has no interest in human life, or that God has some purpose we cannot understand in his infliction of destruction upon us. The first two answers were unacceptable to even the most tolerant authorities of the eighteenth-century church, and perhaps to Voltaire himself. He could reject Leibnitz' dogma with the simple declaration *"Le mal est sur la terre,"* but he could not decide how to bring his poem to a conclusion. His first version was the best: *"Que faut-il, O Mortels! Mortels, il faut souffrir, / Se soumettre en silence, adorer et mourir."* (What must we do, O mortals? We must suffer, submit in silence, worship and die.) He worried about this conclusion, however. Heretics were still subject to imprisonment, or worse, and Voltaire had experienced the miseries of French prisons. But aside from the danger of punishment, was this bleak couplet really what he wanted as the conclusion of his sermon? Several friends to whom he sent this first draft urged him to reconsider. And so he began making an interesting series of compromises. *"Mortels, il faut souffrir,"* the second version ended, with an added note of hope: *"Se soumettre, adorer, espérer, et mourir."* That was still too depressing, Voltaire's friends told him, and so when the poem was finally printed in Geneva in February of 1756, the last two lines had been chopped off, leaving the poem to end on a note of mysticism: *"Au sein de l'infini, nous élançons notre être,/ Sans pouvoir un moment nous voir et nous connaître."*

He was still dissatisfied, understandably enough. So he composed an entirely new ending, introducing the image of a dying caliph who sought to address the maker about to receive him. " *'Je t'apporte, ô seul roi, seul être illimité, Tout ce que tu n'as pas dans ton immensité,/ Les défauts, les regrets, les maux, et l'ignorance,'/ mais il pouvait encore ajouter l'espérance."* Smollett's version: " 'Being supreme, whose greatness knows no bound,/ I bring Thee all that can't in Thee be found;/ Defects and sorrows, ignorance and woe.'/ Hope he omitted, man's sole bliss below." Still, still it wasn't right, still too definite. There has been found a copy on which Voltaire altered in his own hand the last line into a question: *"Mais pouvait-il encore ajouter l'espérance?"*

Voltaire had a neighbor in Geneva, almost twenty years his junior, a onetime footman, schoolteacher, apprentice engraver, seminarian, music copyist, and lately celebrated author of a *Discourse on the Arts and Sciences.* Jean-Jacques Rousseau envied the older man and even considered leaving Geneva because of Voltaire's arrival. "What could I, timid, and a poor speaker, have done unaided against one who was arrogant, wealthy, supported by the credit of the great, brilliantly eloquent, and already the idol of the women and young men?" Rousseau later wrote in his *Confessions.* Voltaire sent Rousseau a copy of his poem on Lisbon, and Rousseau gloated at the prospects of reprisal. "Surprised to hear this poor man, overwhelmed, so to speak, by fame and prosperity, declaim bitterly against the miseries of this life, and declare everything to be bad," Rousseau wrote, "I formed the senseless plan of bringing him to himself again, and proving to him that everything was good. Voltaire, while always appearing to believe in God, has never really believed in anything but the Devil . . ."

To Voltaire himself, Rousseau began on an almost fawning note, describing the older man as his brother and his master. "It is in order to make my admiration more worthy of your works," he wrote, "that I force myself not to admire everything." His first objection—and his letter runs to twenty printed pages, more than twice the length of Voltaire's poem—was equally disingenuous. He claimed that Voltaire had worsened the whole problem by trying to deprive him of his optimism. "This optimism that you find so cruel consoles me in the same sorrows that you portray as unsupportable," he wrote. "The poem of Pope softens my ills and brings me to patience . . . ; yours reduces me to despair."

If the basic paradox was the conflict between God's omnipotence and his benevolence, why must Voltaire insist on "his power at the expense of his goodness?" God is good, and nature is good, Rousseau insisted. It could be stated as a law, self-evident and indisputable. And if a natural force destroyed tens of thousands of human beings, that did not invalidate the law. Why were all those people crowded together in Lisbon in the first place? "Nature did not gather together twenty thousand houses of six or seven stories," Rousseau wrote, "and if the inhabitants of this great city had been more equally dispersed and more lightly housed, the damage would have been much less, and perhaps nil." And then, having unnaturally crowded themselves into this unnatural city, the inhabitants of Lisbon failed even at the last moment to obey the natural instinct of survival. "How many perished in this disaster because they wanted to carry things away," Rousseau asked, "the one his clothes, another his papers, another his money?" And then, is death really so terrible? "Among so many men crushed under the ruins of this unhappy city, several doubtless escaped still worse miseries. . . . It is not sure that a single one of these unfortunates suffered more than he would have, in the ordinary course of things, if he had waited in long anguish for the death that came by surprise." And then, if philosophers interpret such disasters to mean that life is not worth living, it is because they "always forget the sweet pleasures of existence."

Does he contradict himself? Very well, then, he contradicts himself. Rousseau nonetheless kept returning to his dogma that nature was good, and therefore no natural event could be evil. Even earthquakes must have their role in the natural order. "Is it up to us to say that the order of the world must change according to our caprices," he demanded, "and to forbid an earthquake in some place where we have chosen to build a city?" Voltaire had ridiculed the idea that a man's meaningless death could be justified as part of nature's cycle, but Rousseau insisted on exactly that. "That the body of a man feeds worms, wolves or plants is not, I admit, a compensation for the death of that man," he wrote, "but if in the system of this universe, it is necessary for the conservation of the human race that there be a circulation of substances among men, animals and plants, then the particular ill of one individual contributes to the general good."

Rousseau admitted that the statement that *"tout est bien"* might be challenged, but he insisted on the truth of *"le tout est bien,"* an alteration that might be translated by changing "everything is good" to "the whole is good." He insisted just as fervently that this was self-evident despite all the destruction of the Lisbon earthquake. "The true principles of optimism cannot be drawn from the properties of matter, or from the mechanism of the universe, but only by induction from the perfections of God who presides over all," he wrote. "Thus one does not prove the existence of God by Pope's system but Pope's system by the existence of God."

Rousseau presumably knew that such arguments would not convince a man of Voltaire's skeptical turn of mind, and so he reinforced his argument with personal criticisms. Seizing on one of Voltaire's gloomier statements, that "nobody would want to be reborn," Rousseau demanded to know whom he had interviewed as the basis for such a judgment. "Rich men, perhaps," he went on in answer to his own question, "sated with false pleasures but ignorant of the true ones . . . , perhaps men of letters, of all orders of men the most sedentary, the most unhealthy, the most reflective and consequently the most unhappy." For a more accurate view of the human condition, Rousseau plunged on, Voltaire should talk to "an honest merchant, who has spent an obscure and tranquil life, . . . a good artisan, . . . even a peasant." In a final burst of impertinence, Rousseasu undertook to compare Voltaire and himself. "Surfeited with glory, disillusioned with vain grandeur, you live freely in the midst of abundance; certain of immortality, you philosophize calmly on the nature of the soul . . . and yet you find nothing but evil on the earth. And I, an obscure man, poor, alone, tormented by an incurable illness, I meditate with pleasure in my retreat and find that all is good. Whence come these apparent contradictions? You yourself have explained: You enjoy, but I hope, and hope embellishes everything."

Voltaire responded to Rousseau's outburst in a manner that can only be described as philosophical. He addressed his bumptious critic as *"mon cher philosophe"* and called his letter "very fine" but added that he would have to "drop these philosophical discussions, which are merely pastimes," because a niece who was staying at his house had fallen ill. Rousseau, who had been somewhat nervous about Voltaire's reactions, wrote with relief to a friend that "a man who is able to take my letter as he did deserves to be called a philosopher." But Voltaire had by no means abandoned the battlefield. He was simply declining to debate with a neighbor who showed so little understanding of the meaning of the disaster at Lisbon. If Rousseau was determined to echo Leibnitz' claim that God in his goodness had created the best of all possible worlds, then Voltaire could only acquiesce—and portray to the world this best of all possible worlds. His portrait was, of course, *Candide,* which Rousseau characteristically proclaimed as purely an answer to his own letter, adding that it was an answer "of which I cannot speak, because I have not read it."

Candide, a foundling brought up in the castle of a Westphalian baron, believes entirely in the Leibnitzian views of the family tutor, Dr. Pangloss, a teacher of "metaphysico-theologo-cosmolonigology," and it seems perfectly natural that the best of all possible worlds should bring him the kisses of the Baron's daughter Cunegonde, who was "rosy-cheeked, fresh, plump and tempting." He clings to Dr. Pangloss' philosophy even when the Baron expels him for kissing Cunegonde, even after he is forcibly recruited into the Bulgarian Army (an army remarkably like the Prussian Army of the philosopher-king Frederick the Great), even after he watches the "heroic butchery" of the Bulgarians sacking a town, even after he encounters Dr. Pangloss as a beggar, "covered with sores, dull-eyed, with the end of his nose fallen away," even after Dr. Pangloss tells him that Cunegonde is dead, "disemboweled by Bulgarian soldiers, after having been raped to the limit of possibility." Dr. Pangloss explains that all these disasters were inevitable, that "private misfortunes make the public good, so that the more private misfortunes there are, the more everything is well."

Even as he speaks, Candide and Dr. Pangloss are sailing into Lisbon harbor, which gives Voltaire another chance to describe the disaster: "They had scarcely set foot in the town when they felt the earth tremble under their feet; the sea rose in foaming masses in the port and smashed the ships which rode at anchor. Whirlwinds of flame and ashes covered the streets and squares; the houses collapsed, the roofs were thrown upon the foundations, and the foundations were scattered; thirty thousand inhabitants of every age and both sexes were crushed under the ruins . . . 'It is the last day!' cried Candide." Several falling stones injure the young optimist, and he cries out for help, but Dr. Pangloss only rebukes him for false reasoning. "This earthquake is not a new thing," he says. He cites an earthquake in Lima the previous year and argues that there "must certainly be a train of sulphur underground from Lima to Lisbon."

" 'Nothing is more probable,' replied Candide; 'but for God's sake, a little oil and wine.'

" 'What do you mean, probable?' replied the philosopher. 'I maintain that it is proved.' "

Dr. Pangloss continues arguing his view later that same evening, "that all this is for the best; for, if there is a volcano at Lisbon, it cannot be anywhere else; for it is impossible that things should not be where they are; for all is well." As he continues arguing, he encounters an agent of the Inquisition, who asks whether he does not believe in free will and then cuts short his elaborate answer by arresting him.

"After the earthquake which destroyed three-quarters of Lisbon," Voltaire bitterly continues, "the wise men of that country could discover no more efficacious way of preventing a total ruin than by giving the people a splendid *auto-da-fé.*" Dressed in paper miters ornamented with flames and devils, Candide and Dr. Pangloss and three other sinners are led through the streets to the square dedicated to the ritual fires. There is a "most pathetic sermon" and some "lovely" singing. Candide is flogged in time with the music, Dr. Pangloss is hanged, and the other three captives are burned, and then another of the earthquake's aftershocks strikes the square. "Candide, terrified, dumbfounded, bewildered, covered with blood, quivering from head to foot, said to himself, 'If this is the best of all possible worlds, what are the others?' "

Voltaire offers no answer to this, and it is only by following his ferocious narrative that we learn that Dr. Pangloss did not die, nor Cunegonde either. That by the time Candide is reunited with her, Cunegonde "was indeed very ugly, but she became an excellent pastry cook." And that the only purpose in life, as they all finally agree, is to "work without theorizing" and to "cultivate one's garden." Voltaire offered his masterpiece to the world in 1759 under the pseudonym of "Le Docteur Ralph," and when it was suggested that he was the author, Voltaire, like another Galileo denying to the Inquisition his discovery that the earth circled the sun, denied that he had written it. "People must have lost their senses to attribute to me that pack of nonsense," he declared.

*

In Portugal itself, the debate over God's purposes was presided over by Premier Carvalho. It was his view that the priesthood should preach uplifting thoughts and join in the rebuilding of Lisbon, but the saintly Jesuit missionary, Father Malagrida, insisted that God's message was not to rebuild but to repent. Well before his involvement with the Tavora family, Malagrida had openly challenged Carvalho's policy in a series of sermons, and finally in a pamphlet, published in the autumn of 1756, entitled *Juizo da Verdadeira Causa de Terremoto* (*An Opinion on the True Cause of the Earthquake*). "Learn, O Lisbon," wrote Malagrida, "that the destroyers of our houses, palaces, churches, and convents . . . are your abominable sins, and not comets, stars, vapors and exhalations. . . . It is scandalous to pretend the earthquake was just a natural event, for if that be true, there is no need to repent and to try to avert the wrath of God. . . . Now indeed the case of Lisbon is desperate. It is necessary to devote all our strength and purpose to the task of repentance. Would to God we could see as much determination and fervor for this necessary exercise as are devoted to the erection of huts. . . . He is watching, scourge in hand."

Malagrida was not speaking in generalities. He demanded that the government build a series of hostels to house the penitents, and that the entire surviving population of Lisbon go into a six-day retreat. This Quixotic campaign was halted, of course, by Malagrida's arrest in the Tavora conspiracy, but the laws of the time prevented Carvalho from inflicting on Malagrida the ghastly vengeance he wreaked on the Tavora family. He could only imprison him in the fetid dungeon under the Belém Castle, and then wait while the septuagenarian missionary's mind began to crumble. And then finally turn him over to the Inquisition, which was now directed by Carvalho's brother Paul.

The inquisitors took an intense interest in Malagrida's angelic visions, and in the voices that dictated to him his life of Saint Anne. They found his demented fascination with Saint Anne's uterus to be obscene and blasphemous. They decreed that he had consorted with evil spirits. They condemned him to death. And so, on the night of September 21, 1761, after an auto-da-fé that lasted all day, the white-haired priest, by now seventy-two years of age, was dragged out in front of the crowds in the Rossio and publicly strangled. His corpse was flung onto the bonfire, and the ashes were cast into the Tagus.

To Johann Sebastian Bach, the idea of the divine order was embodied in the idea of the fugue. This was as natural to him as it was natural for the architects of Coutances to express their visions in the form of two slender stone towers, or for the sculptors of Moissac to carve their image of God into the startled faces of the twenty-four elders looking up toward the light. When Bach was baptized at the Georgenkirche in Eisenach, at the foot of the famous Wartburg castle where the minstrels once held the competitions that were eventually to be celebrated in *Tannhäuser*, he was baptized into the craft of music. He was the son of Johann Ambrosius Bach, a violinist in the Thuringian court orchestra, and the grandson of Cristoph Bach, the town piper in nearby Arnstadt. His first wife was a cousin, his second a professional singer. Of the five sons who survived him, all were musicians, even Gottfried, who was mentally retarded, and of the four daughters, only one ever married, and she married a musician, one of Sebastian's pupils. And they were devout. All the Bachs were passionate Lutherans, and they took pride in the misfortunes of Veit Bach, Sebastian's great-great-grandfather, a baker who played the cittern and thus was the first of the Bach musicians. He had gone to seek his fortunes in the remote land of Hungary and had been compelled, according to a family chronicle, "to escape from Hungary because of his Lutheran faith." God and music and the raising of children—these were Bach's life.

The fugue is the most ordered form of musical expression, the most systematically organized, and yet it challenges all rigid orthodoxies. It demands flexibility and imagination, and its demands have fascinated composers as diverse as Mozart and Schumann, Liszt and Brahms. Bach was its supreme master, as he was the master of every contrapuntal technique, and it was his unfortunate destiny to be the master of a style that was rapidly passing out of fashion. Counterpoint, in which all voices are equal, was giving way to the accompanied melodies of the *style gallant*. As early as 1737, a twenty-nine-year-old journalist named Adolph Scheibe wrote a stinging attack on Bach in a new periodical, *Critischer Musicus*. Bach could be the wonder of the world, Scheibe wrote with mock deference, "if his compositions displayed more agreeable qualities, were less turgid and sophisticated, more simple and natural in character.... All his parts are equally melodic, so that one cannot distinguish the principal tune among them. In short, ... pomposity diverts [him] from a natural to an artificial style, changing what might have been sublime into the obscure.... We wonder at an effort so labored and, since nothing comes of it, so futile."

It is undeniable that Bach loved complexity, but out of that love came his greatest works. Only Bach could have determined to write a prelude and fugue in each of the twelve halftones of the scale, and in both major and minor, and then, having practically invented modern tonality in the masterpiece that he called *The Well-Tempered Clavier,* calmly repeated the feat with a second set of twenty-four preludes and fugues even more stupendous than the first. Only Bach could have determined to write a set of thirty variations on a beautiful melody without ever quoting any part of that melody, to build instead, on the harmonic substructure of the theme, a gorgeous series of canons at intervals from the second up to the octave, and even the ninth, and all this just so that when the insomniac Count Hermann von Kaiserling couldn't sleep, he could order one of his servants, Johann Theophilus Goldberg, to play him some of Bach's Goldberg Variations.

Now, at the age of sixty-five, Bach decided to build a kind of cathedral of sound, a fortress of his own faith in the craft of his forefathers. It has come down to us under the name *The Art of the Fugue,* but we do not know whether that was Bach's own title or the idea of a fanciful publisher (who ultimately sold a total of fifty copies before deciding to scrap the edition and the engraved plates). We do not even know what instrument Bach planned for his work. Most of it can be played on a piano, but there are sections that require two pianos, and various transcribers have produced versions for organ, string quartet and chamber orchestra. Bach was not concerned about such details. Out of one simple four-measure theme in D minor, he planned to create a vast structure that would display every possibility of his art. It would be a great tower, illuminated by windows of resonance, buttressed by invisible flying arches, and reaching, finally, to the heavens, to a spire surmounted by a gleaming cross. He began, like any master builder of the twelfth century, by digging the foundations. He stated his theme and then composed a handsome, sturdy four-part fugue upon it. Then he stated the theme again, one octave lower, and altered the ending to a dotted rhythm that became the rhythm of the entire fugue. Then he stated the theme a third time, inverted in this appearance, a mirror image of what had gone before. . . .

As he kept working and building, his eyes gave out. He could not see. We do not know the exact symptoms—a general blurring, a graying of everything before him, or dancing spots, or stabbing aches, or sudden rings of light, or the tiny specks and hooks and scratches of his pen swimming before his eyes. The contemporary chronicles tell us only that he strained his eyes through years of overwork, years of staying up much of the night to copy out his compositions by the light of a flickering candle. Now the strain had become too great. He could not see, could not work. The sounds that echoed inside his head could not be captured and transformed into pieces of the cathedral that he was building.

Salvation seemed to appear, at about this time, in the form of a roving English doctor who called himself Chevalier Taylor. He called himself much else besides. In a pamphlet entitled *The Life of the Chevalier John Taylor, Occulist Pontifical, Imperial and Royal,* which he must have subsidized and may even have written, the Chevalier is described as a man "who has been personally known . . . to every crown'd head and sovereign prince now reigning in all Europe, . . . who has also been personally known to all of eminence who lived in his time. . . . With regard to his abilities and extraordinary merit in his profession, it has long been the united voice of the world, that he is the foremost man now living [and] perhaps in any times before us." Taylor boasted of having traveled to "every court, kingdom, province, state, city and town of the least consideration in all Europe," and to have treated "near eighty thousand different persons," including "the kings of England, Poland, Denmark, Sweden &c." These extensive travels may have been prompted by the failures that Taylor left behind him. "The most ignorant man I ever knew, but sprightly," said Dr. Johnson. "He was an example of how far impudence could carry ignorance."

When this charlatan's wanderings brought him to Leipzig, Bach's friends persuaded him to go for treatment. Chevalier Taylor operated on the old man's failing eyes, and after the operation he was worse. Chevalier Taylor operated again, and after the second operation Bach was totally blind. Chevalier Taylor also prescribed some kind of drugs, which, in ways that the contemporary accounts do not make clear,* ruined Bach's previously excellent health. There is

* "Perhaps noxious medicines" is the phrase used by Bach's first biographer, Johann Nikolaus Forkel, whose work appeared in 1802.

little more to tell of Chevalier Taylor, that agent of God's caprices, except that two years later he operated on George Frederick Handel, who had been stricken in the midst of composing a chorus to the text "How dark, oh Lord, are Thy decrees," and Chevalier Taylor succeeded in blinding Handel just as he had blinded Bach.

There had been rage in Bach from the beginning. It never appeared in his music, in contrast to the self-pitying indignation of Beethoven or the noisy grumbling of Brahms, for he never knew the Romantic view of art as an expression of personality. His art was partly a craft, partly a form of worship. But now, blinded, helpless, unable to work, unable even to find his way through the streets of Leipzig, he could hardly help feeling a surge of the anger that he had contained within himself for much of his life. He could hardly help remembering. He had been an orphan at the age of ten, miserably poor, sent to live with an older brother who was almost as poor as he. He had earned his keep by singing in the streets, singing at the funerals of the rich and the ordinations of the powerful, singing in the snowy streets for a few groschen thrown to the boys by the adjutants of the great.

He had found employment as organist at the court of Wilhelm Ernst, Duke of Saxe-Weimar. He was twenty-three and already the transcendent master of the most complex of instruments. "It is as though eternal harmony were conversing with itself," Goethe was later to write of Bach's organ works, "as it may have happened in God's bosom shortly before He created the world." Bach was disinclined to such indulgences. "There is nothing to it," he said of his own virtuosity. "You only have to hit the right notes at the right time, and the instrument plays itself." And again: "I was obliged to work hard. Whoever is equally industrious will succeed just as well."

The same bluntness served him disastrously in the growing conflict between Duke Wilhelm and his eccentric nephew and heir, Duke Ernst August. The old Duke forbade all his musicians to perform at the residence of the young Duke, on pain of a fine of ten thalers. Bach celebrated the young Duke's birthday by conducting a cantata for him. The old Duke did not fine his unruly organist but pointedly passed over him in appointing a new *Kapellmeister*. Bach just as pointedly went and got himself a new position as conductor of the court orchestra in the nearby principality of Cöthen. The Duke of Saxe-Weimar refused to grant permission for Bach to leave. Bach insisted. The Duke again refused. Bach again insisted. The organist, according to the official document, was therefore "put under arrest for too obstinately requesting his dismissal." Not only arrested but imprisoned, from November 6 to December 2, in the year 1717, for the crime of trying to change jobs. Even after a month in prison, Bach refused to give in, so the Duke released him, judging that he had learned his lesson. He undoubtedly had, though he might differ with the Duke on what the lesson was.

Cöthen was a delight. Prince Leopold was a youth of twenty-three who loved music, sang baritone, played the violin, the clavier and the viola de gamba. Here Bach composed much of his best-known instrumental music, the Brandenburg Concertos, the first book of *The Well-Tempered Clavier*, the suites for violin and for cello. But the young Prince married a girl who didn't like music, and Bach soon understood that his future lay elsewhere. He had learned his lesson.

The authorities at Leipzig had been looking for a cantor at the school of the Church of St. Thomas. Bach was by no means their first choice. Their favorite was George Philipp Telemann, newly appointed music director and cantor at Hamburg, and in the course of negotiations Telemann won some important concessions, such as the abolition of the requirement that the cantor teach Latin to the choirboys. Having won these concessions, Telemann went back to Hamburg and negotiated a raise for himself. The frustrated burghers of Leipzig turned to their next choice, one Cristoph Graupner, conductor of the Hessian court orchestra, but the Prince of Hesse would not let him leave. Only then did Leipzig begin to consider hiring Bach. The terms were poor, a salary of one hundred florins a year, one fourth of Bach's salary at Cöthen, to be augmented by what were known as *Accidentien,* a percentage of the fees for weddings, funerals and other ceremonies. And he had to teach Latin. Bach pursued the opening partly because his position at Cöthen was becoming difficult, partly because he wanted greater educational opportunities for his sons, but the job, when he finally got it, was even worse than he expected. Not only did he have to teach Latin but he had to serve as the school disciplinarian for one week in every month, from the reveille at 4 A.M. until he himself turned out all the lights at 8 P.M. As for his music, which he was expected to compose and conduct for all ceremonial occasions, the city authorities heard a tryout and then wrote into his contract a stipulation that he must not be "too theatrical."

Here he wrote a new cantata for every Sunday in the year, then repeated this outpouring until there were five for each Sunday, some three hundred works in all. Here he wrote festive music for weddings, and motets for funerals, and solemn marches for the inauguration of the Leipzig City Council. And here he wrote the *Saint Matthew Passion.* It was a work conceived on a most grand scale, for double choir and double orchestra, and yet Bach had almost nothing to work with. The evidence survives in a pitiful memorandum from Bach to the Leipzig city council entitled *Short but most necessary draft for a well-appointed church music; with certain modest reflections on the decline of the same.* For an orchestra, said Bach, he needed a minimum of eighteen players, and he even specified each one—"two or even three" first violinists, two oboists, one bassoonist, one drummer, and so on. For the chorus, he needed at least three sopranos, altos, tenors and basses. Thus a minimum of twelve singers and eighteen instrumentalists, so that the music could be performed "even if one happens to fall ill (as very often happens, particularly at this time of year, as the prescriptions written by the school physician for the apothecary must show)." But the school had only fifty-four students, and to Bach's despair the authorities kept admitting boys with no musical talent. He even submitted a judgment on them, name by name, and then concluded: "Total: 17 usable, 20 not yet usable, and 17 unfit."

For this ragtag collection, Bach wrote one of the supreme masterpieces of European civilization, and when it was all done—imagine those two dozen snuffling schoolboys struggling through the glories of *Kommt, ihr Töchter* while their classmates sawed away at their fiddles under the terrible glowering of their cantor—when it was all done, nobody seems to have noticed that something had happened. At a meeting of the city council the following August, the councilors considered once again the familiar complaints against Bach, that he had skipped several of his classes, and had delegated others to subordinates. "Not only did the cantor do nothing," said Court Councilor Steger, "but he was not even willing to give an explanation of that fact." Another official identified in the council minutes as Syndic Job added that "the cantor was incorrigible." The council thereupon voted to reduce Bach's share in the fees earned from weddings, funerals and other ceremonies.

The Art of the Fugue would free Bach of all such problems. It didn't matter who played it, or on what instrument, or at what price. The whole wonderful construction grew in his mind, and as he heard it sounding he wrote it down, page after page after page. Until everything suddenly cracked. He couldn't see the paper on which he had written, couldn't see the connections, couldn't connect the sounds in his head to the ruled paper that was separated from him by the gray waste of blindness. He had been working up until the end on the engravers' proofs, but what finally emerged from the publishers in Berlin is a jumble that scholars have never figured out. Nobody knows what the correct sequence of fugues is supposed to be. Nobody knows, for that matter, why Bach suddenly abandoned his fugues and began writing a series of incredibly abstruse canons—the very first, for example, is in augmentation and contrary motion, meaning that the second voice comes in at half the speed of the first, and upside down. Nobody knows, finally, which of these works are drafts that Bach intended to discard or what order he intended to pursue in this ultimate hymn to order.

The reports of Bach's illness reached official quarters, and so the Saxon Court Minister Count Brühl wrote to the Leipzig authorities that they should begin searching for a successor to their obstreperous cantor. He recommended the Dresden conductor Johann Gottlob Harrer, and Harrer was invited to Leipzig to demonstrate his skills. He conducted a performance of one of his cantatas at an inn called Three Swans. The *Chronik Leipzigs* reported that this event was a necessary tryout for the "future position of Thomas cantor, if the *director musices*, Sebastian Bach, should pass away." Bach inevitably heard of the event and was outraged, but now, in contrast to his past rages, there was nothing he could do.

The climax of *The Art of the Fugue* was to be a work of almost unimaginable splendor. "Everything must be possible," Bach liked to say. This final fugue started slowly and majestically with a rather abbreviated version of the main theme, but after 114 bars of rich elaboration Bach introduced an entirely new subject, a nervous, running theme that changed the whole course of the fugue. After seventy-eight more bars of these two subjects working together, Bach introduced yet another new subject, the haunting chromatic theme based on the letters of his own name (in German musical terminology, B stands for B flat and H for B natural). As he began building the fugue around himself, and then combining the three themes into a sky-scraping thrust that recalls the pride and ambition of the Tower of Babel, everything suddenly stopped. The manuscript simply ends, in the middle of a bar. The music, when performed, halts as if the composer had been struck by lightning. As, in fact, he had been.

No scholars have ever figured out exactly how Bach planned to complete his masterpiece, and it puzzled them that this last fugue, if indeed it was the last fugue, did not include any restatement of the original theme that underlay the whole work. Only in 1880 did a German expert named M. G. Nottebohm discover that this main theme could be superimposed on the three subjects of the final fugue to form a stupendous quadruple fugue. This discovery led several contemporary composers, notably Ferrucio Busoni and Donald Francis Tovey, to write imaginary reconstructions of how Bach might have reached his conclusion. This passion for resolution and order might have won Bach's approval, but no ending could possibly be so dramatic, so powerful, so awe-inspiring as the abrupt halt that destiny ordained.

Bach lived some weeks longer, and he too naturally worried about an ending. He could not create it, could not write, could not see. He tried dictating to his son-in-law Johann Christoph Altnikol. He had in his mind an organ chorale that he had written some years previously and entitled "Wenn wir in höchsten Nöthen sein" (When we are in direst need), and now he wanted to make some changes, refinements, and he finally gave it a new title: "Vor deinen Thron tret ich hiemit" (Before thy throne with this I come).

And then, on the morning of July 18, 1750, Bach suddenly and mysteriously regained his eyesight. Saw. Saw the hot sun shining over the tiled rooftops of Leipzig. Saw the linden trees rustling their pale leaves in the breeze. Saw the girls in their red and white dresses chasing each other down the street. Saw the sleeping shepherd dog and the wasp under the eave and the old woman beating the carpet and the water wagon creaking over the cobblestones. Saw all of God's creation, at once and together, and then, that very same day, fell to the floor with an apoplectic stroke, and saw nothing more, and never recovered again. There was a high fever, and he died ten days later, Tuesday, July 28, 1750, at 8:45 P.M. He was buried three days afterward in St. Thomas' churchyard, near the church itself. In the nineteenth century, however, they moved the graveyard farther away from the church, in order to make space for a highway, and so the remains of Bach were obliterated.

And what does all this have to do with the Lisbon earthquake, or the end of the world? It raises, as did the discovery of Pompeii, but in much more concentrated form, many of the questions that Voltaire was to raise in his celebrated poem about the disaster in Portugal. The people of Lisbon were praying on the morning of All Saints' Day, and Bach, in his way, was performing an act of worship in creating The Art of the Fugue. So if God does not strike down the guilty in the midst of their evil, why does he strike down the innocent as they worship him? Or if sudden death is not mere annihilation, a return to nothingness, what is it? Struck blind, did Bach then pray for his sight to be restored? And was it restored, that one day, on condition that Bach give up his life? All of Bach's music preaches acceptance of God's will, so when he gave up life, did he do so willingly, or did he cry out, like the devout Portuguese buried under tons of fallen rock, against the divine order?

BOOK III

—

IN

OUR TIME

—

My flesh is clothed with worms and clods of dust; my skin is broken and become loathsome. My days are swifter than a weaver's shuttle, and are spent without hope. O remember that my life is wind: mine eye shall no more see good. ... What is man, that thou shouldest magnify him? and that thou shouldest set thine heart upon him?

—JOB, 7:5–17

The Coming Revolution

1905

"We can live like this no longer."

Anton Chekhov passionately wanted to write a funny play. His next work would be "gay and lighthearted," he told his new wife, Olga. "I shall call my play a comedy," he wrote to his producers at the Moscow Art Theater. To a friend, he described it as "not a drama but a comedy and even in places a farce," And to Olga, again, he promised that it would "definitely be funny, very funny."

When Chekhov finally sent his manuscript of *The Cherry Orchard* to the Moscow Art Theater, the whole company gathered for a reading. The gay and lighthearted comedy overwhelmed them. "All wept after last act," Konstantin Stanislavsky reported in a telegram to Chekhov at his retreat in Yalta. As for himself, Stanislavsky declared, he was exalted: "Shaken. Cannot come to senses. In unprecedented ecstasy." Chekhov was dismayed by such reactions. He did not answer Stanislavsky's effusive telegram, but when another of the theater's directors commented on the pervasive sadness of *The Cherry Orchard,* he protested, "Why do you say ... that there are many tearful people in my play? Where are they?"

There actually are quite a few of them, and Chekhov could not resist adding an almost tearful description of his own spirits: "I lead a lonely life, keeping to a diet, coughing, and losing my temper from time to time." Despite Chekhov's intentions, *The Cherry Orchard* was indeed written under difficult circumstances. At forty-three, the playwright was not only spitting blood from tuberculosis but also suffering from a whole congeries of other afflictions: emphysema, pleurisy, hemorrhoids, rheumatism, chronic diarrhoea, insomnia, recurrent eye aches and toothaches. A friend who visited him in Yalta during these last months described him as "a little man with narrow shoulders, with a narrow bloodless face ... , thin, emaciated, unrecognizable."

In this state, Chekhov dragged himself to Moscow in December of 1903 to attend the rehearsals of *The Cherry Orchard* and to try to prevent Stanislavsky from turning it into an epic of melancholia. In vain. Stanislavsky was determined to explore what he called "the secret treasure house of the human spirit." And on opening night, Chekhov's forty-fourth birthday, the playwright suffered a fate that he might have considered "very funny" if only it had happened to someone else. During the last intermission of this performance that he believed to be a ruinous misinterpretation, he was surprised to be summoned to the stage and heaped with gifts and sonorous praises. He looked so pale and coughed so badly that someone in the audience cried, "A chair for Anton Pavlovich!" but he patiently remained on his feet as the speeches rolled on. Stanislavsky saw that Chekhov was "far from happy" about the ceremony,* and he attributed this at least partly to the possibility that he "foresaw his own end." Chekhov blamed his interpreter. "All I can say," he wrote bitterly to a friend, "is, Stanislavsky has wrecked my play."

In theory, the artist is the best judge of his own creation, but there occasionally are times when he creates something that is deeper, richer, more complex and more powerful than even he himself realizes, and so it was with *The Cherry Orchard*. The dying Chekhov had a prescient sense not only of his own death, which occurred six months later, but of the death of the whole society that was imperceptibly crumbling all around him. He had acquired a poetic vision of death itself, death as loss, death as transfiguration. In his youth he had been deeply wounded by the bankruptcy of his father, who had been forced to close his grocery store, abandon his home and flee to Moscow in disgrace. Now he transformed that lost home into Madame Ranyevskaya's country estate, where the rows of cherry trees bloomed white just outside the windows of the long-unused nursery.

Everyone sees different shadows among the cherry trees. To Madame Ranyevskaya, they are symbols of romance. "My beautiful orchard!" she cries. "My life, my youth, my happiness!" But in her search for romance—she ran off to France with a lover—she has wasted all the family resources and now faces the loss of the mortgaged estate. She and her feeble brother Gayev can only hope vaguely for a miraculous loan from somewhere, but as Gayev keeps puzzling over the possible solutions, he remarks, "You know, if a lot of cures are suggested for a disease, it means that the disease is incurable." It takes the student revolutionary Trofimov to tell Madame Ranyevskaya's daughter Anya what that disease really is: "Your grandfather, your great-grandfather and all your forefathers were serf owners—they owned living souls. . . . And it has perverted you all . . . so that your mother, your uncle and even you yourself no longer realize that you're living in debt, at other people's expense, at the expense of people you don't admit further than the kitchen." The only man who can pay off these debts is Lopakhin, the son of a serf, now a millionaire, and his plan for salvation is ruinous. "Just you wait and see Yermolai Lopakhin take an ax to the cherry orchard . . . ," he cries after buying the whole estate at auction. "We're going to build a whole lot of new villas . . ."

When Anya dreads the prospect of leaving the estate and its orchard, Trofimov tries to encourage her by saying, "The whole of Russia is our orchard." The reverse is equally true, for although Chekhov was not a writer of solemn

---

* When Chekhov later complained about the banality of various presents that had been given to him, including some embroidered cloth from Stanislavsky, the actor asked him what he would have really liked. Chekhov reflected for some time and then said, "A rat trap." Stanislavsky thought he was joking, but Chekhov gravely defended his choice: "Listen, mice must be destroyed." Then he began laughing.

allegories, and although he could not have specifically foretold the imminent downfall of the Romanov empire, the doomed cherry orchard is in many ways an emblem of Russia itself. A natural treasure, beautiful beyond telling, ever bountiful and ever renewed, it lies at the mercy of its masters. This ruling caste, the former slaveholders, has become weak, feckless, inept, helpless. It is already being challenged by a new class of traders who care only for money. As for the intellectuals, they "care for nothing, do nothing, and are incapable of work." There are revolutionaries who preach a future triumph of the people, but the servants who represent these lower orders seem to be concerned only with their daily routine. "Yes," says Madame Ranyevskaya's adopted daughter, Varya, "life in this house has come to an end. There won't be any more." At the end of Chekhov's lighthearted comedy, the only sound is the distant thud of an ax beginning the destruction of the orchard.

The orchard empire ruled by the house of Romanov was a place of almost unimaginable size. From the perpetually frozen Arctic Ocean to the frontier outposts along the rugged Hindu Kush, from the rebellious territories of occupied Poland to the prison camps on the fog-wrapped island of Sakhalin, it covered nearly 8.5 million square miles, nearly half of the entire Eurasian land mass, a world in itself. Acquired by centuries of migrations into the wilderness and then by a series of colonial conquests, it was the largest empire ever governed from one throne. Yet this vast empire was so isolated and so primitive, so thinly veined with telegraph lines or railways or even dirt roads, and so diverse in its conglomeration of Cossacks and Tartars and Armenians and Kalmucks—the true Russians numbering less than half of the Tsar's 130 million subjects—that it was hardly governed at all. It rather resembled that nightmarish Chinese Empire imagined by Franz Kafka, in which messages announcing imperial victories and defeats have already become history and even legend before they finally reach the remote villages. "Our people do not know what emperor is reigning," Kafka wrote in *The Great Wall of China*, "and there exist doubts regarding even the name of the dynasty. . . . Long-dead emperors are set on the throne in our villages . . . and with a loud cry of woe our village eventually hears how an empress drank her husband's blood in long drafts thousands of years ago."

Nicholas II, who became Emperor and Autocrat of All the Russias in 1894 and placed on his own head a nine-pound crown surmounted by a huge cross of diamonds, thereby acquired seven palaces, millions of acres of land and an annual income of 24 million gold rubles (about $12 million). The imperial jewelry collection also included the Orlov diamond of 194.5 carats and the Moon of the Mountain diamond of 120 carats. But the Tsar, whose title derived from a corruption of "Caesar," felt obliged to support some fifteen thousand court officials and servants, five theaters, the 226 dancers of the Imperial Ballet, and an assortment of hospitals and orphanages and other good works, so he ran out of money in the autumn of every year and thereafter lived on credit. As Trofimov said, the owners of the orchard lived at other people's expense.

Nicholas II nonetheless ruled everything. Russia was approaching the twentieth century without a constitution or a legislature or an independent judiciary. Its religious leaders, hostile toward both the Vatican and Constantinople, liked to call their capital of St. Petersburg—built by Peter the Great at a cost of 200,000 laborers' lives—"the third Rome." But this claim to Orthodox supremacy also led to the imperial palace, where the Tsar appointed the procurator who dominated the Holy Synod. "To the Emperor of all the Russias belongs the supreme and unlimited power," said Article I of the Fundamental Laws of Imperial Russia. "Not only fear, but also conscience commanded by God Himself, is the basis of obedience to this power." Nicholas himself stated the *Führerprinzip* more succinctly: "I am absolute and I answer only to God."

Nicholas was in almost every way unqualified for his position. Almost purely German by blood, he had the virtues of the lesser nobility. He was noted for his quiet courtesy and his dedication to his duties. He was a devoted father. He would have made an admirable successor to his father-in-law, the Grand Duke of Hesse-Darmstadt. He might have served capably as an ambassador somewhere, in a time of peace. He had a very ordinary intelligence, very little understanding of politics or economics or any of the problems facing Russia, very little gift for leadership of any kind. He was weak, timorous, vacillating, and, like many such people, resentful of advice and sometimes irrationally stubborn.

As a boy growing up in the nine-hundred-room Gatchina Palace, Nicholas had been taught by royal tutors all the usual royal subjects: French, geography, dancing, shooting. He had a protracted affair with an ambitious ballerina. He was sent on a trip around the world, inspected the Pyramids, went tiger hunting in India ("How stifling to be surrounded by the British," he wrote, an opinion that he amplified on another occasion by saying, "An Englishman is a *Zhid* [Yid].") He was attacked and slightly wounded, for no clear reason, by a sword-wielding Japanese, and he customarily referred to the Japanese thereafter as *macaques,* or monkeys.

His father, Alexander III, made very little effort to prepare Nicholas to govern his millions of subjects. When it was suggested that the Tsarevich might gain some administrative experience by becoming president of the new Trans-Siberian Railroad, Alexander protested, "He is still absolutely a child, he has only infantile judgments, how would he be able to become president of a committee?" Both of them were surprised shortly thereafter when the robust Tsar Alexander, who was not yet fifty, suddenly began suffering from headaches and a weakness in the legs. Within three months he was dead of nephritis, and the twenty-six-year-old Nicholas tearfully cried out to one of his uncles, "What am I going to do? What is going to happen to me . . . ? I am not prepared to be a tsar. I never wanted to become one. I know nothing of the business of ruling." Yet when a group of local officials ventured in the opening days of the new reign to express a hope that the young Tsar might take counsel with representatives of the people, he declared that he would "maintain the principle of autocracy just as firmly and unflinchingly as it was preserved by my unforgettable dead father," and that anyone who presumed to favor representative government was indulging in "senseless dreams."

The new Tsar, who stood only five feet seven, was overshadowed at the start by the towering grand dukes: Great-Uncle Mikhail, chairman of the State Council; Uncle Vladimir, commander of the Imperial Guards and of the St. Petersburg Military District; Uncle Alexis, the admiral who administered naval affairs; Uncle Sergei, governor general of Moscow. Not only were they about half a foot taller than Nicholas, and two decades older, but they were inclined to shout and pound their fists when they wanted to get their way. Nicholas, on gaining the throne, hoped to get married immediately to his betrothed, Princess Alix Victoria of Hesse-Darmstadt, a prim but handsome girl of twenty-two, "but," as he noted in his diary, "all the uncles are against it, saying that I should marry in Petersburg after the funeral." Nicholas bowed to his uncles.

Princess Alix was upset. She inscribed in Nicholas' diary, in the peculiar English by which they communicated, an exhortation: "Darling boysy, me loves you oh so very tenderly and deep. Be firm. . . . Show your own mind and don't let others forget *who you are*. Forgive me lovy." It was probably good advice for Nicholas to be urged to stand up against his uncles, but Alexandra, as she came to call herself, soon proved to be even more autocratic than the Tsar, and to have even less sense. In hundreds of emotional messages that she wrote him over the years, she repeatedly urged her mild husband to rule with Teutonic severity, to reject all compromises and punish all critics. "Be the master . . . ," she wrote. And again: "Russia loves to feel the whip—it's their nature—tender love & then the iron hand to punish & guide—How I wish I could pour my will into your veins." And again: "Be Peter the Great, be Ivan the Terrible, be Tsar Paul—crush them all under your feet."

Nicholas inherited from his father not only the grand dukes but several of his most important ministers. Preeminent among these was Sergius Witte, a burly and assertive man of Dutch ancestry, who had once hoped to become a mathematician but turned to railroading instead. Alexander III had made him minister of communications, then, in 1892, minister of finance. "As minister of finance, I was also in charge of our commerce and industry," Witte later wrote. "As such, I increased our industry threefold. This is held against me. Fools!" Both the accomplishment and the announcement of it were typical of the man. Witte believed passionately in Russia's need to modernize, and that meant to industrialize, whatever the cost. He started by putting Russia on the gold standard and stabilizing its currency. He began pushing railroad tracks across the wastes of Siberia. He organized all sales of vodka into an immensely profitable government monopoly. He invited in German and English capital to build steel mills and textile works. This too encountered resistance from the traditionalists. "Oh, folly and ignorance!" cried Witte. But Witte's forced marches into the twentieth century were not painless. Russia industrialized at the expense of its peasants, who were driven off the land by starvation, and driven into the pestilential new slums outside St. Petersburg and Moscow. Their anger would someday become torrential, but Witte saw nothing of that.

The other key minister inherited from Alexander III mistrusted progress as strongly as Witte believed in it. He was Konstantin P. Pobedonostsev, a withered septuagenarian zealot who had been tutor to young Nicholas and to his father before him. A former law professor at Moscow University and now chief procurator of the Holy Synod, and thus the highest official responsible for the nation's moral and spiritual life, Pobedonostsev repeatedly warned his imperial protégé against the perils of constitutional government, trials by jury, a free press and other Western innovations. "Among the falsest of political principles," he wrote, "is the principle of the sovereignty of the people ... which has unhappily infatuated certain foolish Russians. ... Parliament is an institution serving for the satisfaction of the personal ambition, vanity and self-interest of its members. [It] is indeed one of the greatest illustrations of human delusion." Pobedonostsev was also a resolute anti-Semite, as were the two tsars he tutored. He once urged a drastic solution to the "Jewish problem": "One third will convert, one third will emigrate, and one third will die out." The new Tsar was not a man who particularly liked advice, and he followed it only when he felt like it, but it is notable that his principal economic and spiritual advisers, among the most capable men in his entourage, both gave him advice that helped lead to disaster.

It took eighteen months to organize the magnificent coronation for Nicholas, and then there occurred, in the midst of the celebrations, a debacle that served both as a demonstration of how the new Tsar ruled Russia and as an omen of how that rule would end. On the outskirts of Moscow lay a military training ground known as Khodynka Fields, and here swarms of citizens gathered from all over Russia to honor the newly crowned Tsar with songs and dances and free beer. The authorities knew that the crowd would be enormous—they had already ordered 400,000 enameled iron mugs to be distributed as souvenirs— but the mob that assembled around bonfires and tents on the night before the ceremony was beyond all counting, perhaps 600,000 or 700,000.

Clim Samghin, the hero of Maxim Gorki's autobiographical novel *Bystander,* was watching the scene through a rooftop telescope: "There, afar off on an enormous field, under the dirty cap of the fog, the closely compressed roemass of people stood rooted. It seemed a single body; only by straining one's eyes could the barely perceptible waverings of the tiny grains be distinguished. Occasionally a wave of movement seemed to swell the multitudes, only to sink again. ... From thence, too, a noise came floating to the roof—not the rejoicing clamor of the city, but a sound that was wintry, like the howling of a blizzard. ... Gluing his eye to the brass circle of the telescope, Samghin looked on, bewitched. The countless throng reminded him of the Crusades. ... A picture came to his mind: Were this mass to surge suddenly like a wave into the city, its streets would not be able to hold the pressure of the dark torrents of people. The people would overturn the houses, trample their roofs into dust, sweep the entire city away ..."

Early in the morning of the coronation feast, at about 6 A.M., people in the crowds at Khodynka Fields began hearing rumors that there were not enough mugs for the beer, that there would not be enough beer either. The crowd began to move, surging, billowing, toward the flimsy police barriers. Some people could not see that the field was lined with trenches used for military training. They stumbled and fell. Others trampled on them. Still others pushed forward, unable to stop. The wild stampede lasted for less than an hour, and then the crowd gradually subsided, as mysteriously as it had erupted. The trampled corpses were laid out in rows. Some of them were lifted onto carts and carried into the city.

Like most onlookers, Gorki's Clim Samghin had very little idea of what had happened—some kind of brawl, he guessed—and he could only look in wonder at the procession of carts: "An arm protruded from the new tarpaulin covering of the cart. It stretched out like the imploring arm of a beggar, bare to the shoulder, daubed in blue and red colors. On one of the fingers a gold ring glistened. . . . Another small rickety cart passed by, loaded with crumpled forms, uncovered. The clothing they wore was torn into shreds; the exposed parts of their bodies were dusty and muddy. After the carts came an ever greater, denser throng of beggarlike people in tatters, with disheveled hair and swollen faces . . ."

Many of the mangled corpses were still laid out in rows—official figures reported 1,429 dead in all, and countless thousands more injured—when it came time later that morning for the Tsar and Tsarina to receive a dozen delegations of citizens, the Moscow woolen workers, the coachmen, the bakers, the Moscow Racing Club, at the gates of the nearby Petrovsky Palace. Three orchestras and a large chorus performed the national anthem, and the Tsar played host at a feast for an assemblage of village elders. They ate whitefish, veal, roast duckling and a raspberry dessert.

It was said that the Tsar looked pale. It was said that when he had first heard of the disaster at Khodynka Fields, he had wanted to cancel the remaining coronation festivities and retire for a time to a monastery. It was said that he had been dissuaded by the royal uncles, who insisted that the ceremonies were too important to be halted. The major event that same evening was to be a ball at the embassy of Russia's chief ally, France. The French had sent valuable tapestries and silver and 100,000 roses. The Tsar danced the opening quadrille with the Countess Montebello, the ambassador's wife. Only the next day did he and the Tsarina tour the hospitals crowded with the injured survivors of Khodynka Fields and offer money to the families of the dead.

The Russians have a proclivity for apocalyptic visions, and the coming of the new century intensified it. Vladimir Solovyev, the eminent theologian, foresaw the final battle between Christ and Antichrist. "The approaching end of the world," he wrote to a friend, "strikes me like some obvious but quite subtle scent—just as a traveler nearing the sea feels the sea breeze before he sees the sea."

There were investigations of a sort, but they led to very little. The man responsible for all security arrangements at the coronation, who had provided only a handful of police to control the vast crowds at Khodynka Fields, was Grand Duke Sergei, the governor general of Moscow, and he, of course, could hardly be punished. Not only was he the uncle of the Tsar, but he had married the sister of the Tsarina. The official generally in charge of the coronation was the Minister of the Imperial Court, Count I. I. Vorontsov-Dashkov, and he submitted his resignation but remained in the good graces of the Dowager Empress.

What made the Khodynka disaster so symptomatic of the Romanov regime was not simply the official incompetence and irresponsibility but the demonstration that Imperial Russia had virtually no functioning government at all. A vast crowd of more than half a million citizens had gathered and then stampeded like a herd of animals, and the imperial regime that had just crowned itself with such magnificent pomp had anticipated nothing, had exercised no governing control, and finally had offered as its judgment nothing more than a shrug. Confronted by the dragon of chaos, the all-powerful Emperor proved powerless.

But the imperial forms were preserved. In the imperial village of Tsarskoe Selo, a half hour by railroad from St. Petersburg, the Tsar rose at seven-thirty every morning, donned a military uniform, breakfasted on rolls and tea with milk in the rosewood room, and then prepared for the first visitor to be ushered into his office promptly at nine. His cabinet ministers usually reported to him once a week, court chamberlains more often. Beneath the Minister of the Imperial Court, there was a grand marshal of the court, a grand master of the court, a cup bearer, an esquire trenchant, a master of the hunt. Even the assertive Witte served purely at the Tsar's pleasure. All important papers came to Nicholas' desk, and, since he preferred not to have a secretary, he opened them himself, wrote his views neatly in the margins and sent them out again. He also preferred not to have a telephone. Twice a day, he went walking in the palace park with his dogs. There was no national legislature, and the local councils known as zemstvos had no effect on the Tsar's tranquillity. An enormous bureaucracy, notable for both arrogance and inefficiency, stood ready in uniform to carry out every imperial decree. The police suppressed any disturbances and the censors any criticism. Except for a few court intrigues, which acquired an undue importance because of the tradition of autocracy, there was very little in the nature of politics at all. "The Russian autocracy as we see it now is a thing apart . . . ," Joseph Conrad wrote in 1905. "It is like a visitation, like a curse from heaven falling in the darkness of ages upon the immense plains of forest and steppe lying dumbly on the confines of two continents."

Under the soothing influence of his courtiers, Nicholas believed up to the day of his execution that he was loved and admired by the Russian people, but even in the tranquil early years of his reign there were obvious signs of trouble. After a series of droughts and crop failures in the early 1890s, worsened by outbreaks of cholera, a drop in the price of wheat set off a widespread economic decline in 1899, and again in 1902. That meant hunger across the length and breadth of Russia, hunger in the dingy huts of the peasant villages on the Volga, hunger in the cramped barracks that surrounded the Moscow factories—hunger, no bread, no flour to make bread. In the black-earth regions of southern Russia, where the ruined peasants had to watch the wheat being shipped abroad to pay for new industries, mysterious fires began breaking out in isolated barns, and sometimes even under the eaves of an owner's home. "The air is heavy with ominous things," one landowner in Voronezh wrote to a friend. "Every day we see the glare of fires on the horizon; a bloody mist crawls over the ground; breathing and living have become difficult as before a storm. The muzhik is sullenly silent . . ." In Kharkov and Poltava provinces, the plundering of ninety-one estates prompted the authorities to send troops to restore order. More than 1,100 peasants were prosecuted and many publicly flogged. In St. Petersburg and Moscow, the long-suppressed radicals began to organize, first the Marxist Social Democrats, then the more assertive Socialist revolutionaries, and alongside them the Jewish Workmen's Bund. These were small beginnings. No sooner had the Social Democrats held their first secret meeting in 1898 than eight of the nine delegates were arrested.

The police were responsible for keeping order, for regulating all travel and collecting the taxes, but in the absence of any political life (newspapers were forbidden, for example, even to mention the word "constitution") it was hard to discover exactly where the seeds of opposition might be growing. And since the law made little distinction between radicals and liberals, or even disillusioned conservatives, and since the sounds of dissent could be heard in even the wealthiest houses in the capital, the police could only assume that treason might be found anywhere. To root it out, they began to acquire spies and informers inside any group that might be suspected of opposition. Before long, they were spending 2.5 million rubles a year on these agents. Once suspicion fell on someone, he could fully exonerate himself only by joining the police network and adding to its stores of information. Knowledge is power. To evaluate all this information was more difficult than collecting it. Some police spies denigrated the information that came from other spies but remained unaware that still other spies had been set to watch them. Knowledge is power. The mere collection of information is a passive response, however. To control and dominate information, one must create the events being reported. Hence, the *agent provocateur*. "We shall provoke you to acts of terror," Sergei Zubatov, chief of the Okhrana political police in Moscow, once boasted to some leftists, "and then crush you."

Even to provoke revolutionary violence is only a manipulation of existing organizations. As the spy network kept expanding, the more ambitious and imaginative police officials began to think of not simply infiltrating but actually creating opposition movements. Zubatov, who had once been a liberal student and still liked to affect the tinted eyeglasses that were popular among radicals, conceived the idea of creating a whole labor movement under the aegis of the secret police. Some years later, when the Bolshevik wing of the Social Democrats became sufficiently organized to get a number of delegates elected to the fledgling Duma (Parliament), their leader, Roman V. Malinovsky, was a paid agent of the police. The speeches that he delivered to the Duma were often first written by Lenin, in exile in Switzerland, and then edited by S. P. Beletsky, the chief of police in St. Petersburg. Knowledge is power.

In these maneuverings, one can discern the beginnings of the modern totalitarian organization known as the police state. It is as different from the blundering constabularies of the nineteenth century as the Dominican interrogators of the Inquisition were different from their brothers in less-determined orders. The police state is based on the idea that total information can become the basis for total control, of both the elite and the general populace. This idea was to inspire Heinrich Himmler's Gestapo and Lavrenty Beria's NKVD, but its complete fulfillment occurred only in George Orwell's imaginary *1984,* in which the Thought Police of the Ministry of Love enforce belief in the three slogans: War is peace, freedom is slavery, ignorance is strength. One can see the Okhrana of 1900 stumbling around in the foundations of the mighty structure that later generations of Moscow officialdom would actually build, but the Okhrana's efforts were largely doomed to failure. The main reason was that although officials like Zubatov were experimenting with ideas of great potential, the police lacked a guiding spirit with both the authority and the longevity to bring such experiments to fruition. Interior ministers came and went, subject to the attacks of terrorists and the whims of the Tsar, and the most gifted police officials fought with one another for control of the coercive machinery that they only partly understood.

The man who had understood it best was Fyodor Dostoevsky, who had become fascinated with the prosecution of a terrorist named Sergei Nechayev and created out of it his grand novel *The Possessed.* Nechayev was a bewitching figure, a slender youth with curls and fierce blue eyes. The son of a house painter, he did not learn to read until he was sixteen, and when he managed to enroll himself at the University of St. Petersburg, he apparently became a student primarily in order to become a revolutionary. He chewed his fingernails. His idea of a revolution had no goal except destruction, yet within a few months he had persuaded nearly one hundred other students to sign oaths of loyalty to his leadership. He began organizing a student revolt, and talked of an underground network that spanned all of Russia, but as the day of uprising approached, he suddenly quailed. He faked his own arrest and imprisonment, then faked his own escape from prison and fled to Switzerland. He was not yet twenty-two.

In Geneva, he courted the aging Mikhail Bakunin, hero of the barricades of Paris in 1848 and Dresden in 1849. Bakunin had endured a decade in Hapsburg prisons and escaped from a life sentence in Siberia, and he still believed in what he called "the eternal spirit that destroys and annihilates." Now fifty-five and almost toothless, Bakunin was charmed by his new disciple. He presented to Nechayev a document attesting that he was "No. 2771" in the "World Revolutionary Alliance," a fanciful organization that apparently had no other members at all. Bakunin assisted the student in composing a series of incendiary pamphlets, notably *The Revolutionary Catechism.* In this chilling work, which was read and admired by the young Lenin, Nechayev preached the subordination of all human instincts and values to the triumph of the revolution. No friendships, no moral hesitations, no sense of compassion must interfere. "Our task," he wrote, "is terrible, total, universal and merciless destruction." Yet when Nechayev returned to Russia to lead the crusade, he soon got into a quarrel with another student who balked at one of his orders. He accused the student of being a police informer, then led a band of confederates in "executing" him, and bungled the job so crudely that he spent the last ten years of his life in prison.

It was this quality of mindless hysteria that fascinated Dostoevsky, that and the gap between revolutionary actions and ideals. Dostoevsky had once been tempted by socialism—it was for this that he himself had been sent to Siberia—and he wrote of the radicals with the venom of the disillusioned. A number of critics have argued, indeed, that the melodramatic murder at the center of *The Possessed* bears little relationship to the political and economic crisis that was already beginning to shake Russia, yet in the maneuverings of the villainous Pyotr Verhovensky, Dostoevsky captured the psychological essence of many of the terrorists. He copied several of Nechayev's characteristics, his rudeness and slovenliness, his sudden rages, his habit of wolfing his food, but he added far richer touches. Instead of being the son of a provincial craftsman, Pyotr is the son of the liberal intelligentsia, the disastrous embodiment of its vague sentimentalities. And although many of the leading citizens are quite aware that the Mephistophelean Pyotr belongs to a revolutionary underground—indeed, the more truculently he behaves, the more they fawn on him—Dostoevsky repeatedly hints that Pyotr may also be a police spy.

"Listen, Verhovensky," his friend Stavrogin demands of him, "you are not one of the higher police, are you?"

"Anyone who has a question like that in his mind doesn't utter it," says Pyotr.

"I understand, but we are by ourselves."

"No, so far I am not one of the higher police. . . ."

He might be someday, though, for what Pyotr admires, as he later tells Stavrogin, is a theory worked out by another revolutionary named Shigalov. "He suggests a system of spying. Every member of the society spies on the others, and it's his duty to inform against them. Everyone belongs to all and all to everyone. All are slaves and equal in their slavery. In extreme cases, he advocates slander and murder, but the great thing about it is equality. To begin with, the level of education, science and talent is lowered. . . . Copernicus will have his eyes put out, Shakespeare will be stoned—that's Shigalovism."

Shigalovism still lay in the future. *The Possessed* appeared in 1872. Only eleven years had passed since the freeing of the serfs by Alexander II, an act that was supposed to express imperial enlightenment but also brought new controversies and conflicts. The dismayed Tsar invoked the forces of repression. A number of young radicals turned to violence. They ambitiously called themselves Narodnaya Volya, the People's Will. One young woman joined a group of petitioners waiting to see General Fedor F. Trepov, the prefect of St. Petersburg, then pulled a gun from her muff and shot him. Another radical accosted General Nikolai Mezentsev, chief of the political-police organization known as the Third Section, then pulled a knife from inside a folded newspaper, stabbed the general in the back, and escaped in a passing carriage. The harried Tsar Alexander granted sweeping powers to one of his chief generals, Count Mikhail Loris-Melikov, and the police made numerous raids and arrests.

As the police maneuvered to infiltrate the Narodnaya Volya, they did not realize that they themselves had been infiltrated. A confidential clerk in the Third Section, Nikolai Kletochnikov, was responsible for transcribing all the reports of the department's secret agents, and for two years he passed them all on to his friends in the Narodnaya Volya. That was the beginning, in a way, of the remarkable symbiosis of the tsarist secret police and the radical terrorists, bound together by an intertwining network of double agents and undercover informants. By the time Kletochnikov was trapped—he had recklessly gone to warn a confederate who had just been arrested—the Narodnaya Volya had formally condemned Tsar Alexander to death.

It seemed an impudent verdict for a relative handful of young radicals to pass on the Tsar of All the Russias, but the radicals were ready, indeed eager, to risk their lives. They laboriously dug tunnels and planted bombs. Their plans kept going awry. One of their agents got himself a job as a carpenter in the Winter Palace and then began smuggling explosives into a hiding place below the Tsar's private dining room. When he set off his bomb, it killed eleven people and injured more than fifty, but the Tsar had been delayed at an audience with some visitors. The terrorists kept watch on the Tsar's movements around St. Petersburg and saw that he usually followed the same route in riding to the parade ground to review his troops. They rented a store along his route, opened what appeared to be a cheese shop, and began another one of their tunnels in the cellar. Two days before the scheduled attack, the police seized the leader of the band, a former serf named Andrei Zhelyabov, but his mistress, Sophia Perovskaya, took over the command. She was, in many ways, typical of the Narodnaya Volya zealots. A tiny blonde with pale-blue eyes, twenty-eight years old, the daughter of the former governor general of St. Petersburg, she had no hesitation in ordering the attack to proceed on schedule. She herself would act as lookout.

Inside the Winter Palace, meanwhile, General Loris-Melikov had been working to persuade the Tsar that some kind of representative government must be established. By mid-February of 1881, he had worked out a draft of a rudimentary constitution that called for the advisory State Council to be enlarged by delegates from the local zemstvos, the city councils and the nobility. The Tsar's conservative advisers strongly opposed such a conciliatory gesture toward the liberals, but the general argued so persuasively that on the morning of March 1 the Tsar signed the measure. Then he set out for his customary ride.

He bypassed the terrorists' cheese store, but Sophia Perovskaya spotted him riding along the Catherine Quay. She gave the signal by blowing her nose. An eighteen-year-old youth named Nikolai Rysakov threw a bomb under the rear axle of the Tsar's carriage. It killed a baker's boy in the crowd and wounded one of the royal escorts. Rysakov was immediately seized. The Tsar imprudently climbed out of the disabled carriage to question him. A second terrorist, Ivan Grinevitsky, darted forward and threw another bomb that exploded in the snow at the Tsar's feet. It tore off his right leg, shattered his left leg, ripped open his stomach, blinded him in one eye. "To the palace, to die there," he gasped to the aides who rushed to his side. He died about two hours later on a blood-stained sofa. Grinevitsky too died in the explosion, and so did about twenty bystanders.

At this moment of revulsion toward violence, there were a few who urged the new Tsar Alexander III to be magnanimous and pardon his father's murderers. The eminent philosopher Solovyev proposed it in a public address and was promptly dismissed from his position at the University of Moscow. A more powerful appeal came from Leo Tolstoy, who had become a kind of national institution in the decade since *War and Peace* and who was now experiencing the first throes of his tumultuous religious conversion. In a personal letter from his estate at Yasnaya Polyana, he begged the Tsar to "forgive, return good for evil.... Then, as wax melts in the fire, the revolutionaries' opposition will melt in the deed of their emperor, the man who fulfills the law of Christ." Pobedonostsev, the procurator of the Holy Synod, reluctantly forwarded Tolstoy's message with a covering note describing it as a "mental aberration" and a "monstrous scheme." "Rest assured ...," the Tsar answered. "I promise you that all six of them will hang." And so it happened. Just a month after the assassination, Sophia Perovskaya and her confederates died in fetters on a scaffold erected in Semyonov Square, done to death by a drunken executioner who repeatedly botched the hangings while a crowd of eighty thousand spectators, including the foreign diplomatic corps, watched in awe.

One of the new Tsar's first acts of business was to bury Loris-Melikov's quasi-constitution and to reassert the principle of absolute autocracy. One of the next was to reorganize the police and to empower them to smash all resistance by whatever means necessary. At the direction of a crafty Prussian named Vyacheslav K. von Plehve, who gradually came to dominate the Interior Ministry under a series of figurehead ministers, the authorities decreed a series of "emergency" measures that they could impose whenever they saw fit. A governor general henceforth could dissolve local zemstvos, dismiss any elected officials and all but the highest civil servants, close factories and universities, confiscate property, ban all public or private gatherings and imprison anyone for up to three months without trial. And from the ruins of the discredited Third Section, there emerged within the Police Department a new political security force known as the Okhrana (meaning defense or protection), which was ordered to spy on and infiltrate and sabotage every form of opposition. Its powers extended even to Paris, where a suave intriguer named Pyotr Rachkovsky kept watch on exile groups all over Europe. The terrorists had never been numerous, but since they had demonstrated that it required a mere half dozen to kill a tsar, the police pursued every possibility. Some four thousand suspects were interrogated during the 1880s, and 154 of them were convicted, seventeen executed. Among these last was Alexander Ulyanov, whose death shocked and embittered the younger brother who would eventually assume the name of Lenin. And so there descended on Russia a tranquillity that later came to be described as the peace of the graveyard.

It lasted almost twenty years, and then, at the opening of the new century, terrorism suddenly reappeared, as irrationally intense as ever. The violence started over relatively minor causes. The rector of St. Petersburg University, hearing that there might be disturbances at the annual festivities to celebrate the school's founding, banned the festivities themselves. Students poured into the streets to shout their protests. Mounted police charged down on them with whips flying—an unprecedented affront to the educated caste. The students called a national strike. The government then began conscripting striking students, another affront to the privileged. On February 1, 1901, a student named Pyotr Karpovich shot and killed the Minister of Education, N. P. Bogolepov. The next victim, appropriately enough, was the Minister of the Interior, Dmitri Sipyagin. Another student, Stepan Balmashev, disguised himself as an aide to Grand Duke Sergei, obtained an audience with the Minister, handed him a "sentence of execution," and shot him. The organization that had decreed that "sentence" was an autonomous wing of the fledgling Socialist Revolutionary Party. It called itself the Fighting Organization, and its only function was killing.

The death of Sipyagin in April of 1902 finally brought to power that same von Plehve who had drafted the emergency statutes twenty years earlier. A fleshy man with a shaggy mustache and pince-nez, Plehve had acquired a reputation as a merciless opponent of liberals and intellectuals, of the Poles, the Jews and other minorities. Nor was the powerful Interior Ministry the limit to his ambitions. With the police behind him, he saw himself as the rival to Finance Minister Witte in all aspects of the Tsar's government. He also liked to be seen in the company of young actresses and ballerinas. "There exist two Russias . . . ," wrote the liberal leader Pavel Milyukov, "the Russia of Leo Tolstoy [and] that of Plehve. . . . The one spells liberty; the other, despotism."

As his chief of political security, Plehve appointed another key figure, Sergei Zubatov, the imaginative Okhrana chief in Moscow, who had been experimenting with the novel idea of a police-run labor union. Zubatov, then thirty-eight, was a professional. It was he who introduced the new techniques of fingerprinting and photography to Moscow police headquarters. It was he who began keeping dossiers on all political suspects. It was he who organized the first police training school to educate his men on revolutionary theory and tactics.

It was Zubatov, too, who sponsored the Okhrana's most remarkable double agent, Yevno Azef. The son of a poor Jewish tailor, Azef had worked as a clerk, a reporter, a traveling salesman, then offered his services as a police spy. The police financed his studies at an engineering school in Karlsruhe, where he began his reports on emigré students. Zubatov brought him back to Moscow in 1901 and assigned him to join the Socialist Revolutionaries, and there he soon wormed his way into the Fighting Organization. In fact, though he did not tell the police the full extent of his success, he became the deputy to its leader, G. A. Gershuni. When Gershuni almost accidentally walked into a police trap, Azef, the police agent, became the head of the chief terrorist organization.

He was an unattractive figure. A contemporary account describes him as "heavily built with a puffy yellow face, large stuck-out ears, a low forehead narrowing toward the top, thick lips and a flattened nose." But his ability to deceive both the police and the terrorists must have been a measure not only of their inefficiency but of his own cunning and audacity. In his early thirties, he lived well. The police paid him five hundred rubles a month, and he supplemented that by taking a share of whatever the terrorists could acquire by robbery and extortion. He liked to visit Stoyetsky's, the most expensive brothel in Moscow, while plainclothesmen spent the night keeping watch in the streets outside.

The ambiguity of Azef's role became acute when the terrorists decided that their next target should be Azef's superior, Plehve. Azef stalled for time. Then he learned that a splinter group led by a young woman named Sophia Klichoglu had decided to assassinate Plehve on its own. Azef stopped that by informing the police, who promptly arrested the conspirators. The demands for action within his own organization increased. Azef himself was hardly opposed to the scheme, for he hated Plehve for his responsibility in a recent pogrom at Kishinev. But if he made any mistake, it might cost him his life. He assigned the actual attack to a team of six youths, mostly ex-students, headed by a fearless Pole named Boris Savinkov. They would watch over Plehve's movements, organize an ambush, then throw a bomb. Azef would be safely out of the country. But how could he explain the attack to the police? Azef shrewdly devised the idea of telling the head of the police department, Alexei Lopukhin, that there was a plot against him. He even used a few details of the conspiracy against Plehve as evidence of a conspiracy against Lopukhin, not enough evidence to enable the police to prevent the attack on Plehve but enough to make it seem later that Azef had been loyal to his employers.

The date for the assassination was set, March 31, but one of the plotters missed a rendezvous, and everything was called off. Savinkov nervously began arguing that Plehve was too well guarded. He persuaded two other conspirators to give up on Plehve and go south with him to assassinate the governor general of Kiev. The remaining three set a new date, April 14, but on that very morning one conspirator named Pokotilov, who had begged unsuccessfully for a chance to take part in three previous assassinations, accidentally blew himself up in his hotel room. Again a delay. Azef had to return from Paris, argue Savinkov out of his venture in Kiev, and organize a new attack for July 15, 1904. Then he departed again.

It was hardly a secret that Plehve was a prime target for the terrorists, but the Minister remained remarkably calm. He had confidence in his sources of secret information. When a friend asked him why he didn't strengthen his bodyguard in view of the radicals' plots, he serenely answered, "I shall know about all these in good time."

Von Plehve's direct responsibility for the Kishinev pogrom has never been clearly established, but his police looked benignly on the rioters, and it was widely believed that they did so at his suggestion. "Personally he had nothing against the Jews ...," Witte wrote of the Interior Minister. "He possessed enough intelligence to understand that he was following an essentially wrong policy. But it pleased Grand Duke Sergei Alexandrovich and apparently His Majesty ..." The royal hostility toward the Jews was primarily religious in origin. "We must never forget that it was the Jews who crucified our Lord and spilled his precious blood," Alexander had declared. He also had less pious sentiments. "I confess that I myself rejoice when Jews are beaten," he once re-marked. Nicholas II added a note of political paranoia. He once wrote to his mother that his loyal subjects were "outraged by the audacity of the socialists and the revolutionaries, and since nine tenths of them are Jews ... there are anti-Jewish pogroms."

The Jews had been in Russia much longer than the Romanovs. Shortly after Nebuchadnezzar sacked Jerusalem in 586 B.C., the first Jewish settlements appeared in the Caucasus. The Jews were thriving in the Crimea before the birth of Christ. They were not hesitant about proselytizing in those days, and they achieved a triumph in the eighth century when they converted the King of the Khazars, who ruled from the Volga to the Black Sea. Jewish culture and commerce flourished. The Khazars were conquered in the early eleventh century by the Russians, who had already made Orthodox Christianity their state religion, but the Church of Constantinople was considerably more tolerant in those years than the Church of Rome. There were no segregated ghettos in medieval Russia, and there was no systematic mistreatment of the Jews.

Still, the Jews resisted conversion, and the Russian authorities increasingly regarded them as troublesome aliens. King Sigismund of Poland, who had given refuge to thousands of German Jews after the massacres that accompanied the Black Death, asked permission for some Lithuanian Jews to enter Russia on business. Tsar Ivan the Terrible refused on the ground that Jews corrupted Christians and poisoned wells. It became Russian policy to bar all Jews, but this policy came to an ironic end in the late eighteenth century when the partitions of Poland brought 900,000 Polish Jews inside Russia's new frontiers. Catherine the Great immediately issued a decree forbidding them to move out of the region they then inhabited, which became known as the Jewish Pale. Double taxes were imposed on them.

Their situation temporarily improved somewhat during the middle of the nineteenth century, for they had become, like the students and the serfs, a measure of the political climate, beneficiaries of every halting move toward liberalism, victims of every lurch toward repression. And so, scarcely a month after the assassination of Alexander II in 1881, the pogroms began. They were not openly organized by the new government of Alexander III but rather by a secret organization called the Sacred League, founded under the aegis of Pobedonostsev, the new Tsar's tutor. Money was secretly raised and secretly disbursed. Bands of youths were recruited to roam the streets, breaking windows, accosting any Jews they encountered. In the two years from 1881 to 1883, pogroms broke out 224 times. The police generally stood aside; the courts were remarkably lenient.

Alexander blamed the pogroms on the Jews and began imposing a series of new restrictions on them. In 1882, Jews were forbidden to own or manage real estate outside the cities of the Pale. They were forbidden to do business on Sundays or Christian holidays. In 1887, a quota was imposed in all high schools and universities, limiting Jews to no more than five percent of the student body. In 1889, it was decreed that no non-Christian lawyer could be admitted to the bar without special permission from the Minister of Justice. No Jews received that permission.

On the first day of Passover in 1891, Grand Duke Sergei decided to expel any Jews illegally living in Moscow. To check on such illegality, he ordered the police to conduct a night raid on the Zaradie district, where many Jews lived. "The whole quarter was ransacked," Harold Frederic reported to the London *Times*, "apartments forced open, doors smashed, every bedroom without exception searched. . . . As a result, over seven hundred men, women and children were dragged at dead of night through the streets to the *outchastoks*, or police stations. They were not even given time to dress themselves, and they were kept in this noisome and overcrowded confinement for thirty-six hours, almost all without food, and some without water as well . . ." When the police raids were finished, some twenty thousand of Moscow's thirty thousand Jews were summarily expelled from the city and shipped to the Pale, all of them stripped of their possessions, some in chains.

Thousands of Jews fled westward—that was, after all, one of the three elements in Pobedonostsev's "solution"—and many were fortunate enough to reach the slums of New York. In the 1880s, 135,000 Russian Jews migrated to the U.S.; in 1891–92, the number increased to 118,000 from Russia and 130,000 from Galicia; then an economic slump in the U.S. prompted Washington to impose a limit of 30,000 a year. A Hungarian journalist and playwright, Theodor Herzl, argued that the only solution for the Jews was to acquire a homeland of their own. He convoked the first Zionist Congress in Basel in 1897, and the delegates endorsed the idea of asking the Sultan of Turkey to sell part of Palestine. The Sultan was appropriately amused, but he simply used Herzl's offer as a way to raise a new loan in Paris. The British solicitously offered to provide the Zionists with some land in Uganda. The Zionists declined, particularly the Russians, and they were the largest Jewish community in the world—5,189,400 of them, according to the 1897 census.

The accession of Nicholas II brought no improvement. Pobedonostsev remained the administrator of the Holy Synod, and Grand Duke Sergei remained in charge in Moscow. The principal change was that the pogroms, which had usually been limited to plunder, now became increasingly bloody. Tsar Nicholas was quoted as saying to one of his generals, "The Jews deserve a lesson." In Kishinev, the capital of Bessarabia, where fifty thousand Jews lived among sixty thousand gentiles, there had been no troubles during the previous reign. In 1898, however, a reactionary and anti-Semitic St. Petersburg publisher named Pavelachi Krushavan launched a government-subsidized local newspaper, *The Bessarabian*. Its tirades against the Jews reached a climax at Easter of 1902, when it published false reports that a Christian boy found dead in a well had been repeatedly stabbed and then drained of blood as part of a Jewish ritual murder. When that failed to provoke a riot, Krushavan published a similar lie the following Easter, and this time the riot was not left to chance. Everyone seemed to know that there was going to be a pogrom on Easter morning. The police knew, too, because Plehve had pointedly asked them whether, in case of a pogrom, they could protect Christian lives and property. They understood their cue.

On the morning of Easter Sunday, April 6, everything seemed quiet, according to an account published the following week by the newspaper *Viedomosti*.

"All the shops were closed and the town had a holiday air. The crowd . . . was massed on one of the city squares, Chuflino Square, where seesaws and pleasure gardens belonging to private entrepreneurs had been constructed. Mingling with the Christians were some Jews who had come to observe how their fellow citizens were amusing themselves. All at once, toward noon, there was movement in the crowd. Several Jews were seen to separate from it and flee toward their homes. They were pursued by small gangs of Christians, composed for the most part of youngsters who threw rocks at them, crying, 'Kill the Jews!' With the speed of lightning the cry spread in the crowd. . . . Suddenly [the Jews] ran in all directions. Most of them took to Alexandrovskaya Street, heading towards the new market. Loud jeers rising from the throats of thousands of young drunks filled the air. The noise of breaking windows, of doors being smashed in by the pressure of the crowd, mingled with the shouts and whistles of the assailants, the cries of distress from the Jews under attack, and the moans of women and children. . . . In the space of a half hour at most, the mob occupied all of the quarter near the station. . . . All Jews found there were beaten into unconsciousness on the spot. One Jew who was spotted in a tramcar was snatched from his seat and thrashed until they thought he was dead. . . ."

A similar account in *Novosti* provides additional details: "An enraged crowd of Christians . . . killed and wounded many people, among them a great number of women and children. The assassins simply threw the latter from heights of two or three stories onto the pavement below. Several synagogues have been looted, and the rolls of the Torah torn and defiled. In some synagogues when the beadles tried to resist the attackers, they were beaten senseless. All the streets are covered with a thick layer of feathers and down from torn quilts, and often the furniture of the looted houses has been broken into bits and pieces. Even the flooring, the stoves, and the walls have not been spared. . . ."

When the two-day Easter pogrom ended, there were fifty Jews dead and several hundred wounded. According to official statistics, seven hundred Jewish homes and six hundred stores had been ruined. The authorities were pleased. Police Chief Lopukhin was said to have referred to the massacre as "a useful bloodletting." Plehve granted publisher Krushavan an additional subsidy for his new St. Petersburg paper, *Znamya.* When a delegation of Jewish leaders came to Plehve to appeal for justice, he made it clear that he regarded the Kishinev pogrom as a kind of retribution. "Make your people stop their revolutionary activity," he told them, according to Witte's account, "and I will stop the pogroms."

✻

After the birth of four daughters, the Tsarina Alexandra longed desperately for a son and heir, and since her doctors could not promise her one, she was ready to rely on clairvoyants and faith healers. She was not alone in her devotion to the supernatural. Wandering saints and hermits who performed miracles were common enough in nineteenth-century Russia, and it was quite fashionable among the bored aristocrats of St. Petersburg to consult various kinds of conjurers. In court circles, the chief sponsors of this activity were two princesses named Militsa and Anastasia, who were known as the Montenegrins. Daughters of King Nicholas I of Montenegro, they had both married Romanov grand dukes, and they often introduced the latest soothsayer to the royal family. These may seem trivial aberrations, but in a land where all authority resided in the Tsar, the aberrations of his court were by no means trivial.

While Nicholas and Alexandra were on a state visit to France in September of 1901, one of the Montenegrins brought to them a faith healer named Philippe Nizier-Vachod, who called himself Dr. Philippe. The son of a Savoy peasant, Philippe had no education except as a butcher's apprentice in Lyon, but he discovered in adolescence that he had a gift for treating people by means of psychic fluids and astral forces. His fame spread; his clientele grew. Now fifty-two, he was a heavily built man with a thick mustache, a rather ordinary-looking man, according to a Russian diplomat who helped arrange the introduction to the Tsar, "except for his eyes—blue eyes, half hidden by heavy eyelids, but every now and then a curious soft light shone in them." The Tsar was charmed. The Tsarina was charmed. They invited Dr. Philippe to accompany them back to Russia, and when they learned that Philippe had no scientific training, the Tsar grandly asked his hosts to provide Philippe with a medical degree. The French refused, but when the Tsar returned to Russia he had Philippe appointed as a counselor of state and a physician in the Imperial Army, with the rank of general. Once or twice a week, Philippe performed feats of hypnotism and prophecy for the royal couple and held seances for the spirits of the dead. It was said that Nicholas received messages of advice from the ghost of his departed father, Alexander III.

As for Alexandra, who had been having difficulty in becoming pregnant again, she apparently succeeded soon after the arrival of Dr. Philippe. He inspired her to euphoria by promising that the baby would be a boy. "The last months . . . came," according to Witte's malicious account. "Everybody noticed that she had grown considerably stouter. She began to wear loose garments, and ceased to appear at court functions. . . . The population of St. Petersburg expected, from day to day, to hear the cannon shots from the Petropavlovsky Fortress. . . . Finally, the Empress ceased to walk, and the court accoucheur, Professor Ott, came to stay in the palace. But time passed without the confinement taking place. Finally, Professor Ott asked Her Majesty's permission to examine her. She agreed, and the physician, after a thorough examination, declared that the Empress was not pregnant."

Alexandra's hysterical pregnancy (by some accounts, it was a miscarriage) considerably damaged Dr. Philippe's prestige as a prophet, but the whole establishment of occult influences at the court had already aroused jealousy and alarm among those who felt their own importance jeopardized. One of these was the Dowager Empress Maria, Alexander's widow, and another was the Grand Duchess Elizaveta, the Tsarina's older sister, who had married Grand Duke Sergei. These women now turned for help to friends with connections in the secret police, and their message soon found its way to the Paris headquarters of the Okhrana's chief foreign agent, Pyotr Ivanovich Rachkovsky. As a youth, Rachkovsky had been a liberal, but when he was arrested for complicity in one of the assassination attempts of the 1870s, he discovered the benefits of becoming a monarchist and a police spy. As the Okhrana's representative in Paris, a position he held for eighteen years, he not only infiltrated all levels of French political life but also organized networks of informers among Russian exile groups in Germany, England, Switzerland. He thus developed cordial relations with like-minded police officials all over Europe. With a fortune gained by speculating on the Bourse, Rachkovsky enjoyed the pleasures of Paris. "Fat, restless, always with a smile on his lips . . . ," wrote a Frenchman who knew him, "he has one rather noticeable weakness—that he is passionately fond of our little Parisiennes—but he is the most skillful operator to be found in the ten capitals of Europe."

Rachkovsky began making inquiries about Dr. Philippe and soon found that he had been arrested three times and fined each time, in 1887, 1890 and 1892, for the illegal practice of medicine. Rachkovsky happened to have work that brought him back to St. Petersburg, so he brought with him the dossier he had compiled on Dr. Philippe. He showed it to the Minister of the Interior, the soon-to-be-assassinated Sipyagin, and Sipyagin, wise in the ways of the court, gestured toward the fireplace in his office and recommended that Rachkovsky throw his report onto the blazing logs. Rachkovsky was not to be dissuaded. He sent his report to the Dowager Empress Maria, who apparently forwarded it to the Tsar.

The plan of Dr. Philippe's opponents was not just to drive him from the court but to replace him with a more pious soothsayer who would represent the interests of his sponsors. For this complex role, they happened upon the implausible figure of Sergei Alexandrovich Nilus. A landowner in the province of Orel, Nilus had studied law at the University of Moscow (he was also fluent in French, German and English) and became a magistrate in Transcaucasia, but he was so harsh and temperamental that he was forced to resign. After an unsuccessful attempt to manage his own estates, he wandered off to Europe with his mistress—he may also at this time have been in the pay of the Okhrana—and while they were living in Biarritz he learned that his estates had gone bankrupt. The blow seems to have maddened him. Having been an atheist and a Nietzschean, he returned to Russia as a searcher for orthodoxy. At the Troitsky-Sergevsky Monastery, he twice saw visions of Saint Sergei. He began wandering from monastery to monastery. He wrote a book entitled *The Great in the Small,* which recounted his spiritual tribulations and prophesied "the coming of the Antichrist and the rule of Satan on earth." This work, published in 1901, received a modest amount of attention in religious newspapers, and so it came to the attention of the pious Grand Duchess Elizaveta, who apparently concluded that Nilus might make a better adviser to the Tsar than the faith healer from Lyon. Early in 1902, Nilus was invited to the royal compound at Tsarskoe Selo and installed there. A big man, he had a gray beard by now, and deep blue eyes. The plan of the anti-Philippe cabal, apparently, was to have Nilus marry one of the Tsarina's ladies-in-waiting, Yelena Ozerova, then become confessor to the Tsarina and finally to the Tsar.

One of the most interesting aspects of this scheme was that Nilus had mysteriously acquired a document that seemed to him a confirmation of his prophesies of impending apocalypse. The Nazis subsequently helped to publicize all over the world this document known as "The Protocols of the Elders of Zion," but it was apparently the creation of none other than Pyotr Rachkovsky of the Okhrana. Though the exact provenance of the celebrated "Protocols" has never been fully demonstrated, it seems to have sprung, perversely, from the imagination of a French lawyer named Maurice Joly, who wanted to write a satiric attack on the Emperor Napoleon III for his suppression of civil liberties. While walking along the Seine near the Pont Royal one rainy evening in 1864, Joly conceived the idea of composing a dialogue in hell between the spirits of Montesquieu and Machiavelli, in which the latter would ironically extol and defend the methods of autocracy. "What restrains these ravenous animals that we call men?" asks Machiavelli. "In the beginnings of society, it is brute force, without control; later, it is law—that is, force again. . . . Political liberty is only a relative idea; the necessity to live is what dominates states as well as individuals . . ." Joly had to go to Brussels to find a publisher for his *Dialogues aux Enfers,* and within a year of his return he was prosecuted for "inciting hatred and contempt of the government," fined three hundred francs and sentenced to fifteen months in prison. All copies of his book were ordered confiscated, but at least one of them found its way to the Okhrana.

Another copy may have helped inspire a shady German named Hermann Goedsche, a minor postal official who had been dismissed for his involvement in a forgery case and had then taken to writing thrillers. One of these, entitled *Biarritz,* also contained unearthly dialogues. In the sinister darkness of the Jewish cemetery in Prague, according to Goedsche's fancy, representatives of the twelve tribes of Israel gather once every hundred years to conjure up the Devil and report to him on their progress in conquering the world. "Every business in which there is speculation and profit must be in our hands," says, for example, the Son of the Tribe of Dan. "That is our natural right. First of all we must get control of the traffic in liquor, butter, wool and bread." "The natural enemy of the Jews is the Christian church," says the representative of the Tribe of Aaron. "Therefore we must try to humiliate it, we must instill into it freethinking, skepticism and conflicts." "We must demand free marriage between Jews and Christians," says the representative of the Tribe of Asher.

This absurd fantasy, published in 1868, soon aquired a life of its own in the fermenting mulch of European anti-Semitism. It was repeatedly plagiarized and revised and republished, and in the course of its transformations the ominous reports by the various tribal chiefs were amalgamated into a single pronouncement by an anonymous rabbi, who gloatingly described how the Jews were manipulating all the forces of materialism, liberalism and secularism in order to seize power all over the world. This fiction, moreover, gradually came to be purveyed as fact. It was widely known as "The Rabbi's Speech."

Anti-Semitism flourished in the late nineteenth century, partly because of the Jews' emergence from their centuries in the ghetto, partly because of the social stresses that accompanied the Industrial Revolution and the decline of traditional customs. In France, the focal point of these conflicts was the treason trial in 1894 of Captain Alfred Dreyfus. The propaganda battles that swirled

around this case apparently inspired Rachkovsky to provide a contribution of
his own. He may also have been inspired by the first Zionist Congress at Basel
in 1897. And, of course, by the well-known sentiments of the Russian royal
family. Sometime in 1897 or 1898, Rachkovsky hired a still unidentified
scrivener to combine Joly's Machiavellian dialogue and Goedsche's fantasy
into a document that would sound like a charter for Jewish domination of the
world.

The result was "The Protocols of the Elders of Zion," in which an anonymous rabbi told an assembly of Jewish leaders how power would be won.
Under the guise of civil rights, the Jews would infiltrate and undermine all governments. Monarchies would be subverted by republicanism and republics by
socialism. The Jews would establish themselves in the schools to weaken
Christian education, and in the press and the theater to weaken Christian
morals. The church would gradually crumble. The Jews would bargain and
barter to acquire gold; they would tempt the old orders into debt and then
foreclose their mortgages; their growing power would enable them to dominate
all markets and bankrupt anyone who resisted.The Jews would try to avoid
force, but they might have to resort to it. As their ultimate weapon, they would
plant explosives in the new subway lines that were now being built in all major
capitals, and if the Christians tried to resist the final Jewish takeover, everything would be destroyed. Once the Jews were triumphant, they would establish a police state of their own, a world government under a Jewish king. There
would be perpetual peace and prosperity, the rabbi promised, so even the
Christians would benefit, but at the price of giving up their religion and sub-
mitting to their fate.

Rachkovsky's original purpose in fabricating the "Protocols" remains obscure. Though written in French, they were never published in France. Instead,
several handwritten copies—allegedly stolen from delegates to the Zionist Congress in Basel or from other eminent Jewish "conspirators"—began to circulate
among Russians in France, then to drift eastward, and so one of them reached
Sergei Nilus. It may have been quite by accident, therefore, that when Rachkovsky arrived at the imperial court to join in the intrigue against Dr. Philippe,
he discovered one of his own creations, "The Protocols of the Elders of Zion,"
in the hands of the man being regarded as Philippe's rival and replacement. Or
perhaps Rachkovsky was too much a fatalist to regard any such accident as accidental. As for Nilus, he praised Rachkovsky as "a fine man" who had fought
against "the Satanic sects," and when someone suggested that Rachkovsky
might have fabricated the "Protocols," Nilus answered, "Did not the ass
of Balaam utter prophecy?"

The intrigue against Philippe, meanwhile, evolved in a strange way. After
Alexandra's false pregnancy, many of Philippe's former admirers began to
avoid him. "Some went so far as to say that he had the evil eye," according to
the French ambassador, Maurice Paléologue, "and even that he had the mark
of Antichrist upon him." When Philippe heard that Rachkovsky was spreading
the word about his past arrests, he pleaded with Grand Duke Nikolai, father-
in-law of one of the Montenegrin princesses, to intervene with the Tsar. There
was also the new Minister of the Interior, Plehve, a man determined both to

please the Tsar and to assert his own authority over all police maneuvers. Rachkovsky was stunned to find himself suddenly summoned before Plehve and dismissed, without pay or pension.

But Philippe too was doomed. The Tsar had decided that Alexandra's spiritual yearnings should be guided into new directions, so the spring of 1903 was devoted to elaborate ceremonies for the canonization of Saint Seraphin of Sarov, and shortly thereafter the Tsarina became pregnant again. Philippe tried to ingratiate himself by prophesying that the Tsar would win a glorious victory in the impending conflict with Japan, but the Tsar abruptly decided that Philippe's intrusion into foreign policy was an impertinence, and he sent him back to France. But Nilus did not replace him, either. Philippe's supporters informed the Tsar of Nilus' mistresses past and present, and the Tsar dispatched him to a monastery. His chief memorial was a new edition of his book, *The Great in the Small,* published under police auspices in 1905 on the Tsar's own printing press at Tsarskoe Selo, with, as an appendix, the first published version of "The Protocols of the Elders of Zion." "With all the might and terror of Satan, the reign of the triumphant King of Israel is approaching our unregenerate world," Nilus wrote about his discovery. "The King born of the blood of Zion—the Antichrist is near to the throne of universal power."

Tsar Nicholas read Nilus' work and was impressed. He was always impressed by reports of Jewish malefactions, and he naturally accepted the idea that liberalism was a Jewish conspiracy. But when he talked of having the police investigate this conspiracy, he had to be persuaded that the "Protocols" were not a very exact source of information. The Tsar had many other things on his mind, crises both political and economic, and not the least of events was that Alexandra had finally given birth to an heir, Alexei, and this heir was suddenly found to be afflicted with hemophilia. To calm the Tsarina's alarms, the Montenegrins had just discovered a new spiritual guide for her, a mesmerizing holy man named Gregory Rasputin. He had already cured Grand Duke Nikolai's favorite hound of the colic.

Von Plehve cherished another theory on how to deal with opposition to the autocracy. When War Minister Alexei Kuropatkin reproached him for it, he was happy to explain. "Alexei Nikolayevich, you are not familiar with Russia's internal situation," he said to the general. "We need a little victorious war to stem the tide of revolution."

Tsar Nicholas was almost as frivolous as Plehve in the maneuvers by which he blundered into that little victorious war. In hindsight, of course, it appears inevitable that Russia's long *Drang nach Osten* should bring it into conflict with the ambitious Japan newly emerging from centuries of feudalism, but Nicholas saw no obstacles to Russian expansion in the East. Witte's new railroad opened up grand possibilities for the development of Siberia and beyond. The Chinese Empire was decrepit, and the Japanese were mere monkeys. The two had fought in 1894–95, and the Japanese had won easily, forcing China to give up Formosa, the Pescadores, and Liaotung Peninsula with its ice-free harbor at Port Arthur.

At the urging of Witte, Nicholas had threatened to intervene unless Japan gave up the Liaotung Peninsula and stayed off the mainland. The Japanese grudgingly agreed. Witte then signed a secret alliance with the Chinese and began building a section of his Trans-Siberian Railroad across Manchuria. But when a German fleet seized Kiaochow in 1898 in supposed revenge for the death of two German missionaries, Tsar Nicholas honored not the alliance with China but a secret personal agreement with his German cousin, Kaiser Wilhelm II; he not only accepted the seizure of Kiaochow but demanded and got Port Arthur for Russia. And when the Boxers rose in revolt against Europe's depradations on China, Russia protected its interests by "temporarily" moving its army into Manchuria.

Nicholas was urged on in these maneuvers by Kaiser Wilhelm, who regularly wrote him imperial exhortations and advice. It had always been in the Germans' interest to guide their Russian neighbors toward the East. "Russia has nothing to do in the West," Bismarck once declared. "There she can only catch Nihilism and other diseases. Her mission is in Asia. There she represents civilization." The Kaiser, who addressed his cousin as "Nicky" and signed himself "Willy," was even more emphatic in warning of "the Yellow Peril." "Clearly, it is the great task of the future for Russia to cultivate the Asian Continent," he wrote, "and to defend Europe from the inroads of the Great Yellow Race. In this you will always find me on your side, ready to help you as best I can . . . in the Defense of the Cross and the old Christian and European culture against the inroads of the Mongols and Buddhism."

Nicholas was also urged on by a court faction inspired by a former cavalry captain named Alexander Bezobrazov, who talked grandiosely of bringing Korea into the Russian Empire "without a drop of blood." The feudal kingdom of Korea was another crumbling adjunct of crumbling China, and the Russians and Japanese had agreed in 1898 that it should remain autonomous, and that they should have equal influence there. The Russians soon subverted this agreement by persuading the Koreans to take in Russian military and financial advisers. Now Bezobrazov was proposing a scheme to develop a huge timber concession that he had bought along the Yalu River, and to send in demobilized Russian soldiers to help work the land. Bezobrazov was "an impractical dreamer and adventurer," according to War Minister Kuropatkin, but he had shrewdly coaxed the Dowager Empress Maria and the Tsar's brother Mikhail into taking shares in his project. The Tsar ordered Witte to make two million rubles of government funds available for the Yalu scheme. Witte and Kuropatkin opposed this scheme as both impractical and dangerously provocative, but Plehve backed it strongly. At a cabinet meeting, according to Witte, Plehve declared "that the Far Eastern problems must be solved by bayonets, not diplomatic pens." Plehve's support was critical. "It was only then," said Witte, "that the Emperor went over to Bezobrazov." From Berlin, the Kaiser offered his encouragement: "It is evident to every unbiased mind that Korea must and will be Russian."

The Japanese kept protesting and objecting. Their leading statesman, Marquis Ito, came to St. Petersburg to negotiate, but the Russians ignored him. The basic Japanese proposal was that Manchuria become a Russian sphere of influence while the Japanese acquire a similar dominion over Korea. Witte urged the Tsar to accept, but the hawks in St. Petersburg kept assuring the Tsar, who needed little urging, that the Japanese could not stand up to mighty Russia. In May of 1903, the Tsar promoted the disreputable Bezobrazov to the rank of secretary of state; in July, he promoted Admiral E. I. Alexeyev, an inexperienced and incompetent official who was believed to be the illegitimate son of Alexander III, to the ominous position of viceroy in the Far East. In August, he removed Witte from the Finance Ministry and installed him in the largely ceremonial position of chairman of the Committee of Ministers. "I was simply discharged," Witte complained to a friend. "I had become tiresome." The Japanese ambassador asked several times for an audience with the Tsar, then quietly went home.

Japan too had its hawks. For a decade, they had been building a modern army trained by the French and a navy trained by the British. Early in 1904, they were ready to strike, and they struck without warning. Under cover of night, on February 9, ten destroyers steamed into the harbor of Port Arthur, where they could see the Russian fleet silhouetted against the lights of the town. Tsar Nicholas had just returned from the theater when he received a telegram from Admiral Alexeyev: "About midnight, Japanese destroyers made a sudden attack on the squadron anchored in the outer harbor of Port Arthur. The battleships *Tsarovich, Retvizan* and the cruiser *Pallada* were torpedoed . . ." The Tsar noted the news in his diary and added: "May God come to our aid."

The proud Russians had some three million men under arms, more than triple the Japanese forces, but most of them were far from the battlefront. East of Lake Baikal, they had only 80,000 troops, 23,000 garrison forces and 30,000 railway guards. The only supply line from the west was the single-track Siberian railway. It still had a one-hundred mile gap near Lake Baikal, where everything had to be transported by horses or ships. The Japanese had 180,000 combat troops ready for action and fiercely eager to prove themselves in their first war against a white nation. Their strategy, obviously, was to cripple the Russians before any reserves could be brought up; the Russians' strategy, just as obviously, was their traditional one, to delay until they mobilized their huge numbers. While Admiral Heihachiro Togo's fleet kept the Russians bottled up in Port Arthur, a second Japanese force attacked the Korean coast at Chemulpo, near Seoul. It sank two Russian cruisers and enabled Japanese troops to start streaming ashore. The Japanese immediately marched to the Yalu, encountered a Russian force there and smashed it aside, then marched on to cut off Port Arthur.

"Patience, patience, and once more patience, gentlemen!" So said General Kuropatkin as he departed from the War Ministry and went east to build up the armies in the field. His strategy was reasonable, but he had to take orders from the inept Viceroy Alexeyev, headquartered in besieged Port Arthur, and Alexeyev had the support of the royal palace. "Inform General Kuropatkin," wrote the Tsar, "that I impose upon him all the responsibility for the fate of Port Arthur." Kuropatkin, who had hoped to make his stand farther north at

Mukden, reluctantly moved south late in August and collided with the Japanese at Liao-yang. He did not have the numerical superiority he wanted. The two armies were roughly equal, 150,000 men on each side, strung out along a sixty-mile front. For a full week of fighting, the Russians tried to break through, and for a full week the Japanese battled them to a standstill. The Russians retreated behind the Sha Ho River and reorganized. Kuropatkin announced a major offensive. Once again, the Japanese stopped the Russians and pushed them back. It was a gory stalemate. The Russians lost more than 48,000 men in the two battles, the Japanese nearly 44,000. Despite Kuropatkin's failure to relieve Port Arthur, or possibly because of it, the general nonetheless won the satisfaction of being made commander in chief; Admiral Alexeyev gave up his vice regency and abandoned his headquarters in surrounded Port Arthur.

In an absurdly belated move to strengthen the Russian forces, Tsar Nicholas finally decided in October to send the entire Baltic Fleet—eight battleships, twelve cruisers, nine destroyers—on an eighteen-thousand-mile voyage around the world to China. The fleet's officers apparently had visions of being attacked by Japanese torpedo boats as soon as they reached the North Sea, so when they encountered some British fishing trawlers in Dogger Bank one night, they suddenly opened fire, sinking one boat and killing two men. The British government angrily threatened reprisal, but the Tsar dispatched a somewhat conciliatory message to King Edward VII. "I sent a telegram to Uncle Bertie, expressing my regret, but I did not apologize," he wrote to his mother. Eventually, Russia had to pay damages of £65,000.

The Japanese were already closing in on the hills around Port Arthur. Baron Ki-Teu Nogi, who had conquered the fortress in the war against China a decade earlier, was confident that his well-trained Third Army could overwhelm the Russians. He did not realize that the 55,000-man garrison under General A. M. Stoessel had strengthened all the fortifications and possessed enough supplies to hold out for months. On the night of July 26, Nogi attacked the strongly guarded east side of the citadel. The Russians resisted bravely. It took two days of fighting for the Japanese to break through the Russian perimeter and another month of intermittent assaults for them to capture two outlying forts. This opening skirmish cost Nogi no fewer than 6,600 men.

The Japanese gain prompted Tsar Nicholas to order his naval commander in Port Arthur, Admiral Witthoft, to break out of Togo's blockade. On the morning of August 10, he led forth a fleet of six battleships and four cruisers. In almost the first exchange of gunfire, the Japanese crippled the Russian flagship and killed the admiral. The Japanese then swept in and mauled the rest of the Russian warships. Seven of them were driven to internment in neutral ports, one beached, and the rest forced back into Port Arthur. The blockade remained.

By this time, Nogi had brought his artillery into range, and after pounding the fortifications for two days, he ordered his infantry to charge. It was a new and daunting experience for the Russians to encounter an enemy who seemed absolutely without fear. The strongly emplaced defenders cut down the Japanese attackers by the thousands, but still they kept coming. By the time they captured their target, two more outlying forts, they had lost fifteen thousand men. The bloodshed was enough to make even Baron Nogi reconsider his tactics. He decided to bring in sappers and begin a siege of almost medieval intensity.

All through the autumn, the Japanese undermined and bombarded the Russian fortifications. In late November, Nogi again attacked on the east, again was beaten back, then attacked on the northwest. His main target was a height named 203-Meter Hill. Through almost two weeks of continuous fighting, the Japanese crept upward and forward. When they finally blasted their way to the top, they found 400 Russian corpses inside the devastated fortifications. They themselves had lost another 9,000 men, but they now commanded a summit overlooking the town and the harbor. Inside, the Russian defenders argued over their course. They still had considerable supplies of food and ammunition, but there was no prospect of relief, and the Japanese onslaughts seemed irresistible. On December 20, General Stoessel ran up the white flag. The Japanese had lost nearly 60,000 men; the Russians suffered less than half that many casualties, but the 24,000 survivors marched out as prisoners. So the Japanese recaptured by force the prize that the Russians had bullied them into giving up a decade before.

*

Plehve did not live to see this development in the little victorious war that he had so casually encouraged. On the new date that Azef had set for his assassination, July 15, 1904, there were no miscalculations. Boris Savinkov, the leader of the assassination team, assembled his confederates on a streetcorner near the Maryinsky Theater in St. Petersburg and handed out the bombs. He gave the main one to Yegor Sergeyevich Sazonov. A curly-haired youth of twenty-five, Sazonov was the son of a respectable lumber merchant. He had been a medical student at the University of Moscow, devout, uninterested in politics. He had been caught almost by accident in the student strikes of 1901, beaten, expelled, imprisoned, filled with rage. The bomb that Savinkov gave him weighed twelve pounds. It was wrapped in newspaper and tied with a string. Sazonov made no effort to conceal it. He carried it down the street in his hands.

The assassins knew that Plehve's carriage would be taking him to the Baltic Station on his way to see the Tsar at his summer residence, Peterhof. They planned to attack him near the station, on the Izmailovsky Prospect. They walked in single file, forty paces apart. The first of them would let Plehve's carriage pass and then block its retreat. The second, Sazonov, would dash up to the carriage and throw his bomb. If that failed, for any reason, the third man, Ivan Kaliayev, would throw another bomb. If that too failed, the fourth assassin was ready with a gun. Kaliayev crossed himself. It was exactly nine-forty on a bright, sunny morning when the young killers left their last rendezvous at the Pokrov Church and began their march toward the station. Sazonov was wearing the peaked cap and uniform of a railway worker. "I followed them with my eyes," Savinkov later recalled. "The sun's rays played on Sazonov's brass buttons. He carried his bomb in his right hand, between the elbow and the shoulder. It was evident that the thing was too heavy for him . . ."

Savinkov took a shortcut to the Izmailovsky Prospect, where Plehve was to pass, and found the street lined with nervous policemen. He suspected that they had heard some report of an impending attack on the Minister. He couldn't see Sazonov. He wondered whether something had once again gone wrong. Then, just as he spotted Sazonov working his way through the waiting crowds, he saw Plehve's armor-plated carriage lumber past, drawn by two black horses. Just behind it, there was a detective pedaling along on a bicycle, and behind that two more detectives in a cab. He glanced back at Sazonov and again couldn't see him. Plehve saw him. He saw a young railway worker burst forth from the crowd and lift up a package wrapped in a newspaper and throw it right at the window of the carriage.

"Suddenly the monotonous noise of the street was broken by a strange, heavy, ponderous thud," Savinkov reported. "It was as if someone had struck an iron plate with a heavy hammer. At the same moment there was a hail of broken windows round about. From the ground rose a thin column of grayish-yellow smoke, almost black at the edges. It grew thicker and thicker until it covered the whole street, and then disappeared as quickly as it had come. . . . I ran across the street to the Warsaw Hotel . . . When I came to the place of the explosion the smoke had already dispersed. There was a smell of burning. Before me, in the dusty street, about four feet from the pavement, I saw Sazonov. He was on the ground, leaning with his left arm on the stones and his head cocked to the right. His cap had been blown off, and his dark brown hair fell in disorder on his forehead. His face was pale. Here and there on his forehead and cheeks there were little streams of blood. The eyes were dim and half closed. A black spot of blood, beginning at the abdomen, grew wider and wider, ending in a large crimson pool at his feet. . . . A few paces from Sazonov lay von Plehve's mutilated corpse, surrounded by fragments of his carriage."

Kaliayev, who carried the second bomb in a handkerchief, was just crossing a nearby bridge when he heard the explosion and saw Plehve's blood-spattered horses come galloping past him. He never had a chance to throw his bomb.

A few months before his death, Plehve formally endorsed the strangest and most disastrous of the intertwining strategies by which the tsarist police hoped to control Russian life. This was the quasi-fascist scheme variously known as Zubatovshchina and "police socialism." It was the creation of Sergei Zubatov, the Okhrana chief in Moscow. In a memorandum he wrote in 1898 to General Dmitri Trepov, the prefect of Moscow and son of the officer who had been shot in the first outbreak of Narodnaya Volya terrorism, Zubatov argued that the hardships inflicted on the rapidly growing class of industrial workers were turning them against the government. The radicals and intellectuals who preached revolution were a small and powerless faction, easily repressed, but if they could convert the increasingly discontented workers to their cause, then the whole autocracy was in danger. Zubatov's remarkable remedy was to have the police covertly organize a labor union. Since all unions were forbidden by law, Zubatov suggested a simple workers' association, a mutual-benefit society that could provide help with insurance policies, a food cooperative and a housing service combined with lectures and readings on various economic problems. That would provide a controlled channel for the workers' grievances against their employers without embroiling them in the radicals' political campaign against the government. General Trepov worried that such an organization might become difficult to control, but Zubatov was confident. An ardent monarchist, he genuinely believed that the Tsar's officials could and should provide the best guidance for the workers. "Official duty . . . ," he said "obliges the Orthodox-autocratic state to treat equally, justly and completely impartially the workers and the owners, the poor and the rich."

In May 1901, with Trepov's permission, Zubatov organized the Moscow Society for Mutual Aid for Workingmen in the Mechanical Industries. Even though uniformed policemen openly attended and observed the society's meetings, workers flocked to join. By February of 1902, on the anniversary of Alexander's liberation of the serfs, the society was able to muster fifty thousand workers for a commemorative religious service. It was a somewhat ambiguous demonstration. "A damp wind was whirling on the Red Square, threatening a snowstorm . . . ," Gorki wrote in *The Magnet*. "The workers were marching unhurriedly. . . . They talked little, in low voices, grumblingly. . . . The heavy scraping of thousands of feet over crunching snow strangely resembled the sound of clearing an enormous throat, the moist rattle of gargantuan lungs. . . . Without a leader, without a hero, the mob was an inanimate body. Today its leader was an official of the Gendarme Administration, Sergei Zubatov."

This anomaly reflected the contradictory situation that Zubatov was trying to control. The Moscow industrial worker at the turn of the century was apt to be a hungry and illiterate peasant newly come from the country, still bound by the traditional loyalties to Tsar and priest and established order. But the circumstances in which he found himself were appalling. It was only in 1897 that the twelve-hour day had been instituted, and even now that reform was often ignored. The average worker's salary was fifteen rubles ($7.50) per month, about one-third the rate in France. Women workers averaged ten rubles and children five to seven. Even these miserable wages were subject to all manner of fines for tardinesss or slow work or lack of respect or whatever the foreman chose to charge. Most workers had to sleep in dingy company barracks, some with wives and children clustered in a corner, others too poor to bring their families in from their villages. Any protest against these conditions led to dismissal, and to immersion in slums like Khitrovka, where starving beggars slept sprawled in the streets and children offered themselves as prostitutes for a few kopecks.

Once Zubatov had launched his society in Moscow, he commissioned other police agents to organize similar unions in the industrial centers to the south. Soon they appeared in Odessa, Kiev, Nikolaiev and Kharkov. The unions' chief function at the start was to operate community centers where the workers could gather for soft drinks and uplifting lectures. But what brought the workers flocking to these meetings was the hope of help. The more assertive of them talked of demanding better wages and a ten-hour day. Zubatov was sympathetic. He even argued with his superiors that strikes should be permitted as long as the strikers asked only for better working conditions. When a delegation of weavers from Zubatov's union presented a demand for better wages to a French silk-factory owner named Jules Goujon, he refused to make any concessions. Zubatov began paying the weavers for their strike fund, and Trepov threatened to have Goujon ordered back to France. The French ambassador appealed to Witte, the patron of industry, and Witte forced "that sworn anarchist Zubatov" to back down. Zubatov's whole operation in Moscow began to falter, for if it could not give the workers real help, then their support could hardly last long. Already, the radicals were doing their best to disrupt and condemn the union's activities.

At this critical juncture, in April of 1902, the assassination of Sipyagin made Plehve the minister of the interior, and Plehve promoted Zubatov to the head of the Special Section, which dealt with all political investigations for the Police Department in St. Petersburg. Zubatov enthusiastically opened new Okhrana offices in Kiev, Odessa and Vilna. Plehve had misgivings about the police unions, which Zubatov now began organizing in the capital, but he considered them a useful weapon with which to torment Witte. "Take a twig, for example," Plehve beamed to a delegation of workers Zubatov brought to him. "A single twig can be broken with ease, but a whole bundle of twigs cannot be broken at once. The workers should take this as a model."

Zubatov transferred three of his organizers with him from Moscow, but as he began looking about him for new recruits, he received a message from one of his Okhrana assistants recommending a young priest named Georgi Gapon. "Nervous, effusive, ambitious, with the burning eyes of an ascetic, Gapon was a restless and turbulent figure," Zubatov's assistant, A. Spiridovich, later recalled. "He had unbounded love for the Tsar and felt that it was possible to attain through him all that was needed by the people. Romantic at heart, he was much concerned with the unfortunate and poor." Gapon, in turn, saw Zubatov as "a short, strongly built man of about forty years of age, with chestnut-brown hair, winning eyes and simple manners." "I have but one object in life," the police official told the young priest, "and that is to help the workingman."

Gapon came from the Ukraine. His father was a Cossack peasant, a village clerk. His mother was deeply devout. Georgi was the eldest of nineteen children, fragile and bookish, destined from childhood for the priesthood. His was an uncertain vocation. As a young seminarian, he resented the ponderous rituals of the Orthodox Church. He came under the influence of some local admirers of Tolstoy. His theological studies suffered. After a severe case of typhus, he decided to give up the priesthood and study medicine, but he could not enter a university unless he earned high marks from the seminary. On learning that he might not receive them, he threatened to kill his teacher and then commit suicide. Instead, he avoided the final examination, writing to excuse himself because of his "disturbed physical and mental state." He found work as a statistician, then fell in love with a devout girl who shared his vague ambitions to help the poor. Her parents opposed a marriage because of Gapon's poor prospects, but she persuaded him to appeal to the bishop for help. The bishop not only ordained him but interceded with the girl's parents to permit the marriage. After two children were born, Gapon's wife suddenly fell ill and died.

Father Gapon decided to seek his fortunes in St. Petersburg. He got himself enrolled as a graduate student in the prestigious Theological Academy. Even here, he saw sin all around him, greed, lust, gluttony, corruption of the spirit. "A sluggish and depraved life," he called it. He devoted most of his considerable energy to missionary work among the poor. He worked himself to the edge of another breakdown. He talked again of studying medicine but could not see how to afford it. By now he was nearly thirty, a handsome man, tall, with thick, wavy hair, long black eyelashes, a luxuriant beard. He spoke in a rich baritone and loved to sing. Wherever he preached, crowds soon gathered to hear him, but he could find neither a place for himself nor a belief in the efficacy of his work. "Is it not my duty to sacrifice myself . . . ?" he wrote to a friend in the Crimea. "If an individual became permeated with this idea, he could be reconciled with . . . the yoke prepared for him by life."

Gapon repeatedly talked of forming some kind of brotherhood of men who could help one another in leading exemplary Christian lives. He became senior priest at an orphanage, and his sermons in the adjoining church once again attracted large crowds. He drew up a plan to reform the poorhouses of the capital and sent it to the authorities and was thrilled to hear that the Empress Alexandra herself looked on it and him with imperial favor. This promising phase of Gapon's career came to an abrupt end when he abandoned all his priestly duties and went off to the Ukraine with a recent graduate of the orphanage named Sasha Uzdaleva. She became his common-law wife. The board of the orphanage promptly dismissed him, and the academy expelled him.

This mixture of idealism and instability inevitably brought Gapon to the attention of Zubatov's political police. His popularity and influence among the poor made him potentially valuable to them; his vanity and self-destructiveness tainted him, made him vulnerable to their designs. They got him reinstated by the church authorities. Zubatov persuaded Gapon to come to some meetings of his fledgling union, which met in a hall of the Temperance Society, but Gapon remained dubious about Zubatov's control. He argued that only an independent union could win the workers' allegiance. "During the meetings, he would sit quietly, attentively listening all the time, occasionally taking notes," according to another participant named N. M. Varnashev. "But he became very animated when some of the most simple and backward workers got up to speak. He would nod appreciatively, voice his support, and help the speaker find words to express his thoughts."

When Father Gapon graduated from the academy in June of 1903, the ecclesiastical authorities proposed that he accept an assignment far from the political complexities of St. Petersburg, but Gapon objected. Determined to stay in the capital, but unable to find work there, he rented a little room, where he lived, as Zubatov put it, "on black bread and olives." Zubatov was only too willing to help, though how much he actually did help is uncertain. Zubatov himself later claimed that he paid Gapon one thousand rubles a month. Gapon denied this and said he had only been "pretending adherence to Zubatov's policy to attain my own ends." He did admit that on one occasion Zubatov had offered him two hundred rubles for a report he had written, and that he had accepted half that amount "lest I should make him suspicious." *"Le distance ne fait rien,"* as Madame du Deffand remarked on hearing that Saint Denis had walked for a mile after his head had been cut off. *"Il n'y a que le premier pas qui coûte."*

Zubatov's grand design, however, had once again led the designer into trouble. The unions that his agents had organized in the south proved more militant than Zubatov's theories had envisaged, and their distance from the capital made them more difficult to control. The first major trouble occurred in Rostov-on-Don in November of 1902, when the railway workers went out on strike for higher wages and persuaded many other workers to join them. The local authorities called in troops to suppress the strike and arrest the union leaders. The following July, a new wave of strikes swept all across the south, to Odessa, Baku, Tiflis, Kiev, to the railways, the oilfields, the factories and harbors. More than a quarter of a million men walked out, and even after the troops went into action it took a full month before the strike was broken. Throughout that month, Zubatov argued for concessions to the strikers; Plehve insisted on repression. Zubatov began saying openly that Plehve should be dismissed. On August 18, finally, Zubatov was not only dismissed but ordered to get out of St. Petersburg within twenty-four hours. Zubatov silently turned and strode out of Plehve's office, slamming the door behind him. One of the few who came to see him off at the station was Father Gapon. Zubatov wept. He urged the priest to help keep the struggling union alive.

As Gapon watched Zubatov's train steam out of the station, he could see that his own future was clear. Instead of involving himself with Zubatov's union, he could start a union of his own. This was against the law, of course, but Gapon was an artful courtier. In meeting after meeting with the authorities, he argued that no union under direct police leadership could ever win the support of the workers, but that if he were allowed to form an independent union, he would keep it loyal to church and Tsar, dedicated to "a sober, Christian view of life." He would preserve the workers from radicalism, from "the danger of exploitation by others, enemies of Russia." And he would welcome, he said, the continued supervision of the police. "Naturally," he wrote in a long memorandum to Plehve, "there can and must be control . . . by the governmental authorities." Gapon made his headquarters in the clubhouse of Zubatov's union, but he already had a resounding new name for his organization: the Assembly of the Russian Factory and Mill Workers of St. Petersburg.

When Plehve finally gave his blessing, in April of 1904, Father Gapon gathered about 150 of his supporters for a formal ceremony to launch the Assembly. There were prayers and songs and a telegram to the Interior Ministry pledging "zealous love for the throne and the fatherland." In this year of repeated military humiliations and increasingly serious economic disturbances, the police might well compliment themselves on the patriotic tone of Father Gapon's Assembly, for the messages arriving from various political gatherings were much more contentious. This was the year in which the zemstvo leaders tried to hold a national conference and were forbidden to do so. A number of those leaders joined in forming a Union of Liberation to work for a freely elected constitutional government, and they too were forbidden to meet. The left wing of the liberals reached out to join forces with the Social Democrats and Socialist Revolutionaries, who continued to meet underground and in exile.

Father Gapon flourished. He provided the poor and the oppressed with a place to discuss their problems and a means to seek improvements. He began organizing a cooperative to provide cheaper tea and sugar and other supplies. He foresaw an annual profit of 100,000 rubles. He offered insurance plans and lending libraries and dances. He offered, above all, solidarity and hope. The movement kept growing. In May, Gapon opened the first new branch in a renovated inn near the Putilov Works in the Narva district. The city's new governor, General I. A. Fullon, came to the opening ceremony, told the workers that "strength lies in unity," and donated one hundred rubles. "The Assembly of Russian Workers begins to emerge as a desirable social force," according to an Okhrana report that June. "It is beginning to gain increasing support among honest, sensible Russian workers." The Okhrana wanted to help by offering to Father Gapon what he described as "a large sum of money." Gapon did not want to jeopardize his independence, but he also did not want to be considered rebellious. "In order to divert suspicion," he said, "I accepted four hundred rubles and entered them as an anonymous gift."

In June, Father Gapon decided that the Assembly should organize branches in other cities. "We will cover the whole of Russia with a network of our organizations," he said. He set out for Moscow, Kharkov and Kiev. The St. Petersburg authorities had warned him not to proselytize in Moscow, but he ignored them. At meetings of the weakened Zubatov unions there, he urged members to break their ties with the police and to form independent groups under his aegis. When word of Gapon's speeches reached Grand Duke Sergei, he sent an angry account of them to Plehve and pointedly asked what Plehve proposed to do about Gapon. Plehve was apologetic. "I myself now see that it was premature," he said, "to develop such a movement among the Russian workers." Plehve's assassination the following month saved Gapon's movement. It brought to the Interior Ministry a mild and cautious official, Prince Pyotr Svyatopolk-Mirsky, a protégé of Witte's, and under his lenient regime there soon began talk of a political "spring." Father Gapon continued to recruit workers for his Assembly. By October, he had nine branches totaling five thousand members in various parts of St. Petersburg. During November, he added another 2,500 members, and at the end of the year he had twenty thousand.

The inevitable conflict began at the Putilov plant in southwestern St. Petersburg, where the Ekateringofka River flows into the Bay of Finland. The Putilov plant, which made guns, ships, railroad cars, was the biggest factory in

Russia. It had twelve thousand workers, many of them now members of the Assembly. Its manager, S. I. Smirnov, originally looked benignly on the Assembly as a social club for his employees. He became an auxiliary member himself, donated one hundred rubles, loaned the organization an auditorium for a concert. He looked with some suspicion, however, on Father Gapon's occasional attempts to settle differences between workers and the management. On December 4, 1904, in the carpentry shop of the railroad-car division, a workman named Sergunin got his wages and found that various management fines for tardiness had reduced his pay to far less than he expected. When he complained to his foreman, A. Tetiavkin, the foreman responded by firing him. Tetiavkin also made a sneering reference to the Assembly, to which Sergunin belonged. Whether Tetiavkin was acting out of personal arrogance, or whether he was carrying out a new company policy of resisting the Assembly, or whether, for that matter, Sergunin deserved to be fired—all these questions have disappeared in the great flood of events that flowed out of this small incident. Sergunin appealed his dismissal to the Putilov complaint section, and then to the Assembly. By this time, Tetiavkin had fired another Assembly member and threatened two others. "Go to your Assembly," he told one of them. "It will do everything for you."

Father Gapon regarded these dismissals as a challenge to the very existence of his Assembly. "I decided," he said later, "it was the duty of the organization to espouse the cause of these men and to stand up for them until the end, come what may." His campaign began quietly. On December 27, he called a meeting of about 350 delegates from the various branches. He told them that the dismissals were a threat to the Assembly and asked their support in fighting back. The delegates passed a resolution warning that if the dismissed men were not reinstated, the Assembly "cannot be held responsible for any breach of the peace." The next day, Gapon led a delegation bringing the resolution to General Fullon, the governor of the city. Fullon, who had long supported the Assembly, was dismayed by its new belligerence. "You are threatening the peace of the capital," he said. Father Gapon assured him that the workers "do not even contemplate any threat."

Another Assembly delegation went to see Smirnov, the factory manager. He said the dispute was simply a misunderstanding, but he insisted that the Assembly had no right to interfere with his management of the plant. He too complained of being "threatened." On January 2, a Sunday, the Assembly delegates met again—six hundred of them this time—and decided that when the Putilov workers went to the factory the next morning they would all gather at Smirnov's office to demand the reinstatement of the dismissed workers and the removal of the foreman who had fired them. And so it was that 2,500 workmen, orderly but very determined, besieged Smirnov in his office the next morning. All work had stopped. At first, Smirnov refused to talk to the strikers. Then he agreed to investigate their complaints, but he also threatened to shut the factory if they did not return to their jobs. By now General Fullon was warning Gapon about the danger of violence. "Do not be alarmed," Gapon told him. "Everything will be orderly and peaceful. The workers only want to be heard."

Gapon kept increasing the workers' demands, however. On Tuesday afternoon, when he led a delegation of thirty-five workers to see Smirnov, he carried a list that included not just the reinstatement of the dismissed workers but also an increase in minimum daily wages from sixty kopecks to one ruble (fifty cents) for men and from forty to seventy-five kopecks for women, a limit of eight hours on the working day, free medical care and improved sanitation. As he recited each demand, Gapon turned to the workers behind him and asked, "Is that right, comrades?" Each time, he received a chorus of approval. Smirnov was appalled. The demand for a ruble a day, he said, would "make beggars out of the shareholders." Besides, he declared, he "would never permit some outside organization that has nothing to do with the plant to dictate its policies."

By now, the Putilov workers were entering neighboring factories and asking support. On Tuesday, the second day of the strike, the Franco-Russian Machine Works was shut down; then came the huge Nevsky Machine and Shipbuilding Works. "I came to the shop on January 5 at 7 A.M.," one of the Nevsky workers later recalled. "We quietly sang a prayer. I . . . had already begun to saw when a certain turner, N., came in and said, 'Change clothes, comrades! Let us go with the Putilov workers to seek truth and justice.' I listened to him, thinking that he was joking. . . . I started to work again. Suddenly I heard the repeated ringing of the bells. . . . I looked around—the workers were changing, and so did I." That same day, the Yekaterinhof textile plant closed down, and so did the Neva textile plant, and by the end of the week almost four hundred firms employing about 150,000 workers were on strike.

Having begun this enormous wave of protest, Father Gapon could see no way to reach a settlement with the factory workers. At a meeting of the Putilov board that Wednesday, Gapon was told that all the grievances could be considered, but only after the workers went back to their jobs. The city authorities, similarly, had nothing to recommend except a return to work. At another meeting that night with his followers, Gapon proposed a dramatic new approach. "The Tsar does not know of our needs, and we will tell him," said Gapon. "If he loves his people, he will grant them their humble supplications!"

The next day, Thursday, was a major religious holiday, the Feast of the Epiphany. While Father Gapon went to meeting after meeting to explain the Assembly's demands and to work out some kind of petition to the Tsar, the Tsar himself paid hardly any attention to the strike at all. His ministers had told him that it was a dispute of small consequence, and General Fullon added that the obscure priest leading the strikers was a loyal supporter of the monarchy. Besides, the closed factories all lay in the industrial outskirts of St. Petersburg, and when the Tsar saw the holiday crowds gathered in the center of the city, he assumed, quite reasonably, that they had assembled to join him in watching the blessing of the waters. This was a venerable ceremony derived from the coming of the Three Magi to honor the newborn Christ. Tsar Nicholas played his part by leading a delegation of uniformed courtiers from the Winter Palace down to a canopy at the edge of the Neva, where the Metropolitan Anthony gave his blessing. When the ceremony was finished, an artillery battery on Vasilevsky Island fired a salute. To the Tsar's surprise, he heard a charge of grapeshot crash into a nearby wall, for one of the cannons had inadvertently been left fully loaded. One policeman was wounded, but the Tsar remained imperturbable as he led the court procession back to the palace and then returned to Tsarskoe Selo.

By now, Father Gapon was nearly finished with his petition, but he was having difficulty in reaching the Tsar. He tried to make an appointment with the Interior Minister, Prince Svyatopolk-Mirsky, but the Prince refused to see him. Father Gapon was not to be denied. At another meeting that Thursday night, he proposed an even more dramatic step—that all the thousands of strikers join him in carrying the petition to the Tsar. "Let us all go with our wives and children to the Winter Palace on Sunday at 2 P.M.," he declared. "Let us go quietly and peacefully, and we will be heard."

Father Gapon kept working on his petition most of that night. He had been secretly planning for some time a series of political demands to be made of the Tsar, but now that it had come time to formulate a petition on behalf of thousands of workers, the priest kept fussing and revising. He showed various drafts to friends and followers and even to roaming journalists. Several of them wrote drafts, too. Gapon repeatedly noted down some of their ideas, then crossed them out again. Even the next day, Friday, when he began reading his final draft at crowded meetings of the Assembly's branches, he was still listening to suggestions and scribbling in the margins of the creased and increasingly grimy paper that he carried about with him.

In tone and spirit, the petition was uniquely his. It was impassioned and prayerful, rhetorical and slightly false, but nonetheless moving. "We, the workers of St. Petersburg, our wives, our children, and our aged, helpless parents, come to Thee, O Sire, to seek justice and protection," it began. "We are impoverished; we are oppressed, overburdened with excessive toil, contemptuously treated. We are not even recognized as human beings, but are treated like slaves who must suffer their bitter lot in silence. . . . We have reached that frightful moment when death is better than the prolongation of our unbearable sufferings."

The petition then recapitulated the reasons for the strike, omitting the dismissed workers who had started it all but reasserting the demands for an eight-hour day and a minimum wage of one ruble. All these demands had been not only rejected but declared criminal, the petition said. "We do not possesss a single human right," it went on, "not even the right to speak, think, gather, discuss our needs and take steps to improve our conditions." It blamed this not on the Tsar but on "Thy officials." "Russia is too vast, and her needs are too great and manifold to be dealt with exclusively by the bureaucrats," the petition said. "Popular representation is essential; it is essential that the people help themselves and govern themselves. Truly, only they know their real needs."

A freely elected constituent assembly, the petition said, was "our principal request, upon which everything else depends." It then proceeded to list a series of requests that would have done credit to Thomas Jefferson but were still forbidden in the Russian Empire at the threshold of the twentieth century: freedom of speech, press, association and worship, and "inviolability of the person"; free and compulsory public education; equality before the law "without any exceptions"; introduction of the progressive income tax; "termination of the war in accordance with the will of the people"; freedom of "professional worker unions"; an eight-hour working day; and even, despite Gapon's priesthood, separation of church and state. If the Tsar would only grant these requests, the petition concluded, "Thou wilt make Russia happy and glorious, and Thy name will forever be engraved in our hearts. . . . But if Thou witholdest Thy command and failest to respond to our supplications, we will die here on this square before Thy palace. There is no place for us to go, nor is there any reason for us to go any farther."

When the final draft was retyped Friday night, one copy went to the Tsar, one copy to the Interior Ministry and several copies to the press. The original, adorned with about 100,000 workers' signatures, Gapon kept for himself, to be carried through the streets to the Winter Palace on Sunday. Gapon also sent a letter to the Tsar, inviting him to receive his subjects and their petition. "All of the people have faith in Thee. . . . ," he declared, but there was also a note of warning: "If Thou wilt waver and wilt not appear before the people, Thou wilt have broken the moral bond between Thyself and Thy people. Their faith in Thee will have been destroyed."

Although it was generally known that the Tsar was not at the Winter Palace but at Tsarskoe Selo, and although the authorities had posted warnings that "no gatherings or processions on the streets will be tolerated," Gapon seems to have been quite confident that his convocation would persuade the Tsar to keep the appointment that the priest had made for the afternoon of Sunday, January 9. "What if the Tsar refuses to hear us out?" he rhetorically asked his followers over and over again. "Then he is no Tsar to us," they chanted. When the handful of Social Democrats tried to persuade Gapon that the great encounter would never take place, that his march would end in failure at best, and at worst in carnage, the priest refused to believe that the police would resist him. "They wouldn't dare," he said. The methodical Social Democrats were dismayed at Gapon's rejection of both their organizational strategies and their red flags. He insisted that his followers march unarmed, wearing their Sunday clothes, accompanied by their wives and children. "This mixture of naiveté, childish chimeras and realistic observations. . . ," wrote the Menshevik leader S. Sosov, "constituted the complete plan . . . of this mysterious first leader of the proletarian masses of St. Petersburg."

In his way, Father Gapon was right, for he did instinctively know his parishioners of the factories, and the workers trusted him far more than they trusted the radicals. The radicals represented factional politics, whereas Gapon was both the workers' advocate and representative and a man of God. And though he spoke with a Ukrainian accent, and with grammatical errors as well, his natural gift for oratory gave him the tongue of angels, and that is a gift that far surpasses the politics of orthodoxy. Men who possess this gift can see its effect, can see that other men will follow them into the sea, and that knowledge fills them with a completely irrational sense of their own authority. Father Gapon was one of them.

There were, as usual, worthy citizens who felt they should do something to avert a violent confrontation. Maxim Gorki and about a dozen notable lawyers and intellectuals formed a delegation to warn Gapon of a collision. One of his assistants told them that the march could not be stopped. Then they went to see the Interior Minister, Prince Svyatopolk-Mirsky. One of his assistants told them that the authorities had the situation under control. Then they went to see Witte, who held the title of chairman of the Committee of Ministers, and Witte told them there was nothing he could do. Once again, the dragon of chaos had appeared.

The Minister of the Interior had by this time gone to Tsarskoe Selo to report to the Tsar on the preparations that had been made. Military reinforcements had been brought in from outlying districts. There were now nine thousand infantrymen and three thousand cavalry on guard in the capital, under the overall command of Prince Vasilchikov, commander of the Guard Corps. The police were looking for Father Gapon to place him under arrest. The march would be stopped. But just as Gapon believed there would be no serious violence because the authorities would not dare to open fire on thousands of loyal citizens, so the authorities believed there would be no serious violence because the citizenry would not dare to disobey the army's orders. "No one at the conference considered it possible that the demonstration would have to be stopped by force," wrote the new Finance Minister, Count Vladimir Kokovtsov. The Tsar was reassured. "The workers are behaving peacefully so far ...," he wrote in his diary. "The union is led by some socialist priest, Gapon." That socialist priest, hoarse and exhausted after about fifty meetings, ended his last speech to his followers by comparing the coming day to the Resurrection. They would all walk with the Lord and find salvation.

Sunday dawned cold and clear. The rising sun gleamed on the gilded domes and spires of the capital, but frost clung to the windows. The temperature was five degrees. Many of the marchers had been up for hours, some all night. They talked about the coming day. Some prayed. There were five main assembly points in various parts of the city, and the marchers from the farthest points started first so that everyone would reach the Winter Palace at the appointed time, 2 P.M. There were more than anyone could count, perhaps 200,000 in all. The first big column, more than ten thousand strong, set forth at about 9 A.M. from the Neva district in the southeast of the city. So these marchers were the first to encounter the Cossacks, who stopped them at a bridge where the Obvodnoi Canal joined the Neva. A colonel warned the marchers that he had orders not to let them cross the bridge. The marchers' leader, Nikolai Petrov, protested that the workers were peaceful and unarmed. The colonel warned that he would shoot. Pressed from behind, the marchers surged forward. Mounted Cossacks beat them back with their sabers and lead-lined whips. Then the infantry fired a volley of blanks. Some workmen in the vanguard of the march battered down several wooden fences along the road and opened a detour onto the frozen Neva. As the marchers scrambled out onto the ice, the colonel remained at his bridge and let them pass.

The main column assembled in the Narva district in the southwest. That was where the Putilov plant stood. That was where Father Gapon was to lead the

march. He awoke at about eight, after a few hours' sleep in a worker's apartment, surrounded by the bodyguards who now protected him against the arrest
that had already been secretly ordered. As he surveyed the shuffling crowd, he
decided that it needed more religious insignia. He sent an assistant into a
nearby church for help. The sexton refused to cooperate, so Gapon told a
whole platoon of workers to strip the church of its icons and banners. He also
sent to Assembly headquarters for some portraits of the Tsar. One man carried
a large banner that said, "Soldiers: Do not shoot at the people." Some of the
marchers now recited the Lord's Prayer. "Soon after ten we started upon our
journey . . . ," Gapon recalled later. "In the first row were the men carrying a
large framed portrait of the Tsar; then followed another file with the banners
and icons, and I stood in the midst of these. Behind us came a crowd of about
twenty thousand people, men and women, old and young. They all marched
bareheaded, in spite of the bitter cold, full of the simple intention of seeing
their Sovereign . . ."

When they reached the Narva Victory Arch, built at the edge of the capital
to welcome the soldiers home from the Napoleonic Wars, the marchers paused.
Someone asked Gapon whether they should proceed straight through the gates
or take some roundabout route to try to avoid any military barriers. "I shouted
huskily, 'No, straight through them. Courage! Death or freedom!' and the
crowd shouted in return, 'Hurrah!' We then started forward, singing in one
mighty, solemn voice the Tsar's hymn, 'God Save Thy People.' . . . At last we
reached within two hundred paces of where the troops stood. Files of infantry
barred the road, and in front of them a company of cavalry was drawn up, with
their swords shining in the sun. Would they dare to touch us? For a moment we
trembled, and then started forward again. Suddenly the company of Cossacks
galloped rapidly toward us with drawn swords . . ."

Charging over a bridge that crossed the Tarakanovsky Canal, the Horse
Grenadier Guards plunged into the crowd of marchers, flailing to right and left
with their swords and whips. The marchers fell back before them but immediately reformed their lines as soon as the horses had passed. The guardsmen
swept the length of the column, then turned and charged back through the
crowds to the bridge. Still, slowly, the ragged ranks of marchers kept pressing
forward until only about thirty paces separated them from the riflemen of the
Thirteenth Irkutsk Regiment, who stood with their bayonets thrust forward.
The commanding officer ordered his bugler to sound the warning that the
troops would fire, a warning that meant little to the swarm of workers and their
families. Three times the bugle sounded, and then the infantry fired a volley
into the air. Still the workers milled around, pushed forward, shouted slogans
and appeals to the nervous soldiers confronting them. Then came the level volley, point-blank. Then another, and another. Two grizzled workers carrying
the portrait of the Tsar fell wounded. Another bullet struck down a youth carrying one of the religious banners. Many turned to run. Cries of pain and fear
mingled with the cracks of rifle fire. A woman screamed. Smoke drifted slowly
upward in the cold sunlight.

Father Gapon, spiritual leader of the working class of St. Petersburg, suddenly found himself lying in the street. He could see two of his bodyguards lying dead. All around him, the trapped marchers were trying to escape, falling, crying out. He heared the urgent voice of one of his assistants, an engineer named Pyotr Rutenberg. "Are you alive, Father?" asked Rutenberg.

"I'm alive," said Gapon.

"Shall we go?" asked Rutenberg.

"Let's go."

So Father Gapon ran away. Forgot all his pledges, abandoned all his followers, and ran away. Rutenberg led him into a side street, and there he pulled out a pair of scissors and hacked at the thick black beard and long hair that made the priest easy to identify. Gapon was already wearing an anonymous worker's coat over his cassock. He seemed to be in a state of shock. He could not believe that the inevitable had inevitably happened. He kept muttering, "There is no Tsar." Rutenberg told him that he had a friend who lived in an apartment nearby. He led the priest away from the battlefield. "It was idle for me to protest," Gapon wrote later of this flight. "What more could be done . . . ? I gave myself unwillingly into the hands of my rescuers. All those who remained . . . were shot down, or dispersed in terror. We had gone unarmed. There was nothing left but to live for the day when the guilty would be punished."

Gapon had warned the authorities that the march could not be stopped, and his flight did not change that. All over the city, the marching column kept encountering military barricades, kept trying to break through. The worst collision came at the Troitskaya Square, near the Peter and Paul Fortress where so many revolutionaries had been chained. A column of about twenty thousand marchers from the north of the city started out at noon, just as the bells in the fortress tolled. They came marching down the broad Kamenno-Ostrovsky Prospect, sweeping along bystanders into a great mob that filled the riverside square. Among them, once again, was Gorki. "We can't stand any more," one of the marchers told him. "We are going to the Father," said another. "He loves us." Ahead of him, Gorki saw the row of bayonets. He saw a burly stoker wave a white handkerchief and then step forward to argue with the soldiers. An old man limped along at his side. "There was a dry, ripping sound, not very loud—twice, three times," Gorki wrote later in *The Magnet*. "Samghin [Gorki's hero] felt no fear when a bullet whistled over his head, another whined, a board in the wooden wall cracked off a splinter, and one of the three men in front of him, rubbing the wall with his back, fell to the ground." The stoker, standing all alone, waving his cap to encourage the other marchers, fell suddenly, his face buried in the snow. To Samghin the bloodshed and confusion all seemed to take place in slow motion. "Without hurry, the dense mass of workers was retreating. The people, stepping backward and sideways, shook their fists at the soldiers. In some hands white kerchiefs still fluttered. The body of the crowd was breaking up; individual figures, bursting from its sides, ran away, fell to the ground, writhed, crawled. Many lay on the snow. . . . A small woman sat on the ground, pulling a black snow boot off her foot. Suddenly, as if struck on the back of the neck, she thrust her head between her knees, spread out her arms and fell on her side."

Then the wall of soldiers suddenly opened like a gate, and the cavalry charged the crowd. "Rusty-colored horses galloped into the open square, kicking snow into a spray," Gorki wrote. "Riders in white caps roared and yelled, swinging their sabers. The crowd grunted, swayed back, commenced to break up into small groups and individual figures.... [One] horse was prancing. A worker was striking it across the legs with a piece of board. The soldier wheeled the animal sharply, as they do in a circus, and slashed the worker's face with his saber. The man staggered, wept blood, thrust the board into the horse's groin, and dropped under its feet."

Despite all the military barriers, thousands of workers managed to reach the streets around the Winter Palace. The marchers from the Neva region had made their way over the ice. Others simply used side streets. When the elite guards units drawn up around the palace tried to disperse them, the crowds simply flowed from one part of the district to another. They had heard of the shootings on the outskirts of the city, but nothing could make them go home. They were waiting for 2 P.M., when Father Gapon would come marching up the Nevsky Prospect with his petition and his army of followers, and then they would all go to the Winter Palace to see the Tsar. Now women stood and shivered in the cold, waiting. Several children climbed into trees to get a better view. Two o'clock came and went with no sign of Father Gapon and his petition. Police officers once again told the workers to go home. They were answered with jeers.

The guards officers decided to clear the streets. The warning bugle sounded. The riflemen sank to one knee in firing position. Several workers mimicked them, falling to their knees, throwing open their arms, mockingly inviting the guardsmen to shoot. When the bugle had sounded for the third time, the guardsmen fired a volley into the crowds, then another. Some even raised their rifles and shot down the children perched in the trees. Suddenly the sun seemed to go into some strange kind of eclipse. The poet Dmitri Merezhkovsky, who was walking nearby, wrote later that the sun had been encircled by a thick red sphere; other observers claimed they had seen three suns. At about three o'clock, a rainbow shone over the city, and then snow began falling.

Father Gapon had fled to Gorki's apartment. He looked wild, his hair and beard crudely hacked. "Give me something to drink!" he shouted. "Wine, water—it's all the same." His dark face twitched compulsively, and his eyes were glassy. Gorki thought he resembled someone who had "gone insane." Savva Morozov, a millionaire who liked dabbling in radical causes, undertook to shave Gapon, and then the priest retired to a bedroom to draft a new manifesto. The city was full of rumors that Gapon was dead, and so Gorki persuaded him to show himself at a protest meeting being held that evening at the white-pillared headquarters of the Free Economic Society. But because of the danger that Gapon might be arrested, it was decided at the last minute not to disclose his identity after all. So Gorki appeared on the balcony of the hall, accompanied by an agitated young man, and announced that Gapon was alive and had taken shelter in his apartment. Then he read aloud what he described as a letter from Gapon: "There is no Tsar. Between him and the Russian nation torrents of blood have flowed today. It is high time for the Russian workmen to begin without him to carry on the struggle for national freedom. . . . Tomorrow I will be among you."

Several of the assembled intellectuals began to applaud Gapon's sudden transformation into a revolutionary, but Gorki shushed them, then introduced the agitated young man at his side as "a delegate" from Father Gapon. "The workmen have shown to Russia that they know how to die," the young man cried. "But unhappily they are unarmed, and with empty hands you cannot fight bayonets and rifles. It is your turn to help now. Give them the means to procure arms, and the people will do the rest." There were murmurings in the hall that this must be Gapon himself, but the young man said no more, sat silent for a while, then left the hall. The assembled liberals contented themselves with a resolution: "It is impossible to live thus any longer. The Russian people needs bread, it needs enlightenment, it needs liberty. . . ." The departed young man disguised himself further in a pince-nez and a new suit and what he called "a showy overcoat," then went into hiding on the country estate of a wealthy friend, then had himself smuggled across the Prussian border into exile.

The rest of the demonstrations did not last long. On Vasilevsky Island, in the western section of the city, the workers who had been barred from the main bridge across the Neva took to erecting crude barricades out of paving stones and fencing, and some even broke into an arms store, where they outfitted themselves with a few pistols and rusty swords. It did not take the cavalry long to smash their humble barriers. As the sky darkened and the snow kept falling, the marchers all over the city gradually abandoned their hopeless crusade and began trekking home. A few students persisted in shouting the slogans of revolution and indulging in various shows of defiance, smashing street lights, jeering at the soldiery, throwing stones, but the workers went home, defeated, exhausted, many with their clothes torn and bloodied. They no longer carried icons and banners. They were no longer the same workers who had set out that morning. Gorki, who worked as a correspondent for Hearst's *New York Journal,* sent a euphoric cable: "The Russian Revolution has begun."

How many died on what came to be known as Bloody Sunday remains a mystery. The government's official communiqué declared that the toll was 56 dead, then admitted 76, then 96. At best, these were only the figures of the people taken to hospitals, but many were carried home or left lying. Gapon himself estimated the casualties at between 600 and 900 dead and at least 5,000 wounded. Various accounts in British and French newspapers spoke of 1,000 dead and 4,000 injured. The exiled Lenin quoted these accounts as authoritative, and so they have passed into Soviet history books, though one authoritative Soviet investigator reduced these clearly exaggerated estimates to 150 to 200 dead and 450 to 800 wounded. The Tsar's government sealed the confusion by taking the bodies from all the city's hospitals and secretly shipping them under police guard to a mass burial in the Preobrazhensky cemetery. The Tsar himself inscribed a mournful verdict in his diary on the night of the massacre. "A painful day. . . ," he wrote. "The workers tried to come to the Winter Palace. The troops have been forced to fire in several parts of the city. . . ." The Tsarina was even more able to blame the workers for the bloodshed. "Don't believe all the horrors the foreign papers say...," she wrote to her sister Princess Victoria of Battenberg. "Yes, the troops, alas, were obliged to fire. Repeatedly the crowd was told to retreat ... but they would not heed and so blood was shed. ... My poor Nicky's cross is a heavy one to bear."

The Tsarina's view was not widely shared. A wave of protests swept Russia, and Europe too. A student strike closed St. Petersburg University, then the conservatory and the Polytechnic Institute. Lawyers refused to appear in court; medical organizations passed resolutions. Sympathy strikes spread to Moscow and Warsaw, Kharkov, Vilna, Kiev, Tiflis. Georges Clemenceau and Jean Jaurès addressed protest meetings in Paris, and Ramsay MacDonald denounced the Tsar as a "blood-stained creature" and a "common murderer." The Tsar's palaces were well insulated against such noises. His troops ruled the streets. The protest strikes gradually withered, and by the end of two weeks even the men of the Putilov plant returned to their jobs.

The Tsar did finally come to think, though, that perhaps he should receive a delegation of workers after all. He suggested as much to General Trepov, who had once endorsed Zubatov's scheme for a police union and who had now been brought from Moscow to become governor general of St. Petersburg and to supervise the restoration of order in the capital. Trepov made all the arrangements. The police went to several factories and picked out thirty-four workmen who looked reasonably docile. They were taken to a police station, stripped naked and searched, then escorted to the Winter Palace. There, according to one of the delegates, they were inspected by Trepov, who told them, "You are about to be blessed with the joy of conversing with the sovereign. Just hold your tongues when he speaks to you, and keep on bowing." The cowed workers were then loaded onto a heavily guarded train, taken to Tsarkoe Selo, warned not to speak to one another, stripped and searched again, and finally ushered into a hall to await the Tsar. "Suddenly the door opened wide," one delegate recalled, "and there entered the Little Father, the Tsar, with a ring of generals around him, and a little piece of paper in his hands. We all bowed low, but he did not even look at us. He began to read from his little paper...." The Tsar told the delegation that he was sorry about the bloodshed, but that wicked men had misled the workers and that strikes always led to violence. He would, however, be merciful. "I believe in the honest feelings of the working people and in their unshakable loyalty to me," said Nicholas, "and therefore I forgive them their guilt."

So now my soul blazes in a fierce tempest
For my heart shouts with a fierce courage!
Soon we shall see the purple fire of freedom
Piercing the darkness of an ancient violence.

This was the voice of Ivan Kaliayev, then twenty-seven, a Pole, son of a small landowner, a former law student in St. Petersburg. He had been carrying the second bomb when Sazonov threw the one that killed Plehve, so he had to retreat into the crowd and wait until Azef sent him out against the next target. It remains extraordinary that Azef was not caught after the Plehve killing, for the wounded and delirious Sazonov babbled the name of "Valentine" during his weeks of interrogation, and there were at least a few eminent police officials who knew that Valentine was Azef's code name. Azef himself insisted to the police that they could have prevented Plehve's death if they had acted more effectively on his tips. The police investigation, in any case, led to nothing. Perhaps the police too, like Azef, hated their slain master.

The terrorists' next target was no less hated: Grand Duke Sergei, the Tsar's gruff and blustering uncle, who had long served as his proconsul in Moscow. It was Sergei who had presided over the disaster at Khodynka Fields, Sergei who had expelled the Jews, Sergei who harried and scourged all opposition to the autocracy. Once again Azef assigned Savinkov to lead the team of four assassins, and once again they stalked their victim through the streets, learning all his ways and habits. Just a month after Bloody Sunday, the terrorists planned an ambush as the Grand Duke drove to the opera. In the midst of a snowstorm, Kaliayev spotted the royal carriage with its telltale green lights as it labored through the deserted Vozkresensky Square. He darted up to the side of the carriage and raised his arm to throw his bomb. Only then did he see that he was attacking not just the detested Grand Duke in his imperial uniform but also the young niece and nephew who were being taken to the opera. Kaliayev could not kill them. He turned and fled into the snowy night. "How can one kill children?" he asked when he next saw Savinkov. The attack had to be tried again, two days later. This time, Kaliayev took up his watch at the Chapel of the Tverskaya Madonna, for in the glass frame that shielded one of its icons he could watch the reflection of the Kremlin gate through which Grand Duke Sergei emerged from his office.

"I hurled my bomb from a distance of four paces . . . ," Kaliayev later wrote to a friend, "striking as I dashed forward, quite close to my object. I was caught by the storm of the explosion and saw how the carriage was torn to pieces. When the cloud had lifted, I found myself standing before the remains of the back wheels. I remember the smell of smoke. Splinters struck my face, tearing off my cap. . . . About five feet away, near the gate, I saw bits of the Grand Duke's clothing and his nude body. About ten feet behind the Grand Duke's carriage lay my cap. I walked over, picked it up and put it on. . . ."

While the police seized Kaliayev and took him away, the Grand Duke's widow, Elizaveta, came rushing from the nearby palace. She shouted distractedly to the gathering bystanders that they should take their hats off, that they should all go home. Then she began picking up the bloody fragments of Sergei's body, the mangled head, one hand, part of a leg with the foot torn away. She collected them in a little pile in the snow. "Are you not ashamed to be staring?" she cried at one bystander. Her fur coat was flecked with blood. Then somebody brought a litter and put the Grand Duke's remains onto it and covered it with a coat, and somebody else led the Grand Duchess away.

Elizaveta, the Tsarina's sister, had always been devout—she was to spend the rest of her days as the eccentric abbess of the Convent of Mary and Martha—and she considered it her Christian duty to bring her husband's murderer to repentance. She went to his prison cell and asked to be left alone with him. She found him in a state of exaltation.

"You must have suffered so much to have done this terrible thing," she said.

"What does it matter whether I have suffered or not?" Kaliayev retorted, according to his subsequent accounts to his friends. "Yes, I have suffered! But I suffered with millions of other people."

"I'm sorry you did not come to us, and then we would have known you earlier," the Grand Duchess said.

"So you think it is easy to go to you?" Kaliayev answered. "Then look what happened on the ninth of January, when they tried to see the Tsar. . . . Then there is this terrible war which the people hate so violently. Well, you have declared war on the people, and we have accepted the challenge!"

"You think you are the only ones to suffer," the Grand Duchess said. "I assure you we suffer, too, and we want only good things for the people."

"Yes, you are suffering now, but as for giving good things to the people, you give with one hand and take it back 'with the back of the knife.'"

The Grand Duchess sighed. "I came to tell you the Grand Duke forgives you," she said. Then she gave the assassin a small icon and added, "I shall pray for you."

"My conscience is clear," Kaliayev said as he took the icon. "I am deeply pained to have caused you so great a sorrow . . . , but still I did my duty."

What the Grand Duchess later said at court about this encounter remains unknown, but word spread that Kaliayev had begged her for mercy and been rejected. Another version, slightly more plausible, reported that the Grand Duchess had offered to intercede for Kaliayev if he would repent, and that he had refused. On the contrary, Kaliayev felt euphoric, triumphant. "My soul, intoxicated with purest wine, / Drinks from the sweet cup of victory," he declared in a poem written shortly after his arrest. Outraged by the rumors about his pleading for mercy, he wrote several angry letters to the Grand Duchess, accusing her of lying and demanding retractions. She did not answer.

In court, Kaliayev was finally given a chance to plead his cause, and he did so with an almost Byronic rhetoric. He started by denying the judges' right to try him at all. "The judgment of history is upon you," he cried. "It is a wave of new life arising out of the gathering storm—the death agony of autocracy. And a revolutionary . . . hurls his hatred into the enemy's teeth with a single battle cry: *I accuse!*" Kaliayev was no less grandiose in the poetry he kept writing in prison: "Like a proud lion I waged this holy war . . . / O terrible was my impetuous wrath! / I killed . . ." And Savinkov remembered that Kaliayev had once said to him, "Everything is beautiful. The stars and clouds and flowers and people and—death is beautiful, too."

The court had no hesitation about delivering its verdict, and on May 9 Kaliayev was transferred to the Schlüsselberg fortress and hanged.

✳

And in the frozen hills of Manchuria, General Kuropatkin prepared for another great battle. His thirty-five-mile defensive lines before Mukden had been strongly entrenched, mined, and strung with barbed wire, and every week the single-track Siberian railroad brought him new troops from the West, not the best troops, not well trained and not eager for battle but perfectly adequate as fodder. Each side counted slightly more than 300,000 men, the largest military confrontation so far recorded in human history, nearly twice as large as Waterloo.

As Kuropatkin was readying his spring offensive, the Japanese suddenly struck first, on February 23, from the mountains on his left. Kuropatkin had been expecting that. He rushed his reserves over to reinforce his left flank. What he had not expected was that Baron Nogi would then attack his right flank and relentlessly begin pushing it back. Both sides engaged in massive thrusts and counterthrusts, threw in reserves at the wrong places, then pulled back while new forces became engaged at other points in the jagged line. And it went on and on, through the whole last week of February and then into the beginning of March.

"Both armies, hundreds of thousands of men, are standing in front of each other, never flinching, sending explosive, crashing projectiles without stopping, and every instant living men are turned into corpses," Leonid Andreyev wrote in his feverish novella *The Red Laugh*. "The roar and incessant vibration of the air has made the very sky shudder and gather black thunderclouds above their heads—while they continue to stand in front of each other, never flinching and still killing each other. If a man does not sleep for three nights, he becomes ill and loses his memory, but they have not slept for a week, and are all mad. That is why they feel no pain, do not retreat, and go on fighting until they have killed all to the last man. They say that some of the detachments came to the end of their ammunition, but still they fought on, using their fists and stones, and biting each other like dogs. . . ."

But Kuropatkin did retreat, slowly, grudgingly. Nogi almost encircled him, and Kuropatkin's one boast was that he had avoided that. He had to abandon Mukden and Tieling and establish a new line eighty miles to the north. He had lost 60,000 killed and wounded and 25,000 prisoners; Japanese casualties were 70,000. And while the two exhausted armies stood numbly facing each other, Admiral Rozhdestvensky finally reached the Pacific with the Baltic Fleet that had so proudly left St. Petersburg the previous fall. Admiral Togo was waiting for him in the Straits of Tsushima. Rozhdestvensky steamed ahead in three long columns, his battleships in the lead, his support ships in the center. Togo's cruisers opened a withering fire at a range of seven thousand feet, at the very edge of the Russians' range. The Russians had hardly begun to fight back before they were crippled. Within forty-five minutes, the battleships leading the main columns were knocked out of action. The smaller vessels in their wake tried to break through, but the faster Japanese kept driving them back. As night fell, Japanese torpedo boats ravaged the survivors. By the next morning, when the Russians were in full flight, four battleships had been sunk and four others captured. Seven of the twelve Russian cruisers, five out of nine destroyers, and five auxiliary ships had also gone to the bottom. Of Russian naval power, there was virtually nothing left.

✳

One of the most remarkable aspects of the early stirrings of the Russian Revolution was the variety of ways in which different people regarded the great confrontation on Bloody Sunday and the variety of contradictory lessons they thought they had learned from it. To the Tsar and his entourage, the march was largely an unfortunate outbreak of disorder, to be dealt with firmly. The well-meaning but ineffectual Interior Minister, Prince Svyatopolk-Mirsky, was replaced by a sterner man, Count Alexander Bulygin. But the strongest authority was now General Trepov, who placed the capital under martial law and used troops to suppress any sign of disturbances. When the radicals assassinated his old patron, Grand Duke Sergei, Trepov stormed into the office of Police Chief Lopukhin and shouted, "Murderer!" Then, without another word, he stormed out again. Lopukhin resigned shortly thereafter, and Trepov installed as his new chief of the political police that old conspirator from Paris, Rachkovsky. (Trepov also tried to bring back his disgraced protégé Zubatov from exile in the city of Vladimir, but Zubatov refused to return.)

Tsar Nicholas saw, though, in his vague, fumbling way, that the strikes and demonstrations that swept Russia all through that January indicated that something was wrong, and that he was supposed to do something about it. Even his courtiers could see that. One nobleman dined at the Imperial Yacht Club and recorded in his diary that he had encountered four panicky members of the royal family. "The Grand Dukes, dreadfully frightened at the approaching revolution, now are throwing off all pride and reconciling themselves to the end. . . . Among the ministers too there is fear and a search for a way out." One of these officials, the nondescript Agriculture Minister A. S. Yermolov, even had the temerity to tell the Tsar to his face that he had not been warned about the scope of the workers' march because the various officials scurrying in and out of the palace did not really constitute a functioning government. "Permit me openly to tell Your Majesty," he said, "that at the present time we have no government." Yermolov followed that bold warning with a long memorandum in which he declared that all Russia was waiting for the Tsar to accept the authority of a legislature consisting of "freely elected representatives of all levels of the Russian soil."

The Tsar actually had been talking with his ministers about how some such body could be formed, a body that would quiet the public turbulence without in any way diminishing his own authority. The killing of his uncle Sergei naturally shocked the Tsar and apparently convinced him of the need for some gesture soon. On February 18, he issued three documents that contradicted each other and muffled any effect that any of them might have had. One was a manifesto denouncing public disorder and calling on "all right-thinking persons" to rally to the throne. The second was a declaration that all citizens had a right to petition the Tsar about their grievances or about "improving the public well-being." The third, finally, was an announcement that he was going to permit "elected representatives of the people to take part in the preliminary discussion of legislation." He added a warning, however, that "the immutability of the fundamental laws of the Empire shall be preserved." The Tsar regarded all this as a great concession, which it would have been a year earlier, but now, a month after Bloody Sunday and just a week before the carnage at Mukden, it satisfied no one.

To the liberals in the opposition, and among these were most of the educated and professional classes, the great march had been an appeal for the fulfillment of what they considered Russia's greatest need, a freely elected and truly governing legislature. That was the great goal of all the meetings they held that spring, that and the sense of a need to organize to achieve the great goal. The Union of Liberation, barely four years old, held its third congress in March to demand a constituent assembly, democratic government, universal suffrage, separation of church and state. The Second Zemstvo Congress came the following month with a similar demand for the election of a "representative assembly." And after months of effort to organize various professions into political unions, fourteen of these groups, including doctors, teachers, lawyers, engineers, journalists and bookkeepers, plus the Union of Equal Rights for Women and the Union for the Achievement of Full Rights for the Jews, met in Moscow in May to form the Union of Unions and to pledge themselves to work for a constituent assembly. The liberals argued endlessly about the details of their dream, about whether the legislature should be bicameral, and whether illiterate peasants were fit to vote, and whether autonomy should be granted to the Poles. They would spend the next ten years pressing their cause, inch by inch, just as Nicholas would spend the next ten years resisting each advance, inch by inch, and they would never understand why, when they finally achieved their goal, they were almost immediately swept away by the radicals.

The various feuding radical factions, in these early days, were hardly better informed. Lenin learned about Bloody Sunday in the Geneva newspapers. He wrote anxiously to his tiny band of supporters in St. Petersburg to find out what was happening, and whether there were any signs of the armed uprising that he had so long preached. But he stayed in Switzerland, as did the Menshevik leaders, Georgy Plekhanov and Julius Martov. Only the young Lev Bronstein, who called himself Trotsky, and who had managed to quarrel with both the Bolshevik and Menshevik wings of the Social Democrats, decided to return home immediately. It took him until mid-February to reach Kiev with a false passport in the name of Arbuzov. Among the somewhat more numerous Socialist Revolutionaries, who were headquartered in Paris, the principal debate was whether the march meant that they should reconsider or even suspend their strategy of terrorism. They decided to continue with their bombs.

As for the workers who had actually marched on January 9, a legislative assembly was of distinctly secondary interest, and a revolutionary uprising was of hardly any interest at all. They had marched for a living wage of a ruble a day and for an eight-hour work day, for a sense of self-respect and of solidarity. What they learned, in the course of that one long day, was that the Tsar whom they had been taught to revere was not much concerned about their needs. He did announce, after the imperial troops had restored order, that the workers should elect delegates to a governmental commission, to be headed by Senator N. V. Shidlovski, which would look into their grievances. Although these elections were actually held, the delegates began by demanding the release of comrades arrested after the January 9 march. Shidlovski's only response was to say that the delegates would not be prosecuted for making such demands, and that was the end of the Shidlovski Commission. By now, though, the workers had also learned that they needed to organize. They were more willing to listen to the radicals, more willing to see the political and even revolutionary aspect of their aims. They had learned that the government was prepared to shoot unarmed citizens, and that they were unarmed. Leaderless, they were still uncertain what to do now, or how to do it.

As for the peasants, the overwhelming majority of the population, they had not marched on January 9, and they thought no more about the workers' wages than they thought about a legislature. They thought mainly about the grievances that had rankled for decades, the land that they felt had been promised and then denied them in 1861, transferred to them only with mortgages that they could not afford—that and all the local grievances that varied from estate to estate, the unused forests where they were not allowed to cut firewood, the meadows that provided hay only for the master's barns, the fines levied on them by the bailiffs for any violation of the bailiffs' own rules. Slowly, all that summer, province by province, the word of "new times" began to spread. Workmen returning to visit their families brought the word to the peasant villages; wounded veterans from Manchuria brought the word; traders in the village markets brought the word.

Trotsky provided a graphic description, in *1905*, of how the process worked in Samara province. "At first, the peasants would come to farms owned by landlords and take away nothing but cattle food, making a precise count for the cattle belonging to each farm, leaving the exact amount of food necessary to feed it, and removing the rest in their carts. The peasants acted quietly, without violence, trying to reach agreement so that there might be 'no unpleasantness.' They explained to the owner that these were new times and people had to live in a new way, more fairly; those who owned a lot should share with those who owned nothing, etc. . . . Soon the arguments about the 'new times' began to lose their effect on the landowner; he plucked up courage and tried to send the peasants packing. Then the good-natured peasants reared up—and not a stone would be left standing on the master's property."

Sometimes, when the owners resisted, the peasants would leave behind an upright pole with a bundle of straw tied to it, a signal for more peasants to return by night with torches. Sometimes, the peasants came armed with clubs and scythes and pitchforks, more often not. Sometimes, they simply wandered from estate to estate with their wagons, helping themselves to what the frightened owners had left behind. "It begins, and the sky is lit up by fires all night long," one newspaper reported. "It is a terrible picture. In the morning you see long lines of horse carriages filled with people fleeing from the estates. As soon as night falls, it is as though the horizon wore a necklace of fires."

The protests that had seemed to die out in late January had not really died. New demonstrations and local strikes kept breaking out, and because they were too scattered and disorganized to accomplish much, they were also hard to suppress. May Day, which had been decreed a labor holiday by the Socialist

Second International of 1889, brought one-day strikes in many cities, and there were clashes with soldiers in Kharkov. All told, the number of workers on strike that month rose to 220,000, and Grand Duke Konstantin wrote in his diary, "I am afraid to read the newspapers." One of the most interesting walkouts occurred in the textile center of Ivanovo-Voznesensk, two hundred miles northeast of Moscow, where the workers first demanded a twenty-ruble monthly wage, an eight-hour day and other improvements in working conditions, then began to add such political demands as the election of a constituent assembly. Their strike committee, of which one quarter of the members were Social Democrats, gradually began to assume political powers, imposing price controls on local merchants, organizing a workers' militia. They called themselves by a name new to politics, a "soviet" (council).

The worst fighting occurred in Odessa, where strikes had shut down textile mills, food plants and printing shops. One day in early June, a demonstrator outside a plow factory fired at a Cossack officer, and the Cossack ordered his troops to charge into the crowd. Street fighting spread, with the troops and the police supported by a new force of armed vigilantes known as the Black Hundreds. On June 15, with much of the city on fire, the authorities declared martial law and launched a military offensive that killed about two thousand civilians in one night of carnage. In the midst of all this, the sailors on the battle cruiser *Potemkin* mutinied, imprisoned their officers, and ran up red flags to summon the rest of the Black Sea Fleet to revolt. The *Potemkin* tried to join in the fighting for Odessa, but its crew's gunfire was so inaccurate that it had to desist. Its appeal for fleetwide mutiny aroused only one other warship (ironically, the one named after the Tsar's reactionary leader of the Holy Synod, the *Pobedonostsev*), which soon ran aground. Fearing capture and punishment, the mutineers fled burning Odessa, sailed the *Potemkin* to Romania and scuttled her.

In this summer of violence and confusion, it seemed almost incidental that the Japanese war faltered to an end. Theodore Roosevelt offered his services as a mediator, and both wearied enemies agreed to negotiate. The Tsar sent Witte to Portsmouth, New Hampshire, for a month of bargaining that ended on August 23 with Russia giving Japan Port Arthur and the rest of the Liaotung Peninsula plus the southern half of Sakhalin. It also agreed to evacuate Manchuria and to acknowledge Japan's "paramount interests" in Korea. It was hardly the end that Plehve had foreseen for the little victorious war, but the Russians managed to persuade themselves that their repeated defeats had ended in almost a draw. The Tsar, who had once sneered at the Japanese as *"macaques,"* had to profess himself satisfied. He rewarded Witte, whom he had come to dislike intensely, by making him a count. "He went quite stiff with emotion," Nicholas wrote in his diary, "and then tried three times to kiss my hand!" At the beginning of September, the Tsar set out from Peterhof in the imperial yacht for a two-week cruise with his family off the coast of Finland. "I'm happy as a child," he wrote to his mother.

✳

The Great October Strike, as it came to be known, began on September 19 at the Sytin publishing house in Moscow. The illegal Union of Moscow Typographers and Lithographers demanded a shorter working day and a higher piece-work pay rate per one thousand characters set—"not excluding," as Trotsky noted with a sense of wonder, "punctuation marks." The owners agreed to shorter hours but not to higher piecework rates. So the Sytin printers went on strike. The other Moscow printers joined in solidarity. Then the city's bakers all walked out. The authorities, fearing the psychological effects of a bread shortage, sent troops to enforce a continuation of work at one large bakery named Filipov's. The bakers fought back with pots and pans and threw bricks from their roof. Then students began marching and demonstrating. Then came the woodworkers, machine-tool workers, textile workers, tobacco workers. On October 2, the strikers formed a soviet to coordinate their activities. By now, though, the unpaid workers were beginning to go hungry and many of them started drifting back to work.

Just as the strike seemed to be fading in Moscow, it suddenly broke out in St. Petersburg. The printers in the capital called a three-day walkout in support of the Moscow printers. The next morning, they clashed with Izmailovsky Guards who had been ordered to keep the strikers away from the government printing office. Then the Neva Shipbuilding Works shut down, and once again the students began marching. The October strike was no more organized than Father Gapon's march of the previous January—indeed, less so—but one important difference was that the railroad workers had spent the summer building a union. In a vast land in which the only other means of transportation were the horse and the river steamer, the railway workers now had the power to shut down the whole country, which they proceeded to do. The Moscow–Kazan line was the first to close, on October 7, then the lines to Yaroslavl and Nizhni-Novgorod and Kursk, and only one train still connected Moscow and St. Petersburg. The railroad strike also inspired local walkouts all along the lines, to turn the protests, though still leaderless, into a national movement with a life of its own.

"The strike rushed forward along the rails and stopped all movement in its wake," Trotsky wrote. "It announced its coming over the wires of the railway telegraph. 'Strike!' was the order of the day in every corner of the land. . . . Where the telegraph refused to serve it, it cut the wires or overturned the telegraph poles. It halted railway engines and let off their steam. It brought the electric power stations to a standstill, and where this was difficult it damaged electric cables and plunged railway stations into darkness. . . .

"Only for its own purposes did the strike allow itself to break the vow of immobility. When it needed news bulletins of the revolution, it opened a printing works; it used the telegraph to send out strike instructions. . . . Nothing else was exempt: the strike closed down industrial plants, chemists' and grocers' shops, courts of law, everything. . . . It used every possible means. It appealed, convinced, implored; it begged on its knees—that is what a woman orator did at the Kursky Station in Moscow—it threatened, terrorized, threw stones, finally fired off its Brownings. It wanted to achieve its aim at whatever cost. . . ."

By the second week in October, St. Petersburg was paralyzed. No factories or stores were open, food was not delivered, bills could not be paid, for the banks were closed, and so were the courts and the stock market, and so was the Maryinsky Ballet. There was not even light at night, except for one searchlight on top of the Admiralty Building. Not only were St. Petersburg and Moscow shut down but also Kharkov, Smolensk, Lodz, Kursk, Poltava, Minsk. Even in Tsarskoe Selo, the Tsar's village, the secondary-school children refused to go to classes, and the primary-school children responded to the obligatory morning prayers by whistling. It was the first truly general strike the world had ever seen, and it had happened all by itself. "One can truthfully say that Russia's soul cried out in agony for relief from the torment of chaos," Witte later wrote. "The universal exclamation was: 'We can live like this no longer.'"

The Tsar's government, which rarely functioned well, ceased to function at all. As in Moscow, the St. Petersburg strikers established a soviet not only to manage the strike but also to provide rudimentary government services. It was the local Menshevik faction of the Social Democrats who first proposed an elected council of workers' delegates (the Bolsheviks, who were ultimately to win power through the soviets, originally boycotted the whole idea). The machinery was already in place, fortuitously, because of the abortive election of worker delegates, at a ratio of roughly one per five hundred workers, to the Tsar's Shidlovski Commission on grievances. About thirty delegates came to the preliminary meeting at the Technological Institute on October 13, and within two days the soviet had become a rival government, the only one the workers obeyed. Its chairman was a frail Jewish intellectual named Georgi Nosar; its flaming spirit was another Jew who had just arrived from Finland and now called himself Yanovsky. He had been known in Switzerland as Trotsky. He wore a pince-nez and a goatee to make himself look older. He was not quite 26.

The newly ennobled Count Witte, who had been chafing at the powerlessness of his post as chairman of the Committee of Ministers, decided to tell the Tsar that he must give in. At six o'clock in the evening of October 9, he was granted an audience and boldly read out to the Tsar a memorandum advocating a constitutional monarchy, implicitly with himself as prime minister. "The first task of the government," he said, "is to fulfill the wish for the establishment of a legal order based on personal inviolability and the freedom of the press, conscience, assembly and association." The Tsar listened gravely to this impertinent proposal and, as Witte later wrote, "refrained from revealing his opinion." Witte grandly said that he might be mistaken and urged the Tsar to consult other officials about his memorandum. Three days later, the Tsar gave General Trepov dictatorial powers to crush the strike. Trepov posted all over the capital the readiness order that he gave to his troops: "Spare no cartridges and use no blanks."

But the Tsar hesitated. He once again summoned Witte to the palace, together with his soldierly cousin, Grand Duke Nikolai Nikolaievich, and Baron Fredericks, the Minister of the Court. He once again asked Witte for his views. Witte, as he recalled, "stated that to the best of his knowledge and belief there were but two ways out of existing difficulties, either to institute a dictatorship or to grant a constitution. [He] recommended the second." The Tsar then called in Trepov—"the honest Trepov," as he called him—and asked him whether he had enough troops to suppress an armed uprising by the strikers. Trepov said that he did, but that such a move would cost what the Tsar later called "rivers of blood." Baron Fredericks, however, strongly opposed any concessions. "I was hoping that the situation would end in a dictatorship with Grand Duke Nikolai Nikolaiovich as dictator," he recalled later, "for it seems to me that he was brave and absolutely devoted to the Emperor." The Baron even appealed directly to the Grand Duke: "It is necessary to set up a dictatorship and you must be appointed dictator." The Grand Duke was appalled (his "rational powers," Witte later claimed, "had long since been befogged by an inordinate passion for occultism"). The Grand Duke took a pistol out of his pocket, Fredericks told Witte, and cried, "Do you see this gun? I will now go to the Emperor and beg him to sign the manifesto and Witte's program. He will either do it or I will blow my brains out with this very weapon."

On October 17, at six in the evening, Tsar Nicholas signed the manifesto that formally proclaimed the end of absolute monarchy. The strikes and demonstrations "fill our heart with a great and painful grief," he said. To "quiet the life of the nation," he had decided "to grant the people the unshakable foundations of civic freedom on the basis of genuine personal inviolability, freedom of conscience, speech, assembly and association," and "to establish as an inviolable rule that no law may go into force without the consent of the State Duma." "Dear Mother, you cannot imagine the anguish this has caused me . . . ," Nicholas wrote to the Dowager Empress. "There was no way out but to make the sign of the cross and do what the world demanded."

✳

Young Trotsky was not satisfied. As soon as the Tsar's manifesto was proclaimed, he went to the university, where he found a crowd already gathering. Many people had torn down the Tsar's tricolored flags and ripped off the blue and white strips, leaving only red on the banners they waved. From a balcony, several speakers took turns addressing the crowd. Trotsky decided to attempt the first major speech of his life. "This tireless hangman on the throne," he shouted from the balcony, had finally been forced by the workers to "promise us freedom," but no such promises could be trusted. "Look around, citizens," he cried. "Has anything changed since yesterday? Have the gates of our prisons been opened. . . ?"

"Amnesty!" someone shouted in the crowd below. "Amnesty!"

"But, citizens, is an amnesty all?" Trotsky demanded. "Today they will let out hundreds of political fighters, tomorrow they will seize thousands of others. . . . Isn't Trepov, the hangman, master of Petersburg?"

"Down with Trepov!" someone yelled.

"Yes, down with Trepov! But is he the only one . . . ? Citizens! Let our demand be the withdrawal of troops from Petersburg!"

"Out with the troops!"

"As for the Tsar's manifesto, look, it's only a scrap of paper.... Here it is crumpled in my fist.... Today they have issued it, tomorrow they will take it and tear it into pieces, just as I am now tearing up this paper freedom before your eyes."

Trotsky's warnings were largely ignored. The Tsar's manifesto set off a nationwide outburst of celebration. People marched joyfully through the streets, embraced each other, waved their banners, sang the "Marseillaise," and invaded public buildings to proclaim their triumph with speeches and chanted slogans. For the most part, they treated the soldiery as friends and allies, but occasionally there were clashes, and then came huge funeral processions, and more speeches and flag-waving. But Trotsky was right: The Tsar still had the guns. The autocracy, though weakened and humiliated, was still in power. And the police were still at work.

Their newest scheme was to organize their own mobs out of the gangs of "patriots" known as the Black Hundreds. In the general birth of new political parties during 1905, the reactionaries too had created organizations, to fight for autocracy and orthodoxy. The Union of the Russian People, headed by Dr. Alexander Dubrovin and V. M. Purishkevich, was the political wing of this movement, and the Black Hundreds were its storm troopers. Some of these street fighters acted on their own beliefs, of course, for any nation at any time contains a certain number of right-wing radicals, bellicose anti-Semites, ultranationalists and what Witte called "plain thieves and hooligans." The support that came from the Orthodox Church was also a natural expression of the clergy's alarm at the spread of rebellion. But to the threatened government, and to Rachkovsky of the secret police, these were fundamentally the soldiers of counterrevolution. Rachkovsky's police supplied them with pistols and vodka, to strengthen their fighting spirits; police presses printed their appeals for action, and police funds helped subsidize them with about 200,000 rubles a year. When one official went to warn the Tsar of the spread of this supposedly secret society, which had been growing all year, he was startled to see that the Tsar was wearing the organization's emblem on his lapel.

Within a day of the celebrations over the Tsar's manifesto, the Black Hundreds turned out to parade for the monarchy and to brawl with anyone they regarded as a student or a Jew or a socialist. There were clashes in Tiflis, Kiev, Baku, Tomsk. The worst occurred in Odessa, where a nationalist demonstration was fired on, supposedly by Jewish radicals. It so happened that the police prefect had just ordered his own men off the streets. The marchers immediately sent up the familiar cry *"Bei zhidov!* Beat the Yids!" and started rampaging through the Jewish quarters of the city. They set stores on fire, broke into houses, attacked anyone they saw. One Gentile physician later testified that he had seen a Jewish girl murdered and several children thrown from windows, but both the police prefect and the military commander refused to take any action. One army captain who tried to stop a gang of looters encountered a policeman who said that he had been ordered not to interfere, that the rioting was "not his business," and that it would continue for three days. And so it did. More than five hundred people were killed, according to official figures, and there were 289 wounded. "It is amazing," the Tsar wrote to his mother, "how the pogroms took place simultaneously in all the towns of Russia."

But if the Tsar and his lieutenants had no intention of yielding power, neither did the radical leaders of the fifty or more soviets around the country make much effort toward an accommodation. Though the October general strike petered out soon after the Tsar's manifesto, the St. Petersburg soviet proclaimed the eight-hour day and answered the employers' opposition with new strikes. There was a mutiny at the naval base in Kronstadt, and when the mutineers were arrested, the soviet called yet another strike in support of them. Then there was a mutiny in Sevastopol, and a nationalist outbreak in Lithuania, and continuing reports of arson and looting in the countryside. "Everything disintegrated," said Trotsky. "Everything turned to chaos."

Witte, who thought he had finally acquired the authority to create a national coalition, soon found he had no such thing. He managed to dismiss General Trepov, and to force the aged Pobedonostsov into retirement, but Trepov soon found shelter in the royal palace as commandant of the imperial court. Witte tried to recruit the zemstvo leader Dmitri Shipov and the chiefs of the newly formed Constitutional Democratic Party (Cadets), but they argued about the conditions of the nascent government and finally refused to join. Witte himself was no liberal; he was a technocrat and an industrialist; he mistrusted his own constitution and yearned only to serve the Tsar who despised him. For the critical office of interior minister, he chose a veteran police official, Pyotr Durnovo. The Tsar demanded movement. The new cabinet ministers "talk a lot but do little," he wrote to his mother. "Everybody is afraid of taking courageous action."

The reports from the countryside were even more alarming than the turbulence in the cities. All over the south and center of European Russia, in the seven provinces of Voronezh, Kursk, Poltava, Chernigov, Saratov, Tambov and Penza, the peasants were burning barns, stealing cattle and grain, attacking landlords. On November 3, an imperial manifesto pleaded for peace and promised that the government would aid the peasants in whatever way it could do so "without injustice." It started by cutting in half the payments that the peasants owed for their land. The measures had little effect. The fledgling Peasants Union, which was dominated by the Socialist Revolutionaries and now claimed 200,000 members, met in Moscow the following week and demanded both a constituent assembly and the transfer of all land to the peasants. The government decided to strike back. Durnovo ordered all the union's leaders arrested. Three prominent military leaders were sent south to begin a systematic campaign of "pacification." Their troops proceeded from village to village, flogging and sometimes hanging anyone even suspected of violence. "Rioters to be exterminated immediately by force of arms," Durnovo ordered, "their dwellings to be burned down in the event of resistance. Arbitrary self-rule must be eradicated once and for all—now. Arrests would not serve any purpose at present, and anyway it is impossible to try hundreds of thousands of peasants. It is essential that the troops should fully understand the above instructions."

In the cities, the next challenge came when the postal and telegraph workers held their first congress and announced a strike to begin November 15. Witte's government retaliated by ordering the arrest of all strike leaders. The following week, it struck directly against the St. Petersburg soviet by arresting its chairman, Nosar. Trotsky and two others promptly assumed the leadership and issued a manifesto calling on all workers to put economic pressure on the government by refusing to pay any taxes, demanding all wages in gold, and withdrawing any savings they had in government banks. Now Witte confiscated all newspapers that published the soviet's manifesto and then sent the Izmailovsky Guards to the temple of the Free Economics Society where the soviet held its meetings. "The whole place was filled with the noise of trampling feet, the ringing of spurs, the clatter of arms," Trotsky later recalled. "Delegates were heard protesting vociferously downstairs. The chairman [i.e., Trotsky] opened a first-floor window, leaned out and called, 'Comrades, don't offer resistance! We declare in advance that if any shots are fired, they will have to come from the police or an *agent provocateur!*' A few minutes later the soldiers climbed the stairs to the first floor and took up a position at the door of the room in which the Executive Committee was meeting. The chairman (addressing an officer): 'I suggest you close the door and do not disturb our business.' " A few minutes after that display of *chutzpah,* Trotsky was on his way to the Peter and Paul Fortress and ultimately to Siberia.

The survivors of the raid appealed for yet another general strike, but the only place where their appeal had any considerable effect was in Moscow. The soviet there, partly under the influence of Lenin, who had finally returned to Russia to take command of his Bolsheviks, called for not only a strike but an insurrection. It was the only time in the whole year of revolution that the leftists tried to resort to armed force, and since they had only about eighty rifles and a few bombs and pistols, they were doomed to utter failure. Indeed, there were no more than a few hundred Bolsheviks and other radicals ready for action in Moscow, but on the morning of December 9 they boldly seized control of the northwest sector of the city, which contained the Government House and the Prefecture of Police. It was an almost festive uprising, like a noisy series of New Year's Eve parties. "The first barricades on the Tverskaya," said Gorki, who lived nearby in an apartment atwitter with his collection of pet birds, "were built gaily with jokes and laughter, and the widest possible variety of people took part in this cherful labor, from the respectable gentleman wearing an expensive greatcoat to the cook-general and the janitor."

Moscow's new governor general, Admiral F. V. Dubasov, one of the three military leaders who had been engaged in suppressing the peasant disorders in the south, commanded a garrison of about fifteen thousand troops, but he was so doubtful of their loyalty that he limited himself to confining the rebels within their northwest sector while he appealed to St. Petersburg for reinforcements. For a week, the two sides skirmished from windows and rooftops, neither able to gain much ground from the other. On December 15, the crack Semyonov Guards finally arrived at the Brest Railroad Station and swept almost unopposed through the center of the city. Then they established their artillery at five points surrounding the rebels' chief stronghold in the factory district of Presnya. At dawn the next morning, the artillery began a systematic shelling of the encircled district. The Schmidt furniture factory soon burst into flames. Then the Marmentov varnish factory. Its blazing storage tanks sent up thick geysers that hung over the area all day. The shelling went on. A brick barracks filled with workers' families collapsed in a cloud of reddish smoke and dust. A row of wooden cottages caught fire. In one of them, nine old men and women who had huddled in an attic for safety were burned to death. "It was about as leisurely and safe a piece of slaughter as ever was seen . . . ," said Henry W. Nevinson, who watched the assault as a correspondent for the London *Daily Chronicle*. "As the wooden houses caught fire, and the work-people were driven out in helpless crowds from their barracks by the crash of shells, the soldiers came crowding in with rifle and sword. . . ." It was hardly a battle at all, merely a mopping-up. The next day, Nevinson finally got inside the smoldering wreckage to find white flags hanging on the ruins. "Arms were being surrendered," he wrote, "and the dead were collected in rows upon the frozen surface of a pond. In one place was a mutilated child of nine; in another a baby's arm, cut off at the shoulder and across the fingers, lay on the snow. Law and order were being restored."

And so, after another 1,000 to 1,500 deaths, with about ten times that many wounded, the Moscow uprising came to an end. Among the buildings in ruins was the Sytin publishing house, where the printers who wanted to be paid more for their punctuation marks had started the great strike three months before. With the collapse of the Moscow insurrection, the entire Russian Revolution of 1905 was over. From this point on, there was only pacification. The hangman and the firing squad claimed about 150 victims a week at first, then gradually less and less as pacification dragged on for more than a year (even as late as 1908 there were 1,059 death sentences for political offenses). Some 20,000 people a year were sentenced to hard labor in the prison camps of Siberia. And all of it was done "in the name of the protection and tranquillity of the people of Russia," as Tolstoy wrote in a great roar of protest, *I Cannot Be Silent*. "For me, therefore, exists the destitution of the people; . . . for me these hundreds of thousands of unfortunates dying of typhus and scurvy in the fortresses and prisons which are insufficient for such a multitude; for me the mothers, wives and fathers of the exiles, the prisoners, and those who are hanged are suffering; for me are these spies and this bribery; for me the interment of those dozens and hundreds of men who have been shot; for me the horrible work of these hangmen goes on. . . . It is impossible to live so! I, at any rate, cannot and will not live so." But he did. The pacification continued.

"I have always been opposed to repression myself," Witte told a delegation of visitors, "but am now compelled to resort to it, merely as the result of having trusted my countrymen." Nobody put much faith in his protestations. "Now he wants to hang and shoot everybody," the Tsar remarked. "I have never seen such a chameleon of a man." The Tsar kept Witte in office only long enough to finish negotiating a large loan from France, then replaced him in April of 1906 with an elderly retainer named Ivan Goremykin. And into the Interior Ministry came Pyotr Stolypin, a shrewd and tough provincial administrator whose right arm had been crippled by a dueling wound. When the first Duma was finally elected on a very restricted franchise that spring, and proved to be full of fractious liberals who imagined themselves at the Jeu de Paume, Stolypin connived with the Tsar to send troops and dissolve the Duma after a session of just seventy-three days. Stolypin himself became prime minister the day of the dissolution and henceforth governed by decree. "Order first, reform later," said Stolypin.

So the Tsar had finally won. And the police had won. The dragon of chaos had been vanquished. The Romanov monarchy, in all its imperial glory, was safe.

*

In exile, Father Gapon had become a great celebrity. All the radical factions in Switzerland courted him, and when he joined the Menshevik wing of the Social Democrats, it was announced as a great coup. But Gapon wanted to become the party leader, and the Mensheviks' admiration did not extend that far. Gapon then turned and joined the Socialist Revolutionaries, tried to become their leader, and was once again rejected. He finally announced that he wanted to unify all radical groups in a Revolutionary Combat Committee, and he invited all the rivals to a meeting. They came and listened and shook their heads and departed again. "He alone had to be in the center of everything," the SR leader Victor Chernov told a friend.

Gapon went to London for two months with his common-law wife, Sasha Uzdaleva, and collaborated with an anonymous Fleet Street scrivener on a lucrative autobiography. And donations kept pouring in from admirers in Russia. He returned to Paris and began appearing in cafés. He was spotted at the gambling casino in Monte Carlo. "Gapon loved life in all its elementary forms," Boris Savinkov, the terrorist leader, said contemptuously. "He loved comfort, luxury, brilliance, in short everything that could be bought for money.... Gapon lacked courage, he feared for his life, he was afraid of the scaffold." But Gapon also felt frustrated and homesick. "I want to go to Russia," he told a friend. "There is no air to breathe here."

Gapon cherished the dream that he could somehow return to Russia and simply pick up again his abandoned role as the leader of the working class. This time there would be no illusions about nonviolence. The priest took fencing lessons and riding lessons, bought himself a pistol and engaged in target practice. He finally returned to Russia in the autumn of 1905 aboard a gunrunning ship named the *John Grafton,* which mysteriously ran aground and had to be abandoned just off Finland. But though he now regarded himself as a radical, he was soon in touch with the police. In fact, he was in touch with Rachkovsky, now chief of all the political police. Rachkovsky entertained Gapon at the Café de Paris and other expensive restaurants and engaged in an almost Mephistophelean seduction. He not only promised Gapon money and power but even hinted that when he, Rachkovsky, retired, Gapon might become his successor. Rachkovsky asked only one thing: Could Gapon inform on and help trap the leadership of the terrorist Fighting Organization, which had murdered Plehve and Grand Duke Sergei and the rest?

Gapon seems to have thought that he could once again engage in a deceptive collaboration with the police, pretending to do what they said while privately pursuing independent plans of his own. For these plans to revive his disintegrated Assembly, he knew he would need a great deal of money. He promised Rachkovsky that he would betray the Fighting Organization, about which he actually knew very little. He said he could organize the trap by recruiting his friend Rutenberg, who had marched at his side on Bloody Sunday. But the price would be high. Gapon demanded of Rachkovsky 100,000 rubles. Rachkovsky, somewhat shocked, relayed the proposal to Interior Minister Durnovo, and Durnovo even relayed it to Witte. Witte indicated that the police should pay whatever they thought was needed, but he himself refused to officially authorize anything. Durnovo authorized 25,000 rubles. Gapon, who had once scrupled at accepting two hundred rubles from Zubatov, agreed.

Gapon went and told Rutenberg of the scheme. Rutenberg was incredulous. "I would deal not only with Rachkovsky but with the Devil himself," the priest said. Rutenberg, however, was more loyal to the Socialist Revolutionary Party than to Gapon. He promptly repeated Gapon's proposal to the head of the Fighting Organization, Yevno Azef. Seeing his long masquerade as a double agent once again in jeopardy, Azef called in Savinkov to decide what to do. Savinkov said Gapon should be put to death immediately. Azef was more cautious. He said that Gapon still had many supporters who would never believe that he had been killed for his treachery. They finally took the problem to the Socialist Revolutionaries' central committee, which decided that if Rutenberg could demonstrate Gapon's guilt by arranging a meeting with both Gapon and Rachkovsky, then he should kill them both. Rutenberg agreed, but reluctantly. He had never undertaken to be a terrorist. Besides, Rachkovsky would be hard to trap. Azef was sympathetic. He privately told Rutenberg that if he couldn't bring Gapon and Rachkovsky together, he should kill Gapon alone. Rutenberg made several nervous attempts to arrange the meeting with Rachkovsky, then gave up and decided to concentrate on Gapon.

A deserted villa was rented in the little village of Ozerki, near the Finnish border. Rutenberg asked Gapon to go there with him for a last discussion on the terms of the deal with Rachkovsky. He also asked four of his friends who had marched on Bloody Sunday to go to the villa first, to hide themselves in one of the rooms, and prepare for the execution. Rutenberg led the unsuspecting Gapon to an adjoining room with an open door. Through the open door, Rutenberg's friends could hear him question Gapon about Rachkovsky's plan to trap the Fighting Organization. Rutenberg asked Gapon why he was willing to join Rachkovsky. "Twenty-five thousand rubles is good money," said the priest. Rutenberg said he was worried that if the police caught the leaders of the Fighting Organization, they might be hanged. "Well, what of it?" said Gapon. "You can't cut down a tree without splinters flying."

At that, Rutenberg signaled the four jurors to come in, and they came with a noose. From one look at their angry faces, Gapon saw immediately what had happened. He fell to his knees and begged for mercy.

"Brothers, forgive me, for the sake of the past," he pleaded.

"Rachkovsky is your brother," said one of the executioners.

They threw their noose over Gapon's head and then flung the other end onto an iron hook that had been used for a clothesline. Gapon was too tall to be hanged there. The executioners had to clutch at his legs and his shoulders until he choked. They left the body and locked up the villa and went back to St. Petersburg. It was a month before the corpse was discovered rotting in the May sunshine.

*

On the early morning of June 30, 1908, a strange light could be seen in the skies to the east. As far away as London, citizens telephoned the police to ask if a whole district of the city was on fire. Six British weather stations recorded mysterious oscillations in barometric pressure, and a similar installation in Potsdam recorded atmospheric shock waves traveling around the world in both directions. Something extraordinary had happened in the remote wilderness of Siberia, in the forest region inhabited only by a few Tunguska tribesmen and their reindeer. The newspaper *Sibir* (*Siberia*), published in Irkutsk, carried a report from a correspondent in the town of Nizhne-Karelinsk, about six hundred miles southeast of the explosion. He quoted some tribal villagers as saying that a cylindrical column of flame had suddenly appeared in the sky, followed by a huge cloud of black smoke and then a thunderous crash. "All the buildings shook and at the same time a forked tongue of flame broke through the cloud," he reported. "All the inhabitants of the village ran out into the streets in panic. The old women wept. Everyone thought the end of the world was approaching."

The Russians had lived so near to the abyss for so long that they were inherently inclined to regard each new disaster as a portent of the ultimate cataclysm. Besides, they were a religious people, and had not the Bible repeatedly foretold the coming of the Final Days in terms of plague and famine, war and anarchy? The Symbolist poet Valeri Bryusov took his inspiration from the sixth chapter of Revelation when he wrote his most popular poem, *The Pale Horse:* "The street was like a storm. The crowds passed by as if pursued by inevitable Fate. Cars, cabs, buses roared amid the furious endless stream of people. . . . Suddenly amid the storm—a hellish whisper. There sounds a strange dissonant footfall, a deadening shriek, a tremendous crash. And the flaming Horseman appears. The horse flies headlong. The air still trembles and the echo rolls. Time quivers and the Look is Terror. In letters of fire the Horseman's scroll spells Death . . ." Boris Savinkov also used *The Pale Horse* as the title of his bleak novel about the terrorists he had led. "Where there is no law there is no crime . . . ," his hero reflects on the ethos of his vocation, and after citing the image from Revelation he adds: "Wherever that horse stamps its feet there the grass withers, and where the grass withers there is no life and consequently no law. For Death recognizes no law."

Visions of the apocalypse usually have an element of the fustian, but the Russian poets and novelists at the turn of the century were genuinely trying to convey a widespread sense of impending disaster. Andrei Bely, for example, claimed that he had been born "under the sign of the death of the old world," and in one of his poems he wrote: "There is nothing. And there will be nothing. . . . / The world has vanished and God will forget it." Leonid Andreyev ended *The Red Laugh* with a ghastly vision of all the corpses killed in Manchuria suddenly being disgorged from the earth, as on Judgment Day: "Behind us on the floor lay a naked, light-pink body with its head thrown back. And instantly at its side there appeared a second, and a third. And the earth threw them up one after the other. . . . And suddenly they stirred and swayed and rose up in the same orderly rows: the earth was throwing up new bodies, and they were lifting the first ones upward. . . ."

The most extraordinary of these apocalyptic visions was a work called *Mysterium,* by the supreme musical genius of the era, Alexander Scriabin. It was to be grand beyond all imagining, to be performed by an orchestra of one thousand and a chorus of one thousand and troops of white-robed dancers all assembled around Scriabin at his piano. He was composing not only poetry and music but various bursts of colored lights and incenses, and there were to be bells hanging from the clouds. Scriabin was afflicted, of course, with a megalomania bordering on the absurd. In the prerevolutionary year 1904, he was already writing in one of his Swiss notebooks: "I am, and there is nothing outside of me. . . . I am all. I am one, and within me is multiplicity. . . . I am fire. I am chaos. . . . I am God." The verses that he wrote for *Mysterium* are similar ("I am the ineffable bliss of dissolution/ I am the joy of death . . ."), but Scriabin actually bought land in Darjeeling for the construction of the vast amphitheater where *Mysterium* would receive its one and only performance, and he seems to have actually believed that when that performance was achieved, the entire human race would disappear. "The one Father flashes into the consciousness of all," he wrote. "All would experience voluntary sonhood, divine essence. . . ."

Before the coming of the reign of Christ, according to prophets of the Final Days, there must come the reign of Antichrist, and it was this that many Russians foresaw in the portents of diaster. In one of his last works before his death in 1900, *War, Progress, and the End of History,* the philosopher Solovyev foretold a war with the Japanese, which the Japanese would win. Indeed, the Japanese would conquer much of the world, but eventually the Europeans would drive them back, and then there would arise a brilliant writer and thinker who would unite the world and decree everlasting peace, and finally he would summon the religious leaders of the world and would promise them everything they wanted if only they would bow down and accept his sovereignty. The Jews too would accept him as the Messiah, until they learned that he was not a Jew, and then they would begin the revolt that would lead to the final battle north of Jerusalem and the eruption of a volcano from the bottom of the Dead Sea. . . .

But for nineteen years nobody knew what had happened to cause that mysterious light in the skies over Siberia, and nobody had even gone to find out. Not until 1927 did an expedition sent forth with dogsleds by the Soviet Academy of Sciences finally search the area. At a point about halfway between the Chunya and Stony Tunguska rivers, nearly fifty miles from either, anthropologist I. M. Suslov and mineralogist Leonid A. Kulik discovered a scene of almost unbelievable devastation. Within a radius of about twenty-five miles, almost all trees had been knocked down and were still lying flat, charred, their roots facing toward the center of the explosion. The few trees that were still standing had all been stripped bare of all bark, like telephone poles. "I still cannot sort out my chaotic impressions . . . ," Kulik wrote in his diary. "From our observation point no sign of forest can be seen, for everything has been devastated and burned."

Searching for witnesses in villages in the region, the two scientists found a few who could still remember what had happened two decades earlier. "I was sitting on the porch facing north," said S. B. Semenov, who lived in Vanavara, about forty miles from the blast, "when in the northwest a fiery blaze appeared for a moment, which sent out such heat it was impossible to stay seated—why, my shirt was almost burned off me. . . . I just had time to glance over and see how big it was, and then . . . an explosion came that threw me from the porch. . . . I was not unconscious very long. I came to, and then this kind of sound came that shook the whole house." A farmer named Bryukhanov, who lived near Kezhma, about 150 miles to the south, recalled that he had been plowing when he heard the explosion. "My horse fell onto its knees," he recalled. "From the north side above the forest a flame shot up. . . . Then I saw that the fir forest had been bent over by the wind and I thought of a hurricane. . . . The hurricane drove a wall of water up the Angara [River]. I saw it all quite clearly because my land was on a hillside."

It was all so long ago. Nearly twenty years. Who would have thought, when that great explosion lighted the skies, that after twenty years the Soviet Academy of Sciences would send Dr. Suslov and Dr. Kulik to investigate? Not Prime Minister Stolypin, the great believer in order, who was shot down in the Kiev opera house in September of 1911 by a Jewish student named D. G. Bogrov, who mysteriously happened to have been a paid police informer. The Tsar did not go to his Prime Minister's funeral, for the loyal Stolypin had lately incurred royal displeasure by trying to curb the increasing influence at court of the monk Rasputin, and the Tsarina said of his death that "those who have offended God may no longer count on divine protection." And not Rasputin himself, who, after acquiring nearly dictatorial authority because of his power over the neurotic Tsarina, was finally poisoned and shot and then thrown into the Neva in 1916 by a band of zealots who hoped that the assassination would save the monarchy.

And not Count Witte, builder of railroads and author of the Tsar's October manifesto, who died of a stroke in 1915. "Count Witte's death has been a great relief to me," the Tsar said. "I also regard it as a sign from God." And not Sergei Zubatov of the Okhrana, who had more of the loyalty that the Tsar prized so highly. When Zubatov heard that the Tsar had been forced to abdicate in 1917, he got up from the family dinner table, strode into the next room, and shot himself. And not the Tsar himself, who was shot by a Bolshevik execution squad the following year, together with his proud wife and all his young children and several servants. The bodies were cut up, burned, covered with acid, and finally thrown down an abandoned well.

And not the great revolutionaries, who fared hardly better. Yevno Azef was finally exposed in 1908 by a left-wing journalist, but the Socialist Revolutionary leaders could not decide whether to kill him immediately, as Savinkov urged, or give him one last chance to refute the accusation. While they equivocated, Azef fled to Germany, then toured the Aegean and Egypt with a lady known as Madame N., and then established himself in Berlin as a highly successful stockbroker. But the German police finally found him and held him for questioning by the Okhrana, and after being kept in prison throughout the war, he reemerged only after the armistice because the Okhrana no longer existed, and by now he was fatally ill with kidney disease. As for Savinkov, he rose to become deputy minister of war in the Kerensky regime of 1917, then turned violently against the usurping Lenin and was again plotting terror when the Bolsheviks trapped him and put him on trial. Savinkov confessed everything but pleaded for a chance to help the revolution, then finally leaped to his death from the second floor of a Cheka prison in 1924. That was the same year in which the all-victorious Lenin, who had done so little in the great days of 1905, died, paralyzed in the right arm and leg, unable to speak. Lenin's death in turn doomed Trotsky, who had done so much, to exile and assassination.

And not the seekers after truth. Scriabin, who thought of himself as the creator and destroyer of the universe, died in the first year of the World War from an infected pimple on his lip. Crowds lined the stairs to his apartment in Moscow as doctors kept coming to cut open the pimple. Scriabin told one of his last visitors that the pain was not bad. Then he suddenly started screaming, "This pain is unbearable!" Only then did he realize what was happening. "This means the end!" he cried. "But this is a catastrophe!" At about midnight, he became delirious, and perhaps he saw some strange new vision, for his last out cry was "Who's there?" The young Osip Mandelstam was greatly moved by Scriabin's death and saw it as another sign of the fate that awaited everyone in the apostate capital: "In translucent Petropolis we shall die .../ With every sigh we drink the deadly air,/ And every hour is our dying day." "Poetry ...," his wife, Nadezhda, added many years later in her own old age, "is a preparation for death. Death encompasses all the fullness of life, its essence, its real pith and substance. Death is the apex of life."

Tolstoy lived to be eighty-two and finally tottered off in flight from his wife and family and ended as an absurd spectacle: huddled in a blanket on a bench in a country railroad station, surrounded by doctors and disciples and officials and even his pursuing family, hiccoughing, his ears and lips turning blue, receiving whiffs of oxygen and injections of camphor while his reverent audience watched him cough and shiver. Ten years earlier, when he had been desperately ill, he had written in his diary: "When I am dying I should like to be asked whether I still see life as before, as a progression toward God, an increase of love. If I should not have the strength to speak, and the answer is yes, I shall close my eyes; if it is no, I shall look up." Now nobody asked him whether he saw life as a progression toward God, and as he tried to speak, his last words to the assembled audience were just a series of mutterings: "The truth ... I care a great deal ... How they ..."

Dr. Suslov and Dr. Kulik could not figure out what had happened in the wilds of Siberia in 1908, and neither have any of their successors. All the trees had been burned, but no mere forest fire could cause an explosion that would level everything. A meteorite could have caused the destruction, but there was no sign of a crater. The tail of a comet might have caused the tiny globules of magnetic iron and silicate found in the area, but how could a comet reach Siberia without anyone on earth spotting it? All the evidence points to an explosion well above the earth's surface, several miles high, and much of that evidence suggests an atomic explosion yielding about ten megatons. But how could such an event occur? There are fanciful theories about an accident involving a nuclear-powered spaceship from some other planet, about a black hole in space or a mysterious appearance of antimatter. We remain as ignorant as the Tunguska tribesmen who first saw a tower of fire.

Perhaps because of our fear of death as the end, the catastrophe, we imagine the end of the world as something terrible, and we imagine Judgment Day as a day of wrath and of condemnation to hellfire. The earliest Christians apparently saw it quite differently, and the tone at the end of Revelation is one of serenity and salvation. And many of those rebels and heretics who regarded the world as dominated by evil viewed the end of that evil as a blessing. No one who saw light in the skies at the dawn of the revolution could know that what would follow would be just as bad, just as unbearable, and just as inevitable. They saw only that everything must end, and they believed that everything must be transfigured. Anton Chekhov, who died with a smile just after drinking a glass of champagne, spoke in several of his plays about that transfiguration and wondered what form it would take. In the closing scene of *Uncle Vanya,* he used the abandoned Sonya to express the hopes of all those who would be betrayed by the coming revolutions: "Well, what can we do? We must go on living. We shall live through a long, long succession of days and dull evenings. We shall patiently suffer the trials that Fate imposes on us. We shall work for others, now and in our old age, and we shall have no rest. When our time comes, we shall die submissively, and over there, beyond the grave, we shall say that we've suffered, that we've wept, that we've had a bitter life, and God will take pity on us. And . . . we shall have rest."

The Kingdom of Auschwitz

1940–45

"In Auschwitz, everything was possible."

In a remote corner of southern Poland, in a marshy valley where the Sola River flows into the Vistula about thirty miles west of Cracow, Heinrich Himmler decided in the spring of 1940 to build a new prison camp. The site chosen by some of his underlings had little to recommend it. Outside a bleak little town named Oswiecim, there stood an abandoned Austrian artillery barracks, a collection of about twenty single-story brick buildings, most of them dark and dirty. The surrounding countryside in the foothills of the Carpathians was strangely beautiful, a mosaic of meadows speckled with wild flowers, but a committee of Himmler's adjutants reported back to Berlin that the prospects for a large prison camp were forbidding. The water supply was polluted, and there were mosquitoes everywhere, and the barracks themselves were virtually useless.

Himmler was undaunted. In this first year of the subjugation of Poland, the need for new detention camps to help establish German law and order in the east was overwhelming. One of Himmler's most dedicated subordinates, SS Major Rudolf Hoess, commandant of the "protective custody camp" at Sachsenhausen, differed from his skeptical colleagues. He reported to Berlin that hard work could transform the marshes along the Vistula into a valuable outpost of the Reich. The place had two important qualities: it had good railroad connections, but it was isolated from outside observation. Himmler promptly assigned Hoess to take charge of the project. On April 29, 1940, Hoess and five other SS officers from Sachsenhausen descended from the Breslau train and surveyed the prospect before them. "It was far away, in the back of beyond, in Poland," Hoess later recalled in the memoir that he wrote shortly before he was hanged in 1947. The Poles called the place Oswiecim; the Germans called it Auschwitz.

Hoess was a remarkable man, as anyone who confesses to personal responsibility for the death of about three million people presumably must be.* It was

---

* Perhaps the most terrible single fact about Auschwitz is that nobody knows, even to the nearest hundred thousand, how many people died there. Hoess acknowledged responsibility for the execution of 2.5 million, plus "another half million who succumbed to starvation and disease," but he then added: "I myself never knew the total number and I have nothing to help me make an estimate of it." He got the figure of 2.5 million from Adolf Eichmann, but

he, apparently, who devised the famous steel sign that mockingly welcomed the trainloads of prisoners to Auschwitz: *Arbeit Macht Frei.* Work makes you free. He seems not to have intended it as a mockery, nor even to have intended it literally, as a false promise that those who worked to exhaustion would eventually be released, but rather as a kind of mystical declaration that self-sacrifice in the form of endless labor does in itself bring a kind of spiritual freedom. "All my life I have thoroughly enjoyed working," Hoess wrote on the eve of his hanging. "I have done plenty of hard, physical work, under the severest conditions, in the coal mines, in oil refineries, and in brickyards. I have felled timbers, cut railroad ties, and stacked peat.... Work in prison [is] a means of training for those prisoners who are fundamentally unstable and who need to learn the meaning of endurance and perseverance...."

He was not a mere brute. One of the few surviving photographs shows a man with a high forehead, large, searching eyes, a full-lipped and rather prissy mouth. His devout parents had been determined that he should become a priest. His father and his grandfather had been soldiers, and though the father retired from the Army to become a salesman in Baden-Baden, he passed on to his only son his belief in military discipline. And piety. He took his son on pilgrimages to shrines as far away as Einsiedeln and Lourdes. "I was taught," Hoess wrote, "that my highest duty was to help those in need. It was constantly impressed on me in forceful terms that I must obey promptly the wishes and commands of my parents, teachers and priests...."

Such commands sometimes conflicted. Shortly after Hoess' father died, the World War broke out, and despite his mother's pleadings that he continue his studies, he lied about his age and managed to enlist at sixteen in the Twenty-first Regiment of Dragoons. He was sent to Turkey, then to the Iraqi front, then to Palestine. At eighteen he was already the commander of a cavalry unit. When the war ended, he refused to surrender and marched his own troops home through Turkey, Bulgaria, Romania, to Austria. He found his mother dead, his household dispersed. He took up arms again in one of the *Freikorps* units that fought in the Baltic states, and when the *Freikorps* became violently involved in the domestic battles of the Weimar Republic, Hoess too took part in an absurd political murder. He and a band of his comrades got drunk and then beat to death a schoolteacher whom they suspected of having informed on another nationalist. It was all a mistake. The schoolteacher had done nothing. Hoess was surprised to find himself arrested, prosecuted, and sentenced to life imprisonment.

By his own account, he was a model prisoner. "I had been taught since childhood to be absolutely obedient and meticulously tidy and clean," he

---

he said that it seemed to him "far too high," and at his trial he reduced it to 1,135,000. The scholars now working at the Auschwitz museum estimate the total at 4 million. Some other scholars differ. Gerald Reitlinger, whose figures are perhaps the lowest, argues in *The Final Solution* that the total of 4 million is "absurd," that Hoess and Eichmann were both boasting, and that the true total is slightly less than 1 million. The Nazis, who began by keeping detailed records of all the killings, ended by burning every document they could, and so the dead remain uncounted.

wrote, "so in these matters I did not find it difficult to conform to the strict discipline of the prison." When the worthy liberals of Weimar devised a system in which meritorious prisoners might pass a series of tests and trials that would lead to their freedom, Hoess was proud to become the first of eight hundred prisoners to reach the top rating, and to wear three stripes on his sleeve. *Arbeit macht frei.* But as a political prisoner, he could not be freed. He began to go mad. He could not eat, could not get to sleep. "I had to ... walk round and round my cell, and was unable to lie still," he wrote. "Then I would sink exhausted onto the bed and fall asleep, only to wake again after a short time bathed in sweat from my nightmares. In these confused dreams, I was always being pursued and killed, or falling over a precipice. Two hours of darkness became a torment. Night after night I heard the clocks strike the hour. As morning approached, my dread increased. I feared the light of day and the people I should have to see once more. . . ."

A prison doctor finally told Hoess that he was suffering from "prison psychosis," and that he would get over it, and he did. But it was not until 1928, when a left-right coalition came to power in Berlin, that an amnesty freed Hoess and an army of others who had committed political crimes. After five years in prison, Hoess passionately wanted to become a farmer. He discovered a right-wing group called the League of Artamanen, which was establishing a network of agricultural communes. He found a girl who shared his views, and they got married and worked the land and had three children (there were ultimately to be five). He learned in due time that one of the leaders of the Artamanen was Heinrich Himmler, scarcely thirty, a thoughtful young man who wore a pince-nez and loved birds and flowers and held a degree in agronomy and owned a chicken farm outside Munich. With the rise of Hitler, Himmler became the commander of the Führer's private guard, the Schutzstaffel, or SS, and when Himmler called for recruits, Hoess answered the call. He claims to have had "many doubts and hesitations" about leaving the farm, claims to have known almost nothing about the new concentration camps that Hitler was building. "To me it was just a question of being an active soldier again, or resuming my military career," Hoess wrote. "I went to Dachau."

Hoess' memoirs are full of lies and evasions, of course, but they also provide a remarkable illustration of the whole process of self-delusion. Having joined the SS for a quasi-military career, Hoess seems to have been surprised and strangely thrilled, at Dachau, the first time he saw a prisoner flogged. "When the man began to scream," he recalled, "I went hot and cold all over. . . . I am unable to give an explanation of this." Hoess dutifully regarded the prisoners as enemies of the state, regarded their forced labor as a justified punishment, regarded all the beatings and torments as a justified enforcement of discipline. He claims, nonetheless, to have had misgivings, and to have suppressed them. "I should have gone to [Himmler] and explained that I was not suited to concentration-camp service, because I felt too much sympathy for the prisoners. I was unable to find the courage to do this. . . . I did not wish to reveal my weakness. . . . I became reconciled to my lot."

Hoess worked hard, enforced orders, won promotions, first at Dachau, then at Sachsenhausen. Then came the war, and the lightning conquest of Poland. Himmler, who by now gloried in the title of *Reichsführer SS,* recognized Hoess' extraordinary dedication and ordered him to create the first concentration camp beyond the original frontiers of the Reich. Hoess sensed from the start that he was being assigned to a project of unprecedented dimensions. At the outbreak of the war, there had been six concentration camps* in Germany, containing about 25,000 prisoners. Himmler told Hoess that he was to build, in the marshy valley of the Vistula, a camp for 10,000 prisoners, and that would be only the beginning. There might someday be 50,000 prisoners, or even more. "The numbers envisioned were at this time something entirely new in the history of concentration camps . . . ," Hoess recalled. "Before the war the concentration camps had served the purposes of self-protection, but during the war, according to the will of the Reichsführer SS, they became a means to an end. They were now to serve the war effort, the munitions production. As many prisoners as possible were to become armaments workers. Every commandant had to run his camp ruthlessly with this end in view."

At Auschwitz, however, there was no camp, only a few dilapidated barracks and stables. On May 20, 1940, a month after Hoess' arrival, an SS officer named Gerhard Pallitzsch, who held the title of *Rapportführer* and thus was responsible for camp discipline, brought to Hoess thirty German criminals whom he had selected from Sachsenhausen. To one of them, a man of Polish ancestry named Bruno Brodniewicz, belonged the sad distinction of being given the number one, the first of perhaps four million prisoners who were to be shipped to Auschwitz. These thirty German criminals were to start the building of the camp, and Pallitzsch had chosen them partly for their various technical skills. They were also destined to become the camp's first *Kapos,*† or trusties, the men who upheld and carried out the orders of the SS and thus became not only the Nazis' representatives but in some cases the worst of oppressors.

The town council of Oswiecim, acting on behalf of a population of twelve thousand, cooperated. It ordered a roundup of two hundred local Jews and assigned them to start work on the building of the new camp. The SS office in Cracow sent fifteen cavalrymen to guard the prisoners as they worked. This work had barely begun when the police headquarters in Breslau sent a message to ask when the camp would be ready to take in prisoners. Before the message had even been answered, a passenger train arrived with 728 Polish political prisoners. The date was June 14, 1940. Most of these first prisoners were young men who had been caught trying to escape across the border into Hungary.

---

* The first was Dachau, just northwest of Munich, built in the spring of 1933, Hitler's first year. The others were Buchenwald, near Weimar; Sachsenhausen, north of Berlin; Mauthausen, near Linz; Flossenburg, in the Sudetenland; and Ravensbrück, the women's prison, also north of Berlin. The SS rated these in three categories, with Dachau and Buchenwald being in Category I, the most lenient.

† The origin of the word is unknown. According to one account, Italian workmen building roads in southern Germany used the Italian term for "head," *capo,* to address their foremen. Prisoners in the work gangs at Dachau overheard them and picked up their slang. From there, the word spread through all the concentration camps. Other accounts suggest that it may be a contraction of *Kamp Polizei* or *Kameradschafts Polizei.*

There were also a few priests and schoolteachers and Jews. They were assigned to some buildings that belonged to the Polish Tobacco Monopoly and were then ordered to join in the building of the camp.

Not many witnesses of those early days of Auschwitz survived the long years of the war, and so the details remain obscure, like the legends of the founding of some mythical city. Hoess himself described the labors in terms of his own dedication ("If I was to get the maximum effort out of my officers and men, I had to set them a good example. When reveille sounded for the SS men in the ranks, I too must get out of bed. . . .") Among the prisoners, however, Hoess' guards applied from the beginning every technique that would terrorize and subjugate their victims. The day began with a roll call that sometimes lasted for hours. The prisoners were ordered to do their work on the run, and when they faltered they were beaten with clubs. They sometimes had to line up on their knees for their rations, a chunk of dark bread and a bowl of watery soup. They were kicked and beaten at the whim of any guard. If they complained or resisted, they were beaten again, or simply shot.

On July 6, a prisoner named Tadeusz Wiejowski escaped. Hoess ordered the other prisoners to stand at attention for a roll call that lasted twenty hours. For three days, the SS men hunted the fugitive but failed to find him. Hoess seized the opportunity to order the expulsion of all Polish civilians from seven peasant villages near Auschwitz. An area extending six miles from north to south and almost three miles from west to east was now decreed to be solely the property of the Auschwitz prison camp.

More Polish prisoners kept streaming in. The first shipment from Warsaw arrived on August 15—513 political prisoners and 1,153 men caught in various roundups. Another shipment followed on September 21. The first snow fell in early October, and although the construction had been going on all summer, there had been little preparation for winter. Polish winters are hard. In that November of 1940, the temperature remained near zero. Icy mists rose from the Vistula every night and seeped through the unfinished barracks at Auschwitz. Many of these barracks had no windows. There was no heat. The prisoners had no winter clothes. Some worked barefoot in the snow.

When another captive escaped, Hoess decided to strengthen camp discipline by making all the other prisoners stand at roll call until 9 P.M. "From dawn heavy rain or sleet had been driving down and a strong northeast wind was blowing," one of the victims later recalled. "From noon onwards frozen men began to be carried or brought in on barrows . . . , half conscious, crawling, reeling like drunks, babbling incoherently and with difficulty, covered with spittle and foaming at the mouth, dying, gasping their last breath." And those were the early days, when Auschwitz was still being built, and still served not as a death camp but just as a minor detention center for various categories of Polish prisoners.

In the midst of these difficulties, however, Hoess nourished grand plans to make Auschwitz a kind of Utopia. As early as January of 1941, while the prisoners were dying of cold, he decided to organize an Auschwitz symphony orchestra. Himmler, the former chicken farmer, indulged in similarly benign fantasies about his outpost on the Vistula. "Auschwitz was to become *the* agricultural research station for the eastern territories," Hoess recalled Himmler saying at a meeting in Berlin. "Opportunities were opened up to us, which we had never before had in Germany. Sufficient labor was available. All essential agricultural research must be carried out there. Huge laboratories and plant nurseries were to be set out. All kinds of stock-breeding was to be pursued there. . . ."

Sufficient labor was available. In that one sentence, that euphemism for the herds of emaciated prisoners in their tattered blue and white stripes, Hoess illuminated the most seductive element of Auschwitz in its first phase. It had been founded as a detention camp, a place to confine undesirable people, Polish army officers, dissidents and heretics of all sorts, people who must be prevented from infecting the new order that the Nazis were trying to build in the disorganized east. But once these thousands of people were stripped of their possessions and confined behind barbed wire, they represented a resource that Himmler was just beginning to appreciate: labor. That basic unit of human value was now available for any use to which the Reichsführer SS might choose to put it, whether an agricultural research laboratory or a symphony orchestra or an armaments factory. "In Auschwitz," said Hoess, "everything was possible."

Though the "sufficient labor" at Auschwitz could never really be sufficient to Himmler's fantasies, his primary imperative was to protect and enlarge this new resource. When he paid his first visit to the year-old outpost on the Vistula on March 1, 1941, he told Hoess that the camp he was building was to contain not 10,000 or 50,000 prisoners, as previously agreed, but 100,000. In fact, Auschwitz itself was too small. A new camp, Auschwitz II, would have to be built in the birch woods outside what had once been the village of Brzezinka, two miles west of Auschwitz. The Germans called it Birkenau. This expansion was not mere SS imperialism, Himmler told Hoess, but a contribution to the war effort. He had brought with him several executives of I. G. Farben, the great chemical cartel, which was proposing to build a synthetic-rubber factory near Auschwitz in order to use the prisoners to make truck tires for the victorious Wehrmacht.

Hoess was appalled, not by the vastness of Himmler's plans but by the lack of means to carry them out. He had been officially warned in advance against reporting anything "disagreeable" to Himmler, but he could not prevent himself from an outpouring of bureaucratic protest. Auschwitz was already overcrowded by the trainloads of prisoners that kept rolling in, and there were no materials with which to build a new camp at Birkenau. The whole region lacked sufficient fresh water and drainage. There was a serious danger of disease. The local gauleiter joined in the protest, but Himmler was unmoved. The creation of Birkenau was an order. "Gentlemen, it will be built," said Himmler. "My reasons for constructing it are far more important than your objections. Ten thousand prisoners are to be provided for the I. G. Farben industries. . . ." As for the lack of building materials, the SS had now acquired its own brick and cement factories, which "will have to be made more productive." As for the lack of fresh water and drainage, Himmler dismissed these as "purely technical problems." In summation, he told Hoess, "I do not appreciate the difficulties in Auschwitz. It is up to you to manage somehow."

Hoess did manage. I. G. Farben began building its Buna synthetic-rubber factory in April in the nearby town of Dwory, and gangs of prisoners trudged there every morning to play their part in the war effort, but that summer changed the whole nature of the war, and therefore of the camp at Auschwitz. On the night of June 22, one of the prisoners heard on a clandestine radio that Hitler's panzer divisions were streaming across the Russian frontier. For a few days, the prisoners were jubilant, for they thought that the widened war and the new alliance among Hitler's enemies would inevitably lead to their liberation. But as the Wehrmacht swept across western Russia, the prisoners saw their future darken. Then came the first Russian captives, thousands and thousands of them. "They had been given hardly any food on the march," Hoess wrote, "during the halts on the way being simply turned out into the nearest fields and there told to 'graze' like cattle on anything edible they could find. In the Lamsdorf camp there must have been about 200,000 Russian prisoners of war. . . . Most of them huddled as best they could in earth hovels they had built themselves. . . . It was with these prisoners, many of whom could hardly stand, that I was now supposed to build the Birkenau prisoner-of-war camp."

It is not easy to compare the Nazis' treatment of different groups of prisoners, but the Russians seem to have received even more abuse than the Poles. Both groups were regarded as subhuman *Untermenschen,* but perhaps the Russians seemed more threatening, soldiers of a great power, now captives under the control of these uniformed Germans who had never been in combat. There was little thought of assigning the Russians to any project like the I. G. Farben plant; they were entirely expendable. Hoess ascribed the Russians' fate to their own weakness, or to a larger destiny. "They died like flies from general physical exhaustion," he recalled, "or from the most trifling maladies which their debilitated constitutions could no longer resist. I saw countless Russians die while in the act of swallowing root vegetables or potatoes. . . . Overcome by the crudest instinct of self-preservation, they came to care nothing for one another, and in their selfishness now thought only of themselves. Cases of cannibalism were not rare in Birkenau. I myself came across a Russian lying between piles of bricks, whose body had been ripped open and the liver removed. They would beat each other to death for food. . . . They were no longer human beings."

Hoess seems to have persuaded himself that this process occurred all by itself, but one of his subordinates, Perry Broad, an SS man of Brazilian parentage, wrote out for the trial of twenty-two Auschwitz officials in Frankfurt in 1964 a vivid account of how the Russians were finally dispatched. "Thousands of prisoners of war were shot in a copse near Birkenau and buried in mass graves," Broad recalled. "The graves were about 150–200 feet long, 15 feet deep, and perhaps just as wide. The camp administration had solved the Russian problem to its satisfaction. Then . . . the fisheries began to complain that the fish in the ponds in the vicinity of Birkenau were dying. Experts said this was due to the pollution of the ground water through cadaveric poisoning. But that was not all. The summer sun was beating down on Birkenau, the bodies, which had not yet decomposed but had only rotted, started to swell up, and a dark red mass began to seep through the cracks of the earth, spreading an indescribable stench throughout. Something had to be done quickly. . . . SS Sergeant Franz Hössler was ordered to dig up the bodies in all possible secrecy and have them burned. . . ." Of the 12,000 Russians sent to build Birkenau in the fall of 1941, only about 150 were still alive the following summer. "Those who did remain were the best," said Hoess. "They were splendid workers."

*

While the authorities at Auschwitz were killing Russians, the authorities in Berlin were making new plans. In the summer of 1941—the exact date is unknown—Himmler summoned Hoess to Berlin for a secret meeting. Not even Himmler's adjutant was present. "The Führer has ordered that the Jewish question be solved once and for all," Himmler said, according to Hoess, "and that we, the SS, are to implement that order." Himmler had considered using various camps in the east, he said, and only Auschwitz would serve as the center of destruction, only Auschwitz was sufficiently big, sufficiently isolated, sufficiently organized to carry out Himmler's plan. "I have now decided to entrust this task to you," Himmler said. "It is difficult and onerous and calls for complete devotion notwithstanding the difficulties that may arise. . . . You will treat this order as absolutely secret, even from your superiors. . . . The Jews are the sworn enemies of the German people and must be eradicated. Every Jew that we can lay our hands on is to be destroyed now during the war, without exception. . . ."

Hoess, the onetime pilgrim to Lourdes, seems by now to have reached such a state of official docility that he did not even question this incredible order, much less dispute it. The only question in his mind, apparently, was how such a gigantic enterprise could be carried out. Himmler did not explain. He said he would send Hoess an emissary, Major Adolf Eichmann, head of Section B-4 of Bureau IV of the Reich Security Office (RSHA), to discuss the details. Shortly afterward, Eichmann arrived in Auschwitz—a lean, wiry man with a sharp nose and a nervous manner. He and Hoess seemed to recognize something in each other that made them friends. Eichmann already had a plan, a geographic sequence for the shipment of Jews to Auschwitz, first those from the eastern part of Upper Silesia, then those from the neighboring Polish areas now under German rule, then those from Czechoslovakia, then a great sweep of Western Europe. . . .

But the two officials seemed unable to decide on the most fundamental question—how to kill the victims. The first bands of *Einsatzgruppen* who had prowled through Eastern Europe in the wake of the advancing German Army had simply shot any Jews they had found, but this was an inefficient way of carrying out mass executions. It was expensive. It was also bad for the morale of the executioners. This may seem a minor aspect of the problem, but the Germans gave it due weight. "It would have placed too heavy a burden on the

SS men who had to carry it out," said Hoess, "especially because of the women and children among the victims."

Eichmann and Hoess agreed that poison gas was the solution, but the technology of gassing was only beginning to be explored. As early as 1939, the Nazis had started a series of experiments on the most feared and despised of all minorities, the mentally defective and the insane. In a dozen mental institutions in various parts of Germany, the Nazis built fake shower rooms into which they could pipe carbon-monoxide gas. Over the course of a year or more, they killed about fifty thousand mental patients in this way, but the technique was generally regarded as unsatisfactory. There were constant breakdowns in the gassing machinery, and the shower rooms could accommodate only about fifty victims at a time, and the disposal of the corpses caused unpleasant rumors in the surrounding towns.

There were also economic problems in applying such techniques on the grand scale envisaged at Auschwitz. Carbon-monoxide sprays "would necessitate too many buildings," as Hoess put it, "and it was also very doubtful whether the supply of gas for such a vast number of people would be available." The question was left open. Eichmann told Hoess that he would try to find a poisonous gas that was both cheap and plentiful, and then they would meet again. In the meantime, they strolled together through the idle farmlands that had been expropriated in the village of Brzezinka. They were looking for a place where the gas, once it was found, might be applied. They finally saw an abandoned farmhouse that they considered, as Hoess said, "most suitable." It was near the northern corner of the still-expanding camp. "It was isolated and screened by woods and hedges," Hoess wrote, "and it was also not far from the railroad. The bodies could be placed in the long deep pits in the nearby meadows. . . . We calculated that after gasproofing the premises then available, it would be possible to kill about eight hundred people simultaneously with a suitable gas."

The search for a suitable gas took Hoess to the other death camps that were now being built.* To Chelmno, about 150 miles north of Auschwitz, where the inhabitants of the Lodz ghetto were herded into a crumbling château known as "the palace," then loaded onto trucks that had been specially equipped so that the exhaust fumes could be piped up into the rear compartment. By the time the trucks arrived at a burial ground in the surrounding forest, the prisoners in the back were dead. This system had its flaws, however. The trucks could not handle large numbers of prisoners, and the gas from the exhaust pipes flowed in so unevenly that some of the victims were still gasping with life when the trucks reached the burial ground. Hoess moved on to Treblinka, near Byalystok, where the plan was to park the trucks filled with prisoners outside three small gas chambers, each about fifteen feet square, and to pipe the exhaust fumes in among the prisoners assembled there. Hoess was still dissatisfied. All these methods were too unreliable, too small in scale.

* Auschwitz was by far the biggest of the death camps, but there were five others, all in Poland, put into operation between December of 1941 and the middle of 1942. They were: Chelmno (Kulmhof), Belzec, Sobibor, Maidanek, and Treblinka.

Hoess apparently was not aware, nor was Eichmann, that the suitable gas was already available. It was called Zyklon B,* a commercial form of hydrocyanic acid, which became active on contact with air. It was manufactured by a firm called Degesch, which was largely owned by I. G. Farben, and it had been brought to Auschwitz in the summer of 1941 as a vermin-killer and disinfectant. It was very dangerous. Two civilians came from Hamburg with their gas masks to show the Auschwitz authorities how to use the poison. Prisoners who worked in the munitions plant had to hang up their vermin-infested clothes, and then the barracks were sealed, and the gas was released.

One of the judges who presided at the 1964 Auschwitz trial in Frankfurt wanted to know exactly how the gas worked. "Was it granular?" he asked.

"Zyklon B was packed in small, two-pound containers which at first resembled cardboard disks, something like beer coasters, always a bit damp and gray," said one of the defendants, Arthur Breitweiser, who had worked in the Auschwitz administrative office. He told how the gas containers had to be pried open with a hammer. "Then we went into the rooms and scattered the stuff . . . ," Breitweiser said. "Zyklon B worked terribly fast. I remember one of the SS men going into a house that had already been disinfected. The ground floor had been aired out in the evening, and the next morning the man wanted to open the windows on the first floor. He must have inhaled some fumes, because he collapsed immediately and rolled down the steps, unconscious, out into the fresh air. Had he fallen the other way, he wouldn't have lived."

On September 3, 1941, while Hoess was away on business, Deputy Commandant Karl Fritzsch decided, apparently on his own authority, to experiment in using Zyklon B on six hundred Russian prisoners of war and 250 tubercular patients in the Auschwitz hospital. He sealed up some of the underground bunkers of Block 11, headquarters of the Gestapo's Politische Abteilung, or Political Department. There he packed in the prisoners, then put on a gas mask and flung one of the disinfectant containers into the midst of the victims. Within a few minutes, they were all dead. "Those who were propped against the door leaned with a curious stiffness and then fell right at our feet, striking their faces hard against the concrete floor," recalled a Pole named Zenon Rozanski, who served in the penal detail assigned to clear out the bunker. "Corpses! Corpses standing bolt upright and filling the entire corridor of the bunker, till they were packed so tight it was impossible for more to fall."

Almost by accident, Captain Fritzsch had discovered the technology that Hoess and Eichmann were seeking, a technology that was "suitable." And Birkenau, where the giant crematoria were to arise, had not yet even been built. It was not until October 15, 1941, that Hoess approved a plan designed by one of the prisoners in the Auschwitz Building Office. To house 100,000 prisoners, as Himmler had ordered, the plan called for a series of two-story barracks to be built in a rectangle 400 feet in width by 2,300 feet in length. Each barracks was to contain three tiers of bunks, with four to six prisoners in each bunk. No sooner had the building been started than Hans Kammler, an engineer in the

---

* The term comes from the first letters of the German names for the three main ingredients, cyanide, chlorine and nitrogen.

SS administrative headquarters in Berlin, arrived in Auschwitz with the news that Birkenau was to house not 100,000 prisoners but 200,000.

The Final Solution lurched into existence. It was perfectly clear in Himmler's meeting with Hoess in the summer of 1941, but there were endless details to be worked out, regulations to be drafted and distributed, meetings and elaborations. The most important of these was the secret Wannsee Conference convened by Himmler's alter ego, Reinhard Heydrich, at a villa in the beautiful lakeside suburb on the southwestern edge of Berlin. It was originally scheduled for December 9, 1941, but the Japanese attack on Pearl Harbor caused a certain amount of confusion, and so the conference was rescheduled for January 20, 1942. Lunch and drinks were served. There were thirteen officials representing the Foreign Office, the Ministry of Justice, the Polish occupation authorities, all the main departments of the German government and the Nazi Party. Heydrich spoke at length of "the coming Final Solution of the Jewish question." Everything was explained. Eichmann kept the minutes.

Yet there were still further delays. It was not until August 3, 1942, that the working plans for the four great crematoria, which could take in as many as ten thousand prisoners per day, were approved by the Auschwitz authorities and the engineers at Toepf A. G. in Erfurt. In January and February of 1943, there were still complaints of work delayed by freezing weather, and only on March 13 was Crematorium II finally ready to operate. Until then, as Himmler had ordered, it was up to Hoess "to manage somehow." Hoess managed with the farmhouse that he and Eichmann had discovered. There and in an abandoned barn about three hundred prisoners a day could be gassed. Hundreds more were killed by lethal injections of phenol, or by simple shooting. Throughout the confusions of 1942, the impossible orders kept pouring in, and Hoess kept improvising. "I cannot say," he wrote in his memoir, "on what date the extermination of the Jews began . . ."

The first *Transport Juden,* consisting of 999 Jewish women from Slovakia, arrived on March 26, 1942, at the Auschwitz railroad station. "A cheerful little station," as a prisoner named Tadeusz Borowski later wrote, "very much like any other provincial railway stop: a small square framed by tall chestnuts and paved with yellow gravel . . ." Since the Birkenau gas chambers had not yet been built, the women were stripped, their heads shaved, and then they were confined in Blocks 1 to 10 of the main camp, separated by a high fence from the men's barracks. Then they were made to stand for hours at roll call, and beaten, and then sent out in work gangs, and beaten again.

And at the little station lined with chestnut trees, the trains kept arriving. On April 17, 1942, another shipment of 973 Slovakian Jews appeared at Auschwitz, and on April 19, another 464. The SS men and their snarling guard dogs met them at the railroad ramp. Prisoner Borowski, who had been a poet of incandescent talent,* appeared at the ramp occasionally to watch the arrivals. "The ramp has become increasingly alive with activity, increasingly noisy," he later wrote of one such scene. "The crews are being divided into those who will open

* Borowski survived three years in Auschwitz, published three collections of stories and a volume of poetry after the war. He committed suicide in 1951 at the age of twenty-nine.

and unload the arriving cattle cars and those who will be posted by the wooden steps. . . . Motorcycles drive up, delivering SS officers, bemedaled, glittering with brass, beefy men with highly polished boots and shiny, brutal faces. Some have brought their briefcases, others hold thin, flexible whips. . . . Some stroll majestically on the ramp, the silver squares on their collars glitter, the gravel crunches under their boots, their bamboo whips snap impatiently. . . . The train rolls slowly alongside the ramp. In the tiny barred windows appear pale, wilted, exhausted human faces, terror-stricken women with tangled hair, unshaven men. They gaze at the station in silence. And then, suddenly, there is a stir inside the cars, and a pounding against the wooden boards. 'Water! Air!' "

The SS men routed the starving and terrified prisoners out of the freight cars, ordered them to abandon all their possessions, and then whipped them into line to prepare for the process known as "selection." Two SS doctors had been assigned by rotation to choose a few of the hardiest prisoners to be preserved for the Auschwitz labor *Kommandos.* These doctors—the most notable was Josef Mengele, who liked to wear white gloves and to whistle themes from Wagner's operas as he worked—surveyed each newcomer for a few seconds and then waved him on in one direction or another. A wave to the right meant—though most of the newcomers did not realize it—survival, an assignment to hard labor in the construction gangs. A wave to the left meant the gas chamber. Anyone more than about forty years of age was waved to the left. Most women went to the left. Almost all children under fifteen went to the left. Families that asked to stay together were reunited and sent to the left. Only about ten percent of each transport, on the average, went to the right. Sometimes more, sometimes less, according to the whim of the SS doctors.

The May 12 transport that brought 1,500 Jews from Sosnowiec marked a turning point in the short history of Auschwitz, for this was the first trainload of Jews who were not imprisoned, not shorn, not sent out in work gangs, not beaten or shot. This time, there was no selection on the ramp at the railroad station, no division of families, no separation of those who were fit to work from the old and the sick and the children. These 1,500 Jews from Sosnowiec were the first to be sent directly to the gas chamber, all of them. And with that, Auschwitz finally became what it had always been destined to become, not just a prisoner-of-war camp, not just a slave-labor camp, but a *Vernichtungslager,* an extermination camp. *Vernichtung* means more than that. It means to make something into nothing. Annihilation.

That summer of 1942, the trains to Auschwitz began bringing the Jews from France, Belgium and Holland. Also the Jews from Croatia. In November came the Jews of Norway. In March of 1943, when the great crematoria finally began operating, came the first of the Jews of Greece, from Macedonia and Thrace. That same spring, after the destruction of the rebellious Warsaw ghetto, the SS began the systematic liquidation of all the remaining Polish ghettos. Lwow was one of the first, then Byalystok. In September, the ghettos of Minsk and Vilna were destroyed. In October, Auschwitz received the Jews of southern France and Rome, in December the Jews of northern Italy, then, early in 1944, the Jews of Athens . . .

"What for Hitler . . . was among the war's main objectives . . . and what for Eichmann was a job. . . ," Hannah Arendt wrote in *Eichmann in Jerusalem,* "was for the Jews quite literally the end of the world."

Despite the annihilation of the 1,500 Jews from Sosnowiec, the selections on the ramp continued, for there was never a consistent policy on anything at Auschwitz, not even on killing. The basic orders from Berlin were completely contradictory. Eichmann and his cohorts at police headquarters, the RSHA, continually demanded more killings, but the SS administrative offices, the WVHA, demanded just as adamantly that the prisoners be made to work for the war effort. So the Auschwitz authorities carried out their orders, murdering or sparing their victims, by a strange mixture of bureaucracy and impulse. "We were all tormented by secret doubts," said Hoess, "[but] I myself dared not admit to such doubts. . . . Often at night, I would walk through the stables and seek relief among my beloved animals."

In the midst of all the killing, according to Ella Lingens, a Viennese doctor who was sent to Auschwitz in 1943 for helping Jews to escape from Austria, there remained one place that Dr. Lingens called an "island of peace," the Babice labor camp. "That was the work of one man alone," Dr. Lingens testified at the Frankfurt trial in 1964. His name was Flacke. "How he did it, I don't know. His camp was clean, and the food also. The women called him 'Daddy,' and he even got eggs from outside. . . . I don't know what happened to him. I once talked to him. 'You know, sir,' I said. 'Everything we do is so horrible, so pointless. Because when this war ends we'll all be murdered. No witnesses will be allowed to survive.' And Flacke answered, 'I hope there will be enough among us to prevent that.' "

The Frankfurt judge, who had heard endless protestations about irresistible orders from higher authorities, was amazed by Dr. Lingens' testimony. "Do you wish to say," he asked, "that everyone could decide for himself to be either good or evil in Auschwitz?"

"That is exactly what I wish to say," Dr. Lingens answered.

The Auschwitz hospital illustrates the central paradox. In theory, there was no reason why a death camp should have a hospital at all, and yet the one at Auschwitz grew to considerable size, with about sixty doctors and more than three hundred nurses. It had a surgical department and an operating theater, and special sections for infectious diseases, internal injuries and dentistry. Yet the lord of this domain was Dr. Mengele (now believed to be a fugitive in Paraguay), who labored long hours on testing and then killing captive twins in a futile effort to find new ways of increasing the German birth rate. Olga Lengyel, the wife of a Romanian psychiatrist, served as a prisoner-nurse in Auschwitz and recalled after the war that Mengele once insisted on personally delivering the baby of a pregnant prisoner. "I saw him take every precaution during the accouchement," she wrote, "watching to see that all aseptic principles were rigorously observed and that the umbilical cord was cut with care. Half an hour later he sent the mother and child to the crematory oven."

The hospital facilities for prisoners were extremely primitive at first, operated by the prisoners themselves and lacking even basic medicines, but the Nazis soon realized that the prisoners' diseases were a danger to their guardians as well. The worst of these was typhus, which invaded the camp with a shipment of prisoners from Lublin in April of 1941. The Nazis' favored remedy was to gas anyone who came to the hospital for treatment. The result was that stricken prisoners avoided the hospital, and so, by the summer of 1942, typhus had become epidemic, killing as many as three hundred prisoners a day. The SS authorities, feeling threatened themselves, could not decide what to do. They periodically wandered through the wards of the hospital, checking the patients' records and making their own diagnoses. Many of those whom they judged unfit were dragged off to the gas chambers. Others were subjected to a lethal injection of phenol, directly into the heart.

Yet although thousands were murdered in the Auschwitz hospital, thousands more were saved. It became, in fact, one of the camp's chief sanctuaries. Its staff, headed by a German homosexual criminal named Hans Bock, was infiltrated and even dominated by the Polish underground that had begun to organize resistance in Auschwitz. And just as the SS doctors had the right to murder anyone, they also had the right to forbid the Gestapo to seize their patients. "I know of almost no SS man who could not claim to have saved someone's life," Dr. Lingens testified in an attempt to explain the myriad contradictions of Auschwitz. "There were few sadists. Not more than five or ten percent were pathological criminals in the clinical sense. The others were all perfectly normal men who knew the difference between right and wrong. They all knew what was going on."

No less paradoxical was the system of justice at Auschwitz. In principle, there was no system except that of force, no rule that could not be broken. The SS men and the *Kapos* who served them could beat or torment or murder the prisoners for any reason they chose, or for no reason at all. And so it was up to the prisoners themselves to institute a crude form of justice, crude and inadequate, but nonetheless justice. Though much of camp life was based on the principle of survival, kangaroo courts met at night. A prisoner accused of stealing another prisoner's food could be sentenced to twenty-five lashes; an informer could be sentenced to death.

And then there appeared, in the middle of 1943, the implausible figure of Dr. Konrad Morgen, an SS judge assigned to investigate the corruption that infested the concentration camps. The incoming prisoners had been stripped of all their possessions—even their shorn hair was destined to make pillows—and everything of value was supposed to be sent to SS headquarters in Berlin. In actual fact, it was stored, piled up to the ceilings, in a row of thirty barracks known as "Canada,"* and Canada soon became the largest black market in Europe. Everything that accumulated there could be "organized," as the

---

* The Polish prisoners originally gave it this name because it evoked that land of legendary wealth to which many of their relatives had emigrated before the war.

Auschwitz slang called it, meaning stolen, sold, traded. Canada had everything, not just the basic supplies of food and clothing but diamonds, tapestries, silk underwear, the finest cognac. In the last days of Auschwitz, in January of 1945, the SS men who were evacuating the camp set Canada afire and burned all but six of its thirty barracks, but even in that charred ruin the Russians found an almost incredible quantity of things that had once belonged to the dead: 836,-255 women's outfits, 38,000 pairs of men's shoes, 13,964 carpets . . .

Judge Morgen, assigned to the absurd task of imposing law on the lawless SS, proved to be a fanatic about carrying out his mission. His first inquiries into corruption had been so diligent that his superiors had shipped him off to fight on the Russian front, but then other officials had maneuvered to bring him back. Morgen personally investigated the financial operations of Karl Koch, commandant at Buchenwald, and had Koch arrested, prosecuted and executed. What brought him to Auschwitz was an intercepted packet of gold that an SS man there had sent home to his wife. Morgen wandered into one of the crematoria and was startled to find half-drunk SS men lolling about in a lounge and being served potato pancakes by attractive female prisoners. "They were being waited on like pashas," he later testified at the Frankfurt trial. Although Morgen was supposed to limit himself to the question of corruption, he returned to Berlin and filed a murder charge against the chief Gestapo officer at Auschwitz, Lieutenant Maximilian Grabner. Such a move naturally amazed the police bureaucracy, but if an SS judge filed a murder charge, then the bureaucracy had to deal with it. Grabner was thereupon removed from his post at Auschwitz and brought back to Berlin for questioning about all the killings in Block 11, about the corruption in Canada, and even about the affair he was having with a woman prisoner. He was eventually sentenced to twelve years in prison (and later retried and executed by the Poles). Morgen survived everything and resumed the practice of law in postwar Germany.

"Do you wish to say that everyone could decide for himself whether to be good or evil in Auschwitz?"

"That is exactly what I wish to say."

SS Sergeant Josef Schillinger was a short, stocky man with light-blond hair and bright-blue eyes. A stern disciplinarian, he liked to make surprise inspections and to punish the prisoners for the slightest infraction of camp rules. He liked to stand at the entrance to the gas chambers and watch as the prisoners filed in. He also liked to appear at the railroad ramp and watch the arriving prisoners being divided, assigned to the work gangs or to the gas chambers.

On October 23, 1943, Sergeant Schillinger was marching up and down this ramp, pistol in hand, when he spotted an attractive Jewish woman who had just arrived in one of the cattle cars. When she saw that he was watching her, she provocatively returned his look. Sergeant Schillinger reached out and seized her by the arm. The woman twisted away, reached down and threw a handful of gravel into his face. Schillinger raised his arms to protect himself, and that made him drop his pistol. The woman pounced on it. Then she shot Sergeant Schillinger in the abdomen, several times. Other SS men soon tore the gun away from her and clubbed her onto the truck bound for the gas chamber.

Sergeant Schillinger lay face down on the ramp, dying, his fingers clawing in the gravel. *"O Gott, mein Gott,"* he groaned, *"was hab' ich getan, das ich so leiden muss?"* Which means "Oh God, my God, what have I done that I must suffer so?"

"That," said Dr. Lingens, *"is exactly what I wish to say."*

*

This Auschwitz that arose out of the swamps and wastelands on the Vistula ultimately grew to a prison empire of nearly 150,000 inhabitants. Out of nothing, Hoess built a city comparable in size to Tangier or Aberdeen or Cedar Rapids, Iowa. But its importance was that it represented a microcosm of Nazi Europe, and thus a microcosm of what twentieth-century Europe itself had become. The civilized world that had once been ruled from Rome was now ruled from Berlin, and the principles of that Nazi civilization were the governing principles of Auschwitz.

These principles sometimes seemed to involve nothing more than the ceaseless conflict between the lust for destruction and the lust for survival, and yet Auschwitz was a society of extraordinary complexity. It had its own soccer stadium, its own library, its own photographic lab, and its own symphony orchestra. It had its own Polish nationalist underground and its own Polish Communist underground—not to mention separate Russian, Slovakian, French and Austrian resistance groups—whose members fought and sometimes killed one another. It also had its underground religious services, Catholic, Protestant and Jewish alike. Auschwitz even had its own brothel, known as "the puff," which favored prisoners could enter by earning chits for good behavior. Crafty veterans of the camp would gather at the office where the chits were handed out, and if any model prisoner failed to claim his due, one of the old-timers would quickly step forward to claim it for him.

"Concentration-camp existence . . . taught us that the whole world is really like a concentration camp," wrote Tadeusz Borowski. "The weak work for the strong, and if they have no strength or will to work—then let them steal, or let them die. . . . There is no crime that a man will not commit in order to save himself. And, having saved himself, he will commit crimes for increasingly trivial reasons; he will commit them first out of duty, then from habit, and finally—for pleasure. . . . The world is ruled by neither justice nor morality; crime is not punished nor virtue rewarded, one is forgotten as quickly as the other. The world is ruled by power. . . ."

The Nazis had established that doctrine when they first rounded up the Jews of the occupied territories into a series of ghettos, but even when the victims huddled in their new captivity, they could still hope for some kind of reprieve. "The barbed wire which fenced us in did not cause us any real fear," Elie Wiesel wrote of his native town in *Night*. "We even thought ourselves rather well off; we were entirely self-contained. A little Jewish republic." For every warning of impending deportations, there was some rumor of explanation. Why would the Germans waste military resources in deporting people to the east? Besides, how long could the war last? When the deportation orders finally

came, the victims yearned to believe the official announcements about resettlement colonies in the east. "The women were cooking eggs," Wiesel wrote of the
last day before the departure to Auschwitz, "roasting meat, baking cakes and
making knapsacks. The children wandered all over . . ."

The trip to Auschwitz served as a kind of initiation. The Nazis crowded the
victims into freight cars, usually about one hundred people to each car, and
then locked them in. There was no food or water, no toilet, no air. Those who
had brought a few sandwiches or pieces of fruit soon found themselves fighting
to defend their treasures. When their supplies were gone, there was nothing.
Children cried endlessly. The old weakened and died. Corpses lay where they
fell, among the battered suitcases held together with rope.

The freight cars came from as far as Bordeaux and Rome and Salonika, voyages of a week or more, stifling in summer, arctic in winter. Sometimes the
trains were shunted onto sidings for days on end, nights on end. The prisoners'
cries for water went unheeded. When they banged their fists on the doors, their
guards usually ignored them. Occasionally, they answered by banging the out-
sides of the doors with their gun butts. Sometimes, by the time the sealed trains
finally reached southern Poland, the dead outnumbered the living. (The trip
from Corfu took twenty-seven days, and when the train came to a stop, no survivors emerged at all.) To arrive at the unknown town of Auschwitz, then,
seemed a kind of liberation.

"A huge, multicolored wave of people loaded down with luggage pours from
the train," Borowski continued his description of the scene on the ramp, "like a
blind, mad river trying to find a new bed. But before they have a chance to recover, before they can draw a breath of fresh air and look at the sky, bundles
are snatched from their hands, coats ripped off their backs, their purses and
umbrellas taken away. . . . *"Verboten!"* one of us barks through clenched teeth.
There is an SS man standing behind your back, calm, efficient, watchful. Meine
Herrschaften, this way, ladies and gentlemen, try not to throw your things
around, please. . . ."

Such courtliness occasionally suited the SS sense of humor, but the Nazis
had whips and used them freely. The arrival on the ramp was usually a chaos
of screams and shouts, barking guard dogs, pandemonium. The *Begrüssung*
(welcome), the Nazis called it. When the train was emptied, a thin, pock-
marked SS man ordered Borowski and his fellow prisoners to clean out the debris. "In the corners," Borowski wrote, "amid human excrement and abandoned wristwatches, lie squashed, trampled infants, naked little monsters with
enormous heads and bloated bellies."

Once the prisoners were assembled on the ramp, the two SS doctors made
their selection, a wave here, a gesture there. While those on the right remained
standing on the ramp, the rest, including most of the women and children, were
pushed onto trucks and driven off. One of the trucks was reassuringly marked
with a large red cross. That was the one that carried the sealed canisters of
Zyklon B. When the newcomers arrived at their destination, officially known as
Bunker No. 1, they saw two neat little farmhouses, with thatched roofs and
whitewashed walls, surrounded by fruit trees and shrubbery. Teams of

Jewish prisoners who had been assigned to the *Sonderkommando*, or special command, shepherded the victims onward, urging them to move along quietly into the shower rooms and to take off all their clothes. Some of them may have guessed what lay ahead. Most of them, in a state of terror, shock and exhaustion, simply did as they were told. They had heard that terrible things would happen to them in the resettlement camps of the east, but so many terrible things had already happened in the railroad cars and on the ramp that they found it hard to imagine anything worse to come. Few of them noticed, as they crowded naked in the shower room, that although there were water pipes and sprays along the ceiling, there were no water drains in the floor.

Here, and later in the four new crematoria at Birkenau, the Final Solution took place. What happened can best be described in the detached tones of Rudolf Hoess, who was in command of all this: "The door would now be quickly screwed up and the gas discharged by the waiting disinfectors through vents in the ceilings of the gas chambers, down a shaft that led to the floor. This insured the rapid distribution of the gas. It could be observed through the peephole in the door that those who were standing nearest to the induction vents were killed at once. It can be said that about one third died straightaway. The remainder staggered about and began to scream and struggle for air. The screaming, however, soon changed to the death rattle and in a few minutes all lay still. . . . The door was opened half an hour after the induction of the gas, and the ventilation switched on. . . . The special detachment now set about removing the gold teeth and cutting the hair from the women. After this, the bodies were taken up by elevator and laid in front of the ovens, which had meanwhile been stoked up. Depending on the size of the bodies, up to three corpses could be put into one oven at the same time. The time required for cremation . . . took twenty minutes."

There were some prisoners who cherished the idea that Hoess had somehow exceeded his orders and begun these massacres on his own authority, and that if the authorities in Berlin knew what was really happening, they would stop it. Such speculations ended with Heinrich Himmler's second visit to Auschwitz in July of 1942. He stayed for two days and inspected everything. He started, according to Hoess' account, with the more benign parts of the camp, "the agricultural areas, the building of the dam, the laboratories and plant-breeding establishments, . . . the stock-breeding centers and the tree nurseries." Then he "watched the whole process of destruction of a transport of Jews, which had just arrived." He started by watching the selections on the railroad ramp, then watched the victims being taken to the gas chambers, then watched them die. He could smell the awful smell of burning flesh, which lingered in the air after the cremations. "He made no remark regarding the process of extermination," Hoess recalled, "but remained quite silent."

Hoess repeatedly complained of his difficulties, pointing out the overcrowding and the shortages, the emaciation and illness among the prisoners. "I want to hear no more about difficulties," Himmler finally snapped at him. "An SS officer does not recognize difficulties." That evening, the Reichsführer SS was "extremely amiable" at a dinner for his officers and their wives. "He discussed the education of children and new buildings and books and pictures," Hoess reported. The next night, shortly before departing, Himmler told Hoess, "I have seen your work and the results you have achieved, and I am satisfied and thank you for your services."

The following January, 1943, Himmler paid a third visit to inspect the progress of the Final Solution. He arrived at Auschwitz at 8 A.M., and by 8:45 one of the gas chambers was packed with victims so that the Reichsführer SS could watch a gassing at 9 o'clock sharp. At 8:55, however, a telephone rang, and the executioners learned that Himmler and Hoess were still having breakfast. "Inside the chamber itself," according to the recollections of a Czech prisoner named Rudolf Vrba, "frantic men and women, who knew by that time what a shower in Auschwitz meant, began shouting, screaming, and pounding weakly on the door . . ." Nobody paid any attention. The SS men waited for orders. At 10 A.M., they were told to wait some more. At 11 A.M., an official car finally arrived, bringing Himmler and Hoess, who paused to chat with the senior officers present. Hoess invited Himmler to observe through a peephole the naked mass sealed inside the gas chamber. Himmler obliged. Then the gassing began. "Hoess courteously invited his guest to have another peep through the observation window," Vrba recalled. "For some minutes, Himmler peered into the death chamber, obviously impressed. . . . What he had seen seemed to have satisfied him and put him in good humor. Though he rarely smoked, he accepted a cigarette from an officer, and, as he puffed at it rather clumsily, he laughed and joked."

Those happy few who survived the selections on the ramp were marched off to the quarantine barracks, where they were initiated into a series of rituals designed to destroy their identity and their personality and thus their capacity for resistance. First they were taken to the yard between Blocks 15 and 16 and ordered to strip off all their clothes. All their hair was shaved off. Then they had to run to a nearby bathhouse and take a cold shower. Then they had to run to another yard where they were provided with ill-fitting blue-and-white striped prison uniforms and wooden clogs. Their uniforms bore triangles of different colors, according to the categories of prisoners—green for professional criminals, red for political opposition, black for prostitutes and other "asocials," pink for homosexuals, purple for fundamentalist "exponents of the Bible." (Jews who fitted any of these categories had their yellow triangle superimposed on the other triangle to form a Star of David.) Finally, the prisoners were tattooed on the left forearm with their prison number. Henceforth, they were told, they were to be known only by this number, not by name. This whole procedure normally took all day, but if the prisoners had arrived in the afternoon, it took all night. Throughout it, they were given no food or water.

Just as the arrival in Auschwitz seemed a relief after days in the crowded freight cars, the arrival in the quarantine barracks seemed a relief after the process of selection and registration. It was, however, a new kind of ordeal, designed to test whether the SS doctors on the ramp had been correct in their

choice of survivors. Roll call was at 4:30 A.M., and sometimes the prisoners had
to stand there all day long. They were drilled in camp routine, trained to form
ranks of five and to take off their caps on command, to perform such drudgery
as digging ditches and moving rocks, and to take part in "physical training."
This physical training, also known as "sport," consisted of running in position
until a *Kapo* ordered the prisoners to drop to the ground and start hopping like
frogs, until a *Kapo* ordered the prisoners to get up and start running again.
"Sport" is a fairly common form of gymnastic drill, but the Auschwitz version
lasted for hours, and anyone who faltered was kicked and beaten. After a fif-
teen-minute break for lunch, the SS training continued with, for example,
singing classes. Jews were taught to chorus an anti-Semitic song called "O Du
mein Jerusalem"; prisoners of all kinds were taught a song in praise of their
own imprisonment, "Im Lager Auschwitz war Ich zwar so manchen Monaten
... In Camp Auschwitz I have spent so many months ..." At 3 P.M., the
"sport" resumed, until 6:30. Then came another roll call, sometimes two hours
long. Those who failed to satisfy their guards had to stand at attention all night
long. Lagerführer Fritzsch, the man who had first tried out Zyklon B on the
Russian prisoners, liked to tell the newcomers, "You have come to a concentration camp, not to a sanatorium, and there is only one way out—through the
chimney. Anyone who does not like it can try hanging himself on the wires.* If
there are Jews in this draft, they have no right to live longer than a fortnight; if
there are priests, their period is one month—the rest, three months."

After four to eight weeks in quarantine, the prisoners came to believe that
life might be better if they could only reach the main camp. Once again, they
were deluded. Auschwitz was designed, just as Fritzsch warned, to work its
victims to death. More than one thousand prisoners were herded into brick
barracks built for four hundred. They slept in three-tiered wooden bunks, half
a dozen men to a bunk, often with no mattresses or blankets. There was little
heat and less ventilation. The place stank. The prisoners' only consolation was
that Birkenau was even worse. Instead of overcrowded brick barracks, there
were overcrowded wooden huts, with leaking roofs and dirt floors that turned
to mud. Auschwitz had yellowish running water and a primitive sewage system; Birkenau had only a few privies. At least half of the prisoners—and often
two thirds or more—suffered the miseries and humiliations of chronic diarrhea.
At night, the only facilities were a few overflowing buckets. And the rats were
everywhere. When a prisoner died during the night, according to a prisoner
named Judith Sternberg Newman, the rats "would get at the body before it was
cold, and eat the flesh in such a way that it was unrecognizable before
morning."

In both camps, the first ordeal of the day was, as always, the *Appell*, or roll
call, which began at about 4:30 A.M., somewhat before dawn, rain or shine, or
frost or snow. Everyone had to stand in line, in rows of five, while the counting

---

* An Auschwitz slang phrase that described the most easily available form of suicide. Anyone who ran toward the electrified wire fence that surrounded the camp was instantly fired on
by SS men in the watch towers. If he succeeded in reaching the wire fence, he was immediately electrocuted by 6,000 volts.

began. No exceptions or excuses were permitted. The sick were dragged from their bunks to take part. Even those who had died during the night were carried out and propped up in position so that they could be counted. As the dawn brightened, the *Kapos* sauntered up and down the ranks of the prisoners, counting, and hitting anyone they felt like hitting. Sometimes they insisted that the shortest prisoners fill the ranks at the front; sometimes the positions were reversed, with the shortest prisoners in the back. Anyone who didn't move quickly enough was clubbed. And there were always the dogs, snarling and straining at their leashes. At any interruption or disturbance, any break or error in the counting, the process began all over again. The roll call generally lasted three or four hours—punitive roll-calls lasted much longer—and only at about eight o'clock did the SS officers arrive to review the roll-call numbers and send the prisoners out to work.

Arbeit macht frei. The prisoners marched off to the booming accompaniment of the Auschwitz band, but without food, or only with the food they had saved from the previous night's ration, or bought or bartered or stolen during the night. Officially, the prisoners were given just enough food to survive. The rations provided for a breakfast of one-half liter of grain coffee or herb tea. The main meal at noon theoretically consisted of one liter of meat soup four times a week and vegetable soup three times a week. The ingredients were carefully listed in the regulations: The meat soup was supposed to contain 150 grams of potatoes, 150 grams of cabbage, kale or beetroot, 20 grams of meat. At night, the ration was 350 grams of black bread, sometimes with a sliver of margarine or a dab of beet-sugar jam. In fact, the prisoners never got more than a fraction of their rations. The authorities who bought the supplies regularly saved money by acquiring rotten meat and spoiled vegetables. The guards and the cooks took the best share for themselves, to eat or to trade. What the prisoners actually received was a bread made partly of sawdust and a soup made of thistles, or worse. Sometimes, according to Olga Lengyel, it was simply called "surprise soup" because it contained such unexpected ingredients as buttons, keys, tufts of hair, dead mice and, on one occasion, a small metal sewing kit complete with needles and thread.

Awful as the food was, the prisoners fought over their shares, and even over the crude bowls from which to eat. Among the 1,500 women in Mrs. Lengyel's barracks, the Nazis distributed just twenty bowls, each containing about two liters, and one pail. "The barracks chief ... immediately commandeered the pail as a chamber pot," Mrs. Lengyel recalled. "Her cronies quickly snatched the other bowls for the same use. What could the rest of us do? It seemed as though the Germans constantly sought to pit us against each other, to make us competitive, spiteful, and hateful. In the morning, we had to be content with rinsing the bowls as well as we could before we put in our minute rations. . . . The first days our stomachs rose at the thought of what were actually chamber pots at night. But hunger drives, and we were so starved that we were ready to eat any food. . . ."

An average man needs about 4,800 calories per day to perform heavy labor, about 3,600 calories for ordinary work. The average Auschwitz prisoner, by official postwar estimates that remain very uncertain, received about 1,500. Many often got no more than half that amount. Apart from calories, of course, there were gross shortages of vitamins and minerals. Scurvy and skin diseases soon became commonplace. Starving children suffered strange afflictions like noma, a gangrenous ulceration that creates gaping holes through the cheek. "I saw diseases which you find only in textbooks," Dr. Lingens testified at the Frankfurt trial. "I never thought I'd see any of them—for example, phemphicus, a very rare disease, in which large areas of the skin become detached and the patient dies within a few days."

The basic effect of starvation, though, is simply emaciation and exhaustion. The body feeds on itself, first on the fat and then on the muscles, which become soft and waste away. "The face looked like a mask," Nutrition Professor J. Olbrycht testified on the condition of these prisoners at Hoess' trial in Cracow, "with a faraway look in the eyes and the pupils unnaturally enlarged. There was apathy and sleepiness, the slowing down and weakening of all life processes." The Auschwitz prisoners easily recognized these marks of coming death, and with the stinging acerbity of the death camps, they likened the numbed victims to the starving beggars of India and named them *Musselmänner,* or Moslems. "Such sick people saw and heard badly," Dr. Olbrycht's testimony continued, "perception, thinking, and all reactions were slowed down, . . . hence, also, lethargy in carrying out instructions, wrongly interpreted as evidence of passive resistance." What Dr. Olbrycht meant was that the starving "Moslems" couldn't carrry out or even understand the orders barked at them by their guardians, and so they were frequently punished for insubordination and beaten to death.

As a self-contained universe, Auschwitz required and provided work of every sort. The camp had its own bakery and its own tannery and its own tinsmithy. Most of the work, however, was simply brute labor, devoted to the constant expansions of the camp for the constant acquisition of new prisoners. One huge earth-rolling machine required sixty prisoners to haul it along for the building of new roadbeds, and when all the horses at the Babice farm were requisitioned by the military in the spring of 1944, teams of women prisoners were harnessed like animals to the plows. The building went on unremittingly until the very end; a new set of barracks known as "Mexico" was still under construction when the SS dynamited the camp and departed. "We work beneath the earth and above it," Borowski wrote, "under a roof and in the rain, with the spade, the pickax and the crowbar. We carry huge sacks of cement, lay bricks, put down rails, spread gravel, trample the earth . . . We are laying the foundation for some new, monstrous civilization. Only now do I realize what price was paid for building ancient civilizations. . . . How much blood must have poured onto the Roman roads, the bulwarks, and the city walls. Antiquity—the tremendous concentration camp where the slave was branded on the forehead by his master, and crucified for trying to escape . . . ! Roman law! Yes, today too there is a law!"

Under the New Order, as in the slave states of the past, such labor could be sold. Many prominent German corporations—among them Krupp, Siemens and Bayer—were interested in what might be negotiated. Auschwitz began developing a network of outlying subcamps, thirty-four in all. The prisoners worked at a cement plant in Goleszow, a coal mine in Wesola, a steel factory in Gliwice, a shoe factory in Chelmek. In the subcamp called Tschechowitz I, the prisoners' main occupation was to remove the fuses from bombs that had failed to explode during Allied air raids. Working conditions in all these places were unbearable. "For interminable days on end, I pushed coal-laden carts up those long, dimly lit corridors, beaten like a donkey en route," a French boxer named Sim Kessel recalled of the coal mines at Jaworzno. The prisoners' only breakfast was a bowl of hot water, divided among four men, before the descent into the sweltering mines. "In the intense heat of those galleries, our raging thirst often drove us to drink our own urine," Kessel said. "We all did. We would urinate into our cupped hands and then drink it. . . ."

The biggest of these Auschwitz subcamps was the I. G. Farben plant first started at Dwory and then headquartered in Monowitz. The plant was known as Buna because its principal purpose was to produce synthetic rubber; its other main installation was a hydrogenation plant designed to convert coal into oil at a rate of nearly 800,000 tons a month. The Farben directors were so impressed with the possibilities of their Auschwitz factories—particularly when they contemplated the victorious end of the war and the whole East European market lying open before them—that they insisted on turning aside all government grants and financing the Auschwitz plants themselves. They committed 900 million marks (about $225 million) to the project, which made the Auschwitz factories the largest in the Farben empire. The SS agreed to provide all necessary labor, for a modest fee. It charged Farben four marks ($1) per day for each skilled worker, three marks for each unskilled one. Later in the war, the SS agreed to provide child laborers for one and a half marks.

Conditions at Monowitz were much like those at Auschwitz—the dawn roll calls, the starvation rations, the labor gangs sent out for twelve hours at a time, forced to work at the double, beaten by guards, harried by giant dogs. The prisoners who died of overwork—dozens of them every day—had to be hauled back to camp at nightfall so that they could be propped up and counted at the next morning's roll call. About 25,000 people, ultimately, were killed in the construction of the I. G. Farben plant at Monowitz. One of the enduring mysteries of Auschwitz is that this plant, built at such cost and such suffering, never actually produced one ounce of synthetic rubber.*

Of the three or four marks paid daily to the SS for a prisoner's labor, the prisoner, of course, never received a pfennig. The stripped and plundered Auschwitz prisoners were not allowed to own anything. And so, inevitably, the desire to possess things became a passion exceeded only by the desire to eat and the desire to be safe. "I badly needed a waistband to hold up my drawers," Olga Lengyel later recalled. "At the garbage dump, by a wonderful stroke of

---

* One section of the Monowitz plant did start producing four truckloads per day of synthetic gasoline early in 1944, but the facility was knocked out by a U.S. air raid that summer. The damage was repaired in a month. A second air raid soon after that halted production permanently.

luck, I found three fragments of twine which could be pieced together for the purpose. I also found a flat piece of wood, which I could sharpen into a knife. . . . These new acquisitions filled me with pride. I felt that I had become a rich woman in the camp."

From the instinct to possess comes the instinct to trade, and so there arose the vast black market around "Canada," with its canned hams, its carpets, its stamp collections, perfumes and antique clocks. Since the SS men were corrupt, and the *Kapo*s were corrupt, and the prisoners who had survived would do almost anything to go on surviving, everything was for sale. Even the gold bars melted down from the teeth of the victims of the crematoria, supposedly destined for the national bank in Berlin, often ended on the black market. But the chief black-market areas were the latrines and the garbage dump, where prisoners bargained over pieces of stale bread.

"The Market is always very active," wrote Primo Levi, an Italian lawyer who arrived in bewilderment at this northern hell. "Although every exchange (in fact, every form of possession) is explicitly forbidden . . . , the northeast corner of the *Lager* . . . is permanently occupied by a tumultuous throng, in the open during the summer, in a washroom during the winter, as soon as the squads return from work. Here scores of prisoners driven desperate by hunger prowl around, with lips half open and eyes gleaming . . ." Olga Lengyel has even preserved some of the prices quoted in the latrines of Auschwitz: A kilo of margarine was worth 250 gold marks, or about $100. One kilo of butter: 500 marks. One kilo of meat: 1,000 marks. A cigarette cost seven marks, but the price of a single puff could be negotiated. So could the price of sex. Officially, none was permitted; unofficially, life continued. Primo Levi watched closely the fluctuations of supply and demand. "While there is a virtually stable price for soup (half a ration of bread for two pints)," he wrote, "the quotations for turnips, carrots, potatoes are extremely variable and depend greatly, among other factors, on the diligence and corruptibility of the guards at the stores."

Since the official rations, reduced by SS thievery, condemned every prisoner to eventual death by starvation, survival depended on a prisoner's ability to "organize" extra supplies for himself and to find himself a sanctuary in the hospital or the kitchens or in some other relatively protected quarter. Assignment to the coal mines at Jaworzno meant almost certain death; assignment to some administrative office meant at least the possibility of survival. "No prisoner who came to Auschwitz before the summer of 1944 survived unless he held a special job," Dr. Lingens testified.

Out of this struggle for survival, therefore, emerged a prison hierarchy, a hierarchy in which men who lived on the brink of death managed to edge away from that brink by edging past other prisoners.

The hierarchy expressed itself in symbols, all designed to contradict the symbolism of the SS. Just as the SS degraded the prisoners by ordering them to wear shapeless rags, the most resilient and imaginative prisoners fought back by commissioning captive tailors to dress them in the most beautifully fitted prison costumes. Among the women, similarly, prestige attended anyone whose shaved skull began to grow hair again, or who appeared at work in a handsome skirt. All these self-assertions were forbidden, of course, and therefore anyone who appeared in full-grown hair or attractive clothing was assumed to be under someone's protection, a member of the hierarchy. Fania Fénelon, a French girl who played in the women's orchestra at Birkenau, has described an extraordinary night on which the prostitutes who dominated the prisoner hierarchy in the women's camp gave a big party for themselves. They hired the whole orchestra to play dance music in exchange for leftover sausages and sauerkraut. Some of the women, Mademoiselle Fénelon recalled, had arrayed themselves in their Berlin street finery, black lace underwear and transparent blouses, while others had dressed up as men, sporting silk pajamas. Then they danced and drank and pawed at each other. "Everywhere women were hugging, kissing and caressing," she wrote, "lying flat out on tables, sliding to the floor . . ." The night of these festivities was the night on which the SS suddenly liquidated the gypsy compound.

The hierarchy extended from such privileged prisoners upward through the bellicose block seniors and barracks overseers and on to the mighty *Kapos*, who had once been, most of them, common criminals. "These *Kapos* . . . were the aristocrats of the camps," recalled one Auschwitz prisoner, Rudolf Vrba. "They had their own rooms in each barracks, and there they entertained their friends to splendid meals. They cooked steaks and chips on their stoves, while the smell wafted through thin partitions to starving prisoners, and they washed it down occasionally with slivovitz stolen from victims of the gas chambers."

The *Kapos* were never safe, however, from the ferocity of the SS. If any of them faltered, he could be instantly reduced to the ranks of common prisoners, and he knew very well what revenge awaited him in the barracks at night. ("We . . . dragged him onto the cement floor under the stove," Borowski wrote of one such retribution, "where the entire block, grunting and growling, trampled him to death.") In the eyes of the Nazis, the *Kapos* who strutted about with their clubs remained no more than criminals, useful in performing the disciplinary chores in whatever way best suited the camp's reigning aristocracy, the SS.

The SS was the self-proclaimed elite not only of Auschwitz but of Nazi Germany and thus all Europe. Founded in 1925 as a kind of bodyguard for Hitler, the SS had only 280 members when Himmler took it over in 1929. He emphasized its supposedly privileged status, its preference for blond and blue-eyed recruits, its exotic black uniforms. "I swear to you, Adolf Hitler, loyalty and valor," each of the SS men vowed. "I pledge to you . . . obedience unto death, so help me God." Himmler took charge of the concentration camps almost from the beginning, and by the time the war began he had created a private army of 250,000 men, including more than a few of the petty criminals he professed to despise. The SS forces at Auschwitz were never large—about 3,000 men to oversee a prison camp of nearly 150,000—but their immaculate uniforms, their guns and whips, and their guard dogs, gave them an aura of invincibility.

To the SS men themselves, duty at Auschwitz was chiefly an unpleasant assignment that kept them from the far more unpleasant prospect of combat on the Russian front. In the east, one could get killed; at Auschwitz, one got extra rations for taking part in one of the gassings known as "special actions"—one fifth of a liter of vodka, five cigarettes, one hundred grams of sausage. At more elevated levels of the SS hierarchy, the rewards were even more generous. Dr. Johann Paul Kremer, a professor of anatomy in the onetime Anabaptist strong-hold of Münster, kept a diary of his service in Poland in the fall of 1942, devot-ing only a few sentences to his role in the "special actions" but savoring the good life at Auschwitz, particularly the good food served at the Waffen SS club. Thus: "September 6, 1942: Today an excellent Sunday dinner: tomato soup, one half of chicken with potatoes and red cabbage, and magnificent va-nilla ice cream. . . . September 17: Have ordered a casual coat from Berlin. . . . September 20: This Sunday afternoon I listened from 3 P.M. till 6 P.M. to a con-cert of the prisoners' band in glorious sunshine; the bandmaster was a conduc-tor of the State Opera from Warsaw. Eighty musicians. Roast pork for din-ner. . . . September 23: . . . a truly festive meal. We had baked pike, as much of it as we wanted, real coffee, excellent beer and sandwiches. . . . September 27: This Sunday afternoon, from 4 till 8, a party in the club with supper, free beer and cigarettes. Speech of Commandant Hoess and a musical and theatrical program. . . . October 11: For dinner roast hare, a whole fat haunch, with dumplings and red cabbage. . . . October 31: Very beautiful autumn weather for the last fourteen days, so that every day one has the opportunity of sun-bathing in the garden of the Waffen SS clubhouse. . . . November 8: . . . we had Bulgarian red wine and plum brandy from Croatia. . . . November 14: Today, Saturday, a variety theater performance in the mess room (quite grand!). The dancing dogs excited great enthusiasm and so did the bantam cocks which crowed in unison. . . ."

The isolation of the SS men, who lived above and beyond all the rules of sur-vival that governed the starving prisoners, enabled them to act on whim, to de-cide questions of life and death on impulse. Thus the strange salvation of Sim Kessel, the French boxer, who had been selected for the gas chambers. "Now we were ordered to take off our clothes and lay them neatly folded along the wall," Kessel later recalled. "We did so. There we skeletons stood barefoot in the snow . . ." A detachment of SS men roared up on motorcycles, simply to oversee the shipment of these walking corpses to the gas chambers. The naked prisoners stood in the snow and waited. Then Kessel noticed that one of the SS men, a noncom, had a broken nose, and ridges of scar tissue over the eyes, and all the other marks of the ring. "I hesitated for a second and then thought, Oh, what the hell! Naked and shivering, I walked up to him [and] simply blurted out in German, 'Boxer?'

" ' Boxer? Ja!'

"He didn't wait for me to explain, he understood. I too had a broken nose." The SS man asked Kessel where he had fought, and Kessel named a series of second-rate places, Pacra, Central, Delbor, Japy. The SS man gave a quick smile of recognition, then ordered Kessel to climb aboard his motorcycle so that he could drive him to the sanctuary of the hospital. "It must have been a weird and unforgettable sight," Kessel observed, "the pathetic nude prisoner riding behind an SS on the back seat of a motorcycle, running right through the center of Auschwitz. . . . I never saw him again."

This same whimsical turn of fate, once the SS had decided to break all its own rules, touched an Austrian leftist named Rudolf Friemel, who had fought in the defense of Madrid, then escaped to France, then been arrested and eventually shipped to Auschwitz. While in France, he had become involved with a French woman named Margarita Ferrer Rey, who had borne him a son, and who now demanded that he marry her. Her demand somehow penetrated the machinery of the Nazi state and floated upward to the highest levels, perhaps to Himmler, perhaps to Hitler himself. From the highest levels, the order came down, decreeing that Mademoiselle Rey and her son should be taken to the "labor camp" at Auschwitz so that she could be married and her son legitimized. Such sponsorship inspired the Auschwitz authorities to the most elaborate preparations. Friemel was stripped of his prison rags and outfitted with a new suit that had been specially ironed by the *Kapo* in the laundry room. He was even issued a necktie and matching socks. Somewhere a priest was found to marry the Austrian and his bride. Then they had their matrimonial picture taken by a technician from the Auschwitz photo lab, she with a bouquet of hyacinths in her arms. A group of musicians from the Auschwitz orchestra played appropriate tunes. The newlyweds then went to the camp brothel, which had been emptied of its regular inhabitants in honor of the wedding night. The next day, the Frenchwoman and her son were shipped back to France, and the Austrian was put back into his prison uniform and returned to his work gang.

At the top of the hierarchy, of course, was the camp commandant, who lived with his wife, Hedwig, and their five children in a tree-shaded stucco house known as Villa Hoess. It stood just outside the northeastern corner of the camp, separated from the neighboring barracks by a concrete wall high enough so that nothing inside the camp could actually be seen by Hoess' family. Near the wall, Frau Hoess grew rose hedges, and begonias in blue flowerboxes. "My wife's garden was a paradise of flowers . . . ," the commandant recalled. "No former prisoner can ever say that he was in any way or at any time badly treated in our house. My wife's greatest pleasure would have been to give a present to every prisoner who was in any way connected with our household. The children were perpetually begging me for cigarettes for the prisoners. . . . The children always kept animals in the garden, creatures the prisoners were forever bringing them. Tortoises, martens, cats, lizards . . . Their greatest joy was when Daddy bathed with them [in the swimming pool]. He had, however, so little time for all these childish pleasures . . ."

The image of the Villa Hoess as a plantation tended by devoted prisoners is about as accurate as Hoess' image of himself as a sternly incorruptible soldier. Stanislaw Dubiel, who somehow managed to remain a gardener to the rulers of Auschwitz from 1940 to 1945, testified that the Hoesses limited themselves neither to their rations nor to their incomes but rather extorted everything they wanted from the SS hierarchy. "I took from the [prisoners' food] magazine for the Hoess household: sugar, flour, margarine, various baking powders, condiments for soup, macaroni, oat flakes, cocoa, cinnamon, cream of wheat, peas and other foodstuffs. Frau Hoess never had enough of them. . . . I also supplied the Hoess kitchen with meat from the butcher's, and always with milk. . . . Frau Hoess would very often also demand cream. . . . Hoess never paid for the provisions taken from the prisoners' food store, or from the camp butcher's. . . . The equipment and furnishings of the Hoess home were of similar origin. Everything was made by prisoners from camp materials. The rooms were furnished with the most magnificent furniture, the desk drawers were covered with leather. . . . Two Jewish dressmakers were employed in the Hoess home [to make] dresses for Frau Hoess and her daughters. . . . Hoess settled down in such a well-appointed and magnificent home that his wife remarked, '*Hier will ich leben und sterben* (I want to live here till I die).' "

Hoess' self-portrait as a devoted paterfamilias is also somewhat exaggerated. He had an affair with an Italian prisoner named Eleonore Hodys, who worked for several months in the Villa Hoess. He tried then to get rid of her by assigning her to the penal company, in which death within a few weeks by overwork and mistreatment was taken for granted. Then she was mysteriously transferred to the stifling dungeons of Block 11. There Hoess secretly visited her. There she became pregnant. When Hoess heard of her pregnancy, he ordered her gassed. "Into the chimney with her," he commanded, according to a witness at the Frankfurt trial. But the chief of Block 11, Max Grabner, who was already being investigated for having an affair with a prisoner, became interested in Eleonore Hodys and informed on Hoess to that same SS Judge Morgen who was pursuing the Grabner case. Morgen apparently rescued Eleonore Hodys from Auschwitz and sent her to Munich, though the SS killed her toward the end of the war.

But Hoess' children, to whom the servile prisoners brought presents, understood their father and the world he ruled. A French prisoner named Charlotte Delbo caught a glimpse of that understanding and recorded a matchless image of the commandant's sons at play. She saw two boys, aged about eleven and seven, both blond and blue-eyed. The older one had a sword in his belt, and he screwed an imaginary monocle into his eye as he ordered the younger one, who represented all the prisoners in the camp, to march faster and faster. "Soon the prisoners to whom these orders are addressed can no longer follow. They stumble on the ground, lose their footing. Their commandant is pale with rage. With his switch, he strikes, strikes, strikes. He screams in rage, '*Schnell! Schneller!*' . . . The little boy staggers, spins around, and falls flat on the grass. The commandant looks at the prisoner that he has knocked to the ground with contempt, saliva on his lips. And his fury subsides. He feels only disgust. He kicks him—a fake kick, he is barefoot and he's just playing. But the little boy knows the game. The kick turns him over like a limp bag. He lies there, mouth open, eyes glazed over. Then the big boy, with a sign of the stick to the invisible prisoners that surround him, commands, '*Zum Krematorium,*' and moves on. Stiff, satisfied, and disgusted."

✳

In theory, there were no children in Auschwitz. All of them were supposed to be singled out on the railroad ramp, judged unfit for hard labor, and sent directly to the gas chambers. Some survived that process, for various reasons, but eventually the process caught them.

Dunja Wasserstrom, a Russian woman who ended as a language teacher in Mexico, testified at the Frankfurt trial about one such case. As a prisoner, she had the misfortune to work for Friedrich Wilhelm Boger, Grabner's deputy in the Auschwitz Gestapo, who made her watch while he interrogated suspects on a whirling contraption known as "the Boger swing." One day, there was an interlude.

"A truck came and stopped for a moment in front of the Political Section," Mrs. Wasserstrom testified. "A little boy jumped off. He held an apple in his hand. Boger and Draser [another SS man] were standing in the doorway. I was standing at the window. The child was standing next to the car with his apple and was enjoying himself. Suddenly Boger went over to the boy, grabbed his legs, and smashed his head against the wall. Then he calmly picked up the apple. And Draser told me to wipe 'that' off the wall. About an hour later I was called to Boger to interpret in an interrogation, and I saw him eating the child's apple."

The Frankfurt court had heard a good deal of testimony about the enormities of Auschwitz, but it found this small scene hard to believe.

"You saw this with your own eyes?" the witness was asked.

"I saw it with my own eyes," she said.

"You can swear to it in good conscience?"

"Absolutely."

The children who survived the ramp at Auschwitz soon learned and understood what was going to happen to them. The first Auschwitz prisoner to testify at Frankfurt, Dr. Otto Wolken, sixty, a general practitioner in Vienna, told of having encountered a boy in the dispensary and of having asked him, "Well, boy, how are you? Are you afraid?" The boy answered, "I am not afraid. Everything here is so terrible it can only be better up there."

Then Wolken told of having heard an SS man talking to a boy of about ten through a barbed-wire barrier. The SS man said, "Well, my boy, you know a lot for your age." The boy answered, "I know that I know a lot, and I also know that I won't learn any more."

Then Wolken told of a group of ninety children who arrived in Auschwitz and were placed in quarantine for several days and then were loaded onto trucks to go to the gas chambers.

"There was one boy, a little older than the rest," Wolken testified, "who called out to them when they resisted, 'Climb into the car, don't scream. You saw how your parents and grandparents were gassed. We'll see them again up there.' And then he turned to the SS men and shouted, 'But don't think you'll get away with it. You'll die the way you let us die.' He was a brave boy. In this moment he said what he had to say."

∗

At Christmastime, a large Christmas tree was erected opposite one of the crematoria. It was decorated with colored lights. The prisoners were ordered to sing "Silent Night." Anyone who did not sing it correctly got no evening rations.

*

The gas chamber was, in a sense, the easiest fate. Life ended quickly there, whereas the various punishments devised by the SS achieved the same end more slowly and more painfully. Aside from the routine starvation and mistreatment, the most standard of these punishments was public flogging, usually a minimum of twenty-five blows on the bared buttocks with a whip or wooden club. The victim was sometimes forced to count each blow aloud, and if he failed to keep count the flogging started again from the beginning. When the ordeal ended, the prisoner was often unconscious, and the bruises on his thighs were frequently so severe that he never recovered.

Even flogging might be considered preferable to the torments inflicted in Block 11. The Gestapo had endless questions to ask, about the camp underground, about escape attempts, about links to the resistance movement, and it accepted no pleas of ignorance. "The atmosphere was oppressive," recalled Sim Kessel, who had originally been arrested while smuggling guns for the French resistance. "Almost bare walls with only a picture of Der Führer and the swastika, plus a few shelves holding books and files. For furniture, two massive tables, some straight-backed chairs. Seated at the tables were four men smoking. The youngest, short and blond, was drinking a cup of steaming coffee. . . ."

There came then the standard questioning, and then the standard beating, until the blood poured from Kessel's ears and nose. Then the guards flung him into a chair facing the short, blond SS man, who held a medical kit in his lap. "With finicky deliberation he took out pliers and scalpels of various sizes," Kessel recalled, "looking at me at the same time, he smiled gently as if he were setting up a game. . . . Finally he took a small pair of pliers, picked up my left hand and applied the instrument to the nail of my middle finger, driving one tong of the tool under the nail to get a better grip. Then he pulled. I screamed. He paused for an instant, smiling all the while, then pulled again. I watched the nail come out slowly, millimeter by millimeter. He never stopped smiling. . . . 'Well, Kessel, had enough?' "

Gestapo Deputy Boger's favorite method involved the so-called Boger swing, a device of his own invention. "My talking machine will make you talk," he used to tell the prisoners. The swing consisted of a steel bar to which the prisoner was tied by his wrists and ankles. As Boger lunged at him with his club, usually aiming for the genitals, the prisoner swung head over heels, round and round. One prisoner named Breiden, who came to testify at the Frankfurt trial, burst into tears on the witness stand when he saw a replica of the machine to which he had once been bound. "Murderer!" he shouted at Boger.

"Terrible cries could be heard," said another witness, Maryla Rosenthal, who had to work in an adjoining room. "After an hour or more the victims would be carried out on a stretcher. They no longer looked human. I could not recognize them." One reasonably typical victim was a prisoner from Munich named Gustl Berger. He and another prisoner named Rohmann were accused of having acquired some alcohol from the SS canteen. Rohmann was confined to one of the *Stehzelle,* or standing cells. These were vertical tubes, about three feet by three feet across, in which the prisoner could neither sit nor lie. Nor was he fed. "The door never opened," said a Polish prisoner named Josef Kral, who actually survived the standing cells. "One could shout and curse Hitler and everybody else. Nobody would come. Death from hunger is not an easy death. . . . The prisoners screamed, begged, pleaded, licked the walls . . ."

Rohmann lasted nineteen days, according to the testimony of a Munich businessman named Paul Leo Scheidel, and then he "starved to death, finis, gone." But from Berger the Gestapo wanted to know how the alcohol had been obtained, and so he was tied to the Boger swing. After forty-five minutes, according to Scheidel's testimony, "the skin on his hands was gone, his buttocks were ripped open, his face was smeared with blood." After his interrogation, Berger was led out into the yard outside Block 11, where the Nazis had built a wall of black cork as the background for thousands of summary executions. In front of the wall lay a bed of sand to soak up the blood that gushed from the victims. "You murderers! You criminals!" Berger shouted. Then Boger shot him.

It might seem that nothing could be worse that Block 11, but Block 10 may have been even worse. This was where the SS doctors assembled the prisoners who had been selected for various medical experiments. There seems to have been very little purpose or coherence to these experiments. Anyone in Germany who had some quasi-scientific proposal that might benefit the state could send his suggestion to Himmler's headquarters in Berlin, and in due time authorizations of one sort or another would be issued. Some of these proposals were relatively innocuous, and so we find the pharmaceutical firm of Bayer asking for "a number of women in connection with our intended experiments with a new sleeping drug." Other schemes were both lethal and utterly pointless, like the request from Professor Hirt of the University of Strasbourg that the heads of 150 "Jewish-Bolshevist commissars, who embody a repulsive but characteristic subhumanity," be cut off and sent to Strasbourg for study. Or like Dr. Mengele's obsessive efforts to explore the mysteries of twins. Dr. Miklos Nyiszli, a Hungarian prisoner who served as Mengele's pathologist, reported that "several hundred sets of twins" turned up in Auschwitz. Mengele, who seems to have thought that he was seeking methods to increase the German birth rate, ordered each pair carefully examined and then killed. Since twins do not ordinarily die simultaneously, Mengele considered himself blessed with a rare research opportunity, and he rushed the results of all the autopsies to the Institute of Biological, Racial and Evolutionary Research in Berlin.

The main medical experiments in Auschwitz dealt with sterilization. Officially, the goal was to refine the program of genocide by not simply killing the members of "inferior races" but first sterilizing them and then putting them to work. As early as March 28, 1941, before the Final Solution was decreed, an SS official named Viktor Brack was urging Himmler to have all able-bodied Jews sterilized by X rays. Brack's theory was that the unwitting victims should be made to line up at a counter. "There," he wrote, "they would be asked questions or handed a form to fill in, keeping them at the counter for two or three minutes. The clerk behind the counter would . . . start an X-ray apparatus with two tubes to irradiate the persons at the counter . . ." At Auschwitz, as Hoess said, everything was possible. Dr. Horst Schumann of Berlin exposed a batch of several hundred Dutch and Greek Jews to fifteen minutes of radiation of the genital area at a rate of thirty prisoners a day. Many victims suffered severe burns. After three months, Dr. Schumann removed parts of the women's sexual organs to be sent to Berlin for analysis. The men were castrated. Records of these experiments were partially destroyed, but one surviving report from one day in the surgical ward, December 16, 1943, records ninety castrations.

Himmler had meanwhile met Professor Carl Clauberg of the University of Königsberg, who ran a clinic for the treatment of sterile women. Himmler asked Dr. Clauberg whether he could turn his knowledge to the opposite side of the problem and devise a technique of mass sterilization. Clauberg was delighted with the prospect of official support for his research and unlimited numbers of patients to work on. When he arrived at Auschwitz in the spring of 1943, more than two hundred women were installed in Block 10 and placed at his disposal. Clauberg injected various chemicals into their Fallopian tubes. His formulas were kept secret, but the main ingredient was apparently a formalin solution. This stopped the women's menstruation. Clauberg pronounced his system a great success. He boasted to Himmer that his method would enable one skilled physician with ten assistants to sterilize several hundred women a day.

After the completion of these experiments, the subjects were generally sent to the gas chambers.

✳

The worst crime that a prisoner could commit at Auschwitz, and therefore the crime most sternly punished, was to attempt an escape. There were more than six hundred cases. Once the roll call disclosed that someone was missing, the sirens began wailing, and everything stopped. The prisoners had to stand at attention for hours while detachments of SS men set forth with their dogs to hunt for the fugitive. For three days, the hunt continued through all the fields and marshes that surrounded Auschwitz. About two thirds of the time, the pursuers soon found their prey. After torturing him to make him confess who had helped him escape, the SS made him parade around the camp with a sign that said, "Hurrah! I'm back!" Then they gathered all the other prisoners to watch his punishment, and they hanged him.

There was a remarkable girl in Birkenau named Mala Zimetbaum, aged twenty-four, tattooed with the number 19880. She was Polish by birth, but her family migrated to Belgium, to Antwerp, and there, after her father went blind, she dropped out of school to help support him and the four other children. When the Germans overran Belgium, she joined the resistance but was soon arrested and shipped to Auschwitz. There she became a *Läuferin,* or runner, someone who carried messages and ran errands all over the camp. That enabled her to do favors and to tip off the prisoners whenever a selection was planned. Everybody loved her for her courage and independence, for a spirit that even the SS men respected.

Now Mala fell in love with a young Pole named Edek Galiński, also a member of the resistance, and Edek figured out a scheme to escape from Auschwitz. He found a way to steal an SS uniform, but he needed an SS pass, which only Mala, making her rounds of the camp, could find and acquire. Mala was perfectly willing to get him the pass but pleaded with him to take her along. He agreed.

On June 24, 1944, Edek Galiński marched out of Auschwitz in the uniform of an SS man. At the gate, he displayed documents declaring that he was authorized to take with him the female prisoner who was in his custody. Having performed this impossible feat, Mala and Edek seem to have lost all sense of who and where they were. Although accounts of their wanderings differ, they seem to have stopped in the nearby town of Auschwitz, which still harbored a few shops and cafés and an illusory sense of tranquillity, and there they found themselves a room and made love. They apparently thought that their SS papers made them invisible, or immune to the laws of Auschwitz. For several weeks, they survived in this absurd defiance, and then an SS man accosted them in a café and asked to see their papers and refused to accept the faked papers that they offered him.

So the prisoners were assembled on August 22 to watch Mala, battered and bloodied by the Gestapo, go to the gallows. She refused to carry the sign rejoicing in her recapture. They could not make her do that. But the commander of the Birkenau women's camp, Marie Mandel, looked triumphant as she began reading out the death sentence. While she read, Mala suddenly produced from somewhere a razor blade and slashed her wrist. An SS man named Riters grabbed her arm and tried to stop her. Mala managed to strike one last blow in her own defense: She smashed the SS man in the face with her bloody fist.

"You want to be a heroine!" the SS man gasped as he struggled with her. "You want to kill yourself! But that's what we're here for!"

"Murderers!" Mala cried out. "You will soon pay for our suffering! Don't be afraid, girls! Their end is near. I am certain of that. I know. I was free!"

A half-dozen SS men threw themselves on Mala, clubbed her to the ground, kicked her prostrate body and flung her into the back of a waiting truck that took her to the crematorium.

On the other side of the camp, a similar ceremony awaited Edek Galiński. He was bloodied almost beyond recognition by the Gestapo men in Block 11, but in the middle of the reading of the death sentence he leaped onto a bench, thrust his head into the waiting noose, and then kicked over the bench. The SS men rescued him too, then hanged him themselves. His last words were an unfinished cry of defiance: "Long live the Po—"

*

It may seem absurd to report that life in hell could gradually improve, but there is much testimony to confirm that conditions in Auschwitz did get somewhat better during 1943 and early 1944. "At the beginning, beating and killing were the rule, but later this became only sporadic," Borowski wrote as he listed the new comforts. "At first you had to sleep on the floor lying on your side because of the lack of space, and could turn over only on command; later you slept in bunks, or wherever you wished, sometimes even in bed. Originally, you had to stand at roll call for as long as two days at a time, later only until the second gong, until nine o'clock. In the early years, packages were forbidden, later you could receive five hundred grams, and finally as much as you wanted ... Life in the camp became 'better and better' all the time—after the first three or four years. We felt certain that the horrors could never again be repeated, and we were proud that we had survived."

One reason for the change may be that Rudolf Hoess won a promotion in November of 1943 and was summoned back to Berlin to become inspector of concentration camps. Into his place as commandant at Auschwitz stepped SS Lieutenant Colonel Arthur Liebehenschel. He was a rather small, pudgy man with bulging eyes and a weak, dissolute face, and yet he asserted from the beginning a series of modest changes and reforms. He made an inspection tour of Block 11 and ordered fifty-six of the captives released from their dark cells and returned to the regular camp. He abolished the standing cells. He canceled the rule decreeing the death penalty for any attempt at escape, and the rule imposing collective responsibility on all prisoners for any such attempt. He reduced the power of the professional criminals who wore the green triangles, and gave more authority to the leftists and other political prisoners who wore the red triangles. Whether these mild reforms were the result of his own wishes or of orders from Berlin remains uncertain, but his arrival was only part of an organizational upheaval at Auschwitz. While Hoess himself went on to a bigger job in Berlin, his chief deputies were brought down by the strange subterranean currents of SS politics. Not only was Gestapo Chief Max Grabner embroiled in an SS investigation, but so was Rapportführer Gerhard Pallitzsch, one of the five SS officers from Sachsenhausen who accompanied Hoess on his original trip to Auschwitz. Pallitsch was suddenly shipped off to be commandant of a small subcamp in Brno, Czechoslovakia, then arrested three weeks later on a charge of having had an affair with a Jewish prisoner at Birkenau, then sent to join an SS combat unit fighting Hungarian partisans. He was killed near Budapest.

Though these upheavals may all have been a matter of SS politics, those politics themselves were changing as a consequence of one increasingly important fact: The German victory, on which everything was predicated, no longer seemed so certain. General Paulus' Sixth Army had been surrounded and besieged in Stalingrad, and after nearly three months of house-to-house combat in the ruins of the snow-covered city, Paulus surrendered on January 31, 1943. The retreat from Russia was irreversible. At the other end of Hitler's empire, the Americans and the British had invaded Morocco in November of 1942 and conquered all of North Africa by the following May, then invaded Sicily in

July. Such events forced even the most dedicated of SS officers to wonder about their own futures, to wonder how their own actions might someday be judged, and who might survive to bear witness against them. The *Kapos*, who actually ran the concentration camps much of the time and inflicted much of the hardship on the ordinary prisoners, must have felt similar misgivings.

There has been speculation, particularly among East Europeans, that the slaughter of the Jews was only the first stage of an extermination campaign that would eventually extend to the Poles and the Slavs and all other "inferior" peoples who interfered with Hitler's dream of German colonization of the east. If that was indeed Hitler's plan, the changing fortunes of war necessarily stayed his hand, but they did not by any means bring a modification of the Final Solution. On the contrary, the difficulties caused by the war, the shortages of transportation and fuel—all these inspired the SS officers in command of the annihilation not to reduce their efforts but to intensify them, to get their assignment finished before they could be prevented from carrying it out at all. What this meant at Auschwitz was that life got better for the camp inmates because the inmates were mostly Gentiles (about three quarters of them), and after about June of 1943 the Nazis stopped gassing Gentiles. They could still be shot, of course, for any number of offenses, from attempting escape to stealing a piece of bread. But the SS now concentrated its efforts on the destruction of the Jews.

For this, Auschwitz was reorganized again. In May of 1944, Rudolf Hoess reassumed command of the camp he had created, but he exercised only a general supervision. Direct command over Auschwitz was delegated to Richard Baer, and over Birkenau to Josef Kramer, two killers worthy of the task ahead. The milder Liebehenschel was transferred to Majdanek, which was already in the process of closing down.

The next step was to renovate the giant crematoria, to repair all cracks in the brickwork, to reinforce the chimneys with steel bands, to repaint the "changing rooms," to prepare all the machinery for maximum use. The railroad line was extended into Birkenau so that prisoners could be unloaded within two hundred yards of the crematoria, rather than being trucked over from the main camp at Auschwitz. The culmination of the Holocaust, the annihilation of the Jews of Hungary, was about to begin.

Until this last year of the war, Hungary had provided a kind of haven for the Jews of Eastern Europe. The septuagenarian Miklós Horthy, who had served since 1920 as admiral of Hungary's nonexistent navy and as regent for its nonexistent monarchy, joined the war on Hitler's side mainly in order to expand Hungary's sovereignty over the territories to its east. Though anti-Semitism was official Hungarian policy, Jewish businessmen still controlled a large number of Hungarian firms, eleven Jews continued to sit in the Hungarian parliament, and some 130,000 Jews actually served as auxiliary military forces on the Russian front. In contrast to the roundups in Poland, Hungary offered some hope of sanctuary to any fugitive who could slip across its borders, and the

Jewish population consequently increased from about 500,000 at the start of the war to more than 800,000 (there were also about 150,000 converted Jews, whose status was disputed according to the conflicting theories of the Nazis and the Catholic Church). They lived in a state of constant fear, but they lived.

By March of 1944, when the Red Army was only a few days' march from the Hungarian border, the Hungarians began talking of surrender. The Nazis' reaction was harsh. Horthy was summoned to a conference in Germany, placed under virtual arrest, and handed an ultimatum: A German plenipotentiary would immediately take charge in Budapest, and German troops would move in to support him. By the time that plenipotentiary arrived at the German Embassy in Budapest on March 19, Adolf Eichmann had already established his headquarters at the Majestic Hotel. The first step, as usual, was to invite the Jewish leaders of Budapest to establish a *Judenrat,* or Jewish Council, that ugly institution by which the Germans assigned the Jews to organize themselves for the execution of orders from Berlin, assigned them to decide for themselves who should be the first to be deported and who should be spared until the next order came. "Do you know what I am?" Eichmann asked at his first meeting with the Jewish Council of Hungary on March 31. "I am a bloodhound."

On May 15, the deportations to Auschwitz began. It was an operation in which Eichmann took considerable pride. In the middle of a major military campaign—in the middle, in fact, of a catastrophic retreat from the battlefields of the east—Eichmann managed to bargain and negotiate for enough trains to ship half a million Hungarian Jews to their death. There were three trains a day, on the average, each hauling between forty and fifty freight cars, each car carrying about eighty to one hundred people. As on the transports from Germany and France and Holland and everywhere else, the prisoners were given no food or water, but they had been encouraged to bring with them whatever personal possessions might prove valuable in the resettlement camps of the east, and so they embarked with sandwiches and blankets and prayer books and carpets and the family silver and even pouches filled with diamonds, all of it ultimately useless. In less than two months, about 400,000 of these Hungarian Jews found themselves on the ramp at Auschwitz.

"It was ten o'clock one morning that the first of the trains were unloaded," recalled Kitty Hart, a teen-age Polish girl who worked among the mountains of confiscated goods in "Canada." "From the distance we could see masses of people standing, waiting. . . . Their column stretched as far as the eye could see. It seemed as though they were disposing of the whole of Europe. . . ." From the incoming trains, the prospect was ominous. "Peering through a crack in the side of the car . . . ," one of the Hungarians, Dr. Miklós Nyiszli, later wrote, "I saw a desertlike terrain: the earth was a yellowish clay . . . broken here and there by a green thicket of trees. Concrete pylons stretched in even rows to the horizon, with barbed wire strung between them from top to bottom. . . . One object immediately caught my eye: an immense square chimney built of red bricks, tapering toward the summit. It towered above a two-story building and looked like a strange factory chimney. I was especially struck by the enormous tongues of flame rising between the lightning rods. . . ."

Even as the trainloads of Hungarian prisoners began rolling into Auschwitz, the Nazis were exploring a new tactic, not to kill the Jews but to sell them. The idea had been born, apparently, in the first days of the German move into Hungary, when the Wehrmacht discovered two directors of the Manfred Weiss steel empire hiding in a monastery. In exchange for their own freedom to emigrate, along with forty-five of the corporation's chief executives and their relatives, they gave the SS a twenty-five-year lease on the whole empire. Officials in Berlin were fascinated. The ghettos of Poland had offered very few opportunities like this. On April 5, one of the top Nazi officials in Budapest suggested informally to the Jewish leaders an advance deposit of $2 million for the ransom of 100,000 Jews. While this possibility was being explored, Eichmann went a step further. On May 5, just ten days before the first freight cars headed north to Auschwitz, he summoned Joel Brand, a representative of the American-sponsored Joint Distribution Committee, and made what was apparently an official proposal: All the Jews of Hungary could emigrate if the Allies would provide ten thousand heavy military trucks in return. "I was surprised, amazed, happy and confused, all at the same time," Brand testified at Eichmann's trial in Jerusalem. Leaving behind his wife and children as hostages, Brand went to Istanbul on May 19 to establish contact with the British. The Allied answer was harsh but not surprising: No military supplies could be sent to the enemy, no matter what the price might be. Perhaps the Nazis had expected that answer. Even while Brand's hopeless negotiations continued, there was no interruption in the trains to Auschwitz.

On the new ramp at Birkenau, very few selections were made now. The SS men and their dogs herded the prisoners along a cinder path, surrounded by neatly mowed lawns, toward a concrete stairway. A dozen steps led downward to the brightly lit "changing room." Each of these rooms, some three hundred square yards in size, could accommodate as many as one thousand people at a time. There were signs in German, French, Greek and Hungarian, all saying, "Baths and Disinfecting Room." Other signs warned of diseases: "Cleanliness Brings Freedom" and "One Louse Can Kill You." There were wooden benches along the walls, and above these benches there were pegs and coat hangers. More signs told the prisoners to hang up their clothes, and to tie their shoes together by the laces. The pegs were numbered, and the signs told the prisoners to remember their numbers so that they could retrieve their clothes after the baths. Once the prisoners had undressed, they were herded on into another large room, also brightly lit. Once they were all inside, the doors were bolted shut, and the lights were switched off. Some of the prisoners embraced each other as they waited. Some simply waited, numb. The gas had a smell of something burning.

"Twenty minutes later, the electric ventilators were set going in order to evacuate the gas," Dr. Nyiszli later wrote as a medical witness to these scenes. "The doors opened. . . . The bodies were not lying here and there throughout the room but piled in a mass to the ceiling. The reason for this was that the gas first inundated the lower layers of air and rose but slowly toward the ceiling. This forced the victims to trample one another in a frantic effort to escape the gas. . . . I noticed that the bodies of the women, the children and the aged were at the bottom of the pile; at the top, the strongest. Their bodies, which were covered with scratches and bruises from the struggle which had set them against each other, were often interlaced. Blood oozed from their noses and mouths; their faces, bloated and blue, were so deformed as to be almost unrecognizable. . . . The *Sonderkommando* squad, outfitted with large rubber boots, lined up around the hill of bodies and flooded it with powerful jets of water. This was necessary because the final act of those who die by drowning or by gas is an involuntary defecation. Each body was befouled and had to be washed. Once the 'bathing' of the dead was finished . . . they knotted thongs around the wrists . . . and with these thongs they dragged the slippery bodies to the elevators in the next room."

Each crematorium had four large elevators. Each elevator could hold about twenty-five bodies. When it was filled, a bell rang and the elevator rose to the incineration room. Sliding doors opened automatically. The *Sonderkommando* prisoners again seized the thongs around the wrists of the corpses and hauled them onto a chute that carried them toward the furnaces. One last rite still had to be administered. All the victims' hair was shaved off and stored. Then the Tooth Kommando, eight prisoners who had once been dental surgeons, set to work. They pried open the corpses' mouths and yanked out any gold teeth or bridgework they could find. The gold teeth were dropped into buckets filled with an acid that burned away all flesh and bone. According to Dr. Nyiszli's calculations, these operations recovered about eighteen to twenty pounds of gold per crematorium per day. The bodies were then loaded onto pushcarts, three to a cart, and slid into the ovens. The ashes were raked out and loaded onto trucks and dumped into the Vistula.

Even the most elaborate plans proved insufficient for the liquidation of the Hungarians that summer. Though the crematoria worked night and day, there were still too many bodies to be destroyed (the highest number actually gassed within twenty-four hours, Hoess estimated, was nine thousand). The Nazis had to resort once again to the more primitive means that they had previously abandoned. In the fields of wild flowers that were now blooming behind the crematoria, Hoess ordered nine gigantic pits dug. There he had thousands more bodies dumped in and set afire. It is not easy to burn bodies, particularly emaciated bodies. The first attempts, long before the crematoria were built, had used up a lot of scarce coke. The Nazis had therefore conducted a series of experiments to find out how to save fuel. They soon found that if a fat man was burned along with a thin one, the fat man's fat would serve as fuel to consume the thin one. In due time, they discovered a still more efficient combination: a fat man and a thin woman (or vice versa) and a child. By the time of the slaughter of the Jews of Hungary, they had reached even higher levels of efficiency. The pits to be filled with corpses, up to two thousand at a time, had been dug with slanted bottoms so that the fat could flow into containers and be scooped up and poured back over the burning bodies.

"The corpses in the pit looked as if they had been chained together," according to Filip Müller, a Czech Jew who worked in the *Sonderkommando*.

"Tongues of a thousand tiny blue-red flames were licking at them. . . . Blisters which had formed on their skin burst one by one. Almost every corpse was covered with black scorch marks and glistened as if it had been greased. The searing heat had burst open their bellies: There was the violent hissing and sputtering of frying in great heat. . . . Fanned by the wind, the flames, dark red before, now took on a fiery-white hue. . . . The process of incineration took five to six hours. What was left barely filled a third of the pit. The shiny whitish-gray surface was strewn with countless skulls. . . ."

*

While the fires were burning in the summer of 1944—fires that could be seen as far as thirty miles away—the advancing Allied armies finally acquired the ability to destroy the railroad lines from Budapest to Auschwitz, and, for that matter, to destroy Auschwitz itself. Specifically, the U.S. Eighth Air Force based in Britain and the Fifteenth Air Force based in southern Italy were already beginning to bomb military targets in Poland. On April 4, 1944, U.S. reconnaissance planes flying over Auschwitz took some remarkably clear photographs (stowed away in the CIA archives until 1979) that show all the essential evidence—the gas chambers and crematoria, the prisoners standing in line—yet even the experts trained to interpret such photographic evidence apparently saw nothing here but a large prison camp.

What was happening at Auschwitz could not be imagined, therefore could not be believed, not even when photographed, could not be believed even when reported in detail by escaping prisoners, could not be believed and therefore could not be stopped. There certainly was nothing secret about the existence of Hitler's concentration camps. The Nazis almost boasted of them. The very names of Dachau and Buchenwald, and the reports of terrible things that happened there, served to cow the population. The Final Solution, however, was officially a state secret, and the SS went to considerable effort to keep it a secret. Even though it was widely known that deportation to the east meant great hardship and often death, anyone who spoke of the Auschwitz crematoria faced severe punishment.

The prisoners tried, at great risk and sacrifice, to tell the world. As early as November of 1940, a brave Polish officer named Witold Pilecki, who voluntarily got himself sent to Auschwitz in order to organize a resistance movement there, smuggled out a message describing the appalling conditions at the camp. Appalling conditions are still not the same as systematic extermination, however. By the summer of 1942, the Allied capitals had received reports of mass slaughters, from the camps themselves, from neutral observers, even from anti-Nazi Germans. The London *Daily Telegraph* reported that June that more than one million Jews had been killed in the east. The report was just part of the flood of war news. In the spring of 1944, finally, Rudolf Vrba and Alfred Weczler escaped from Auschwitz, reached Czechoslovakia, and produced a sixty-page report on all the details of the gassing and burning at Birkenau, a report that managed to get to the White House, the Vatican, the Red Cross, and the Jewish community leaders in Budapest. Allied leaders remained doubtful, skeptical, preoccupied with military strategy. There was a certain amount of anti-Semitism in Washington, and in the United States at large (not to mention Britain and Russia), and even those who heard the recurrent reports from Poland tended to regard them as propaganda, wildly exaggerated. Even those who were inclined to intervene on behalf of the Jews feared being accused of diverting resources from the overall war effort. As late as November of 1944, just six months before the war ended, Elmer Davis, head of the Office of War Information, tried to suppress a report on Auschwitz out of concern that it would weaken Allied credibility.

In January of 1944, President Roosevelt did establish a War Refugee Board that was supposed to "take all measures within its power to rescue the victims of enemy oppression," but it had very little power to take any such measures. Proposals for military action against the Hungarian deportations attracted little attention or support. One of the first was an open letter by Isaac Rosengarten in the May issue of the magazine *Jewish Forum,* demanding that Budapest be bombed "off the face of the earth." Nobody responded. The War Department issued a statement of policy: "It is not contemplated that units or individuals of the armed forces will be employed for the purpose of rescuing victims of enemy oppression unless such rescues are the direct result of military operations."

In late June, when the killing of the Hungarians had been going on for more than a month, the U.S. legation in Bern reported that both the Jewish deportations and some considerable German troop movements followed five specific railroad lines. "It is urged by all sources of this information . . . ," the Bern cable said, "that vital sections of these lines, especially bridges along one, be bombed as the only possible means of slowing down or stopping future deportations." John W. Pehle, executive director of the War Refugee Board, sent a copy of this message to John J. McCloy at the War Department. On July 4, McCloy sent Pehle a message saying that the War Department was opposed to any raid on the railroad lines to Auschwitz. "It could be executed only by the diversion of considerable air support essential to the success of our forces now engaged in decisive operations and would in any case be of such doubtful efficacy that it would not amount to a practical project."

The WRB representative in Bern kept sending Pehle more accounts of the killings. One, apparently the Vrba-Weczler report, provided two eyewitness descriptions of the gas chambers at Birkenau. Pehle's horror presumably reflects Washington's ignorance. "These were the first real verifications we'd had about what was going on in those camps," he later said. With this new evidence, Pehle sent McCloy a more drastic message: "I strongly recommend that the War Department give serious consideration to the possibility of destroying the execution chambers in Birkenau through direct bombing action." McCloy answered simply by passing along a memo prepared by the office of the Chief of Staff, which said once more that such a raid would be an impractical diversion of bombers needed for the war effort. As it happened, U.S. bombers actually did raid Auschwitz in August and again in September, aiming at the synthetic-oil plant affiliated with the camp. They accidentally dropped a few bombs on Auschwitz itself and killed fifteen German soldiers.

Though the Allies refused to strike at the gas chambers of Auschwitz, this was one of the rare occasions when strong words partially made up for the lack of action. The first protest came from the papal nuncio to Budapest, Angelo Rotta, who warned the Hungarian government on the day that the first train left for Auschwitz: "The whole world knows what the deportations mean in practice." The Hungarian bishops complained, too, partly because Eichmann's forces were making no distinctions between Orthodox Jews and those who had converted to Christianity, and finally Monsignor Rotta delivered a gentle protest from Pope Pius XII. The next day, June 25, the aged Admiral Horthy issued instructions that the deportations were to cease. Horthy's authority, particularly over the Germans, was limited. Eichmann's roundups continued. The protests increased. U.S. Secretary of State Cordell Hull delivered a note via the Swiss Legation on June 26 threatening reprisals, and President Roosevelt publicly warned: "Hungary's fate will not be like any other civilization . . . unless deportations are stopped." Sweden sent Raoul Wallenberg as a special envoy to Budapest, authorized to issue thousands of Swedish visas to the threatened Jews, and the Swiss and the Portuguese joined in establishing shelters where Jews could find haven.

Hungary itself stood at the edge of collapse. The Red Army was at its frontiers, and the various authorities in Budapest issued contradictory orders. Premier Dome Sztojay assured the papal nuncio on July 8 that all transports to Auschwitz had stopped. Eichmann still commanded a unit of 150 men, and he sent them to round up another 1,450 Jews on July 14 and pack them aboard a train. An order from Horthy stopped the train before it left Hungary, but two more of Eichmann's trains carried more than 2,000 more Jews to Auschwitz on July 19 and 24. They were the last. By now, the Nazi regime itself was crumbling. In the same week that the last transports left Budapest, Count Klaus von Stauffenberg planted a bomb next to Hitler at his command post in East Prussia, and for a few hours it seemed as though the Wehrmacht had finally rid Germany of its tyrant. Even though the July 20 plotters ended dangling from wires in the prison at Plötzensee, Hitler's closest lieutenants began wondering how they might save themselves. Himmler had been evacuating prisoners from the Majdanek death camp near Lublin, sending most of them westward to Auschwitz, but a Polish resistance group seized control of Majdanek on July 24 and turned it over to the advancing Russians. Allied war correspondents got their first look at gas chambers, crematoria, canisters of Zyklon B, piles of human bones. Allied broadcasts spoke of atrocities and the prosecution of war criminals, and still Hitler shouted that all Germans would fight on to the death.

At Auschwitz, the halting of the trains from Budapest did not halt the gassings, not yet. The extermination machinery appeared to be running on its own momentum, and the camp was crowded with prisoners, ready to be fed into the machinery. First came the destruction of the so-called Family Camp, the remnant of the prisoners brought from Theresienstadt. This ancient fortress near the Czech-German frontier had originally been a showplace camp, where the Nazis sent distinguished prisoners like Germany's venerable Chief Rabbi Leo Baeck, where they sent decorated Jewish military heroes of the World War, where they sent people who couldn't simply be made to disappear. They and their families, wives, mothers-in-law, lived under prison discipline but under conditions so much better than those in any other prison camp that the Nazis regularly invited in the Red Cross and other international observers to show that the rumors about the concentration camps were greatly exaggerated. Wartime changed all that, however, and thousands of Theresienstadt prisoners were shipped to Auschwitz, where they lived apart, and somewhat better, in the Family Camp.

When the new orders decreed the extermination of the Family Camp, the victims couldn't believe it. They thought that because they had survived so long, they were somehow immune. Even inside the changing room, they shouted their disbelief, "We want to live! We want to work!" The SS men, with their truncheons and their police dogs, herded them toward the gas chambers. "Husbands, helpless themselves, crowded round their wives and children to protect them from blows and also from the savage teeth of the dogs," according to Filip Müller, who was there as one of the *Sonderkommando*. "There was chaos as in the narrow space people pushed and shoved each other, SS men shouted and used their truncheons, and the dogs barked and snapped ferociously. Suddenly a voice began to sing. Others joined in, and the sound swelled into a mighty choir. They sang first the Czechoslovak national anthem and then the Hebrew song 'Hatikvah.' And all this time the SS men never stopped their brutal beatings. It was as if they regarded the singing as a last kind of protest which they were determined to stifle if they could." Four thousand people from the Family Camp were killed on March 9, the last four thousand on July 12.

Hoess turned over his command to Richard Baer on July 29 and returned to Berlin, but the gassing went on. Next came the turn of the gypsies. Himmler had originally rounded them up and sent them to Auschwitz not for extermination but for scientific examination. He had been fascinated for years by the imagery of prehistoric Germany, its Nordic gods and runic inscriptions, its legends of unconquerable Goths and Vandals, and he somehow imagined that the mysterious gypsies were the descendants of these lost tribes. Many of them were shot and beaten in the course of the roundups, but when they finally reached Auschwitz they were isolated and observed and encouraged to carry on their folk traditions. The men were not required to work. A *tzigeuner* orchestra formed, and everybody danced. The women tended the children, and the children clambered all over one another. They too felt themselves immune. Nobody was immune. As that last summer wore on, Himmler lost interest in the gypsies and decreed their annihilation. On the night of August 2, all of them, some four thousand, went to the gas chambers.

∗

Himmler himself seemed to have acquired illusions that he could somehow supplant Hitler and negotiate an armistice. He sent envoys to suggest these illusions in neutral Stockholm. He seemed to have denied to himself the fact that Auschwitz would be discovered, and that the discovery would damn him. Very few of the Nazi leaders acted rationally in these last months of the war. Hitler himself rarely emerged from his underground bunker. To the contradictory orders of gassing prisoners or saving them for labor was now added a third policy of moving them from camp to camp, often without food or shelter. While thousands were still being shipped to Auschwitz (one of the very last transports from Holland brought Anne Frank and her family), thousands more were being shipped from Auschwitz back to Germany to work in armaments factories.

At some point during the early fall of 1944—probably between mid-September and mid-October—Himmler decided to end the gassings. They did not end immediately, for the machinery was not easy to stop, but on October 28, when yet another 1,700 Jews from Theresienstadt were crowded into the gas chambers and put to death, they became the last victims of Zyklon B. A trainload of Slovakian Jews who arrived from Bratislava five days later were sent directly to the quarantine camp, with all their luggage. Even this did not mean that the killing had stopped entirely—SS courts still imposed sentences of summary execution, and prisoners still died of starvation and dysentery—but the new edict did mean that the wholesale slaughter had ended. On November 26, an order from Himmler declared: "The crematoria at Auschwitz are to be dismantled ..."

The prospect of an end of the gassing was terrifying news to one group of prisoners, the *Sonderkommando*. The whole camp swarmed with rumors that everyone in Auschwitz would be killed, but the *Sonderkommando* had always been, as its name indicated, special. Its whole function, its whole existence, depended on the crematoria, and each new squad began by taking part in an essential ritual, the killing of its predecessors. For performing their degrading work in the gas chambers, the men of the *Sonderkommando* were remarkably well treated. They lived in special quarters in the crematoria buildings, and all the plunder of "Canada" was theirs. "The table awaiting us," one of the few survivors later wrote of his arrival at the *Sonderkommando* barracks, "was covered with a heavy silk brocade tablecloth, fine initialed porcelain dishes, and place settings of silver; ... all sorts of preserves, bacon, jellies, several kinds of salami, cakes and chocolate." They drank fine cognac until they could no longer stand up, and then they fell into bed on linen sheets. Some of the *Sonderkommando* went mad, and some committed suicide, but most of them struggled on for three months or so, and then they ended as they had begun, in a ritual of replacement. Their successors steered them, unprotesting, willing and perhaps even eager to die, into the gas chambers.

The last *Sonderkommando*, however, was not ready to die. The prospect of their imminent annihilation in the last days of the camp suddenly filled them with a passion to rebel. They turned to the Polish underground for help, but the prospect of the end of Auschwitz, the same prospect that inspired the *Sonderkommando* to rebellion, inspired the Polish underground to caution. To some extent, the Polish underground always emphasized caution. Its primary goal was to organize and defend itself, and to that end its agents maneuvered themselves into relatively safe positions in the hospital and the administrative offices. Open rebellion remained a distant possibility. In the view of the underground leaders, these self-protective maneuvers justified themselves as a matter of survival, and, as the Red Army drew nearer to Auschwitz, survival seemed all the more to require that everyone lie low.

The last *Sonderkommando* had been expanded, in order to deal with the Hungarians, from about two hundred to seven hundred men, a fairly formidable force, and as these men realized that they themselves were doomed they began to arm. By theft and bribery, and with infinite stealth, they smuggled into their luxurious quarters, one by one, a pistol, then a grenade, then more grenades. As early as June, the *Sonderkommando* planned a full-scale uprising. The prisoners would attack their SS guards, seize their weapons and uniforms, then bluff their way past the sentries, escape into the woods and join forces with Polish partisan units. But the Polish underground kept warning that it was too early, too dangerous. Then the SS men began to sense trouble. One of the ringleaders of the *Sonderkommando*, a *Kapo* named Kamiński, who was in charge of Crematorium II, was suddenly arrested, tortured, and shot. The other rebel leaders turned cautious.

On October 7, the Polish underground agents in the Auschwitz administrative office sent word to the *Sonderkommando* that the SS had decided on their liquidation, and that it might come at any moment. The ringleaders gathered inside Crematorium IV to decide what to do. That same day, an SS officer named Busch had told the *Kapos* of Crematorium IV that he needed three hundred men from the *Sonderkommando* to go and clear rubble in a town in Upper Silesia. The *Kapos* suspected that this was a ruse that would lead to their death. Filip Müller, who was one of the prisoners standing at roll call in the yard, noted that some prisoners didn't answer when their numbers were called. Busch sent several guards into the crematorium to look for them. "The guards were just leaving," Müller recalled, "when quite suddenly from out of the ranks of selected prisoners they were pelted with a hail of stones. Some SS men were wounded, but others managed to dodge the stones and were drawing their guns and starting to shoot wildly into the crowd of prisoners. Two more SS men had managed to get away to the camp street, where they grabbed two bicycles leaning against the camouflage fence and sped off . . . ."

Inside the crematorium itself, the assembled ringleaders had been surprised by a *Kapo* who was not in on the plot, and so they killed him. Then they packed the hated crematorium with their precious store of explosives, and some oil-soaked rags, and blew it up. "I saw the red-tiled roof and supporting beams of [the] crematorium blow off," Dr. Nyiszli recalled, "followed by an immense spiral of flame and black smoke. No sooner than a minute later, machine-gun fire broke out. . . . The dismal wail of sirens began. . . . From the window I saw eighty to one hundred trucks arriving. The first one pulled up in front of our crematorium. Half a company jumped out and formed up in battle formation in front of the barbed-wire fences. . . . The *Sonderkommando* men . . . were spraying the SS troops with bullets and grenades. . . . I saw several soldiers drop, either dead or wounded. Seeing this, the besiegers . . . brought up fifty well-trained police dogs and unleashed them. . . ."

The explosion in Crematorium IV signaled the *Sonderkommando* in the other installations that the revolt had begun. In Crematorium II, the rebels quickly seized control. They threw one SS man and one German *Kapo* into the furnace and burned them alive. They also beat one German soldier to death. Then they poured out into the prison yard, cut holes in the surrounding fence, and fled toward the woods. But they ran in the wrong direction, not northeast toward the Vistula but southwest toward the Rajsko subcamp. That kept them within the confines of the camp's outer fences.

In fact, the *Sonderkommando* did almost everything wrong. The uprising had originally been planned for the night but started in broad daylight. All the crematoria were supposed to rebel at once, and in silence, so that the rebels could secretly organize a mass escape, but the shooting at Crematorium IV warned the SS men of trouble, and they quickly secured the three other crematoria. And since the uprising had not been coordinated with the Polish underground, there were no partisan units to help anyone who escaped.

"Prisoners were now milling about aimlessly and panic-stricken while from all sides they were met by a shower of bullets," according to Müller's account of the pandemonium in the yard of Crematorium IV. "One by one they fell to the ground fatally injured. Finally a large number raced toward the barbed wire to try and break through." Müller decided on a different course. He sought refuge inside the ruins. "The crematorium was still burning fiercely. The wooden doors were ablaze, several of the wooden beams were charred and dangling from the ceiling, and there was a fire raging in the coke store. The windows on the opposite wall were riddled with bullet holes. Outside, the firing continued. . . . In a flash I remembered a place where I would be safe from bullets: inside the flue leading from the ovens to the chimney. I lifted one of the cast-iron covers, climbed down and closed the cover behind me. . . . As I glanced up I glimpsed, framed by the four soot-blackened chimney walls, a small square of deep-blue sky. . . ."

Outside, the sound of machine gun fire slowly died down. That was because the truckloads of SS men had surrounded the woods where the prisoners had fled, and now they were slowly closing in. Other SS men with dogs headed southward in pursuit of the prisoners who had escaped from Crematorium II. They trapped most of them in a barn near Rajsko. Partly out of caution, partly for sport, the SS men did not attack the barn but set fire to it. As the prisoners fled the flames, the SS men shot them down.

When the shooting was over, the SS men brought all the corpses back to the yard outside Crematorium IV. They counted some 250 of them, but when they checked their lists and records they found that twelve of the *Sonderkommando* were missing. They were about to set out in search of them when the air-raid sirens began sounding. That forced a halt to the search, for everyone was supposed to take cover. Before they did so, the SS men rounded up every prisoner they could find from the *Sonderkommando* in Crematoria II and IV. They forced them to their knees, then shot them, about two hundred men in all. When the all-clear finally sounded at sundown, the SS men and their dogs started their search for the twelve missing prisoners. They trapped them in a building on the far side of the Vistula, where they had taken refuge for the night. The SS men shot them all and then dragged their bodies back to be piled up next to the corpses lying outside Crematorium IV. The SS casualties: three dead, 12 wounded.

After the revolt, the remnants of the *Sonderkommando* consisted of 198 men, who still hoped that they could somehow survive. The SS had other plans. At about two in the afternoon of November 17, they were all marched to Crematorium II, and the doors were locked behind them. They were not ordered to undress, for there was no need for any pretense of showers. They all knew they were going to die, and they attempted neither protest nor revolt. As they stood silently awaiting their execution, they suddenly heard the voice of a man whom they knew only as "the dayyan" (judge). He was a thin, bespectacled Pole of about thirty, who devoted himself to the study of Scripture. The Nazis often amused themselves by assigning such people to the most degrading work in the camp, particularly the latrine-cleaning detail known as the *Scheisskommando,* but this dayyan, assigned to the crematoria, absolutely refused to take any part in the mutilation and burning of the corpses. He also rejected the luxuries of the *Sonderkommando,* eating only the bread rations of the ordinary prisoners. Such insubordination should have led quickly to his execution, but there was something about this unworldly dayyan that prompted the Nazis to spare him. He was assigned to a detail that sorted out the hair shaved from the dead, and even here he spent his time arguing with prisoners who raged at the God who had consigned them to such a fate. "Listen, Dayyan, not once have I felt even a breath of divine justice here," one twenty-year-old youth named Menachem charged. "Absolutely everything that you stuffed into my head in school is just nonsense. There is no God, and if there is one, he is an ox and a bastard!" The SS men guffawed at such disputation, according to Müller, who recorded this one, but the dayyan did his best to uphold the faith even in these disastrous circumstances. "If the Haggadah commands man in each generation to look at himself as if he himself had migrated from Egypt," he said, "the brothers who perhaps by a miracle will manage to survive will read the Haggadah, made whole by their experiences in Auschwitz."

Now, sealed into their underground tomb, the last *Sonderkommando* heard once again the voice of the dayyan.

"Brothers!" he called out. "Fellow Jews . . . Fate has allotted us the cruelest of tasks, that of participating in our own destruction, of witnessing our own disappearance, down to the very ashes to which we are reduced. . . . We must accept, resignedly, as sons of Israel should, that this is the way things must be. God has so ordained it. Why? It is not for us, miserable humans, to seek the answer. This is the fate that has befallen us. Do not be afraid of death. What is life worth, even if, by some strange miracle, we should manage to remain alive? We would return to our cities and towns to find cold and pillaged homes. . . . We would wander like the restless, shuffling shadows of our former selves, of our completed pasts, finding nowhere any peace or rest."

A few minutes after this impassioned sermon in the underground mausoleum, three SS men with machine guns opened the door and ordered all doctors to return to their quarters to await further assignment, and that was how Dr. Nyiszli, one of three doctors who emerged into the sunlight, survived to record this scene. The next time he saw the last *Sonderkommando,* they were charred beyond recognition. The SS had taken them all out into the fields outside the camp and turned flame-throwers on them.

This was part of Himmler's deluded attempt to destroy all the evidence of what had happened at Auschwitz and the other Polish death camps. Once Himmler had ordered that the crematoria were to be dismantled, teams of prisoners happily began taking apart Crematoria II and III, but, just like the building of those installations, the dismantling took time. One set of furnaces was kept burning to deal with the camp's routine deaths and with the destruction of papers (and one of the SS men, who liked to raise rabbits, kept several of his hutches in an unused gas chamber). The Auschwitz authorities seemed confused about how to start the obliteration of evidence. Clerks began going through the voluminous files that had so carefully been kept for so long—the official police dossiers on thousands of interrogations, the carefully falsified death certificates on hundreds of thousands of killings—trying to decide what was incriminating, what should be burned and what should be saved. First they burned the lists of those incoming prisoners who had gone directly from the railroad ramp to the gas chambers, and then the files of the Political Department, and then the hospital records of the thousands who had been murdered by phenol injections. Then came the great sorting out of Canada. Carloads of clothes and furniture and jewelry and musical instruments were shipped to Berlin, carloads more were judged worthless and consigned to the flames. And then the crematorium equipment. Details of prisoners worked all through December, through Christmas, to dismantle the furnaces and pack the supplies for shipment to Mauthausen and Gross-Rosen. And finally the funeral pits. Squads of prisoners dug them up, sifted out the bones and ashes to be dumped in the Vistula, then replanted the desecrated earth with grass.

The last spasms of killing were relentlessly legal. On January 6, 1945, when the camp was covered with a heavy blanket of snow, the prisoners in the women's camp at Birkenau were assembled to watch a hanging. The SS had been working for three months to discover who had provided the explosives used in the revolt of the *Sonderkommando,* and after subjecting certain suspects to torture they had identified four young Jewish girls who worked at I. G. Farben's Union munitions factory. These four were thereupon convicted of smuggling and sentenced to death. Two of them were marched up to a specially erected gallows. "They were wearing their regular clothes, except that they did not have their coats on," recalled Judith Sternberg Newman, an eyewitness and a good friend of one of the victims, Aline Gärtner. "They walked calmly, their faces composed. . . . An SS man bound their hands behind their backs. . . . Aline was then pulled up on the table, and her last words were, 'You'll pay for this. I shall die now, but your turn will come soon.' The executioner fixed the noose around her neck, and she was pulled up by the rope. Now a noose was put around the other girl's neck. . . . All she said when they lifted her up on the table was, 'I hope all my comrades will get their freedom.' They hung there like two marionettes, turning in the breeze. It was a horrible sight."

The second girl, a Pole, had a younger sister who was also among the condemned, but her hanging had been delayed. "She had been left behind in her block, for she had suffered a complete nervous breakdown," Mrs. Newman reported. "Her wild screams could be heard from afar." The execution was not delayed for long. Just after dark, that same night, the mad girl and the fourth condemned prisoner were both taken out to the gallows and hanged. Those were the last official executions at Auschwitz.

*

The Red Army, which had been stalled for weeks within about fifty miles of Auschwitz, finally launched a surprise offensive on January 12, 1945. Within a week, its artillery was pounding the outskirts of the camp, and shortly after midnight of January 18 the Nazis ordered a general evacuation. They dynamited the brick walls of Crematorium V, the last one still standing. They set fire to Canada. It was about ten degrees below zero when the SS began routing the ragged prisoners out onto the snow-covered fields and bullying them into the customary ranks of five. Even then, there were long delays, roll calls, shouts and confusion. Several thousand prisoners in the camp hospital argued about whether to join the evacuation, and those who wanted to flee fought over the few pairs of wooden clogs that the authorities had left them to use in going to the latrines. Among the SS too there were arguments about whether to kill everyone who couldn't march. There had been various plans drawn up for the complete annihilation of the camp and all remaining prisoners, but nobody had ever formally issued the orders to carry out this final massacre. By now, the SS men were thinking mainly of flight from the dreaded Russians, so they decided simply to leave the sick and injured behind. Or perhaps no one decided anything, and the sick were just abandoned in the chaos of the four-day evacuation.

"Order and discipline had disappeared," Olga Lengyel recalled of her last round through the hospital wards. "Most of the sick had left their beds and were massing around the stove in the middle of the room." Several patients had broken into the supervisor's quarters and stolen some food, and now they were frying *plazki* on the stove. Mrs. Lengyel led a band of patients in attacking the hospital storehouse with pickaxes; inside, they seized a large supply of bread. When she had wrapped up her few possessions in a blanket roll that she knotted at both ends, she joined the stream of prisoners heading out into the snowy night.

"Thirty guards stood at the gate," she reported. "Before letting us out, they examined us one by one under a pocket flashlight, in what became another selection. Those who were judged to be too old or too feeble were driven back into the camp. Once we were outside the camp, we had to line up, as always, in columns of five. A new period of waiting began. This lasted for about two hours, for the whole convoy was to consist of six thousand women. Then the SS closed the gates. An order was barked. Our column was under way.... After we had traveled some distance, we came to a turn in the road. Here we looked back for our last glimpse of Birkenau.... Everything was plunged into darkness; and only burning embers, where the crematory records were being incinerated, feebly lighted the barracks and the barbed-wire fences."

Dr. Nyiszli, who had gone to bed early in the barracks of the crematoria, was wakened shortly after midnight by machine-gun fire and flashes of light and the thud of footsteps running past his door. He prudently outfitted himself with a warm overcoat, a two-pound can of food, even some cigarettes, and as he left the barracks he passed the room where the gold torn from the prisoners' teeth was stored. "We did not even think of stopping to take some of it. What was money when one's life was at stake? We had learned that nothing lasts and that no value is absolute."

Nyiszli simply walked unchallenged through the main gate, past the deserted ramp where all the doomed transports had come to a halt. Outside the firelit Birkenau gate, he saw a crowd of about three thousand prisoners waiting docilely for the SS to tell them what to do. He decided to join this crowd in the hope that their numbers would provide him some security during the flight to the west. At about 1 A.M. the last SS man left Birkenau. "He closed the iron gates and cut off the lights from the main switchboard, which was located near the entrance.... Birkenau sank into darkness." Even as the prisoners started their march, a Russian advance guard opened fire. "They were using submachine guns and had the support of a light tank," Nyiszli reported. "The SS returned the fire and shouted for us to take cover on the ground. The fire was heavy on both sides. Then, in a little while, all grew quiet again and we resumed our journey across the sterile, snow covered earth of Silesia."

To be leaving Birkenau under any circumstances seemed a kind of liberation, but this trek to the west was to be cruel. The sixty thousand prisoners who were marched off into the snow and darkness had been issued only one day's ration of bread. Most of them had no coats or blankets. They were heading vaguely toward the Gross-Rosen camp, some 150 miles to the west, but most of the prisoners did not know where they were going, and many of their guards did not know how to get there. "An icy wind blew in violent gusts," according to the narrator of Elie Wiesel's *Night*. "But we marched without faltering. The SS made us increase our pace. 'Faster, you swine, you filthy sons of bitches ...' We were no longer marching; we were running. Like automatons. The SS were running, too, their weapons in their hands. We looked as though we were fleeing before them. Pitch darkness. Every now and then, an explosion in the night. They had orders to fire on any who could not keep up.... I repeated to myself, 'Don't think. Don't stop. Run.' Near me, men were collapsing in the dirty snow. Shots ..."

As the first dawn broke, Dr. Nyiszli's unit had gone about ten miles from Auschwitz. "All along the way I noticed pots and blankets and wooden shoes that had been abandoned by a convoy of women who had preceded us. A few miles farther on we came upon a much sadder sight: every forty or fifty yards, a bloody body lay in a ditch beside the road. For miles and miles it was the same story: bodies everywhere. Exhausted, they had been unable to walk any farther; when they had strayed from the ranks an SS man had dispatched them with a bullet in the back."

In the opposite direction came, of all people, Rudolf Hoess, the creator of Auschwitz, now frantic and enraged at this spectacle of disorderly flight. Driving eastward from his headquarters in Berlin, he had stopped at Gross-Rosen, where he found his successor, Baer, bumbling around in an effort to make what Hoess called "preparations for the reception of the prisoners." Of the prisoners themselves, Baer seemed to know very little. "He had no idea where his camp might be wandering," Hoess reported.

Hoess climbed back into his car and drove eastward. His main purpose was to check on "the order for the destruction of everything important." The carrying out of every order was important to Hoess, of course, but this particular order for the burning of evidence was one that he hoped might ultimately save him from the hangman. "I was only able to get as far as the Oder, near Ratibor," Hoess wrote, "for the Russian armored spearheads were already fanning out on the far side of that river. On all the roads and tracks in Upper Silesia west of the Oder I now met columns of prisoners, struggling through the deep snow. They had no food. Most of the noncommissioned officers in charge of these stumbling columns of corpses had no idea where they were supposed to be going. They only knew that their final destination was Gross-Rosen. But how to get there was a mystery."

Since Himmler had by now issued orders against the wanton killing of prisoners, Hoess claimed that he too "gave strict orders to the men in charge of all these columns that they were not to shoot prisoners incapable of further marching." He found the new orders ignored. "On the road near Leobschütz," he said, "I constantly came upon the bodies of prisoners who had just been shot, and which were therefore still bleeding. On one occasion, as I stopped my car by a dead body, I heard revolver shots quite near. I ran toward the sound, and saw a soldier in the act of stopping his motorcycle and shooting a prisoner leaning against a tree. I shouted at him, asking him what he thought he was doing, and what harm the prisoner had done him. He laughed impertinently in my face, and asked me what I proposed to do about it. I drew my pistol and shot him forthwith. He was a sergeant major in the Air Force."

Tramping through the snow, famished and exhausted, the prisoners clung to the idea that they would eventually reach a railroad line that would carry them to the west. Those who actually survived long enough to reach such a lifeline soon discovered, once again, still further ordeals ahead. Sim Kessel, the French boxer, who was now missing a finger, marched for a week before reaching a switching yard, and there the SS troops clubbed the prisoners onto a string of open-topped freight cars. Kessel was one of seventy. "We were forced to lie down, one on top of another, all tangled and mixed together . . . ," he recalled. "Not a hair showed above the edge. The SS guaranteed this by firing machine guns over our heads. . . . For five days we lay there almost motionless and without as much as a crust, or a drop of water. . . . In the terrible cold many of the inert bodies slowly gave up what remained of life in them. . . . I spent the last two days in an on-again-off-again coma. Noticing that my two nearest neighbors were dead, I took their blankets and then snuggled under their stiff bodies for warmth. On the evening of the fifth day we reached Mauthausen. We were ordered to get off the freight car, and I was strong enough to get down. In the few minutes we waited on the platform, I tried to count the men who had survived and could still walk. There were nine of us."

Far to the east, the grim and partly gutted ruins of Auschwitz lay abandoned in the snow. At 3 P.M. on January 27, 1945, more than a week after the SS evacuation, some white-caped reconnaissance scouts of the First Ukrainian Front emerged from the woods and saw the rows and rows of barracks, the miles of barbed wire, the empty guardposts. Inside the camp, they found some 7,650* of those half-dead prisoners whom the SS had judged too feeble to be worth evacuating. "There was a mad rush to shake them by the hand and shout out our gratitude," said one of the survivors, Karel Ornstein. "Several prisoners waved red scarves. The shouts of joy [could] have gone on forever...."

Of those last sixty thousand prisoners who marched west from Auschwitz, about one third died along the way. And for the survivors, survival meant to arrive, starving and frozen and exhausted, at some new destination like Mauthausen, a hilltop fortress near Linz where tens of thousands of prisoners had been worked to death in the nearby granite quarries. Yet, in a way, the 8,365 Auschwitz prisoners who reached Mauthausen were lucky. Most of them got some food and new clothing and then were shipped to smaller camps in the area. A far worse fate awaited the largest contingent, perhaps ten thousand in all, which finally arrived at Bergen-Belsen.

Bergen-Belsen, near the old Hanseatic town of Hannover, was once a Wehrmacht camp for wounded prisoners of war. It was quite small, designed for seven thousand men, who lived in a series of neat little buildings connected by neat little pathways. Not until 1943 did the SS get control of half the camp, and even then it remained a relatively "model" camp. Many of the prisoners confined here were rich or eminent Jews whom the SS hoped to ransom in one way or another. As the war drew to an end, however, Bergen-Belsen was first crowded, then swamped, then engulfed by the hordes streaming westward from the slave camps of Poland.

First came the SS men themselves, notably Captain Josef Kramer. A brutal professional who had served in the SS since 1932, Kramer had gone with Hoess in 1940 to join in the building of Auschwitz and had been made commandant of Birkenau in the spring of 1944 to preside over the gassing of the Hungarians. He was a heavyset man, with large ears and crew-cut brown hair and an aloof manner that one prisoner described as his "Buddhalike air." Dr. Lingens, however, remembered once seeing him in a rage, "his bull neck lowered, his thick

---

* This number, like so many Auschwitz statistics, is hardly more than an official approximation. Indeed, the total number of Auschwitz survivors is almost as cloudy as the number of dead. The estimates generally run around 30,000. The essential fact in all these estimates is that of all the prisoners shipped to Auschwitz, fewer than 1% survived.

head and jowls purple." This was the man who brought to Bergen-Belsen in December of 1944 the harshest Auschwitz methods. "We had suddenly the feeling that Belsen was going to become a second Auschwitz," a prisoner named Ada Bimke testified when Kramer and forty-four other Belsen officials came before a British military court at Lüneburg in the autumn of 1945. "They started with roll calls, *Appelle,* and those SS men who previously did not hit the prisoners started now to do so. . . . I worked in the hospital at Belsen, and many prisoners were admitted suffering from beating."

Like Hoess at Auschwitz, Kramer found himself flooded with new prisoners, but, unlike Hoess, he was not supposed to gas them. He protested to Berlin that he had no room, no food, no supplies, and yet the transports from the East kept streaming in, a grotesque reversal of the transports from the West that Kramer had once received at Birkenau. In the week of April 4–13 alone, 28,000 new prisoners arrived. Kramer hardly even attempted to combat the impending famine but simply accepted it as some incomprehensible and unavoidable vagary of war. "It was hardly possible to get any potatoes or vegetables," he testified at the Lüneburg trial, "and although I had been getting bread from Celle and Hannover the air raids destroyed part of the bakeries and the road and rail system. It was when the air raids started that, for the first time, bread did not arrive in the camp. . . . At last I lost patience, and told them [the authorities in Hannover], through my administrative officials, that if I did not get any potatoes or vegetables sent I would hold them responsible for any sort of catastrophe which might happen." In actual fact, Kramer knew that there was a Wehrmacht training school just two miles away which had eight hundred tons of food and a bakery capable of producing sixty thousand loaves of bread a day, but Kramer did not ask for help, he testified, because that would have required "special papers." And so the catastrophe happened.

Guns and clubs can kill people, but nothing is more lethal than simply keeping fifty thousand prisoners confined behind barbed wire with no food, almost no water, and just a few latrines. Within a few weeks, typhus and dysentery were everywhere, and so were the rats. The famished prisoners, who knew the war was almost over, ambled about or sat in a stupor, waiting for someone to rescue them. "There was no bread for four weeks before the arrival of the British troops," an Auschwitz prisoner named Dora Szafran testified at the Lüneburg trial. "During the whole time I was at Belsen, people were not taken for baths nor were their clothes changed. Toward morning there were several hundred corpses in the blocks and around the blocks. When the commandant . . . came along to inspect people, the corpses were cleared away from the front of the blocks, but inside they were full of corpses." Some of the survivors even resorted to cannibalism. "I actually saw a prisoner whip out a knife," Harold Le Druillenec testified, "cut a portion out of the leg of a dead body, and quickly put it in his mouth, naturally frightened of being seen in the act of doing so."

The first man from the outside world to enter this inferno was a British psychological-warfare officer named Captain Derek Sington, who had been ordered to negotiate the takeover of the camp. He could hardly believe what he saw. Along with 28,000 women and 12,000 men, all haggard and emaciated, there were 13,000 unburied corpses, some stacked in piles like pieces of fire-wood, many just lying around wherever they had fallen. (Among the dead was Anne Frank, who succumbed here during the last weeks of the war.) The half-mad Commandant Kramer proved to be "genial and friendly," said Sington. He described his prisoners to the British as "habitual criminals, felons, and homosexuals." He accompanied Sington on a tour of the camp in a British armored car, and the British repeatedly announced through bullhorns that the camp was now liberated. The prisoners too could hardly believe what they saw. Many of them simply stared numbly at their liberators. Some of the women began sobbing. A few ceremoniously scattered twigs and leaves in the path of the armored car. Kramer became alarmed. "Now the tumult is beginning," he said to Sington. The orderly camp had been "disrupted." Behind him, Sington heard the sound of gunfire as the Germans attempted even after their surrender to enforce their authority. Sington strode up to a Wehrmacht officer who was firing just over the heads of some prisoners and ordered him at gunpoint to stop. Sington then told Kramer that if any prisoners were shot for any reason whatever, the British would immediately shoot an equal number of SS men. The SS grudgingly acquiesced.

"Feed the living and bury the dead," the Marquis of Pombal had proposed as his prescription for healing the ravages of the Lisbon earthquake. The British did just that. As gently as soldiers can, they fed and cared for the starving prisoners and brought most of them back to life. Many of them, however, were beyond all help. An estimated ten thousand inmates liberated at Bergen-Belsen died shortly after their liberation. As for the mountains of decaying corpses, the British simply brought in bulldozers and pushed the bodies into vast pits and then covered them with lime. Then they bulldozed the rest of the camp, everything. All that remains of Bergen-Belsen today is a series of swollen graves, covered with grass.

Auschwitz remains. It is a museum now, and the marshy grass grows tall alongside the rusting railroad tracks that end at the haunted ramp of Birkenau. The Poles wanted to keep everything just as it was—"a monument of the martyrdom of the Polish nation," according to the official decree, "and of other nations"—and so they left the giant brick crematoria in ruins, just as the SS men had left them in their frenzy to escape. At the same time, the Poles wanted to preserve and demonstrate and explain, and so they repaired and repainted some of the grimmest barracks and filled them with educational exhibitions.

Here in Block 4 is a "hall of nations," outfitted with the flags of all the occupied lands that gave up their citizens to Auschwitz. And here an artfully constructed model of the destroyed gas chambers, and here a mountain of the hair cut from the women who were murdered. The Soviet troops who liberated Auschwitz found more than fifteen thousand pounds of this hair awaiting shipment back to Germany. And here in Block 5 is a display case containing all the artificial arms and legs, dozens and dozens of them, that were stripped from crippled prisoners before their execution. Here in Block 6 is another glass case

332 THE END OF THE WORLD

in which the tattered rags of the prisoners are neatly hung up for observation, like the costumes of a tribe that has long since vanished. And here, forever preserved, is the daily food ration that so many prisoners never got, the bowl of soup, the chunk of bread, the dab of margarine, the shriveled slice of sausage. Here in Block 7 are the three-tiered bunks, all neat and clean now, and empty.

In the cellar of Block 11 the "standing cells" are available for inspection, and the benches on which prisoners were flogged, and the clubs that were used to flog them. And here, next to the camp kitchen, is the long wooden gallows, where Rudolf Hoess, having confessed and testified and explained, was brought back to be hanged. "I too must now be destroyed," he had written. "The world demands it." And at Birkenau, finally, a rough stone pathway leads past the series of plaques that attempt to commemorate the dead. "Four million people suffered and died here," they say in a score of languages, "at the hands of the Nazi murderers between the years 1940 and 1945."

It is a great place for wreaths, for official visits by statesmen bearing wreaths. They pause to write worthy sentiments in the official visitors' book. West German Foreign Minister Walter Scheel, who was a Luftwaffe navigator during World War II, was the first German cabinet minister to make the pilgrimage and deposit a wreath. "It will be our task to preserve these highest values— dignity of man, peace among people," he wrote in the visitors' book. Gerald Ford was the first American President to come, and two U.S. Marines deposited his wreath of red and white carnations. "This monument . . . ," he wrote in the official book, "inspires us further to the dedicated pursuit of peace, cooperation and security for all peoples."

And the first Polish Pope, John Paul II, who was studying in his seminary during most of the Auschwitz years, arrived at the camp by means of a white helicopter and then a limousine, its path strewn with flowers. He fell to his knees in prayer. "Peace!" he cried. "Only peace! Only peace!" The carefully preserved barbed wire was strung with TV cables that day, and some of the reporters on the scene were impressed by other peculiarities. "It was a day of pitiless heat," recalled one of them, Neal Ascherson. "The Polish crowds poured into the vast Birkenau enclosures hour after hour, buying Catholic souvenirs, memorial postcards, soft drinks, and chocolate from the stalls set up along the way. . . . The Papal dais stood astride the blackened rails which led to the ramp. . . . Much had given way to time and nature since my last visit. Stout trees had grown out of soil composed of what had been human ash. . . . The poplars planted by the Nazis to screen the crematoria have grown enormously tall and graceful, stirring their tips against the blue sky. . . ."

The Polish purpose in all this commemoration is to make sure that the world remembers what happened at Auschwitz, and that it learns the lesson of what happened. To Polish officialdom—Józef Cyrankiewicz, who became premier in 1947, had been a prisoner at Auschwitz from 1941 to 1945—what happened and what it meant appeared perfectly clear. That is evident in the plaque mourning "the martyrdom of the Polish nation" and warning against "international fascism."

To others, neither the meaning of the event nor the lesson to be learned from it is quite so obvious. None of us can approach Auschwitz—neither the museum standing in the ruins nor the very idea of the great death camp on the Vistula—without all the intellectual and spiritual burdens that we carry with us. We see Auschwitz and we judge Auschwitz according to the way we see and judge the human race, and life, and God.

Auschwitz was a world unlike any other because it was created and governed according to the principles of absolute evil. Its only function was death. The first question, then, is whether we see Auschwitz as the epitome of life itself, an incarnation of the darkest principles of Machiavelli and Hobbes, or whether we see it as a mirror image of the true life, a Satanic perversion of some divine plan that we have not yet discovered. From that central enigma flow all the lesser contradictions that still bedevil anyone who seeks to understand the mystery of Auschwitz. Did it represent the ultimate evil of the German nation, and was that the evil of German rationality or of German irrationality? Or did it represent, conversely, the apotheosis of Jewish suffering? And was that suffering simply the result of centuries of anti-Semitism, or was it part of the fulfillment of the prophecy that the tormented Jews would someday return to Palestine, return, as Ezekiel had written, to "the land that is restored from the ravages of the sword, where people are gathered out of many nations upon the mountains of Israel?"

It can be argued that Auschwitz proves there is no God, neither for the Jews nor for the Catholics, neither for atheists nor for Jehovah's Witnesses, who all went equally helpless to their death. "If all this was possible," wrote one Hungarian survivor, Eugene Heimler, "if men could be herded like beasts toward annihilation, then all that I had believed in before must have been a lie. There was not, there could not be, a God, for he could not condone such godlessness." But such declarations have been made at every moment of extreme crisis by those who see God only in success and happiness. Since all efforts to prove or explain God's purposes demonstrate only the futile diligence of worker ants attempting to prove the existence of Mozart, Auschwitz can just as well prove a merciful God, an indifferent God, or, perhaps best, an unknowable God. William Styron, in *Sophie's Choice*, suggested the answer as a riddle: "At Auschwitz, tell me, where was God?" The answer is only another question: "Where was man?"

The evidence of Auschwitz has demonstrated many things about humanity. It has demonstrated that men (and women too) are capable of committing every evil the mind can conceive, that there is no natural or unwritten law that says of any atrocity whatever: This shall not be done. It has demonstrated that men can also bear and accept every evil, and that they will do so in order to survive. To survive, even just from one day to the next, they will kill and let kill, they will rob and betray their friends, steal food rations from the dying, inform on neighbors, do anything at all, just for one more day. The evidence of Auschwitz has demonstrated just as conclusively that men will sacrifice themselves for others, sometimes quite selflessly. Franciszek Gajnowiczek, for example, is a stooped, gray-haired man, who has survived Auschwitz to testify that when he was selected at random for execution one day in 1941, a Franciscan priest named Maximilian Kolbe stepped forward and volunteered to take his place, and did take his place and did die. (The Vatican in due time proclaimed Kolbe to be a saint.) The evidence has demonstrated, moreover, that those who are ready to sacrifice themselves for one another, those who share a commmitment to some political or spiritual purpose, are at least as likely to survive as those who make survival their only goal. The evidence, in other words, is as contradictory as human nature itself. "The truth about Auschwitz?" Józef Cyrankiewicz once reflected. "There is no person who could tell the whole truth about Auschwitz."

Elie Wiesel, who was sent to Auschwitz as a boy, remembered the place as hellish, and when he finally revisited it in 1979 he was overwhelmed by its beauty. "The low clouds, the dense forest, the calm solemnity of the scenery," he wrote. "The silence is peaceful, soothing. Dante understood nothing. Hell is a setting whose serene splendor takes the breath away." When Wiesel tried to decipher the meaning of that serene graveyard, he was helpless. "How was it possible?" he wrote. "We shall never understand. Even if we manage somehow to learn every aspect of that insane project, we will never understand it. . . . I think I must have read all the books—memoirs, documents, scholarly essays and testimonies written on the subject. I understand it less and less." That is the survivor's message on the mystery of survival, but the nameless dayyan may have been preaching a richer variation of the same message when he urged the men of the last *Sonderkommando* not to be afraid as they waited in the underground chamber for the fulfillment of God's incomprehensible will.

The Great War

"We would perform our function"

*... and fire came down from God out of heaven
and devoured them.*
—REVELATION, 20:9

At almost the exact center of the United States, vibrant with pride in being at the heart of the heartland, lies the city of Omaha, Nebraska. Lewis and Clark paused here, before the city was even founded, and so did the Mormon caravans searching for salvation in the wilds of Utah. Omaha was created in 1845 by some land speculators in Council Bluffs, Iowa, just across the Missouri River, who named it after a dispossessed Indian tribe and touted it as the prospective capital of the newly created Nebraska Territory and thus the logical starting point for the main railroad to California. They succeeded. Omaha became one of the great railroad centers of the Middle West, one of the great grain markets and cattle stockyards. With commerce came finance, and Omaha became home to a large number of insurance companies. With prosperity came culture, the Joslyn Art Museum and the Omaha Symphony Orchestra. Also the celebrated Boys Town operated by Father Edward Flanagan, who declared it to be his belief that "there is no such thing as a bad boy."

To protect all this, Omaha looked toward Fort Crook, long the home of the Twenty-second U.S. Infantry Regiment. Over the years, military systems changed. During World War I, Fort Crook served as the home base of the nation's first air unit, the Sixty-first Balloon Company, and after the war it was renamed Offutt Field in honor of First Lieutenant Jarvis J. Offutt, Nebraska's first air casualty, who had been killed in 1918 while flying for the Royal Air Force. During World War II, Martin B-24 and B-29 bombers were manufactured here, including the *Enola Gay,* which dropped the first atomic bomb on Hiroshima, and in 1948 the newly independent Air Force established in Offutt the headquarters of its Strategic Air Command. Omaha is thus at the center not only of the United States, not only of cattle and grain and life insurance, but of the planning for World War III.

When the Columbia Broadcasting System decided in 1981 to devote five prime-time hours and about $1 million to a documentary report entitled *The Defense of the United States,* it seemed logical to begin by simulating the devastating effects of a fifteen-megaton thermonuclear bomb on Omaha. The narrator's voice recited all the usual statistics, the radius of the blast area, the number of deaths by fire, but what was unforgettable to anyone who saw it was the monstrous image of the mushroom cloud rising over the office buildings of Omaha. It was the ordinariness of Omaha that made the image so powerful. The spectacle of a nuclear fireball rising over the Empire State Building in New York would probably have looked like another Hollywood epic, like *King Kong* or *The Beast from 20,000 Fathoms,* but the sight of that cloud over the office towers of Omaha made the viewer feel, as one feels at the onset of any commonplace disaster, an automobile collision or a heart attack: *So this is the way it is.*

But this is not the way it is. This is the way CBS imagined it, and simulated it, and then filmed the simulation. "Even if you staged an explosion yourself, it might not look real," says the CBS producer who managed the show. He and his technicians looked at hundreds of nuclear explosions on Pentagon film, but those films were just the raw material from which the special-effects technicians created their special effects.

"It's a little hard to explain the technical process," the CBS producer says. He reaches for a memo pad and begins sketching a mushroom cloud with a long stem, then another with a shorter stem. "It might look like this, when you need something more like this," he says, gesturing at the two clouds. "So you use artwork, and you superimpose that on the film, and you shoot it again, and you may have to do that four or five times until you get film that's compatible with what you need."

The producer is smooth and well tanned, in his mid-thirties. He wears a blue shirt, a striped necktie, a macrame belt and a heavy gold ring. He takes a certain pride in having spent $85,000 on one minute of broadcast film. That is "an unheard-of amount," he says. Ordinarily, a complete documentary costs about $200,000. The producer recalls working on his one minute over the course of four months. He began with Pentagon statistics, then organized meetings with MIT scientists, then joined in drafting a script, "what we call the story boards." Then there were more meetings with special-effects producers in California. "I said, 'This is what we want to do, and we've got $85,000, so what can you do for that?'" And finally there was a week in Omaha, with two camera crews, one to shoot in 35-millimeter film and one in 16-millimeter.

The budget of $85,000 was an irritating restriction, the producer remembers. There were so many possibilities that had to be left out. "We only showed one explosion by a fifteen-megaton weapon," he says. "It would have been interesting to show what would have happened if they'd fired fifteen different one-megaton weapons. Or if there had been different weather conditions. There are hundreds of different types of renderings. It's a Rubik's cube!"

Was he satisfied, finally, with the one minute of apocalypse that he had produced for television?

"No! How could I be satisfied?" the producer cries. Then he pauses. Behind him, a benign sunlight streams through white Venetian blinds. "Well, it was the best I could do for the money. You know, the Pentagon has a saying about getting the most bang for a buck. We got the most bang we could get for the bucks."

The appearance of people was . . . well, they all had skin blackened by burns. . . . They had no hair because their hair was burned, and at a glance you couldn't tell whether you were looking at them from in front or in back. . . . They held their arms bent like this . . . and their skin—not only on their hands, but on their faces and bodies too—hung down. . . . Wherever I walked I met these people. . . . Many of them died along the road—I can still picture them in my mind: like walking ghosts. . . . They didn't look like people of this world. . . . They had a special way of walking—very slowly. . . . I myself was one of them.

—A grocer in Hiroshima

If the Gallup Poll is to be believed, and there is no particular reason why it shouldn't be, most Americans now think that World War III may break out during the 1980s, that they themselves may not survive the atomic attack, and that they would rather not think about the prospects. Specifically, according to a Gallup Poll commissioned by *Newsweek* and published in its issue of October 5, 1981, a representative sampling of 671 adults was asked about the likelihood of an all-out nuclear war between the United States and the Soviet Union within the next ten years. Thirty-eight percent, the largest group, thought there was "some chance it will happen," 24 percent foresaw "a good chance," and 6 percent thought it "almost certain."

Though much of the press was reporting at the time that the public supported President Reagan in proclaiming a tougher military policy, the Gallup Poll asked whether the Reagan policy was increasing or reducing the chances of war, or not changing those chances. Thirty-five percent saw the dangers unchanged, 28 percent thought Reagan was increasing them, while 23 percent thought he was reducing them. Asked whether they themselves favored using nuclear weapons if the Soviets attacked and seemed likely to conquer Western Europe—one of the foundations of U.S. policy for many years—a solid 49 percent said they were opposed, while only 37 percent were in favor.

And what do you think your chances of living through a Soviet atomic attack? Good: 9 percent. Poor: 43 percent. Just fifty-fifty: 43 percent.

As for their own attitudes, 47 percent, the largest category, subscribed to the view that "while I am concerned about the chances of a nuclear war, I try to put it out of my mind."

The feeling I had was that everyone was dead. The whole city was destroyed. . . . I thought all of my family must be dead—it doesn't matter if I die. . . . I thought this was the end of Hiroshima, of Japan—of humankind. . . . This was God's judgment on man.

—A Protestant minister in Hiroshima

Despite the widespread desire to avoid thinking about an impending catastrophe, that sense of catastrophe itself exists mainly in the popular imagination. No nuclear-armed strategic missile has ever been fired, after all, though both the superpowers have actually possessed for many years the weapons capable of inflicting the destruction that so many people dread. The intensity of public anxiety therefore varies not according to changes in Soviet military power, nor even changes in the East–West political climate, but according to official manipulations of public opinion. The idea of the end of the world has finally become an instrument of international propaganda.

Today, that idea seems strong, yet the students who demonstrate against the threat of nuclear war appear quite unaware that the threat was probably greater twenty years ago than it is now. Soviet and American nuclear tests in those days really did fill the atmosphere with a radioactive fallout of strontium 90 and iodine 131, and these half-forgotten carcinogens really did appear in the food chain, first in grass and cattle fodder, then in the cows' milk destined for babies.

Both sides brandished their new weapons with an almost reckless pugnacity. When Nikita Khrushchev shipped ballistic missiles to Cuba in 1962, President Kennedy threatened to retaliate with all the military forces at his command. There were supporting moves of extreme belligerence. Kennedy not only organized a national bomb-shelter program but urged all homeowners to start building their own fallout shelters in their own backyards. The basic purpose was less to protect American lives than to persuade the Russians that Americans were ready to fight.

The strain was too great. Khrushchev backed down, then was deposed and disgraced. But to many Americans too, the nuclear threats were terrifying, making the risks seem greater than any reward. Swarms of mothers marched through Washington, and there arose a national debate on whether it would really be justifiable to shoot a neighbor who was trying to force his way into one's bomb shelter. Faced with such public scruples, the Pentagon planners began fretting over the problem of what they called "credibility." Of what value was American military strength if the Soviets did not believe Washington would use it?

During the Vietnam years, this question was tested at a lower level of danger, the level of infantry combat, and both sides kept accumulating more and more nuclear weapons. Critics of these gigantic arsenals periodically observed that each superpower had enough atomic bombs to destroy the other ten times over, or a hundred times. But in that swollen excess of destructive power—by now about eight or nine thousand warheads on each side—the generals saw a kind of stability, which they named with one of their aptest acronyms, MAD, for "mutually assured destruction." Behind the apparent stability of MAD, however, the American defeat in Vietnam caused new uncertainties about whether Washington could ever bring itself to use its nuclear weapons. The Minuteman intercontinental missiles were officially judged to be vulnerable to increasingly accurate Soviet ICBMs, but all the remedies seemed too expensive. In the long-forgotten bomb shelters of New York, teams of young blacks were paid three dollars an hour to haul the food caches of the Kennedy era out into the sunlight. An entrepreneur named Jack Jordan agreed to buy the decaying provisions for $1.06 per ton and grind them up into chicken feed. "This stuff," said Jordan, "should have been taken out years ago."

Everything that reassures Americans that there will not be a nuclear war, however, reassures the rulers of Russia that they have relatively little to fear from Washington. When the Russians sent troops into Afghanistan early in

1980, Carter seemed to lack either the means or the will to use force. Apart from scrapping the Strategic Arms Limitation Treaty (SALT) that he and the Russians had recently signed, he limited his indignation to such gestures as restricting wheat sales to Russia and boycotting the Moscow Olympics.

Washington once again felt a need, then, to persuade the world that it was really preparing for the prospect of nuclear war. If MAD was no longer credible—and was it ever really credible that the United States could protect itself by threatening suicide?—then President Carter wanted it known that he was altering United States policy by aiming American missiles at the Soviets' military bases rather than their cities. The implication of Presidential Directive No. 59, officially approved in the summer of 1980, was that Washington was ready not simply to deter war but to wage it.

And since the Minuteman missiles were reputed to be vulnerable to surprise attack, Carter asked Congress to approve a $34 billion program to build two hundred mobile MX missiles as well as a series of huge "racetracks" in Utah and Nevada to disguise the missiles' location. Although Carter did not go so far as to replenish the canned goods in the bomb shelters, he did ask $2 billion to plan the evacuation of American cities in case of attack. (By coincidence, the Pentagon added to the public anxiety that summer by disclosing that there had been at least three recent false alarms, three occasions on which military computers had mistakenly announced a Soviet missile attack. Air Force bombers had actually started their engines before the computer errors were diagnosed, but a Pentagon spokesman coolly declared that "we weren't remotely close to World War Three.")

Ronald Reagan's defeat of Carter in 1980 canceled all these maneuvers, for Reagan wanted to begin maneuvers of his own. The ridiculous MX racetracks were canceled as too expensive, but to the MX missile itself Reagan added a long list of other weapons, a revival of the B-1 bomber that Carter had abandoned, further work on the so-called "neutron bomb," even the de-mothballing of the battleships of World War II. He also requested $4 billion for a revival of civil defense. Washington announced that this showy military buildup would cost more than $1 trillion over the course of five years, but as a deteriorating economy brought large budget deficits, it remained uncertain how many such defense moves would ever be completed. None of these measures had much effect on the essential danger, which had remained basically unchanged for many years, but Reagan, like his predecessors, did his best to impress the world with a rhetoric of strength. He talked loudly of Soviet threats and let it be known that he could imagine a limited nuclear exchange in Europe. His excitable Secretary of State Alexander Haig said there was a NATO contingency plan to detonate a nuclear bomb somewhere in Europe as a warning. U.S. officials pressed plans to deploy more than 500 new Pershing II and cruise missiles in Europe, and Europeans responded with a wave of protest demonstrations.

Whatever its practical effects, the new policy revived the public fear of apocalypse. The prestigious *Bulletin of the Atomic Scientists,* which has expressed its concern over the years by publishing on the cover of each issue a clock with the hands nearing the midnight of Doomsday, moved those hands forward at the beginning of 1980 from nine minutes to seven minutes before midnight. In January of 1981, it moved them forward again to four minutes to midnight. "Both sides willfully delude themselves that a nuclear war can remain limited or even be won," it said. "In 1980 both sides officially declared nuclear war 'thinkable.' "

> *I saw blue phosphorescent flames rising from the dead bodies—and there were plenty of them. These were quite different from the orange flames coming from the burning buildings. . . . These blue phosphorescent flames are what we Japanese look upon as spirits rising from dead bodies—in former days we called them fireballs. And yet, at that time I had no sense of fear, not a bit, but merely thought, "Those dead bodies are still burning."*
> —A noncommissioned officer in Hiroshima

Would it now be possible to see an actual missile? The much-discussed and much-feared thing itself? What does a nuclear-armed Minuteman III, ready for launching, really look like?

The United States Air Force would like to oblige. It offers to welcome the inquiring visitor to the Minot Air Force Base, in Minot, North Dakota, and to demonstrate all its capabilities. Minot has a large new hospital, and a base library with thirty thousand books, and a nine-hole golf course, and a Hustlers Square Dancing Club. Handel's *Messiah* is performed every Christmas. The actual missiles, unfortunately, cannot be seen. Each of them is hidden away in an underground silo that is ninety feet deep, and each silo is plugged up with a concrete "door" that weighs 110 tons. Only about once a year, says the Air Force spokesman, is the door opened by a compressed-air pump so that maintenance men can check whether the missile is still in working order. The snows are heavy in North Dakota, and sometimes water seeps into the silos.

For inquiring visitors, however, the Air Force has built a Potemkin missile inside a Potemkin silo. It looks exactly like a real Minuteman III—and color photographs of it appear occasionally in national magazines—but it is quite harmless. It is an optical illusion, a *trompe l'oeil*. But come and look. Underneath the concrete door, propped open now on a large ratchet bar, there is a second stopper known as a B-plug. It weighs seven tons, and it takes thirty minutes to open—long enough, according to Air Force calculation, for the Air Police to catch any saboteurs or terrorists who try to open it. The Air Force is acutely sensitive to the idea of saboteurs interfering with its plans, and there is talk of electronic sensors and savage guard dogs, though no one can recall an instance of an actual sabotage attempt.

The tip of the missile, which has no warhead, is sheathed in aluminum. The bottom section, sixty feet below, is made of concrete and painted apple green. Steel scaffolding encircles the missile, and teams of electricians labor over its wiring with screwdrivers, shining their lights into the innards of the vehicle, occasionally calling out instructions to one another. The gigantic missile is a strange and impressive object, but it does not arouse any emotion. It is only there to be looked at. It cannot fly. It cannot kill.

Would it, then, be possible to see, if not a real missile, a real missile man?

One of those legendary officers who sits in an underground command post, eternally waiting for the message that will order him to insert the key in the lock and send the missiles on their way?

Ever obliging, the Air Force provides a gray helicopter to carry a visitor across the flat, bare, brown fields of North Dakota. This is fertile land, scarred by the marks of the harrow, but in May there are still patches of snow under the trees, and greenish puddles reflect the sky that bears one northward toward Manitoba. "This is the spring time/ But not in time's covenant ...," Eliot wrote. "If you came this way,/ Taking any route, starting from anywhere,/ At any time or at any season,/ It would always be the same. ...."

About forty miles north of Minot, the helicopter reaches a little encampment designated as Oscar One. A high chain-link fence surrounds a plain one-story wooden building painted in the familiar apple green. Nearby stands a garage with a basketball hoop screwed into its side. There is no other building in any direction as far as the horizon. The Ninety-first Strategic Missile Wing has fifteen such units scattered over eight thousand square miles of farmland. (Each launch command facility [LCF] controls ten missile silos from three to seven miles away. Each LCF and its ten missiles form a flight; five flights make a squadron, three squadrons a wing.) Inside Oscar One, there is a lounge with a pool table on one side and a few small pots of philodendron in the window. "The boys do what they can to make these places look different," says the colonel who is guiding the tour.

Has anyone ever gone mad here? The colonel smiles and shakes his head. (How many times has the question been asked?) All precautions have been taken. The missile men have been tested again and again, questioned, examined, reassessed and reassured. Once here, says the colonel, anyone who develops a "personal problem" is immediately transferred. Anyone who wants to leave the missile program for any reason whatever is not only permitted but requested to do so. There is no Catch-22 here in Minot, North Dakota.

So strong is the Air Force image of efficiency that one imagines the subterranean command post will resemble a gleaming Martian headquarters in a science-fiction movie. It is almost reassuringly decrepit. It resembles not a Martian headquarters so much as the basement of some elementary school that one attended long ago, a place where the janitor kept old rags and half-empty cans of paint behind the asbestos-covered heating pipes. The elevator that creaks slowly downward to the command module has the scissored gates of an antique freight elevator in an abandoned warehouse. At the bottom of the shaft, a sergeant gives a heave, and an enormous eight-ton blast door grudgingly swings open.

The subterranean capsule that contains the two missile officers is little better than a prison cell. One enters past a toilet, unscreened by any wall, and then a cot with a khaki blanket. Here the two men must serve a twenty-four-hour shift, about eight times a month, each man taking a turn on the cot while the other maintains the vigil. They usually cannot sleep more than four or five hours a night, but they can read or watch television. They can even study for an M.B.A. degree under a program specially worked out for them by the University of North Dakota. Their two red easy chairs, from which the two men must simultaneously insert their keys in the locks that control the missiles, stand exactly twelve feet apart because the Air Force has determined that no demented or traitorous missile officer, after overpowering his partner, could dash the twelve feet from one chair to the other within the two seconds that the Air Force defines as simultaneity. The Air Force seems to have thought of everything. But the two red chairs are rather worn and shabby, and each one is missing an arm.

The two officers, a captain and a lieutenant, are of average size, though perhaps a little heavy, as uniformed men in confined spaces tend to be. They both wear a kind of orange foulard scarf around the neck, designed as a gallant emblem of *esprit de corps,* but the foulards are pre-tied, like a waiter's bow tie and dickey. Both officers look about twenty-five. One forgets that wars are fought by one's children.

This is undoubtedly not the first time that the captain has received official visitors. Poised and articulate, he recites the drill, the series of steps he would take as soon as he receives an order to launch his ten missiles. First the order must be elaborately corroborated and confirmed. "We format it," he says. The message must come by several different systems, by telephone, by computer printout, by high-frequency and low-frequency radio. There must be a "launch vote," corroboration by another missile team.

"Then what?" a visitor asks as the captain pauses.

"Then we would perform our function."

If any part of the countdown violates any of the myriad regulations, the missile is not fired; everything must go exactly according to plan. The plan leads inexorably toward one action, the insertion of the key.

"Where is the key right now?" the visitor asks.

"Over there, in that red box," the captain says.

The box has two padlocks. Each of the officers has one combination. The combinations are changed whenever a new shift comes on duty. The lock into which the key fits is sealed with blue-and-white tape.

One cannot resist asking, finally, the obvious question that has been asked again and again: What do they think they would think at the moment when the launching order comes? The captain is ready with his answer. The question has been part of his training from the start. Each new officer is made to sign a statement declaring that he knows what his task will be, that he knows what is involved, that he will push the button when ordered to do so. At the end of his training, he signs another statement declaring once again that he understands what he is to do and agrees to do it.

But has he actually tried to imagine what the moment of decision would be like?

"If you had a lot of time, you'd probably think about it—that's only human—" the captain says, then pauses. "But we're trained not to think about it. There are lots of things that have to be done, and you concentrate on that. You're trying to do the job."

He turns to the lieutenant and asks him if he has anything to add.

"I assume that if the launch order was given it would be a matter of national survival," the lieutenant says. "I'd have no qualms."

My daughter . . . had no burns and only minor external wounds, so I took her with me to my country house. She was quite all right for a while, but on the fourth of September she suddenly became sick. . . . She had spots all over her body. . . . Her hair began to fall out. She vomited small clumps of blood many times. Finally she began to bleed all over her mouth. And at times her fever was very high. . . . We didn't know what it was. I thought it was a kind of epidemic—something like cholera. So I told the rest of my family not to touch her and to disinfect all utensils and everything she used. . . . Even the doctor didn't know what it was. . . . After ten days of agony and torture she died. . . . I thought it was very cruel that my daughter, who had nothing to do with the war, had to be killed in this way.

—A manufacturer in Hiroshima

When one talks with military men for any length of time, one realizes that they speak a unique language. It is partly the language of bureaucracy, freighted with acronyms and technical terminology, and those who use it tend to use jargon for even the most ordinary concepts. "In the 1976-type time frame" is simply an Air Force officer's way of saying "1976." Another one says, "You can go to a standoff mode," when a civilian would say, "It's a draw." Quite often, though, military men use military terminology to avoid the words that would convey the realities of nuclear warfare. LUA means launch under attack, and DE means damage estimate. "The enemy threat area" means Russia. "The button-up period" is the POI, or period of interest, during which the survivors of a nuclear attack would be huddled in their fallout shelters. Such word games are natural enough to people who play war games and who use the language of games even to describe real wars. "It depends," says an officer at Minot, "on what kind of war you're playing."

"But it's not just those military words that don't mean anything anymore," says a middle-aged journalist back in New York. "The real words we keep using for that kind of disaster—*holocaust, apocalypse, Doomsday*—what do any of them mean?

"About twenty years ago, I used to write for the foreign-news section of *Newsweek*," he goes on, "and every week I had to describe whatever happened that week as 'momentous,' 'epic,' 'history changed last week.' There was a lot of atomic strategy going on in those days, and I began to get the feeling that none of the epic stories I wrote meant much of anything. The words were all getting worn out.

"So I thought up a sort of test. I said to my boss, the foreign editor, 'Suppose World War Three really started right now, and the Russians and the Americans fired a lot of nuclear missiles at each other, and there were more than a hundred million dead on each side, but for some reason New York was spared, and *Newsweek* wanted to keep right on publishing, and you had to write the lead story. What would your first sentence say?'

"He sort of smiled and hesitated, as though he suspected a trick, and then he said, 'What would *yours* be?' I said I didn't know. Then he got a kind of glassy-eyed look, the way he did when he started writing inside his head, and he went over to his typewriter and began hammering away. After a while, he cranked this piece of copy paper out of his typewriter and showed it to me. Quite proud of it he was, too. And I looked at it, and it was just like any other *Newsweek* lead, the kind of thing I wrote every week. I still remember, it began: 'At last, it had happened. The unthinkable tragedy that mankind had feared for so long ...' And so on and so on and so on."

I climbed Hijiyama Hill and looked down. I saw that Hiroshima had disappeared. ... What I felt then and still feel now I just can't explain with words. Of course I saw many dreadful scenes after that, but that experience—looking down and finding nothing left of Hiroshima—was so shocking that I simply can't express what I felt. ... Hiroshima didn't exist—that was mainly what I saw: Hiroshima just didn't exist.

—A history professor in Hiroshima

It is difficult for the nation's official experts to confront the menacing prospect of nuclear war without attempting to predict what would actually happen. How many would die in the first attack? How would the survivors survive? What would they have to eat? Would there be any electricity? Would money still serve as money? Would the victims all help one another or prey on one another?

Large amounts of information have been fed into various computers, and many reemerging statistics have been weighed and puzzled over. The answers are largely guesswork, of course, because even the simplest results of the first attack would depend on a large number of variables. Who can predict whether the attack would be large or small, aimed at missile bases in the remote prairies or at oil refineries near big cities, whether the enemy warheads would be detonated in midair or at ground level, whether the radioactive fallout from a ground-level explosion would be carried near or far by various winds?

All that the experts can do, then, is to suggest a series of hypotheses. When the Senate Foreign Relations Committee asked Congress' Office of Technology Assessment in 1978 to study "the impact which various levels of attack would have on populations and economies of the United States and the Soviet Union," the OTA experts somewhat arbitrarily decided on four basic sets of hypotheses. Even within each set, the estimates of the dead varied by tens of millions. Still, if thinking about the unthinkable has any value, then one must begin somewhere.

Begin by imagining, the OTA said, that the Soviets decide to retaliate against some unspecified provocation by attacking just one American city with just one of their estimated eight thousand warheads. Imagine Detroit, to be specific, hit by a one-megaton weapon, a relatively small weapon but still about fifty times the size of the Hiroshima bomb. Imagine that it explodes at ground level, at night, in front of the civic center at the intersection of Highways I-75 and I-94.

Where the civic center now stands, there would be nothing but a crater about two hundred feet deep and one thousand feet in diameter, surrounded by a rim of highly radioactive earth. Out to a distance of .6 miles from this crater, the OTA says, "there will be nothing recognizable remaining, with the exception of some massive concrete bridge abutments and building foundations." From .6 to 1.3 miles out, there will remain only "a few very strongly constructed buildings ... with the interiors totally destroyed." About 1.7 miles is "the closest range where any significant structure will remain standing." That 1.7-mile ring, encircling the area that would be subjected to blast pressure of more than 12 pounds per square inch (psi), extends from Grosse Point Park in the east to Ferndale in the northwest and River Rouge in the southwest. By day, there are about 200,000 people at work within that ring, in central Detroit; by night, when the hypothetical attack occurs, the number drops to 70,000. Of these, says the OTA report, "there will be virtually no survivors."

Outside the 12-psi ring, as the blast pressure decreases, the OTA provides estimates of what might remain. Between 1.7 and 2.7 miles from the explosion, pressure will drop to 5 psi. Although most walls will be blown out, "at the greater distances the skeletal structures will remain standing." The streets will be a mass of rubble, from tens of feet in depth in downtown Detroit to a few inches here. About 250,000 people live in this outer ring by night, and the OTA estimates that 130,000 will be killed, 100,000 injured. Most of the deaths will be caused by collapsing buildings, but here also begin the deaths from burns and radiation. These casualties would vary widely according to the time of year and the weather conditions, which would alter the number of people caught out in the open. Eventual deaths from burns could range from 1,200 to 30,000. Many fires would start in the rubble, but most would die down after the blast wave passed.

From 2.7 to 4.7 miles out, under a pressure of 2 psi, the nature of the destruction changes considerably. The planes and hangars at the Detroit City Airport would be destroyed, and major industrial buildings like the Cadillac plant would be severely damaged. Of the 400,000 inhabitants, about 20,000 would be killed and perhaps 200,000 injured. Only about five percent of the buildings would catch fire, but the fires would spread much more extensively through the surviving buildings than in the devastated central areas of the city. The fires would go on spreading for at least twenty-four hours and would destroy half of all buildings. In the outermost damaged areas, up to 7.4 miles from the center, there would be "only an insignificant number killed," but about 150,000 of the 600,000 inhabitants would be injured. Damage to buildings would be "light" to "moderate," and "fires would be comparatively rare."

All in all, then, the OTA portrays a scene of almost unimaginable devastation and yet not one of apocalyptic annihilation. Of Detroit's population of 1.3 million, some 220,000 would be dead, 430,000 injured, and 670,000 uninjured. The question then is how the survivors would survive in the ruins. Very few of the injured would ever get to hospitals. In Detroit, specifically, Wayne, Macomb and Oakland counties have sixty-three hospitals containing about 18,000 beds, but more than half of them would be destroyed. But as the OTA experts tried to predict the overall process of recovery, they sketched a surprisingly optimistic picture. Electricity would immediately be cut off throughout the city, but the main electrical power plants at Grosse Point Park and Zug Island should receive "only superficial damage." Power could be restored as far as the 1-psi ring within twenty-four hours, to the 2-psi ring within a few days. The water supply should remain usable, and service could resume as soon as the electric pumps were restored to duty. . . .

Such estimates of recovery, however, are based on several implausibilities: that the Soviets attack only Detroit, in some kind of symbolic reprisal, and only with a single one-megaton warhead, that radioactive fallout would be correspondingly limited, and that the surrounding regions stand ready and able to provide help. The OTA would not disagree about the unlikelihood of these circumstances; it is trying only to examine some of the possibilities.

I kept screaming, "Mother!" very loudly, and then I saw my mother staggering toward me. . . . She pulled the debris away from my body and then there was a hole I could crawl out through. . . . But my mother was very weak and began to collapse and fall on her side. So I helped her up and tried to drag her along. But the road was cluttered with pieces of destroyed houses and I couldn't move her at all. . . . The fire was all around us. . . . I was suffocating from the smoke and I thought if we stayed like this then both of us would be killed. . . . I found a neighbor and told him my mother was lying in there and asked him to please fetch her. . . . My mother [was] found dead, face down in a water tank, very close to the spot where I left her. . . . If I had been a little older or stronger I could have rescued her.

—A student in Hiroshima

Imagine now a slightly more plausible scenario of Soviet attack. Imagine that instead of limiting themselves to one city, the Soviets decide to cripple the entire United States economy by destroying one essential industry. The OTA picked the oil-refining industry, since it is highly concentrated and highly vulnerable. The experts arbitrarily hypothesized that the Soviets would launch this "limited" attack with ten intercontinental missiles, each armed with eight one-megaton warheads. They also assumed that the Soviets would aim only at the refineries, without attempting either to kill civilians or to avoid killing civilians. The sixty-five principal refineries are all located near major cities, however, so the eighty Soviet warheads would devastate the New York–Philadelphia area, the Detroit–Chicago area, the Kansas City area, the Gulf Coast from New Orleans to Houston, and most of California.

The attack would kill more than five million people if the warheads were detonated in the air, the OTA estimated, and just over three million if they were detonated at ground level. It would also destroy sixty-four percent of U.S. refinery capacity for many months. Again, the OTA tried to illustrate the effects of the attack by concentrating on one city, Philadelphia, where two warheads would land near an Exxon refinery on the Schuylkill River. About 135,000 of the 155,000 people within two miles of the explosion would be killed immediately; so would 410,000 of the 785,000 within five miles. Here, the oil fires would be disastrous. "Some oil tanks would rupture and the oil would leak onto rivers or harbors, where it would ignite and spread fire," the OTA report says. "Fires at refineries could not be extinguished because of intense heat, local fallout, an inadequate supply of chemicals to use on petroleum fires, and roads blocked by rubble and evacuees. . . ." Again, this scenario assumes that there is only one limited raid, and that the survivors will care for the casualties and repair the damages.

Most U.S. official planners believe that a "limited" Soviet attack would be aimed not against economic installations, however, but against American strategic forces, the missiles and bombers that threaten Russia. They call this a "counterforce attack." In one of the OTA's rare ventures in making judgments, it reports that "some observers" believe such a counterforce attack would be "the least irrational way of waging strategic war." The Pentagon has already attempted several studies of a raid against its forty-eight strategic-bomber bases and eight intercontinental-missile bases, scattered across thirty-four states, plus the nuclear submarine base at Charleston, South Carolina. Some cities like Charleston and Little Rock would suffer major damage, but, since most of the bases are in fairly remote areas, the deaths caused by the blast waves would be fewer than in an urban attack. Since more missiles would be used, however, fallout casualties might well be higher. This would depend on variables ranging from wind conditions to the amount of shelter available. Combining the various Pentagon studies, the OTA could conclude only that civilian deaths would total between one million and twenty million, but it added that any estimate lower than eight million "requires quite optimistic assumptions."

The most optimistic of all assumptions, once again, is that any limited attack could remain limited. One authoritative study, compiled by Dr. Desmond Ball of Australia and published in 1981 by the Institute of Strategic Studies in London, took considerable pains to refute that idea. The standard Pentagon theory that "escalation can be controlled" by the military command structure is "most unrealistic," said Ball. His own estimates of deaths in Europe sounded much like the OTA figures on deaths in the U.S.: two million to twenty million. But that would be only in the "unrealistic" case of the military maintaining restraints. An unrestrained nuclear war in Europe, said Ball, would kill 200 million, or about one third of the population, a figure that echoes once again the Book of Revelation and the Black Death.

The American estimates of death in an all-out nuclear war are hardly less nebulous. The OTA cited a 1977 Pentagon study that estimated a death toll of 155 to 165 million if no civil-defense measures were taken. It claimed that the use of existing shelters could reduce that figure to 110 to 145 million. The OTA cited a similar analysis by the Arms Control and Disarmament Agency, however, which computed the death toll at 105 to 131 million without shelters and 76 to 85 million with shelters. Deaths could be still further reduced to 40 to 55 million, the Pentagon suggested hopefully, if civilians could somehow be evacuated from major cities.

Another congressional report, published in 1979 by the Senate Committee on Banking, Housing and Urban Affairs, offered considerable detail on not only the casualties but the economic consequences of an all-out attack. It said that a strike with five hundred megatons "would be adequate for effective urban-industrial attacks" on the seventy-one largest metropolitan areas in the United States. That would extend from New York and Los Angeles down to such places as West Palm Beach, Albuquerque and Fresno. These seventy-one areas contain 62 percent of the nation's population and 68 percent of its manufacturing capacity. Between 50 and 65 percent of the people in these areas would be killed and wounded, the Senate report said, and more than 80 percent of the industry would be destroyed. Indeed, there would be 98 percent destruction of such basic industries as iron and steel, petroleum and nonferrous metals.

Having cited all its statistics, the OTA study made a modest attempt to portray what the first hours of nuclear attack would be like: "Fires will be raging, water mains will be flooding, power lines will be down, bridges will be gone, freeway overpasses will be collapsed, and debris will be everywhere." It even attempted to speculate on the social chaos that would follow. "While some degree of law and order could probably be maintained in localities where a fairly dense population survived," it said, "the remaining highways might become quite unsafe, which would reduce trade over substantial distances. . . . There is a possibility that the country might break up into several regional entities. If these came into conflict with each other there would be further waste and destruction. . . . Such an attack would place in question whether the United States would ever recover its position as an organized, industrial, and powerful country."

After considering all these official assessments, the only conclusion that one can safely draw is that the reality would be much worse. Statistics on millions of deaths come to seem abstract—"acceptable" is the military term—unless one can imagine one's own children with their faces burned away, and one cannot. As is clear in Robert Jay Lifton's interviews with Hiroshima survivors, several of which have been quoted in this chapter, the shock of nuclear attack surpasses anyone's capacity for comprehending catastrophe. The mutilated and the uninjured seem equally unable to realize what has happened to them. They wander about in a numbed state of near-madness. Even several decades after the explosion, they are still haunted by guilt and anxiety. And the scars of their burns have not healed.

Yet one must keep remembering that the Hiroshima bomb was a little thing, about one-fiftieth the size of the one-megaton weapons that are the smallest to figure in the OTA report. No less important is the fact that Hiroshima and Nagasaki were the only cities attacked, and that the rest of Japan stood ready to help. Doctors and ambulances soon arrived from other areas. Hiroshima's electricity was partially restored the day after the raid, and train service to the city resumed on the day after that. In all disasters, the knowledge that help is on the way, that there is normal life outside the disaster area, provides critical support to the victims. In an all-out nuclear attack on the United States, the victims could know only that they were helpless.

Some of them would take refuge in fallout shelters, but Pentagon statistics on the value of such shelters give no idea of what life there would be like. Many of the shelters that do exist have neither sufficient food nor adequate ventilation. Many of the victims seeking safety in these overcrowded dens would already be suffering the effects of radiation. The symptoms include nausea, vomiting, bleeding from mouth and rectum, diarrhea with large amounts of blood in the stool. Whether the people jammed into such pestilential places for days on end would help each other or attack each other is impossible to predict. The prediction depends heavily on the forecaster's philosophy of human nature, on whether Rousseau's view of life was truer than that of Hobbes, on whether men are animals. Presumably the circumstances would vary considerably. After the first major New York blackout in 1968, there was much self-congratulation about the altruism and aplomb with which New Yorkers had reacted to the crisis; in the second blackout a decade later, looting soon became epidemic. And those were only disturbances of a few hours, with nobody injured and the full police force in action. Even more unpredictable, then, is the broader question of what might happen when the survivors of a nuclear attack emerged from their shelters into a ruined and poisoned world.

Thinking about the unthinkable usually includes one final illusion, that the generals in charge of the missiles would themselves be thinking. While popular fantasies sometimes predict a total extinction of the human race, almost every official scenario of World War III assumes that after one or two nuclear exchanges, the firing would stop. Both sides would then try to figure out who had won, or else declare a stalemate and begin the process of recovery. It seems just as plausible, however, to argue that if the generals were that rational, they would never fire the missiles at all. The mentality required to launch a nuclear attack does not by any means necessarily imply a cool ability to cease firing. On the contrary, it is at least as easy to imagine that once one's own side has suffered millions of casualties, a general who still controls some of the remaining missiles might well consider it his sacred duty to continue firing at any remaining sign of life.

> *I tried to take some things out of the house, but everything was buried . . . and so, carrying only the baby's diapers . . . and myself wearing only a panty and slip, the three of us, a mother with two children—what should we do? In what direction should we escape? . . . I had no clear destination, but I felt we had to run away. . . . The eight-year-old began to complain that her stomach was hot, and she threw up—a dark liquid like coal tar . . . and then the baby began to throw up also. . . . I tried to go over a nearby bridge, but it was on fire, so we couldn't go that way. . . . And then I lost consciousness. . . . It was not so much my bodily injuries, but the feeling of helpless desperation . . . the things I saw around me. . . . I didn't know what I could do about caring for my children, what would happen to us. . . .*
>
> —A housewife in Hiroshima

Just as the prospect of a major nuclear war is inherently absurd—a contradiction of any goal that might inspire it—all reactions to it are also absurd.

It is absurd, to begin with, for governments that spend billions of dollars on the weapons of destruction to spend almost nothing on defending their own citizens from attack. Bomb shelters are absurd, but the lack of bomb shelters is also absurd. The idea of evacuating major cities in a time of crisis is absurd, but if such evacuations could save millions of lives, then the absence of any evacuation plan is absurd. It is absurd that the United States government claims to have built antimissile missiles that could destroy all incoming warheads, but it is equally absurd that such purely defensive missiles are the only ones now forbidden by Soviet-American treaty. According to the logic of strategic thinking, any effective defensive measure, like the building of defensive missiles or bomb shelters, is by definition provocative and threatening. It implies a dangerously increased readiness to fight because it reduces, no matter how slightly, the absurdity of war. In absurdity, therefore, lies safety. That statement too is absurd.

And what is to become of Western civilization? In 1954, a number of nations gathered at The Hague and signed a "convention for the protection of cultural objects in case of armed conflict." The United States did not sign—though it had signed a similar treaty in 1935—but West Germany was among the seventy nations that did, and after the Bundestag finally ratified the agreement about one hundred German officials and experts began in 1979 the process of listing, labeling and, where possible, duplicating some fifteen thousand objects that were considered essential parts of the national heritage. The selections included the Cologne Cathedral, the Arnsberg Monastery, various medieval tax records, and the speeches of Adolf Hitler. Such efforts to save old buildings and records in the midst of a nuclear war seem absurd, but so does the reckless willingness to leave the treasures of civilization lying exposed to ruin on the battlefields of the future.

Since both Washington and Moscow seem unwilling to renounce their nuclear weapons, various eminent citizens have felt themselves obliged to protest and demonstrate against the official obduracy. Peace marches and newspaper advertisements have made the same impassioned arguments for many years, but each new demonstrator needs to believe that this gesture of protest is the one that will finally have some effect. Dr. Howard Hiatt, dean of Harvard's School of Public Health, used data that had been compiled nearly twenty years earlier to warn a Harvard symposium in 1981 of the infectious diseases that would follow a nuclear attack. And speaking of his own efforts to organize doctors and scientists against nuclear weapons, he said, "We didn't have the luxury of simply doing nothing." The implication was that he had done something, achieved some purpose. To protest is absurd; not to protest is absurd.

Since protests seem to have as little effect as disarmament conferences, a number of citizens have decided in recent years to undertake absurd protective measures of their own. They call themselves "survivalists," and they have built little fortresses for themselves in remote areas of the country, filling their cellars with canned food and medicines and guns. One of them, a bearded young man named Bruce Clayton, wrote a guidebook entitled *Life After Doomsday* and dedicated it "to the memory of a few sensible Romans who in 79 AD fled from Pompeii in the middle of the night while their neighbors laughed at them." Clayton's book is a comprehensive catalogue of provisions and supplies, what kind of water purifier to buy (The Waterpik Portable Instapur) and what kind of guns (Heckler & Koch HK 91). Clayton also provides a rationale for acquiring such supplies: "Nuclear war will be the greatest social and biological catastrophe our world has ever known . . . but it will not be difficult to survive it." And for those guns: "Are you justified in using force to protect [your] supplies? I think you are fully justified. . . . Anyone who attempts to steal or sabotage those supplies is attempting to murder you or your family."

It is one of the permanent rules of the American system that whenever a sufficient number of people acquire a fixation, vendors and dealers will materialize and start selling them whatever their fantasy requires. As of 1981, according to an account in *The New York Times,* a real-estate office in La Verkin, Utah, was offering for $39,000 a one-bedroom, twelve-by-thirty-foot "unit" with blastproof doors and eight-inch reinforced-concrete ceilings, as well as a four-year supply of food. The Survival Homes Corporation of Hoodville, Oregon, reported that its architects had designed twenty "survival homes" costing $100,000 to $800,000 in various parts of the country. "My guess is that it's a $150 million business, just in physical survival," said Bill Pier, owner of a California mail-order firm called Survival Inc. He said he had sold in the previous year more than $1 million worth of dried food and other supplies, "everything from washboards to vaults to radiation suits."

While there is an element of amiable play-acting in all this buying and selling of survival equipment, an element of tree houses and king-of-the-castle, the survival fantasy can become, just like king-of-the-castle, more ominous. Mike McKinney, for example, is a former Los Angeles police officer who now describes himself as a "survival counselor." He told the *Times* correspondent that he himself maintained a cache of one hundred weapons, including thirty rifles to be used for bartering with other survivors of the nuclear holocaust. He had his own ideas of bartering, however. "If you came to me with a month's worth of freeze-dried goods to trade to me for my M-1A rifle," he said, "I'd end up with both my M-1A and the food."

It is clear that the survivalists are not really preparing to defend themselves against a Soviet missile attack, much less against a Soviet army of occupation, but rather against their neighbors. It is the neighbors who threaten, in a struggle for survival, to become the enemy. The actual outcome of such a confrontation might well be that a horde of neighbors would strip the survivalist of his guns and his food and then tear him limb from limb. But in all the public anxiety about the dangers of World War III, it becomes apparent that the impending disaster we call World War III may not finally be a nuclear war at all. In the nightmares of the would-be survivors, and of many others who have done nothing in particular to save themselves, the anticipated catastrophe takes a number of different forms, all reflecting in one way or another the dreamer's own anxieties. To some, Armageddon will be a racial conflagration, a final orgy of hatred and revenge. Others imagine a total economic collapse, the loss of all savings and all security, the ruin of all conventional values (hence the need for stored supplies). Or else some vast natural disaster, a new flood, a new earthquake, a new epidemic of something, a new poisoning of air and water, some recurrence of those mystifying scourges that modern technology only seems to have conquered. "Something," said Roger Oie, who moved 110 miles north of Phoenix to find shelter on a twelve-acre ranch, "has to collapse."

Those who survived the atom bomb were the people who ignored their friends crying out in extremis; or who shook off wounded neighbors who clung to them, pleading to be saved. . . . In short, those who survived the bomb were, if not merely lucky, in a greater or lesser degree selfish, self-centered, guided by instinct and not civilization . . . and we know it, we who have survived. Knowing it is a dull ache.

—A physician at Nagasaki

The Scriptures have no answer, either. Or rather, they have answers of many kinds. Jesus Christ prophesied that the sun would darken and the stars would fall, and though he said that no man could tell when the apocalypse was coming, he promised that it would come within that same generation. "Take ye heed, watch and pray," he said, "for ye know not when the time is." In the later days of Saint Peter, there were already murmurings about the failure of Christ's prediction. Peter explained that "one day is with the Lord as a thousand years," but Christians must continue watching, for the Lord would come "as a thief in the night." Then, at last, the heavens would turn to fire and "the earth and the works that are therein shall be burned up."

The watching never ceases. The coming of the millennial year 1000 is thought to have caused widespread alarm, and the first Protestants foresaw on several occasions an imminent Armageddon. In the nineteenth century, a Massachusetts farmer named William Miller declared after a series of Biblical computations that the world would end on March 21, 1843. Many of his followers donned white muslin robes and took to the hills to await the event. When nothing happened, Miller corrected his computations and announced the end on October 22, 1844. When he died in 1845, his followers organized themselves as Seventh Day Adventists and kept watch. Charles Taze Russell, founder of the Jehovah's Witnesses, first announced that the Last Days had imperceptibly begun in 1874, then that the end could come in 1914. Russell's follower J. F. Rutherford changed the date to 1925. Other prophets of one sort or another have announced the apocalypse in 1936, 1953, 1973 . . .

Then there periodically occur sad little scenes of expectation. On May 25, 1981, for example, about fifty white-robed members of a group called the Assembly of Yahweh gathered at New York's Coney Island and waited for God to lift them into heaven when the world ended between 3 P.M. and sundown. Rumors that the faithful might wade out to sea brought in the police, with two launches and two ambulances. "Anyone can walk into the water and swim," a police lieutenant declared. "But if they go in with the intent to kill themselves, we'll stop them." While a crowd of about three hundred onlookers waited for something to happen, the faithful played bongo drums and chanted prayers until sundown. Then they went home.

It is easy enough to ridicule such sects, as the earliest Christians and their apocalyptic expectations also were ridiculed, but there remain millions of people who believe that the Bible is literally true, and that even the most phantasmagorical prophecies in Revelation must soon be fulfilled. And the pain will be real pain. "The Age of Utopia will be preceded by unparalleled events of suffering for the human race . . . ," as Billy Graham put it in *Angels,* "but it will be a victorious day for the universe, and especially planet earth, when the devil and his angels are thrown into the lake of fire."

One of the most elaborate recent explanations of such prophecies is a book entitled *The Late Great Planet Earth,* by Hal Lindsey (with C. C. Carlson), which has sold several million copies and inspired half a dozen sequels (*1980's Countdown to Armageddon, The World's Final Hour, The Terminal Generation,* and more). Lindsey, a traveling speaker for an evangelical movement called the Campus Crusade for Christ, provides up-to-date identities for all the legendary figures. Gog and Magog, which once seemed to represent Alaric and his Goths, or the Turkish invaders at the time of the Reformation, have now become the Soviets. The King of the South has become Egypt, still threatening Israel as it did two millennia ago. Though Rome no longer seems a major force in power politics, Lindsey artfully points out that the European Common Market was created by the Treaty of Rome, and thus "Rome" may be considered a term for the united forces of Western Europe. The essential precondition for the last great war, according to the fundamentalist interpretation, is the prophesied return of the Jews to their homeland. Armageddon is the Mount of Megiddo, not far from Haifa. The Russians will start the war by attacking Israel, says Lindsey, and Ezekiel's "description of torrents of fire and brimstone raining down upon the Red Army . . . could well be describing the use of tactical nuclear weapons against them." And so on.

Not everyone takes the prophets so literally, of course, and there are many who consider their warnings only a series of metaphors. Still, the metaphoric warnings parallel the realistic ones that emanate from both the Pentagon and the demonstrators who parade against the Pentagon. The forces of religious orthodoxy now seem increasingly inclined to join that parade. They are less ready to accept the Biblical prophecies of catastrophe, or to reflect on the religious meaning of catastrophe, than they are to attempt a resistance. The National Council of Churches, for one, responded to the apparent dangers of a nuclear-arms race by formally appealing to both Washington and Moscow in the spring of 1981 for "a mutual freeze on all further testing, production, and deployment of . . . nuclear weapons." Later that year, the three-million-member United Presbyterian Church and the 1.6-million-member American Baptist Churches both issued a similar call for an end to the nuclear-arms race. "There is no justification," the Baptists said, "for the use of nuclear weapons on any people under any circumstances."

The principal tower of orthodoxy nowadays is probably once again the Vatican, and the Vatican wants to be reasonable. There is no talk here of apocalypse. Nuclear war would be a disaster of monstrous dimensions, but there would be survivors, as always, and among them would be priests, as always. The church would go on, somehow. Life would go on, somehow. It is the duty of Christ's vicar on earth, however, to sound the alarm and to keep sounding it. "If someone goes crazy and he is the head of a nation which has these arms, what will happen to humanity?" the late Pope Paul VI asked in 1978 on the fifteenth anniversary of his accession. On another occasion, he answered his own question: "A war ... would not be the end of difficulties but the end of civilization."

Pope John Paul II went even further when he asked "whether the very destruction of humanity is not a real possibility." He said as much in an address to the United Nations General Assembly, and then in February of 1981 he went on a pilgrimage to Hiroshima. As at Auschwitz, the white-robed Roman Pontiff seemed an incongruous figure in the Peace Memorial Park, but he did his best to consecrate the haunted place. "To remember what the people of this city suffered," he said, "is to renew our faith in men. . . . One must affirm, again and again, that the waging of war is not inevitable or unchangeable. Humanity is not destined to self-destruction."

Perhaps not, but it is not "humanity" that controls the nuclear warheads but rather a number of officials who stand ready to "perform our function." Fully aware of that, the Pope then addressed himself to the authorities of both East and West: "To the heads of state and government, to those who hold political and economic power, I say: Let us pledge ourselves to peace through justice; let us take a solemn decision, now, that war will never be tolerated or sought as a means of resolving differences; . . . let us replace violence and hate with confidence and caring." That, of course, is exactly what the rulers on both sides repeatedly do. Almost daily they pledge themselves to peace through justice. And when they finally decide that war is unavoidable, as it has repeatedly appeared to be, they will launch the missiles not out of violence and hate but to defend their own people, with confidence and caring, against the violence and hate that seem to threaten them.

Knowing that these words too were just words, the Vicar of Christ concluded his address to the Japanese by turning to prayer and invoking the divine power to change men's ways. "Hear my voice, for I speak for the multitudes in every country . . . ," said the Pope. "O God, hear my voice and grant unto the world your everlasting peace."

Is that the answer, finally, or is it the final demonstration that there is no answer?

*

Six weeks after the nuclear bomb hit Hiroshima, a flood struck the city.

The city looked like a huge lake. Beneath its waves it was possible to detect tiled roofs and the outline of much else as well. I felt as though this were the final burial. For what reason had the citizens of Hiroshima been condemned to such frightful sufferings? Suppose the flood waters were never to recede, and it [Hiroshima] were all to remain drowned forever? In that case, I thought, so much the better.

—Shinzo Hamai, mayor of Hiroshima

PEACE IS OUR PROFESSION, says the sign at the entrance to the Strategic Air Command, just outside Omaha. The headquarters building itself is a nondescript rectangle of brown bricks, surrounded by an expanse of neatly clipped crabgrass. It could be a post office or a public library. On a concrete platform outside the front door stands a Minuteman I missile, bright white and sleek as Brancusi's bird. It is obsolete now, a relic; the missiles waiting in their silos are called Minuteman III. A small brown rabbit incongruously hops out from behind the missile, pauses for a moment, nibbling, and then hops away. Peace is our profession.

It is a sunny Sunday morning in May. It is, in fact, Mother's Day, and the Strategic Air Command is welcoming the mothers of its men to Offutt Air Force Base. At the officers' club just across from the headquarters building, the line of mothers and men waiting to get their breakfast extends almost the length of the building. Behind the officers' club, there are a swimming pool and a golf course and a neatly trimmed field reaching all the way to the highway. "And the wind shall say: 'Here were decent godless people: / Their only monument the asphalt road / And a thousand lost golf balls.' "

Despite its pastoral surroundings, the interior of the SAC headquarters building is closely guarded. There is an elaborate protocol of signing in and receiving an identity card, which must be affixed to the lapel. The military police, elaborately outfitted in berets and white braid, watch closely at each checkpoint. The guide leads the way downward, three stories underground, through a maze of bleak corridors. Food and supplies for thirty days have been stored here, the guide says, though the headquarters building itself has never been "hardened." A warhead anywhere nearby would obliterate it. The survivors in some other headquarters would have to carry on.

In the control center itself, finally, the commanding general's easy chair dominates a long balcony overlooking banks of computers. A sign in front of the vacant chair announces the commander's official identity: "CinC SAC." A touch of awe enters the guide's voice as he pronounces the title: "Sink Sack." Would the visitor like to sit on the throne for a moment? The visitor would. In front of him now stand the CinC SAC's seven telephones. The news of the apocalypse would come in on the yellow telephone and go out on the red one.

On the far wall, four clocks announce Omaha time, Zulu time (Greenwich Mean Time), Moscow time and Guam time. The wall's twenty giant video screens can provide, in seven different colors, any kind of information the CinC SAC would like. Within a minute, the Air Force can produce a report on weather conditions, for example, anywhere in the world. Would the visitor like to test the system? Would the visitor choose a place, any place in the world? The visitor chooses Guam. In about twenty seconds, letters flicker onto one of the screens to announce that the temperature is eighty-four degrees in Guam.

As a last touch, the Air Force would like to present its PACC, which means Post Attack Command Control. The voice now speaking on the telephone is that of General W., who greets the visitor by name and reports that he is calling from an airplane now flying "somewhere over the central United States." Ever since 1961, every day and night, a plane of this type has been circling somewhere over the United States. There is always a general on duty, like the Flying Dutchman, waiting at the controls of the devices that could launch the missiles from their underground silos. This means, says the general, that even if an enemy surprise attack destroyed Washington, even if an enemy surprise attack destroyed Omaha, and New York and Chicago and Los Angeles, there would still be a general circling through the skies, ready to perform his function, to retaliate.

After explaining his mission, the general politely asks if there are any questions.

"No, thanks," says the visitor.

"Well, goodbye, then," says the general, "and happy Mother's Day."

A Note on Sources

This book has become, in a way, a history of the world. Each chapter represents a major area of scholarly study, and to master the accomplishments of the many experts would require a mastery of two millennia of history, philosophy, art and literature, not to mention a dozen languages ranging from Greek to Provençal to Yiddish. Having failed all these requirements, I offer here simply a rough summary of the main sources on which I have based my work.

The Great Flood. The best way to imagine the eruption of Santorini is to go there and look. The view from a café on the rim of the crater is one of the most beautiful sights in the world. After one has absorbed it for an hour or two, one begins to search for a shop that might have a guidebook. And so one discovers *Santorini,* by Artemios M. Mitropias; *Santorini,* by Christos G. Doumos, and even such specialized guides as *Wild Flowers of Greece,* by George Sfikas, which identifies all the strange blossoms that cover the volcanic slopes. More serious and more comprehensive is *Greece,* by Stuart Rossiter, in the Blue Guide series.

Here too one can begin looking into the legends of Atlantis. My acquisitions at the Santorini bookshop included two stirring paperbacks, *The End of Atlantis,* by J. V. Luce (1969) and *The Mystery of Atlantis,* by Charles Berlitz (1969). Back in New York, much more can be found. The classic compendium of legends, *Atlantis: The Antediluvian World,* by Ignatius Donnelly, was originally published in 1882, but a revised edition appeared in 1949. For a contemporary account by an oceanographic engineer who engaged in one of the many searches, see *Voyage to Atlantis,* by James W. Mavor, Jr. (1969).

In quoting from the Gilgamesh Epic, I have relied on the version published in *The Gilgamesh Epic and Old Testament Parallels,* by Alexander Heidel (1946). The flood legends around the world come from *Myth, Legend, and Custom in the Old Testament, A Comparative Study with Chapters from Sir James G. Frazer's Folklore in the Old Testament,* by Theodore H. Gaster (1969). For Plato's *Timaeus* and *Critias* on the Atlantis legend, I have used the standard two-volume translation by B. Jowett (1882, republished 1937). For some of the details of Cretan civilization, I am indebted to *The House of the Double Axe: The Palace at Knossos,* by Agnes Carr Vaughan (1959). But I end as I came, looking out at the Aegean from the top of the crater in Santorini.

The Sack of Rome. The ultimate source, of course, is Edward Gibbon's glorious *History of the Decline and Fall of the Roman Empire* (I use the seven-volume version edited by J. B. Bury and published in 1900). But as Gibbon himself said, he was only as good as his sources, and the confused history of the Gothic invasions is therefore not among his greatest chapters. The two main Roman sources are the *Histories* of Ammianus Marcellinus (tr. John Rolfe, 1935, in three volumes of the Loeb Classical Library), which unfortunately break off at Ammianus' death in about 380, three decades before Alaric's triumph, and the various heroic poems of Claudian (tr. Maurice Platnauer, 1922, in two volumes of the Loeb Library), which are sycophantic and unreliable. See also *The History of Count Zosimus, Chancellor of the Roman Empire,* which was translated and published in London in 1814. On the Gothic side, the main source is the rather simple but engaging *Gothic History of Jordanes,* tr. Charles Christopher Mierow (1915, republished in 1960). We have also entered the era of ecclesiastical histories, in which theological controversy takes precedence over mere political narrative. The one masterpiece is Saint Augustine's *The City of God;* I have used the Modern Library translation by Marcus Dods (1950). The sixty-volume *Fathers of the Church* contains *Seven Books of History Against the Pagans* by Paulus Orosius, and the fourteen-volume *Select Library of Nicene and Post-Nicene Fathers of the Christian Church* contains the ecclesiastical chronicles of Sozomen, Theodoretus and Socrates Scholasticus.

The best general history of the Gothic wars, I think, is the pleasantly old-fashioned *Italy and Her Invaders,* by Thomas Hodgkin (eight volumes, 1880, republished in 1967). See also J. B. Bury's *History of the Later Roman Empire* (1923) and his *The Invasion of Europe by the Barbarians* (1967). The most detailed account of Gothic life, though somewhat before the reign of Alaric, is *The Visigoths in the Time of Ulfila,* by E. A. Thompson (1966). And here I should acknowledge a reference work of endless value for this and subsequent chapters, *The Cambridge Mediaeval History,* ed. H. M. Gwatkin *et al.* (8 volumes, 1922 and thereafter).

On the sack of Jerusalem, virtually the only source is *The Jewish Wars,* by Marcus Flavius Josephus, tr. G. A. Williamson (1959). See also Williamson's *The World of Josephus,* which includes a valuable comparison of *The Jewish Wars* with Josephus' other works.

For an explication of the Book of Revelation, I have relied chiefly on the commentaries by Martin Rist and Lynn Harold Hough in Volume 12 of *The Interpreter's Bible,* ed. George Arthur Buttrick *et al.* (1957). See also *The Revelation of Saint John the Divine,* by G. B. Caird (1966).

The Birth of the Inquisition. The best contemporary account of the Albigensian Crusade is *La Canzon de la Crozada,* which was begun by Guilhem de Tudela, then carried on by an anonymous poet. Guilhem tries to be fair to both sides, but his sympathies clearly lie with the Albigensians even though he disapproves of their heresy. Eugène Martin-Chabot's French translation, on alternating pages facing the original text, appeared in three volumes in Paris in 1931. The other two main contemporary accounts are the ardently anti-Albigensian *Hystoria Albigensis* or *Histoire Albigeois,* by Pierre des Vaux-de-Cernay, tr. Pascal Guébin and Henri Maisonneuve (1951) and the *Cronica* or

Chronique de Guillaume de Puy-Laurens, ed. M. Guizot (1824). See also *Heresies of the High Middle Ages, Selected Sources,* ed. and tr. Walter L. Wakefield and Austin P. Evans (1969).

The best modern account of the crusade is *Massacre at Mont-Ségur* by Zoé Oldenburg, tr. Peter Green (1961), an excellent work that can be faulted only for its extreme partisanship in favor of the Albigensians. For other good modern studies, see *The Albigensian Crusade,* by Jacques Madaule, tr. Barbara Wall (1967), *Heresy, Crusade and Inquisition in Southern France, 1100-1250,* by Walter L. Wakefield (1974), and *Histoire de la Croisade contre les Albigeois,* by Jean-Pierre Cartier (1968). The classic work on the Inquisition is *The Inquisition of the Middle Ages,* by Henry Charles Lea (1888). See also *The Mediaeval Manichee,* by Steven Runciman (1947).

We now encounter, and will encounter again, the unusually interesting works of Norman Cohn, professor at the University of Sussex, who devoted years to studying the antecedents to the Nazi holocaust. The relevant books here are *The Pursuit of the Millennium* (1957, revised 1970), a history of the recurrent appearances of millenarian prophets during the Middle Ages, and *Europe's Inner Demons* (1975), which deals with the evolution of the fear of sorcery and witchcraft, originally attributed to Christians and only much later to heretics and Jews.

The troubadors are a subject apart. Of the numerous anthologies, the best collection I have found is *Songs of the Troubadors,* ed. Anthony Bonner (1972). Ezra Pound's *Spirit of Romance* (1910) and *Literary Essays* (1954) are valuable simply because Pound is Pound. See also *Love in the Western World,* by Denis de Rougemont (1940, revised 1956).

The Black Death. Our fragmentary knowledge of the Great Plague is chiefly based on about a score of contemporary chronicles that keep reappearing over and over again, and no account of the catastrophe would be complete without the wonderful tales of Gabriel de Mussis, Michael of Piazza, and the rest. The best modern synthesis of these materials is generally thought to be *The Black Death,* by Philip Ziegler (1969), though the disproportionate emphasis on events in England takes up roughly half the book. Similarly useful is *The Black Death,* by George Deaux (1969). See also *Mediaeval Panorama,* by G. G. Coulton (1938, republished 1974), *Plagues and Peoples,* by William H. McNeill (1976), *Epidemics,* by Geoffrey Marks and William K. Beatty (1976), and *A Distant Mirror: The Calamitous 14th Century,* by Barbara Tuchman (1978). The standard older sources are *The Black Death,* by J. F. C. Hecker (1844, republished 1972), *The Black Death of 1348 and 1349,* by Francis Aidan Gasquet (1893), *A Chronicle of the Black Death,* by Johannes Nohl, tr. G. H. C. Clarke (1926, republished 1961), and *The Black Death,* by G. G. Coulton (1929).

In quoting Boccaccio's *Decameron* at length, I have relied on the translation by G. H. McWilliam (1972). Among other contemporary accounts, I have used *Villani's Chronicle,* tr. Rose E. Selfe (1906), and *The Chronicle of Jean de Venette,* tr. Jean Birdsall (1953).

Cohn's previously cited *Pursuit of the Millennium* provides one of the best accounts of the persecution of the Jews during the Black Death. See also *The History of Anti-Semitism,* by Léon Poliakov, tr. Richard Howard (1965), and *The Jew in the Mediaeval World, A Source Book: 315-1791,* by Jacob R. Marcus (1938, republished 1969). On the Avignon Papacy, see *Avignon in Flower, 1309-1403,* by Marion Gail (1965), *The Popes at Avignon, 1305-1378,* by G. Mollat, tr. Janet Love (1949), and *Petrarch and His World,* by Morris Bishop (1963).

Every account of the plague makes an effort to assess its meaning, of course, but perhaps the most detailed account of its economic effects can be found in the first volume of *The Cambridge Economic History of Europe,* ed. M. M. Postan (6 volumes, 1966). See also *Before the Industrial Revolution, European Society and Economy, 1000-1700,* by Carlo M. Cipolla (1976); *The Economic and Social History of Mediaeval Europe,* by Henri Pirenne (1933), and *The Mediaeval Machine: The Industrial Revolution of the Middle Ages,* by Jean Gimpel (1976).

The Theater and Its Double, by Antonin Artaud, tr. Mary Caroline Richards (1958), contains Artaud's strange essay "The Theater and the Plague." I have also relied on *Antonin Artaud, Poet without Words,* by Naomi Greene (1970). Camus' life and work are well portrayed in *Albert Camus: A Biography,* by Herbert Lottman (1979). For more analytic studies, see *Camus,* by Germaine Brée (1959), and *Albert Camus and the Literature of Revolt,* by John Cruickshank (1959).

The New Jerusalem. The story of the Anabaptists has been distorted by partisan convictions from the very beginning. One of the first and fullest accounts of life inside Münster was set down by Heinrich Gresbeck, one of the two defectors who betrayed the city to its besiegers. The traditional view of the Anabaptists as demented zealots began to change in the mid-nineteenth century, when Friedrich Engels and Karl Kautsky both portrayed them as the precursors of socialism. In this century, by contrast, a whole school of dedicated Mennonite historians has emphasized the peaceful teachings of the Swiss and German Anabaptists and tried to dissociate them from the excesses of Münster.

Probably the fullest and best modern account of the Anabaptists is in *The Radical Reformation,* by George H. Williams (1962), which presents in sometimes exhausting detail the various sects on the left, or fundamentalist, wing of the Reformation. Williams is also the editor of *Spiritual and Anabaptist Writers* (1957), a valuable anthology that includes George Blaurock's report on the first baptism, Conrad Grebel's letters to Thomas Müntzer, and Müntzer's sermon to the Saxon princes. Two good but more specialized studies are *Anabaptists and the Sword,* by James N. Stayer (1972), which concentrates on the Anabaptists' controversies over the use of force, and *Anabaptism, A Social History,* by Claus-Peter Clasen (1972), which unfortunately limits itself to Switzerland, Austria and southern Germany.

The fullest account of the movement's origins in Zurich is still *A History of the Anabaptists in Switzerland,* by Henry S. Burrage (1882, republished 1973).

See also *The Anabaptist Story,* by William R. Estep (1963). Of the founding fathers, the only biography is *Conrad Grebel,* by Harold S. Bender (1950), longtime editor of *The Mennonite Quarterly Review.* It was for Bender that the most notable Mennonite historians compiled an interesting collection of essays, *The Recovery of the Anabaptist Vision,* ed. Guy F. Hershberger (1957).

The most detailed account of the siege of Münster is in *The Rise and Fall of the Anabaptists,* by E. Belfort Bax (1903, republished 1966), the concluding volume of a three-volume study of Germany during the Reformation. An admirer of socialism, and of Kautsky's *Communism in Central Europe in the Time of the Reformation,* Bax went to great effort to justify every extreme of the Münsterites. By contrast, Norman Cohn's spirited account in *The Pursuit of the Millennium* portrays the Anabaptist leaders as fanatics. For a similar recent view, see *Antichrist and the Millennium,* by E. R. Chamberlin (1976).

To fit the Anabaptists into the framework of their time, the best guide is probably Roland Bainton, a scholar both judicious and graceful. His *The Reformation of the Sixteenth Century* (1952) presents the whole period with considerable skill, and his *Here I Stand: A Life of Martin Luther* (1950) is still the best biography of Luther in English. Among the many other studies, I have been helped by *Young Man Luther,* by Erik Erikson (1958); *Luther, His Life and Work,* by Gerhard Ritter, tr. John Riches (1959); *Luther: A Biography,* by Richard Marius (1964), and *Luther Alive,* by Edith Simon (1968). For good accounts of several other key figures, see *Zwingli, Third Man of the Reformation,* by Jean Rilliet (1964), *Reformer without a Church: The Life and Thought of Thomas Müntzer,* by Eric W. Gritsch (1967), and *Erasmus and the Age of Reformation,* by Johan Huizinga (1924).

The Lisbon Earthquake. The English have long taken a special interest in Portugal and therefore in this disaster. The only thorough modern study is *The Lisbon Earthquake,* by T. D. Kendrick (1956). For contemporary reports, perhaps the best collection is in the surviving files of *The Gentleman's Magazine,* a lively London monthly, which published a dozen anonymous eyewitness accounts in its issue of December 1755. Equally anonymous, unfortunately, is a vivid pamphlet entitled *An Account of the Late Dreadful Earthquake and Fire Which Destroyed the City of Lisbon, the Metropolis of Portugal, in a Letter from a Merchant Resident There, to his Friend in England* (1755). The splendid narrative by Mr. Braddock can be found quoted in *Letters Addressed Chiefly to a Young Gentleman Upon Subjects of Literature,* by Charles Davy (1787). See also *The Private Correspondence of Sir Benjamin Keene,* ed. Sir Richard Lodge (1933); *They Went to Portugal,* by Rose Macaulay (1946), and *La Désastre de Lisbonne,* by G. Gastinal (1913, republished 1970).

For the background on life in Portugal in the eighteenth century, everyone has relied on the sprightly little volume entitled *Description de la Ville de Lisbonne* (1730), published anonymously in Paris but attributed to a Monsieur Gaillardie. There is a good biography of Carvalho, *Dictator of Portugal: A Life of the Marquis de Pombal,* by Marcus Cheke (1938, republished 1969). See also *Memoirs of the Marquis de Pombal, with Extracts from his Writings,* by John

Smith (1843). For an account of the Inquisition, I have relied once again on Henry Charles Lea, *A History of the Inquisition of Spain* (1906–7, republished 1922). More generally, I have consulted *Portugal, Old and Young, an Historical Study*, by Sir George Young (1917), and *A History of Spain and Portugal*, by Stanley G. Payne (1973).

As for the controversy about the significance of the disaster, the best general account of this period probably is *The Enlightenment: An Interpretation*, by Peter Gay (1966). See also Gay's *Voltaire's Politics: The Poet as Realist* (1959). I have quoted Smollett's version of the famous poem on Lisbon from *The Portable Voltaire*, ed. Ben Ray Redman (1949), and I have also relied on *Selected Letters of Voltaire*, ed. Richard A. Brooks (1973), and *Voltaire*, by Theodore Bestermann (1969). Rousseau's preposterous letter to Voltaire can be found in *Religious Writings*, by Jean-Jacques Rousseau, ed. Ronald Grimsley (1970). Whitefield's account of Lisbon is in the six-volume *Works of the Reverend George Whitefield* (1771), and John Wesley's reflections were published anonymously as *Serious Thoughts Occasioned by the Late Earthquake at Lisbon* (1755). For further accounts of this controversy, see *Some Contemporary Reactions to the Lisbon Earthquake of 1775*, by C. R. Boxer (1956), and *The Lisbon Earthquake: A Study in Religious Evaluation*, by Edgar S. Brightman (in *The American Journal of Theology*, 1919).

There have been many accounts of the disaster at Vesuvius and the rediscovery of the buried ruins at its foot. I have particularly relied on *Cities of Vesuvius, Pompeii and Herculaneum*, by Michael Grant (1971); *Pompeii—A.D. 79, The Treasure of Rediscovery*, by Richard Brilliant (1979); *The Destruction and Resurrection of Pompeii and Herculaneum*, by Egon Caesar Conte Corti, tr. K. and R. Gregor Smith (1951). I am also indebted to *The Rediscovery of Herculaneum and Pompeii*, by G. W. Bowersock, in *The American Scholar* (1978).

The best biography of Bach, I think, is *Johann Sebastian Bach, The Culmination of an Era*, by Karl Geiringer (1966). The first biography, by J. N. Forkel (1802), can be found, along with a great deal else of value, in *The Bach Reader*, ed. Hans David and Arthur Mendel (1945), and the classic three-volume biography by Philipp Spitta was republished in 1951. As for Bach's nemesis, I found in the New York Public Library an anonymous and wholly unreliable pamphlet, probably written by its subject, entitled *The Life of the Chevalier John Taylor, Oculist, Pontifical, Imperial, and Royal . . .* (1754).

The Coming of Revolution. There are a number of good histories of pre-revolutionary Russia, and despite or perhaps because of the mountains of documentary material to be evaluated, the best of these works have been produced by journalists. For an overall view of the grand confrontations of 1905, I have relied particularly on *Black Night, White Snow: Russia's Revolution, 1905–1917*, by Harrison Salisbury (1978); *The Shadow of the Winter Palace: Russia's Drift to Revolution, 1825–1917*, by Edward Crankshaw (1976); *The Twilight of Imperial Russia*, by Richard Charques (1958), and *Years of the Golden Cockerel*, by Sidney Harcave (1968). Harcave, the only academic among these four, has also written an excellent account of the 1905 Revolution alone, *First Blood*

(1964). The standard older authority is Sir Bernard Pares, whose *History of Russia* was originally published in 1926 and has been updated several times since then. See also his *Fall of the Russian Monarchy* (1939).

A special category must be reserved for those personal chronicles that have gone past being outdated and now seem like artifacts of a vanished age. The most notable of these is *Russia: On the Eve of War and Revolution,* by Sir Donald MacKenzie Wallace, longtime correspondent for *The Times* of London, whose account was originally published in 1877, then updated after the 1905 Revolution and finally condensed in a paperback edition of 1961. No less remarkable is *The Dawn in Russia, or Scenes in the Russian Revolution,* by Henry W. Nevinson (1906). Arriving in St. Petersburg in November of 1905 to report on the crisis for the London *Daily Chronicle,* Nevinson was unabashedly partisan toward the revolutionaries and not only covered the street fighting but helped the wounded. Henri Troyat has read many more such memoirs to compile his fascinating *Daily Life in Russia under the Last Tsar* (1962), which suffers from being written as a quasi-fictional narrative but provides rich detail on many usually overlooked aspects of pre-revolutionary life.

Cultural historians tend to treat their subject separately from politics. The best of these studies is probably *The Icon and the Axe: An Interpretive History of Russian Culture,* by James H. Billington (1966). Two useful literary chronicles are *A History of Russian Literature from Its Beginnings to 1900,* by D. S. Mirsky (1926), and *From Chekhov to the Revolution: Russian Literature from 1900 to 1917,* by Marc Slonim (1962). See also *The Russian Experiment in Art: 1863-1922,* by Camilla Gray (1962).

Of the many editions of Chekhov, I have relied mainly on the Penguin edition of the plays, translated by Elisaveta Fen (1954). Of the several collections of Chekhov's letters, I have used the one translated and edited by Michael Henry Heim and Simon Karlinsky (1973). Probably the best general biography is *A New Life of Anton Chekhov,* by Ronald Hingley (1976), a major revision, based on new materials, of the work he published in 1950. For a rather pugnacious analysis of Chekhov's dramas, see *The Real Chekhov: An Introduction to Chekhov's Last Plays,* by David Magarshack (1973). Stanislavsky's account of *The Cherry Orchard* is in his autobiography, *My Life in Art* (1924).

Personal memoirs and biographies on this period are almost endless. The basic documents on Tsar Nicholas became available after the revolution, notably his journals (1925), the letters from and to his wife (1923 and 1929), and his correspondence with his mother (1938). I have made use of Robert K. Massie's dramatic biography, *Nicholas and Alexandra* (1967), though I do not share his sympathy for his subject. The *Memoirs of Count Witte* (1921) are continuously self-serving and sometimes clearly false, but he is an engagingly rambunctious narrator and often at the center of action. For more impartial views, see *Sergei Witte and the Industrialization of Russia,* by Theodore H. von Laue (1963), and *Count Witte and the Tsarist Government in the 1905 Revolution,* by Howard D. Mehlinger and John M. Thompson (1972). Among other recollections, I should single out the gossipy and sometimes malicious *An Ambassador's Memoirs,* by the French envoy, Maurice Paléologue (1925).

The most interesting account, in some ways, is Maxim Gorki's interminable autobiographical novel, *The Life of Olim Sanghin,* which includes major scenes of the revolution in three of its four volumes, *Bystander* (1930), *The Magnet* (1931) and *Other Fires* (1933). Gorki's work is very undistinguished as fiction, and colored by a rather simpleminded proletarianism, but it conveys a strong sense of his presence at the scenes he describes. I know of no really good biography of Gorki, but see *Maxim Gorki and His Russia,* by Alexander Kaun (1931), and *Stormy Petrel,* by Dan Levin (1965).

I first encountered the idea of the Okhrana as the originator of the police state in Konrad Heiden's brilliant portrait of Hitler, *Der Führer* (1944). It flickers through several other studies of the Tsarist police (for a detailed listing, see *The Okhrana, The Russian Police: A Bibliography,* by Edward Ellis Smith [1967]), but I have found no major exploration of the interesting implications. For a straightforward history of the Okhrana, a good account is *The Russian Secret Police: Muscovite, Imperial Russian and Soviet Political Security Operations,* by Ronald Hingley (1970). The last tsarist chief of police, A. T. Vassilyev, produced a self-justification entitled *Ochrana, The Russian Secret Police,* ed. René Fülöp-Miller (1930). The most authoritative study of the experiment with police unions is Jerome Schneiderman's *Sergei Zubatov and Revolutionary Marxism: The Struggle for the Working Class in Tsarist Russia* (1976).

The extraordinary story of the Okhrana's double agents is well told in *Aseff the Spy, Russian Terrorist and Police Stool,* by Boris Nicolaievsky, tr. George Reavey (1934). Like many writers in this cloudy field, Nicolaievsky often drifts close to the border between speculation and fiction, but his narrative is still unmatched. No less enigmatic is the work of Boris Savinkov, whose *Memoirs of a Terrorist,* tr. Joseph Shaplen (1931), provides the definitive description of the assassinations of Plehve and Grand Duke Sergei and then abruptly breaks off in 1909 with a declaration of more underground work to be done. So vivid is Savinkov's account that one suspects the presence of an unidentified ghost writer, and it has been reported that the fashionable Symbolist poet Hippius Zinaida "helped" Savinkov to write his pseudonymous early novel, *The Pale Horse,* by "V. Ropshin," tr. Z. Vengerova (1917), a bleak narrative of the killing of a provincial governor.

Probably the best general work on the terrorists is *The Fortress,* by Robert Payne (1967), which includes detailed portraits of Nechaev, Sazonov and Kaliayev. For a closely focused chronicle of the terrorists' greatest victory, see *Nihilists, Russian Radicals and Revolutionaries in the Reign of Alexander II,* by Ronald Hingley (1967). One of the participants, Vera Figner, has left a wonderfully guileless version of the plot in *Memoirs of a Revolutionist* (1927). On Bakunin and his heirs, see *To the Finland Station: A Study in the Writing and Acting of History,* by Edmund Wilson (1940), *The Anarchists,* by James Joll (1979), and *The Russian Anarchists,* by Paul Avrich (1967).

The Jews in Russia, by Louis Greenburg (1944, the second volume completed by Mark Wischnitzer in 1951) seems to me the most authoritative history of the subject. I have also made use of *The Jews in Russia,* by Gerard Israel (1975). The first full account of the so-called "Protocols of the Elders of Zion" is *The Truth about 'The Protocols of Zion': A Complete Exposure,* by Herman Bernstein (1935, republished 1971). This includes not only the text of the "Protocols" but a detailed comparison with the relevant passages from the works of Joly and Goedsche. The most thorough recent analysis is *Warrant for Genocide: The Myth of the Jewish World-Conspiracy and the Protocols of the Elders of Zion,* by Norman Cohn (1967), the English scholar we previously encountered among the Albigensians and the Anabaptists. On the later influences of the "Protocols," see again Heiden's *Der Führer* and also *Russia and Germany: A Century of Conflict,* by Walter Laqueur (1965).

For the saga of Father Gapon, the basic text is his own autobiography, *The Story of My Life,* but it is transparently unreliable. At the time of its creation by a Fleet Street ghost, the mercurial priest still felt the euphoria of the great march and envisioned himself as a revolutionary leader; he thus minimized both his relationship with the police and the eccentricity of his behavior. The most detailed study of Gapon, to which I am much indebted, is *The Road to Bloody Sunday: Father Gapon and the St. Petersburg Massacre of 1905,* by Walter Sablinsky (1976).

Leon Trotsky is an incomparable narrator of his own adventures, partisan almost to the point of mendacity but vivid and impassioned. He told and retold his experiences and the theories he drew from them, notably in *1905* (written in 1909 and often reprinted, most recently in a 1972 paperback) and *My Life* (1930, republished in a 1970 paperback). The definitive biography is Isaac Deutscher's three-volume work, which starts with *The Prophet Armed: Trotsky: 1879-1921,* published in 1954. See also *Three Who Made a Revolution,* by Bertram D. Wolfe (1948).

The novels of Tolstoy, Dostoevsky and various other literary witnesses hardly need bibliographical citation. On Dostoevsky, though, I should mention the series of workbooks published by the University of Chicago, notably *The Notebooks for the Possessed,* ed. Edward Wasiolek (1968). On Tolstoy, I have made use of Henri Troyat's admirable biography, *Tolstoy* (1965). Worthy of note, too, are Boris Pasternak's 1925 cycle of poems, *The Year 1905,* and Vladimir Solovyev's *War, Progress and the End of History, Including a Short Story of the Anti-Christ* (1915).

My chief source on the details of the Tunguska explosion is Walter Sullivan's *Black Holes, the Edge of Space, the End of Time (1979).*

The Kingdom of Auschwitz. Much of what happened at Auschwitz remains somewhat mysterious, for many of the Nazi records were falsified with terms like "special handling," and many of even these falsified records were destroyed in the evacuation of the camp. The most valuable source of information is the testimony of the prisoners who were there, who have done their best to bear witness to what they experienced. This testimony is fallible, however, partly because most of the survivors saw only a small part of this huge institution; partly because they had no way of recording events as they happened, under conditions of great hardship; partly because memory itself is fallible, and half-stifled recollections are still emerging forty years after the war; partly because many of these memoirs have been worked on by interviewers, ghost writers and editors, whose contributions to the process are now inextricably intertwined with the raw material of raw memory.

One ends by making very subjective judgments about the spirit and reliability of each witness. Among the accounts I have found particularly impressive are: (1) *I Cannot Forgive,* by Rudolf Vrba and Alan Bestic (1964). Vrba, an intelligent and indomitable man, a chemist by profession, survived two years in Auschwitz, saw a great deal, finally escaped and brought important evidence to the Allies. (Bestic is the writer.) (2) *Five Chimneys, The Story of Auschwitz,* by Olga Lengyel (1947). A trained nurse and the wife of a Romanian psychiatrist, Mrs. Lengyel combines a rather sketchy account of the camp as a whole (one of the first to be published) with the much stronger story of her own efforts to organize the prisoner hospital. (3) *This Way for the Gas, Ladies and Gentlemen,* by Tadeusz Borowski, tr. Barbara Vedder (originally published in two collections of stories in Poland in 1948, translated into English in 1967, and now available in a Penguin paperback, 1976). A poet of considerable power, Borowski presented his stories as fiction, but they are clearly based on fact. The fictionalization enabled Borowski to blur the element of his own collaboration with the camp hierarchy, but that in turn strengthens the verisimilitude of the stories. Borowski became a police official in Poland's Stalinist regime before committing suicide in 1951. (4) *Hanged at Auschwitz,* by Sim Kessel, tr. Melville and Delight Wallace (1972). A tough and likable French boxer, arrested while smuggling arms, Kessel offers no remarkable insights but epitomizes the will to fight on.

Also extremely valuable in different ways are: (1) *The Death Factory: Documents on Auschwitz,* by Ota Kraus and Erich Kulka, tr. Stephen Jolly (originally written in Czech and published in 1946 but revised and reprinted several times, most recently in London in 1966). Kraus and Kulka made a niche for themselves in Auschwitz as skilled craftsmen and repairmen. Then they began gathering other prisoners' recollections, which they assembled into an important though somewhat disorganized account of camp life. (2) *Survival in Auschwitz: The Assault on Humanity,* by Primo Levi, tr. Stuart Woolf (1961, originally entitled *If This Is a Man*), and *Man's Search for Meaning: An Introduction to Logotherapy,* by Viktor Frankl (1962, originally entitled *From Death-Camp to Existentialism*). These two accounts, by an Italian chemist and an Austrian psychiatrist, are perceptive analyses of how the SS methods destroyed the prisoners' identities and how that destruction could be resisted. (3) *Auschwitz: A Doctor's Eyewitness Account,* by Dr. Miklos Nyiszli, tr. Tibere Kremer and Richard Seaver (1960), and *Eyewitness Auschwitz: Three Years in the Gas Chambers,* by Filip Müller, ed. Helmut Freitag, tr. Susanne Flatauer (1979). A Hungarian pathologist, who was made an assistant to Dr. Mengele, and a Czech member of the *Sonderkommando* provide unique accounts of their coerced participation in the Final Solution. (4) *Fighting Auschwitz: The Resistance Movement in the Concentration Camp,* by Józef Garliński (1975). A prisoner himself but not a member of the underground, Garliński subsequently recreated the story of the Polish nationalist resistance.

Other noteworthy prisoner memoirs include (in alphabetical order): *At the Mind's Limits: Contemplations by a Survivor of Auschwitz,* by Jean Améry, tr. Sidney Rosenfeld and Stella P. Rosenfeld (1980); *Hope Is the Last to Die: A Personal Documentation of Nazi Terror,* by Halina Birenbaum, tr. David Walsh

(1971); *None of Us Will Return*, by Charlotte Delbo, tr. John Githens (1968); *Playing for Time*, by Fania Fénelon with Marcelle Routier, tr. Judith Landry (1977); *I Am Alive*, by Kitty Hart (1961); *Night of the Mist*, by Eugène Heimler, tr. André Ungar (undated); *Anus Mundi: 1500 Days in Auschwitz/Birkenau*, by Wieslaw Kielar (1980); *In the Hell of Auschwitz: The Wartime Memoirs of Judith Sternberg Newman* (1963); *Night*, by Elie Wiesel, tr. Stella Rodway (1960).

More fragmentary but hardly less important are the statements of the survivors who testified in court against their persecutors. The most important collection is *Auschwitz: A Report on the Proceedings Against Robert Karl Mulka and Others before the Court at Frankfurt*, by Bernd Naumann, tr. Jean Steinberg (1966). This is an excellent account by a German journalist of the 1964 trial of two dozen Auschwitz officials, and I have quoted extensively from such witnesses as Ella Lingens and Otto Wolken. An impressive dramatic arrangement of this testimony was devised by Peter Weiss under the title *The Investigation* (1966). See also *Trial of Josef Kramer and Forty-Four Others* (*The Belsen Trial*), ed. Raymond Phillips (1949). (Another noteworthy collection of memoirs, though not court testimony, is *Voices from the Holocaust*, ed. Sylvia Rothschild (1981) for the William E. Wiener Oral History Library of the American Jewish Committee.)

There is far less testimony from the Nazi side, of course, but Rudolf Hoess left a unique confession. Originally published in a Polish translation entitled *Wspomnienia* (1951), Hoess' story appeared in English as *Commandant of Auschwitz: The Autobiography of Rudolf Hoess*, tr. Constantine Fitzgibbon (1959). The chapters dealing with Auschwitz (about two thirds of the book) also appear in a valuable collection, *KZ Auschwitz as seen by the SS*, ed. Jadwiga Bezwińska and Danuta Czech (1972), which further includes the confessions of Perry Broad and the journal of Dr. Johann Paul Kremer. This book was published by the museum at Auschwitz, which continues to study and report on the documentary remnants of the camp, notably in fifteen volumes of records, analyses and recollections entitled *Zeszyty Oswiecimskie*, translated into German by Herta Henschel *et al.* under the title *Hefte von Auschwitz*. The museum's English-language works also include *Selected Problems from the History of KZ Auschwitz*, by Kazimierz Smoleń *et al.* (1979), and Smoleń's detailed *Guide-Book* (1978).

Despite the quantity of memoirs on Auschwitz, there is as yet no comprehensive book on the camp (though William Craig, author of *The Fall of Japan*, has been working on one for several years). Perhaps the nearest thing to it is *Concentration Camp Oswiecim-Brzezinka, Based on Documentary Evidence and Sources*, by Jan Sehn, tr. Klemens Keplics (1957). Sehn was the presiding judge at Hoess' trial before the Polish Supreme National Tribunal and at the subsequent trial of forty Auschwitz officials. Though rather terse and dry, his account gives considerable detail on Gestapo activities and general living conditions in the camp.

Since Auschwitz was the center of the holocaust, it naturally forms a major part in the many books on the disaster as a whole. On this, probably the most valuable studies are *The War Against the Jews, 1933-1945*, by Lucy S. Dawidowicz (1975); *The Destruction of the European Jews*, by Raul Hilberg (1961);

The Holocaust: The Destruction of European Jewry, 1933–1945, by Nora Levin, and *The Final Solution: The Attempt to Exterminate the Jews of Europe, 1939–1945,* by Gerald Reitlinger (1953).

On various specific aspects of the Holocaust, I am indebted to *Eichmann in Jerusalem: A Report on the Banality of Evil,* by Hannah Arendt (1963, revised 1964); *The Crime and Punishment of I. G. Farben,* by Joseph Borkin (1976); *Less than Slaves: Jewish Forced Labor and the Quest for Compensation,* by Benjamin B. Ferencz (1979); *The Terrible Secret: Suppression of the Truth about Hitler's 'Final Solution,'* by Walter Laqueur (1980); *Auschwitz and the Allies,* by Martin Gilbert (1981); *They Fought Back: The Story of the Jewish Resistance in Nazi Europe,* ed. and tr. Yuri Suhl (1967), and *The Murderers Among Us,* by Simon Wiesenthal, ed. Joseph Wechsberg (1967).

The Great War. As in the opening chapter, I have been impressionistic here rather than comprehensive. The literature on the plans and predictions for nuclear war is not only large (100 books since 1980, by one account) but so constantly changing that no bibliographic reckoning can remain accurate for long.

Among the numerous publications by the United States government, the best overall study that I could find is *The Effects of Nuclear War,* produced in 1979 by the Congressional Office of Technology Assessment (OTA) under the supervision of Daniel de Simone, acting director. The standard older work, with exhaustive detail, is *The Effects of Nuclear Weapons,* edited by Samuel Glasstone and Philip J. Dolan, published by the Defense Department in 1957 and revised several times, most recently in 1977. Among new works, the most spectacular success has been *The Fate of the Earth,* by Jonathan Schell (1982), which I find quite exaggerated in both its analysis and its recommendations.

Quotations from various people generally come from *The New York Times,* clipped and saved over the course of the past few years. A few such stories from periodicals should perhaps be specifically cited (in chronological order): "Fearing Society's Collapse, 'Survivalists' Cache Goods," by Wayne King, *New York Times,* Jan. 14, 1981; "Rethinking the Unthinkable," by Wade Green, *New York Times Magazine,* March 15, 1981; " 'Unacceptable Damage,' " by Lewis Thomas, *New York Review of Books,* Sept. 24, 1981; "The Nuclear Arms Race," by Peter McGrath *et al., Newsweek,* Oct. 5, 1981; "Medical Problems of Survivors of Nuclear War," by Herbert L. Abrams and William E. Von Kaenel, *New England Journal of Medicine,* Nov. 12, 1981, and "Thinking the Unthinkable" by Strobe Talbott *et al., Time,* March 29, 1982.

All the italic quotations from survivors of the nuclear attacks on Hiroshima and Nagasaki come from the brilliant study *Death in Life: Survivors of Hiroshima,* by Robert Jay Lifton (1967).

Finally, when history has not yet been written or has not yet happened, one ventures to the prospective scene to take a look, and to listen. So as I began by hearing a cock crow at dawn on the island of Santorini, I end by recording for myself (in 1979) the good wishes of an Air Force general flying high over Omaha.

Locust Valley, N.Y.
February 7, 1982

Index